D1338061

INTERNATIONAL CHILDREN'S BIBLE

My child, pay attention to my words.
Listen closely to what I say.
Don't ever forget my words.
Keep them within your heart.
These words are the secret to life
for those who find them.

THE GREATEST COMMANDMENT

"'Love the Lord your God with all your heart, soul and mind'. This is the first and most important command. And the second command is like the first: 'Love your neighbour as you love yourself'. All the law and the writings of the prophets depend on these two commands."

Holy Bible

INTERNATIONAL CHILDREN'S BIBLE

NEW TESTAMENT

PRESENTED TO . . :

. . . .

FROM . . .

. . . .

DATE . . .

. . . .

Jesus said, "Those who hear the teaching of God and obey it – they are the ones that are truly blessed."
LUKE 11:28

THE ICB FAMILY TREE

Tree diagram showing the relationships between Bible versions:

HEBREW OT — GREEK NT
SEPT OT c132BC
TYNDALE 1526
LATIN VUL c400
GB 1539
WYC 1384
GVA 1560
MAT 1537
BEDE 735
AV 1611
DOUAI 1610
COV 1535
KNX 1956
LIND 698-721
BISH 1568
JBP 1972
MOF 1935
NASB 1971
RSV 1962
NAB 1970
LVB 1969
NEB 1970
AMB 1964
NKJ 1982
ASV 1901
TNT 1973
JER 1966
NRSV 1990
GNB 1976
LVB 1971
RV 1885
NIV 1978
NLT 1996
REB 1989
NJB 1985
ICB NCV 1991

AMB	Amplified Bible	**HEBREW OT**	Original Hebrew – Old Testament	**NJB**	New Jerusalem Bible
ASV	American Standard Version	**ICB**	International Children's Bible	**NKJ**	New King James Bible
AV	The Authorised Version/	**JBP**	JB Phillips' New Testament		Revised Authorised Version
	King James Bible	**JER**	Jerusalem Bible	**NLT**	New Living Translation
BEDE	Part of John's Gospel in Anglo-Saxon	**KNX**	Knox. Roman Catholic version	**NRSV**	New Revised Standard Version
BISH	The Bishop's Bible	**LATIN**	Latin Vulgate	**REB**	Revised English Bible
COV	Coverdale. First printed English Bible	**VUL**	Translated by Jerome, using Greek	**RSV**	Revised Standard Version
DOUAI	The Douai-Rheims Bible		and Hebrew texts	**RV**	English Revised Version
	Roman Catholic Version	**LIND**	The Lindisfarne Gospels in Latin	**SEPT/OT**	Septuagint Old Testament (Greek)
GB	The Great Bible	**LVB**	Living Bible		– the first translation from Hebrew
GNB/TEV	Good News Bible/Today's	**MAT**	Matthew's Bible	**TNT**	Translator's New Testament
	English Version	**MOF**	Moffat Bible	**TYND**	Tyndale. First printed English
GREEK/NT	Original Greek New Testament	**NAB**	New American Bible		New Testament
GVA	The Geneva Bible –	**NASB**	New American Standard Bible	**WB**	William Barclay. New Testament.
	First small edition in Roman Type	**NEB**	New English Bible	**WYC**	Wycliffe. First Bible in English.
		NIV	New International Version		

CONTENTS AND FEATURES

List of Maps

NEW CENTURY VERSION

Holy Bible

INTERNATIONAL CHILDREN'S BIBLE

NEW TESTAMENT

NEW CENTURY VERSION

Holy Bible

INTERNATIONAL CHILDREN'S BIBLE

NEW TESTAMENT

Authentic
BIBLES

PREFACE

The International Children's Bible (ICB), unlike any other editions, is neither a book of Bible stories nor a paraphrased version. This is the children's edition of the New Century Version, which is the only translation solely for children from the original Hebrew and Greek texts. This is the first time that a translation of God's Word has been specifically prepared for children. Children have had to grapple with story books and adult translations, leaving them flummoxed, confused and, at the worst, with the wrong ideas. God spoke because he wanted *everyone* to understand him and his purposes. The earliest scriptures were spoken to and written for a fairly uneducated society. Words were short and simple and fully understandable. The New Testament was written by fishermen in simple Greek phrases. Jesus used teaching ideas that were easily understood, parables of the land, and comparisons with everyday living.

An Accurate Translation?

This translation was put together by a team from the World Bible Translation Centre, and another twenty-one experienced scholars of the Bible were brought together to work on this project for thirteen years to ensure accuracy. These are people who have had experience translating texts to be used in the New International Version, the New American Standard Bible and the New King James Version. This International Children's Bible is based on the best available Greek and Hebrew texts and quality up-to-date scholarship.

A Clear Translation

One of the reasons for producing this Bible was to make the language easy enough for children to read and understand for themselves. Guidelines were drawn up to maintain simplicity, such as keeping sentences short, using appropriate children's vocabulary and where the words are complicated, there are references, marked "d", to the dictionary which is at the back of the Bible. Otherwise, footnotes, marked "n", are provided at the bottom of the page.

The International Children's Bible helps a child by putting biblical concepts into modern terms. Measurements are now in metric units and the twenty-first century versions of geographical names are now used, such as "Mediterranean Sea" instead of "Great Sea" or "Western Sea". Also, to prevent confusion, one name for one place is used consistently throughout. "Lake Galilee" is used throughout, rather than its variant forms, "Sea of Kinnereth" and "Sea of Tiberias".

Ambiguous words and phrases which would lead children into odd flights of fancy have been avoided to prevent potential misunderstandings.

Rhetorical questions are not understood by children, so rather than implying an answer, we state the meaning quite clearly.

Hebrew idioms have been translated in order to communicate the same meaning to today's children. For example, the Hebrew idiom "he rested with his fathers" is translated as "he died". Wherever possible, we have tried to retain the beauty and poetry of the original in English images.

This anglicised edition of this special Bible for children features new colourful artwork, dynamically presenting biblical scenes with a special emphasis on children, women and different ethnic groups. Full-colour maps of Bible lands and journeys have been provided, and flow charts, prayers, quotes, dictionary and footnotes are there as study aids.

Our Prayer

Realising our own lack of knowledge, we have had to trust in the Lord to guide us throughout, honour him for his steadfastness and pray none of us forget his teaching.

We pray that God through his Spirit will teach and guide you in his truth, and that you will find his love for the whole of your life. To that end we give you his Word.

THE PUBLISHERS
AUTHENTIC BIBLES
UNITED KINGDOM

WHAT IS THE BIBLE?

The Bible is God's holy Word, which he has spoken to help us to find out more about himself, and the life he wants us to lead. The Bible is made up of 66 books, from Genesis through to Revelation. These books have an incredible way of fitting together to form a whole. Each book is special on its own, but put together, all these books give us the history of what God has done in our world and his message of love and hope through his Son, Jesus Christ who came to live, to die, and to save us.

The Bible is not just a book of amazing stories but also a personal guide for us to follow. God has not left us to struggle on our own; instead he has purposefully used history, writing, culture and people to talk to us. Inside is adventure, excitement, battles and mysteries. There is, though, some serious reading and learning – God is the authority and his Word should not ever be distorted, ignored or added to. There are no mistakes in what God has said, and we now have the chance to discover the Truth. The Holy Bible is a reliable book and worth reading all the way through! (More than once!)

This Bible was especially translated for children to read and understand.

There are two major sections of the Bible: the *Old Testament* and the *New Testament*. This edition contains only the *New Testament*.

There are 39 books in the *Old Testament*, mostly written by Jews, in their own language, Hebrew. It begins with the story of how God created the world, the sky, the earth, the animals, the trees and human beings in his image and proved his goodness to us through creation. The history continues through God's special people, the Jews. We learn about prophets and what God has told them to tell us. They spoke a lot about a very special person, the Messiah. It really is quite surprising as to how accurate they were, and it is proof that God really told them what was to come in the future.

The *New Testament* has 27 books, written by Christians, mostly in Greek, which was the language they spoke. This second section starts with the birth of Jesus Christ, God's son. It tells us what Jesus said, how He was killed and then came back to life again. It also explains that one day He will come back. This testament tells us how Jesus' teaching led to the start and continued growth of the Christian church and how to continue within that today.

HOW DO I USE MY BIBLE?

Because this New Testament has 27 books in it, sometimes it is very hard to find what you want. So here is a tip or two . . .

1. Open your Bible and see how at the top of each page there is a name and a number. These are called the books and the chapters.

2. Now look down one page and you can see that there are lots of little numbers in each chapter. Each one is called a verse.

1 JOHN 2

him to do wrong. [11]But whoever hates his brother is in darkness. He lives in darkness and does not know where he is going. The darkness has made him blind.
[12]I write to you dear children,
   because your sins are forgiven
      through Christ.
[13]I write to you, fathers,
   because you know the One who

The chapter and verse numbers help you to find what you need quickly.

Sometimes though there are two books with exactly the same name. Where this happens they have a number first.

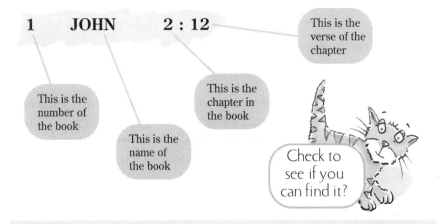

1   JOHN   2 : 12

This is the verse of the chapter

This is the number of the book

This is the name of the book

This is the chapter in the book

Check to see if you can find it?

Everyone who has heard or reads the Gospel must either: accept Jesus and receive his power, or leave him behind. Who is Jesus to you? A name or a friend? If as yet you don't know, at least read and reply to the agreement below.

I ....

promise to read and try to understand that the Bible is from God. If I find that this book tells me the truth and that Jesus Christ is my Saviour and Lord, I will accept him and try to follow him my whole life.

(Signed) ....

(Dated) ....

CONTENTS

THE NEW TESTAMENT

MATTHEW

Matthew Tells the Jews About Jesus

The Family History of Jesus

1 This is the family history of Jesus Christ. He came from the family of David. David came from the family of Abraham.

2 Abraham was the father[n] of Isaac.
Isaac was the father of Jacob.
Jacob was the father of Judah and his brothers.
3 Judah was the father of Perez and Zerah.
(Their mother was Tamar.)
Perez was the father of Hezron.
Hezron was the father of Ram.
4 Ram was the father of Amminadab.
Amminadab was the father of Nahshon.
Nahshon was the father of Salmon.
5 Salmon was the father of Boaz.
(Boaz's mother was Rahab.)
Boaz was the father of Obed.
(Obed's mother was Ruth.)
Obed was the father of Jesse.

6 Jesse was the father of King David.
David was the father of Solomon.
(Solomon's mother had been Uriah's wife.)
7 Solomon was the father of Rehoboam.
Rehoboam was the father of Abijah.
Abijah was the father of Asa.
8 Asa was the father of Jehoshaphat.
Jehoshaphat was the father of Jehoram.
Jehoram was the ancestor of Uzziah.
9 Uzziah was the father of Jotham.
Jotham was the father of Ahaz.
Ahaz was the father of Hezekiah.
10 Hezekiah was the father of Manasseh.
Manasseh was the father of Amon.
Amon was the father of Josiah.
11 Josiah was the grandfather of ¯ Jehoiachin and his brothers.

father "Father" in Jewish lists of ancestors can sometimes mean grandfather or more distant relative.

Matthew 1:1–17 The family history of Jesus

(This was at the time that the people were taken to Babylon.)

[12] After they were taken to Babylon: Jehoiachin was the father of Shealtiel.
Shealtiel was the grandfather of Zerubbabel.
[13] Zerubbabel was the father of Abiud.
Abiud was the father of Eliakim.
Eliakim was the father of Azor.
[14] Azor was the father of Zadok.
Zadok was the father of Akim.
Akim was the father of Eliud.
[15] Eliud was the father of Eleazar.
Eleazar was the father of Matthan.
Matthan was the father of Jacob.
[16] Jacob was the father of Joseph.
Joseph was the husband of Mary, and Mary was the mother of Jesus.
Jesus is called the Christ.[d]
[17] So there were 14 generations from Abraham to David. There were 14 generations from David until the time when the people were taken to Babylon. And there were 14 generations from the time when the people were taken to Babylon until Christ was born.

The Birth of Jesus Christ

[18] The mother of Jesus Christ was Mary. And this is how the birth of Jesus came about. Mary was engaged to marry Joseph. But before they married, she learned that she was going to have a baby. She was pregnant by the power of the Holy Spirit.[d] [19] Mary's husband, Joseph, was a good man. He did not want to disgrace her in public, so he planned to divorce her secretly.

[20] While Joseph thought about this, an angel of the Lord came to him in a dream. The angel said, "Joseph, descendant[d] of David, don't be afraid to take Mary as your wife. The baby in her is from the Holy Spirit. [21] She will give birth to a son. You will name the son Jesus.[n] Give him that name because he will save his people from their sins."

Matthew 1:21 "She will give birth to a son. You will name the son Jesus."

[22] All this happened to make clear the full meaning of what the Lord had said through the prophet:[d] [23] "The virgin[d] will be pregnant. She will have a son, and they will name him Immanuel."[n] This name means "God is with us."

[24] When Joseph woke up, he did what the Lord's angel had told him to do. Joseph married Mary. [25] But he did not have sexual relations with her until she gave birth to a son. And Joseph named the son Jesus.

Jesus The name Jesus means "salvation".
"The virgin . . . Immanuel." Quotation from Isaiah 7:14.

Wise Men Come to Visit Jesus

2 Jesus was born in the town of Bethlehem in Judea during the time when Herod was king. After Jesus was born, some wise men from the east came to Jerusalem. [2]They asked, "Where is the baby who was born to be the king of the Jews? We saw his star in the east. We have come to worship him."

[3]When King Herod heard about this new king of the Jews, he was troubled. And all the people in Jerusalem were worried too. [4]Herod called a meeting of all the leading priests and teachers of the law. He asked them where the Christ[d] would be born. [5]They answered, "In the town of Bethlehem in Judea. The prophet[d] wrote about this in the Scriptures:[d]

[6]'But you, Bethlehem, in the land of Judah,
   you are important among the rulers of Judah.
A ruler will come from you.
He will be like a shepherd for my people, the Israelites'."

Micah 5:2

[7]Then Herod had a secret meeting with the wise men from the east. He learned from them the exact time they first saw the star. [8]Then Herod sent the wise men to Bethlehem. He said to them, "Go and look carefully to find the child. When you find him, come and tell me. Then I can go and worship him too."

[9]The wise men heard the king and then left. They saw the same star they had seen in the east. It went before them until it stopped above the place where the child was. [10]When the wise men saw the star, they were filled with joy. [11]They went to the house where the child was and saw him with his mother, Mary. They bowed down and worshipped the child. They opened the gifts they had brought for him. They gave him treasures of gold, frankincense,[d] and myrrh.[d] [12]But God warned the wise men in a dream not to go back to Herod. So they went home to their own country by a different way.

Jesus' Parents Take Him to Egypt

[13]After they left, an angel of the Lord came to Joseph in a dream. The angel said, "Get up! Take the child and his mother and escape to Egypt. Herod will start looking for the child to kill him. Stay in Egypt until I tell you to return."

[14]So Joseph got up and left for Egypt during the night with the child and his mother. [15]Joseph stayed in Egypt until Herod died. This was to make clear the full meaning of what the Lord had said through the prophet.[d] The Lord said, "I called my son out of Egypt."[n]

Herod Kills the Baby Boys

[16]When Herod saw that the wise men had tricked him, he was very angry. So he gave an order to kill all the baby boys in Bethlehem and in all the area around Bethlehem who were two years old or younger. This was in keeping with the time he learned from the wise men. [17]So what God had said through the prophet[d] Jeremiah came true:

[18]"A sound was heard in Ramah.
   It was painful crying and much sadness.
Rachel cries for her children,
   and she cannot be comforted,
because her children are dead."

Jeremiah 31:15

"I called . . . Egypt." Quotation from Hosea 11:1.

Joseph and Mary Return

¹⁹After Herod died, an angel of the Lord came to Joseph in a dream. This happened while Joseph was in Egypt. ²⁰The angel said, "Get up! Take the child and his mother and go to Israel. The people who were trying to kill the child are now dead." ²¹So Joseph took the child and his mother and went to Israel. ²²But he heard that Archelaus was now king in Judea. Archelaus became king when his father Herod died. So Joseph was afraid to go there. After being warned in a dream, he went to the area of Galilee. ²³He went to a town called Nazareth and lived there. And so what God had said through the prophets*d* came true: "He will be called a Nazarene."*n*

The Work of John the Baptist

3 About that time John the Baptist*d* came and began preaching in the desert area of Judea. ²John said, "Change your hearts and lives because the kingdom of heaven is coming soon." ³John the Baptist is the one Isaiah the prophet*d* was talking about. Isaiah said:

"This is a voice of a man
    who calls out in the desert:
'Prepare the way for the Lord.
    Make the road straight for
        him'." *Isaiah 40:3*

⁴John's clothes were made from camel's hair. He wore a leather belt around his waist. For food, he ate locusts*d* and wild honey. ⁵Many people went to hear John preach. They came from Jerusalem and all Judea and all the area around the Jordan River.

⁶They told of the sins they had done, and John baptised them in the Jordan River.

⁷Many of the Pharisees*d* and Sadducees*d* came to the place where John was baptising people. When John saw them, he said: "You are all snakes! Who warned you to run away from God's anger that is coming? ⁸You must do the things that show that you have really changed your hearts and lives. ⁹And don't think that you can say to yourselves, 'Abraham is our father'. I tell you that God could make children for Abraham from these rocks. ¹⁰The axe is now ready to cut down the trees. Every tree that does not produce good fruit will be cut down and thrown into the fire.*n*

¹¹"I baptise you with water to show that your hearts and lives have changed. But there is one coming later who is greater than I am. I am not good enough to carry his sandals. He will baptise you with the Holy Spirit*d* and with fire. ¹²He will come ready to clean the grain. He will separate the good grain from the chaff.*d* He will put the good part of the grain into his barn. And he will burn the chaff with a fire that cannot be put out."*n*

Jesus Is Baptised by John

¹³At that time Jesus came from Galilee to the Jordan River. He came to John and wanted John to baptise him. ¹⁴But John tried to stop him. John said, "Why do you come to me to be baptised? I should be baptised by you!" ¹⁵Jesus answered, "Let it be this way for now. We should do all things that are right." So John agreed to baptise Jesus.

Nazarene A person from the city of Nazareth, a name probably meaning "branch" (see Isaiah 11:1).
The axe . . . fire. This means that God is ready to punish his people who do not obey him.
He will . . . out. This means that Jesus will come to separate the good people from the bad people, saving the good and punishing the bad.

[16]Jesus was baptised and came up out of the water. Heaven opened, and he saw God's Spirit[d] coming down on him like a dove. [17]And a voice spoke from heaven. The voice said, "This is my Son and I love him. I am very pleased with him."

The Temptation of Jesus

4 Then the Spirit[d] led Jesus into the desert to be tempted by the devil. [2]Jesus ate nothing for 40 days and nights. After this, he was very hungry. [3]The devil came to Jesus to tempt him. The devil said, "If you are the Son of God, tell these rocks to become bread."

[4]Jesus answered, "It is written in the Scriptures,[d] 'A person does not live only by eating bread. But a person lives by everything the Lord says'."[n]

[5]Then the devil led Jesus to the holy city of Jerusalem. He put Jesus on a very high place of the Temple.[d] [6]The devil said, "If you are the Son of God, jump off. It is written in the Scriptures,

'He has put his angels in charge of
   you.
They will catch you with their
   hands.
And you will not hit your foot on a
   rock'."   *Psalm 91:11–12*

[7]Jesus answered him, "It also says in the Scriptures, 'Do not test the Lord your God'."[n]

[8]Then the devil led Jesus to the top of a very high mountain. He showed Jesus all the kingdoms of the world and all the great things that are in those kingdoms. [9]The devil said, "If you will bow down and worship me, I will give you all these things."

[10]Jesus said to the devil, "Go away from me, Satan! It is written in the

Scriptures, 'You must worship the Lord your God. Serve only him!'"[n]

[11]So the devil left Jesus. And then some angels came to Jesus and helped him.

Jesus Begins Work in Galilee

[12]Jesus heard that John had been put in prison. So Jesus went back to Galilee. [13]He left Nazareth and went and lived in Capernaum, a town near Lake Galilee. Capernaum is in the area near Zebulun and Naphtali. [14]Jesus did this to make what the prophet[d] Isaiah had said come true:

[15]"Land of Zebulun and land of
      Naphtali
   are on the way to the sea.
They are along the Jordan River.
This is Galilee where the
      non-Jewish people live.
[16]These people who live in darkness
   will see a great light.
They live in a place that is very
   dark.
But a light will shine on them."
                           Isaiah 9:1–2

Jesus Chooses Some Followers

[17]From that time Jesus began to preach, saying, "Change your hearts and lives, because the kingdom of heaven is coming soon."

[18]Jesus was walking by Lake Galilee. He saw two brothers, Simon (called Peter) and Simon's brother Andrew. The brothers were fishermen, and they were fishing in the lake with a net. [19]Jesus said, "Come and follow me. I will make you fishermen for men." [20]At once Simon and Andrew left their nets and followed him.

[21]Jesus continued walking by Lake Galilee. He saw two other brothers,

'A person . . . says'. Quotation from Deuteronomy 8:3.
'Do . . . God'. Quotation from Deuteronomy 6:16.
'You . . . him!' Quotation from Deuteronomy 6:13.

James and John, the sons of Zebedee. They were in a boat with their father Zebedee, preparing their nets to catch fish. Jesus told them to come with him. 22 At once they left the boat and their father, and they followed Jesus.

Jesus Teaches and Heals People

23 Jesus went everywhere in Galilee. He taught in the synagogues[d] and preached the Good News[d] about the kingdom of heaven. And he healed all the people's diseases and sicknesses. 24 The news about Jesus spread all over Syria, and people brought all the sick to him. These sick people were suffering from different kinds of diseases and pain. Some were suffering very great pain, some had demons,[d] some were epileptics,[n] and some were paralysed. Jesus healed all of them. 25 Many people followed him. They came from Galilee, the Ten Towns,[n] Jerusalem, Judea, and the land across the Jordan River.

Jesus Teaches the People

5 Jesus saw the crowds who were there. He went up on a hill and sat down. His followers came to him. 2 Jesus taught the people and said:
3 "Those people who know they
    have great spiritual needs
    are happy.
The kingdom of heaven belongs
    to them.
4 Those who are sad now are
    happy.
God will comfort them.
5 Those who are humble are happy.
The earth will belong to them.

6 Those who want to do right more
    than anything else are
    happy.
God will fully satisfy them.
7 Those who give mercy to others
    are happy.
Mercy will be given to them.
8 Those who are pure in their
    thinking are happy.
They will be with God.
9 Those who work to bring peace
    are happy.
God will call them his sons.
10 Those who are treated badly for
    doing good are happy.
The kingdom of heaven belongs
    to them.
11 "People will say bad things about you and hurt you. They will lie and say all kinds of evil things about you because you follow me. But when they do these things to you, you are happy. 12 Rejoice and be glad. You have a great reward waiting for you in heaven. People did the same evil things to the prophets[d] who lived before you.

You Are like Salt and Light

13 "You are the salt of the earth. But if the salt loses its salty taste, it cannot be made salty again. It is good for nothing. It must be thrown out for people to walk on.
14 "You are the light that gives light to the world. A city that is built on a hill cannot be hidden. 15 And people don't hide a light under a bowl. They put the light on a lampstand. Then the light shines for all the people in the house. 16 In the same way, you should be a light for other people. Live so that they will see the good things you do.

---

epileptics   People with a disease that causes them sometimes to lose control of their bodies, and maybe faint, shake strongly, or not be able to move.
Ten Towns   In Greek, called "Decapolis". It was an area east of Lake Galilee that once had ten main towns.

Live so that they will praise your Father in heaven.

The Importance of the Law

[17] "Don't think that I have come to destroy the law of Moses or the teaching of the prophets.[d] I have not come to destroy their teachings but to do what they said. [18] I tell you the truth. Nothing will disappear from the law until heaven and earth are gone. The law will not lose even the smallest letter or the smallest part of a letter until all has happened. [19] Whoever refuses to obey any command and teaches other people not to obey that command will be the least important in the kingdom of heaven. But whoever obeys the law and teaches other people to obey the law will be great in the kingdom of heaven. [20] I tell you that you must do better than the teachers of the law and the Pharisees.[d] If you are not better than they are, you will not enter the kingdom of heaven.

Jesus Teaches About Anger

[21] "You have heard that it was said to our people long ago, 'You must not murder anyone.'[n] Anyone who murders another will be judged'. [22] But I tell you, if you are angry with your brother, you will be judged. And if you say bad things to your brother, you will be judged by the Jewish council. And if you call your brother a fool, then you will be in danger of the fire of hell.

[23] "So when you offer your gift to God at the altar, and you remember that your brother has something against you, [24] leave your gift there at the altar. Go and make peace with him. Then come and offer your gift.

Matthew 5:24 "Go and make peace with him."

[25] "If your enemy is taking you to court, become friends with him quickly. You should do that before you go to court. If you don't become his friend, he might turn you over to the judge. And the judge might give you to a guard to put you in jail. [26] I tell you that you will not leave that jail until you have paid everything you owe.

Jesus Teaches About Sexual Sin

[27] "You have heard that it was said, 'You must not be guilty of adultery'.[n] [28] But I tell you that if anyone looks at a woman and wants to sin sexually with her, then he has already done that sin with the woman in his mind. [29] If your right eye causes you to sin, then take it out and throw it away. It is better to lose one part of your body than to have your whole body thrown into hell. [30] If your right hand causes you to sin, then cut it off and throw it

'You . . . anyone'. Quotation from Exodus 20:13; Deuteronomy 5:17.
'You . . . adultery'. Quotation from Exodus 20:14; Deuteronomy 5:18.

away. It is better to lose one part of your body than for your whole body to go into hell.

Jesus Teaches About Divorce

[31] "It was also said, 'Anyone who divorces his wife must give her a written divorce paper'.[n] [32] But I tell you that anyone who divorces his wife is causing his wife to be guilty of adultery.[d] The only reason for a man to divorce his wife is if she has sexual relations with another man. And anyone who marries that divorced woman is guilty of adultery.

Make Promises Carefully

[33] "You have heard that it was said to our people long ago, 'When you make a promise, don't break your promise. Keep the promises that you make to the Lord'.[n] [34] But I tell you, never make an oath. Don't make an oath using the name of heaven, because heaven is God's throne. [35] Don't make an oath using the name of the earth, because the earth belongs to God. Don't make an oath using the name of Jerusalem, because that is the city of the great King. [36] And don't even say that your own head is proof that you will keep your oath. You cannot make one hair on your head become white or black. [37] Say only 'yes' if you mean 'yes', and say only 'no' if you mean 'no'. If you must say more than 'yes' or 'no', it is from the Evil One.

Don't Fight Back

[38] "You have heard that it was said, 'An eye for an eye, and a tooth for a tooth'.[n] [39] But I tell you, don't stand up against an evil person. If someone slaps you on the right cheek, then turn and let him slap the other cheek too. [40] If someone wants to sue you in court and take your shirt, then let him have your coat too. [41] If a soldier forces you to go with him one mile, then go with him two miles. [42] If a person asks you for something, then give it to him. Don't refuse to give to a person who wants to borrow from you.

Love All People

[43] "You have heard that it was said, 'Love your neighbour[n] and hate your enemies'. [44] But I tell you, love your enemies. Pray for those who hurt you. [45] If you do this, then you will be true sons of your Father in heaven. Your Father causes the sun to rise on good people and on bad people. Your Father sends rain to those who do good and to those who do wrong. [46] If you love only the people who love you, then you will get no reward. Even the tax collectors do that. [47] And if you are nice only to your friends, then you are no better than other people. Even people without God are nice to their friends. [48] So you must be perfect, just as your Father in heaven is perfect.

Jesus Teaches About Giving

6 "Be careful! When you do good things, don't do them in front of people to be seen by them. If you do that, then you will have no reward from your Father in heaven.

[2] "When you give to the poor, don't be like the hypocrites.[d] They blow trumpets before they give so that people will see them. They do that in the synagogues[d] and on the streets. They want other people to honour

---

'Anyone . . . divorce paper'.   Quotation from Deuteronomy 24:1.
'When . . . Lord'.   Quotation from Leviticus 19:12; Numbers 30:2; Deuteronomy 23:21.
'An eye . . . tooth'.   Quotation from Exodus 21:24; Leviticus 24:20; Deuteronomy 19:21.
'Love your neighbour'   Quotation from Leviticus 19:18.

them. I tell you the truth. Those hypocrites already have their full reward. ³So when you give to the poor, give very secretly. Don't let anyone know what you are doing. ⁴Your giving should be done in secret. Your Father can see what is done in secret, and he will reward you.

Jesus Teaches About Prayer

⁵"When you pray, don't be like the hypocrites.ᵈ They love to stand in the synagoguesᵈ and on the street corners and pray loudly. They want people to see them pray. I tell you the truth. They already have their full reward. ⁶When you pray, you should go into your room and close the door. Then pray to your Father who cannot be seen. Your Father can see what is done in secret, and he will reward you.

⁷"And when you pray, don't be like those people who don't know God. They continue saying things that mean nothing. They think that God will hear them because of the many things they say. ⁸Don't be like them. Your Father knows the things you need before you ask him. ⁹So when you pray, you should pray like this:
'Our Father in heaven,
we pray that your name will
always be kept holy.
¹⁰We pray that your kingdom will
come.
We pray that what you want will
be done,
here on earth as it is in heaven.
¹¹Give us the food we need for each
day.
¹²Forgive the sins we have done,
just as we have forgiven those
who did wrong to us.
¹³Do not cause us to be tested;
but save us from the Evil One'.

¹⁴Yes, if you forgive others for the things they do wrong, then your Father in heaven will also forgive you for the things you do wrong. ¹⁵But if you don't forgive the wrongs of others, then your Father in heaven will not forgive the wrong things you do.

Jesus Teaches About Worship

¹⁶"When you give up eating,ⁿ don't put on a sad face like the hypocrites.ᵈ They make their faces look strange to show people that they are giving up eating. I tell you the truth, those hypocrites already have their full reward. ¹⁷So when you give up eating, comb your hair and wash your face. ¹⁸Then people will not know that you are giving up eating. But your Father, whom you cannot see, will see you. Your Father sees what is done in secret, and he will reward you.

God Is More Important than Money

¹⁹"Don't store treasures for yourselves here on earth. Moths and rust will destroy treasures here on earth. And thieves can break into your house and steal the things you have. ²⁰So store your treasure in heaven. The treasures in heaven cannot be destroyed by moths or rust. And thieves cannot break in and steal that treasure. ²¹Your heart will be where your treasure is.

²²"The eye is a light for the body. If your eyes are good, then your whole body will be full of light. ²³But if your eyes are evil, then your whole body will be full of darkness. And if the only light you have is really darkness, then you have the worst darkness.

²⁴"No one can be a slave to two masters. He will hate one master and love the other. Or he will follow one

---

give up eating This is called "fasting". The people would give up eating for a special time of prayer and worship to God. It was also done to show sadness.

master and refuse to follow the other. So you cannot serve God and money at the same time.

Don't Worry

25 "So I tell you, don't worry about the food you need to live. And don't worry about the clothes you need for your body. Life is more important than food. And the body is more important than clothes. 26 Look at the birds in the air. They don't plant or harvest or store food in barns. But your heavenly Father feeds the birds. And you know that you are worth much more than the birds. 27 You cannot add any time to your life by worrying about it. 28 "And why do you worry about clothes? Look at the flowers in the field. See how they grow. They don't work or make clothes for themselves. 29 But I tell you that even Solomon with his riches was not dressed as beautifully as one of these flowers. 30 God clothes the grass in the field like that. The grass is living today, but tomorrow it is thrown into the fire to be burned. So you can be even more sure that God will clothe you. Don't have so little faith! 31 Don't worry and say, 'What will we eat?' or 'What will we drink?' or 'What will we wear?' 32 All the people who don't know God keep trying to get these things. And your Father in heaven knows that you need them. 33 The thing you should want most is God's kingdom and doing what God wants. Then all these other things you need will be given to you. 34 So don't worry about tomorrow. Each day has enough trouble of its own. Tomorrow will have its own worries.

Be Careful About Judging Others

7 "Don't judge other people, and you will not be judged. 2 You will be judged in the same way that you judge others. And the forgiveness you give to others will be given to you.

3 "Why do you notice the little piece of dust that is in your brother's eye, but you don't notice the big piece of wood that is in your own eye? 4 Why do you say to your brother, 'Let me take that little piece of dust out of your eye'? Look at yourself first! You still have that big piece of wood in your own eye. 5 You are a hypocrite!^{d} First, take the wood out of your own eye. Then you will see clearly enough to take the dust out of your brother's eye.

6 "Don't give holy things to dogs. Don't throw your pearls before pigs. Pigs will only trample on them. And the dogs will only turn to attack you.

Ask God for What You Need

7 "Continue to ask, and God will give to you. Continue to search, and you will find. Continue to knock, and the door will open for you. 8 Yes, everyone who continues asking will receive. He who continues searching will find. And he who continues knocking will have the door opened for him.

9 "What would you do if your son asks for bread? Which of you would give him a stone? 10 Or if your son asks for a fish, would you give him a snake? 11 Even though you are bad, you know how to give good gifts to your children. So surely your heavenly Father will give good things to those who ask him.

The Most Important Rule

12 "Do for other people the same things you want them to do for you. This is the meaning of the law of Moses and the teaching of the prophets.^{d}

The Way to Heaven Is Hard

13 "Enter through the narrow gate. The road that leads to hell is a very

easy road. And the gate to hell is very wide. Many people enter through that gate. [14] But the gate that opens the way to true life is very small. And the road to true life is very hard. Only a few people find that road.

People Know You by Your Actions

[15] "Be careful of false prophets.[d] They come to you and look gentle like sheep. But they are really dangerous like wolves. [16] You will know these people because of the things they do. Good things don't come from bad people, just as grapes don't come from thorn bushes. And figs don't come from thorny weeds. [17] In the same way, every good tree produces good fruit, and bad trees produce bad fruit. [18] A good tree cannot produce bad fruit, and a bad tree cannot produce good fruit. [19] Every tree that does not produce good fruit is cut down and thrown into the fire. [20] You will know these false prophets by what they produce.

[21] "Not everyone who says that I am his Lord will enter the kingdom of heaven. The only people who will enter the kingdom of heaven are those who do the things that my Father in heaven wants. [22] On the last day many people will say to me, 'You are our Lord! We spoke for you. And through you we forced out demons[d] and did many miracles'.[d] [23] Then I will tell them clearly, 'Get away from me, you who do evil. I never knew you'.

Two Kinds of People

[24] "Everyone who hears these things I say and obeys them is like a wise man. The wise man built his house on rock. [25] It rained hard and the water rose. The winds blew and hit that house. But the house did not fall, because the house was built on rock. [26] But the person who hears the

things I teach and does not obey them is like a foolish man. The foolish man built his house on sand. [27] It rained hard, the water rose, and the winds blew and hit that house. And the house fell with a big crash."

[28] When Jesus finished saying these things, the people were amazed at his teaching. [29] Jesus did not teach like their teachers of the law. He taught like a person who had authority.

Jesus Heals a Sick Man

8 When Jesus came down from the hill, great crowds followed him. [2] Then a man sick with a harmful skin disease came to Jesus. The man bowed down before him and said, "Lord, you have the power to heal me if you want."

[3] Jesus touched the man and said, "I want to heal you. Be healed!" And immediately the man was healed from his skin disease. [4] Then Jesus said to him, "Don't tell anyone about what

Matthew 8:3 Jesus touched the man and said, "I want to heal you. Be healed!"

happened. But go and show yourself to the priest.ⁿ And offer the gift that Moses commandedⁿ for people who are made well. This will show people that you are healed."

Jesus Heals a Soldier's Servant

5 Jesus went to the city of Capernaum. When he entered the city, an army officer came to Jesus and begged for help. 6 The officer said, "Lord, my servant is at home in bed. He can't move his body and is in much pain."

7 Jesus said to the officer, "I will go and heal him."

8 The officer answered, "Lord, I am not good enough for you to come into my house. All you need to do is command that my servant be healed, and he will be healed. 9 I myself am a man under the authority of other men. And I have soldiers under my command. I tell one soldier, 'Go', and he goes. I tell another soldier, 'Come', and he comes. I say to my servant, 'Do this', and my servant obeys me.

10 When Jesus heard this, he was amazed. He said to those who were with him, "I tell you the truth. This man has more faith than any other person I have found, even in Israel. 11 Many people will come from the east and from the west. They will sit and eat with Abraham, Isaac, and Jacob in the kingdom of heaven. 12 And those people who should have the kingdom will be thrown outside into the darkness. In that place people will cry and grind their teeth with pain."

13 Then Jesus said to the officer, "Go home. Your servant will be healed just as you believed he would." And at that same time his servant was healed.

Jesus Heals Many People

14 Jesus went to Peter's house. There Jesus saw that Peter's mother-in-law was in bed with a high fever. 15 Jesus touched her hand, and the fever left her. Then she stood up and began to serve Jesus.

16 That evening people brought to Jesus many who had demons.ᵈ Jesus spoke and the demons left them. Jesus healed all the sick. 17 He did these things to make what Isaiah the prophetᵈ had said come true:

"He took our suffering on him.
And he felt our pain for us."

Isaiah 53:4

People Want to Follow Jesus

18 When Jesus saw the crowd around him, he told his followers to go to the other side of the lake. 19 Then a teacher of the law came to Jesus and said, "Teacher, I will follow you wherever you go."

20 Jesus said to him, "The foxes have holes to live in. The birds have nests to live in. But the Son of Manᵈ has no place where he can rest his head."

21 Another man, one of Jesus' followers, said to Jesus, "Lord, let me go and bury my father first."

22 But Jesus said to him, "Follow me, and let the people who are dead bury their own dead."

Jesus Stops a Storm

23 Jesus got into a boat, and his followers went with him. 24 A very bad storm arose on the lake. The waves covered the boat. But Jesus was sleeping. 25 The followers went to Jesus and woke him. They said, "Lord, save us! We will drown!"

---

show . . . priest The law of Moses said a priest must say when a Jew who had a harmful skin disease was well.
Moses commanded Read about this in Leviticus 14:1–32.

[26] Jesus answered, "Why are you afraid? You don't have enough faith." Then Jesus got up and gave a command to the wind and the sea. The wind stopped, and the sea became very calm. [27] The men were amazed. They said, "What kind of man is this? Even the wind and the sea obey him!"

Jesus Heals Two Men with Demons

[28] Jesus arrived at the other side of the lake in the country of the Gadarene[n] people. There, two men came to Jesus. They had demons[d] in them. These men lived in the burial caves. They were so dangerous that people could not use the road by those caves. [29] The two men came to Jesus and shouted, "What do you want with us, Son of God? Did you come here to punish us before the right time?" [30] Near that place there was a large herd of pigs feeding. [31] The demons begged Jesus, "If you make us leave these men, please send us into that herd of pigs." [32] Jesus said to them, "Go!" So the demons left the men and went into the pigs. Then the whole herd of pigs ran down the hill into the lake and were drowned. [33] The men who were caring for the pigs ran away and went into town. They told about all of this and what had happened to the men who had demons. [34] Then the whole town went out to see Jesus. When they saw him, they begged him to leave their area.

Jesus Heals a Paralysed Man

9 Jesus got into a boat and went back across the lake to his own town. [2] Some people brought to Jesus a man who was paralysed. The man was lying on his mat. Jesus saw that these people had great faith, so he said to the paralysed man, "Be happy, young man. Your sins are forgiven." [3] Some of the teachers of the law heard this. They said to themselves, "This man speaks as if he were God – that is blasphemy!"[n] [4] Jesus knew what they were thinking. So he said, "Why are you thinking evil thoughts? [5] Which is easier: to tell this paralysed man, 'Your sins are forgiven', or to tell him, 'Stand up and walk'? [6] But I will prove to you that the Son of Man[d] has power on earth to forgive sins." Then Jesus said to the paralysed man, "Stand up. Take your mat and go home." [7] And the man stood up and went home. [8] The people saw this and were amazed. They praised God for giving power like this to men.

Jesus Chooses Matthew

[9] When Jesus was leaving, he saw a man named Matthew. Matthew was sitting in the tax office. Jesus said to him, "Follow me." And Matthew stood up and followed Jesus. [10] Jesus had dinner at Matthew's house. Many tax collectors and "sinners" came and ate with Jesus and his followers. [11] The Pharisees[d] saw this and asked Jesus' followers, "Why does your teacher eat with tax collectors and 'sinners'?" [12] Jesus heard the Pharisees ask this. So he said, "Healthy people don't need a doctor. Only the sick need a doctor. [13] Go and learn what this means: 'I want faithful love more than I want animal sacrifices'.[n] I did not

---

Gadarene From Gadara, an area southeast of Lake Galilee.
blasphemy Saying things against God.
'I want . . . sacrifices'. Quotation from Hosea 6:6.

come to invite good people. I came to invite sinners".

Jesus Is Not like Other Jews

[14]Then the followers of John[n] came to Jesus. They said to Jesus, "We and the Pharisees[d] often give up eating.[n] But your followers don't. Why?" [15]Jesus answered, "The friends of the bridegroom are not sad while he is with them. But the time will come when the bridegroom will leave them. Then his friends are sad, and they will give up eating.

[16]"When someone sews a patch over a hole in an old coat, he never uses a piece of cloth that is not yet shrunk. If he does, the patch will shrink and pull away from the coat. Then the hole will be worse. [17]Also, people never pour new wine into old leather bags for holding wine. If they do, the old bags will break. The wine will spill, and the wine bags will be ruined. But people always pour new wine into new wine bags. Then the wine and the wine bags will continue to be good."

Jesus Gives Life to a Dead Girl and Heals a Sick Woman

[18]While Jesus was saying these things, a ruler of the synagogue[d] came to him. The ruler bowed down before Jesus and said, "My daughter has just died. But come and touch her with your hand, and she will live again." [19]So Jesus stood up and went with the ruler. Jesus' followers went too. [20]Then a woman who had been bleeding for 12 years came behind Jesus and touched the edge of his coat. [21]She was thinking, "If I can touch his coat, then I will be healed." [22]Jesus turned and saw the woman. He said, "Be happy, dear woman. You are made well because you believed." And the woman was healed at once. [23]Jesus continued along with the ruler and went into the ruler's house. Jesus saw people there who play music for funerals. And he saw many people there crying. [24]Jesus said, "Go away. The girl is not dead. She is only asleep." But the people laughed at Jesus. [25]After the crowd had been put outside, Jesus went into the girl's room. He took her hand, and she stood up. [26]The news about this spread all around the area.

Jesus Heals More People

[27]When Jesus was leaving there, two blind men followed him. They cried out, "Show kindness to us, Son of David!"[d] [28]Jesus went inside, and the blind men went with him. He asked the men, "Do you believe that I can make you see again?"

They answered, "Yes, Lord."

[29]Then Jesus touched their eyes and said, "You believe that I can make you see again. So this will happen." [30]Then the men were able to see. But Jesus warned them very strongly, saying, "Don't tell anyone about this." [31]But the blind men left and spread the news about Jesus all around that area.

[32]When the two men were leaving, some people brought another man to Jesus. This man could not talk because he had a demon[d] in him. [33]Jesus forced the demon to leave the man. Then the man who couldn't talk was able to speak. The crowd was amazed

---

John John the Baptist, who preached to people about Christ's coming (Matthew 3, Luke 3).
give up eating This is called "fasting". The people would give up eating for a special time of prayer and worship to God. It was also done to show sadness.

and said, "We have never seen anything like this in Israel."

[34] But the Pharisees[d] said, "The leader of demons is the one that gives him power to force demons out."

[35] Jesus travelled through all the towns and villages. He taught in their synagogues[d] and told people the Good News[d] about the kingdom. And he healed all kinds of diseases and sicknesses. [36] He saw the crowds of people and felt sorry for them because they were worried and helpless. They were like sheep without a shepherd. [37] Jesus said to his followers, "There are many people to harvest, but there are only a few workers to help harvest them. [38] God owns the harvest. Pray to him that he will send more workers to help gather his harvest."[n]

Jesus Sends Out His Apostles

10 Jesus called his 12 followers together. He gave them power to drive out evil spirits and to heal every kind of disease and sickness. [2] These are the names of the 12 apostles:[d] Simon (also called Peter) and his brother Andrew; James son of Zebedee, and his brother John; [3] Philip and Bartholomew; Thomas and Matthew, the tax collector; James son of Alphaeus, and Thaddaeus; [4] Simon the Zealot[d] and Judas Iscariot. Judas is the one who turned against Jesus.

[5] These 12 men he sent out with the following order: "Don't go to the non-Jewish people. And don't go into any town where the Samaritans[d] live. [6] But go to the people of Israel. They are like sheep that are lost. [7] When you go, preach this: 'The kingdom of heaven is coming soon'. [8] Heal the sick. Give dead people life again. Heal those who have harmful skin diseases. Force demons[d] to leave people. I give you these powers freely. So help other people freely. [9] Don't carry any money with you – gold or silver or copper. [10] Don't carry a bag. Take for your trip only the clothes and sandals you are wearing. Don't take a walking stick. A worker should be given the things he needs.

[11] "When you enter a city or town, find some worthy person there and stay in his home until you leave. [12] When you enter that home, say, 'Peace be with you'. [13] If the people there welcome you, let your peace stay there. But if they don't welcome you, take back the peace you wished for them. [14] And if a home or town refuses to welcome you or listen to you, then

"**There are . . . harvest.**"   As a farmer sends workers to harvest the grain, Jesus sends his followers to bring people to God.

Matthew 10:1 Jesus called his 12 followers together.

leave that place. Shake its dust off your feet.[n] [15]I tell you the truth. On the Judgement Day it will be worse for that town than for the towns of Sodom and Gomorrah.[n]

Jesus Warns His Apostles

[16]"Listen! I am sending you out, and you will be like sheep among wolves. So be as clever as snakes. But also be like doves and do nothing wrong. [17]Be careful of people. They will arrest you and take you to court. They will whip you in their synagogues.[d] [18]Because of me you will be taken to stand before governors and kings. You will tell them and the non-Jewish people about me. [19]When you are arrested, don't worry about what to say or how you should say it. At that time you will be given the things to say. [20]It will not really be you speaking. The Spirit of your Father will be speaking through you.

[21]"Brothers will turn against their own brothers and give them over to be killed. Fathers will turn against their own children and give them to be killed. Children will fight against their own parents and have them killed. [22]All people will hate you because you follow me. But the person who continues strong until the end will be saved. [23]When you are treated badly in one city, go to another city. I tell you the truth. You will not finish going through all the cities of Israel before the Son of Man[d] comes.

[24]"A student is not better than his teacher. A servant is not better than his master. [25]A student should be satisfied to become like his teacher. A servant should be satisfied to become like his master. If the head of the family is called Beelzebul,[d] then the other members of the family will be called worse names!

Fear God, Not People

[26]"So don't be afraid of those people. Everything that is hidden will be shown. Everything that is secret will be made known. [27]I tell you these things in the dark, but I want you to tell them in the light. I speak these things only to you, but you should tell them to everyone. [28]Don't be afraid of people. They can only kill the body. They cannot kill the soul. The only one you should fear is the One who can destroy the body and the soul in hell. [29]When birds are sold, two small birds cost only a penny. But not even one of the little birds can die without your Father's knowing it. [30]God even knows how many hairs are on your head. [31]So don't be afraid. You are worth much more than many birds.

Tell People About Your Faith

[32]"If anyone stands before other people and says he believes in me, then I will say that he belongs to me. I will say this before my Father in heaven. [33]But if anyone stands before people and says he does not believe in me, then I will say that he does not belong to me. I will say this before my Father in heaven.

[34]"Don't think that I have come to bring peace to the earth. I did not come to bring peace, but a sword. [35]I have come to make this happen:
'A son will be against his father,
   a daughter will be against her mother,
a daughter-in-law will be against her mother-in-law.

Shake . . . feet. A warning. It showed that they had finished talking to these people.
Sodom and Gomorrah Two cities that God destroyed because the people were so evil.

36 A person's enemies will be members of his own family'.

Micah 7:6

37 "Whoever loves his father or mother more than he loves me is not worthy to be my follower. Whoever loves his son or daughter more than he loves me is not worthy to be my follower. 38 Whoever is not willing to die on a cross and follow me is not worthy of me. 39 Whoever tries to hold on to his life will give up true life. Whoever gives up his life for me will hold on to true life. 40 Whoever accepts you also accepts me. And whoever accepts me also accepts the One who sent me. 41 Whoever meets a prophet*d* and accepts him will receive the reward of a prophet. And whoever accepts a good man because that man is good will receive the reward of a good man. 42 Whoever helps one of these little ones because they are my followers will truly get his reward. He will get his reward even if he only gave my follower a cup of cold water."

Jesus and John the Baptist

11 Jesus finished telling these things to his 12 followers. Then he left there and went to the towns in Galilee to teach and preach.

2 John the Baptist*d* was in prison, but he heard about the things Christ was doing. So John sent some of his followers to Jesus. 3 They asked Jesus, "Are you the man who John said was coming, or should we wait for another one?"

4 Jesus answered, "Go back to John and tell him about the things you hear and see: 5 The blind can see. The crippled can walk. People with harmful skin diseases are healed. The deaf can hear. The dead are raised to life. And the Good News*d* is told to the poor. 6 The person who does not lose faith because of me is blessed."

7 As John's followers were leaving, Jesus began talking to the people about John. Jesus said, "What did you go out to the desert to see? A reed*n* blown by the wind? No. 8 Really, what did you go out to see? A man dressed in fine clothes? No. Those people who wear fine clothes live in kings' palaces. 9 So what did you go out to see? A prophet?*d* Yes, and I tell you, John is more than a prophet. 10 This was written about John in the Scriptures:*d*

'I will send my messenger ahead
     of you.
He will prepare the way for you'.

Malachi 3:1

11 I tell you the truth: John the Baptist is greater than any other man who has ever lived. But even the least important person in the kingdom of heaven is greater than John. 12 Since the time John the Baptist came until now, the kingdom of heaven has been going forwards in strength. People using force have been trying to take the kingdom. 13 All the prophets and the law of Moses spoke until the time John came. They told about the things that would happen. 14 And if you will believe the things the law and the prophets said, then you will believe that John is Elijah. The law and the prophets said he would come. 15 You people who hear me, listen!

16 "What can I say about the people who live today? What are they like? They are like children sitting in the market place. One group calls to the other,

17 'We played music for you, but you
     did not dance;
we sang a sad song, but you did
     not cry'.

18 John came, and he did not eat like

---

reed It means that John was not weak like grass blown by the wind.

other people or drink wine. And people say, 'He has a demon'.[d] [19]The Son of Man[d] came, eating and drinking wine, and people say, 'Look at him! He eats too much and drinks too much. He is a friend of tax collectors and "sinners".' But wisdom is proved to be right by the things it does."

Jesus Warns Unbelievers

[20]Then Jesus criticised the cities where he did most of his miracles.[d] He criticised them because the people there did not change their lives and stop sinning. [21]Jesus said, "How terrible for you, Korazin! How terrible for you, Bethsaida! I did many miracles in you. If those same miracles had happened in Tyre and Sidon,[n] then the people there would have changed their lives a long time ago. They would have worn rough cloth and put ashes on themselves to show that they had changed. [22]But I tell you, on the Judgement Day it will be worse for you than for Tyre and Sidon. [23]And you, Capernaum,[n] will you be lifted up to heaven? No. You will be thrown down to the depths. I did many miracles in you. If those same miracles had happened in Sodom,[n] its people would have stopped sinning, and it would still be a city today. [24]But I tell you it will be worse for you on the Judgement Day than for Sodom."

Jesus Offers Rest to People

[25]Then Jesus said, "I thank you, Father, Lord of heaven and earth. I praise you because you have hidden these things from the people who are wise and clever. But you have shown them to those who are like little children. [26]Yes, Father, this is what you really wanted.

[27]"My Father has given me all things. No one knows the Son – only the Father knows the Son. And no one knows the Father – only the Son knows the Father. And the only people who will know about the Father are those whom the Son chooses to tell. [28]"Come to me, all of you who are tired and have heavy loads. I will give you rest. [29]Accept my work and learn from me. I am gentle and humble in spirit. And you will find rest for your souls. [30]The work that I ask you to accept is easy. The load I give you to carry is not heavy."

Jesus Is Lord of the Sabbath

12 About that same time, Jesus was walking through some fields of grain on a Sabbath[d] day. His followers were with him, and they were hungry. So they began to pick the grain and eat it. [2]The Pharisees[d] saw this, and they said to Jesus, "Look! Your followers are doing something that is against the Jewish law to do on the Sabbath day."

[3]Jesus answered, "Have you not read what David did when he and the people with him were hungry? [4]David went into God's house. He and those with him ate the bread that was made holy for God. It was against the law for them to eat that bread. Only the priests were allowed to eat it. [5]And have you not read in the law of Moses that on every Sabbath day the priests in the Temple[d] break this law about the Sabbath day? But the priests are not wrong for doing that. [6]I tell you that there is something here that is greater than the Temple. [7]The

---

Tyre and Sidon   Towns where wicked people lived.
Korazin, Bethsaida, Capernaum   Towns by Lake Galilee where Jesus preached to the people.
Sodom   City that God destroyed because the people were so evil.

Scripture[d] says, 'I want faithful love more than I want animal sacrifices'.[n] You don't really know what those words mean. If you understood them, you would not judge those who have done nothing wrong. [8]"The Son of Man[d] is Lord of the Sabbath day."

Jesus Heals a Man's Crippled Hand

[9]Jesus left there and went into their synagogue.[d] [10]In the synagogue, there was a man with a crippled hand. Some Jews there were looking for a reason to accuse Jesus of doing wrong. So they asked him, "Is it right to heal on the Sabbath[d] day?"[n]

[11]Jesus answered, "If any of you has a sheep, and it falls into a ditch on the Sabbath day, then you will take the sheep and help it out of the ditch. [12]Surely a man is more important than a sheep. So the law of Moses allows people to do good things on the Sabbath day."

[13]Then Jesus said to the man with the crippled hand, "Let me see your hand." The man put his hand out, and the hand became well again, the same as the other hand. [14]But the Pharisees[d] left and made plans to kill Jesus.

Jesus Is God's Chosen Servant

[15]Jesus knew what the Pharisees[d] were doing, so he left that place. Many people followed him, and he healed all who were sick. [16]But Jesus warned the people not to tell who he was. [17]He did these things to make what Isaiah the prophet[d] had said come true:
[18]"Here is my servant whom I have chosen.

I love him, and I am pleased with him.
I will put my Spirit[d] in him.
Then he will tell how I will judge all people fairly.
[19]He will not argue or shout.
No one will hear his voice in the streets.
[20]He will not break a crushed blade of grass.
He will not put out even a weak flame.
He will continue until he makes fair judgement win the victory.
[21]   In him will the nations find hope."   *Isaiah 42:1-4*

Jesus' Power Is from God

[22]Then some people brought a man to Jesus. This man was blind and could not talk, because he had a demon.[d] Jesus healed the man, and the man could talk and see. [23]All the people were amazed. They said, "Perhaps this man is the Son of David!"[d]

[24]The Pharisees[d] heard the people saying this. The Pharisees said, "Jesus uses the power of Beelzebul[d] to force demons out of people. Beelzebul is the ruler of demons."

[25]Jesus knew what the Pharisees were thinking. So he said to them, "Every kingdom that is fighting against itself will be destroyed. And every city that is divided will fall. And every family that is divided cannot succeed. [26]So if Satan forces out his own demons, then Satan is divided, and his kingdom will not continue. [27]You say that I use the power of Satan when I force out demons. If that is true, then what power do your people use when they force out demons? So your own people prove that you are

---

'I . . . sacrifices'. Quotation from Hosea 6:6.
"Is it right . . . day?" It was against Jewish law to work on the Sabbath day.

wrong. [28] But if I use the power of God's Spirit[d] to force out demons, this shows that the kingdom of God has come to you.

[29] "If anyone wants to enter a strong man's house and steal his things, first he must tie up the strong man. Then he can steal the things from the strong man's house.

[30] "If anyone is not with me, then he is against me. He who does not work with me is working against me. [31] So I tell you, people can be forgiven for every sin they do. And people can be forgiven for every bad thing they say. But if anyone speaks against the Holy Spirit, then he will not be forgiven. [32] Anyone who says things against the Son of Man[d] can be forgiven. But anyone who says things against the Holy Spirit will not be forgiven. He will not be forgiven now or in the future.

People Know You by Your Words

[33] "If you want good fruit, you must make the tree good. If your tree is not good, then it will have bad fruit. A tree is known by the kind of fruit it produces. [34] You snakes! You are evil people! How can you say anything good? The mouth speaks the things that are in the heart. [35] A good person has good things in his heart. And so he speaks the good things that come from his heart. But an evil person has evil in his heart. So he speaks the evil things that come from his heart. [36] And I tell you that people will have to explain about every careless thing they have said. This will happen on the Judgement Day. [37] The words you have said will be used to judge you. Some of your words will prove you right, but some of your words will prove you guilty."

The Leaders Ask for a Miracle

[38] Then some of the Pharisees[d] and teachers of the law answered Jesus. They said, "Teacher, we want to see you work a miracle[d] as a sign."

[39] Jesus answered, "Evil and sinful people are the ones who want to see a miracle for a sign. But no sign will be given to them. The only sign will be what happened to the prophet[d] Jonah. [40] Jonah was in the stomach of the big fish for three days and three nights. In the same way, the Son of Man[d] will be in the grave three days and three nights. [41] And on the Judgement Day the men from Nineveh[n] will stand up with you people who live today. They will show that you are guilty because when Jonah preached to them, they were sorry and changed their lives. And I tell you that someone greater than Jonah is here! [42] On the Judgement Day, the Queen of the South[n] will stand up with you people who live today. She will show that you are guilty because she came from far away to listen to Solomon's wise teaching. And I tell you that someone greater than Solomon is here!

People Today Are Full of Evil

[43] "When an evil spirit comes out of a man, it travels through dry places looking for a place to rest. But it finds no place to rest. [44] So the spirit says, 'I will go back to the home I left'. When the spirit comes back to the man, the spirit finds the home still empty. The home is swept clean and made neat. [45] Then the evil spirit goes out and brings seven other spirits even more

Nineveh   The city where Jonah preached to warn the people. Read Jonah 3.
Queen of the South   The Queen of Sheba. She travelled 1,000 miles to learn God's wisdom from Solomon. Read 1 Kings 10:1–13.

evil than it is. Then all the spirits go into the man and live there. And that man has even more trouble than he had before. It is the same way with the evil people who live today."

Jesus' True Family

⁴⁶While Jesus was talking to the people, his mother and brothers stood outside. They wanted to talk to him. ⁴⁷Someone told Jesus, "Your mother and brothers are waiting for you outside. They want to talk to you." ⁴⁸He answered, "Who is my mother? Who are my brothers?" ⁴⁹Then he pointed to his followers and said, "See! These people are my mother and my brothers. ⁵⁰My true brothers and sisters and mother are those who do the things that my Father in heaven wants."

A Story About Planting Seed

13 That same day Jesus went out of the house and sat by the lake. ²Large crowds gathered around him. So Jesus got into a boat and sat, while the people stayed on the shore. ³Then Jesus used stories to teach them many things. He said: "A farmer went out to plant his seed. ⁴While he was planting, some seed fell by the road. The birds came and ate all that seed. ⁵Some seed fell on rocky ground, where there wasn't enough soil. That seed grew very fast, because the ground was not deep. ⁶But when the sun rose, the plants dried up because they did not have deep roots. ⁷Some other seed fell among thorny weeds. The weeds grew and choked the good plants. ⁸Some other seed fell on good ground where it grew and became grain. Some plants made 100 times more grain. Other plants made 60 times more grain, and some made 30 times more grain. ⁹You people who hear me, listen!"

Matthew 13:4 "The birds came and ate all that seed."

Why Jesus Used Stories to Teach

¹⁰The followers came to Jesus and asked, "Why do you use stories to teach the people?"

¹¹Jesus answered, "Only you can know the secret truths about the kingdom of heaven. Other people cannot know these secret truths. ¹²The person who has something will be given more. And he will have all he needs. But the person who does not have much, even what he has will be taken from him. ¹³This is why I use stories to teach the people: they see, but they don't really see. They hear, but they don't really understand. ¹⁴So they show that the things Isaiah said about them are true:

'You will listen and listen, but you
    will not understand.
You will look and look, but you
    will not learn.
¹⁵For these people have become
    stubborn.

They do not hear with their
ears.
And they have closed their
eyes.
Otherwise they might really
understand
what they see with their eyes
and hear with their ears.
They might really understand in
their minds.
If they did this, they would
come back to me and be
forgiven'.   *Isaiah 6:9–10*
[16] But you are blessed. You understand
the things you see with your eyes. And
you understand the things you hear
with your ears. [17] I tell you the truth.
Many prophets[d] and good people
wanted to see the things that you now
see, but they did not see them. And
many prophets and good people
wanted to hear the things that you now
hear, but they did not hear them.

Jesus Explains the Seed Story

[18] "So listen to the meaning of that
story about the farmer. [19] What is the
seed that fell by the road? That seed
is like the person who hears the teaching about the kingdom but does not
understand it. The Evil One comes
and takes away the things that were
planted in that person's heart. [20] And
what is the seed that fell on rocky
ground? That seed is like the person
who hears the teaching and quickly
accepts it with joy. [21] But he does not
let the teaching go deep into his life.
He keeps it only a short time. When
trouble or persecution comes because
of the teaching he accepted, then he
quickly gives up. [22] And what is the
seed that fell among the thorny
weeds? That seed is like the person
who hears the teaching but lets
worries about this life and love of

money stop that teaching from growing. So the teaching does not produce
fruit[n] in that person's life. [23] But what
is the seed that fell on the good
ground? That seed is like the person
who hears the teaching and understands it. That person grows and produces fruit, sometimes 100 times
more, sometimes 60 times more, and
sometimes 30 times more."

A Story About Wheat and Weeds

[24] Then Jesus told them another
story. He said, "The kingdom of
heaven is like a man who planted good
seed in his field. [25] That night, when
everyone was asleep, his enemy came
and planted weeds among the wheat.
Then the enemy went away. [26] Later,
the wheat grew and heads of grain
grew on the wheat plants. But at the
same time the weeds also grew.
[27] Then the man's servants came to
him and said, 'You planted good seed in
your field. Where did the weeds come
from?' [28] The man answered, 'An
enemy planted weeds'. The servants
asked, 'Do you want us to pull up the
weeds?' [29] The man answered, 'No,
because when you pull up the weeds,
you might also pull up the wheat. [30] Let
the weeds and the wheat grow together
until the harvest time. At harvest time
I will tell the workers this: first gather
the weeds and tie them together to be
burned. Then gather the wheat and
bring it to my barn'."

Stories of Mustard Seed and Yeast

[31] Then Jesus told another story:
"The kingdom of heaven is like a mustard seed. A man plants the seed in
his field. [32] That seed is the smallest
of all seeds. But when it grows, it is

produce fruit To produce fruit means to have in your life the good things God wants.

one of the largest garden plants. It becomes a tree, big enough for the wild birds to come and make nests in its branches."

³³Then Jesus told another story: "The kingdom of heaven is like yeast that a woman mixes into a big bowl of flour. The yeast makes all the dough rise."

³⁴Jesus used stories to tell all these things to the people. He always used stories to teach people. ³⁵This is as the prophet^d said:

"I will speak using stories;
I will tell things that have been
    secret since the world was
    made."   *Psalm 78:2*

Jesus Explains About the Wheat and Weeds

³⁶Then Jesus left the crowd and went into the house. His followers came to him and said, "Explain to us the meaning of the story about the weeds in the field."

³⁷Jesus answered, "The man who planted the good seed in the field is the Son of Man.^d ³⁸The field is the world. And the good seed is all of God's children in the kingdom. The weeds are those people who belong to the Evil One. ³⁹And the enemy who planted the bad seed is the devil. The harvest time is the end of the world. And the workers who gather are God's angels.

⁴⁰"The weeds are pulled up and burned in the fire. It will be this way at the end of the world. ⁴¹The Son of Man will send out his angels. They will gather out of his kingdom all who cause sin and all who do evil. ⁴²The angels will throw them into the blazing furnace. There the people will cry and grind their teeth with pain. ⁴³Then the good people will shine like the sun in the kingdom of their Father. You people who hear me, listen!

Stories of a Treasure and a Pearl

⁴⁴"The kingdom of heaven is like a treasure hidden in a field. One day a man found the treasure, and then he hid it in the field again. The man was very happy to find the treasure. He went and sold everything that he owned to buy that field.

⁴⁵"Also, the kingdom of heaven is like a man looking for fine pearls. ⁴⁶One day he found a very valuable pearl. The man went and sold everything he had to buy that pearl.

A Story of a Fishing Net

⁴⁷"Also, the kingdom of heaven is like a net that was put into the lake. The net caught many different kinds of fish. ⁴⁸When it was full, the fishermen pulled the net to the shore. They sat down and put all the good fish in baskets. Then they threw away the bad fish. ⁴⁹It will be this way at the end of the world. The angels will come and separate the evil people from the good people. ⁵⁰The angels will throw the evil people into the blazing furnace. In that place the people will cry and grind their teeth with pain."

⁵¹Jesus asked his followers, "Do you understand all these things?"

They answered, "Yes, we understand."

⁵²Then Jesus said to them, "So every teacher of the law who has been taught about the kingdom of heaven is like the owner of a house. He has both new things and old things saved in his house. And he brings out both those new things and old things."

Jesus Goes to His Home Town

⁵³When Jesus finished teaching with these stories, he left there. ⁵⁴He went to the town where he grew up. He taught the people in the synagogue,^d and they were amazed. They

said, "Where did this man get this wisdom and this power to do miracles?[d] [55]He is only the son of the carpenter. And his mother is Mary. His brothers are James, Joseph, Simon and Judas. [56]And all his sisters are here with us. So where does this man get all these things?" [57]And the people refused to accept Jesus.

But Jesus said to them, "A prophet[d] is honoured everywhere except in his own town or in his own home."

[58]The people there did not believe in Jesus. So Jesus did not do many miracles there.

How John the Baptist Was Killed

14 At that time Herod, the ruler of Galilee, heard the reports about Jesus. [2]So Herod said to his servants, "Jesus is really John the Baptist.[d] He has risen from death. That is why he is able to do these miracles."[d]

[3]Sometime before this, Herod had arrested John, tied him up, and put him into prison. Herod did this because of Herodias. Herodias was the wife of Philip, Herod's brother. [4]Herod arrested John because he told Herod: "It is not right for you to have Herodias." [5]Herod wanted to kill John, but he was afraid of the people. They believed that John was a prophet.[d]

[6]On Herod's birthday, the daughter of Herodias danced for Herod and his guests. Herod was very pleased with her, [7]so he promised he would give her anything she wanted. [8]Herodias told her daughter what to ask for. So she said to Herod, "Give me the head of John the Baptist here on a platter." [9]King Herod was very sad. But he had promised to give her anything she wanted, and the people eating with him had heard his promise. So Herod ordered that what she asked for be done. [10]He sent men to the prison to cut off John's head. [11]And the men brought John's head on a platter and gave it to the girl. She took it to her mother, Herodias. [12]John's followers came and got his body and buried it. Then they went and told Jesus what happened.

More than 5,000 People Fed

[13]When Jesus heard what happened to John, Jesus left in a boat. He went to a lonely place by himself. But when the crowds heard about it, they followed him on foot from the towns. [14]When Jesus arrived, he saw a large crowd. He felt sorry for them and healed those who were sick.

[15]Late that afternoon, his followers came to Jesus and said, "No one lives in this place. And it is already late. Send the people away so they can go to the towns and buy food for themselves."

[16]Jesus answered, "They don't need to go away. You give them some food to eat."

[17]The followers answered, "But we have only five loaves of bread and two fish."

[18]Jesus said, "Bring the bread and the fish to me." [19]Then he told the people to sit down on the grass. He took the five loaves of bread and the two fish. Then he looked to heaven and thanked God for the food. Jesus divided the loaves of bread. He gave them to his followers, and they gave the bread to the people. [20]All the people ate and were satisfied. After they finished eating, the followers filled 12 baskets with the pieces of food that were not eaten. [21]There were about 5,000 men there who ate, as well as women and children.

Jesus Walks on the Water

[22]Then Jesus made his followers get into the boat. He told them to go ahead of him to the other side of the lake. Jesus stayed there to tell the people

they could go home. ²³After he said good bye to them, he went alone up into the hills to pray. It was late, and Jesus was there alone. ²⁴By this time, the boat was already far away on the lake. The boat was having trouble because of the waves, and the wind was blowing against it.

²⁵Between three and six o'clock in the morning, Jesus' followers were still in the boat. Jesus came to them. He was walking on the water. ²⁶When the followers saw him walking on the water, they were afraid. They said, "It's a ghost!" and cried out in fear.

²⁷But Jesus quickly spoke to them. He said, "Have courage! It is I! Don't be afraid."

²⁸Peter said, "Lord, if that is really you, then tell me to come to you on the water."

²⁹Jesus said, "Come."

And Peter left the boat and walked on the water to Jesus. ³⁰But when Peter saw the wind and the waves, he became afraid and began to sink. He shouted, "Lord, save me!"

³¹Then Jesus reached out his hand and caught Peter. Jesus said, "Your faith is small. Why did you doubt?"

³²After Peter and Jesus were in the boat, the wind became calm. ³³Then those who were in the boat worshipped Jesus and said, "Truly you are the Son of God!"

³⁴After they crossed the lake, they came to the shore at Gennesaret. ³⁵The people there saw Jesus and knew who he was. So they told people all around there that Jesus had come. They brought all their sick to him. ³⁶They begged Jesus to let them just touch the edge of his coat to be healed. And all the sick people who touched it were healed.

Obey God's Law Not Men's

15 Then some Pharisees[d] and teachers of the law came to Jesus from Jerusalem. They asked him, ²"Why do your followers not obey the rules given to us by the great people who lived before us? Your followers don't wash their hands before they eat!"

³Jesus answered, "And why do you refuse to obey God's command so that you can follow those rules you have? ⁴God said, 'Honour your father and mother'.[n] And God also said, 'Anyone who says cruel things to his father or mother must be put to death'.[n] ⁵But you say that a person can tell his father or mother, 'I have something I could

---

'Honour . . . mother'.   Quotation from Exodus 20:12; Deuteronomy 5:16.
'Anyone . . . death'.   Quotation from Exodus 21:17.

Matthew 14:19 Then he looked to heaven and thanked God for the food.

use to help you. But I will not use it for you. I will give it to God'. ⁶You teach that person not to honour his father. You teach that it is not important to do what God said. You think that it is more important to follow the rules you have. ⁷You are hypocrites!ᵈ Isaiah was right when he spoke about you:

⁸'These people show honour to me with words,
but their hearts are far from me.
⁹Their worship of me is worthless.
The things they teach are nothing
but human rules they have memorised'."   *Isaiah 29:13*

¹⁰Jesus called the crowd to him. He said, "Listen and understand what I am saying. ¹¹It is not what a person puts into his mouth that makes him unclean.ᵈ It is what comes out of his mouth that makes him unclean."

¹²Then his followers came to Jesus and asked, "Do you know that the Pharisees are angry because of what you said?"

¹³Jesus answered, "Every plant that my Father in heaven has not planted himself will be pulled up by the roots. ¹⁴Stay away from the Pharisees. They are blind leaders. And if a blind man leads another blind man, then both men will fall into a ditch."

¹⁵Peter said, "Explain the story to us."

¹⁶Jesus said, "You still have trouble understanding? ¹⁷Surely you know that all the food that enters the mouth goes into the stomach. Then that food goes out of the body. ¹⁸But what a person says with his mouth comes from the way he thinks. And these are the things that make him unclean. ¹⁹Out of his mind come evil thoughts, murder, adultery,ᵈ sexual sins, stealing, lying, and saying bad things

against other people. ²⁰These things make a person unclean. But eating with unwashed hands does not make him unclean."

Jesus Helps a Non-Jewish Woman

²¹Jesus left that place and went to the area of Tyre and Sidon. ²²A Canaanite woman from that area came to Jesus. The woman cried out, "Lord, Son of David,ᵈ please help me! My daughter has a demon,ᵈ and she is suffering very much."

²³But Jesus did not answer the woman. So the followers came to Jesus and begged him, "Tell the woman to go away. She is following us and shouting."

²⁴Jesus answered, "God sent me only to the lost sheep, the people of Israel."

²⁵Then the woman came to Jesus again. She bowed before him and said, "Lord, help me!"

²⁶Jesus answered, "It is not right to take the children's bread and give it to the dogs."

²⁷The woman said, "Yes, Lord, but even the dogs eat the pieces of food that fall from their masters' table."

²⁸Then Jesus answered, "Woman, you have great faith! I will do what you asked me to do." And at that moment the woman's daughter was healed.

Jesus Heals Many People

²⁹Then Jesus left that place and went to the shore of Lake Galilee. He went up on a hill and sat there.

³⁰Great crowds came to Jesus. They brought their sick with them: the lame, the blind, the crippled, the dumb and many others. They put them at Jesus' feet, and he healed them. ³¹The crowd were amazed when they saw that people who could not speak were able to speak again. The crippled were made strong again. Those who could

not walk were able to walk again. The blind were able to see again. And they praised the God of Israel for this.

More than 4,000 People Fed

[32]Jesus called his followers to him and said, "I feel sorry for these people. They have been with me for three days, and now they have nothing to eat. I don't want to send them away hungry. They might faint while going home."

[33]His followers asked him, "Where can we get enough bread to feed all these people? We are far away from any town."

[34]Jesus asked, "How many loaves of bread do you have?"

They answered, "We have seven loaves and a few small fish."

[35]Jesus told the people to sit on the ground. [36]He took the seven loaves of bread and the fish and gave thanks to God for the food. Then Jesus divided the food and gave it to his followers. They gave the food to the people. [37]All the people ate and were satisfied. After this, the followers filled seven baskets with the pieces of food that were not eaten. [38]There were about 4,000 men there who ate, besides women and children. [39]After they had eaten, Jesus told the people to go home. He got into the boat and went to the area of Magadan.

The Leaders Ask for a Miracle

16 The Pharisees[d] and Sadducees[d] came to Jesus. They wanted to trap him. So they asked him to show them a miracle[d] to prove that he was from God.

[2]Jesus answered, "When you see the sunset, you know what the weather will be. If the sky is red, then you say we will have good weather. [3]And in the morning if the sky is dark and red, then you say that it will be a rainy day. You see these signs in the sky, and you know what they mean. In the same way, you see the things that are happening now. But you don't know their meaning. [4]Evil and sinful people ask for a miracle as a sign. But they will have no sign – only the sign of Jonah."[n] Then Jesus left them and went away.

Guard Against Wrong Teachings

[5]Jesus and his followers went across the lake. But the followers forgot to bring bread. [6]Jesus said to them, "Be careful! Guard against the yeast of the Pharisees[d] and the Sadducees."[d]

[7]The followers discussed the meaning of this. They said, "Did Jesus say this because we forgot to bring bread?"

[8]Jesus knew that they were talking about this. So he asked them, "Why are you talking about not having bread? Your faith is small. [9]You still don't understand? Remember the five loaves of bread that fed the 5,000 people? And remember that you filled many baskets with bread after the people finished eating? [10]And remember the seven loaves of bread that fed the 4,000 people? Remember that you filled many baskets then also? [11]So I was not talking to you about bread. Why don't you understand that? I am telling you to be careful and guard against the yeast of the Pharisees and the Sadducees." [12]Then the followers understood what Jesus meant. He was not telling them to guard against the yeast used in bread. He was telling them to guard against

---

sign of Jonah Jonah's three days in the big fish are like Jesus' three days in the tomb. The story about Jonah is in the book of Jonah.

the teaching of the Pharisees and the Sadducees.

Peter Says Jesus Is the Christ

[13] Jesus went to the area of Caesarea Philippi. He said to his followers, "I am the Son of Man.[d] Who do the people say I am?"

[14] They answered, "Some people say you are John the Baptist.[d] Others say you are Elijah. And others say that you are Jeremiah or one of the prophets."[d]

[15] Then Jesus asked them, "And who do you say I am?"

[16] Simon Peter answered, "You are the Christ,[d] the Son of the living God."

[17] Jesus answered, "You are blessed, Simon son of Jonah. No person taught you that. My Father in heaven showed you who I am. [18] So I tell you, you are Peter.[n] And I will build my church on this rock. The power of death will not be able to defeat my church. [19] I will give you the keys of the kingdom of heaven. The things you don't allow on earth will be the things that God does not allow. The things you allow on earth will be the things that God allows." [20] Then Jesus warned his followers not to tell anyone that he was the Christ.

Jesus Says that He Must Die

[21] From that time on Jesus began telling his followers that he must go to Jerusalem. He explained that the older Jewish leaders, the leading priests, and the teachers of the law would make him suffer many things. And he told them that he must be killed. Then, on the third day, he would be raised from death.

[22] Peter took Jesus aside and began to criticise him. Peter said, "God save you from those things, Lord! Those things will never happen to you!"

[23] Then Jesus said to Peter, "Go away from me, Satan![n] You are not helping me! You don't care about the things of God. You care only about things that men think are important."

[24] Then Jesus said to his followers, "If anyone wants to follow me, he must say 'no' to the things he wants. He must be willing even to die on a cross, and he must follow me. [25] Whoever wants to save his life will give up true life. And whoever gives up his life for me will have true life. [26] It is worth nothing for a man to have the whole world if he loses his soul. He could never pay enough to buy back his soul. [27] The Son of Man[d] will come again with his Father's glory and with his angels. At that time, he will reward everyone for what he has done. [28] I tell you the truth. There are some people standing here who, before they die, will see the Son of Man coming with his kingdom."

Jesus with Moses and Elijah

17 Six days later, Jesus took Peter, James, and John the brother of James up on a high mountain. They were all alone there. [2] While they watched, Jesus was changed. His face became bright like the sun. And his clothes became white as light. [3] Then two men were there, talking with him. The men were Moses and Elijah.[n]

[4] Peter said to Jesus, "Lord, it is good that we are here. If you want, I will put three tents here – one for you, one for Moses, and one for Elijah."

[5] While Peter was talking, a bright cloud covered them. A voice came from the cloud. The voice said, "This

---

Peter The Greek name "Peter", like the Aramaic name "Cephas", means "rock".
Satan Name for the devil, meaning "the enemy". Jesus means that Peter was talking like Satan.
Moses and Elijah Two of the most important Jewish leaders in the past.

is my Son and I love him. I am very pleased with him. Obey him!" [6]The followers with Jesus heard the voice. They were so frightened that they fell to the ground. [7]But Jesus went to them and touched them. He said, "Stand up. Don't be afraid." [8]When the followers looked up, they saw Jesus was now alone.

[9]When Jesus and the followers were coming down the mountain, Jesus commanded them, "Don't tell anyone about the things you saw on the mountain. Wait until the Son of Man[d] has been raised from death. Then you may tell."

[10]The followers asked Jesus, "Why do the teachers of the law say that Elijah must come first, before the Christ[d] comes?"

[11]Jesus answered, "They are right to say that Elijah is coming. And it is true that Elijah will make everything the way it should be. [12]But I tell you, Elijah has already come. People did not know who he was. They did to him everything they wanted to do. It will be the same with the Son of Man. Those same people will make the Son of Man suffer." [13]Then the followers understood that Jesus was talking about John the Baptist.[d]

Jesus Heals a Sick Boy

[14]Jesus and his followers went back to the crowd. A man came to Jesus and bowed before him. [15]The man said, "Lord, please help my son. He has epilepsy[n] and is suffering very much. He often falls into the fire or into the water. [16]I brought him to your followers, but they could not cure him."

[17]Jesus answered, "You people have no faith. Your lives are all wrong. How long must I stay with you? How long must I continue to be patient with you? Bring the boy here." [18]Jesus gave a strong command to the demon[d] inside the boy. Then the demon came out, and the boy was healed.

[19]The followers came to Jesus when he was alone. They said, "Why couldn't we force the demon out?"

[20]Jesus answered, "You were not able to drive out the demon because your faith is too small. I tell you the truth. If your faith is as big as a mustard seed,[n] you can say to this mountain, 'Move from here to there'. And the mountain will move. All things will be possible for you." [21] [n]

Jesus Talks About His Death

[22]Later, the followers met together in Galilee. Jesus said to them, "The Son of Man[d] will be given into the control of some men. [23]They will kill him, but on the third day he will be raised from death." And the followers were filled with sadness.

Jesus Talks About Paying Taxes

[24]Jesus and his followers went to Capernaum. There some men came to Peter. They were the men who collected the Temple[d] tax. They asked, "Does your teacher pay the Temple tax?"

[25]Peter answered, "Yes, Jesus pays the tax."

Peter went into the house where Jesus was. Before Peter could speak, Jesus said to him, "The kings on the earth collect different kinds of taxes. But who are the people who pay the taxes? Are they the king's children?

epilepsy A disease that causes a person sometimes to lose control of his body, and maybe faint, shake strongly, or not be able to move.
mustard seed This seed is very small, but the plant grows taller than a man.
Verse 21 Some Greek copies add verse 21: "That kind of spirit comes out only if you use prayer and give up eating."

Or do others pay the taxes? What do you think?"

26 Peter answered, "Other people pay the taxes."

Jesus said to Peter, "Then the children of the king don't have to pay taxes. 27 But we don't want to make

Matthew 17:27 "Inside its mouth you will find a coin."

these tax collectors angry. So go to the lake and fish. After you catch the first fish, open its mouth. Inside its mouth you will find a coin. Take that coin and give it to the tax collectors. That will pay the tax for you and me."

Who Is the Greatest?

18 At that time the followers came to Jesus and asked, "Who is greatest in the kingdom of heaven?"

2 Jesus called a little child to him. He stood the child before the followers. 3 Then he said, "I tell you the truth. You must change and become like little children. If you don't do this, you will never enter the kingdom of heaven. 4 The greatest person in the kingdom of heaven is the one who makes himself humble like this child. 5 "Whoever accepts a little child in my name accepts me. 6 If one of these little children believes in me, and someone causes that child to sin, then it will be very bad for that person. It would be better for him to have a large stone tied around his neck and be drowned in the sea. 7 How terrible for the people of the world because of the things that cause them to sin. Such things will happen. But how terrible for the one who causes them to happen. 8 If your hand or your foot causes you to sin, cut it off and throw it away. It is better for you to have only part of your body but have life for ever. That is much better than to have two hands and two feet but be thrown into the fire that burns for ever. 9 If your eye causes you to sin, take it out and throw it away. It is better for you to have only one eye but have life for ever. That is much better than to have two eyes but be thrown into the fire of hell.

A Lost Sheep

10 "Be careful. Don't think these little children are worth nothing. I tell you that they have angels in heaven who are always with my Father in heaven.11 *n*

12 "If a man has 100 sheep, but one of the sheep gets lost, he will leave the other 99 sheep on the hill. He will go to look for the lost sheep. 13 And if he finds it, he is happier about that one sheep than about the 99 that were never lost. I tell you the truth. 14 In the same way, your Father in heaven does

---

Verse 11   Some Greek copies add verse 11: "The Son of Man came to save lost people."

not want any of these little children to be lost.

When a Person Sins Against You

15 "If your brother sins against you, go and tell him what he did wrong. Do this in private. If he listens to you, then you have helped him to be your brother again. 16 But if he refuses to listen, then go to him again and take one or two other people with you. 'Every case may be proved by two or three witnesses'. *n* 17 If he refuses to listen to them, then tell it to the church. If he refuses to listen to the church, then treat him as you would one who does not believe in God. Treat him as if he were a tax collector.

18 "I tell you the truth. The things you don't allow on earth will be the things God does not allow. The things you allow on earth will be the things that God allows.

19 "Also, I tell you that if two of you on earth agree about something, then you can pray for it. And the thing you ask for will be done for you by my Father in heaven. 20 This is true because if two or three people come together in my name, I am there with them."

An Unforgiving Servant

21 Then Peter came to Jesus and asked, "Lord, when my brother sins against me, how many times must I forgive him? Should I forgive him as many as seven times?"

22 Jesus answered, "I tell you, you must forgive him more than seven times. You must forgive him even if he does wrong to you 77 times.

23 "The kingdom of heaven is like a king who decided to collect the money his servants owed him. 24 So the king

began to collect his money. One servant owed him several million pounds. 25 But the servant did not have enough money to pay his master, the king. So the master ordered that everything the servant owned should be sold, even the servant's wife and children. The money would be used to pay the king what the servant owed.

26 "But the servant fell on his knees and begged, 'Be patient with me. I will pay you everything I owe'. 27 The master felt sorry for his servant. So the master told the servant he did not have to pay. He let the servant go free.

28 "Later, that same servant found another servant who owed him a few pounds. The servant grabbed the other servant around the neck and said, 'Pay me the money you owe me!'

29 "The other servant fell on his knees and begged him, 'Be patient with me. I will pay you everything I owe'.

30 "But the first servant refused to be patient. He threw the other servant into prison until he could pay everything he owed. 31 All the other servants saw what happened. They were very sorry. So they went and told their master all that had happened.

32 "Then the master called his servant in and said, 'You evil servant! You begged me to forget what you owed. So I told you that you did not have to pay anything. 33 I had mercy on you. You should have had the same mercy on that other servant'. 34 The master was very angry, and he put the servant in prison to be punished. The servant had to stay in prison until he could pay everything he owed.

35 "This king did what my heavenly Father will do to you if you do not forgive your brother from your heart."

'Every . . . witnesses'. Quotation from Deuteronomy 19:15.

Jesus Teaches About Divorce

19 After Jesus said all these things, he left Galilee. He went into the area of Judea on the other side of the Jordan River. [2] Large crowds followed Jesus, and he healed them there.

[3] Some Pharisees[d] came to Jesus and tried to trick him. They asked, "Is it right for a man to divorce his wife for any reason he chooses?"

[4] Jesus answered, "Surely you have read in the Scriptures[d] that when God made the world, 'he made them male and female'.[n] [5] And God said, 'So a man will leave his father and mother and be united with his wife. And the two people will become one body'.[n] [6] So the two are not two, but one. God joined the two people together. No person should separate them."

[7] The Pharisees asked, "Why then did Moses give a command for a man to divorce his wife by giving her divorce papers?"

[8] Jesus answered, "Moses allowed you to divorce your wives because you refused to accept God's teaching. But divorce was not allowed in the beginning. [9] I tell you that anyone who divorces his wife and marries another woman is guilty of adultery.[d] The only reason for a man to divorce and marry again is if his first wife has sexual relations with another man."

[10] The followers said to him, "If that is the only reason a man can divorce his wife, then it is better not to marry."

[11] Jesus answered, "Not everyone can accept this truth about marriage. But God has made some able to accept it. [12] There are different reasons why some men cannot marry. Some men were born without the ability to become fathers. Others were made that way later in life by other people. And other men have given up marriage because of the kingdom of heaven. But the person who can marry should accept this teaching about marriage."[n]

Jesus Welcomes Children

[13] Then the people brought their little children to Jesus so that he could put his hands on them[n] and pray for them. When his followers saw this, they told the people to stop bringing their children to Jesus. [14] But Jesus said, "Let the little children come to me. Don't stop them, because the kingdom of heaven belongs to people who are like these children." [15] After Jesus put his hands on the children, he left there.

A Rich Young Man's Question

[16] A man came to Jesus and asked, "Teacher, what good thing must I do to have life for ever?"

[17] Jesus answered, "Why do you ask me about what is good? Only God is good. But if you want to have life for ever, obey the commands."

[18] The man asked, "Which commands?"

Jesus answered, " 'You must not murder anyone. You must not be guilty of adultery.[d] You must not steal. You must not tell lies about your neighbour in court. [19] Honour your father and mother.[n] Love your neighbour as you love yourself'."[n]

'he made . . . female'.   Quotation from Genesis 1:27 or 5:2.
'So . . . body'.   Quotation from Genesis 2:24.
But . . . marriage.   This may also mean, "The person who can accept this teaching about not marrying should accept it."
put his hands on them   Showing that Jesus gave special blessings to these children.
'You . . . mother.'   Quotation from Exodus 20:12–16; Deuteronomy 5:16–20.
'Love . . . yourself '.   Quotation from Leviticus 19:18.

20The young man said, "I have obeyed all these things. What else do I need to do?" 21Jesus answered, "If you want to be perfect, then go and sell all the things you own. Give the money to the poor. If you do this, you will have a treasure in heaven. Then come and follow me!" 22But when the young man heard this, he became very sad because he was very rich. So he left Jesus.

23Then Jesus said to his followers, "I tell you the truth. It will be very hard for a rich person to enter the kingdom of heaven. 24Yes, I tell you that it is easier for a camel to go through the eye of a needle than for a rich person to enter the kingdom of God."

25When the followers heard this, they were very surprised. They asked, "Then who can be saved?"

26Jesus looked at them and said, "This is something that men cannot do. But God can do all things."

27Peter said to Jesus, "We left everything we had and followed you. So what will we have?"

28Jesus said to them, "I tell you the truth. When the new age comes, the Son of Man^d will sit on his great throne. And all of you who followed me will also sit on 12 thrones. And you will judge the 12 tribes^d of Israel. 29And everyone who has left houses, brothers, sisters, father, mother, children, or farms to follow me will get much more than he left. And he will have life for ever. 30Many who have the highest place in life now will have the lowest place in the future. And many who have the lowest place now will have the highest place in the future.

A Story About Vineyard Workers

20 "The kingdom of heaven is like a man who owned some land. One morning, he went out very early to hire some people to work in his vineyard. 2The man agreed to pay the workers one silver coin^n for working that day. Then he sent them into the vineyard to work. 3About nine o'clock the man went to the marketplace and saw some other people standing there, doing nothing. 4So he said to them, 'If you go and work in my vineyard, I will pay you what your work is worth'. 5So they went to work in the vineyard. The man went out again about twelve o'clock and again at three o'clock. Both times he hired people to work in his vineyard. 6About five o'clock the man went to the marketplace again. He saw others standing there. He asked them, 'Why did you stand here all day doing nothing?' 7They answered, 'No one gave us a job'. The man said to them, 'Then you can go and work in my vineyard'.

8"At the end of the day, the owner of the vineyard said to the foreman, 'Call the workers and pay them. Start by paying the last people I hired. Then pay all of them, ending with the workers I hired first'.

9"The workers who were hired at five o'clock came to get their pay. Each worker received one silver coin. 10Then the workers who were hired first came to get their pay. They thought they would be paid more than the others. But each one of them also received one silver coin. 11When they got their silver coin, they complained to the man who owned the land. 12They said, 'Those people were hired last and worked only one hour. But you paid them the same as you paid

---

silver coin   A Roman denarius. One coin was the average pay for one day's work.

us. And we worked hard all day in the hot sun'. ¹³But the man who owned the vineyard said to one of those workers, 'Friend, I am being fair to you. You agreed to work for one silver coin. ¹⁴So take your pay and go. I want to give the man who was hired last the same pay that I gave you. ¹⁵I can do what I want with my own money. Are you jealous because I am good to those people?'

¹⁶"So those who have the last place now will have the first place in the future. And those who have the first place now will have the last place in the future."

Jesus Talks About His Own Death

¹⁷Jesus was going to Jerusalem. His 12 followers were with him. While they were on the way, Jesus gathered the followers together and spoke to them privately. He said to them, ¹⁸"We are going to Jerusalem. The Son of Man*d* will be turned over to the leading priests and the teachers of the law. They will say that he must die. ¹⁹They will give the Son of Man to the non-Jewish people. They will laugh at him and beat him with whips, and then they will kill him on a cross. But on the third day after his death, he will be raised to life again."

A Mother Asks Jesus a Favour

²⁰Then the wife of Zebedee came to Jesus. Her sons were with her. The mother bowed before Jesus and asked him to do something for her.

²¹Jesus asked, "What do you want?"

She said, "Promise that one of my sons will sit at your right side in your kingdom. And promise that the other son will sit at your left side."

²²But Jesus said, "You don't understand what you are asking. Can you accept the kind of suffering that I must suffer?"*n*

The sons answered, "Yes, we can!"

²³Jesus said to them, "Truly you will suffer the same things that I will suffer. But I cannot choose who will sit at my right side or my left side. Those places belong to those for whom my Father has prepared them."

²⁴The other ten followers heard this and were angry with the two brothers.

²⁵Jesus called all the followers together. He said, "You know that the rulers of the non-Jewish people love to show their power over the people. And their important leaders love to use all their authority. ²⁶But it should

accept . . . suffer Literally, "drink the cup that I must drink". Jesus used the idea of drinking from a cup to mean accepting the terrible things that would happen to him.

Matthew 20:9 "Each worker received one silver coin."

not be that way among you. If one of you wants to become great, then he must serve the rest of you like a servant. [27]If one of you wants to become first, then he must serve the rest of you like a slave. [28]So it is with the Son of Man.[d] The Son of Man did not come for other people to serve him. He came to serve others. The Son of Man came to give his life to save many people."

Jesus Heals Two Blind Men

[29]When Jesus and his followers were leaving Jericho, a great many people followed Jesus. [30]There were two blind men sitting by the road. The blind men heard that Jesus was going by, so they shouted, "Lord, Son of David,[d] please help us!"

[31]All the people criticised the blind men. They told them to be quiet. But the blind men shouted more and more, "Lord, Son of David, please help us!"

[32]Jesus stopped and said to the blind men, "What do you want me to do for you?"

[33]They answered, "Lord, we want to be able to see."

[34]Jesus felt sorry for the blind men. He touched their eyes, and at once they were able to see. Then the men followed Jesus.

Jesus Enters Jerusalem as a King

21 Jesus and his followers were coming closer to Jerusalem. But first they stopped at Bethphage at the hill called the Mount of Olives.[d] From there Jesus sent two of his followers into the town. [2]He said to them, "Go to the town you can see there. When you enter it, you will find a donkey tied there with its colt. Untie them

and bring them to me. [3]If anyone asks you why you are taking the donkeys, tell him, 'The Master needs them. He will send them back soon'."

[4]This was to make clear the full meaning of what the prophet[d] said:

[5]"Tell the people of Jerusalem,
    'Your king is coming to you.
He is gentle and riding on a
        donkey.
He is on the colt of a donkey'."

Isaiah 62:11; Zechariah 9:9

[6]The followers went and did what Jesus told them to do. [7]They brought the donkey and the colt to Jesus. They laid their coats on the donkeys, and Jesus sat on them. [8]Many people spread their coats on the road before Jesus. Others cut branches from the trees and spread them on the road. [9]Some of the people were walking ahead of Jesus. Others were walking behind him. All the people were shouting,

"Praise[n] to the Son of David![d]
God bless the One who comes in
        the name of the Lord!

Psalm 118:26

Praise to God in heaven!"

[10]Then Jesus went into Jerusalem. The city was filled with excitement. The people asked, "Who is this man?" [11]The crowd answered, "This man is Jesus. He is the prophet from the town of Nazareth in Galilee."

Jesus Goes to the Temple

[12]Jesus went into the Temple.[d] He threw out all the people who were buying and selling there. He turned over the tables that belonged to the men who were exchanging different kinds of money. And he upset the benches of those who were selling doves. [13]Jesus said to all the people there, "It is

---

Praise Literally, "Hosanna", a Hebrew word used at first in praying to God for help. At this time it was probably a shout of joy used in praising God or his Messiah.

written in the Scriptures,[d] 'My Temple will be a house where people will pray'.[n] But you are changing God's house into a 'hideout for robbers'. "[n]

[14] The blind and crippled people came to Jesus in the Temple, and Jesus healed them. [15] The leading priests and the teachers of the law saw that Jesus was doing wonderful things. They saw the children praising him in the Temple. The children were saying, "Praise[n] to the Son of David."[d] All these things made the priests and the teachers of the law very angry.

[16] They asked Jesus, "Do you hear the things these children are saying?"

Jesus answered, "Yes. Haven't you read in the Scriptures, 'You have taught children and babies to sing praises'?"[n]

[17] Then Jesus left and went out of the city to Bethany, where he spent the night.

The Power of Faith

[18] Early the next morning, Jesus was going back to the city. He was very hungry. [19] He saw a fig tree beside the road. Jesus went to it, but there were no figs on the tree. There were only leaves. So Jesus said to the tree, "You will never again have fruit!" The tree immediately dried up.

[20] His followers saw this and were amazed. They asked, "How did the fig tree dry up so quickly?"

[21] Jesus answered, "I tell you the truth. If you have faith and do not doubt, you will be able to do what I did to this tree. And you will be able to do more. You will be able to say to this mountain, 'Go, mountain, fall into the sea'. And if you have faith, it will

happen. [22] If you believe, you will get anything you ask for in prayer."

Leaders Doubt Jesus' Authority

[23] Jesus went to the Temple.[d] While he was teaching there, the leading priests and the older leaders of the people came to Jesus. They said to him, "Tell us! What authority do you have to do these things? Who gave you this authority?"

[24] Jesus answered, "I will ask you a question, too. If you answer me, then I will tell you what authority I have to do these things. [25] Tell me: when John baptised people, did that come from God or from man?"

The priests and the leaders argued about Jesus' question. They said to each other, "If we answer, 'John's baptism was from God', then Jesus will say, 'Then why didn't you believe John?' [26] But if we say, 'It was from man', we are afraid of what the people will do because they all believe that John was a prophet."[d]

[27] So they answered Jesus, "We don't know."

Then Jesus said, "Then I won't tell you what authority I have to do these things!

A Story About Two Sons

[28] "Tell me what you think about this: there was a man who had two sons. He went to the first son and said, 'Son, go and work today in my vineyard'. [29] The son answered, 'I will not go'. But later the son decided he should go, and he went. [30] Then the father went to the other son and said, 'Son, go and work today in my vineyard'. The son answered, 'Yes, sir, I

'My Temple . . . pray'. Quotation from Isaiah 56:7.
'hideout for robbers'. Quotation from Jeremiah 7:11.
Praise Literally, "Hosanna", a Hebrew word used at first in praying to God for help. At this time it was probably a shout of joy used in praising God or his Messiah.
'You . . . praises' Quotation from the Septuagint (Greek) version of Psalm 8:3.

will go and work'. But he did not go. ³¹Which of the two sons obeyed his father?"

The priests and leaders answered, "The first son."

Jesus said to them, "I tell you the truth. The tax collectors and the prostitutes*ᵈ* will enter the kingdom of God before you do. ³²John came to show you the right way to live. And you did not believe him. But the tax collectors and prostitutes believed John. You saw this, but you still refused to change and believe him.

God Sends His Son

³³"Listen to this story: there was a man who owned a vineyard. He put a wall around the vineyard and dug a hole for a winepress.*ᵈ* Then he built a tower. He leased the land to some farmers and left for a trip. ³⁴Later, it was time for the grapes to be picked. So the man sent his servants to the farmers to get his share of the grapes. ³⁵But the farmers grabbed the servants, beat one, killed another, and then killed a third servant with stones. ³⁶So the man sent some other servants to the farmers. He sent more servants than he sent the first time. But the farmers did the same thing to the servants that they had done before. ³⁷So the man decided to send his son to the farmers. He said, 'The farmers will respect my son'. ³⁸But when the farmers saw the son, they said to each other, 'This is the owner's son. This vineyard will be his. If we kill him, then his vineyard will be ours!' ³⁹So the farmers grabbed the son, threw him out of the vineyard, and killed him. ⁴⁰So what will the owner of the vineyard do to these farmers when he comes?"

⁴¹The priests and leaders said, "He will surely kill those evil men. Then he will lease the vineyard to some other farmers. They will give him his share of the crop at harvest time."

⁴²Jesus said to them, "Surely you have read this in the Scriptures:*ᵈ*

'The stone that the builders did
    not want
became the cornerstone.*ᵈ*
The Lord did this,
and it is wonderful to us'.

Psalm 118:22–23

⁴³"So I tell you that the kingdom of God will be taken away from you. It will be given to people who do the things God wants in his kingdom. ⁴⁴The person who falls on this stone will be broken. But if the stone falls on him, he will be crushed."

⁴⁵The leading priests and the Pharisees*ᵈ* heard these stories that Jesus told. They knew he was talking about them. ⁴⁶They wanted to arrest him, but they were afraid of the people, because the people believed that Jesus was a prophet.*ᵈ*

A Story About a Wedding Feast

22 Jesus used stories to tell other things to the people. He said, ²"The kingdom of heaven is like a king who prepared a wedding feast for his son. ³The king invited some people to the feast. When the feast was ready, the king sent his servants to tell the people to come. But they refused to come to the feast.

⁴"Then the king sent other servants. He said to them, 'Tell those who have been invited that my feast is ready. I have killed my best bulls and calves for the dinner. Everything is ready. Come to the wedding feast'.

⁵"But the people refused to listen to the servants. They went to do other things. One went to work in his field, and another went to his business. ⁶Some of the other people grabbed the servants, beat them, and killed them. ⁷The king was very angry. He sent his

army to kill the people who had killed his servants. And the army burned their city.

[8] "After that, the king said to his servants, 'The wedding feast is ready. I invited those people, but they were not worthy to come. [9] So go to the street corners and invite everyone you see. Tell them to come to my feast'. [10] So the servants went into the streets. They gathered all the people they could find, both good and bad. And the wedding hall was filled with guests.

[11] "Then the king came in to see all the guests. He saw a man there who was not dressed in the right clothes for a wedding. [12] The king said, 'Friend, how were you allowed to come in here? You are not wearing the right clothes for a wedding'. But the man said nothing. [13] So the king told some servants, 'Tie this man's hands and feet. Throw him out into the darkness. In that place, people will cry and grind their teeth with pain'.

[14] "Yes, many people are invited. But only a few are chosen."

The Pharisees Try to Trap Jesus

[15] Then the Pharisees[d] left the place where Jesus was teaching. They made plans to trap Jesus with a question. [16] They sent some of their own followers and some men from the group called Herodians.[n] These men said, "Teacher, we know that you are an honest man. We know that you teach the truth about God's way. You are not afraid of what other people think about you. All men are the same to you. [17] So tell us what you think. Is it right to pay taxes to Caesar[d] or not?" [18] But Jesus knew that these men were trying to trick him. So he said, "You hypocrites![d] Why are you trying

to trap me? [19] Show me a coin used for paying the tax." The men showed him a silver coin.[n] [20] Then Jesus asked, "Whose picture is on the coin? And whose name is written on the coin?"

Matthew 22:20 "Whose picture is on the coin?"

[21] The men answered, "Caesar's."

Then Jesus said to them, "Give to Caesar the things that are Caesar's. And give to God the things that are God's."

[22] The men heard what Jesus said, and they were amazed. They left him and went away.

Sadducees Try to Trick Jesus

[23] That same day some Sadducees[d] came to Jesus. (Sadducees believe that no person will rise from death.) The Sadducees asked Jesus a question. [24] They said, "Teacher, Moses told us that a married man might die without having children. Then his

---

Herodians   A political group that followed Herod and his family.
silver coin   A Roman denarius. One coin was the average pay for one day's work.

brother must marry the widow and have children for him. [25]There were seven brothers among us. The first one married but died. He had no children. So his brother married the widow. [26]Then the second brother also died. The same thing happened to the third brother and all the other brothers. [27]The woman was last to die. [28]But all seven men had married her. So when people rise from death, whose wife will she be?"

[29]Jesus answered, "You don't understand because you don't know what the Scriptures[d] say. And you don't know about the power of God. [30]When people rise from death, there will be no marriage. People will not be married to each other. They will be like the angels in heaven. [31]Surely you have read what God said to you about the rising from death? [32]God said, 'I am the God of Abraham, the God of Isaac, and the God of Jacob'.[n] God is the God of living people, not dead people."

[33]All the people heard this. They were amazed at Jesus' teaching.

The Most Important Command

[34]The Pharisees[d] learned that the Sadducees[d] could not argue with Jesus' answers to them. So the Pharisees met together. [35]One Pharisee was an expert in the law of Moses. That Pharisee asked Jesus a question to test him. [36]The Pharisee asked, "Teacher, which command in the law is the most important?"

[37]Jesus answered, " 'Love the Lord your God with all your heart, soul and mind'.[n] [38]This is the first and most important command. [39]And the second command is like the first:

'Love your neighbour as you love yourself'.[n] [40]All the law and the writings of the prophets[d] depend on these two commands."

Jesus Questions the Pharisees

[41]While the Pharisees[d] were together, Jesus asked them a question. [42]He asked, "What do you think about the Christ?[d] Whose son is he?"

The Pharisees answered, "The Christ is the Son of David."[d]

[43]Then Jesus said to them, "Then why did David call him 'Lord'? David was speaking by the power of the Holy Spirit.[d] David said,

[44]'The Lord said to my Lord:
Sit by me at my right side,
until I put your enemies under
    your control.'   Psalm 110:1

[45]David calls the Christ 'Lord'. So how can he be David's son?"

[46]None of the Pharisees could answer Jesus' question. And after that day no one was brave enough to ask Jesus any more questions.

Jesus Accuses the Leaders

23 Then Jesus spoke to the crowds and to his followers. Jesus said, [2]"The teachers of the law and the Pharisees[d] have the authority to tell you what the law of Moses says. [3]So you should obey and follow whatever they tell you. But their lives are not good examples for you to follow. They tell you to do things, but they don't do the things themselves. [4]They make strict rules and try to force people to obey them. But they themselves will not try to follow any of those rules.

[5]"The reason they do good things is so other people will see them. They

---

'**I am . . . Jacob'.**   Quotation from Exodus 3:6.
'**Love . . . mind'.**   Quotation from Deuteronomy 6:5.
'**Love . . . yourself '.**   Quotation from Leviticus 19:18.

make the boxes[n] of Scriptures[d] that they wear bigger and bigger. And they make their special prayer clothes very long so that people will notice them. [6]Those Pharisees and teachers of the law love to have the most important seats at the feasts. And they love to have the most important seats in the synagogues.[d] [7]They love people to show respect to them in the marketplaces. And they love to have people call them 'Teacher'.

[8]"But you must not be called 'Teacher'. You are all brothers and sisters together. You have only one Teacher. [9]And don't call any person on earth 'Father'. You have one Father. He is in heaven. [10]And you should not be called 'Master'. You have only one Master, the Christ.[d] [11]He who serves you as a servant is the greatest among you. [12]Whoever makes himself great will be made humble. Whoever makes himself humble will be made great.

[13]"How terrible for you, teachers of the law and Pharisees! You are hypocrites![d] You close the door for people to enter the kingdom of heaven. You yourselves don't enter, and you stop others who are trying to enter. [14][n]

[15]"How terrible for you, teachers of the law and Pharisees! You are hypocrites! You travel across land and sea to find one person who will follow your ways. When you find that person, you make him more fit for hell than you are.

[16]"How terrible for you, teachers of the law and Pharisees! You guide the people, but you are blind. You say, 'If anyone swears by the Temple[d] when he makes a promise, that means nothing. But if anyone swears by the gold that is in the Temple, then he must keep that promise'. [17]You are blind fools! Which is greater: the gold or the Temple? The Temple makes that gold holy. [18]And you say, 'If anyone swears by the altar when he makes a promise, that means nothing. But if he swears by the gift on the altar, then he must keep his promise'. [19]You are blind! Which is greater: the gift or the altar? The altar makes the gift holy. [20]The person who swears by the altar is really using the altar and also everything on the altar. [21]And the person who uses the Temple to make a promise is really using the Temple and also everything in the Temple. [22]The person who uses heaven to make a promise is also using God's throne and the One who sits on that throne.

[23]"How terrible for you, teachers of the law and Pharisees! You are hypocrites! You give to God one-tenth of everything you earn – even your mint, dill, and cumin.[n] But you don't obey the really important teachings of the law – being fair, showing mercy, and being loyal. These are the things you should do, as well as those other things. [24]You guide the people, but you are blind! You are like a person who picks a fly out of his drink and then swallows a camel![n]

[25]"How terrible for you, teachers of the law and Pharisees! You are hypocrites! You wash the outside of your

---

boxes Small leather boxes containing four important Scriptures. Some Jews tied these to the forehead and left arm, probably to show they were very religious.
Verse 14 Some Greek copies add verse 14: "How terrible for you, teachers of the law and Pharisees. You are hypocrites. You take away widows' houses, and you make long prayers so that people can see you. So you will have a worse punishment."
mint, dill, and cumin Small plants grown in gardens and used for spices. Only very religious people would be careful enough to give a tenth of these plants.
You ... camel! Meaning, "You worry about the smallest mistakes but commit the biggest sin."

cups and dishes. But inside they are full of things that you got by cheating others and pleasing only yourselves. [26] Pharisees, you are blind! First make the inside of the cup clean and good. Then the outside of the cup can be truly clean.

[27] "How terrible for you, teachers of the law and Pharisees. You are hypocrites! You are like tombs that are painted white. Outside, those tombs look fine. But inside, they are full of the bones of dead people, and all kinds of unclean things are there. [28] It is the same with you. People look at you and think you are good. But on the inside you are full of hypocrisy and evil.

[29] "How terrible for you, teachers of the law and Pharisees! You are hypocrites! You build tombs for the prophets.[d] You show honour to the graves of people who lived good lives. [30] And you say, 'If we had lived during the time of our fathers, we`would not have helped them kill the prophets'. [31] But you give proof that you are children of those people who murdered the prophets. [32] And you will complete the sin that your fathers started! [33] "You are snakes! A family of poisonous snakes! You will not escape God. You will all be judged guilty and be sent to hell! [34] So I tell you this: I am sending to you prophets and wise men and teachers. You will kill some of these people. You will nail some of them to crosses. You will beat some of them in your synagogues. You will chase them from town to town. [35] So you will be guilty for the death of all the good people who have been killed on earth. You will be guilty for the murder of that good man Abel. And you will be guilty for the murder of Zechariah[n] son of Berakiah. He was murdered when he was between the Temple and the altar. [36] I tell you the truth. All of these things will happen to you people who are living now.

Jesus Feels Sorry for Jerusalem

[37] "Jerusalem, Jerusalem! You kill the prophets[d] and kill with stones those men God sent to you. Many times I wanted to help your people! I wanted to gather them together as a hen gathers her chicks under her wings. But you did not let me. [38] Now your home will be left completely empty. [39] I tell you, you will not see me again until that time when you will say, 'God bless the One who comes in the name of the Lord'."[n]

The Temple Will Be Destroyed

24 Jesus left the Temple[d] and was walking away. But his followers came to show him the Temple's buildings. [2] Jesus asked, "Do you see all these buildings? I tell you the truth. Every stone will be thrown down to the ground. Not one stone will be left on another."

[3] Later, Jesus was sitting on the Mount of Olives.[d] His followers came to be alone with him. They said, "Tell us when these things will happen. And what will happen to show us that it is time for you to come again and for the world to end?"

[4] Jesus answered: "Be careful that no one fools you. [5] Many people will come in my name. They will say, 'I am the Christ'.[d] And they will fool many people. [6] You will hear about wars and stories of wars that are coming. But don't be afraid. These things must happen before the end comes. [7] Nations will fight against other nations. Kingdoms will fight against

---

Abel . . . Zechariah In the Hebrew Old Testament, the first and last men to be murdered.
God . . . Lord Quotation from Psalm 118:26.

Matthew 24:4 "Be careful that no one fools you."

other kingdoms. There will be times when there is no food for people to eat. And there will be earthquakes in different places. [8] These things are like the first pains when something new is about to be born.

[9] "Then men will arrest you and hand you over to be hurt and kill you. They will hate you because you believe in me. [10] At that time, many who believe will lose their faith. They will turn against each other and hate each other. [11] Many false prophets[d] will come and cause many people to believe false things. [12] There will be more and more evil in the world. So most people will stop showing their love for each other. [13] But the person who continues to be strong until the end will be saved. [14] The Good News[d] about God's kingdom will be preached in all the world, to every nation. Then the end will come.

[15] "Daniel the prophet spoke about 'the horrible thing that destroys'.[n] You will see this terrible thing standing in the holy place." (You who read this should understand what it means.) [16] "At that time, the people in Judea should run away to the mountains. [17] If a person is on the roof[n] of his house, he must not go down to get anything out of his house. [18] If a person is in the field, he must not go back to get his coat. [19] At that time, it will be hard for women who are pregnant or have nursing babies! [20] Pray that it will not be winter or a Sabbath[d] day when these things happen and you have to run away. [21] This is because at that time there will be much trouble. There will be more trouble than has ever happened since the beginning of the world. And nothing as bad as that will ever happen again. [22] God has decided to make that terrible time short. If that time were not made short, then no one would go on living. But God will make that time short to help the people he has chosen. [23] At that time, someone might say to you, 'Look, there is the Christ!' Or another person might say, 'There he is!' But don't believe them. [24] False Christs and false prophets will come and perform great things and miracles.[d] They will do these things to the people God has chosen. They will fool them, if that is possible. [25] Now I have warned you about this before it happens.

[26] "If people tell you, 'The Christ is in the desert' – don't go there. If they say, 'The Christ is in the inner room'

'horrible . . . destroys'. Mentioned in Daniel 9:27; 12:11 (cf. Daniel 11:31).

roof In Bible times houses were built with flat roofs. The roof was used for drying things such as flax and fruit. It was also used as an extra room, as a place for worship and as a place to sleep in the summer.

– don't believe it. [27]When the Son of Man[d] comes, he will be seen by everyone. It will be like lightning flashing in the sky that can be seen everywhere. [28]Wherever there is a dead body, there the vultures will gather.

[29]"Soon after the trouble of those days, this will happen:

'The sun will grow dark.
And the moon will not give its
    light.
The stars will fall from the sky.
And everything in the sky will
    be changed'. *Isaiah 13:10; 34:4*

[30]"At that time, there will be something in the sky that shows the Son of Man is coming. All the peoples of the world will cry. They will see the Son of Man coming on clouds in the sky. He will come with great power and glory. [31]He will use a loud trumpet to send his angels all around the earth. They will gather his chosen people from every part of the world.

[32]"The fig tree teaches us a lesson. When its branches become green and soft, and new leaves begin to grow, then you know that summer is near. [33]So also, when you see all these things happening, you will know that the time is near, ready to come. [34]I tell you the truth. All these things will happen while the people of this time are still living! [35]The whole world, earth and sky, will be destroyed, but the words I have said will never be destroyed!

When Will Jesus Come Again?

[36]"No one knows when that day or time will be. Even the Son and the angels in heaven don't know. Only the Father knows. [37]When the Son of Man[d] comes, it will be the same as what happened during Noah's time. [38]In those days before the flood,

people were eating and drinking. They were marrying and giving their children to be married. They were still doing those things until the day Noah entered the boat. [39]They knew nothing about what was happening. But then the flood came, and all those people were destroyed. It will be the same when the Son of Man comes. [40]Two men will be working together in the field. One man will be taken and the other left. [41]Two women will be grinding grain with a hand mill.[n] One woman will be taken and the other will be left.

[42]"So always be ready. You don't know the day your Lord will come. [43]Remember this: if the owner of the house knew what time a thief was coming, then the owner would be ready for him. The owner would watch and not let the thief enter his house. [44]So you also must be ready. The Son of Man will come at a time you don't expect him.

[45]"Who is the wise and trusted servant? The master trusts one servant to give the other servants their food at the right time. [46]When the master comes and finds the servant doing his work, the servant will be very happy. [47]I tell you the truth. The master will choose that servant to take care of everything the master owns. [48]But what will happen if the servant is evil and thinks his master will not come back soon? [49]Then that servant will begin to beat the other servants. He will feast and get drunk with others like him. [50]And the master will come when the servant is not ready and is not expecting him. [51]Then the master will punish that servant. He will send him away to be among the hypocrites.[d] There people will cry and grind their teeth with pain.

---

mill Two large, round, flat rocks used for grinding grain to make flour.

A Story About Ten Girls

25 "At that time the kingdom of heaven will be like ten girls who went to wait for the bridegroom. They took their lamps with them. ²Five of the girls were foolish and five were wise. ³The five foolish girls took their lamps, but they did not take more oil for the lamps to burn. ⁴The wise girls took their lamps and more oil in jars. ⁵The bridegroom was very late. All the girls became sleepy and went to sleep.

⁶"At midnight someone cried out, 'The bridegroom is coming! Come and meet him!' ⁷Then all the girls woke up and got their lamps ready. ⁸But the foolish girls said to the wise, 'Give us some of your oil. Our lamps are going out'. ⁹The wise girls answered, 'No! The oil we have might not be enough for all of us. Go to the people who sell oil and buy some for yourselves'.

¹⁰"So the five foolish girls went to buy oil. While they were gone, the bridegroom came. The girls who were ready went in with the bridegroom to the wedding feast. Then the door was closed and locked.

¹¹"Later the others came back. They called, 'Sir, sir, open the door to let us in'. ¹²But the bridegroom answered, 'I tell you the truth, I don't know you'.

¹³"So always be ready. You don't know the day or the time the Son of Man*ᵈ* will come.

A Story About Three Servants

¹⁴"The kingdom of heaven is like a man who was going to another place for a visit. Before he left, he talked with his servants. The man told them to take care of his things while he was gone. ¹⁵He decided how much each servant would be able to care for. He gave one servant five bags of money.

He gave another servant two bags of money. And he gave a third servant one bag of money. Then the man left. ¹⁶The servant who got five bags went quickly to invest the money. The five bags of money earned five more. ¹⁷It was the same with the servant who had two bags of money. He invested the money and earned two more. ¹⁸But the servant who got one bag of money went out and dug a hole in the ground. Then he hid his master's money in the hole.

¹⁹"After a long time the master came home. He asked the servants what they did with his money. ²⁰The servant who got five bags of money brought five more bags to the master. The servant said, 'Master, you trusted me to care for five bags of money. So I used your five bags to earn five more'. ²¹The master answered, 'You did well. You are a good servant who can be trusted. You did well with small things. So I will let you care for much greater things. Come and share my happiness with me'.

²²"Then the servant who got two bags of money came to the master. The servant said, 'Master, you gave me two bags of money to care for. So I used your two bags to earn two more'. ²³The master answered, 'You did well. You are a good servant who can be trusted. You did well with small things. So I will let you care for much greater things. Come and share my happiness with me'.

²⁴"Then the servant who got one bag of money came to the master. The servant said, 'Master, I knew that you were a hard man. You harvest things you did not plant. You gather crops where you did not sow any seed. ²⁵So I was afraid. I went and hid your money in the ground. Here is the bag of money you gave me'. ²⁶The master answered, 'You are a bad and lazy ser-

vant! You say you knew that I harvest things I did not plant, and that I gather crops where I did not sow any seed? ²⁷So you should have put my money in the bank. Then, when I came home, I would get my money back with interest'.

²⁸"So the master told his other servants, 'Take the bag of money from that servant and give it to the servant who has ten bags of money. ²⁹Everyone who uses what he has will get more. He will have much more than he needs. But the one who does not use what he has will have everything taken away from him'. ³⁰Then the master said, 'Throw that useless servant outside, into the darkness! There people will cry and grind their teeth with pain'.

The King Will Judge All People

³¹"The Son of Man*d* will come again in his great glory. All his angels will come with him. He will be King and sit on his great throne. ³²All the people of the world will be gathered before him. Then he will separate them into two groups as a shepherd separates the sheep from the goats. ³³The Son of Man will put the sheep, the good people, on his right and the goats, the bad people, on his left.

³⁴"Then the King will say to the good people on his right, 'Come. My Father has given you his blessing. Come and receive the kingdom God has prepared for you since the world was made. ³⁵I was hungry, and you gave me food. I was thirsty, and you gave me something to drink. I was alone and away from home, and you invited me into your house. ³⁶I was without clothes, and you gave me something to wear. I was sick, and you cared for me. I was in prison, and you visited me'.

³⁷"Then the good people will answer, 'Lord, when did we see you hungry and give you food? When did we see you thirsty and give you something to drink? ³⁸When did we see you alone and away from home and invite you into our house? When did we see you without clothes and give you something to wear? ³⁹When did we see you sick or in prison and care for you?'

⁴⁰"Then the King will answer, 'I tell you the truth. Anything you did for any of my people here, you also did for me'.

⁴¹"Then the King will say to those on his left, 'Go away from me. God has said that you will be punished. Go into the fire that burns for ever. That fire was prepared for the devil and his helpers. ⁴²I was hungry, and you gave me nothing to eat. I was thirsty, and you gave me nothing to drink. ⁴³I was alone and away from home, and you did not invite me into your house. I was without clothes, and you gave me nothing to wear. I was sick and in prison, and you did not care for me'.

⁴⁴"Then those people will answer, 'Lord, when did we see you hungry or thirsty? When did we see you alone and away from home? Or when did we see you without clothes or sick or in prison? When did we see these things and not help you?'

⁴⁵"Then the King will answer, 'I tell you the truth. Anything you refused to do for any of my people here, you refused to do for me'.

⁴⁶"These people will go off to be punished for ever. But the good people will go to live for ever."

The Plan to Kill Jesus

26 After Jesus finished saying all these things, he told his followers, ²"You know that the day after tomorrow is the day of the Passover*d* Feast. On that day the Son of Man*d* will be given to his enemies to be killed on a cross."

³Then the leading priests and the older Jewish leaders had a meeting at the palace of the high priest. The high priest's name was Caiaphas. ⁴At the meeting, they planned to set a trap to arrest Jesus and kill him. ⁵But they said, "We must not do it during the feast. The people might cause a riot."

A Woman with Perfume for Jesus

⁶Jesus was in Bethany. He was at the house of Simon, who had a harmful skin disease. ⁷While Jesus was there, a woman came to him. She had an alabaster*d* jar filled with expensive perfume. She poured this perfume on Jesus' head while he was eating.

⁸His followers saw the woman do this and were upset. They asked, "Why waste that perfume? ⁹It could be sold for a great deal of money, and the money could be given to the poor."

¹⁰But Jesus knew what happened. He said, "Why are you troubling this woman? She did a very beautiful thing for me. ¹¹You will always have the poor with you. But you will not always have me. ¹²This woman poured perfume on my body to prepare me for burial. ¹³I tell you the truth. The Good News*d* will be told to people in all the world. And in every place where it is preached, what this woman has done will be told. And people will remember her."

Judas Becomes an Enemy of Jesus

¹⁴Then one of the 12 followers went to talk to the leading priests. This was the follower named Judas Iscariot. ¹⁵He said, "I will give Jesus to you. What will you pay me for doing this?"

The priests gave Judas 30 silver coins. ¹⁶After that, Judas waited for the best time to give Jesus to the priests.

Jesus Eats the Passover Feast

¹⁷On the first day of the Feast*d* of Unleavened Bread, the followers came to Jesus. They said, "We will prepare everything for you to eat the Passover*d* Feast. Where do you want to have the feast?"

¹⁸Jesus answered, "Go into the city to a certain man. Tell him that the Teacher says, 'The chosen time is near. I will have the Passover Feast with my followers at your house'." ¹⁹The followers did what Jesus told them to do, and they prepared the Passover Feast.

²⁰In the evening Jesus was sitting at the table with his 12 followers. ²¹They were all eating. Then Jesus said, "I tell you the truth. One of you 12 will turn against me."

²²This made the followers very sad. Each one said to Jesus, "Surely, Lord, I am not the one who will turn against you. Am I?"

²³Jesus answered, "The man who has dipped his hand with me into the bowl is the one who will turn against me. ²⁴The Son of Man*d* will die. The Scriptures*d* say this will happen. But how terrible it will be for the person who gives the Son of Man to be killed. It would be better for him if he had never been born."

²⁵Then Judas said to Jesus, "Teacher, surely I am not the one. Am I?" (Judas is the one who would give Jesus to his enemies.)

Jesus answered, "Yes, it is you."

The Lord's Supper

²⁶While they were eating, Jesus took some bread. He thanked God for it and broke it. Then he gave it to his

followers and said, "Take this bread and eat it. This bread is my body."

²⁷Then Jesus took a cup. He thanked God for it and gave it to the followers. He said, "Every one of you drink this. ²⁸This is my blood which begins the new agreement that God makes with his people. This blood is poured out for many to forgive their sins. ²⁹I tell you this: I will not drink of this fruit of the vine*ⁿ* again until that day when I drink it new with you in my Father's kingdom."

³⁰They sang a hymn. Then they went out to the Mount of Olives.*ᵈ*

Jesus' Followers Will All Leave Him

³¹Jesus told the followers, "Tonight you will lose your faith because of me. It is written in the Scriptures:*ᵈ*

'I will kill the shepherd,
    and the sheep will scatter'.

Zechariah 13:7

³²But after I rise from death, I will go ahead of you into Galilee."

³³Peter said, "All the other followers may lose their faith because of you. But I will never lose my faith."

³⁴Jesus said, "I tell you the truth. Tonight you will say you don't know me. You will say this three times before the cock crows."

³⁵But Peter said, "I will never say that I don't know you! I will even die with you!" And all the other followers said the same thing.

Jesus Prays Alone

³⁶Then Jesus went with his followers to a place called Gethsemane. He said to them, "Sit here while I go over there and pray." ³⁷He told Peter and the two sons of Zebedee to come with him. Then Jesus began to be very sad and troubled. ³⁸He said to Peter and the two sons of Zebedee, "My heart is full of sorrow and breaking with sadness. Stay here with me and watch."

³⁹Then Jesus walked a little further away from them. He fell to the ground and prayed, "My Father, if it is possible, do not give me this cup*ⁿ* of suffering. But do what you want, not what I want." ⁴⁰Then Jesus went back to his followers and found them asleep. Jesus said to Peter, "You men could not stay awake with me for one hour? ⁴¹Stay awake and pray for strength against temptation. Your spirit wants to do what is right. But your body is weak."

fruit of the vine Product of the grapevine; this may also be translated "wine".
cup Jesus is talking about the bad things that will happen to him. Accepting these things will be very hard, like drinking a cup of something that tastes very bitter.

Matthew 26:26 Jesus took some bread. He thanked God for it and broke it.

⁴²Then Jesus went away a second time. He prayed, "My Father, if it is not possible for this painful thing to be taken from me, and if I must do it, then I pray that what you want will be done."

⁴³Then Jesus went back to the followers. Again he found them asleep, because their eyes were heavy. ⁴⁴So Jesus left them and went away one more time and prayed. This third time he prayed, he said the same thing.

⁴⁵Then Jesus went back to the followers and said, "You are still sleeping and resting? The time has come for the Son of Man[d] to be given to sinful people. ⁴⁶Get up. We must go. Here comes the man who has turned against me."

Jesus Is Arrested

⁴⁷While Jesus was still speaking, Judas came up. Judas was one of the 12 followers. He had many people with him. They had been sent from the leading priests and the older leaders of the people. They carried swords and clubs. ⁴⁸Judas had planned to give them a signal. He had said, "The man I kiss is Jesus. Arrest him." ⁴⁹At once Judas went to Jesus and said, "Greetings, Teacher!" Then Judas kissed him.

⁵⁰Jesus answered, "Friend, do the thing you came to do."

Then the men came and grabbed Jesus and arrested him. ⁵¹When that happened, one of Jesus' followers reached for his sword and pulled it out. The follower struck the servant of the high priest with the sword and cut off his ear.

⁵²Jesus said to the man, "Put your sword back in its place. All who use swords will be killed with swords. ⁵³Surely you know I could ask my Father, and he would give me more than 12 armies of angels. ⁵⁴But this thing must happen this way so that it will be as the Scriptures[d] say."

⁵⁵Then Jesus said to the crowd, "You came to get me with swords and clubs as if I were a criminal. Every day I sat in the Temple[d] teaching. You did not arrest me there. ⁵⁶But all these things have happened so that it will be as the prophets[d] wrote." Then all of Jesus' followers left him and ran away.

Jesus Before the Jewish Leaders

⁵⁷Those men who arrested Jesus led him to the house of Caiaphas, the high priest. The teachers of the law and the older Jewish leaders were gathered there. ⁵⁸Peter followed Jesus but did not go near him. He followed Jesus to the courtyard of the high priest's house. He sat down with the guards to see what would happen to Jesus.

⁵⁹The leading priests and the Jewish council tried to find something false against Jesus so that they could kill him. ⁶⁰Many people came and told lies about him. But the council could find no real reason to kill Jesus. Then two people came and said, ⁶¹"This man said, 'I can destroy the Temple[d] of God and build it again in three days'."

⁶²Then the high priest stood up and said to Jesus, "Aren't you going to answer? Don't you have something to say about their charges against you?" ⁶³But Jesus said nothing.

Again the high priest said to Jesus, "You must swear to this. I command you by the power of the living God to tell us the truth. Tell us, are you the Christ,[d] the Son of God?"

⁶⁴Jesus answered, "Yes, I am. But I tell you, in the future you will see the Son of Man[d] sitting at the right hand of God, the Powerful One. And you will see him coming in clouds in the sky."

⁶⁵When the high priest heard this, he was very angry. He tore his clothes

and said, "This man has said things that are against God! We don't need any more witnesses. You all heard him say these things against God. [66]What do you think?"

The people answered, "He is guilty, and he must die."

[67]Then the people there spat in Jesus' face and beat him with their fists. Others slapped Jesus. [68]They said, "Prove to us that you are a prophet,[d] you Christ! Tell us who hit you!"

Peter Says He Doesn't Know Jesus

[69]At that time, Peter was sitting in the courtyard. A servant girl came to him and said, "You were with Jesus, that man from Galilee."

[70]But Peter said that he was never with Jesus. He said this to all the people there. Peter said, "I don't know what you are talking about."

[71]Then he left the courtyard. At the gate, another girl saw him. She said to the people there, "This man was with Jesus of Nazareth."

[72]Again, Peter said that he was never with Jesus. Peter said, "I swear that I don't know this man Jesus!"

[73]A short time later, some people standing there went to Peter. They said, "We know you are one of those men who followed Jesus. We know this because of the way you talk."

[74]Then Peter began to curse. He said, "May a curse fall on me if I'm not telling the truth. I don't know the man." After Peter said this, a cock crowed. [75]Then he remembered what Jesus had told him: "Before the cock crows, you will say three times that you don't know me." Then Peter went outside and cried painfully.

Jesus Is Taken to Pilate

27 Early the next morning, all the leading priests and older leaders of the people decided to kill Jesus. [2]They tied him, led him away, and turned him over to Pilate, the governor.

Judas Kills Himself

[3]Judas saw that they had decided to kill Jesus. Judas was the one who gave Jesus to his enemies. When Judas saw what happened, he was very sorry for what he had done. So he took the 30 silver coins back to the priests and the leaders. [4]Judas said, "I sinned. I gave you an innocent man to be killed."

The leaders answered, "What is that to us? That's your problem, not ours."

[5]So Judas threw the money into the Temple.[d] Then he went off and hanged himself.

[6]The leading priests picked up the silver coins in the Temple. They said, "Our law does not allow us to keep this money with the Temple money. This money has paid for a man's death." [7]So they decided to use the coins to buy a field called Potter's Field. This field would be a place to bury strangers who died while visiting Jerusalem. [8]That is why that field is still called the Field of Blood. [9]So the thing came true that Jeremiah the prophet[d] had said: "They took 30 silver coins. That is how little the Israelites thought he was worth. [10]They used those 30 silver coins to buy the potter's field, as the Lord commanded me."[n]

Pilate Questions Jesus

[11]Jesus stood before Pilate the governor. Pilate asked him, "Are you the King of the Jews?"

"They . . . commanded me."   See Zechariah 11:12–13 and Jeremiah 32:6–9.

Jesus answered, "Yes, I am."

[12] When the leading priests and the older leaders accused Jesus, he said nothing.

[13] So Pilate said to Jesus, "Don't you hear these people accusing you of all these things?"

[14] But Jesus said nothing in answer to Pilate. Pilate was very surprised at this.

Pilate Tries to Free Jesus

[15] Every year at the time of Passover[d] the governor would free one person from prison. This was always a person the people wanted to be set free. [16] At that time there was a man in prison who was known to be very bad. His name was Barabbas. [17] All the people gathered at Pilate's house. Pilate said, "Which man do you want me to free: Barabbas, or Jesus who is called the Christ?"[d] [18] Pilate knew that the people gave Jesus to him because they were jealous.

[19] Pilate said these things while he was sitting on the judge's seat. While he was sitting there, his wife sent a message to him. The message said, "Don't do anything to that man. He is not guilty. Today I had a dream about him, and it troubled me very much."

[20] But the leading priests and older leaders told the crowd to ask for Barabbas to be freed and for Jesus to be killed.

[21] Pilate said, "I have Barabbas and Jesus. Which do you want me to set free for you?"

The people answered, "Barabbas!"

[22] Pilate asked, "What should I do with Jesus, the one called the Christ?"

They all answered, "Kill him on a cross!"

[23] Pilate asked, "Why do you want me to kill him? What wrong has he done?"

But they shouted louder, "Kill him on a cross!"

[24] Pilate saw that he could do nothing about this, and a riot was starting. So he took some water and washed his hands[n] in front of the crowd. Then he said, "I am not guilty of this man's death. You are the ones who are causing it!"

[25] All the people answered, "We will be responsible. We accept for ourselves and for our children any punishment for his death."

[26] Then Pilate freed Barabbas. Pilate told some of the soldiers to beat Jesus with whips. Then he gave Jesus to the soldiers to be killed on a cross.

[27] Pilate's soldiers took Jesus into the governor's palace. All the soldiers gathered around Jesus. [28] They took off his clothes and put a red robe on him. [29] Then the soldiers used thorny branches to make a crown. They put this crown of thorns on Jesus' head. They put a stick in his right hand. Then the soldiers bowed before Jesus and made fun of him. They said, "Hail, King of the Jews!" [30] They spat on Jesus. Then they took his stick and hit him on the head many times. [31] After they finished making fun of Jesus, the soldiers took off the robe and put his own clothes on him again. Then they led Jesus away to be killed on a cross.

Jesus Is Killed on a Cross

[32] The soldiers were going out of the city with Jesus. They forced another man to carry the cross to be used for Jesus. This man was Simon, from Cyrene. [33] They all came to the place called Golgotha. (Golgotha means the

---

washed his hands   He did this as a sign to show that he wanted no part in what the people did.

Place of the Skull.) [34] At Golgotha, the soldiers gave Jesus wine to drink. This wine was mixed with gall.[n] He tasted the wine but refused to drink it. [35] The soldiers nailed Jesus to a cross. They threw lots[d] to decide who would get his clothes. [36] The soldiers sat there and continued watching him. [37] They put a sign above Jesus' head with the charge against him written on it. The sign read: "THIS IS JESUS, THE KING OF THE JEWS." [38] Two robbers were nailed to crosses beside Jesus, one on the right and the other on the left. [39] People walked by and insulted Jesus. They shook their heads, [40] saying, "You said you could destroy the Temple[d] and build it again in three days. So save yourself! Come down from that cross, if you are really the Son of God!"

[41] The leading priests, the teachers of the law, and the older Jewish leaders were also there. These men made fun of Jesus [42] and said, "He saved other people, but he can't save himself! People say he is the King of Israel! If he is the King, then let him come down now from the cross. Then we will believe in him. [43] He trusts in God. So let God save him now, if God really wants him. He himself said, 'I am the Son of God'." [44] And in the same way, the robbers who were being killed on crosses beside Jesus also insulted him.

Jesus Dies

[45] At noon the whole country became dark. This darkness lasted for three hours. [46] About three o'clock Jesus cried out in a loud voice, "Eli, Eli, lema sabachthani?" This means,

"My God, my God, why have you left me alone?"

[47] Some of the people standing there heard this. They said, "He is calling Elijah."

[48] Quickly one of them ran and got a sponge. He filled the sponge with vinegar and tied it to a stick. Then he used the stick to give the sponge to Jesus to drink from it. [49] But the others said, "Don't bother him. We want to see if Elijah will come to save him."

[50] Again Jesus cried out in a loud voice. Then he died.

[51] Then the curtain in the Temple[n] split into two pieces. The tear started at the top and tore all the way down to the bottom. Also, the earth shook and rocks broke apart. [52] The graves opened, and many of God's people who had died were raised from death. [53] They came out of the graves after Jesus was raised from death. They went into the holy city, and many people saw them.

[54] The army officer and the soldiers guarding Jesus saw this earthquake and everything else that happened. They were very frightened and said, "He really was the Son of God!"

[55] Many women were standing at a distance from the cross, watching. These were women who had followed Jesus from Galilee to care for him. [56] Mary Magdalene, and Mary the mother of James and Joseph, and the mother of James and John were there.

Jesus Is Buried

[57] That evening a rich man named Joseph came to Jerusalem. He was a follower of Jesus from the town of Arimathea. [58] Joseph went to Pilate

---

gall Probably a drink of wine mixed with drugs to help a person feel less pain.
curtain in the Temple A curtain divided the Most Holy Place from the other part of the Temple. That was the special building in Jerusalem where God commanded the Jews to worship him.

and asked to have Jesus' body. Pilate gave orders for the soldiers to give it to Joseph. ⁵⁹ Then Joseph took the body and wrapped it in a clean linen cloth. ⁶⁰ He put Jesus' body in a new tomb that he had cut in a wall of rock. He rolled a very large stone to block the entrance of the tomb. Then Joseph went away. ⁶¹ Mary Magdalene and the other woman named Mary were sitting near the tomb.

The Tomb of Jesus Is Guarded

⁶² That day was the day called Preparation^d Day. The next day, the leading priests and the Pharisees^d went to Pilate. ⁶³ They said, "Sir, we remember that while that liar was still alive he said, 'After three days I will rise from death'. ⁶⁴ So give the order for the tomb to be guarded closely till the third day. His followers might come and steal the body. Then they could tell the people that he has risen from death. That lie would be even worse than the first one."

⁶⁵ Pilate said, "Take some soldiers and go and guard the tomb the best way you know." ⁶⁶ So they all went to the tomb and made it safe from thieves. They did this by sealing the stone in the entrance and then putting soldiers there to guard it.

Jesus Rises from Death

28 The day after the Sabbath^d day was the first day of the week. At dawn on the first day, Mary Magdalene and another woman named Mary went to look at the tomb.

² At that time there was a strong earthquake. An angel of the Lord came down from heaven. The angel went to the tomb and rolled the stone away from the entrance. Then he sat on the stone. ³ He was shining as bright as lightning. His clothes were

Matthew 28:2 An angel of the Lord came down from heaven.

white as snow. ⁴ The soldiers guarding the tomb were very frightened of the angel. They shook with fear and then became like dead men.

⁵ The angel said to the women, "Don't be afraid. I know that you are looking for Jesus, the one who was killed on the cross. ⁶ But he is not here. He has risen from death as he said he would. Come and see the place where his body was. ⁷ And go quickly and tell his followers. Say to them: 'Jesus has risen from death. He is going into Galilee. He will be there before you. You will see him there'." Then the angel said, "Now I have told you."

⁸ The women left the tomb quickly. They were afraid, but they were also very happy. They ran to tell Jesus' followers what had happened. ⁹ Suddenly, Jesus met them and said, "Greetings." The women came up to Jesus, took hold of his feet, and worshipped him. ¹⁰ Then Jesus said to

LUKE 2:16
And the shepherds saw the baby lying in a feeding box.

MATTHEW 2:9–10
They saw the same star they had seen in the east. It went before them until it stopped above the place were the child was.

LUKE 2:47
*All who heard him were
amazed at his understanding
and wise answers.*

them, "Don't be afraid. Go and tell my brothers to go on to Galilee. They will see me there."

The Soldiers Report to the Jewish Leaders

[11]The women went to tell Jesus' followers. At the same time, some of the soldiers who had been guarding the tomb went into the city. They went to tell the leading priests everything that had happened. [12]Then the priests met with the older Jewish leaders and made a plan. They paid the soldiers a large amount of money. [13]They said to the soldiers, "Tell the people that Jesus' followers came during the night and stole the body while you were asleep. [14]If the governor hears about this, we will satisfy him and save you from trouble." [15]So the soldiers kept the money and obeyed the priests. And that story is still spread among the Jews even today.

Jesus Talks to His Followers

[16]The 11 followers went to Galilee. They went to the mountain where Jesus told them to go. [17]On the mountain they saw Jesus and worshipped him. But some of them did not believe that it was really Jesus. [18]Then Jesus came to them and said, "All power in heaven and on earth is given to me. [19]So go and make followers of all people in the world. Baptise them in the name of the Father and the Son and the Holy Spirit.[d] [20]Teach them to obey everything that I have told you. You can be sure that I will be with you always. I will continue with you until the end of the world."

MARK

Mark Tells About the Power of Jesus

John Prepares for Jesus

1 This is the beginning of the Good News*d* about Jesus Christ, the Son of God,*n* 2 as the prophet*d* Isaiah wrote:

"I will send my messenger ahead of you.
He will prepare your way."
Malachi 3:1

3 "There is a voice of a man who calls out in the desert:
'Prepare the way for the Lord.
Make the road straight for him'." *Isaiah 40:3*

4 John was baptising people in the desert. He preached a baptism of changed hearts and lives for the forgiveness of sins. 5 All the people from Judea and Jerusalem were going out to John. They told about the sins they had done. Then they were baptised by him in the Jordan River. 6 John wore clothes made from camel's hair and had a leather belt around his waist. He ate locusts*d* and wild honey. 7 This is what John preached to the people: "There is one coming later who is greater than I. I am not good enough even to kneel down and untie his sandals. 8 I baptise you with water. But the one who is coming will baptise you with the Holy Spirit."*d*

Jesus Is Baptised

9 At that time Jesus came from the town of Nazareth in Galilee to the place where John was. John baptised Jesus in the Jordan River. 10 When Jesus was coming up out of the water, he saw heaven open. The Holy Spirit*d* came down on him like a dove. 11 A voice came from heaven and said: "You are my Son and I love you. I am very pleased with you."

12 Then the Spirit sent Jesus into the desert alone. 13 He was in the desert 40 days and was there with the wild animals. While he was in the desert, he was tempted by Satan. Then angels came and took care of Jesus.

Jesus Chooses Some Followers

14 After John was put in prison, Jesus went into Galilee and preached the Good News*d* from God. 15 Jesus said, "The right time has come. The kingdom of God is near. Change your hearts and lives and believe the Good News!"

16 When Jesus was walking by Lake Galilee, he saw Simon*n* and Simon's brother, Andrew. They were fishermen and were throwing a net into the lake to catch fish. 17 Jesus said to them, "Come and follow me. I will make you fishermen for men." 18 So Simon and Andrew immediately left their nets and followed him.

19 Jesus continued walking by Lake Galilee. He saw two more brothers, James and John, the sons of Zebedee. They were in their boat, preparing their nets to catch fish. 20 Their father Zebedee and the men who worked for him were in the boat with the brothers. When Jesus saw the brothers, he called them to come with

---

the Son of God Some Greek copies omit these words.
Simon Simon's other name was Peter.

him. They left their father and followed Jesus.

Jesus Removes an Evil Spirit

[21] Jesus and his followers went to Capernaum. On the Sabbath[d] day Jesus went to the synagogue[d] and began to teach. [22] The people there were amazed at his teaching. He did not teach like their teachers of the law. He taught like a person who had authority. [23] While he was in the synagogue, a man was there who had an evil spirit in him. The man shouted, [24] "Jesus of Nazareth! What do you want with us? Did you come to destroy us? I know who you are – God's Holy One!"

[25] Jesus said strongly, "Be quiet! Come out of the man!" [26] The evil spirit made the man shake violently. Then the spirit gave a loud cry and came out of him.

[27] The people were amazed. They asked each other, "What is happening here? This man is teaching something new. And he teaches with authority. He even gives commands to evil spirits, and they obey him." [28] And the news about Jesus spread quickly everywhere in the area of Galilee.

Jesus Heals Many People

[29] Jesus and his followers left the synagogue.[d] They all went at once with James and John to the home of Simon[n] and Andrew. [30] Simon's mother-in-law was sick in bed with a fever. The people there told Jesus about her. [31] So Jesus went to her bed, took her hand, and helped her up. Immediately the fever left her, and she was healed. Then she began serving them.

[32] That night, after the sun went down, the people brought to Jesus all who were sick. They also brought those who had demons[d] in them. [33] The whole town gathered at the door of the house. [34] Jesus healed many who had different kinds of sickness. He also forced many demons to leave people. But he would not allow the demons to speak, because they knew who he was.

[35] Early the next morning, Jesus woke and left the house while it was still dark. He went to a place to be alone and pray. [36] Later, Simon and his friends went to look for Jesus. [37] They found him and said, "Everyone is looking for you!"

[38] Jesus answered, "We should go somewhere else, to other towns around here. Then I can preach there too. That is the reason I came." [39] So he travelled everywhere in Galilee. He preached in the synagogues and forced demons to leave people.

Jesus Heals a Sick Man

[40] A man who had a harmful skin disease came to Jesus. The man fell to his knees and begged Jesus, "I know that you can heal me if you will."

[41] Jesus felt sorry for the man. So he touched him and said, "I want to heal you. Be healed!" [42] At once the disease left the man, and he was healed.

[43] Jesus told the man to go at once. But Jesus warned him strongly, [44] "Don't tell anyone about what I did for you, but go and show yourself to the priest. And offer a gift to God because you have been healed. Offer the gift that Moses commanded.[n] This will show the people that you are healed." [45] The man left there, but he told everyone he saw that Jesus had healed him. So the news about Jesus

Simon   Simon's other name was Peter.
Moses commanded   Read about this in Leviticus 14:1–32.

spread. That is the reason Jesus could not enter a town if people saw him. He stayed in places where nobody lived. But people came from all the towns to wherever he was.

Jesus Heals a Paralysed Man

2 A few days later, Jesus came back to Capernaum. The news spread that he was home. ²So many people gathered to hear him preach that the house was full. There was nowhere to stand, not even outside the door. Jesus was teaching them. ³Some people came, bringing a paralysed man to Jesus. Four of them were carrying the paralysed man. ⁴But they could not get to Jesus because of the crowd. So they went to the roof above Jesus and made a hole in the roof. Then they lowered the mat with the paralysed man on it. ⁵Jesus saw that these men had great faith. So he said to the paralysed man, "Young man, your sins are forgiven."

⁶Some of the teachers of the law were sitting there. They saw what Jesus did, and they said to themselves, ⁷"Why does this man say things like that? He is saying things that are against God. Only God can forgive sins."

⁸At once Jesus knew what these teachers of the law were thinking. So he said to them, "Why are you thinking these things? ⁹Which is easier: to tell this paralysed man, 'Your sins are forgiven', or to tell him, 'Stand up. Take your mat and walk'? ¹⁰But I will prove to you that the Son of Man*d* has authority on earth to forgive sins." So Jesus said to the paralysed man, ¹¹"I tell you, stand up. Take your mat and go home." ¹²Immediately the paralysed man stood up. He took his mat and walked out while everyone was watching him.

The people were amazed and

Mark 2:5 "Young man, your sins are forgiven."

praised God. They said, "We have never seen anything like this!"

¹³Jesus went to the lake again. A crowd followed him there, and he taught them. ¹⁴While he was walking beside the lake, he saw a tax collector named Levi son of Alphaeus. Levi was sitting in the tax office. Jesus said to him, "Follow me". And Levi stood up and followed Jesus.

¹⁵Later that day, Jesus ate at Levi's house. There were many tax collectors and "sinners" eating there with Jesus and his followers. Many people like this followed Jesus. ¹⁶The teachers of the law who were Pharisees*d* saw Jesus eating with the tax collectors and "sinners". They asked his followers, "Why does he eat with tax collectors and 'sinners'?"

¹⁷Jesus heard this and said to them, "Healthy people don't need a doctor. It is the sick who need a doctor. I did not come to invite good people. I came to invite sinners."

Jesus' Followers Are Criticised

[18] One day the followers of John[n] and the Pharisees[d] were giving up eating.[n] Some people came to Jesus and said, "John's followers and the followers of the Pharisees give up eating, but your followers don't. Why?"

[19] Jesus answered, "When there is a wedding, the friends of the bridegroom are not sad while he is with them. They do not give up eating while the bridegroom is still there. [20] But the time will come when the bridegroom will leave them. Then the friends will be sad and will give up eating.

[21] "When a person sews a patch over a hole on an old coat, he never uses a piece of cloth that is not yet shrunk. If he does, the patch will shrink and pull away from the coat. Then the hole will be worse. [22] Also, no one ever pours new wine into old leather bags for holding wine. If he does, the new wine will break the bags, and the wine will be ruined along with the bags for the wine. People always put new wine into new leather bags."

Jesus Is Lord of the Sabbath

[23] On the Sabbath[d] day, Jesus was walking through some grainfields. His followers were with him and picked some grain to eat. [24] The Pharisees[d] saw this and said to Jesus, "Why are your followers doing what is not lawful on the Sabbath?"

[25] Jesus answered, "You have read what David did when he and those with him were hungry and needed food. [26] It was during the time of Abiathar the high priest. David went into God's house and ate the bread that was made holy for God. The law of Moses says that only priests may eat that bread. But David also gave some of the bread to those who were with him."

[27] Then Jesus said to the Pharisees, "The Sabbath day was made to help people. They were not made to be ruled by the Sabbath day. [28] The Son of Man[d] is Lord even of the Sabbath."

Jesus Heals a Man's Crippled Hand

3 Another time when Jesus went into a synagogue,[d] a man with a crippled hand was there. [2] Some people there wanted to see Jesus do something wrong so they could accuse him. They watched him closely to see if he would heal the man on the Sabbath[d] day.

[3] Jesus said to the man with the crippled hand, "Stand up here in front of everyone."

[4] Then Jesus asked the people, "Which is right on the Sabbath day: to do good, or to do evil? Is it right to save a life or to destroy one?" But they said nothing to answer him.

[5] Jesus was angry as he looked at the people. But he felt very sad because they were stubborn. Then he said to the man, "Let me see your hand." The man put his hand out for Jesus, and it was healed. [6] Then the Pharisees[d] left and began making plans with the Herodians[n] about a way to kill Jesus.

Many People Follow Jesus

[7] Jesus left with his followers for the lake. A large crowd from Galilee followed him. [8] Also many people came from Judea, from Jerusalem, from Idumea, from the lands across the Jordan River, and from the area of

---

John John the Baptist who preached to the Jews about Christ's coming (Mark 1:4–8).
giving up eating This is called "fasting". The people would give up eating for a special time of prayer and worship to God. It was also done to show sadness.
Herodians A political group that followed Herod and his family.

Tyre and Sidon. They came because they had heard about all the things Jesus was doing. ⁹Jesus saw the crowds. So he told his followers to get a boat ready for him. He wanted the boat so that the many people would not crowd themselves against him. ¹⁰He had healed many people. So all the sick were pushing toward him to touch him. ¹¹Some had evil spirits in them. When the evil spirits saw Jesus, they fell down before him and shouted, "You are the Son of God!" ¹²But Jesus strongly commanded the spirits not to tell who he was.

Jesus Chooses His 12 Apostles

¹³Then Jesus went up on a hill and called some men to come to him. These were the men Jesus wanted, and they went up to him. ¹⁴Jesus chose 12 men and called them apostles.ᵈ He wanted these 12 to be with him, and he wanted to send them to other places to preach. ¹⁵He also wanted them to have the power to force demonsᵈ out of people. ¹⁶These are the 12 men he chose: Simon (Jesus gave him the name Peter); ¹⁷James and John, the sons of Zebedee (Jesus gave them the name Boanerges, which means "Sons of Thunder"); ¹⁸Andrew, Philip, Bartholomew, Matthew, Thomas, James the son of Alphaeus, Thaddaeus, Simon the Zealot,ᵈ ¹⁹and Judas Iscariot. Judas is the one who gave Jesus to his enemies.

People Say Jesus Has a Devil

²⁰Then Jesus went back home. But again a crowd gathered. There were so many people that Jesus and his followers could not eat. ²¹His family heard about all these things. They went to get him because people were saying that Jesus was out of his mind. ²²And the teachers of the law from Jerusalem were saying, "Beelzebulᵈ is

living inside him! He uses power from the ruler of demonsᵈ to force demons out."

²³So Jesus called the people together and used stories to teach them. He said, "Satan will not force his own demons out of people. ²⁴A kingdom that fights against itself cannot continue, ²⁵and a family that is divided cannot continue. ²⁶And if Satan is against himself and fights against his own people, then he cannot continue. And that is the end of Satan. ²⁷If a person wants to enter a strong man's house and steal his things, first he must tie up the strong man. Then the thief can steal the things from the strong man's house. ²⁸I tell you the truth. All sins that people do can be forgiven. And all the bad things people say against God can be forgiven. ²⁹But any person who says bad things against the Holy Spiritᵈ will never be forgiven. He is guilty of a sin that continues for ever."

³⁰Jesus said this because the teachers of the law said that Jesus had an evil spirit inside him.

Jesus' True Family

³¹Then Jesus' mother and brothers arrived. They stood outside and sent someone in to tell him to come out. ³²Many people were sitting around Jesus. They said to him, "Your mother and brothers are waiting for you outside."

³³Jesus asked, "Who is my mother? Who are my brothers?" ³⁴Then Jesus looked at those sitting around him. He said, "Here are my mother and my brothers! ³⁵My true brother and sister and mother are those who do the things God wants."

A Story About Planting Seed

4 Another time Jesus began teaching by the lake. A great crowd

gathered around him. So he got into a boat and went out on the lake. All the people stayed on the shore close to the water. [2]Jesus used many stories to teach them. He said, [3]"Listen! A farmer went out to plant his seed. [4]While the farmer was planting, some seed fell by the road. The birds came and ate all that seed. [5]Some seed fell on rocky ground where there wasn't much soil. The seed grew very fast there because the ground was not deep. [6]But when the sun rose, the plants withered. The plants died because they did not have deep roots. [7]Some other seed fell among thorny weeds. The weeds grew and choked the good plants. So those plants did not make grain. [8]Some other seed fell on good ground. In the good ground, the seed began to grow. It grew and made a crop of grain. Some plants made 30 times more grain, some 60 times more grain, and some 100 times more grain."

[9]Then Jesus said, "You people who hear me, listen!"

Jesus Tells Why He Used Stories

[10]Later, when Jesus was alone, the 12 apostles[d] and others around him asked him about the stories.

[11]Jesus said, "Only you can know the secret truth about the kingdom of God. But to other people I tell everything by using stories. [12]I do this so that:

'They will look and look, but they will not learn.

They will listen and listen, but they will not understand.

If they did learn and understand, they would come back to me and be forgiven'."

Isaiah 6:9–10

Jesus Explains the Seed Story

[13]Then Jesus said to the followers, "Do you understand this story? If you don't, then how will you understand any story? [14]The farmer is like a person who plants God's teaching in people. [15]Sometimes the teaching falls on the road. This is like some people. They hear the teaching of God. But Satan quickly comes and takes away the teaching that was planted in them. [16]Others are like the seed planted on rocky ground. They hear the teaching and quickly accept it with joy. [17]But they don't allow the teaching to go deep into their lives. They keep it only a short time. When trouble or persecution comes because of the teaching, they quickly give up. [18]Others are like the seed planted among the thorny weeds. They hear the teaching. [19]But then other things come into their lives: worries, the love of money, and wanting all kinds of other things. These things stop the teaching from growing. So that teaching does not produce fruit[n] in their lives. [20]Others are like the seed planted in the good ground. They hear the teaching and accept it. Then they grow and produce fruit – sometimes 30 times more, sometimes 60 times more, and sometimes 100 times more."

Use What You Have

[21]Then Jesus said to them, "Do you hide a lamp under a bowl or under a bed? No! You put the lamp on a lampstand. [22]Everything that is hidden will be made clear. Every secret thing will be made known. [23]You people who hear me, listen!

[24]"Think carefully about the things you hear. The way you give to others is the way God will give to you. But

produce fruit To produce fruit means to have in your life the good things God wants.

God will give you more than you give. 25The person who has something will be given more. But the person who does not have much, even what he has will be taken from him."

Jesus Uses a Story About Seed

26Then Jesus said, "The kingdom of God is like a man who plants seed in the ground. 27The seed comes up and grows night and day. It doesn't matter whether the man is asleep or awake; the seed still grows. The man does not know how it grows. 28Without any help, the earth produces grain. First the plant grows, then the head, and then all the grain in the head. 29When the grain is ready, the man cuts it. This is the harvest time."

A Story About Mustard Seed

30Then Jesus said, "How can I show you what the kingdom of God is like? What story can I use to explain it? 31The kingdom of God is like a mustard seed. The mustard seed is the smallest seed you plant in the ground. 32But when you plant this seed, it grows and becomes the largest of all garden plants. It produces large branches. Even the wild birds can make nests in it and be protected from the sun."

33Jesus used many stories like these to teach them. He taught them all that they could understand. 34He always used stories to teach them. But when he and his followers were alone together, Jesus explained everything to them.

Jesus Stops a Storm

35That evening, Jesus said to his followers, "Come with me across the lake." 36He and the followers left the people there. They went in the boat that Jesus was already sitting in. There were also other boats with them. 37A very strong wind came up on the lake.

The waves began coming over the sides and into the boat. It was almost full of water. 38Jesus was at the back of the boat, sleeping with his head on a pillow. The followers went to him and woke him. They said, "Teacher, do you care about us? We will drown!"

39Jesus stood up and commanded the wind and the waves to stop. He said, "Quiet! Be still!" Then the wind stopped, and the lake became calm.

40Jesus said to his followers, "Why are you afraid? Do you still have no faith?"

41The followers were very afraid and asked each other, "What kind of man is this? Even the wind and the waves obey him!"

A Man with Demons Inside Him

5 Jesus and his followers went across the lake to the region of the Gerasene people. 2When Jesus got out of the boat, a man came to him from the caves where dead people were buried. This man, who lived in the caves, had an evil spirit living in him. 3No one could tie him up, not even with a chain. 4Many times people had used chains to tie the man's hands and feet. But he always broke the chains off. No one was strong enough to control him. 5Day and night he would wander around the burial caves and on the hills, screaming and cutting himself with stones. 6While Jesus was still far away, the man saw him. He ran to Jesus and knelt down before him. 7-8Jesus said to the man, "You evil spirit, come out of that man."

But the man shouted in a loud voice, "What do you want with me, Jesus, Son of the Most High God? I beg you, promise God that you will not punish me!"

9Then Jesus asked the man, "What is your name?"

The man answered, "My name is

Legion,[n] because I have many spirits in me." [10]The man begged Jesus again and again not to send the spirits out of that area.

[11]A large herd of pigs was eating on a hill near there. [12]The evil spirits begged Jesus, "Send us to the pigs. Let us go into them." [13]So Jesus allowed them to do this. The evil spirits left the man and went into the pigs. Then the herd of pigs rushed down the hill into the lake and were drowned. There were about 2,000 pigs in that herd.

Mark 5:13 Then the herd of pigs rushed down the hill into the lake and were drowned.

[14]The men who took care of the pigs ran away. They went to the town and to the countryside, telling everyone about this. So people went out to see what had happened. [15]They came to Jesus and saw the man who had had the many evil spirits. The man was sitting there, clothed and in his right mind. The people were frightened. [16]Some people were there who saw what Jesus had done. They told the others what had happened to the man who had the demons[d] living in him. And they also told about the pigs. [17]Then the people began to beg Jesus to leave their area.

[18]Jesus was getting ready to leave in the boat. The man who was freed from the demons begged to go with him.

[19]But Jesus would not allow the man to go. Jesus said, "Go home to your family and friends. Tell them how much the Lord has done for you and how he has had mercy on you." [20]So the man left and told the people in the Ten Towns[n] about the great things Jesus had done for him. All the people were amazed.

Jesus Gives Life to a Dead Girl and Heals a Sick Woman

[21]Jesus went in the boat back to the other side of the lake. There, a large crowd gathered around him. [22]A ruler from the synagogue,[d] named Jairus, came to that place. Jairus saw Jesus and bowed before him. [23]The ruler begged Jesus again and again. He said, "My little daughter is dying. Please come and put your hands on her. Then she will be healed and will live." [24]So Jesus went with the ruler, and many people followed Jesus. They were pushing very close around him.

[25]A woman was there who had been bleeding for the past 12 years. [26]She had suffered very much. Many doctors had tried to help her. She had spent all the money she had, but she

Legion Means very many. A legion was about 5,000 men in the Roman army.
Ten Towns In Greek, called "Decapolis". It was an area east of Lake Galilee that once had ten main towns.

was not improving. She was getting worse. [27]When the woman heard about Jesus, she followed him with the people and touched his coat. [28]The woman thought, "If I can even touch his coat, that will be enough to heal me." [29]When she touched his coat, her bleeding stopped. She could feel in her body that she was healed.

[30]At once Jesus felt power go out from him. So he stopped and turned around. Then he asked, "Who touched my clothes?"

[31]The followers said, "There are so many people pushing against you! And you ask, 'Who touched me?'"

[32]But Jesus continued looking around to see who had touched him. [33]The woman knew that she was healed. So she came and bowed at Jesus' feet. Shaking with fear, she told him the whole story. [34]Jesus said to the woman, "Dear woman, you are made well because you believed. Go in peace. You will have no more suffering."

[35]Jesus was still speaking to her when some men came from the house of Jairus, the synagogue ruler. The men said, "Your daughter is dead. There is now no need to bother the teacher."

[36]But Jesus paid no attention to what the men said. He said to the synagogue ruler, "Don't be afraid; only believe."

[37]Jesus let only Peter, James, and John the brother of James go with him to Jairus's house. [38]They came to the house of the synagogue ruler, and Jesus found many people there crying loudly. There was much confusion. [39]Jesus entered the house and said to the people, "Why are you crying and making so much noise? This child is not dead. She is only asleep." [40]But they only laughed at Jesus. He told all the people to leave. Then he went into the room where the child was. He took the child's father and mother and his three followers into the room with him. [41]Then he took hold of the girl's hand and said to her, "Talitha, koum!" (This means, "Little girl, I tell you to stand up!") [42]The girl stood right up and began walking. (She was 12 years old.) The father and mother and the followers were amazed. [43]Jesus gave the father and mother strict orders not to tell people about this. Then he told them to give the girl some food.

Jesus Goes to His Home Town

6 Jesus left there and went back to his home town. His followers went with him. [2]On the Sabbath[d] day he taught in the synagogue.[d] Many people heard him and were amazed. They said, "Where did this man get these teachings? What is this wisdom that has been given to him? And where did he get the power to work miracles?[d] [3]He is only the carpenter. His mother is Mary. He is the brother of James, Joseph, Judas, and Simon. And his sisters are here with us." The people did not accept Jesus.

[4]Jesus said to them, "Other people give honour to a prophet.[d] But in his own town with his own people and in his own home, a prophet does not receive honour." [5]Jesus was not able to work many miracles there. The only miracles he did were to heal some sick people by putting his hands on them. [6]Jesus was amazed that they had no faith.

Then Jesus went to other villages in that area and taught. [7]He called the 12 followers together and sent them out in groups of two. He gave them authority over evil spirits. [8]This is what Jesus told them: "Take nothing for your trip except a walking stick. Take no bread, no bag, and no money in your pockets. [9]Wear sandals, and take only the clothes you are wearing.

[10]When you enter a house, stay there until you leave that place. [11]If any town refuses to accept you or its people refuse to listen to you, then leave that town. Shake its dust off your feet.[n] This will be a warning to them."

[12]The followers went out and preached to the people to change their hearts and lives. [13]The followers forced many demons[d] out and poured olive oil on many sick people and healed them.

How John the Baptist Was Killed

[14]King Herod heard about Jesus, because Jesus was now well-known. Some people said, "He is John the Baptist.[d] He is risen from death. That is the reason he can work these miracles."[d]

[15]Others said, "He is Elijah."[n]

Other people said, "Jesus is a prophet.[d] He is like the prophets who lived long ago."

[16]Herod heard all these things about Jesus. He said, "I killed John by cutting off his head. Now he has been raised from death!"

[17]Herod himself had ordered his soldiers to arrest John, and John was put in prison. Herod did this to please his wife, Herodias. Herodias was the wife of Philip, Herod's brother. But then Herod married her. [18]John told Herod that it was not lawful for him to be married to his brother's wife. [19]So Herodias hated John and wanted to kill him. But she could not because of Herod. [20]Herod was afraid to kill John because he knew John was a good and holy man. So Herod protected John. Also, Herod enjoyed listening to John preach. But John's preaching always bothered him.

[21]Then the perfect time came for Herodias to cause John's death. It happened on Herod's birthday. Herod gave a dinner party for the most important government leaders, the commanders of his army, and the most important people in Galilee. [22]The daughter of Herodias came to the party and danced. When she danced, Herod and the people eating with him were very pleased.

So King Herod said to the girl, "I will give you anything you want." [23]He promised her, "Anything you ask for I will give to you. I will even give you half of my kingdom."

[24]The girl went to her mother and asked, "What should I ask the king to give me?"

Her mother answered, "Ask for the head of John the Baptist."[d]

[25]Quickly the girl went back to the king. She said to him, "Please give me the head of John the Baptist. Bring it to me now on a platter."

[26]The king was very sad. But he had promised to give the girl anything she wanted. And the people eating there with him had heard his promise. So Herod could not refuse what she asked. [27]Immediately the king sent a soldier to bring John's head. The soldier went and cut off John's head in the prison [28]and brought it back on a platter. He gave it to the girl, and the girl gave it to her mother. [29]John's followers heard about what happened. So they came and got John's body and put it in a tomb.

More than 5,000 People Fed

[30]The apostles[d] that Jesus had sent out to preach returned. They gathered around him and told him about all the things they had done and taught. [31]Crowds of people were coming and

---

Shake . . . feet A warning. It showed that they had finished talking to these people.
Elijah A man who spoke for God. He lived hundreds of years before Christ.

going. Jesus and his followers did not even have time to eat. He said to them, "Come with me. We will go to a quiet place to be alone. There we will get some rest."

[32] So they went in a boat alone to a place where there were no people. [33] But many people saw them leave and recognised them. So people from all the towns ran to the place where Jesus was going. They got there before Jesus arrived. [34] When he landed, he saw a great crowd waiting. Jesus felt sorry for them, because they were like sheep without a shepherd. So he taught them many things.

[35] It was now late in the day. Jesus' followers came to him and said, "No one lives in this place. And it is already very late. [36] Send the people away. They need to go to the farms and towns around here to buy some food to eat."

[37] But Jesus answered, "You give them food to eat."

They said to him, "We can't buy enough bread to feed all these people! We would all have to work a month to earn enough money to buy that much bread!"

[38] Jesus asked them, "How many loaves of bread do you have now? Go and see."

When they found out, they came to him and said, "We have five loaves and two fish."

[39] Then Jesus said to the followers, "Tell all the people to sit in groups on the green grass." [40] So all the people sat in groups. They sat in groups of 50 or groups of 100. [41] Jesus took the five loaves and two fish. He looked up to heaven and thanked God for the bread. He divided the bread and gave it to his followers for them to give to the people. Then he divided the two fish among them all. [42] All the people ate and were satisfied. [43] The followers filled 12 baskets with the pieces of bread and fish that were not eaten. [44] There were about 5,000 men there who ate.

Jesus Walks on the Water

[45] Then Jesus told his followers to get into the boat and go to Bethsaida on the other side of the lake. Jesus said that he would come later. He stayed there to tell the people they could go home. [46] After sending them away, he went into the hills to pray.

[47] That night, the boat was in the middle of the lake. Jesus was alone on the land. [48] He saw the followers working hard to row the boat because the wind was blowing against them. At some time between three and six o'clock in the morning, Jesus came to them, walking on the water. He continued walking until he was almost past the boat. [49] But when his followers saw him walking on the water, they thought he was a ghost and cried out. [50] They all saw him and were terrified. But Jesus spoke to them and said, "Have courage! It is I! Do not be afraid." [51] Then he got into the boat with them. And the wind became calm. The followers were greatly amazed. [52] They had seen Jesus make more bread from the five loaves. But they did not understand what it meant. Their minds were closed.

[53] When they had crossed the lake, they came to shore at Gennesaret. They tied the boat there. [54] When they got out of the boat, the people saw Jesus and immediately recognised him. [55] They ran to tell others everywhere in that area that Jesus was there. They brought sick people on mats to every place Jesus went. [56] Jesus went into towns and cities and farms around that area. And everywhere he went, the people brought the sick to the marketplaces. They begged him to let them just touch the edge of

his coat. And all who touched him were healed.

Obey God's Law Not Men's

7 Some Pharisees*d* and some teachers of the law came from Jerusalem. They gathered around Jesus. ²They saw that some of Jesus' followers ate food with hands that were not clean.*d* ("Not clean" means that they did not wash their hands in the way the Pharisees said people must. ³The Pharisees and all the Jews never eat before washing their hands in this special way. They do this to follow the teaching given to them by their great people who lived before them. ⁴And when the Jews buy something in the market, they never eat it until they have washed it in a special way. They also follow other rules of their great people who lived before them. They follow rules about the washing of cups, pitchers, and pots.)

⁵The Pharisees and the teachers of the law said to Jesus, "Your followers don't follow the rules given to us by our great people who lived before us. Your followers eat their food with hands that are not clean. Why do they do this?"

⁶Jesus answered, "You are all hypocrites!*d* Isaiah was right when he spoke about you. Isaiah wrote,

'These people show honour to me
    with words.
But their hearts are far from
    me.
⁷Their worship of me is worthless.
    The things they teach are
        nothing
    but human rules they have
        memorised'.   *Isaiah 29:13*

⁸You have stopped following the commands of God. Now you only follow the teachings of men."

⁹Then Jesus said to them: "You think you are clever! You ignore the commands of God so that you can follow your own teachings! ¹⁰Moses said, 'Honour your father and mother'.*n* Then Moses also said, 'Anyone who says cruel things to his father or mother must be put to death'.*n* ¹¹But you teach that a person can say to his father or mother, 'I have something I could use to help you. But I will not use it for you. I will give it to God'. ¹²You are telling that person that he does not have to do anything for his father or mother. ¹³So you are teaching that it is not important to do what God said. You think that it is more important to follow your own rules,

---

'Honour your father and mother'. Quotation from Exodus 20:12; Deuteronomy 5:16.
'Anyone . . . death'. Quotation from Exodus 21:17.

Mark 7:5 "Your followers eat their food with hands that are not clean."

which you teach people. And you do many things like that."

[14] Jesus called the people to him again. He said, "Every person should listen to me and understand what I am saying. [15] There is nothing a person puts into his body that makes him unclean. A person is made unclean by the things that come out of him." [16] [n]

[17] When Jesus left the people and went inside, his followers asked him about this story. [18] Jesus said, "Do you still have trouble understanding? Surely you know that nothing that enters a man from the outside can make him unclean. [19] Food does not go into a person's mind. Food goes into his stomach. Then that food goes out of his body." (When Jesus said this, he meant that there is no food that is unclean for people to eat.)

[20] And Jesus said, "The things that come out of a man are the things that make him unclean. [21] All these evil things begin inside a person, in his mind: evil thoughts, sexual sins, stealing, murder, adultery,[d] [22] selfishness, doing bad things to other people, lying, doing sinful things, jealousy, saying bad things about people, pride, and foolish living. [23] All these evil things come from within a person. These things make a person unclean."

Jesus Helps a Non-Jewish Woman

[24] Jesus left that place and went to the area around Tyre. He went into a house and did not want anyone to know he was there. But Jesus could not stay hidden. [25] A woman heard that he was there. Her little daughter had an evil spirit in her. So the woman quickly came to Jesus and fell at his

feet. [26] She was not Jewish. She was Greek, born in Phoenicia, in Syria. She begged Jesus to force the demon[d] out of her daughter.

[27] Jesus told the woman: "It is not right to take the children's bread and give it to the dogs. First let the children eat all they want."

[28] She answered, "That is true, Lord. But the dogs under the table can eat the pieces of food that the children don't eat."

[29] Then Jesus said, "That is a very good answer. You may go. The demon has left your daughter."

[30] The woman went home and found her daughter lying in bed. The demon was gone.

Jesus Heals a Deaf Man

[31] Then Jesus left the area around Tyre. He went through Sidon to Lake Galilee, to the area of the Ten Towns.[n] [32] While he was there, some people brought a man to him. This man was deaf and could not talk. The people begged Jesus to put his hand on the man to heal him.

[33] Jesus led the man away from the crowd, to be alone with him. Jesus put his fingers in the man's ears. Then Jesus spat and touched the man's tongue. [34] Jesus looked up to heaven and took a deep breath. He said to the man, "Ephphatha!" (This means, "Be opened".) [35] When Jesus did this, the man was able to hear. He was also able to use his tongue, and he spoke clearly.

[36] Jesus commanded the people not to tell anyone about what happened. But the more he commanded them, the more they told about it. [37] They were really amazed. They said, "Jesus does everything well. He makes the

---

Verse 16   Some Greek copies add verse 16: "You people who hear me, listen!"
Ten Towns   In Greek, called "Decapolis". It was an area east of Lake Galilee that once had ten main towns.

deaf hear! And those who can't talk – Jesus makes them able to speak."

More than 4,000 People Fed

8 Another time there was a great crowd with Jesus. They had nothing to eat. So Jesus called his followers to him. He said, [2]"I feel sorry for these people. They have been with me for three days, and now they have nothing to eat. [3]I cannot send them home hungry. If they leave without eating, they will faint on the way home. Some of them live a long way from here."

[4]Jesus' followers answered, "But we are far away from any towns. Where can we get enough bread to feed all these people?"

[5]Jesus asked, "How many loaves of bread do you have?"

They answered, "We have seven loaves."

[6]Jesus told the people to sit on the ground. Then he took the seven loaves and gave thanks to God. Jesus divided the bread and gave the pieces to his followers. He told them to pass out the bread to the people, and they did so. [7]The followers also had a few small fish. Jesus gave thanks for the fish and told his followers to give the fish to the people. [8]All the people ate and were satisfied. Then the followers filled seven baskets with the pieces of food that were not eaten. [9]There were about 4,000 men who ate. After they had eaten, Jesus told them to go home. [10]Then he went in a boat with his followers to the area of Dalmanutha.

The Leaders Ask for a Miracle

[11]The Pharisees[d] came to Jesus and asked him questions. They wanted to trap him. So they asked Jesus to do a miracle[d] to show that he was from God. [12]Jesus sighed deeply. He said, "Why do you people ask for a miracle as proof? I tell you the truth. No miracle will be given to you." [13]Then Jesus left the Pharisees. He went in the boat to the other side of the lake.

Guard Against Wrong Teachings

[14]The followers had only one loaf of bread with them in the boat. They had forgotten to bring more bread. [15]Jesus warned them, "Be careful! Guard against the yeast of the Pharisees[d] and the yeast of Herod."

[16]Among themselves, his disciples discussed the meaning of this. They said, "He said this because we have no bread."

[17]Jesus knew what his followers were talking about. So he asked them, "Why are you talking about having no bread? You still don't see or understand? Are your minds closed? [18]You have eyes, but you don't really see. You have ears, but you don't really listen. Remember what I did before, when we did not have enough bread? [19]I divided five loaves of bread for 5,000 people. Remember how many baskets you filled with pieces of food that were not eaten?"

They answered, "We filled 12 baskets."

[20]"And remember that I divided seven loaves of bread for 4,000 people. Remember how many baskets you filled with pieces of food that were not eaten?"

They answered, "We filled seven baskets."

[21]Then Jesus said to them, "You remember these things I did, but you still don't understand?"

Jesus Heals a Blind Man

[22]Jesus and his followers came to Bethsaida. Some people brought a blind man to Jesus and begged him to touch the man. [23]So Jesus took the blind man's hand and led him out of the village. Then he spat on the man's

eyes. He put his hands on the blind man and asked, "Can you see now?"

24 The man looked up and said, "Yes, I see people, but they look like trees walking around."

25 Again Jesus put his hands on the man's eyes. Then the man opened his eyes wide. His eyes were healed, and he was able to see everything clearly. 26 Jesus told him to go home, saying, "Don't go into the town."

Peter Says Jesus Is the Christ

27 Jesus and his followers went to the towns around Caesarea Philippi. While they were travelling, Jesus asked them, "Who do people say I am?"

28 They answered, "Some people say you are John the Baptist.[d] Others say you are Elijah.[n] And others say that you are one of the prophets."[d]

29 Then Jesus asked, "Who do you say I am?"

Peter answered, "You are the Christ."[d]

30 Jesus ordered his followers, "Don't tell anyone who I am."

31 Then Jesus began to teach them that the Son of Man[d] must suffer many things. He taught that the Son of Man would not be accepted by the older Jewish leaders, the leading priests, and the teachers of the law. He taught that the Son of Man must be killed and then rise from death after three days. 32 Jesus told them plainly what would happen. Then Peter took Jesus aside and began to criticise him. 33 But Jesus turned and looked at his followers. Then he criticised Peter and said, "Go away from me, Satan![n] You don't care about the things of God. You care only about things men think are important."

34 Then Jesus called the crowd to him, along with his followers. He said, "If anyone wants to follow me, he must say 'no' to the things he wants. He must be willing to die on a cross, and he must follow me. 35 Whoever wants to save his life will give up true life. But whoever gives up his life for me and for the Good News[d] will have true life for ever. 36 It is worth nothing for a person to have the whole world, if he loses his soul. 37 A person could never pay enough to buy back his soul. 38 The people who live now are living in a sinful and evil time. If anyone is ashamed of me and my teaching, then I will be ashamed of him. I will be ashamed of him when I come with the glory of my Father and the holy angels."

9 Then Jesus said to the people, "I tell you the truth. Some of you standing here will see the kingdom of God come with power before you die."

Jesus with Moses and Elijah

2 Six days later Jesus took Peter, James, and John and went up on a high mountain. They were all alone there. While these followers watched, Jesus was changed. 3 His clothes became shining white, whiter than any person could make them. 4 Then two men appeared, talking with Jesus. The men were Moses and Elijah.[n]

5 Peter said to Jesus, "Teacher, it is good that we are here. We will put three tents here – one for you, one for Moses, and one for Elijah." 6 Peter did not know what to say, because he and the others were so frightened.

7 Then a cloud came and covered them. A voice came from the cloud.

Elijah   A man who spoke for God. He lived hundreds of years before Christ.
Satan   Name for the devil meaning "the enemy". Jesus means that Peter was talking like Satan.
Moses and Elijah   Two of the most important Jewish leaders in the past.

The voice said, "This is my Son, and I love him. Obey him!"

⁸Then Peter, James, and John looked around, but they saw only Jesus there alone with them.

⁹As Jesus and his followers were walking back down the mountain, he commanded them, "Don't tell anyone about the things you saw on the mountain. Wait till the Son of Man*ᵈ* rises from death. Then you may tell."

¹⁰So the followers obeyed Jesus and said nothing about what they had seen. But they discussed what Jesus meant about rising from death.

¹¹They asked Jesus, "Why do the teachers of the law say that Elijah must come first?"

¹²Jesus answered, "They are right to say that Elijah must come first. Elijah makes all things the way they should be. But why does the Scripture*ᵈ* say that the Son of Man will suffer much and that people will treat him as if he were nothing? ¹³I tell you that Elijah has already come. And people did to him whatever they wanted to do. The Scriptures said this would happen to him."

Jesus Heals a Sick Boy

¹⁴Then Jesus, Peter, James, and John went to the other followers. They saw a great crowd around them. The teachers of the law were arguing with them. ¹⁵But when the crowd saw Jesus, they were surprised and ran to welcome him.

¹⁶Jesus asked, "What are you arguing about with the teachers of the law?"

¹⁷A man answered, "Teacher, I brought my son to you. He has a spirit from the devil in him. This spirit stops him from talking. ¹⁸The spirit attacks him and throws him on the ground. My son foams at the mouth, grinds his teeth, and becomes very stiff. I asked your followers to force the evil spirit out, but they couldn't."

¹⁹Jesus answered, "You people don't believe! How long must I stay with you? How long must I go on being patient with you? Bring the boy to me!"

²⁰So the followers brought him to Jesus. As soon as the evil spirit saw Jesus, it attacked the boy. He fell down and rolled on the ground, foaming from his mouth.

²¹Jesus asked the boy's father, "How long has this been happening?"

The father answered, "Since he was very young. ²²The spirit often throws him into a fire or into water to kill him. If you can do anything for him, please have pity on us and help us."

²³Jesus said to the father, "You said, 'If you can!' All things are possible for him who believes."

²⁴Immediately the father cried out, "I do believe! Help me to believe more!"

²⁵Jesus saw that a crowd was running there to see what was happening. So he spoke to the evil spirit, saying, "You deaf and dumb spirit – I command you to come out of this boy and never enter him again!"

²⁶The evil spirit screamed and caused the boy to fall on the ground again. Then the spirit came out. The boy looked as if he were dead. And many people said, "He is dead!" ²⁷But Jesus took hold of the boy's hand and helped him to stand up.

²⁸Jesus went into the house. His followers were alone with him there. They said, "Why couldn't we force that evil spirit out?"

²⁹Jesus answered, "That kind of spirit can only be forced out by prayer."

Jesus Talks About His Death

³⁰Then Jesus and his followers left that place and went through Galilee.

Jesus did not want anyone to know where he was [31]because he wanted to teach his followers alone. He said to them, "The Son of Man[d] will be given to men who will kill him. After three days, he will rise from death." [32]But the followers did not understand what Jesus meant. And they were afraid to ask.

Who Is the Greatest?

[33]Jesus and his followers went to Capernaum and went into a house there. Then Jesus said to them, "What were you arguing about on the road?" [34]But the followers did not answer, because their argument on the road was about which one of them was the greatest. [35]Jesus sat down and called the 12 apostles[d] to him. He said, "If anyone wants to be the most important, then he must be last of all and servant of all."

[36]Then Jesus took a small child and had him stand among them. He took the child in his arms and said, [37]"If anyone accepts children like these in my name, then he is also accepting me. And if he accepts me, then he is also accepting the One who sent me."

Anyone Not Against Us Is For Us

[38]Then John said, "Teacher, we saw a man using your name to force demons[d] out of a person. We told him to stop, because he does not belong to our group."

[39]Jesus said, "Don't stop him. Anyone who uses my name to do powerful things will not say evil things about me. [40]He who is not against us is with us. [41]I tell you the truth. If anyone

Mark 9:37 "If anyone accepts children . . . he is also accepting me."

helps you by giving you a drink of water because you belong to the Christ,[d] then he will truly get his reward.

[42]"If one of these little children believes in me, and someone causes that child to sin, then it will be very bad for him. It would be better for him to have a large stone tied around his neck and be drowned in the sea. [43]If your hand causes you to sin, cut it off. It is better for you to lose part of your body but have life for ever. That is much better than to have two hands and go to hell. In that place the fire never goes out. [44] n [45]If your foot causes you to sin, cut it off. It is better for you to lose part of your body but have life for ever. That is much better than to have two feet and be thrown into hell. [46] n [47]If your eye causes you to sin, take it out. It is better for you

Verse 44 Some Greek copies of Mark add verse 44, which is the same as verse 48.
Verse 46 Some Greek copies of Mark add verse 46, which is the same as verse 48.

to have only one eye but have life for ever. That is much better than to have two eyes and be thrown into hell. [48]In hell the worm does not die; the fire is never stopped. [49]Every person will be salted with fire.

[50]"Salt is good. But if the salt loses its salty taste, then you cannot make it salty again. So, be full of goodness. And have peace with each other."

Jesus Teaches About Divorce

10 Then Jesus left that place. He went into the area of Judea and across the Jordan River. Again, crowds came to him. And Jesus taught them as he always did.

[2]Some Pharisees[d] came to Jesus and tried to trick him. They asked, "Is it right for a man to divorce his wife?"

[3]Jesus answered, "What did Moses command you to do?"

[4]They said, "Moses allowed a man to write out divorce papers and send her away."[n]

[5]Jesus said, "Moses wrote that command for you because you refused to accept God's teaching. [6]But when God made the world, 'he made them male and female'.[n] [7]'So a man will leave his father and mother and be united with his wife. [8]And the two people will become one body'.[n] So the people are not two, but one. [9]God has joined the two people together. So no one should separate them."

[10]Later, the followers and Jesus were in the house. They asked Jesus again about the question of divorce. [11]He answered, "Anyone who divorces his wife and marries another woman is guilty of adultery[d] against her. [12]And the woman who divorces her husband and marries another man is also guilty of adultery."

Jesus Accepts Children

[13]Some people brought their small children to Jesus so he could touch them. But his followers told the people to stop bringing their children to him. [14]When Jesus saw this, he was displeased. He said to them, "Let the little children come to me. Don't stop them. The kingdom of God belongs to people who are like these little children. [15]I tell you the truth. You must accept the kingdom of God as a little child accepts things, or you will never enter it." [16]Then Jesus took the children in his arms. He put his hands on them and blessed them.

A Rich Young Man's Question

[17]Jesus started to leave, but a man ran to him and fell on his knees before Jesus. The man asked, "Good teacher, what must I do to get the life that never ends?"

[18]Jesus answered, "Why do you call me good? No one is good except God alone. [19]You know the commands: 'You must not murder anyone. You must not be guilty of adultery.[d] You must not steal. You must not tell lies about your neighbour in court. You must not cheat. Honour your father and mother'."[n]

[20]The man said, "Teacher, I have obeyed all these commands since I was a boy."

[21]Jesus looked straight at the man and loved him. Jesus said, "There is still one more thing you need to do. Go and sell everything you have, and give the money to the poor. You will

---

"Moses . . . away." Quotation from Deuteronomy 24:1.
'he made . . . female'. Quotation from Genesis 1:27.
'So . . . body'. Quotation from Genesis 2:24.
'You . . . mother'. Quotation from Exodus 20:12–16; Deuteronomy 5:16–20.

have a reward in heaven. Then come and follow me."

²²He was very sad to hear Jesus say this, and he left. The man was sad because he was very rich.

²³Then Jesus looked at his followers and said, "How hard it will be for those who are rich to enter the kingdom of God!"

²⁴The followers were amazed at what Jesus said. But he said again, "My children, it is very hard to enter the kingdom of God! ²⁵And it will be very hard for a rich person to enter the kingdom of God. It would be easier for a camel to go through the eye of a needle!"

²⁶The followers were even more amazed and said to each other, "Then who can be saved?"

²⁷Jesus looked straight at them and said, "This is something that men cannot do. But God can do it. God can do all things."

²⁸Peter said to Jesus, "We left everything to follow you!"

²⁹Jesus said, "I tell you the truth. Everyone who has left his home, brothers, sisters, mother, father, children, or fields for me and for the Good News*d* ³⁰will get a hundred times more than he left. Here in this world he will have more homes, brothers, sisters, mothers, children, and fields. And with those things, he will also suffer for his belief. But in the age that is coming he will have life for ever. ³¹Many who have the highest place now will have the lowest place in the future. And those who have the lowest place now will have the highest place in the future."

Jesus Talks About His Own Death

³²Jesus and the people with him were on the road to Jerusalem. Jesus

was leading the way. The followers were amazed, but those who followed behind them were afraid. Jesus took the 12 apostles*d* aside and talked with them alone. He told them what would happen in Jerusalem. ³³He said, "We are going to Jerusalem. The Son of Man*d* will be given to the leading priests and teachers of the law. They will say that he must die. They will give him to the non-Jewish people, ³⁴who will laugh at him and spit on him. They will beat him with whips and kill him. But on the third day after his death, he will rise to life again."

Two Followers Ask Jesus a Favour

³⁵Then James and John, sons of Zebedee, came to Jesus. They said, "Teacher, we want to ask you to do something for us."

³⁶Jesus asked, "What do you want me to do for you?"

³⁷They answered, "You will have glory in your kingdom. Let one of us sit at your right, and let one of us sit at your left."

³⁸Jesus said, "You don't understand what you are asking. Can you drink the cup that I must drink? And can you be baptised with the same kind of baptism that I must have?"*n*

³⁹They answered, "Yes, we can!"

Jesus said to them, "You will drink the same cup that I will drink. And you will be baptised with the same baptism that I must have. ⁴⁰But I cannot choose who will sit at my right or my left. These places are for those for whom they are prepared."

⁴¹The ten followers heard this. They began to be angry with James and John.

⁴²Jesus called all the followers

Can you . . . have? Jesus was asking if they could suffer the same terrible things that would happen to him.

together. He said, "The non-Jewish people have men they call rulers. You know that those rulers love to show their power over the people. And their important leaders love to use all their authority. ⁴³But it should not be that way among you. If one of you wants to become great, then he must serve you like a servant. ⁴⁴If one of you wants to become the most important, then he must serve all of you like a slave. ⁴⁵In the same way, the Son of Man*ᵈ* did not come to be served. He came to serve. The Son of Man came to give his life to save many people."

Jesus Heals a Blind Man

⁴⁶Then they came to the town of Jericho. As Jesus was leaving there with his followers and a large crowd, a blind beggar named Bartimaeus (son of Timaeus) was sitting by the road. ⁴⁷He heard that Jesus from Nazareth was walking by. The blind man cried out, "Jesus, Son of David,*ᵈ* please help me!"

⁴⁸Many people scolded the blind man and told him to be quiet. But he shouted more and more, "Son of David, please help me!"

⁴⁹Jesus stopped and said, "Tell the man to come here."

So they called the blind man. They said, "Cheer up! Get to your feet. Jesus is calling you." ⁵⁰The blind man stood up quickly. He left his coat there and went to Jesus.

⁵¹Jesus asked him, "What do you want me to do for you?"

The blind man answered, "Teacher, I want to see again."

⁵²Jesus said, "Go. You are healed because you believed." At once the man was able to see again, and he followed Jesus on the road.

Jesus Enters Jerusalem as a King

11 Jesus and his followers were coming closer to Jerusalem. They came to the towns of Bethphage and Bethany near the Mount of Olives.*ᵈ* There Jesus sent two of his followers. ²He said to them, "Go to the town you see there. When you enter it, you will find a colt tied which no one has ever ridden. Untie it and bring it here to me. ³If anyone asks you why you are doing this, tell him, 'The Master needs the colt. He will send it back soon'."

⁴The followers went into the town. They found a colt tied in the street near the door of a house, and they untied it. ⁵Some people were standing there and asked, "What are you doing? Why are you untying that colt?" ⁶The followers answered the way Jesus told them to answer, and the people let them take the colt.

⁷The followers brought the colt to Jesus. They put their coats on the colt, and Jesus sat on it. ⁸Many people spread their coats on the road. Others cut branches in the fields and spread the branches on the road. ⁹Some of the people were walking ahead of Jesus. Others were following him. All of them were shouting,

"Praise*ⁿ* God!
God bless the One who comes in
     the name of the Lord!
                              Psalm 118:26
¹⁰ God bless the kingdom of our
     father David!
     That kingdom is coming!
     Praise to God in heaven!"

¹¹Jesus entered Jerusalem and went into the Temple.*ᵈ* When he had looked at everything, and since it was already late, he went out to Bethany with the 12 apostles.*ᵈ*

Praise Literally, "Hosanna", a Hebrew word used at first in praying to God for help, but at this time it was probably a shout of joy used in praising God or his Messiah.

[12]The next day as Jesus was leaving Bethany, he was hungry. [13]He saw a fig tree in leaf. So he went to the tree to see if it had any figs on it. But he found no figs, only leaves. It was not the right season for figs to grow. [14]So Jesus said to the tree, "May no one ever eat fruit from you again." Jesus' followers heard him say this.

Jesus Goes to the Temple

[15]Jesus returned to Jerusalem and went into the Temple.[d] He began to throw out those who were buying and selling things there. He overturned the tables that belonged to the men

Mark 11:15 He overturned the tables . . .

who were exchanging different kinds of money. And he turned over the benches of the men who were selling doves. [16]Jesus refused to allow anyone to carry goods through the Temple courts. [17]Then Jesus taught the people. He said, "It is written in the Scriptures,[d] 'My Temple will be a house where people from all nations will pray'.[n] But you are changing God's house into a 'hideout for robbers'."[n]

[18]The leading priests and the teachers of the law heard all this. They began trying to find a way to kill Jesus. They were afraid of him because all the people were amazed at his teaching. [19]That night, Jesus and his followers left the city.

The Power of Faith

[20]The next morning, Jesus was passing by with his followers. They saw the fig tree, and it was dry and dead, even to the roots. [21]Peter remembered the tree and said to Jesus, "Teacher, look! Yesterday, you cursed the fig tree. Now it is dry and dead!"

[22]Jesus answered, "Have faith in God. [23]I tell you the truth. You can say to this mountain, 'Go, mountain, fall into the sea'. And if you have no doubts in your mind and believe that the thing you say will happen, then God will do it for you. [24]So I tell you to ask for things in prayer. And if you believe that you have received those things, then they will be yours. [25]When you are praying, and you remember that you are angry with another person about something, then forgive him. If you do this, then your Father in heaven will also forgive your sins." [26][n]

Leaders Doubt Jesus' Authority

[27]Jesus and his followers went again to Jerusalem. Jesus was walking in the

---

'My Temple . . . pray'. Quotation from Isaiah 56:7.
'hideout for robbers'. Quotation from Jeremiah 7:11.
Verse 26 Some early Greek copies add verse 26: "But if you don't forgive other people, then your Father in heaven will not forgive your sins."

Temple.[d] The leading priests, the teachers of the law, and the older Jewish leaders came to him. [28]They said to him, "Tell us! What authority do you have to do these things? Who gave you this authority?"

[29]Jesus answered, "I will ask you one question. You answer it. Then I will tell you whose authority I use to do these things. [30]Tell me: when John baptised people, was that from God or from man? Answer me!"

[31]They argued about Jesus' question. They said to each other, "If we answer, 'John's baptism was from God', then Jesus will say, 'Then why didn't you believe John?' [32]But if we say, 'From man', then the people will be against us." (These leaders were afraid of the people. All the people believed that John was a prophet.[d])

[33]So the leaders answered Jesus, "We don't know."

Jesus said, "Then I will not tell you what authority I use to do these things."

God Sends His Son

12 Jesus used stories to teach the people. He said, "A man planted a vineyard. He put a wall around it and dug a hole for a winepress.[d] Then he built a tower. He leased the vineyard to some farmers and left for a trip. [2]Later, it was time for the grapes to be picked. So the man sent a servant to the farmers to get his share of the grapes. [3]But the farmers grabbed the servant and beat him. They sent him away with nothing. [4]Then the man sent another servant. They hit him on the head and showed no respect for him. [5]So the man sent another servant. They killed this servant. The man sent many other servants. The farmers beat some of them and killed others.

[6]"The man had one person left to send, his son whom he loved. He sent him last of all, saying, 'The farmers will respect my son'.

[7]"But they said to each other, 'This is the owner's son. This vineyard will be his. If we kill him, then it will be ours'. [8]So they took the son, killed him, and threw him out of the vineyard.

[9]"So what will the man who owns the vineyard do? He will go to the vineyard and kill those farmers. Then he will give the vineyard to other farmers. [10]Surely you have read this Scripture:[d]

'The stone that the builders did
    not want
  became the cornerstone.[d]
[11]The Lord did this,
  and it is wonderful to us'."

Psalm 118:22–23

[12]The Jewish leaders knew that the story was about them. So they wanted to find a way to arrest Jesus, but they were afraid of the people. So the leaders left him and went away.

The Leaders Try to Trap Jesus

[13]Later, the Jewish leaders sent some Pharisees[d] and some men from the group called Herodians[n] to Jesus. They wanted to catch Jesus saying something wrong. [14]They came to him and said, "Teacher, we know that you are an honest man. You are not afraid of what other people think about you. All men are the same to you. And you teach the truth about God's way. Tell us: is it right to pay taxes to Caesar?[d] Should we pay them, or not?"

[15]But Jesus knew what these men were really trying to do. He said, "Why are you trying to trap me? Bring me a silver coin. Let me see it." [16]They gave Jesus a coin, and he asked,

---

Herodians   A political group that followed Herod and his family.

"Whose picture is on the coin? And whose name is written on it?"

They answered, "Caesar's."

[17] Then Jesus said to them, "Give to Caesar the things that are Caesar's. And give to God the things that are God's." The men were amazed at what Jesus said.

Sadducees Try to Trick Jesus

[18] Then some Sadducees[d] came to Jesus. (Sadducees believe that no person will rise from death.) The Sadducees asked Jesus a question. [19] They said, "Teacher, Moses wrote that a man's brother might die. He leaves a wife but no children. Then that man must marry the widow and have children for the dead brother. [20] There were seven brothers. The first brother married but died. He had no children. [21] So the second brother married the widow. But he also died and had no children. The same thing happened with the third brother. [22] All seven brothers married her and died. None of the brothers had any children. The woman was last to die. [23] But all seven brothers had married her. So at the time people rise from death, whose wife will the woman be?"

[24] Jesus answered, "Why did you make this mistake? Is it because you don't know what the Scriptures[d] say? Or is it because you don't know about the power of God? [25] When people rise from death, there will be no marriage. People will not be married to each other but will be like angels in heaven. [26] Surely you have read what God said about people rising from death. In the book in which Moses wrote about the burning bush,[n] it says that God told

Moses this: 'I am the God of Abraham, the God of Isaac, and the God of Jacob'.[n] [27] God is the God of living people, not dead people. You Sadducees are wrong!"

The Most Important Command

[28] One of the teachers of the law came to Jesus. He heard Jesus arguing with the Sadducees[d] and the Pharisees.[d] He saw that Jesus gave good answers to their questions. So he asked Jesus, "Which of the commands is most important?"

[29] Jesus answered, "The most important command is this: 'Listen, people of Israel! The Lord our God, he is the only Lord. [30] Love the Lord your God. Love him with all your heart, all your soul, all your mind, and all your strength'.[n] [31] The second most important command is this: 'Love your neighbour as you love yourself'.[n] These two commands are the most important commands."

[32] The man answered, "That was a good answer, Teacher. You were right when you said these things. God is the only Lord, and there is no other God besides him. [33] A person must love God with all his heart, all his mind, and all his strength. And he must love his neighbour as he loves himself. These commands are more important than all the animals and sacrifices we offer to God."

[34] Jesus saw that the man answered him wisely. So Jesus said to him, "You are close to the kingdom of God." And after that, no one was brave enough to ask Jesus any more questions.

[35] Jesus was teaching in the Temple.[d] He asked, "Why do the

burning bush   Read Exodus 3:1–12 in the Old Testament.
'I am . . . Jacob'.   Quotation from Exodus 3:6.
'Listen . . . strength'.   Quotation from Deuteronomy 6:4–5.
'Love . . . yourself '.   Quotation from Leviticus 19:18.

teachers of the law say that the Christ*d*
is the son of David? ³⁶David himself,
speaking by the Holy Spirit,*d* said:

'The Lord said to my Lord:
  Sit by me at my right side,
  until I put your enemies under
    your control'.   *Psalm 110:1*
³⁷David himself calls the Christ 'Lord'.
So how can the Christ be David's
son?" The large crowd listened to
Jesus with pleasure.

³⁸Jesus continued teaching. He
said, "Beware of the teachers of the
law. They like to walk around wearing
clothes that look important. And they
love people to show respect to them in
the marketplaces. ³⁹They love to have
the most important seats in the synagogues.*d* And they love to have the
most important seats at the feasts.
⁴⁰They cheat widows and steal their
homes. Then they try to make themselves look good by saying long
prayers. God will punish these people
terribly."

True Giving

⁴¹Jesus sat near the Temple*d* money
box where people put their gifts. He
watched the people put in their money.
Many rich people gave large sums of
money. ⁴²Then a poor widow came
and gave two very small copper coins.
These coins were not worth even a
penny.

⁴³Jesus called his followers to him.
He said, "I tell you the truth. This poor
widow gave only two small coins. But
she really gave more than all those
rich people. ⁴⁴The rich have plenty;
they gave only what they did not need.
This woman is very poor, but she gave
all she had. And she needed that
money to help her live."

The Temple Will Be Destroyed

13 Jesus was leaving the Temple.*d*
One of his followers said to him,
"Look, Teacher! This Temple has
beautiful buildings with very big
stones."

²Jesus said, "Do you see all these
great buildings? Every stone will be
thrown to the ground. Not one stone
will be left on another."

³Later, Jesus was sitting on the
Mount of Olives.*d* He was alone with
Peter, James, John, and Andrew. They
could all see the Temple. They asked
Jesus, ⁴"Tell us, when will all these
things happen? And what will show us
that the time has come for them to
happen?"

⁵Jesus said to them: "Be careful that
no one fools you. ⁶Many people will
come and use my name. They will say,
'I am the One'. And they will fool many.
⁷You will hear about wars and stories
of wars that are coming. But don't be
afraid. These things must happen
before the end comes. ⁸Nations will
fight against other nations. Kingdoms
will fight against other kingdoms.
There will be times when there is no
food for people to eat. And there will
be earthquakes in different places.
These things are like the first pains
when something new is about to be
born.

⁹"You must be careful. People will
arrest you and take you to court. They
will beat you in their synagogues.*d* You
will be forced to stand before kings
and governors, to tell them about me.
This will happen to you because you
follow me. ¹⁰But before these things
happen, the Good News*d* must be told
to all people. ¹¹When you are arrested
and judged, don't worry about what
you should say. Say the things God
gives you to say at that time. It will
not really be you speaking. It will be
the Holy Spirit.*d*

¹²"Brothers will turn against their
own brothers and give them over to
be killed. Fathers will turn against

their own children and give them over to be killed. Children will fight against their own parents and cause their parents to be killed. [13] All people will hate you because you follow me. But the person who continues to be strong until the end will be saved.

[14] "You will see 'the horrible thing that destroys'.[n] You will see this thing standing in the place where it should not be." (You who read this should understand what it means.) "At that time, the people in Judea should run away to the mountains. [15] If a person is on the roof[n] of his house, he must not go down to take anything out of his house. [16] If a person is in the field, he must not go back to get his coat. [17] At that time, it will be hard for women who are pregnant or have nursing babies. [18] Pray that these things will not happen in winter. [19] This is because those days will be full of trouble. There will be more trouble than there has ever been since the beginning, when God made the world. And nothing as bad will ever happen again. [20] God has decided to make that terrible time short. If that time were not made short, then no one would go on living. But God will make that time short to help his special people whom he has chosen. [21] At that time, someone might say to you, 'Look, there is the Christ!'[d] Or another person might say, 'There he is!' But don't believe them. [22] False Christs and false prophets[d] will come and perform great wonders and miracles.[d] They will do these things to the people God has chosen. They will do these things to try to fool them, if that is possible. [23] So be careful. For I have warned you about all this before it happens.

[24] "During the days after this trouble comes,

'The sun will grow dark.
    And the moon will not give its
        light.
[25] The stars will fall from the sky.
    And everything in the sky will
        be changed'.   *Isaiah 13:10; 34:4*

[26] "Then people will see the Son of Man[d] coming in clouds with great power and glory. [27] The Son of Man will send his angels all around the earth. They will gather his chosen people from every part of the earth.

[28] "The fig tree teaches us a lesson: when its branches become green and soft, and new leaves begin to grow, then you know that summer is near. [29] So also when you see all these things happening, then you will know that the time is near, ready to come. [30] I tell you the truth. All these things will happen while the people of this time are still living. [31] The whole world, earth and sky, will be destroyed, but the words I have said will never be destroyed.

[32] "No one knows when that day or time will be. The Son and the angels in heaven don't know. Only the Father knows. [33] Be careful! Always be ready! You don't know when that time will be. [34] It is like a man who goes on a trip. He leaves his house and lets his servants take care of it. He gives each servant a special job to do. One servant has the work of guarding the door. The man tells this servant always to be watchful. This is what I am now telling you. [35] You must always be ready. You don't know when the

---

'horrible . . . destroys.'   Mentioned in Daniel 9:27; 12:11 (cf. Daniel 11:31).

roof   In Bible times houses were built with flat roofs. The roof was used for drying things, such as flax and fruit. It was also used as an extra room, as a place for worship and as a place to sleep in the summer.

owner of the house will come back. He might come in the evening, or at midnight, or in the early morning, or when the sun rises. ³⁶He might come back quickly. If you are always ready, then he will not find you sleeping. ³⁷I tell you this, and I say this to everyone: 'Be ready!'"

The Plan to Kill Jesus

14 It was now only two days before the Passover*d* and the Feast*d* of Unleavened Bread. The leading priests and teachers of the law were trying to find a way to use some trick to arrest Jesus and kill him. ²But they said, "We must not do it during the feast. The people might cause a riot."

A Woman with Perfume for Jesus

³Jesus was in Bethany. He was at dinner in the house of Simon, who had a harmful skin disease. While Jesus was there, a woman came to him. She had an alabaster*d* jar filled with very expensive perfume, made of pure nard.*d* The woman opened the jar and poured the perfume on Jesus' head.

⁴Some of those who were there saw this and became angry. They complained to each other, saying, "Why waste that perfume? ⁵It was worth a full year's work. It could be sold, and the money could be given to the poor." They spoke to the woman sharply.

⁶Jesus said, "Don't bother the woman. Why are you troubling her? She did a beautiful thing for me. ⁷You will always have the poor with you. You can help them whenever you want. But you will not always have me. ⁸This woman did the only thing she could do for me. She poured perfume on my body. She did this before I die to prepare me for burial. ⁹I tell you the truth. The Good News*d* will be told to people in all the world. And in every

Mark 14:3 The woman opened the jar and poured the perfume on Jesus' head.

place it is preached, what this woman has done will be told. And people will remember her."

Judas Becomes an Enemy of Jesus

¹⁰One of the 12 followers, Judas Iscariot, went to talk to the leading priests. Judas offered to give Jesus to them. ¹¹The leading priests were pleased about this. They promised to pay Judas money. So he waited for the best time to give Jesus to them.

Jesus Eats the Passover Feast

¹²It was now the first day of the Feast*d* of Unleavened Bread. This was a time when the Jews always sacrificed the Passover*d* lambs. Jesus' followers came to him. They said, "We will go and prepare everything for the Passover Feast. Where do you want to eat the feast?"

¹³Jesus sent two of his followers and said to them, "Go into the city. A man

carrying a jar of water will meet you. Follow him. [14] He will go into a house. Tell the owner of the house, 'The Teacher asks that you show us the room where he and his followers can eat the Passover Feast'. [15] The owner will show you a large room upstairs. This room is ready. Prepare the food for us there."

[16] So the followers left and went into the city. Everything happened as Jesus had said. So they prepared the Passover Feast.

[17] In the evening, Jesus went to that house with the 12. [18] While they were all eating, Jesus said, "I tell you the truth. One of you will give me to my enemies – one of you eating with me now."

[19] The followers were very sad to hear this. Each one said to Jesus, "I am not the one, am I?"

[20] Jesus answered, "The man who is against me is one of the 12. He is the one who dips his bread into the bowl with me. [21] The Son of Man[d] must go and die. The Scriptures[d] say this will happen. But how terrible it will be for the person who gives the Son of Man to be killed. It would be better for that person if he had never been born."

The Lord's Supper

[22] While they were eating, Jesus took some bread. He thanked God for it and broke it. Then he gave it to his followers and said, "Take it. This bread is my body."

[23] Then Jesus took a cup. He thanked God for it and gave it to the followers. All the followers drank from the cup.

[24] Then Jesus said, "This is my blood which begins the new agreement that God makes with his people.

This blood is poured out for many. [25] I tell you the truth. I will not drink of this fruit of the vine[n] again until that day when I drink it new in the kingdom of God."

[26] They sang a hymn and went out to the Mount of Olives.[d]

Jesus' Followers Will All Leave Him

[27] Then Jesus told the followers, "You will all lose your faith in me. It is written in the Scriptures:[d]

'I will kill the shepherd,
and the sheep will scatter'.

Zechariah 13:7

[28] But after I rise from death, I will go ahead of you into Galilee."

[29] Peter said, "All the other followers may lose their faith. But I will not."

[30] Jesus answered, "I tell you the truth. Tonight you will say you don't know me. You will say this three times before the cock crows twice."

[31] But Peter answered strongly, "I will never say that I don't know you! I will even die with you!" And all the other followers said the same thing.

Jesus Prays Alone

[32] Jesus and his followers went to a place called Gethsemane. He said to his followers, "Sit here while I pray." [33] Jesus told Peter, James, and John to come with him. Then Jesus began to be very sad and troubled. [34] He said to them, "I am full of sorrow. My heart is breaking with sadness. Stay here and watch."

[35] Jesus walked a little further away from them. Then he fell on the ground and prayed. He prayed that, if possible, he would not have this time of suffering. [36] He prayed, "Abba,[n] Father! You can do all things. Let me

---

fruit of the vine   Product of the grapevine; this may also be translated "wine".
Abba   Name that a child called his father.

not have this cup[n] of suffering. But do what you want, not what I want."

[37]Then Jesus went back to his followers. He found them asleep. He said to Peter, "Simon, why are you sleeping? You could not stay awake with me for one hour? [38]Stay awake and pray that you will not be tempted. Your spirit wants to do what is right, but your body is weak."

[39]Again Jesus went away and prayed the same thing. [40]Then he went back to the followers. Again he found them asleep because their eyes were very heavy. And they did not know what to say to Jesus.

[41]After Jesus prayed a third time, he went back to his followers. He said to them, "You are still sleeping and resting? That's enough! The time has come for the Son of Man[d] to be given to sinful people. [42]Get up! We must go. Here comes the man who has turned against me."

Jesus Is Arrested

[43]While Jesus was still speaking, Judas came up. Judas was one of the 12 followers. He had many people with him. They were sent from the leading priests, the teachers of the law, and the older Jewish leaders. Those with Judas had swords and clubs.

[44]Judas had planned a signal for them. He had said, "The man I kiss is Jesus. Arrest him and guard him while you lead him away." [45]So Judas went to Jesus and said, "Teacher!" and kissed him. [46]Then the men grabbed Jesus and arrested him. [47]One of the followers standing near drew his sword. He struck the servant of the high priest with the sword and cut off his ear.

[48]Then Jesus said, "You came to get me with swords and clubs as if I were a criminal. [49]Every day I was with you teaching in the Temple.[d] You did not arrest me there. But all these things have happened to make the Scriptures[d] come true." [50]Then all of Jesus' followers left him and ran away.

[51]A young man, wearing only a linen cloth, was following Jesus. The people also grabbed him. [52]But the cloth he was wearing came off, and he ran away naked.

Jesus Before the Leaders

[53]The people who arrested Jesus led him to the house of the high priest. All the leading priests, the older Jewish leaders, and the teachers of the law were gathered there. [54]Peter followed far behind and entered the courtyard of the high priest's house. There he sat with the guards, warming himself by the fire.

[55]The leading priests and all the Jewish council tried to find something that Jesus had done wrong so they could kill him. But the council could find no proof against him. [56]Many people came and told false things about him. But all said different things – none of them agreed.

[57]Then some men stood up and lied about Jesus. They said, [58]"We heard this man say, 'I will destroy this Temple[d] that men made. And three days later, I will build another Temple – a Temple not made by men'." [59]But even the things these men said did not agree.

[60]Then the high priest stood before them and said to Jesus, "Aren't you going to answer the charges these men bring against you?" [61]But Jesus said nothing. He did not answer.

The high priest asked Jesus another

---

cup Jesus is talking about the bad things that will happen to him. Accepting these things will be very hard, like drinking a cup of something that tastes very bitter.

question: "Are you the Christ,[d] the Son of the blessed God?"

[62] Jesus answered, "I am. And in the future you will see the Son of Man[d] sitting at the right side of the Powerful One. And you will see the Son of Man coming on clouds in the sky."

[63] When the high priest heard this, he was very angry. He tore his clothes and said, "We don't need any more witnesses! [64] You all heard him say these things against God. What do you think?"

They all said that Jesus was guilty and should be killed. [65] Some of the people there spat at Jesus. They covered his eyes and hit him with their fists. They said, "Prove that you are a prophet!"[d] Then the guards led Jesus away and beat him.

Peter Says He Doesn't Know Jesus

[66] Peter was still in the courtyard when a servant girl of the high priest came there. [67] She saw Peter warming himself at the fire. She looked closely at him.

Then the girl said, "You were with Jesus, that man from Nazareth."

[68] But Peter said that he was never with Jesus. He said, "I don't know or understand what you are talking about." Then Peter left and went toward the entrance of the courtyard.[n]

[69] The servant girl saw Peter there. Again she said to the people who were standing there, "This man is one of those who followed Jesus." [70] Again Peter said that it was not true.

A short time later, some people were standing near Peter. They said, "We know you are one of those who followed Jesus. You are from Galilee, too."

[71] Then Peter began to curse. He said, "I swear that I don't know this man you're talking about!"

[72] As soon as Peter said this, the cock crowed the second time. Then Peter remembered what Jesus had told him: "Before the cock crows twice, you will say three times that you don't know me." Then Peter was very sad and began to cry.

Pilate Questions Jesus

15 Very early in the morning, the leading priests, the older Jewish leaders, the teachers of the law, and all the Jewish council decided what to do with Jesus. They tied him, led him away, and turned him over to Pilate, the governor.

[2] Pilate asked Jesus, "Are you the king of the Jews?"

Jesus answered, "Yes, I am."

[3] The leading priests accused Jesus of many things. [4] So Pilate asked Jesus another question. He said, "You can see that these people are accusing you of many things. Why don't you answer?"

[5] But Jesus still said nothing. Pilate was very surprised at this.

Pilate Tries to Free Jesus

[6] Every year at the Passover[d] time the governor would free one person from prison. He would free any person the people wanted him to free. [7] At that time, there was a man named Barabbas in prison. He was a rebel and had committed murder during a riot. [8] The crowd came to Pilate and asked him to free a prisoner as he always did.

[9] Pilate asked them, "Do you want me to free the king of the Jews?" [10] Pilate knew that the leading priests had given Jesus to him because they were jealous of Jesus. [11] And the leading

Verse 68 Many Greek copies add: "And the cock crowed."

priests had persuaded the people to ask Pilate to free Barabbas, not Jesus.

¹²Pilate asked the crowd again, "So what should I do with this man you call the king of the Jews?"

¹³They shouted, "Kill him on a cross!"

¹⁴Pilate asked, "Why? What wrong has he done?"

But they shouted louder and louder, "Kill him on a cross!"

¹⁵Pilate wanted to please the crowd. So he freed Barabbas for them. And Pilate told the soldiers to beat Jesus with whips. Then he gave Jesus to the soldiers to be killed on a cross.

¹⁶Pilate's soldiers took Jesus into the governor's palace (called the Praetorium). They called all the other soldiers together. ¹⁷They put a purple robe on Jesus. Then they used thorny branches to make a crown. They put it on his head. ¹⁸Then they called out to him, "Hail, King of the Jews!" ¹⁹The soldiers beat Jesus on the head many times with a stick. They also spat on him. Then they made fun of him by bowing on their knees and worshipping him. ²⁰After they had finished making fun of him, the soldiers took off the purple robe and put his own clothes on him again. Then they led Jesus out of the palace to be killed on a cross.

Jesus Is Killed on a Cross

²¹There was a man from Cyrene coming from the fields to the city. The man was Simon, the father of Alexander and Rufus. The soldiers forced Simon to carry the cross for Jesus. ²²They led Jesus to the place called Golgotha. (Golgotha means the Place of the Skull.) ²³At Golgotha the soldiers tried to give Jesus wine to drink. This wine was mixed with myrrh.ᵈ But he refused to drink it. ²⁴The soldiers nailed Jesus to a cross. Then they divided his clothes among themselves. They threw lotsᵈ to decide which clothes each soldier would get.

²⁵It was nine o'clock in the morning when they nailed Jesus to the cross. ²⁶There was a sign with the charge against Jesus written on it. The sign read: "THE KING OF THE JEWS". ²⁷They also put two robbers on crosses beside Jesus, one on the right, and the other on the left. ²⁸ ⁿ ²⁹People walked by and insulted Jesus. They shook their heads, saying, "You said you could destroy the Templeᵈ and build it again in three days. ³⁰So save yourself! Come down from that cross!"

Verse 28 Some Greek copies add verse 28: "And the Scripture came true that says, 'They put him with criminals'."

Mark 15:20 Then they led Jesus out of the palace to be killed on a cross.

[31]The leading priests and the teachers of the law were also there. They made fun of Jesus just as the other people did. They said among themselves, "He saved other people, but he can't save himself. [32]If he is really the Christ,[d] the king of Israel, then let him come down from the cross now. We will see this, and then we will believe in him." The robbers who were being killed on the crosses beside Jesus also insulted him.

Jesus Dies

[33]At noon the whole country became dark. This darkness lasted for three hours. [34]At three o'clock Jesus cried in a loud voice, "Eloi, Eloi, lama sabachthani." This means, "My God, my God, why have you left me alone?"

[35]Some of the people standing there heard this. They said, "Listen! He is calling Elijah."

[36]One man there ran and got a sponge. He filled the sponge with vinegar and tied it to a stick. Then he used the stick to give the sponge to Jesus to drink from it. The man said, "We should wait now and see if Elijah will come to take him down from the cross."

[37]Then Jesus cried in a loud voice and died.

[38]When Jesus died, the curtain in the Temple[n] split into two pieces. The tear started at the top and tore all the way to the bottom. [39]The army officer that was standing there before the cross saw what happened when Jesus died. The officer said, "This man really was the Son of God!"

[40]Some women were standing at a distance from the cross, watching. Some of these women were Mary Magdalene, Salome, and Mary the mother of James and Joseph. (James was her youngest son.) [41]These were the women who followed Jesus in Galilee and cared for him. Many other women were also there who had come with Jesus to Jerusalem.

Jesus Is Buried

[42]This was Preparation[d] Day. (That means the day before the Sabbath[d] day.) It was becoming dark. [43]A man named Joseph from Arimathea was brave enough to go to Pilate and ask for Jesus' body. Joseph was an important member of the Jewish council. He was one of the people who wanted the kingdom of God to come. [44]Pilate wondered if Jesus was already dead. Pilate called the army officer who guarded Jesus and asked him if Jesus had already died. [45]The officer told Pilate that he was dead. So Pilate told Joseph he could have the body. [46]Joseph bought some linen cloth, took the body down from the cross and wrapped it in the linen. He put the body in a tomb that was cut in a wall of rock. Then he closed the tomb by rolling a very large stone to cover the entrance. [47]And Mary Magdalene and Mary the mother of Joseph saw the place where Jesus was laid.

Jesus Rises from Death

16 The day after the Sabbath[d] day, Mary Magdalene, Mary the mother of James, and Salome bought some sweet-smelling spices to put on Jesus' body. [2]Very early on that day, the first day of the week, the women were on their way to the tomb. It was soon after sunrise. [3]They said to each

---

curtain in the Temple A curtain divided the Most Holy Place from the other part of the Temple. That was the special building in Jerusalem where God commanded the Jews to worship him.

other, "There is a large stone covering the entrance of the tomb. Who will move the stone for us?"

[4] Then the women looked and saw that the stone had already been moved. The stone was very large, but it had been moved away from the entrance. [5] The women entered the tomb and saw a young man wearing a white robe. He was sitting on the right side, and the women were afraid.

[6] But the man said, "Don't be afraid. You are looking for Jesus from Nazareth, the one who was killed on a cross. He has risen from death. He is not here. Look, here is the place they laid him. [7] Now go and tell his followers and Peter, 'Jesus is going into Galilee. He will be there before you. You will see him there as he told you before'."

[8] The women were confused and shaking with fear. They left the tomb and ran away. They did not tell anyone about what happened, because they were afraid.[n]

Some Followers See Jesus

[9] Jesus rose from death early on the first day of the week. He showed himself first to Mary Magdalene. Once in the past, he had forced seven demons[d] to leave Mary. [10] After Mary saw Jesus, she went and told his followers. They were very sad and were crying. [11] But Mary told them that Jesus was alive. She said that she had seen him, but the followers did not believe her.

[12] Later, Jesus showed himself to two of his followers while they were walking in the country. But Jesus did not look the same as before. [13] These followers went back to the others and told them what had happened. Again, the followers did not believe them.

Jesus Talks to the Apostles

[14] Later Jesus showed himself to the 11 followers while they were eating. He criticised them because they had little faith. They were stubborn and refused to believe those who had seen him after he had risen from death.

[15] Jesus said to the followers, "Go everywhere in the world. Tell the Good News[d] to everyone. [16] Anyone who believes and is baptised will be saved. But he who does not believe will be judged guilty. [17] And those who believe will be able to do these things as proof: they will use my name to force demons[d] out of people. They will speak in languages[n] they never learned. [18] They will pick up snakes without being hurt. And they will drink poison without being hurt. They will touch the sick, and the sick will be healed."

[19] After the Lord Jesus said these things to the followers, he was carried up into heaven. There, Jesus sat at the right side of God. [20] The followers went everywhere in the world and told the Good News to people. And the Lord helped them. The Lord proved that the Good News they told was true by giving them power to work miracles.[d]

Verse 8   Some early Greek copies end the book with verse 8.
languages   This can also be translated "tongues".

LUKE

Luke Tells the Non-Jews About Jesus

Luke Writes About Jesus' Life

1 To Theophilus:
  Many have tried to give a history of the things that happened among us. [2] They have written the same things that we learned from others – the people who saw those things from the beginning and served God by telling people his message. [3] I myself studied everything carefully from the beginning, your Excellency.[n] I thought I should write it out for you. So I put it in order in a book. [4] I write these things so that you can know that what you have been taught is true.

Zechariah and Elizabeth

[5] During the time Herod ruled Judea, there was a priest named Zechariah. He belonged to Abijah's group.[n] Zechariah's wife came from the family of Aaron. Her name was Elizabeth. [6] Zechariah and Elizabeth truly did what God said was good. They did everything the Lord commanded and told people to do. They were without fault in keeping his law. [7] But Zechariah and Elizabeth had no children. Elizabeth could not have a baby; and both of them were very old.

[8] Zechariah was serving as a priest before God for his group. It was his group's time to serve. [9] According to the custom of the priests, he was chosen to go into the Temple[d] of the Lord and burn incense.[d] [10] There were a great many people outside praying at the time the incense was offered.

[11] Then, on the right side of the incense table, an angel of the Lord came and stood before Zechariah. [12] When he saw the angel, Zechariah was confused and frightened. [13] But the angel said to him, "Zechariah, don't be afraid. Your prayer has been heard by God. Your wife, Elizabeth, will give birth to a son. You will name him John. [14] You will be very happy. Many people will be happy because of his birth. [15] John will be a great man for the Lord. He will never drink wine or beer. Even at the time John is born, he will be filled with the Holy Spirit.[d] [16] He will help many people of Israel return to the Lord their God. [17] He himself will go first before the Lord. John will be powerful in spirit like Elijah. He will make peace between fathers and their children. He will bring those who are not obeying God back to the right way of thinking. He will make people ready for the coming of the Lord."

[18] Zechariah said to the angel, "How can I know that what you say is true? I am an old man, and my wife is old, too."

[19] The angel answered him, "I am Gabriel. I stand before God. God sent me to talk to you and to tell you this good news. [20] Now, listen! You will not be able to talk until the day these things happen. You will lose your speech because you did not believe what I told you. But these things will really happen."

Excellency This word was used to show respect to an important person like a king or ruler.
Abijah's group The Jewish priests were divided into 24 groups. See 1 Chronicles 24.

²¹Outside, the people were still waiting for Zechariah. They were surprised that he was staying so long in the Temple. ²²Then Zechariah came outside, but he could not speak to them. So they knew that he had seen a vision in the Temple. Zechariah could not speak. He could only make signs to them. ²³When his time of service as a priest was finished, he went home.

²⁴Later, Zechariah's wife, Elizabeth, became pregnant. She did not go out of her house for five months. Elizabeth said, ²⁵"Look what the Lord has done for me! My people were ashamed[n] of me, but now the Lord has taken away that shame."

The Virgin Mary

²⁶⁻²⁷During Elizabeth's sixth month of pregnancy, God sent the angel Gabriel to a virgin[d] who lived in Nazareth, a town in Galilee. She was engaged to marry a man named Joseph from the family of David. Her name was Mary. ²⁸The angel came to her and said, "Greetings! The Lord has blessed you and is with you."

²⁹But Mary was very confused by what the angel said. Mary wondered, "What does this mean?"

³⁰The angel said to her, "Don't be afraid, Mary, because God is pleased with you. ³¹Listen! You will become pregnant. You will give birth to a son, and you will name him Jesus. ³²He will be great, and people will call him the Son of the Most High. The Lord God will give him the throne of King David, his ancestor. ³³He will rule over the people of Jacob for ever. His kingdom will never end."

³⁴Mary said to the angel, "How will this happen? I am a virgin!"

³⁵The angel said to Mary, "The

Luke 1:28 The angel came to her and said, "Greetings!"

Holy Spirit[d] will come upon you, and the power of the Most High will cover you. The baby will be holy. He will be called the Son of God. ³⁶Now listen! Elizabeth, your relative, is very old. But she is also pregnant with a son. Everyone thought she could not have a baby, but she has been pregnant for six months. ³⁷God can do everything!"

³⁸Mary said, "I am the servant girl of the Lord. Let this happen to me as you say!" Then the angel went away.

Mary's Visit

³⁹Mary got up and went quickly to a town in the mountains of Judea. ⁴⁰She went to Zechariah's house and greeted Elizabeth. ⁴¹When Elizabeth heard Mary's greeting, the unborn baby inside Elizabeth jumped. Then Elizabeth was filled with the Holy Spirit.[d] ⁴²She cried out in a loud voice, "God

---

ashamed   The Jews thought it was a disgrace for women not to have children.

has blessed you more than any other woman. And God has blessed the baby which you will give birth to. ⁴³You are the mother of my Lord, and you have come to me! Why has something so good happened to me? ⁴⁴When I heard your voice, the baby inside me jumped with joy. ⁴⁵You are blessed because you believed what the Lord said to you would really happen."

Mary Praises God

⁴⁶Then Mary said,

"My soul praises the Lord;
⁴⁷   my heart is happy because God
        is my Saviour.
⁴⁸I am not important, but God has
        shown his care for me, his
        servant girl.
    From now on, all people will say
        that I am blessed,
⁴⁹   because the Powerful One has
        done great things for me.
    His name is holy.
⁵⁰God will always give mercy
        to those who worship him.
⁵¹God's arm is strong.
    He scatters the people who are
        proud
    and think great things about
        themselves.
⁵²God brings down rulers from their
        thrones,
    and he raises up the humble.
⁵³God fills the hungry with good
        things,
    but he sends the rich away with
        nothing.
⁵⁴God has helped his people Israel
        who serve him.
    He gave them his mercy.
⁵⁵God has done what he promised
        to our ancestors,
    to Abraham and to his children
        for ever."

⁵⁶Mary stayed with Elizabeth for about three months and then returned home.

The Birth of John

⁵⁷When it was time for Elizabeth to give birth, she had a boy. ⁵⁸Her neighbours and relatives heard how good the Lord was to her, and they rejoiced. ⁵⁹When the baby was eight days old, they came to circumcise*ᵈ* him. They wanted to name him Zechariah because this was his father's name. ⁶⁰But his mother said, "No! He will be named John."

⁶¹The people said to Elizabeth, "But no one in your family has this name!" ⁶²Then they made signs to his father, "What would you like to name him?"

⁶³Zechariah asked for something to write on. Then he wrote, "His name is John." Everyone was surprised. ⁶⁴Then Zechariah could talk again. He began to praise God. ⁶⁵And all their neighbours became alarmed. In all the mountains of Judea people continued talking about all these things. ⁶⁶The people who heard about these things wondered about them. They thought, "What will this child be?" They said this because the Lord was with him.

Zechariah Praises God

⁶⁷Then Zechariah, John's father, was filled with the Holy Spirit.*ᵈ* He told the people what would happen:
⁶⁸"Let us thank the Lord, the God of
        Israel.
    God has come to help his
        people and has given them
        freedom.
⁶⁹God has given us a powerful
        Saviour
    from the family of God's servant
        David.
⁷⁰God said that he would do this.
    He said it through his holy
        prophets*ᵈ* who lived long
        ago.
⁷¹God will save us from our enemies

and from the power of all those who hate us.

[72] God said he would give mercy to our fathers.

And he remembered his holy promise.

[73] God promised Abraham, our father,

[74]   that he would free us from the power of our enemies,

so that we could serve him without fear.

[75] We will be righteous and holy before God as long as we live.

[76] "Now you, child, will be called a prophet of the Most High God.

You will go first before the Lord to prepare the people for his coming.

[77] You will make his people know that they will be saved.

They will be saved by having their sins forgiven.

[78] With the loving mercy of our God, a new day from heaven will shine upon us.

[79] God will help those who live in darkness,

in the fear of death.

He will guide us into the path that goes toward peace."

[80] And so the child grew up and became strong in spirit. John lived away from other people until the time when he came out to preach to Israel.

The Birth of Jesus

2 At that time, Augustus Caesar[d] sent an order to all people in the countries that were under Roman rule. The order said that they must list their names in a register. [2] This was the first registration[n] taken while Quirinius was governor of Syria. [3] And everyone went to their own towns to be registered.

[4] So Joseph left Nazareth, a town in Galilee. He went to the town of Bethlehem in Judea. This town was known as the town of David. Joseph went there because he was from the family of David. [5] Joseph registered with Mary because she was engaged to marry him. (Mary was now pregnant.) [6] While Joseph and Mary were in Bethlehem, the time came for her to have the baby. [7] She gave birth to her first son. There were no rooms left in the inn. So she wrapped the baby in cloths and laid him in a box where animals are fed.

Some Shepherds Hear About Jesus

[8] That night, some shepherds were in the fields nearby watching their sheep. [9] An angel of the Lord stood before them. The glory of the Lord was shining around them, and suddenly they became very frightened. [10] The angel said to them, "Don't be afraid, because I am bringing you some good news. It will be a joy to all the people. [11] Today your Saviour was born in David's town. He is Christ,[d] the Lord. [12] This is how you will know him: you will find a baby wrapped in cloths and lying in a feeding box."

[13] Then a very large group of angels from heaven joined the first angel. All the angels were praising God, saying: [14] "Give glory to God in heaven,

and on earth let there be peace to the people who please God."

[15] Then the angels left the shepherds and went back to heaven. The shepherds said to each other, "Let us go to Bethlehem and see this thing

registration   Census. A counting of all the people and the things they own.

that has happened. We will see this thing the Lord told us about."

[16] So the shepherds went quickly and found Mary and Joseph. [17] And the shepherds saw the baby lying in a feeding box. Then they told what the angels had said about this child. [18] Everyone was amazed when they heard what the shepherds said to them. [19] Mary hid these things in her heart; she continued to think about them. [20] Then the shepherds went back to their sheep, praising God and thanking him for everything that they had seen and heard. It was just as the angel had told them.

[21] When the baby was eight days old, he was circumcised,[d] and he was named Jesus. This name had been given by the angel before the baby began to grow inside Mary.

Jesus Is Presented in the Temple

[22] The time came for Mary and Joseph to do what the law of Moses taught about being made pure.[n] They took Jesus to Jerusalem to present him to the Lord. [23] It is written in the law of the Lord: "Give every firstborn[d] male to the Lord."[n] [24] Mary and Joseph also went to offer a sacrifice, as the law of the Lord says: "You must sacrifice two doves or two young pigeons."[n]

Simeon Sees Jesus

[25] A man named Simeon lived in Jerusalem. He was a good man and very religious. He was waiting for the time when God would help Israel. The Holy Spirit[d] was in him. [26] The Holy Spirit told Simeon that he would not die before he saw the Christ[d]

promised by the Lord. [27] The Spirit led Simeon to the Temple.[d] Mary and Joseph brought the baby Jesus to the Temple to do what the law said they must do. [28] Then Simeon took the baby in his arms and thanked God:

[29] "Now, Lord, you can let me, your
        servant,
    die in peace as you said.
[30] I have seen your Salvation[n] with
        my own eyes.
[31]   You prepared him before all
        people.
[32] He is a light for the non-Jewish
        people to see.
    He will bring honour to your
        people, the Israelites."

[33] Jesus' father and mother were amazed at what Simeon had said about him. [34] Then Simeon blessed them and said to Mary, "Many in Israel will fall and many will rise because of this child. He will be a sign from God that many people will not accept. [35] The things they think in secret will be made known. And the things that will happen will make your heart sad, too."

Anna Sees Jesus

[36] Anna, a prophetess,[d] was there at the Temple.[d] She was from the family of Phanuel in the tribe[d] of Asher. Anna was very old. She had once been married for seven years. [37] Then her husband died and she lived alone. She was now 84 years old. Anna never left the Temple. She worshipped God by going without food and praying day and night. [38] She was standing there at that time, thanking God. She talked about Jesus to all who were waiting for God to free Jerusalem.

pure The law of Moses said that 40 days after a Jewish woman gave birth to a baby, she must be cleansed by a ceremony at the Temple. Read Leviticus 12:2–8.
"Give . . . Lord." Quotation from Exodus 13:2.
"You . . . pigeons." Quotation from Leviticus 12:8.
Salvation Simeon was talking about Jesus. The name Jesus means "salvation".

Joseph and Mary Return Home

³⁹Joseph and Mary finished doing everything that the law of the Lord commanded. Then they went home to Nazareth, their own town in Galilee. ⁴⁰The little child began to grow up. He became stronger and wiser, and God's blessings were with him.

Jesus As a Boy

⁴¹Every year Jesus' parents went to Jerusalem for the Passover*ᵈ* Feast. ⁴²When Jesus was 12 years old, they went to the feast as they always did. ⁴³When the feast days were over, they went home. The boy Jesus stayed behind in Jerusalem, but his parents did not know it. ⁴⁴Joseph and Mary travelled for a whole day. They thought that Jesus was with them in the group. Then they began to look for him among their family and friends, ⁴⁵but they did not find him. So they went back to Jerusalem to look for him there. ⁴⁶After three days they found him. Jesus was sitting in the Temple*ᵈ* with the religious teachers, listening to them and asking them questions. ⁴⁷All who heard him were amazed at his understanding and wise answers. ⁴⁸When Jesus' parents saw him, they were amazed. His mother said to him, "Son, why did you do this to us? Your father and I were very worried about you. We have been looking for you."

⁴⁹Jesus asked, "Why did you have to look for me? You should have known that I must be where my Father's work is!" ⁵⁰But they did not understand the meaning of what he said.

⁵¹Jesus went with them to Nazareth and obeyed them. His mother was still thinking about all that had happened. ⁵²Jesus continued to learn more and to grow physically. People liked him, and he pleased God.

The Preaching of John

3 It was the fifteenth year of the rule of Tiberius Caesar.*ᵈ* These men were under Caesar: Pontius Pilate was the ruler of Judea. Herod was the ruler of Galilee. Philip, Herod's brother, was the ruler of Iturea and Trachonitis. And Lysanias was the ruler of Abilene. ²Annas and Caiaphas were the high priests. At this time, a command from God came to John son of Zechariah. John was living in the desert. ³He went all over the area around the Jordan River and preached to the people. He preached a baptism of changed hearts and lives for the forgiveness of their sins. ⁴As it is written in the book of Isaiah the prophet:*ᵈ*

"This is a voice of a man
  who calls out in the desert:
'Prepare the way for the Lord.
  Make the road straight for
    him.
⁵Every valley should be filled in.
  Every mountain and hill should
    be made flat.
Roads with turns should be made
    straight,
  and rough roads should be
    made smooth.
⁶And all people will know about the
    salvation of God!'" *Isaiah 40:3–5*

⁷Crowds of people came to be baptised by John. He said to them, "You poisonous snakes! Who warned you to run away from God's anger that is coming? ⁸You must do the things that will show that you really have changed your hearts. Don't say, 'Abraham is our father'. I tell you that God can make children for Abraham from these rocks here. ⁹The axe is now ready to cut down the trees. Every tree that does not produce good fruit

Luke 3:7 Crowds of people came to be baptised by John.

will be cut down and thrown into the fire."[n]

[10]The people asked John, "What should we do?"

[11]John answered, "If you have two shirts, share with the person who does not have one. If you have food, share that too."

[12]Even tax collectors came to John to be baptised. They said to John, "Teacher, what should we do?"

[13]John said to them, "Don't take more taxes from people than you have been ordered to take."

[14]The soldiers asked John, "What about us? What should we do?"

John said to them, "Don't force people to give you money. Don't lie about them. Be satisfied with the pay you get."

[15]All the people were hoping for the Christ[d] to come, and they wondered about John. They thought, "Maybe he is the Christ."

[16]John answered everyone, "I baptise you with water, but there is one coming later who can do more than I can. I am not good enough to untie his sandals. He will baptise you with the Holy Spirit[d] and with fire. [17]He will come ready to clean the grain. He will separate the good grain from the chaff.[d] He will put the good part of the grain into his barn. Then he will burn the chaff with a fire that cannot be put out."[n] [18]And John continued to preach the Good News,[d] saying many other things to encourage the people.

[19]But John spoke against Herod, the governor, because of his sin with Herodias, the wife of Herod's brother. John also criticised Herod for the many other evil things Herod did. [20]So Herod did another evil thing: he put John in prison.

Jesus Is Baptised by John

[21]When all the people were being baptised by John, Jesus also was baptised. While Jesus was praying, heaven opened and [22]the Holy Spirit[d] came down on him. The Spirit was in the form of a dove. Then a voice came from heaven and said, "You are my Son and I love you. I am very pleased with you."

The Family History of Jesus

[23]When Jesus began to teach, he was about 30 years old. People thought that Jesus was Joseph's son. Joseph was the son[n] of Heli.

The axe . . . fire. This means that God is ready to punish his people who do not obey him.
He will . . . out. This means that Jesus will come to separate the good people from the bad people, saving the good and punishing the bad.
son "Son" in Jewish lists of ancestors can sometimes mean grandson or more distant relative.

24 Heli was the son of Matthat.
Matthat was the son of Levi.
Levi was the son of Melki.
Melki was the son of Jannai.
Jannai was the son of Joseph.
25 Joseph was the son of Mattathias.
Mattathias was the son of Amos.
Amos was the son of Nahum.
Nahum was the son of Esli.
Esli was the son of Naggai.
26 Naggai was the son of Maath.
Maath was the son of Mattathias.
Mattathias was the son of
Semein.
Semein was the son of Josech.
Josech was the son of Joda.
27 Joda was the son of Joanan.
Joanan was the son of Rhesa.
Rhesa was the son of Zerubbabel.
Zerubbabel was the grandson of
Shealtiel.
Shealtiel was the son of Neri.
28 Neri was the son of Melchi.
Melchi was the son of Addi.
Addi was the son of Cosam.
Cosam was the son of Elmadam.
Elmadam was the son of Er.
29 Er was the son of Joshua.
Joshua was the son of Eliezer.
Eliezer was the son of Jorim.
Jorim was the son of Matthat.
Matthat was the son of Levi.
30 Levi was the son of Simeon.
Simeon was the son of Judah.
Judah was the son of Joseph.
Joseph was the son of Jonam.
Jonam was the son of Eliakim.
31 Eliakim was the son of Melea.
Melea was the son of Menna.
Menna was the son of Mattatha.
Mattatha was the son of Nathan.
Nathan was the son of David.
32 David was the son of Jesse.
Jesse was the son of Obed.
Obed was the son of Boaz.
Boaz was the son of Salmon.
Salmon was the son of Nahshon.

33 Nahshon was the son of
Amminadab.
Amminadab was the son of
Admin.
Admin was the son of Arni.
Arni was the son of Hezron.
Hezron was the son of Perez.
Perez was the son of Judah.
34 Judah was the son of Jacob.
Jacob was the son of Isaac.
Isaac was the son of Abraham.
Abraham was the son of Terah.
Terah was the son of Nahor.
35 Nahor was the son of Serug.
Serug was the son of Reu.
Reu was the son of Peleg.
Peleg was the son of Eber.
Eber was the son of Shelah.
36 Shelah was the son of Cainan.
Cainan was the son of Arphaxad.
Arphaxad was the son of Shem.
Shem was the son of Noah.
Noah was the son of Lamech.
37 Lamech was the son of
Methuselah.
Methuselah was the son of
Enoch.
Enoch was the son of Jared.
Jared was the son of Mahalalel.
Mahalalel was the son of Kenan.
38 Kenan was the son of Enosh.
Enosh was the son of Seth.
Seth was the son of Adam.
Adam was the son of God.

Jesus Is Tempted by the Devil

4 Jesus, filled with the Holy Spirit,*d*
returned from the Jordan River.
The Spirit led Jesus into the desert
2 where the devil tempted Jesus for 40
days. Jesus ate nothing during that
time. When those days were ended,
he was very hungry.
3 The devil said to Jesus, "If you are
the Son of God, tell this rock to
become bread."
4 Jesus answered, "It is written in the

Scriptures:[d] 'A person does not live only by eating bread'."[n]

[5] Then the devil took Jesus and showed him all the kingdoms of the world in a moment of time. [6] The devil said to Jesus, "I will give you all these kingdoms and all their power and glory. It has all been given to me, and I can give it to anyone I wish. [7] If you worship me, all will be yours."

[8] Jesus answered, "It is written in the Scriptures: 'You must worship the Lord your God. Serve only him!'"[n]

[9] Then the devil led Jesus to Jerusalem and put him on a high place of the Temple.[d] He said to Jesus, "If you are the Son of God, jump off! [10] It is written in the Scriptures:

'He has put his angels in charge of you.
They will watch over you'.
Psalm 91:11

[11] 'They will catch you with their hands.
And you will not hit your foot on a rock'."
Psalm 91:12

[12] Jesus answered, "But it also says in the Scriptures: 'Do not test the Lord your God'."[n]

[13] After the devil had tempted Jesus in every way, he went away to wait until a better time.

Jesus Teaches the People

[14] Jesus went back to Galilee with the power of the Holy Spirit.[d] Stories about Jesus spread all through the area. [15] He began to teach in the synagogues,[d] and all the people praised him.

[16] Jesus travelled to Nazareth, where he had grown up. On the Sab-

bath[d] day he went to the synagogue as he always did. Jesus stood up to read. [17] The book of Isaiah the prophet[d] was given to him. He opened the book and found the place where this is written:

[18] "The Spirit of the Lord is in me.
This is because God chose me
to tell the Good News[d] to
the poor.
God sent me to tell the prisoners
of sin that they are free,
and to tell the blind that they
can see again.   *Isaiah 61:1*
God sent me to free those who
have been treated unfairly,
Isaiah 58:6
[19]   and to announce the time when
the Lord will show kindness
to his people."   *Isaiah 61:2*

[20] Jesus closed the book, gave it back, and sat down. Everyone in the synagogue was watching Jesus closely. [21] He began to speak to them. He said, "While you heard these words just now, they were coming true!"

[22] All the people praised Jesus. They were amazed at the beautiful words he spoke. They asked, "Isn't this Joseph's son?"

[23] Jesus said to them, "I know that you will tell me the old saying: 'Doctor, heal yourself'. You want to say, 'We heard about the things you did in Capernaum. Do those things here in your own town!'" [24] Then Jesus said, "I tell you the truth. A prophet is not accepted in his own town. [25] What I say is true. During the time of Elijah it did not rain in Israel for three and a half years. There was no food anywhere in the whole country. And there were many widows in Israel during

---

'A person . . . bread'. Quotation from Deuteronomy 8:3.
'You . . . him!' Quotation from Deuteronomy 6:13.
'Do . . . God'. Quotation from Deuteronomy 6:16.

that time. [26]But Elijah was sent to none of those widows. He was sent only to a widow in Zarephath, a town in Sidon. [27]And there were many with a harmful skin disease living in Israel during the time of the prophet Elisha. But none of them were healed except Naaman, who was from the country of Syria."

[28]When all the people in the synagogue heard these things, they became very angry. [29]They got up and forced Jesus out of town. The town was built on a hill. They took Jesus to the edge of the hill and wanted to throw him off. [30]But Jesus walked through the crowd and went on his way.

Jesus Removes an Evil Spirit

[31]Jesus went to Capernaum, a city in Galilee. On the Sabbath[d] day, Jesus taught the people. [32]They were amazed at his teaching, because he spoke with authority. [33]In the synagogue[d] there was a man who had an evil spirit from the devil inside him. The man shouted in a loud voice, [34]"Jesus of Nazareth! What do you want with us? Did you come here to destroy us? I know who you are – God's Holy One!"

[35]But Jesus warned the evil spirit to stop. He said, "Be quiet! Come out of the man!" The evil spirit threw the man down to the ground before all the people. Then the evil spirit left the man and did not hurt him.

[36]The people were amazed. They said to each other, "What does this mean? With authority and power he commands evil spirits, and they come out." [37]And so the news about Jesus spread to every place in the whole area.

Jesus Heals Many People

[38]Jesus left the synagogue[d] and went to Simon's[n] house. Simon's mother-in-law was very sick with a high fever. They asked Jesus to do something to help her. [39]He stood very close to her and commanded the fever to leave. It left her immediately, and she got up and began serving them.

[40]When the sun went down, the people brought their sick to Jesus. They had many different diseases. Jesus put his hands on each sick person and healed every one of them. [41]Demons[d] came out of many people. The demons would shout, "You are the Son of God." But Jesus gave a strong command for the demons not to speak. They knew Jesus was the Christ.[d]

[42]At daybreak, Jesus went to a place to be alone, but the people looked for him. When they found him, they tried to keep him from leaving. [43]But Jesus said to them, "I must tell the Good News[d] about God's kingdom to other towns, too. This is why I was sent."

[44]Then Jesus kept on preaching in the synagogues[d] of Judea.

Jesus' First Followers

5 One day Jesus was standing beside Lake Galilee. Many people were pressing all around him. They wanted to hear the word of God. [2]Jesus saw two boats at the shore of the lake. The fishermen had left them and were washing their nets. [3]Jesus got into one of the boats, the one which belonged to Simon.[n] Jesus asked Simon to push off a little from the land. Then Jesus sat down in the boat and continued to teach the people on the shore.

[4]When Jesus had finished speaking,

Simon   Simon's other name was Peter.

he said to Simon, "Take the boat into deep water. If you will put your nets in the water, you will catch some fish."

[5] Simon answered, "Master, we worked hard all night trying to catch fish, but we caught nothing. But you say to put the nets in the water; so I will." [6] The fishermen did as Jesus told them. And they caught so many fish that the nets began to break. [7] They called to their friends in the other boat to come and help them. The friends came, and both boats were filled so full that they were almost sinking.

[8-9] The fishermen were all amazed at the many fish they caught. When Simon Peter saw what had happened, he bowed down before Jesus and said, "Go away from me, Lord. I am a sinful man!" [10] James and John, the sons of Zebedee, were amazed too. (James and John were Simon's partners.)

Jesus said to Simon, "Don't be afraid. From now on you will be fishermen for men." [11] When the men brought their boats to the shore, they left everything and followed Jesus.

Jesus Heals a Sick Man

[12] Once Jesus was in a town where a very sick man lived. The man was covered with a harmful skin disease. When he saw Jesus, he bowed before Jesus and begged him, "Lord, heal me. I know you can if you want to."

[13] Jesus said, "I want to. Be healed!" And Jesus touched the man. Immediately the disease disappeared. [14] Then Jesus said, "Don't tell anyone about what happened. But go and show yourself to the priest.[n] And offer a gift to God for your healing as Moses commanded.[n] This will prove to everyone that you are healed."

[15] But the news about Jesus was spreading more and more. Many people came to hear Jesus and to be healed of their sicknesses. [16] But Jesus often slipped away to other places to be alone so that he could pray.

Jesus Heals a Paralysed Man

[17] One day Jesus was teaching the people. The Pharisees[d] and teachers of the law were there, too. They had come from every town in Galilee and from Judea and Jerusalem. The Lord was giving Jesus the power to heal people. [18] There was a man who was paralysed. Some men were carrying him on a mat. They tried to bring him in and put him down before Jesus.

show . . . priest The law of Moses said a priest must say when a Jew with a harmful skin disease was well.
Moses commanded Read about this in Leviticus 14:1–32.

Luke 5:6 They caught so many fish that the nets began to break.

¹⁹But because there were so many people there, they could not find a way to Jesus. So the men went up on the roof and made a hole in the ceiling. They lowered the mat so that the paralysed man was lying right before Jesus. ²⁰Jesus saw that these men believed. So he said to the sick man, "Friend, your sins are forgiven."

²¹The Jewish teachers of the law and the Pharisees thought to themselves, "Who is this man? He is saying things that are against God! Only God can forgive sins."

²²But Jesus knew what they were thinking. He said, "Why do you have thoughts like that in your hearts? ²³Which is easier: to tell this paralysed man, 'Your sins are forgiven', or to tell him, 'Stand up and walk'? ²⁴But I will prove to you that the Son of Man^d has authority on earth to forgive sins." So Jesus said to the paralysed man, "I tell you, stand up! Take your mat and go home."

²⁵Then the man stood up before the people there. He picked up his mat and went home, praising God. ²⁶All the people were totally amazed and began to praise God. They were filled with much respect and said, "Today we have seen amazing things!"

Levi Follows Jesus

²⁷After this, Jesus went out and saw a tax collector named Levi sitting in the tax office. Jesus said to him, "Follow me!" ²⁸Levi got up, left everything, and followed Jesus.

²⁹Then Levi gave a big dinner for Jesus. The dinner was at Levi's house. At the table there were many tax collectors and other people, too. ³⁰But the Pharisees^d and the men who taught the law for the Pharisees began to complain to the followers of Jesus. They said, "Why do you eat and drink with tax collectors and 'sinners'?"

³¹Jesus answered them, "Healthy people don't need a doctor. It is the sick who need a doctor. ³²I have not come to invite good people. I have come to invite sinners to change their hearts and lives!"

Jesus Answers a Question

³³They said to Jesus, "John's followers often give up eating^n and pray, just as the Pharisees^d do. But your followers eat and drink all the time."

³⁴Jesus said to them, "When there is a wedding, you cannot make the friends of the bridegroom give up eating while he is still with them. ³⁵But the time will come when he will be taken away from them. Then his friends will give up eating."

³⁶Jesus told them this story: "No one takes cloth off a new coat to cover a hole in an old coat. If he does, he ruins the new coat, and the cloth from the new coat will not be the same as the old cloth. ³⁷People never pour new wine into old leather bags for holding wine. If they do, the new wine will break the bags, and the wine will spill out. Then the leather bags for holding wine will be ruined. ³⁸People always put new wine into new leather bags. ³⁹No one after drinking old wine wants new wine because he says, 'The old wine is better'."

Jesus Is Lord over the Sabbath

6 One Sabbath^d day Jesus was walking through some grainfields. His followers picked the heads of grain, rubbed them in their hands, and ate them. ²Some Pharisees^d said, "Why are you doing that? It is against the

---

give up eating   This is called "fasting". The people would give up eating for a special time of prayer and worship to God. It was also done to show sadness.

law of Moses to do that on the Sabbath day."

³Jesus answered, "Haven't you read about what David did when he and those with him were hungry? ⁴David went into God's house. He took the bread that was made holy for God and ate it. And he gave some of the bread to the people with him. This was against the law of Moses. It says that only priests can eat that bread." ⁵Then Jesus said to the Pharisees, "The Son of Man*d* is Lord of the Sabbath day."

Jesus Heals a Man's Crippled Hand

⁶On another Sabbath*d* day Jesus went into the synagogue*d* and was teaching. A man with a crippled right hand was there. ⁷The teachers of the law and the Pharisees*d* were watching to see if Jesus would heal on the Sabbath day. They wanted to see Jesus do something wrong so that they could accuse him. ⁸But he knew what they were thinking. He said to the man with the crippled hand, "Get up and stand before these people." The man got up and stood there. ⁹Then Jesus said to them, "I ask you, which is it right to do on the Sabbath day: to do good, or to do evil? Is it right to save a life or to destroy one?" ¹⁰Jesus looked around at all of them. He said to the man, "Let me see your hand." The man stretched out his hand, and it was completely healed.

¹¹The Pharisees and the teachers of the law became very angry. They said to each other, "What can we do to Jesus?"

Jesus Chooses His Apostles

¹²At that time Jesus went off to a mountain to pray. He stayed there all night, praying to God. ¹³The next morning, Jesus called his followers

to him. He chose 12 of them, whom he named "apostles".*d* They were ¹⁴Simon (Jesus named him Peter) and Andrew, Peter's brother; James and John, Philip and Bartholomew; ¹⁵Matthew, Thomas, James son of Alphaeus, and Simon (called the Zealot*d*), ¹⁶Judas son of James and Judas Iscariot. This Judas was the one who gave Jesus to his enemies.

Jesus Teaches and Heals

¹⁷Jesus and the apostles*d* came down from the mountain. Jesus stood on level ground where there was a large group of his followers. Also, there were many people from all around Judea, Jerusalem, and the sea-coast cities of Tyre and Sidon. ¹⁸They all came to hear Jesus teach and to be healed of their sicknesses. He healed those who were troubled by evil spirits. ¹⁹All the people were trying to touch Jesus, because power was coming from him and healing them all!

²⁰Jesus looked at his followers and said,

"Poor people, you are happy,
    because God's kingdom belongs
        to you.
²¹You people who are now hungry
        are happy,
    because you will be satisfied.
You people who are now crying
        are happy,
    because you will laugh with joy.
²²"You are happy when people hate you and are cruel to you. You are happy when they say that you are evil because you belong to the Son of Man.*d* ²³At that time be full of joy, because you have a great reward in heaven. Their fathers were cruel to the prophets*d* in the same way these people are cruel to you.
²⁴"But how terrible it will be for you
        who are rich,

because you have had your easy
life.
25 How terrible it will be for you who
are full now,
because you will be hungry.
How terrible it will be for you who
are laughing now,
because you will be sad and
cry.
26 "How terrible when all people say
only good things about you. Their
fathers always said good things about
the false prophets.

Love Your Enemies

27 "I say to you who are listening to
me, love your enemies. Do good
to those who hate you. 28 Ask God to
bless those who say bad things to you.
Pray for those who are cruel to you.
29 If anyone slaps you on one cheek,
let him slap the other cheek too. If
someone takes your coat, do not stop
him from taking your shirt. 30 Give to
everyone who asks you. When a
person takes something that is yours,
don't ask for it back. 31 Do for other
people what you want them to do for
you. 32 If you love only those who love
you, should you get some special
praise for doing that? No! Even sinners love the people who love them!
33 If you do good only to those who
do good to you, should you get some
special praise for doing that? No! Even
sinners do that! 34 If you lend things
to people, always hoping to get something back, should you get some
special praise for that? No! Even sinners lend to other sinners so that they
can get back the same amount! 35 So
love your enemies. Do good to them,
and lend to them without hoping to
get anything back. If you do these
things, you will have a great reward.
You will be sons of the Most High
God. Yes, because God is kind even
to people who are ungrateful and full

of sin. 36 Show mercy just as your
father shows mercy.

Look at Yourselves

37 "Don't judge other people, and
you will not be judged. Don't accuse
others of being guilty, and you will not
be accused of being guilty. Forgive
other people, and you will be forgiven.
38 Give, and you will receive. You will
be given much. It will be poured into
your hands – more than you can hold.
You will be given so much that it will
spill into your lap. The way you give
to others is the way God will give to
you."

39 Jesus told them this story: "Can a
blind man lead another blind man? No!
Both of them will fall into a ditch. 40 A
student is not better than his teacher.
But when the student has fully learned
all that he has been taught, then he
will be like his teacher.

41 "Why do you notice the little piece
of dust that is in your brother's eye,
but you don't see the big piece of wood
that is in your own eye? 42 You say to
your brother, 'Brother, let me take that
little piece of dust out of your eye'.
Why do you say this? You cannot see
that big piece of wood in your own
eye! You are a hypocrite!*d* First, take
the piece of wood out of your own eye.
Then you will see clearly to take the
dust out of your brother's eye.

Two Kinds of Fruit

43 "A good tree does not produce
bad fruit. Also, a bad tree does not
produce good fruit. 44 Each tree is
known by its fruit. People don't gather
figs from thorn bushes. And they don't
get grapes from bramble bushes. 45 A
good person has good things saved up
in his heart. And so he brings good
things out of his heart. But an evil
person has evil things saved up in his
heart. So he brings out bad things. A

person speaks the things that are in his heart.

Two Kinds of People

46 "Why do you call me, 'Lord, Lord', but do not do what I say? 47 Everyone who comes to me and listens to my words and obeys 48 is like a man building a house. He digs deep and lays his foundation on rock. The floods come, and the water tries to wash the house away. But the flood cannot move the house, because the house was built well. 49 But the one who hears my words and does not obey is like a man who builds his house on the ground without a foundation. When the floods come, the house quickly falls down. And that house is completely destroyed."

Jesus Heals a Soldier's Servant

7 When Jesus finished saying all these things to the people, he went to Capernaum. 2 In Capernaum there was an army officer. He had a servant who was so sick he was nearly dead. The officer loved the servant very much. 3 When the officer heard about Jesus, he sent some older Jewish leaders to him. The officer wanted the leaders to ask Jesus to come and heal his servant. 4 The men went to Jesus and begged him saying, "This officer is worthy of your help. 5 He loves our people, and he built us a synagogue."*d*

6 So Jesus went with the men. He was getting near the officer's house when the officer sent friends to say, "Lord, you don't need to come into my house. I am not good enough for you to be under my roof. 7 That is why I did not come to you myself. You only need to say the word, and my servant will be healed. 8 I, too, am a man under the authority of other men, and I have soldiers under my command. I tell one soldier, 'Go', and he goes. And I tell

another soldier, 'Come', and he comes. And I say to my servant, 'Do this', and my servant obeys me."

9 When Jesus heard this, he was amazed. He turned to the crowd following him and said, "I tell you, this is the greatest faith I have seen anywhere, even in Israel."

10 The men who had been sent to Jesus went back to the house. There they found that the servant was healed.

Jesus Brings a Man Back to Life

11 The next day Jesus went to a town called Nain. His followers and a large crowd were travelling with him. 12 When he came near the town gate, he saw a funeral. A mother, who was a widow, had lost her only son. A large crowd from the town was with the mother while her son was being carried out. 13 When the Lord saw her, he felt very sorry for her. Jesus said to her, "Don't cry." 14 He went up to the coffin and touched it. The men who

Luke 7:14 "Young man, I tell you, get up!"

were carrying it stopped. Jesus said, "Young man, I tell you, get up!" 15 And the son sat up and began to talk. Then Jesus gave him back to his mother.

16 All the people were amazed. They began praising God. They said, "A great prophet*d* has come to us! God is taking care of his people."

17 This news about Jesus spread through all Judea and into all the places around there.

John Asks a Question

18 John's followers told him about all these things. He called for two of his followers. 19 He sent them to the Lord to ask, "Are you the One who is coming, or should we wait for another?"

20 So the men came to Jesus. They said, "John the Baptist*d* sent us to you with this question: 'Are you the One who is coming, or should we wait for another?'"

21 At that time, Jesus healed many people of their sicknesses, diseases, and evil spirits. He healed many blind people so that they could see again. 22 Then Jesus said to John's followers, "Go and tell John the things that you saw and heard here. The blind can see. The crippled can walk. People with a harmful skin disease are healed. The deaf can hear, and the dead are given life. And the Good News*d* is told to the poor. 23 The person who does not lose faith is blessed!"

24 When John's followers left, Jesus began to tell the people about John: "What did you go out into the desert to see? A reed*n* blown by the wind? 25 What did you go out to see? A man dressed in fine clothes? No. People who have fine clothes live in kings' palaces. 26 But what did you go out to see? A prophet?*d* Yes, and I tell you, John is more than a prophet. 27 This was written about John:

'I will send my messenger ahead
      of you.
He will prepare the way for you'.
                              Malachi 3:1

28 I tell you, John is greater than any other man ever born. But even the least important person in the kingdom of God is greater than John."

29 (When the people heard this, they all agreed that God's teaching was good. Even the tax collectors agreed. These were people who were already baptised by John. 30 But the Pharisees*d* and teachers of the law refused to accept God's plan for themselves; they did not let John baptise them.)

31 Then Jesus said, "What shall I say about the people of this time? What are they like? 32 They are like children sitting in the marketplace. One group of children calls to the other group and says,

'We played music for you, but you
      did not dance.
We sang a sad song, but you did
      not cry'.

33 John the Baptist came and did not eat like other people or drink wine. And you say, 'He has a demon*d* in him'. 34 The Son of Man*d* came eating like other people and drinking wine. And you say, 'Look at him! He eats too much and drinks too much wine! He is a friend of the tax collectors and "sinners"!' 35 But wisdom is shown to be right by the things it does."

Simon the Pharisee

36 One of the Pharisees*d* asked Jesus to eat with him. Jesus went into the Pharisee's house and sat at the table. 37 A sinful woman in the town learned that Jesus was eating at the Pharisee's house. So she brought an alabaster*d* jar of perfume. 38 She stood at Jesus' feet, crying, and began to wash his feet with her tears. She dried his feet

---

reed   It means that John was not weak like grass blown by the wind.

.

with her hair, kissed them many times and rubbed them with the perfume. [39]The Pharisee who asked Jesus to come to his house saw this. He thought to himself, "If Jesus were a prophet,[d] he would know that the woman who is touching him is a sinner!"

[40]Jesus said to the Pharisee, "Simon, I have something to say to you."

Simon said, "Teacher, tell me."

[41]Jesus said, "There were two men. Both men owed money to the same banker. One man owed the banker 500 silver coins.[n] The other man owed the banker 50 silver coins. [42]The men had no money; so they could not pay what they owed. But the banker told the men that they did not have to pay him. Which one of the two men will love the banker more?"

[43]Simon, the Pharisee, answered, "I think it would be the one who owed him the most money."

Jesus said to Simon, "You are right." [44]Then Jesus turned towards the woman and said to Simon, "Do you see this woman? When I came into your house, you gave me no water for my feet. But she washed my feet with her tears and dried my feet with her hair. [45]You did not kiss me, but she has been kissing my feet since I came in! [46]You did not rub my head with oil, but she rubbed my feet with perfume. [47]I tell you that her many sins are forgiven. This is clear because she showed great love. But the person who has only a little to be forgiven will feel only a little love."

[48]Then Jesus said to her, "Your sins are forgiven."

[49]The people sitting at the table began to think to themselves, "Who is this man? How can he forgive sins?"

[50]Jesus said to the woman, "Because you believed, you are saved from your sins. Go in peace."

The Group with Jesus

8 The next day, while Jesus was travelling through some cities and small towns, he preached and told the Good News[d] about God's kingdom. The 12 apostles[d] were with him. [2]There were also some women with him who had been healed of sicknesses and evil spirits. One of the women was Mary, called Magdalene, from whom seven demons[d] had gone out. [3]Also among the women were Joanna, the wife of Chuza (Herod's helper), Susanna, and many other women. These women used their own money to help Jesus and his apostles.

A Story About Planting Seed

[4]A great crowd gathered. People were coming to Jesus from every town. He told them this story:

[5]"A farmer went out to plant his seed. While he was planting, some seed fell beside the road. People walked on the seed, and the birds ate all this seed. [6]Some seed fell on rock. It began to grow but then died because it had no water. [7]Some seed fell among thorny weeds. This seed grew, but later the weeds choked the good plants. [8]And some seed fell on good ground. This seed grew and made 100 times more grain."

Jesus finished the story. Then he called out, "You people who hear me, listen!"

[9]Jesus' followers asked him, "What does this story mean?"

[10]Jesus said, "You have been chosen to know the secret truths of the kingdom of God. But I use stories to speak to other people. I do this so that:

'They will look, but they may not
    see.
They will listen, but they may
    not understand'.   *Isaiah 6:9*

---

silver coins A Roman denarius. One coin was the average pay for one day's work.

[11] "This is what the story means: The seed is God's teaching. [12] What is the seed that fell beside the road? It is like the people who hear God's teaching, but then the devil comes and takes it away from their hearts. So they cannot believe the teaching and be saved. [13] What is the seed that fell on rock? It is like those who hear God's teaching and accept it gladly. But they don't have deep roots. They believe for a while, but then trouble comes. They stop believing and turn away from God. [14] What is the seed that fell among the thorny weeds? It is like those who hear God's teaching, but they let the worries, riches, and pleasures of this life keep them from growing. So they never produce good fruit. [15] And what is the seed that fell on the good ground? That is like those who hear God's teaching with a good, honest heart. They obey God's teaching and patiently produce good fruit.

Use What You Have

[16] "No one lights a lamp and then covers it with a bowl or hides it under a bed. Instead, he puts the lamp on a lampstand so that those who come in will have enough light to see. [17] Everything that is hidden will become clear. Every secret thing will be made known. [18] So be careful how you listen. The person who has something will be given more. But to the person who has nothing, this will happen: even what he thinks he has will be taken away from him."

Jesus' True Family

[19] Jesus' mother and brothers came to see him. There was such a crowd that they could not get to him. [20] Someone said to Jesus, "Your mother and your brothers are standing outside. They want to see you."

[21] Jesus answered them, "My mother and my brothers are those who listen to God's teaching and obey it!"

Jesus Stops a Storm

[22] One day Jesus and his followers got into a boat. He said to them, "Come with me across the lake." And so they started across. [23] While they were sailing, Jesus fell asleep. A big storm blew up on the lake. The boat began to fill with water, and they were in danger. [24] The followers went to Jesus and woke him. They said, "Master! Master! We will drown!"

Jesus got up and gave a command to the wind and the waves. The wind stopped, and the lake became calm. [25] Jesus said to his followers, "Where is your faith?"

The followers were afraid and amazed. They said to each other, "What kind of man is this? He commands the wind and the water, and they obey him!"

A Man with Demons Inside Him

[26] Jesus and his followers sailed across the lake from Galilee to the area where the Gerasene people live. [27] When Jesus got out of the boat, a man from the town came to Jesus. This man had demons[d] inside him. For a long time he had worn no clothes. He lived in the burial caves, not in a house. [28] When he saw Jesus, he cried out and fell down before him. The man said with a loud voice, "What do you want with me, Jesus, Son of the Most High God? Please don't punish me!" [29] He said this because Jesus had commanded the evil spirit to come out of him. Many times it had taken hold of him. He had been kept under guard and chained hand and foot. But he had broken his chains and had been driven by the demon out into the desert.

[30] Jesus asked him, "What is your name?"

The man answered, "Legion".[n] (He said his name was "Legion" because many demons were in him.) [31]The demons begged Jesus not to send them into eternal darkness.[n] [32]On the hill there was a large herd of pigs eating. The demons begged Jesus to allow them to go into the pigs. So Jesus allowed them to do this. [33]Then the demons came out of the man and went into the pigs. The herd of pigs ran down the hill and into the lake. All the pigs drowned.

[34]The men who took care of the pigs ran away. They told about this in the town and the countryside. [35]And people went to see what had happened. They came to Jesus and found the man sitting there at Jesus' feet. The man was clothed and in his right mind because the demons had gone. But the people were frightened. [36]The men who saw these things happen told the others all about how Jesus had made the man well. [37]All the people of the Gerasene country asked Jesus to go away. They were all very afraid. So Jesus got into the boat and went back to Galilee.

[38]The man that Jesus had healed begged to go with him. But Jesus sent him away, saying, [39]"Go back home and tell people what God did for you." So the man went all over town telling how much Jesus had done for him.

Jesus Gives Life to a Dead Girl and Heals a Sick Woman

[40]When Jesus got back to Galilee, a crowd welcomed him. Everyone was waiting for him. [41]A man named Jairus came to Jesus. Jairus was a ruler of the synagogue.[d] He bowed down at Jesus' feet and begged him to come to his house. [42]Jairus had only one daughter. She was 12 years old, and she was dying.

While Jesus was on his way to Jairus' house, the people were crowding all around him. [43]A woman was there who had been bleeding for 12 years. She had spent all her money on doctors, but no doctor was able to heal her. [44]The woman came up behind Jesus and touched the edge of his coat. At that moment, her bleeding stopped. [45]Then Jesus said, "Who touched me?"

All the people said they had not touched Jesus. Peter said, "Master, the people are all around you and are pushing against you."

[46]But Jesus said, "Someone did touch me! I felt power go out from me." [47]When the woman saw that she could not hide, she came forward, shaking. She bowed down before Jesus. While all the people listened, she told why she had touched him. Then, she said, she was healed immediately. [48]Jesus said to her, "Dear woman, you are healed because you believed. Go in peace."

[49]While Jesus was still speaking, someone came from the house of the synagogue ruler and said to the ruler, "Your daughter has died! Don't bother the teacher now."

[50]When Jesus heard this, he said to Jairus, "Don't be afraid. Just believe, and your daughter will be well."

[51]Jesus went to the house. He let only Peter, John, James, and the girl's father and mother go inside with him. [52]All the people were crying and feeling sad because the girl was dead. But Jesus said, "Don't cry. She is not dead; she is only sleeping."

[53]The people laughed at Jesus because they knew that the girl was

---

"Legion"   Means very many. A legion was about 5,000 men in the Roman army.
eternal darkness   Literally, "the abyss", something like a pit or a hole that has no end.

dead. [54] But Jesus took her by the hand and called to her, "My child, stand up!" [55] Her spirit came back into her, and she stood up immediately. Jesus said, "Give her something to eat." [56] The girl's parents were amazed. Jesus told them not to tell anyone about what happened.

Jesus Sends Out the Apostles

9 Jesus called the 12 apostles[d] together. He gave them power to heal sicknesses and power over all demons.[d] [2] Jesus sent the apostles out to tell about God's kingdom and to heal the sick. [3] He said to them, "When you travel, don't take a walking stick. Also, don't carry a bag, or food, or money. Take for your trip only the clothes you are wearing. [4] When you go into a house, stay there until it is time to leave. [5] If the people in the town will not welcome you, go outside the town and shake the dust off of your feet.[n] This will be a warning to them."

[6] So the apostles went out. They travelled through all the towns. They told the Good News[d] and healed people everywhere.

Herod Is Confused About Jesus

[7] Herod, the governor, heard about all these things that were happening. He was confused because some people said, "John the Baptist[d] is risen from death." [8] Others said, "Elijah has come to us." And still others said, "One of the prophets[d] from long ago has risen from death." [9] Herod said, "I cut off John's head. So who is this man I hear these things about?" And Herod kept trying to see Jesus.

More than 5,000 People Fed

[10] When the apostles[d] returned, they told Jesus all the things they had done on their trip. Then Jesus took them away to a town called Bethsaida. There, Jesus and his apostles could be alone together. [11] But the people learned where Jesus went and followed him. Jesus welcomed them and talked with them about God's kingdom. He healed those who needed to be healed.

[12] Late in the afternoon, the 12 apostles came to Jesus and said, "No one lives in this place. Send the people away. They need to find food and places to sleep in the towns and countryside around here."

[13] But Jesus said to them, "You give them something to eat."

They said, "We have only five loaves of bread and two fish. Do you want us to go and buy food for all these

---

shake . . . feet A warning. It showed that they had finished talking to these people.

Luke 9:13 "We have only five loaves of bread and two fish."

people?" [14] (There were about 5,000 men there.)

Jesus said to his followers, "Tell the people to sit in groups of about 50 people."

[15] So the followers did this, and all the people sat down. [16] Then Jesus took the five loaves of bread and two fish. He looked up to heaven and thanked God for the food. Then Jesus divided the food and gave it to the followers to give to the people. [17] All the people ate and were satisfied. And there was a lot of food left. Twelve baskets were filled with pieces of food that were not eaten.

Jesus Is the Christ

[18] Once when Jesus was praying alone, his followers came together there. Jesus asked them, "Who do the people say I am?"

[19] They answered, "Some say you are John the Baptist.[d] Others say you are Elijah.[n] And others say you are one of the prophets[d] from long ago who has come back to life."

[20] Then Jesus asked, "And who do you say I am?"

Peter answered, "You are the Christ[d] from God."

[21] Jesus warned them not to tell anyone. Then he said, [22] "The Son of Man[d] must suffer many things. He will be rejected by the older Jewish leaders, the leading priests, and the teachers of the law. The Son of Man will be killed. But after three days he will be raised from death."

[23] Jesus went on to say to all of them, "If anyone wants to follow me, he must say 'no' to the things he wants. Every day he must be willing even to die on a cross, and he must follow me.

[24] Whoever wants to save his life will lose it. And whoever gives his life for me will save it. [25] It is worth nothing for a man to have the whole world, if he himself is destroyed or lost. [26] If anyone is ashamed of me and my teaching, then I[n] will be ashamed of him. I will be ashamed of him at the time I come with my glory and with the glory of the Father and the holy angels. [27] I tell you the truth. Some of you people standing here will see the kingdom of God before you die."

Jesus with Moses and Elijah

[28] About eight days after Jesus said these things, he took Peter, James, and John and went up on a mountain to pray. [29] While Jesus was praying, his face was changed, and his clothes became shining white. [30] Then two men were talking with Jesus. The men were Moses and Elijah.[n] [31] They appeared in heavenly glory, talking with Jesus about his death which would happen in Jerusalem. [32] Peter and the others were asleep. But they woke up and saw the glory of Jesus. They also saw the two men who were standing with him. [33] When Moses and Elijah were about to leave, Peter said, "Master, it is good that we are here. We will put three tents here – one for you, one for Moses, and one for Elijah." (Peter did not know what he was saying.)

[34] While Peter was saying these things, a cloud came down all around them. Peter, James, and John became afraid when the cloud covered them. [35] A voice came from the cloud. The voice said, "This is my Son. He is the One I have chosen. Obey him."

[36] When the voice finished speak-

Elijah   A man who spoke for God. He lived hundreds of years before Christ.
I   Literally, "the Son of Man."
Moses and Elijah   Two of the most important Jewish leaders in the past.

ing, only Jesus was there. Peter, James, and John said nothing. At that time they told no one about what they had seen.

Jesus Heals a Sick Boy

37 The next day, Jesus, Peter, James, and John came down from the mountain. A large crowd met Jesus. 38 A man in the crowd shouted to Jesus, "Teacher, please come and look at my son. He is the only child I have. 39 An evil spirit comes into my son, and then he shouts. He loses control of himself, and he foams at the mouth. The evil spirit keeps on hurting him and almost never leaves him. 40 I begged your followers to make the evil spirit leave my son, but they could not do it."

41 Jesus answered, "You people who live now have no faith. Your lives are all wrong. How long must I be with you and be patient with you?" Then Jesus said to the man, "Bring your son here."

42 While the boy was coming, the demon*d* threw him on the ground. The boy lost control of himself. But Jesus gave a strong command to the evil spirit. Then the boy was healed, and Jesus gave him back to his father. 43 All the people were amazed at the great power of God.

Jesus Talks About His Death

The people were all wondering about the things Jesus did. But he said to his followers, 44 "Don't forget the things I tell you now: the Son of Man*d* will be handed over into the control of men." 45 But the followers did not understand what Jesus meant. The meaning was hidden from them so that they could

not understand it. But they were afraid to ask Jesus about what he said.

The Most Important Person

46 Jesus' followers began to have an argument about which one of them was the greatest. 47 Jesus knew what they were thinking. So he took a little child and stood the child beside him. 48 Then Jesus said, "If anyone accepts a little child like this in my name, then he accepts me. And when he accepts me, he accepts the One who sent me. He who is least among you all – he is the greatest."

Anyone Not Against Us Is for Us

49 John answered, "Master, we saw someone using your name to force demons*d* out of people. We told him to stop because he does not belong to our group."

50 Jesus said to him, "Don't stop him. If a person is not against you, then he is for you."

A Samaritan Town

51 The time was coming near when Jesus would leave and be taken to heaven. He was determined to go to Jerusalem 52 and sent some men ahead of him. The men went into a town in Samaria to make everything ready for Jesus. 53 But the people there would not welcome him because he was going toward Jerusalem. 54 James and John, the followers of Jesus, saw this. They said, "Lord, do you want us to call fire down from heaven and destroy those people?"*n*

55 But Jesus turned and scolded

Verse 54 Here, some Greek copies add: ". . . as Elijah did."

them.[n] [56]Then he and his followers went to another town.

Following Jesus

[57]They were all going along the road. Someone said to Jesus, "I will follow you anywhere you go."

[58]Jesus answered, "The foxes have holes to live in. The birds have nests to live in. But the Son of Man[d] has no place to rest his head."

[59]Jesus said to another man, "Follow me!"

But the man said, "Lord, first let me go and bury my father."

[60]But Jesus said to him, "Let the people who are dead bury their own dead! You must go and tell about the kingdom of God."

[61]Another man said, "I will follow you, Lord, but first let me go and say good bye to my family."

[62]Jesus said, "Anyone who begins to plough a field but keeps looking back is of no use in the kingdom of God."

Jesus Sends the 72 Men

10 After this, the Lord chose 72[n] others. He sent them out in pairs. He sent them ahead of him into every town and place where he planned to go. [2]He said to them, "There are a great many people to harvest. But there are only a few workers to harvest them. God owns the harvest. Pray to God that he will send more workers to help gather his harvest. [3]You can go now. But listen! I am sending you, and you will be like sheep among wolves. [4]Don't carry a

purse, a bag, or sandals. Don't stop to talk with people on the road. [5]Before you go into a house, say, 'Peace be with this house'. [6]If a peaceful man lives there, your blessing of peace will stay with him. If the man is not peaceful, then your blessing of peace will come back to you. [7]Stay in the peaceful house. Eat and drink what the people there give you. A worker should be given his pay. Don't move from house to house. [8]If you go into a town and the people welcome you, eat what they give you. [9]Heal the sick who live there. Tell them, 'The kingdom of God is soon coming to you!' [10]But if you go into a town, and the people don't welcome you, then go out into the streets of that town. Say to them, [11]'Even the dust from your town that sticks to our feet we wipe off against you.[n] But remember that the kingdom of God is coming soon'. [12]I tell you, on the Judgement Day it will be worse for the people of that town than for the people of Sodom.[n]

Jesus Warns Unbelievers

[13]"How terrible for you, Korazin! How terrible for you, Bethsaida! I did many miracles[d] in you. If those same miracles had happened in Tyre and Sidon,[n] those people would have changed their lives and stopped sinning long ago. They would have worn rough cloth and put ashes on themselves to show that they had changed. [14]But on the Judgement Day it will be worse for you than for Tyre and Sidon. [15]And you, Capernaum,[n] will you be

---

Verse 55 Here, some copies add: "And Jesus said, 'You don't know what kind of spirit you belong to. [56]The Son of Man did not come to destroy the souls of men but to save them'."
72 Many Greek copies read 70.
dust . . . you A warning. It showed that they had finished talking to these people.
Sodom City that God destroyed because the people were so evil.
Tyre and Sidon Towns where wicked people lived.
Korazin, Bethsaida, Capernaum Towns by Lake Galilee where Jesus preached to the people.

lifted up to heaven? No! You will be thrown down to the depths!

¹⁶"He who listens to you is really listening to me. He who refuses to accept you is really refusing to accept me. And he who refuses to accept me is refusing to accept the One who sent me."

Satan Falls

¹⁷When the 72^n men came back from their trip, they were very happy. They said, "Lord, even the demons^d obeyed us when we used your name!"

¹⁸Jesus said to the men, "I saw Satan falling like lightning from the sky. ¹⁹Listen! I gave you power to walk on snakes and scorpions. I gave you more power than the Enemy has. Nothing will hurt you. ²⁰You should be happy, but not because the spirits obey you. You should be happy because your names are written in heaven."

Jesus Prays to the Father

²¹Then the Holy Spirit^d made Jesus rejoice. He said, "I thank you, Father, Lord of heaven and earth, because you have hidden these things from the people who are wise and clever. But you have shown them to those who are like little children. Yes, Father, you did this because this is what you really wanted.

²²"My Father has given me all things. No one knows the Son – only the Father knows. And only the Son knows the Father. The only people who will know about the Father are those whom the Son chooses to tell."

²³Then Jesus turned to his followers and said privately, "You are blessed to see what you now see! ²⁴I tell you, many prophets^d and kings wanted to see what you now see. But they did not see these things. And many prophets and kings wanted to hear what you now hear. But they did not hear these things."

The Good Samaritan

²⁵Then a teacher of the law stood up. He was trying to test Jesus. He said, "Teacher, what must I do to get life for ever?"

²⁶Jesus said to him, "What is written in the law? What do you read there?"

²⁷The man answered, "Love the Lord your God. Love him with all your heart, all your soul, all your strength, and all your mind."^{n} Also, "You must love your neighbour as you love yourself."^{n}

²⁸Jesus said to him, "Your answer is right. Do this and you will have life for ever."

²⁹But the man wanted to show that the way he was living was right. So he said to Jesus, "And who is my neighbour?"

³⁰To answer this question, Jesus said, "A man was going down the road from Jerusalem to Jericho. Some robbers attacked him. They tore off his clothes and beat him. Then they left him lying there, almost dead. ³¹It happened that a Jewish priest was going down that road. When the priest saw the man, he walked by on the other side of the road. ³²Next, a Levite^n came there. He went over and looked at the man. Then he walked by on the

72   Many Greek copies read 70.
"Love . . . mind."   Quotation from Deuteronomy 6:5.
"You . . . yourself."   Quotation from Leviticus 19:18.
Levite   Levites were men from the tribe of Levi who helped the Jewish priests with their work in the Temple. Read 1 Chronicles 23:24–32.

other side of the road. [33]Then a Samaritan[n] travelling down the road came to where the hurt man was lying. He saw the man and felt very sorry for him. [34]The Samaritan went to him and poured olive oil and wine[n] on his

Luke 10:33 "He saw the man and felt very sorry for him."

wounds and bandaged them. He put the hurt man on his own donkey and took him to an inn. At the inn, the Samaritan took care of him. [35]The next day, the Samaritan brought out two silver coins[n] and gave them to the innkeeper. The Samaritan said, 'Take care of this man. If you spend more money on him, I will pay it back to you when I come again'."

[36]Then Jesus said, "Which one of these three men do you think was a neighbour to the man who was attacked by the robbers?"

[37]The teacher of the law answered, "The one who helped him."

Jesus said to him, "Then go and do the same thing he did!"

Mary and Martha

[38]While Jesus and his followers were travelling, Jesus went into a town. A woman named Martha let Jesus stay at her house. [39]Martha had a sister named Mary. Mary was sitting at Jesus' feet and listening to him teach. [40]Martha became angry because she had so much work to do. She went in and said, "Lord, don't you care that my sister has left me alone to do all the work? Tell her to help me!"

[41]But the Lord answered her, "Martha, Martha, you are getting worried and upset about too many things. [42]Only one thing is important. Mary has chosen the right thing, and it will never be taken away from her."

Jesus Teaches About Prayer

11 Once Jesus was praying in a place. When he had finished, one of his followers said to him, "John taught his followers how to pray. Lord, please teach us how to pray, too."

[2]Jesus said to them, "When you pray, say:
'Father, we pray that your name
    will always be kept holy.
We pray that your kingdom will
    come.
[3]Give us the food we need for each
    day.
[4]Forgive us the sins we have done,
    because we forgive every person
    who has done wrong to us.
And do not cause us to be tested'."

Samaritan   Samaritans were people from Samaria. These people were part Jewish, but the Jews did not accept them as true Jews. Samaritans and Jews hated each other.
olive oil and wine   Oil and wine were used like medicine to soften and clean wounds.
silver coins   A Roman denarius. One coin was the average pay for one day's work.

Continue to Ask

5-6Then Jesus said to them, "Suppose one of you went to your friend's house at midnight and said to him, 'A friend of mine has come into town to visit me, but I have nothing for him to eat. Please lend me three loaves of bread'. 7Your friend inside the house answers, 'Don't bother me! The door is already locked. My children and I are in bed. I cannot get up and give you the bread now'. 8I tell you, perhaps friendship is not enough to make him get up to give you the bread. But he will surely get up to give you what you need if you continue to ask. 9So I tell you, continue to ask, and God will give to you. Continue to search, and you will find. Continue to knock, and the door will open for you. 10Yes, if a person continues asking, he will receive. If he continues searching, he will find. And if he continues knocking, the door will open for him. 11What would you fathers do if your son asks you for a fish? Would any of you give him a snake? 12Or, if your son asks for an egg, would you give him a scorpion? 13Even though you are bad, you know how to give good things to your children. So surely your heavenly Father knows how to give the Holy Spirit*d* to those who ask him."

Jesus' Power Is from God

14Once Jesus was sending a demon*d* out of a man who could not talk. When the demon came out, the man was able to speak. The people were amazed. 15But some of them said, "Jesus uses the power of Beelzebul*d* to force demons out of people. Beelzebul is the ruler of demons."

16Other people wanted to test Jesus. They asked him to give them a sign from heaven. 17But Jesus knew what they were thinking. So he said to them, "Every kingdom that is divided and fights against itself will be destroyed. And a family that fights against itself will break apart. 18So if Satan is fighting against himself, then how will his kingdom last? You say that I use the power of Beelzebul to force out demons. 19But if I use the power of Beelzebul to force out demons, then by what power do your people force out demons? So your own people prove that you are wrong. 20But if I use the power of God to force out demons, the kingdom of God has come to you!

21"When a strong man with many weapons guards his own house, then the things in his house are safe. 22But suppose a stronger man comes and defeats him. The stronger man will take away the weapons that the first man trusted to keep his house safe. Then the stronger man will do what he wants with the first man's things.

23"If anyone is not with me, he is against me. He who does not work with me is working against me.

The Empty Man

24"When an evil spirit comes out of a person, it travels through dry places, looking for a place to rest. But that spirit finds no place to rest. So it says, 'I will go back to the home I left'. 25When the spirit comes back to that person, it finds that home swept clean and made neat. 26Then the evil spirit goes out and brings seven other spirits more evil than itself. Then all the evil spirits go into that person and live there. And he has even more trouble than he had before."

People Who Are Truly Blessed

27When Jesus was saying these things, a woman in the crowd spoke out. She said to Jesus, "Your mother is blessed because she gave birth to you and nursed you."

²⁸But Jesus said, "Those who hear the teaching of God and obey it – they are the ones who are truly blessed."

Give Us Proof!

²⁹The crowd grew larger. Jesus said, "The people who live today are evil. They ask for a miracle^d as a sign from God. But they will have no sign – only the sign of Jonah.^{n} ³⁰Jonah was a sign for those people who lived in Nineveh. In the same way the Son of Man^d will be a sign for the people of this time. ³¹On the Judgement Day the Queen of the South^n will stand up with the men who live now. She will show that they are guilty because she came from far away to listen to Solomon's wise teaching. And I tell you that someone greater than Solomon is here! ³²On the Judgement Day the men of Nineveh will stand up with the people who live now. And they will show that you are guilty, because when Jonah preached to those people, they changed their hearts and lives. And I tell you that someone greater than Jonah is here!

Be a Light for the World

³³"No one takes a light and puts it under a bowl or hides it. Instead, he puts the light on a lampstand so that the people who come in can see. ³⁴Your eye is a light for the body. If your eyes are good, then your whole body will be full of light. But if your eyes are evil, then your whole body will be full of darkness. ³⁵So be careful! Don't let the light in you become darkness. ³⁶If your whole body is full

of light, and none of it is dark, then you will shine bright, as when a lamp shines on you."

Jesus Accuses the Pharisees

³⁷After Jesus had finished speaking, a Pharisee^d asked Jesus to eat with him. So Jesus went in and sat at the table. ³⁸But the Pharisee was surprised when he saw that Jesus did not wash his hands^n before the meal. ³⁹The Lord said to him, "You Pharisees clean the outside of the cup and the dish. But inside you are full of greed and evil. ⁴⁰You are foolish. The same One who made what is outside also made what is inside. ⁴¹So give what is in your cups and dishes to the poor. Then you will be fully clean. ⁴²But how terrible for you Pharisees! You give God one-tenth of even your mint, your rue, and every other plant in your garden. But you forget to be fair to other people and to love God. These are the things you should do. And you should also continue to do those other things – like giving one-tenth. ⁴³How terrible for you Pharisees, because you love to get the most important seats in the synagogues.^{d} And you love people to show respect to you in the marketplaces. ⁴⁴How terrible for you, because you are like hidden graves. People walk on them without knowing it."

Jesus Talks to Teachers of the Law

⁴⁵One of the teachers of the law said to Jesus, "Teacher, when you say these things, you are insulting us, too."

⁴⁶Jesus answered, "How terrible for

---

sign of Jonah   Jonah's three days in the big fish are like Jesus' three days in the tomb.

Queen of the South   The Queen of Sheba. She travelled 1,000 miles to learn God's wisdom from Solomon. Read 1 Kings 10:1–3.

wash his hands   This was a Jewish religious custom that the Pharisees thought was very important.

you, you teachers of the law! You make strict rules that are very hard for people to obey. But you yourselves don't even try to follow those rules. [47]How terrible for you, because you build tombs for the prophets.[d] But these are the prophets that your fathers killed! [48]And now you show that you approve of what your fathers did. They killed the prophets, and you build tombs for the prophets! [49]This is why in his wisdom God said, 'I will send prophets and apostles[d] to them. Some of my prophets and apostles will be killed, and others will be treated cruelly'. [50]So you who live now will be punished for the deaths of all the prophets who were killed since the beginning of the world. [51]You will be punished for the killing of Abel and for the killing of Zechariah.[n] Zechariah was killed between the altar and the Temple.[d] Yes, I tell you that you people who live now will be punished for them all.

[52]"How terrible for you, you teachers of the law. You have hidden the key to learning about God. You yourselves would not learn, and you stopped others from learning, too."

[53]When Jesus was leaving, the teachers of the law and the Pharisees[d] began to give him trouble, asking him questions about many things. [54]They were trying to catch Jesus saying something wrong.

Don't Be Like the Pharisees

12 Many thousands of people had gathered. There were so many people that they were stepping on each other. Before Jesus spoke to them, he said to his followers, "Be careful of the yeast of the Pharisees.[d] They are hypocrites.[d] [2]Everything that is hidden will be shown. Every-thing that is secret will be made known. [3]The things you say in the dark will be told in the light. The things you have whispered in an inner room will be shouted from the top of the house."

Fear Only God

[4]Then Jesus said to the people, "I tell you, my friends, don't be afraid of people. People can kill the body, but after that they can do nothing more to hurt you. [5]I will show you the One to fear. You should fear him who has the power to kill you and also to throw you into hell. Yes, he is the One you should fear.

[6]"When five sparrows are sold, they cost only two pennies. But God does not forget any of them. [7]Yes, God even knows how many hairs you have on your head. Don't be afraid. You are worth much more than many sparrows.

Don't Be Ashamed of Jesus

[8]"I tell you, if anyone stands before others and says that he believes in me, then I will say that he belongs to me. I will say this before the angels of God. [9]But if anyone stands before others and says he does not believe in me, then I will say that he does not belong to me. I will say this before the angels of God.

[10]"If a person says something against the Son of Man,[d] he can be forgiven. But a person who says bad things against the Holy Spirit[d] will not be forgiven.

[11]"When men bring you into the synagogues[d] before the leaders and other important men, don't worry about how to defend yourself or what to say. [12]At that time the Holy Spirit will teach you what you must say."

Abel . . . Zechariah   In the Hebrew Old Testament, the first and last men to be murdered.

Jesus Warns Against Selfishness

¹³One of the men in the crowd said to Jesus, "Teacher, tell my brother to divide with me the property our father left us."

¹⁴But Jesus said to him, "Who said that I should be your judge or decide how to divide the property between you two?" ¹⁵Then Jesus said to them, "Be careful and guard against all kinds of greed. A man's life is not measured by the many things he owns."

¹⁶Then Jesus used this story: "There was a rich man who had some land, which grew a good crop of food. ¹⁷The rich man thought to himself, 'What will I do? I have no place to keep all my crops'. ¹⁸Then he said, 'I know what I will do. I will tear down my barns and build bigger ones! I will put all my grain and other goods together in my new barns. ¹⁹Then I can say to myself, I have enough good things stored to last for many years. Rest, eat, drink, and enjoy life!'

²⁰"But God said to that man, 'Foolish man! Tonight you will die. So who will get those things you have prepared for yourself?'

²¹"This is how it will be for anyone who stores things up only for himself and is not rich towards God."

Don't Worry

²²Jesus said to his followers, "So I tell you, don't worry about the food you need to live. Don't worry about the clothes you need for your body. ²³Life is more important than food. And the body is more important than clothes. ²⁴Look at the birds. They don't plant or harvest. They don't save food in houses or barns. But God takes care of them. And you are worth much more than birds. ²⁵None of you can add any time to your life by worrying about it. ²⁶If you cannot do even the little things, then why worry about the big things? ²⁷Look at the wild flowers. See how they grow. They don't work or make clothes for themselves. But I tell you that even Solomon, the great and rich king, was not dressed as beautifully as one of these flowers. ²⁸God clothes the grass in the field like that. That grass is living today, but tomorrow it will be thrown into the fire. So you know how much more God will clothe you. Don't have so little faith! ²⁹Don't always think about what you will eat or what you will drink. Don't worry about it. ³⁰All the people in the world are trying to get those things. Your Father knows that you need them. ³¹The thing you should seek is God's kingdom. Then

Luke 12:24–27 "Look at the birds . . . Look at the wild flowers."

all the other things you need will be given to you.

Don't Trust in Money

[32] "Don't fear, little flock. Your Father wants to give you the kingdom. [33] Sell the things you have and give to the poor. Get for yourselves purses that don't wear out. Get the treasure in heaven that never runs out. Thieves can't steal it in heaven, and moths can't destroy it. [34] Your heart will be where your treasure is.

Always Be Ready

[35] "Be ready! Be dressed for service and have your lamps shining. [36] Be like servants who are waiting for their master to come home from a wedding party. The master comes and knocks. The servants immediately open the door for him. [37] Those servants will be blessed when their master comes home, because he sees that his servants are ready and waiting for him. I tell you the truth. The master will dress himself to serve and tell the servants to sit at the table. Then the master will serve them. [38] Those servants might have to wait until midnight or later for their master. But they will be happy when he comes in and finds them still waiting.

[39] "Remember this: if the owner of the house knew what time a thief was coming, then the owner would not allow the thief to enter his house. [40] So you also must be ready! The Son of Man[d] will come at a time when you don't expect him!"

Who Is the Trusted Servant?

[41] Peter said, "Lord, did you tell this story for us or for all people?"

[42] The Lord said, "Who is the wise and trusted servant? Who is the ser-vant the master trusts to give the other servants their food at the right time? [43] When the master comes and finds his servant doing the work he gave him, that servant will be very happy. [44] I tell you the truth. The master will choose that servant to take care of everything the master owns. [45] But what will happen if the servant is evil and thinks that his master will not come back soon? That servant will begin to beat the other servants, men and women. He will eat and drink and get drunk. [46] Then the master will come when that servant is not ready. It will be a time when the servant is not expecting him. Then the master will cut him in pieces and send him away to be with the others who don't obey.

[47] "The servant who knows what his master wants but is not ready or does not do what the master wants will be beaten with many blows! [48] But the servant who does not know what his master wants and does things that should be punished will be beaten with few blows. Everyone who has been given much will be responsible for much. Much more will be expected from the one who has been given more."

Jesus Causes Division

[49] Jesus continued speaking, "I came to set fire to the world. I wish it were already burning! [50] I must be baptised with a different kind of bap-tism.[n] I feel very troubled until it is over. [51] Do you think that I came to give peace to the world? No! I came to divide the world! [52] From now on, a family with five people will be divided, three against two, and two against three. [53] A father and son will be divided: the son will be against his

---

I . . . baptism. Jesus was talking about the suffering he would soon go through.

father. The father will be against his son. A mother and her daughter will be divided: the daughter will be against her mother. The mother will be against her daughter. A mother-in-law and her daughter-in-law will be divided: the daughter-in-law will be against her mother-in-law. The mother-in-law will be against her daughter-in-law."

Understanding the Times

[54]Then Jesus said to the people, "When you see clouds coming up in the west, you say, 'It's going to rain'. And soon it begins to rain. [55]When you feel the wind begin to blow from the south, you say, 'It will be a hot day'. And you are right. [56]Hypocrites![d] You can understand the weather. Why don't you understand what is happening now?

Settle Your Problems

[57]"Why can't you decide for yourselves what is right? [58]When someone is suing you, and you are going with him to court, try hard to settle it on the way. If you don't settle it, he may take you to the judge. The judge might turn you over to the officer. And the officer might throw you into jail. [59]You will not get out of there until they have taken everything you have."

Change Your Hearts

13 At that time some people were there with Jesus. They told him about what had happened to some people from Galilee. Pilate[n] killed those people while they were worshipping. He mixed their blood with the blood of the animals they were sacrificing to God. [2]Jesus answered, "Do you think this happened to them because they were more sinful than

all others from Galilee? [3]No, they were not! But if all of you don't change your hearts and lives, then you will be destroyed as they were! [4]What about those 18 people who died when the tower of Siloam fell on them? Do you think they were more sinful than all the others who live in Jerusalem? [5]They were not! But I tell you, if you don't change your hearts and lives, then you will all be destroyed too!"

The Useless Tree

[6]Jesus told this story: "A man had a fig tree planted in his vineyard. He came looking for some fruit on the tree, but he found none. [7]So the man said to his servant who took care of his vineyard, 'I have been looking for fruit on this tree for three years, but I never find any. Cut it down! Why should it waste the ground?' [8]But the servant answered, 'Master, let the tree have one more year to produce fruit. Let me dig up the soil around it and put on some fertiliser. [9]Maybe the tree will produce fruit next year. If the tree still doesn't produce fruit, then you can cut it down'."

Jesus Heals on the Sabbath

[10]Jesus was teaching in one of the synagogues[d] on the Sabbath[d] day. [11]In the synagogue there was a woman who had an evil spirit in her. This spirit had made the woman a cripple for 18 years. Her back was always bent; she could not stand up straight. [12]When Jesus saw her, he called her over and said, "Woman, your sickness has left you!" [13]Jesus put his hands on her. Immediately she was able to stand up straight and began praising God.

[14]The synagogue leader was angry because Jesus healed on the Sabbath day. He said to the people, "There are

---

Pilate   Pontius Pilate was the Roman governor of Judea from A.D. 26 to A.D. 36.

MATTHEW 3:17
*"This is my Son and I love him.
I am very pleased with him."*

Luke 14:21 "Bring in the poor, the crippled, the blind, and the lame."

You Must First Plan

25 Large crowds were travelling with Jesus. He turned and said to them, 26 "If anyone comes to me but loves his father, mother, wife, children, brothers, or sisters more than he loves me, then he cannot be my follower. A person must love me more than he loves himself! 27 If anyone is not willing to die on a cross when he follows me, then he cannot be my follower. 28 If you wanted to build a tower, you would first sit down and decide how much it would cost. You must see if you have enough money to finish the job. 29 If you don't do that, you might begin the work, but you would not be able to finish. And if you could not finish it, then all who would see it would laugh at you. 30 They would say, 'This man began to build but was not able to finish!'

31 "If a king is going to fight against another king, first he will sit down and plan. If the king has only 10,000 men, he will plan to see if he is able to defeat the other king who has 20,000 men. 32 If he cannot defeat the other king, then he will send some men to speak to the other king and ask for peace. 33 In the same way, you must give up everything you have to follow me. If you don't, you cannot be my follower!

Don't Lose Your Influence

34 "Salt is a good thing. But if the salt loses its salty taste, then it is worth nothing. You cannot make it salty again. 35 It is no good for the soil or for manure. People throw it away.

"You people who hear me, listen!"

A Lost Sheep and a Lost Coin

15 Many tax collectors and "sinners" came to listen to Jesus. 2 The Pharisees[d] and the teachers of the law began to complain: "Look! This man welcomes sinners and even eats with them!"

3 Then Jesus told them this story: 4 "Suppose one of you has 100 sheep, but he loses one of them. Then he will leave the other 99 sheep alone and go out and look for the lost sheep. The man will keep on searching for the lost sheep until he finds it. 5 And when he finds it, the man is very happy. He puts it on his shoulders 6 and goes home. He calls to his friends and neighbours and says, 'Be happy with me because I found my lost sheep!' 7 In the same way, I tell you there is much joy in heaven when one sinner changes his heart. There is more joy for that one sinner than there is for 99 good people who don't need to change.

8 "Suppose a woman has ten silver coins,[n] but she loses one of them. She

---

silver coins   A Roman denarius. One coin was the average pay for one day's work.

will light a lamp and clean the house. She will look carefully for the coin until she finds it. ⁹And when she finds it, she will call her friends and neighbours and say, 'Be happy with me because I have found the coin that I lost!' ¹⁰In the same way, there is joy before the angels of God when one sinner changes his heart."

The Son Who Left Home

¹¹Then Jesus said, "A man had two sons. ¹²The younger son said to his father, 'Give me my share of the property'. So the father divided the property between his two sons. ¹³Then the younger son gathered up all that was his and left. He travelled far away to another country. There he wasted his money in foolish living. ¹⁴He spent everything that he had. Soon after that, the land became very dry, and there was no rain. There was not enough food to eat anywhere in the country. The son was hungry and needed money. ¹⁵So he got a job with one of the citizens there. The man sent the son into the fields to feed pigs. ¹⁶The son was so hungry that he was willing to eat the food the pigs were eating. But no one gave him anything. ¹⁷The son realised that he had been very foolish. He thought, 'All of my father's servants have plenty of food. But I am here, almost dying with hunger. ¹⁸I will leave and return to my father. I'll say to him: Father, I have sinned against God and have done wrong to you. ¹⁹I am not good enough to be called your son. But let me be like one of your servants'. ²⁰So the son left and went to his father.

"While the son was still a long way off, his father saw him coming. He felt sorry for his son. So the father ran to him, and hugged and kissed him. ²¹The son said, 'Father, I have sinned against God and have done wrong to you. I am not good enough to be called your son'. ²²But the father said to his servants, 'Hurry! Bring the best clothes and put them on him. Also, put a ring on his finger and sandals on his feet. ²³And get our fat calf and kill it. Then we can have a feast and celebrate! ²⁴My son was dead, but now he is alive again! He was lost, but now he is found!' So they began to celebrate.

²⁵"The older son was in the field. As he came closer to the house, he heard the sound of music and dancing. ²⁶So he called to one of the servants and asked, 'What does all this mean?' ²⁷The servant said, 'Your brother has come back. Your father killed the fat calf to eat because your brother came home safely!' ²⁸The older son was angry and would not go in to the feast. So his father went out and begged him to come in. ²⁹The son said to his father, 'I have served you like a slave for many years! I have always obeyed your commands, but you never even killed a young goat for me to have a feast with my friends. ³⁰But your other son has wasted all your money on prostitutes.ᵈ Then he comes home, and you kill the fat calf for him!' ³¹The father said to him, 'Son, you are always with me. All that I have is yours. ³²We had to celebrate and be happy because your brother was dead, but now he is alive. He was lost, but now he is found'."

True Wealth

16 Jesus also said to his followers, "Once there was a rich man. He had a manager to take care of his business. Later, the rich man learned that his manager was cheating him. ²So he called the manager in and said to him, 'I have heard bad things about you. Give me a report of what you have done with my money. You can't be my manager any longer!' ³Later, the manager thought to himself, 'What will I do? My master is taking my job away from me! I am not strong enough to dig ditches. I am too proud to beg. [4]I know! I'll do something so that when I lose my job, people will welcome me into their homes'.

[5]"So the manager called in everyone who owed the master any money. He said to the first man, 'How much do you owe my master?' [6]The man answered, 'I owe him 3000 litres of olive oil'. The manager said to him, 'Here is your bill; sit down quickly and make the bill less. Write 1500 litres'. [7]Then the manager said to another man, 'How much do you owe my master?' The man answered, 'I owe him 36,000 litres of wheat'. Then the manager said to him, 'Here is your bill; you can make it less. Write 28,000 litres'. [8]Later, the master praised the dishonest manager for being clever. Yes, worldly people are smarter with their own kind than spiritual people are.

[9]"I tell you, make friends for yourselves using worldly riches. Then, when those things are gone, you will be welcomed in that home that continues for ever. [10]Whoever can be trusted with small things can also be trusted with large things. Whoever is dishonest in little things will be dishonest in large things too. [11]If you cannot be trusted with worldly riches, then you will not be trusted with the true riches. [12]And if you cannot be trusted with the things that belong to someone else, then you will not be given things of your own.

[13]"No servant can serve two masters. He will hate one master and love the other. Or he will follow one master and refuse to follow the other. You cannot serve both God and money."

God's Law Cannot Be Changed

[14]The Pharisees[d] were listening to all these things. They made fun of Jesus because they all loved money. [15]Jesus said to them, "You make yourselves look good in front of people. But God knows what is really in your hearts. The things that are important to people are worth nothing to God.

[16]"God wanted the people to live by the law of Moses and the writings of the prophets.[d] But ever since John[n] came, the Good News[d] about the kingdom of God is being told. Now everyone is trying hard to get into the kingdom. [17]Even the smallest part of a letter in the law cannot be changed. It would be easier for heaven and earth to pass away.

Divorce and Remarriage

[18]"If a man divorces his wife and marries another woman, he is guilty of adultery.[d] And the man who marries a divorced woman is also guilty of adultery."

The Rich Man and Lazarus

[19]Jesus said, "There was a rich man who always dressed in the finest clothes. He lived in luxury every day. [20]There was also a very poor man named Lazarus, whose body was covered with sores. Lazarus was often placed at the rich man's gate. [21]He wanted to eat only the small pieces of food that fell from the rich man's table. And the dogs would come and lick his sores! [22]Later, Lazarus died. The angels took Lazarus and placed him in the arms of Abraham.[d] The rich man died, too, and was buried. [23]But he was sent to where the dead are and had much pain. The rich man saw Abraham far away with Lazarus in his

John   John the Baptist, who preached to people about Christ's coming (Matthew 3, Luke 3).

arms. ²⁴He called, 'Father Abraham, have mercy on me! Send Lazarus to me so that he can dip his finger in water and cool my tongue. I am suffering in this fire!' ²⁵But Abraham said, 'My child, remember when you lived? You had all the good things in life, but all the bad things happened to Lazarus. Now Lazarus is comforted here, and you are suffering. ²⁶Also, there is a big pit between you and us. No one can cross over to help you. And no one can leave there and come here'. ²⁷The rich man said, 'Then please send Lazarus to my father's house on earth! ²⁸I have five brothers. Lazarus could warn my brothers so that they will not come to this place of pain'. ²⁹But Abraham said, 'They have the law of Moses and the writings of the prophets^d to read; let them learn from them!' ³⁰The rich man said, 'No, father Abraham! If someone came to them from the dead, they would believe and change their hearts and lives'. ³¹But Abraham said to him, 'No! If your brothers won't listen to Moses and the prophets, then they won't listen to someone who comes back from death'."

Sin and Forgiveness

17 Jesus said to his followers, "Things will surely happen that cause people to sin. But how terrible for the one who causes them to happen. ²It would be better for him to be thrown into the sea with a large stone around his neck than to cause one of these weak people to sin. ³So be careful!

"If your brother sins, tell him he is wrong. But if he is sorry and stops sinning, forgive him. ⁴If your brother sins against you seven times in one day, but he says that he is sorry each time, then forgive him."

How Big Is Your Faith?

⁵The apostles^d said to the Lord, "Give us more faith!"

⁶The Lord said, "If your faith is as big as a mustard seed,ⁿ then you can say to this mulberry tree, 'Dig yourself up and plant yourself in the sea!' And the tree will obey you.

Be Good Servants

⁷"Suppose one of you has a servant who has been ploughing the ground or caring for the sheep. When the servant comes in from working in the field, would you say, 'Come in and sit down to eat'? ⁸No, you would say to your servant, 'Prepare something for me to eat. Then get yourself ready and serve me. When I finish eating and drinking, then you can eat'. ⁹The servant does not get any special thanks for doing what his master told him to do. ¹⁰It is the same with you. When you do everything you are told to do, you should say, 'We don't deserve any special thanks. We have only done the work we should do'."

Be Thankful

¹¹Jesus was on his way to Jerusalem. Travelling from Galilee to Samaria, ¹²he came into a small town. Ten men met him there. These men did not come close to Jesus, because they all had a harmful skin disease. ¹³But they called to him, "Jesus! Master! Please help us!"

¹⁴When Jesus saw the men, he said, "Go and show yourselves to the priests."ⁿ

mustard seed This seed is very small, but the plant grows taller than a man.
show . . . priests The law of Moses said a priest must say when a Jew with a harmful skin disease became well.

MATTHEW 7:28
*The people were amazed
at his teaching.*

LUKE 15:4
*The man will keep on searching
for the lost sheep until he finds it.*

six days for work. So come to be healed on one of those days. Don't come for healing on the Sabbath day."

[15]The Lord answered, "You people are hypocrites![d] All of you untie your work animals and lead them to drink water every day – even on the Sabbath day! [16]This woman that I healed is our Jewish sister. But Satan has held her for 18 years. Surely it is not wrong for her to be freed from her sickness on a Sabbath day!" [17]When Jesus said this, all the men who were criticising him were ashamed. And all the people were happy with the wonderful things Jesus was doing.

Stories of Mustard Seed and Yeast

[18]Then Jesus said, "What is God's kingdom like? What can I compare it with? [19]God's kingdom is like the seed of the mustard plant.[n] A man plants this seed in his garden. The seed grows and becomes a tree. The wild birds build nests on its branches."

[20]Jesus said again, "What can I compare God's kingdom with? [21]It is like yeast that a woman mixes into a big bowl of flour. The yeast makes all the dough rise."

The Narrow Door

[22]Jesus was teaching in every town and village. He continued to travel towards Jerusalem. [23]Someone said to Jesus, "Lord, how many people will be saved? Only a few?"

Jesus said, [24]"Try hard to enter through the narrow door that opens the way to heaven! Many people will try to enter there, but they will not be able. [25]A man gets up and closes the door of his house. You can stand outside and knock on the door. You can say, 'Sir, open the door for us!' But he

will answer, 'I don't know you! Where did you come from?' [26]Then you will say, 'We ate and drank with you. You taught in the streets of our town'. [27]But he will say to you, 'I don't know you! Where did you come from? Go away from me! All of you do evil!' [28]You will see Abraham, Isaac, Jacob, and all the prophets[d] in God's kingdom. But you will be thrown outside. Then you will cry and grind your teeth with pain. [29]People will come from the east, west, north, and south. They will sit down at the table in the kingdom of God. [30]Those who have the lowest place in life now will have the highest place in the future. And those who have the highest place now will have the lowest place in the future."

Jesus Will Die in Jerusalem

[31]At that time some Pharisees[d] came to Jesus and said, "Go away from here! Herod wants to kill you!"

[32]Jesus said to them, "Go and tell that fox Herod, 'Today and tomorrow I am forcing demons[d] out of people and finishing my work of healing. Then, on the third day, I will reach my goal'. [33]Yet I must be on my way today and tomorrow and the next day. Surely it cannot be right for a prophet[d] to be killed anywhere except in Jerusalem.

[34]"Jerusalem, Jerusalem! You kill the prophets. You kill with stones those men that God has sent you. Many times I wanted to help your people. I wanted to gather them together as a hen gathers her chicks under her wings. But you did not let me. [35]Now your home will be left completely empty. I tell you, you will not see me again until that time when you will say, 'God bless the One who comes in the name of the Lord'."[n]

---

mustard plant   The seed is very small, but the plant grows taller than a man.
'God . . . Lord'.   Quotation from Psalm 118:26.

Is It Right to Heal on the Sabbath?

14 On a Sabbath*d* day, Jesus went to the home of a leading Pharisee*d* to eat with him. The people there were all watching Jesus very closely. [2] A man with dropsy*n* was brought before Jesus. [3] Jesus said to the Pharisees and teachers of the law, "Is it right or wrong to heal on the Sabbath day?" [4] But they would not answer his question. So Jesus took the man, healed him, and sent him away. [5] Jesus said to the Pharisees and teachers of the law, "If your son or ox falls into a well on the Sabbath day, will you not pull him out quickly?" [6] And they could not answer him.

Don't Make Yourself Important

[7] Then Jesus noticed that some of the guests were choosing the best places to sit. So Jesus told this story: [8] "When someone invites you to a wedding feast, don't take the most important seat. The host may have invited someone more important than you. [9] And if you are sitting in the most important seat, the host will come to you and say, 'Give this man your seat'. Then you will begin to move down to the last place. And you will be very embarrassed. [10] So when you are invited, go and sit in a seat that is not important. Then the host will come to you and say, 'Friend, move up here to a more important place!' Then all the other guests will respect you. [11] Everyone who makes himself great will be made humble. But the person who makes himself humble will be made great."

You Will Be Rewarded

[12] Then Jesus said to the man who had invited him, "When you give a lunch or a dinner, don't invite only your friends, brothers, relatives, and rich neighbours. At another time they will invite you to eat with them. Then you will have your reward. [13] Instead, when you give a feast, invite the poor, the crippled, the lame and the blind. [14] Then you will be blessed, because they cannot pay you back. They have nothing. But you will be rewarded when the good people rise from death."

A Story About a Big Banquet

[15] One of the men sitting at the table with Jesus heard these things. The man said to Jesus, "The people who will eat a meal in God's kingdom are blessed."

[16] Jesus said to him, "A man gave a big banquet and invited many people. [17] When it was time to eat, the man sent his servant to tell the guests, 'Come! Everything is ready!'

[18] "But all the guests said they could not come. Each man made an excuse. The first one said, 'I have just bought a field, and I must go and look at it. Please excuse me'. [19] Another man said, 'I have just bought five pairs of oxen; I must go and try them. Please excuse me'. [20] A third man said, 'I just got married; I can't come'. [21] So the servant returned. He told his master what had happened. Then the master became angry and said, 'Go at once into the streets and alleys of the town. Bring in the poor, the crippled, the blind, and the lame'. [22] Later the servant said to him, 'Master, I did what you told me to do, but we still have places for more people'. [23] The master said to the servant, 'Go out to the roads and country lanes. Tell the people there to come. I want my house to be full! [24] None of those men that I invited first will ever eat with me!'"

dropsy A sickness that causes the body to swell larger and larger.

While the ten men were going, they were healed. [15] When one of them saw that he was healed, he went back to Jesus. He praised God in a loud voice. [16] Then he bowed down at Jesus' feet and thanked him. (This man was a Samaritan.[d]) [17] Jesus asked, "Ten men were healed; where are the other nine? [18] Is this Samaritan the only one who came back to thank God?" [19] Then Jesus said to him, "Stand up and go on your way. You were healed because you believed."

God's Kingdom Is Within You

[20] Some of the Pharisees[d] asked Jesus, "When will the kingdom of God come?"

Jesus answered, "God's kingdom is coming, but not in a way that you will be able to see with your eyes. [21] People will not say, 'Look, God's kingdom is here!' or, 'There it is!' No, God's kingdom is within you."

[22] Then Jesus said to his followers, "The time will come when you will want very much to see one of the days of the Son of Man.[d] But you will not be able to see it. [23] People will say to you, 'Look, there he is!' or, 'Look, here he is!' Stay where you are; don't go away and search.

When Jesus Comes Again

[24] "The Son of Man[d] will come again. On the day he comes he will shine like lightning, which flashes across the sky and lights it up from one side to the other. [25] But first, the Son of Man must suffer many things and be rejected by the people of this time. [26] When the Son of Man comes again, it will be as it was when Noah lived. [27] In the time of Noah, people were eating, drinking, and getting married even on the day when Noah entered the boat. Then the flood came and killed all the people. [28] It will be the same as during the time of Lot. Those people were eating, drinking, buying, selling, planting, and building. [29] They were doing these things even on the day Lot left Sodom.[n] Then fire and sulphur rained down from the sky and killed them all. [30] This is exactly how it will be when the Son of Man comes again.

[31] "On that day, if a man is on his roof, he will not have time to go inside and get his things. If a man is in the field, he cannot go back home. [32] Remember what happened to Lot's wife?[n] [33] Whoever tries to keep his life will give up true life. But whoever gives up his life will have true life. [34] At the time when I come again, there may be two people sleeping in one bed. One will be taken and the other will be left. [35] There may be two women grinding grain together. One will be taken and the other will be left." [36] [n]

[37] The followers asked Jesus, "Where will this be, Lord?"

Jesus answered, "People can always find a dead body by looking for the vultures."

God Will Answer His People

18 Then Jesus used this story to teach his followers that they should always pray and never lose hope. [2] "Once there was a judge in a town. He did not care about God. He also did not care what people thought about him. [3] In that same town there was a widow who kept coming to this judge. She said, 'There is a man who

---

Sodom City that God destroyed because the people were so evil.
Lot's wife A story about what happened to Lot's wife is found in Genesis 19:15–17,26.
Verse 36 A few Greek copies add verse 36: "Two men will be in the same field. One man will be taken, but the other man will be left behind."

is not being fair to me. Give me my rights!' [4]But the judge did not want to help the widow. After a long time, he thought to himself, 'I don't care about God. And I don't care about what people think. [5]But this widow is bothering me. I will see that she gets her rights, or she will bother me until I am worn out!'"

[6]The Lord said, "Listen to what the bad judge said. [7]God's people cry to him night and day. God will always give them what is right, and he will not be slow to answer them. [8]I tell you, God will help his people quickly! But when the Son of Man[d] comes again, will he find those on earth who believe in him?"

Being Right with God

[9]There were some people who thought that they were very good and looked down on everyone else. Jesus used this story to teach them: [10]"One day there was a Pharisee[d] and a tax collector. Both went to the Temple[d] to pray. [11]The Pharisee stood alone, away from the tax collector. When the Pharisee prayed, he said, 'God, I thank you that I am not as bad as other people. I am not like men who steal, cheat, or take part in adultery.[d] I thank you that I am better than this tax collector. [12]I give up eating[n] twice a week, and I give one-tenth of everything I earn!'

[13]"The tax collector stood at a distance. When he prayed, he would not even look up to heaven. He beat on his chest because he was so sad. He said, 'God, have mercy on me. I am a sinner!' [14]I tell you, when this man went home, he was right with God. But the Pharisee was not right with

God. Everyone who makes himself great will be made humble. But everyone who makes himself humble will be made great."

Who Will Enter God's Kingdom?

[15]Some people brought their small children to Jesus so that he could touch them. When the followers saw this, they told the people not to do it. [16]But Jesus called the little children to him and said to his followers, "Let the little children come to me. Don't stop them, because the kingdom of God belongs to people who are like these little children. [17]I tell you the truth. You must accept God's kingdom like a little child, or you will never enter it!"

A Rich Man's Question

[18]A Jewish leader asked Jesus, "Good Teacher, what must I do to get the life that continues for ever?"

[19]Jesus said to him, "Why do you call me good? Only God is good. [20]You know the commands: 'You must not be guilty of adultery.[d] You must not murder anyone. You must not steal. You must not tell lies about your neighbour in court. Honour your father and mother'."[n]

[21]But the leader said, "I have obeyed all these commands since I was a boy!"

[22]When Jesus heard this, he said to him, "But there is still one more thing you need to do. Sell everything you have and give the money to the poor. You will have a reward in heaven. Then come and follow me!" [23]But when the man heard this, he became very sad because he was very rich.

---

give up eating This is called "fasting". The people would give up eating for a special time of prayer and worship to God. It was also done to show sadness.
'You ... mother'. Quotation from Exodus 20:12–16; Deuteronomy 5:16–20.

²⁴When Jesus saw that the man was sad, he said, "It will be very hard for rich people to enter the kingdom of God! ²⁵It would be easier for a camel to go through the eye of a needle than

Luke 18:25 "It would be easier for a camel to go through the eye of a needle ..."

for a rich person to enter the kingdom of God!"

Who Can Be Saved?

²⁶When the people heard this, they asked, "Then who can be saved?"

²⁷Jesus answered, "God can do things that are not possible for men to do!"

²⁸Peter said, "Look, we left everything we had and followed you!"

²⁹Jesus said, "I tell you the truth. Everyone who has left his house, wife, brothers, parents, or children for God's kingdom ³⁰will get much more than he left. He will receive many times more in this life. And after he dies, he will live with God for ever."

Jesus Will Rise from Death

³¹Then Jesus talked to the 12 apostles^d alone. He said to them, "Listen! We are going to Jerusalem. Everything that God told the prophets^d to write about the Son of Man^d will happen! ³²He will be turned over to the non-Jewish people. They will laugh at him, insult him, and spit on him. ³³They will beat him with whips and then kill him. But on the third day after his death, he will rise to life again." ³⁴The apostles tried to understand this, but they could not; the meaning was hidden from them.

Jesus Heals a Blind Man

³⁵Jesus was coming near the city of Jericho. There was a blind man sitting beside the road, begging for money. ³⁶When he heard the people coming down the road, he asked, "What is happening?"

³⁷They told him, "Jesus, the one from Nazareth, is coming here."

³⁸The blind man cried out, "Jesus, Son of David!^d Please help me!"

³⁹The people who were in front, leading the group, told the blind man to be quiet. But the blind man shouted more and more, "Son of David, please help me!"

⁴⁰Jesus stopped and said, "Bring the blind man to me!" When he came near, Jesus asked him, ⁴¹"What do you want me to do for you?"

He said, "Lord, I want to see again."

⁴²Jesus said to him, "Then see! You are healed because you believed."

⁴³At once the man was able to see, and he followed Jesus, thanking God. All the people who saw this praised God.

Zacchaeus

19 Jesus was going through the city of Jericho. ²In Jericho there was a man named Zacchaeus. He was a wealthy, very important tax collector. [3] He wanted to see who Jesus was, but he was too short to see above the crowd. [4] He ran ahead to a place where he knew Jesus would come. He climbed a sycamore tree so he could see Jesus. [5] When Jesus came to that place, he looked up and saw Zacchaeus in the tree. He said to him, "Zacchaeus, hurry and come down! I must stay at your house today."

[6] Zacchaeus came down quickly. He was pleased to have Jesus in his house. [7] All the people saw this and began to complain, "Look at the kind of man Jesus stays with. Zacchaeus is a sinner!"

[8] But Zacchaeus said to the Lord, "I will give half of my money to the poor. If I have cheated anyone, I will pay that person back four times more!"

[9] Jesus said, "Salvation has come to this house today. This man truly belongs to the family of Abraham. [10] The Son of Man[d] came to find lost people and save them."

A Story About Three Servants

[11] Jesus travelled closer to Jerusalem. Some of the people thought that God's kingdom would appear soon. [12] Jesus knew that the people thought this, so he told them this story: "A very important man was preparing to go to a country far away to be made a king. Then he planned to return home and rule his people. [13] So the man called ten of his servants together. He gave a bag of money[n] to each servant. He said, 'Do business with this money till I get back'. [14] But the people in the kingdom hated the man. So they sent a group to follow him and say, 'We don't want this man to be our king!'

[15] "But the man became king. When he came home, he said, 'Call those servants who have my money. I want to know how much they earned with it'.

[16] "The first servant came and said, 'Sir, I earned ten bags of money with the one bag you gave me!' [17] The king said to the servant, 'Fine! You are a good servant. I see that I can trust you with small things. So now I will let you rule over ten of my cities'.

[18] "The second servant said, 'Sir, with your one bag of money I earned five bags!' [19] The king said to this servant, 'You can rule over five cities'.

[20] "Then another servant came in. The servant said to the king, 'Sir, here is your bag of money. I wrapped it in a piece of cloth and hid it. [21] I was afraid of you because you are a hard man. You even take money that you didn't earn and gather food that you didn't plant'. [22] Then the king said to the servant, 'You evil servant! I will use your own words to condemn you. You said that I am a hard man. You said that I even take money that I didn't earn and gather food that I didn't plant. [23] If that is true, then you should have put my money in the bank. Then, when I came back, my money would have earned some interest'.

[24] "Then the king said to the men who were watching, 'Take the bag of money away from this servant and give it to the servant who earned ten bags of money'. [25] They said to the king, 'But sir, that servant already has ten bags of money!' [26] The king said, 'The one who uses what he has will get more. But the one who does not use what he has will have everything taken away from him. [27] Now where are my enemies who didn't want me

---

bag of money One bag of money was a Greek "mina". One mina was enough money to pay a person for working three months.

to be king? Bring them here and kill them before me'."

Jesus Enters Jerusalem as a King

28 After Jesus said this, he went on towards Jerusalem. 29 Jesus came near Bethphage and Bethany, towns near the hill called the Mount of Olives.*d* Then he sent out two of his followers. 30 He said, "Go into the town you can see there. When you enter it, you will find a colt tied there. No one has ever ridden this colt. Untie it, and bring it here to me. 31 If anyone asks you why you are taking it, say, 'The Master needs it'."

32 The two followers went into town. They found the colt just as Jesus told them. 33 The followers untied it, but the owners of the colt came out. They asked the followers, "Why are you untying our colt?"

34 The followers answered, "The Master needs it." 35 So they brought it to Jesus. They threw their coats on the colt's back and put Jesus on it. 36 As Jesus rode toward Jerusalem, the followers spread their coats on the road before him.

37 Jesus was coming close to Jerusalem. He was already near the bottom of the Mount of Olives. The whole crowd of followers was very happy. They began shouting praise to God for all the powerful works they had seen. They said,

38 "God bless the king who comes in
        the name of the Lord!
    There is peace in heaven and
        glory to God!"   *Psalm 118:26*

39 Some of the Pharisees*d* said to Jesus, "Teacher, tell your followers not to say these things!"

40 But Jesus answered, "I tell you, if my followers don't say these things, then the stones will cry out."

Jesus Cries for Jerusalem

41 Jesus came near Jerusalem. He saw the city and began to cry for it.

Luke 19:41 He saw the city and began to cry for it.

42 Jesus said to Jerusalem, "I wish you knew today what would bring you peace! But you can't know it, because it is hidden from you. 43 A time is coming when your enemies will build a wall around you and will hold you in on all sides. 44 They will destroy you and all your people. Not one stone of your buildings will be left on another. All this will happen because you did not know the time when God came to save you."

Jesus Goes to the Temple

45 Jesus went into the Temple.*d* He began to throw out the people who were selling things there. 46 He said, "It is written in the Scriptures,*d* 'My Temple will be a house where people will pray'.*n* But you

'My Temple . . . pray'. Quotation from Isaiah 56:7.

have changed it into a 'hideout for robbers'!"[n]

[47] Jesus taught in the Temple every day. The leading priests, the teachers of the law, and some of the leaders of the people wanted to kill Jesus. [48] But all the people were listening closely to him and were interested in all the things he said. So the leading priests, the teachers of the law, and the leaders did not know how they could kill him.

Jewish Leaders Question Jesus

20 One day Jesus was in the Temple,[d] teaching the people and telling them the Good News.[d] The leading priests, teachers of the law, and older Jewish leaders came up to talk with him. [2] They said, "Tell us! What authority do you have to do these things? Who gave you this authority?"

[3] Jesus answered, "I will ask you a question too. Tell me: [4] when John baptised people, did that come from God or from man?"

[5] The priests, the teachers of the law, and the Jewish leaders all talked about this. They said to each other, "If we answer, 'John's baptism was from God', then Jesus will say, 'Then why did you not believe John?' [6] But if we say, 'John's baptism was from man', then all the people will kill us with stones because they believe that John was a prophet."[d] [7] So they answered, "We don't know the answer."

[8] So Jesus said to them, "Then I will not tell you by what authority I do these things!"

God Sends His Son

[9] Then Jesus told the people this story: "A man planted a vineyard. The man leased the land to some farmers. Then he went away for a long time.

[10] Later, it was time for the grapes to be picked. So the man sent a servant to those farmers to get his share of the grapes. But they beat the servant and sent him away with nothing. [11] Then he sent another servant. They beat this servant too. They showed no respect for him and sent him away with nothing. [12] So the man sent a third servant. The farmers hurt this servant badly and threw him out. [13] The owner of the vineyard said, 'What will I do now? I will send my son whom I love very much. Maybe they will respect him!' [14] When they saw the son, they said to each other, 'This is the owner's son. This vineyard will be his. If we kill him, then it will be ours!' [15] So the farmers threw the son out of the vineyard and killed him.

"What will the owner of this vineyard do? [16] He will come and kill those farmers! Then he will give the vineyard to other farmers."

The people heard this story. They said, "No! Let this never happen!"

[17] But Jesus looked at them and said, "Then what does this verse mean:

'The stone that the builders did
    not want
became the cornerstone'?[d]

                Psalm 118:22

[18] Everyone who falls on that stone will be broken. If that stone falls on you, it will crush you!"

[19] The teachers of the law and the priests heard this story that Jesus told. They knew the story was about them. So they wanted to arrest Jesus at once. But they were afraid of what the people would do.

The Leaders Try to Trap Jesus

[20] So they waited for the right time to get Jesus. They sent some spies

---

'hideout for robbers' Quotation from Jeremiah 7:11.

who acted as if they were good men. They wanted to trap Jesus in what he said so they could hand him over to the authority and power of the governor. ²¹So the spies asked Jesus, "Teacher, we know that what you say and teach is true. You teach the same to all people. You always teach the truth about God's way. ²²Tell us, is it right that we pay taxes to Caesar^d or not?"

²³But Jesus knew that these men were trying to trick him. He said, ²⁴"Show me a coin. Whose name is on the coin? And whose picture is on it?"

They said, "Caesar's."

²⁵Jesus said to them, "Then give to Caesar the things that are Caesar's. And give to God the things that are God's."

²⁶The men were amazed at his answer. They could say nothing. They were not able to trap Jesus in anything he said before the people.

Sadducees Try to Trick Jesus

²⁷Some Sadducees^d came to Jesus. (Sadducees believe that people will not rise from death.) They asked, ²⁸"Teacher, Moses wrote that a man's brother might die. He leaves a wife but no children. Then that man must marry the widow and have children for his dead brother. ²⁹Once there were seven brothers. The first brother married, but died. He had no children. ³⁰Then the second brother married the widow, and he died. ³¹And the third brother married the widow, and he died. The same thing happened with all the other brothers. They all died and had no children. ³²The woman was the last to die. ³³But all seven brothers married her. So when

people rise from death, whose wife will the woman be?"

³⁴Jesus said to the Sadducees, "On earth, people marry each other. ³⁵But those who will be worthy to be raised from death and live again will not marry. ³⁶In that life they are like angels and cannot die. They are children of God, because they have been raised from death. ³⁷Moses clearly showed that the dead are raised to life. When Moses wrote about the burning bush,ⁿ he said that the Lord is 'the God of Abraham, the God of Isaac, and the God of Jacob'.ⁿ ³⁸God is the God of living people, not dead people. All people are alive to God."

³⁹Some of the teachers of the law said, "Teacher, your answer was good." ⁴⁰No one was brave enough to ask him another question.

Is the Christ the Son of David?

⁴¹Then Jesus said, "Why do people say that the Christ^d is the Son of David?^d ⁴²In the book of Psalms, David himself says:

'The Lord said to my Lord:
    Sit by me at my right side,
⁴³until I put your enemies under
        your control'.ⁿ   *Psalm 110:1*
⁴⁴David calls the Christ 'Lord'. But the Christ is also the son of David. How can both these things be true?"

Jesus Accuses the Leaders

⁴⁵While all the people were listening, Jesus said to his followers, ⁴⁶"Be careful of the teachers of the law. They like to walk around wearing clothes that look important. And they love people to show respect to them in the marketplaces. They love to have the most important seats in the syna-

---

burning bush   Read Exodus 3:1–12 in the Old Testament.
'the God of . . . Jacob'.   These words are taken from Exodus 3:6.
until . . . control   Literally, "until I make your enemies a footstool for your feet".

gogues[d] and at the feasts. [47] But they cheat widows and steal their houses. Then they try to make themselves look good by saying long prayers. God will punish these men very much."

True Giving

21 Jesus saw some rich people putting their gifts into the Temple[d] money box.[n] [2] Then Jesus saw a poor widow. She put two small copper coins into the box. [3] He said, "I tell you the truth. This poor widow gave only two small coins. But she really gave more than all those rich people. [4] The rich have plenty; they gave only what they did not need. This woman is very poor, but she gave all she had. And she needed that money to live on."

The Temple Will Be Destroyed

[5] Some of the followers were talking about the Temple[d] and how it was decorated with beautiful stones and gifts offered to God.

[6] But Jesus said, "The time will come when all that you see here will be destroyed. Every stone will be thrown down to the ground. Not one stone will be left on another!"

[7] Some followers asked Jesus, "Teacher, when will these things happen? What will show us that it is time for them to take place?"

[8] Jesus said, "Be careful! Don't be fooled. Many people will come using my name. They will say, 'I am the Christ'[d] and, 'The right time has come!' But don't follow them. [9] When you hear about wars and riots, don't be afraid. These things must happen first. Then the end will come later."

[10] Then he said to them, "Nations will fight against other nations. Kingdoms will fight against other kingdoms. [11] There will be great earthquakes, sicknesses, and other terrible things in many places. In some places there will be no food for the people to eat. Fearful events and great signs will come from heaven.

[12] "But before all these things happen, people will arrest you and treat you cruelly. They will judge you in their synagogues[d] and put you in jail. You will be forced to stand before kings and governors. They will do all these things to you because you follow me. [13] But this will give you an opportunity to tell about me. [14] Don't worry about what you will say. [15] I will give you the wisdom to say things so that none of your enemies will be able to show that you are wrong. [16] Even your parents, brothers, relatives and friends will turn against you. They will kill some of you. [17] All people will hate you because you follow me. [18] But none of these things can really harm you. [19] You will save yourselves by continuing strong in your faith through all these things.

Jerusalem Will Be Destroyed

[20] "When you see armies all around Jerusalem, then you will know that it will soon be destroyed. [21] At that time, the people in Judea should run away to the mountains. The people in Jerusalem must get out. If you are near the city, don't go in! [22] These are the days of punishment to make all that is written in the Scriptures come true.[d] [23] At that time, it will be hard for women who are pregnant or have nursing babies! Great trouble will come upon this land, and God will be angry with these people. [24] Some will be killed by the sword and taken as prisoners to all nations. Jerusalem will be crushed by non-Jewish people until their time is over.

money box   A special box in the Jewish place for worship where people put their gifts to God.

Don't Fear

25 "Amazing things will happen to the sun, moon, and stars. On earth, nations will be afraid because of the roar and fury of the sea. They will not know what to do. 26 People will be so afraid they will faint. They will wonder what is happening to the whole world. Everything in the sky will be changed. 27 Then people will see the Son of Man*d* coming in a cloud with power and great glory. 28 When these things begin to happen, don't fear. Look up and hold your heads high because the time when God will free you is near!"

My Words Will Live For Ever

29 Then Jesus told this story: "Look at the fig tree and all the other trees. 30 When their leaves appear, you know that summer is near. 31 In the same way, when you see all these things happening, then you will know that God's kingdom is coming very soon.

32 "I tell you the truth. All these things will happen while the people of this time are still living! 33 The whole world, earth and sky, will be destroyed; but the words I have said will never be destroyed!

Be Ready All the Time

34 "Be careful! Don't spend your time feasting and drinking. Or don't be too busy with worldly things. If you do that, you will not be able to think straight. And then that day might come when you are not ready. 35 It will close like a trap on all people on earth. 36 So be ready all the time. Pray that you will be strong enough to escape all these things that will happen. And pray that you will be able to stand before the Son of Man."*d*

37 During the day, Jesus taught the people in the Temple.*d* At night he went out of the city and stayed on the Mount of Olives.*d* 38 Every morning all the people got up early to go to the Temple to listen to him.

Plans to Kill Jesus

22 It was almost time for the Jewish Feast*d* of Unleavened Bread, called the Passover*d* Feast. 2 The leading priests and teachers of the law were trying to find a way to kill Jesus. But they were afraid of the people.

3 One of Jesus' 12 apostles*d* was named Judas Iscariot. Satan entered Judas, and he went to 4 the leading priests and some of the soldiers who guarded the Temple.*d* He talked to them about a way to give Jesus to them. 5 They were pleased and promised to give Judas money. 6 Judas agreed. Then he waited for the best time to turn Jesus over to them without the crowd knowing it.

Preparation of the Passover Meal

7 The Day of Unleavened*d* Bread came. This was the day the Passover*d* lambs had to be sacrificed. 8 Jesus said to Peter and John, "Go and prepare the Passover meal for us to eat."

9 They asked, "Where do you want us to prepare it?"

Jesus said to them, 10 "Listen! After you go into the city, you will see a man carrying a jar of water. Follow him into the house that he enters. 11 Tell the person who owns that house, 'The Teacher asks that you please show us the room where he and his followers may eat the Passover meal'. 12 Then he will show you a large room upstairs. This room is ready for you. Prepare the Passover meal there."

13 So Peter and John left. Everything happened as Jesus had said. So they prepared the Passover meal.

The Lord's Supper

[14]When the time came, Jesus and the apostles[d] were sitting at the table. [15]He said to them, "I wanted very much to eat this Passover[d] meal with you before I die. [16]I will never eat another Passover meal until it is given its true meaning in the kingdom of God."

[17]Then Jesus took a cup. He gave thanks to God for it and said, "Take this cup and give it to everyone here. [18]I will not drink again from the fruit of the vine[n] until God's kingdom comes."

[19]Then Jesus took some bread. He thanked God for it, broke it, and gave it to the apostles. Then Jesus said, "This bread is my body that I am giving for you. Do this to remember me."

Luke 22:19 "Do this to remember me."

[20]In the same way, after supper, Jesus took the cup and said, "This cup shows the new agreement that God makes with his people. This new agreement begins with my blood which is poured out for you."[n]

Who Will Turn Against Jesus?

[21]Jesus said, "One of you will turn against me. His hand is by my hand on the table. [22]The Son of Man[d] will do what God has planned. But how terrible it will be for that man who gives the Son of Man to be killed." [23]Then the apostles[d] asked each other, "Which one of us would do that to Jesus?"

Be Like a Servant

[24]Then the apostles[d] began to argue about which one of them was the most important. [25]But Jesus said to them, "The kings of the world rule over their people. Men who have authority over others are called 'very important'. [26]But you must not be like that. The greatest among you should be like the youngest, and the leader should be like the servant. [27]Who is more important: the one sitting at the table or the one serving him? You think the one at the table is more important. But I am like a servant among you!

[28]"You men have stayed with me through many struggles. [29]My Father has given me the power to rule. I also give you authority to rule with me. [30]You will eat and drink at my table in my kingdom. You will sit on thrones and judge the 12 tribes[d] of Israel.

Don't Lose Your Faith!

[31]"Satan has asked to test all of you as a farmer tests his wheat. Simon, Simon, [32]I have prayed that you will not lose your faith! Help your brothers to be stronger when you come back to me."

fruit of the vine Product of the grapevine; this may also be translated "wine".
Verse 20 A few Greek copies do not have the last part of verse 19 and all of verse 20.

[33] But Peter said to Jesus, "Lord, I am ready to go to prison with you. I will even die with you!"

[34] But Jesus said, "Peter, before the cock crows tonight, you will say you don't know me. You will say this three times!"

Be Ready for Trouble

[35] Then Jesus said to the apostles,[d] "When I sent you out without money, a bag, or sandals, did you need anything?"

They said, "No."

[36] He said to them, "But now if you have money or a bag, carry that with you. If you don't have a sword, sell your coat and buy one. [37] The Scripture[d] says, 'He was treated like a criminal'.[n] This scripture must have its full meaning. It was written about me, and it is happening now."

[38] The followers said, "Look, Lord, here are two swords!"

He said to them, "That's enough."

Jesus Prays Alone

[39-40] Jesus left the city and went to the Mount of Olives.[d] His followers went with him. (Jesus went there often.) He said to his followers, "Pray for strength against temptation."

[41] Then Jesus went about a stone's throw away from them. He kneeled down and prayed, [42] "Father, if it is what you want, then let me not have this cup[n] of suffering. But do what you want, not what I want." [43] Then an angel from heaven appeared to him to help him. [44] Jesus was full of pain; he prayed even more. Sweat dripped from his face as if he were bleeding. [45] When he had finished praying, he went to his followers. They were asleep. (Their sadness had made them very tired.) [46] Jesus said to them, "Why are you sleeping? Get up and pray for strength against temptation."

Jesus Is Arrested

[47] While Jesus was speaking, a crowd came up. One of the 12 apostles[d] was leading them. He was Judas. He came close to Jesus so that he could kiss him.

[48] But Jesus said to him, "Judas, are you using the kiss to give the Son of Man[d] to his enemies?"

[49] The followers of Jesus were standing there too. They saw what was happening. They said to Jesus, "Lord, should we use our swords?" [50] And one of them did use his sword. He cut off the right ear of the servant of the high priest.

[51] Jesus said, "Stop!" Then he touched the servant's ear and healed him.

[52] Those who came to arrest Jesus were the leading priests, the soldiers who guarded the Temple,[d] and the older Jewish leaders. Jesus said to them, "Why did you come out here with swords and sticks? Do you think I am a criminal? [53] I was with you every day in the Temple. Why didn't you try to arrest me there? But this is your time – the time when darkness rules."

Peter Says He Doesn't Know Jesus

[54] They arrested Jesus and took him away. They brought him into the house of the high priest. Peter followed them, but he did not go near Jesus. [55] The soldiers started a fire in the middle of the courtyard and sat together. Peter sat with them. [56] A servant girl saw Peter sitting there near

'**He . . . criminal'.** Quotation from Isaiah 53:12.

cup Jesus is talking about the bad things that will happen to him. Accepting these things will be hard, like drinking a cup of something that tastes very bitter.

the light. She looked closely at Peter's face and said, "This man was also with him!"

[57] But Peter said this was not true. He said, "Girl, I don't know him."

[58] A short time later, another person saw Peter and said, "You are also one of them."

But Peter said, "Man, I am not!"

[59] About an hour later, another man insisted, "It is true! This man was with him. He is from Galilee!"

[60] But Peter said, "Man, I don't know what you are talking about!"

Immediately, while Peter was still speaking, a cock crowed. [61] Then the Lord turned and looked straight at Peter. And Peter remembered what the Lord had said: "Before the cock crows tonight, you will say three times that you don't know me." [62] Then Peter went outside and cried with much pain in his heart.

The People Laugh at Jesus

[63-64] Some men were guarding Jesus. They made fun of him like this: they covered his eyes so that he could not see them. Then they hit him and said, "Prove that you are a prophet,[d] and tell us who hit you!" [65] The men said many cruel things to Jesus.

Jesus Before the Leaders

[66] When day came, the older leaders of the people, the leading priests, and the teachers of the law came together. They led Jesus away to their highest court. [67] They said, "If you are the Christ,[d] then tell us that you are!"

Jesus said to them, "If I tell you I am the Christ, you will not believe me. [68] And if I ask you, you will not answer. [69] But beginning now, the Son of Man[d] will sit at the right hand of the powerful God."

[70] They all said, "Then are you the Son of God?"

Jesus said to them, "Yes, you are right when you say that I am."

[71] They said, "Why do we need witnesses now? We ourselves heard him say this!"

Governor Pilate Questions Jesus

23 Then the whole group stood up and led Jesus to Pilate.[n] [2] They began to accuse Jesus. They told Pilate, "We caught this man telling things that were confusing our people. He says that we should not pay taxes to Caesar.[d] He calls himself the Christ,[d] a king."

[3] Pilate asked Jesus, "Are you the king of the Jews?"

Jesus answered, "Yes, that is right."

[4] Pilate said to the leading priests and the people, "I find nothing wrong with this man."

[5] They said again and again, "But Jesus is making trouble with the people! He teaches all around Judea. He began in Galilee, and now he is here!"

Pilate Sends Jesus to Herod

[6] Pilate heard this and asked if Jesus was from Galilee. [7] If so, Jesus was under Herod's authority. Herod was in Jerusalem at that time; so Pilate sent Jesus to him. [8] When Herod saw Jesus, he was very glad. He had heard about Jesus and had wanted to meet him for a long time. Herod was hoping to see Jesus work a miracle.[d] [9] Herod asked Jesus many questions, but Jesus said nothing. [10] The leading priests and teachers of the law were standing there. They were shouting things against Jesus. [11] Then Herod and his soldiers made fun of Jesus. They dressed him in a kingly robe and then sent him back to Pilate. [12] In the past, Pilate and

---

Pilate   Pontius Pilate was the Roman governor of Judea from A.D. 26 to A.D. 36.

Herod had always been enemies. But on that day they became friends.

Jesus Must Die

[13] Pilate called all the people together with the leading priests and the Jewish leaders. [14] He said to them, "You brought this man to me. You said that he was making trouble among the people. But I have questioned him before you all, and I have not found him guilty of the things you say. [15] Also, Herod found nothing wrong with him; he sent him back to us. Look, he has done nothing for which he should die. [16] So, after I punish him, I will let him go free." [17] *n*

[18] But all the people shouted, "Kill him! Let Barabbas go free!" [19] (Barabbas was a man who was in prison because he started a riot in the city. He was guilty of murder.)

[20] Pilate wanted to let Jesus go free. So he told this to the crowd. [21] But they shouted again, "Kill him! Kill him on a cross!"

[22] A third time Pilate said to them, "Why? What wrong has he done? I can find no reason to kill him. So I will have him punished and set him free."

[23] But they continued to shout. They demanded that Jesus be killed on the cross. Their yelling became so loud that [24] Pilate decided to give them what they wanted. [25] They wanted Barabbas to go free, the man who was in jail for starting a riot and for murder. Pilate let Barabbas go free and gave Jesus to them to be killed.

Jesus Is Killed on a Cross

[26] The soldiers led Jesus away. At that time, there was a man coming into the city from the fields. His name was Simon, and he was from the city of Cyrene. The soldiers forced Simon to carry Jesus' cross and walk behind him.

[27] A large crowd of people were following Jesus. Some of the women were sad and crying. [28] But Jesus turned and said to them, "Women of Jerusalem, don't cry for me. Cry for yourselves and for your children too! [29] The time is coming when people will say, 'Happy are the women who cannot have children! Happy are the women who have no babies to nurse'. [30] Then people will say to the mountains, 'Fall on us!' And they will say to the hills, 'Cover us!' [31] If they act like this now when life is good, what will happen when bad times come?"*n*

[32] There were also two criminals led out with Jesus to be killed. [33] Jesus and the two criminals were taken to a place called the Skull. There the soldiers nailed Jesus to his cross. They also nailed the criminals to their crosses, one beside Jesus on the right and the other beside Jesus on the left. [34] Jesus said, "Father, forgive them. They don't know what they are doing."*n*

The soldiers threw lots*d* to decide who would get his clothes. [35] The people stood there watching. The Jewish leaders made fun of Jesus. They said, "If he is God's Chosen One, the Christ,*d* then let him save himself. He saved other people, didn't he?"

[36] Even the soldiers made fun of him. They came to Jesus and offered him some vinegar. [37] They said, "If you are the king of the Jews, save yourself!" [38] (At the top of the cross these

Verse 17　A few Greek copies add verse 17: "Every year at the Passover Feast, Pilate had to release one prisoner to the people."
If . . . come?　Literally, "If they do these things in the green tree, what will happen in the dry?"
Verse 34　Some early Greek copies do not have this part of the verse.

words were written: "THIS IS THE KING OF THE JEWS.")

[39] One of the criminals began to shout insults at Jesus: "Aren't you the Christ? Then save yourself! And save us too!"

[40] But the other criminal stopped him. He said, "You should fear God! You are getting the same punishment as he is. [41] We are punished justly; we should die. But this man has done nothing wrong!" [42] Then this criminal said to Jesus, "Jesus, remember me when you come into your kingdom!"

[43] Then Jesus said to him, "Listen! What I say is true: today you will be with me in paradise!"[n]

Jesus Dies

[44] It was about noon, and the whole land became dark until three o'clock in the afternoon. [45] There was no sun! The curtain in the Temple[n] was torn into two pieces. [46] Jesus cried out in a loud voice, "Father, I give you my life." After Jesus said this, he died.

[47] The army officer there saw what happened. He praised God, saying, "I know this was a good man!"

[48] Many people had gathered there to watch this thing. When they saw what happened, they returned home. They beat their chests because they were so sad. [49] Those who were close friends of Jesus were there. Some were women who had followed Jesus from Galilee. They all stood far away from the cross and watched.

Joseph of Arimathea

[50-51] A man from the Jewish town of Arimathea was there, too. His name was Joseph. He was a good, religious man. He wanted the kingdom of God to come. Joseph was a member of the Jewish council, but he had not agreed when the other leaders decided to kill Jesus. [52] Joseph went to Pilate to ask for the body of Jesus. [53] So Joseph took the body down from the cross and wrapped it in cloth. Then he put Jesus' body in a tomb that was cut in a wall of rock. This tomb had never been used before. [54] This was late on Preparation[d] Day. When the sun went down, the Sabbath[d] day would begin.

[55] The women who had come from Galilee with Jesus followed Joseph. They saw the tomb and saw inside where the body of Jesus was laid. [56] Then the women left to prepare perfumes and spices.

On the Sabbath day they rested, as the law of Moses commanded.

Jesus Rises from Death

24 Very early on the first day of the week, the women came to the tomb where Jesus' body was laid. They brought the spices they had prepared. [2] They found that the stone had been rolled away from the entrance of the tomb. [3] They went in, but they did not find the body of the Lord Jesus. [4] While they were wondering about this, two men in shining clothes suddenly stood beside them. [5] The women were very afraid; they bowed their heads to the ground. The men said to the women, "Why are you looking for a living person here? This is a place for the dead. [6] Jesus is not here. He has risen from death! Do you remember what he said in Galilee? [7] He said that the Son of Man[d] must be given to evil men, be killed on a cross, and

---

paradise A place where good people go when they die.
curtain in the Temple A curtain divided the Most Holy Place from the other part of the Temple. This was the special building in Jerusalem where God commanded the Jews to worship him.

rise from death on the third day."
⁸Then the women remembered what
Jesus had said.

⁹The women left the tomb and told
all these things to the 11 apostles*d* and
the other followers. ¹⁰These women
were Mary Magdalene, Joanna, Mary
the mother of James, and some other
women. The women told the apostles
everything that had happened at the
tomb. ¹¹But they did not believe the
women. It sounded like nonsense.
¹²But Peter got up and ran to the
tomb. He looked in, but he saw only
the cloth that Jesus' body had been
wrapped in. Peter went away to be
alone, wondering about what had
happened.

On the Road to Emmaus

¹³That same day two of Jesus' followers were going to a town named
Emmaus. It is about 11 kilometres
from Jerusalem. ¹⁴They were talking
about everything that had happened.
¹⁵While they were discussing these
things, Jesus himself came near and
began walking with them. ¹⁶(They
were not allowed to recognise Jesus.)
¹⁷Then he said, "What are these
things you are talking about while you
walk?"

The two followers stopped. Their
faces were very sad. ¹⁸The one named

Cleopas answered, "You must be
the only one in Jerusalem who does
not know what just happened
there."

¹⁹Jesus said to them, "What are you
talking about?"

The followers said, "It is about Jesus
of Nazareth. He was a prophet*d* from
God to all the people. He said and did
many powerful things. ²⁰Our leaders
and the leading priests gave him up
to be judged and killed. They nailed
him to a cross. ²¹But we were hoping
that he would free the Jews. It is now
the third day since this happened.
²²And today some women among us
told us some amazing things. Early
this morning they went to the tomb,
²³but they did not find his body there.
They came and told us that they had
seen a vision of angels. The angels
said that Jesus was alive! ²⁴So some
of our group went to the tomb, too.
They found it just as the women said,
but they did not see Jesus."

²⁵Then Jesus said to them, "You are
foolish and slow to realise what is true.
You should believe everything the
prophets said. ²⁶They said that the
Christ*d* must suffer these things
before he enters his glory." ²⁷Then
Jesus began to explain everything that
had been written about himself in the
Scriptures.*d* He started with Moses,

Luke 24:15 Jesus himself came near and began walking with them.

and then he talked about what all the prophets had said about him.

²⁸They came near the town of Emmaus, and Jesus acted as if he did not plan to stop there. ²⁹But they begged him, "Stay with us. It is late; it is almost night." So he went in to stay with them.

³⁰Jesus sat down with them and took some bread. He gave thanks for the food and divided it. Then he gave it to them. ³¹And then, they were allowed to recognise Jesus. But when they saw who he was, he disappeared. ³²They said to each other, "When Jesus talked to us on the road, it felt like a fire burning in us. It was exciting when he explained the true meaning of the Scriptures."

³³So the two followers got up at once and went back to Jerusalem. There they found the 11 apostles*d* and others gathered. ³⁴They were saying, "The Lord really has risen from death! He showed himself to Simon."

³⁵Then the two followers told what had happened on the road. They talked about how they recognised Jesus when he divided the bread.

Jesus Appears to His Followers

³⁶While the two followers were telling this, Jesus himself stood among those gathered. He said to them, "Peace be with you."

³⁷They were fearful and terrified. They thought they were seeing a ghost. ³⁸But Jesus said, "Why are you troubled? Why do you doubt what you see? ³⁹Look at my hands and my feet. It is I myself! Touch me. You can see

that I have a living body; a ghost does not have a body like this."

⁴⁰After Jesus said this, he showed them his hands and feet. ⁴¹The followers were amazed and very happy. They still could not believe it. Jesus said to them, "Do you have any food here?" ⁴²They gave him a piece of cooked fish. ⁴³While the followers watched, Jesus took the fish and ate it.

⁴⁴He said to them, "Remember when I was with you before? I said that everything written about me must happen – everything in the law of Moses, the books of the prophets,*d* and the Psalms."

⁴⁵Then Jesus opened their minds so that they could understand the Scriptures.*d* ⁴⁶He said to them, "It is written that the Christ*d* would be killed and rise from death on the third day. ⁴⁷⁻⁴⁸You saw these things happen – you are witnesses. You must tell people to change their hearts and lives. If they do this, their sins will be forgiven. You must start at Jerusalem and preach these things in my name to all nations. ⁴⁹Listen! My Father has promised you something; I will send it to you. But you must stay in Jerusalem until you have received that power from heaven."

Jesus Goes Back to Heaven

⁵⁰Jesus led his followers out of Jerusalem almost to Bethany. He raised his hands and blessed them. ⁵¹While he was blessing them, he was separated from them and carried into heaven. ⁵²They worshipped him and then went back to the city very happy. ⁵³They stayed in the Temple*d* all the time, praising God.

JOHN

John Tells About Jesus, the Son of God

Christ Comes to the World

1 Before the world began, there was the Word.[n] The Word was with God, and the Word was God. [2] He was with God in the beginning. [3] All things were made through him. Nothing was made without him. [4] In him there was life. That life was light for the people of the world. [5] The Light shines in the darkness. And the darkness has not overpowered the Light.

[6] There was a man named John[n] who was sent by God. [7] He came to tell people about the Light. Through him all people could hear about the Light and believe. [8] John was not the Light, but he came to tell people about the Light. [9] The true Light was coming into the world. The true Light gives light to all.

[10] The Word was in the world. The world was made through him, but the world did not know him. [11] He came to the world that was his own. But his own people did not accept him. [12] But some people did accept him. They believed in him. To them he gave the right to become children of God. [13] They did not become his children in the human way. They were not born because of the desire or wish of some man. They were born of God.

[14] The Word became a man and lived among us. We saw his glory – the glory that belongs to the only Son of the Father. The Word was full of grace and truth. [15] John told about him. He said, "This is the One I was talking about. I said, 'The One who comes after me is greater than I am. He was living before me'."

[16] The Word was full of grace and truth. From him we all received more and more blessings. [17] The law was given through Moses, but grace and truth came through Jesus Christ. [18] No man has ever seen God, but God the only Son is very close to the Father.[n] And the Son has shown us what God is like.

John Tells People About Jesus

[19] The Jews in Jerusalem sent some priests and Levites to John.[n] The Jews sent them to ask, "Who are you?"

[20] John spoke freely and did not refuse to answer. He said clearly, "I am not the Christ."[d]

[21] So they asked him, "Then who are you? Are you Elijah?"[n]

He answered, "No, I am not Elijah."

Then they asked, "Are you the Prophet?"[n]

Word The Greek word is "logos", meaning any kind of communication. It could be translated "message". Here, it means Christ. Christ was the way God told people about himself.
John John the Baptist, who preached to people about Christ's coming (Matthew 3, Luke 3).
but . . . Father This could be translated, "but the only God is very close to the Father." Also, some Greek copies say, "but the only Son is very close to the Father."
John John the Baptist, who preached to people about Christ's coming (Matthew 3, Luke 3).
Elijah A man who spoke for God. He lived hundreds of years before Christ.
Prophet They probably meant the prophet that God told Moses he would send (Deuteronomy 18:15–19).

He answered, "No, I am not the Prophet."

[22]Then they said, "Who are you? Give us an answer to tell those who sent us. What do you say about yourself?"

[23]John told them in the words of the prophet Isaiah:

"I am the voice of a man
   calling out in the desert:
'Make the road straight for the
   Lord'."   *Isaiah 40:3*

[24]In the group of Jews who were sent, there were some Pharisees.[d] [25]They said to John: "You say you are not the Christ. You say you are not Elijah or the Prophet. Then why do you baptise people?"

[26]John answered, "I baptise people with water. But there is one here with you that you don't know. [27]He is the One who comes after me. I am not good enough to untie the strings of his sandals."

[28]This all happened at Bethany on the other side of the Jordan River. This is where John was baptising people.

[29]The next day John saw Jesus coming toward him. John said, "Look, the Lamb of God.[n] He takes away the sins of the world! [30]This is the One I was talking about. I said, 'A man will come after me, but he is greater than I am, because he was living before me'. [31]Even I did not know who he was. But I came baptising with water so that the people of Israel could know who he is."

[32-33]Then John said, "I did not know who the Christ was. But God sent me to baptise with water. And God told me, 'You will see the Spirit[d] come down and rest on a man. That man is the One who will baptise with the Holy Spirit'." John said, "I saw the Spirit come down from heaven. The Spirit looked like a dove and rested on him. [34]I have seen this happen. So I tell people: 'He is the Son of God'."

The First Followers of Jesus

[35]The next day John[n] was there again with two of his followers. [36]He saw Jesus walking by and said, "Look, the Lamb of God!"[n]

[37]The two followers heard John say this. So they followed Jesus. [38]Jesus turned and saw them following him. He asked, "What do you want?"

They said, "Rabbi, where are you staying?" ("Rabbi" means "Teacher".)

[39]Jesus answered, "Come with me and you will see." So the two men went with Jesus. They saw the place where Jesus was staying and stayed there with him that day. It was then about four o'clock.

[40]These two men followed Jesus after they heard about him from John. One of the men was Andrew. He was Simon Peter's brother. [41]The first thing Andrew did was to find his brother, Simon. He said to Simon, "We have found the Messiah." ("Messiah" means "Christ".[d])

[42]Then Andrew took Simon to Jesus. Jesus looked at Simon and said, "You are Simon son of John. You will be called Cephas." ("Cephas" means "Peter".[n])

[43]The next day Jesus decided to go to Galilee. He found Philip and said to him, "Follow me." [44]Philip was from the town of Bethsaida, where Andrew and Peter lived. [45]Philip found Nathanael and told him, "Remember that Moses wrote in the law about a

---

Lamb of God Name for Jesus. Jesus is like the lambs that were offered as a sacrifice to God.
John John the Baptist, who preached to people about Christ's coming (Matthew 3, Luke 3).
Peter The Greek name "Peter", like the Aramaic name "Cephas", means "rock".

man who was coming, and the prophets[d] also wrote about him. We have found him. He is Jesus, the son of Joseph. He is from Nazareth."

[46]But Nathanael said to Philip, "Nazareth! Can anything good come from Nazareth?"

Philip answered, "Come and see."

John 1:46 "Come and see."

[47]Jesus saw Nathanael coming toward him. He said, "Here is truly a person of Israel. There is nothing false in him."

[48]Nathanael asked, "How do you know me?"

Jesus answered, "I saw you when you were under the fig tree. That was before Philip told you about me."

[49]Then Nathanael said to Jesus, "Teacher, you are the Son of God. You are the King of Israel."

[50]Jesus said to Nathanael, "You believe in me because I told you I saw you under the fig tree. But you will see greater things than that!" [51]And Jesus said to them, "I tell you the truth. You will all see heaven open. You will see 'angels of God going up and coming down'[n] on the Son of Man."[d]

The Wedding at Cana

2 Two days later there was a wedding in the town of Cana in Galilee. Jesus' mother was there. [2]Jesus and his followers were also invited to the wedding. [3]When all the wine was gone, Jesus' mother said to him, "They have no more wine."

[4]Jesus answered, "Dear woman, why come to me? My time has not yet come."

[5]His mother said to the servants, "Do whatever he tells you to do."

[6]In that place there were six stone water jars. The Jews used jars like these in their washing ceremony.[n] Each jar held about 100 litres.

[7]Jesus said to the servants, "Fill the jars with water." So they filled the jars to the top.

[8]Then he said to them, "Now take some out and give it to the master of the feast."

So the servants took the water to the master. [9]When he tasted it, the water had become wine. He did not know where the wine came from. But the servants who brought the water knew. The master of the wedding called the bridegroom [10]and said to him, "People always serve the best wine first. Later, after the guests have been drinking a lot, they serve the cheaper wine. But you have saved the best wine till now."

'angels ... down' These words are from Genesis 28:12.
washing ceremony The Jews washed themselves in special ways before eating, before worshipping in the Temple, and at other special times.

[11] So in Cana of Galilee, Jesus did his first miracle.[d] There he showed his glory, and his followers believed in him.

Jesus in the Temple

[12] Then Jesus went to the town of Capernaum with his mother, brothers and his followers. They all stayed in Capernaum for a few days. [13] But it was almost time for the Jewish Passover[d] Feast. So Jesus went to Jerusalem. [14] In the Temple[d] he found men selling cattle, sheep, and doves. He saw others sitting at tables, exchanging money. [15] Jesus made a whip out of cords. Then he forced all these men, with the sheep and cattle, to leave the Temple. He turned over the tables and scattered the money of the men who were exchanging it. [16] Then he said to those who were selling pigeons, "Take these things out of here! Don't make my Father's house a place for buying and selling!"

[17] When this happened the followers remembered what was written in the Scriptures:[d] "My strong love for your Temple completely controls me."[n]

[18] The Jews said to Jesus, "Show us a miracle[d] for a sign. Prove that you have the right to do these things."

[19] Jesus answered, "Destroy this temple, and I will build it again in three days."

[20] The Jews answered, "Men worked 46 years to build this Temple! Do you really believe you can build it again in three days?"

[21] (But the temple Jesus meant was his own body. [22] After Jesus was raised from death, his followers remembered that Jesus had said this. Then they believed the Scripture[d] and the words Jesus said.)

[23] Jesus was in Jerusalem for the Passover Feast. Many people believed in him because they saw the miracles he did. [24] But Jesus did not trust himself to them because he knew them all. [25] He did not need anyone to tell him about people. Jesus knew what was in a person's mind.

Jesus and Nicodemus

3 There was a man named Nicodemus who was one of the Pharisees.[d] He was an important Jewish leader. [2] One night Nicodemus came to Jesus. He said, "Teacher, we know that you are a teacher sent from God. No one can do the miracles[d] you do, unless God is with him."

[3] Jesus answered, "I tell you the truth. Unless a person is born again, he cannot be in God's kingdom."

[4] Nicodemus said, "But if a man is already old, how can he be born again? He cannot enter his mother's body again. So how can he be born a second time?"

[5] But Jesus answered, "I tell you the truth. Unless a person is born from water and the Spirit,[d] he cannot enter God's kingdom. [6] A person's body is born from his human parents. But a person's spiritual life is born from the Spirit. [7] Don't be surprised when I tell you, 'You must all be born again'. [8] The wind blows where it wants to go. You hear the wind blow. But you don't know where the wind comes from or where it is going. It is the same with every person who is born from the Spirit."

[9] Nicodemus asked, "How can all this be possible?"

[10] Jesus said, "You are an important teacher in Israel. But you still don't understand these things? [11] I tell you the truth. We talk about what we know. We tell about what we have

"**My . . . me.**"   Quotation from Psalm 69:9.

seen. But you don't accept what we tell you. [12] I have told you about things here on earth, but you do not believe me. So certainly you will not believe me if I tell you about the things of heaven! [13] The only one who has ever gone up to heaven is the One who came down from heaven – the Son of Man.[d]

[14] "Moses lifted up the snake in the desert.[n] It is the same with the Son of Man. The Son of Man must be lifted up too. [15] Then everyone who believes in him can have eternal life.

[16] "For God loved the world so much that he gave his only Son. God gave his Son so that whoever believes in him may not be lost, but have eternal life. [17] God did not send his Son into the world to judge the world guilty, but to save the world through him. [18] He who believes in God's Son is not judged guilty. He who does not believe has already been judged guilty, because he has not believed in God's only Son. [19] People are judged by this fact: I am the Light from God that has come into the world. But men did not want light. They wanted darkness because they were doing evil things. [20] Everyone who does evil hates the light. He will not come to the light because it will show all the evil things he has done. [21] But he who follows the true way comes to the light. Then the light will show that the things he has done were done through God."

Jesus and John the Baptist

[22] After this, Jesus and his followers went into the area of Judea. There Jesus stayed with his followers and baptised people. [23] John was also bap-

tising in Aenon, near Salim, because there was plenty of water there. People were going there to be baptised. [24] (This was before John was put into prison.)

[25] Some of John's followers had an argument with a Jew about religious washing.[n] [26] So they came to John and said, "Teacher, remember the man who was with you on the other side of the Jordan River, the one you spoke about? He is baptising, and everyone is going to him."

[27] John answered, "A man can get only what God gives him. [28] You yourselves heard me say, 'I am not the Christ.[d] I am only the one God sent to prepare the way for him'. [29] The bride belongs only to the bridegroom. The friend who helps the bridegroom waits and listens for him. He is glad when he hears the bridegroom's voice. That is the same pleasure I have. And my time of joy is now here. [30] He must become greater. And I must become less important.

The One Who Comes from Heaven

[31] "The One who comes from above is greater than all. He who is from the earth belongs to the earth and talks about things on the earth. But the One who comes from heaven is greater than all. [32] He tells what he has seen and heard, but no one accepts what he says. [33] The person who accepts what he says has proved that God is true. [34] God sent him, and he tells the things that God says. God gives him the Spirit[d] fully. [35] The Father loves the Son and has given him power over everything. [36] He who believes in the

---

Moses . . . desert The people of Israel were dying from snake bites. God told Moses to put a brass snake on a pole. The people who looked at the snake were healed (Numbers 21:4–9).
religious washing The Jews washed themselves in special ways before eating, before worshipping in the Temple, and at other special times.

Son has eternal life. But he who does not obey the Son will never have that life. God's anger stays with him."

Jesus and a Samaritan Woman

4 The Pharisees[d] heard that Jesus was getting and baptising more followers than John. [2] (But really Jesus himself did not baptise people. His followers did the baptising.) Jesus knew that the Pharisees had heard about him. [3] So he left Judea and went back to Galilee. [4] On the way he had to go through the country of Samaria.

[5] In Samaria Jesus came to the town called Sychar. This town is near the field that Jacob gave to his son Joseph. [6] Jacob's well was there. Jesus was tired from his long trip, so he sat down beside the well. It was about six o'clock in the evening. [7] A Samaritan[d] woman came to the well to get some water. Jesus said to her, "Please give me a drink." [8] (This happened while

John 4:7 "Please give me a drink."

Jesus' followers were in town buying some food.)

[9] The woman said, "I am surprised that you ask me for a drink. You are a Jew and I am a Samaritan." (Jews are not friends with Samaritans.[n])

[10] Jesus said, "You don't know what God gives. And you don't know who asked you for a drink. If you knew, you would have asked me, and I would have given you living water."

[11] The woman said, "Sir, where will you get that living water? The well is very deep, and you have nothing to get water with. [12] Are you greater than Jacob, our father? Jacob is the one who gave us this well. He drank from it himself. Also, his sons and flocks drank from this well."

[13] Jesus answered, "Every person who drinks this water will be thirsty again. [14] But whoever drinks the water I give will never be thirsty again. The water I give will become a spring of water flowing inside him. It will give him eternal life."

[15] The woman said to him, "Sir, give me this water. Then I will never be thirsty again. And I will not have to come back here to get more water."

[16] Jesus told her, "Go and get your husband and come back here."

[17] The woman answered, "But I have no husband."

Jesus said to her, "You are right to say you have no husband. [18] Really you have had five husbands. But the man you live with now is not your husband. You told the truth."

[19] The woman said, "Sir, I can see that you are a prophet.[d] [20] Our fathers worshipped on this mountain. But you Jews say that Jerusalem is the place where people must worship."

[21] Jesus said, "Believe me, woman.

Jews . . . Samaritans This can also be translated "Jews don't use things that Samaritans have used".

The time is coming when you will not have to be in Jerusalem or on this mountain to worship the Father. [22] You Samaritans worship what you don't understand. We Jews understand what we worship. Salvation comes from the Jews. [23] The time is coming when the true worshippers will worship the Father in spirit and truth. That time is now here. And these are the kinds of worshippers the Father wants. [24] God is spirit. Those who worship God must worship in spirit and truth."

[25] The woman said, "I know that the Messiah is coming." (Messiah is the One called Christ.[d]) "When the Messiah comes, he will explain everything to us."

[26] Then Jesus said, "He is talking to you now. I am he."

[27] Just then his followers came back from town. They were surprised because they saw Jesus talking with a woman. But none of them asked, "What do you want?" or "Why are you talking with her?"

[28] Then the woman left her water jar and went back to town. She said to the people, [29] "A man told me everything I have ever done. Come and see him. Perhaps he is the Christ!" [30] So the people left the town and went to see Jesus.

[31] While the woman was away, the followers were begging him, "Teacher, eat something!"

[32] But Jesus answered, "I have food to eat that you know nothing about."

[33] So the followers asked themselves, "Has somebody already brought Jesus some food?"

[34] Jesus said, "My food is to do what the One who sent me wants me to do. My food is to finish the work that he gave me to do. [35] You say, 'Four more months to wait before we gather the grain'. But I tell you, open your eyes. Look at the fields that are ready for harvesting now. [36] Even now, the one who harvests the crop is being paid. He is gathering crops for eternal life. So now the one who plants can be happy along with the one who harvests. [37] It is true when we say, 'One person plants, but another harvests the crop'. [38] I sent you to harvest a crop that you did not work for. Others did the work, and you get the profit from their work."[n]

[39] Many of the Samaritans in that town believed in Jesus. They believed because of what the woman said: "He told me everything I have ever done." [40] The Samaritans came to Jesus and begged him to stay with them. So he stayed there two days. [41] Many more believed because of the things he said.

[42] They said to the woman, "First we believed in Jesus because of what you told us. But now we believe because we heard him ourselves. We know that this man really is the Saviour of the world."

Jesus Heals an Officer's Son

[43] Two days later, Jesus left and went to Galilee. [44] (Jesus had said before that a prophet[d] is not respected in his own country.) [45] When Jesus arrived in Galilee, the people there welcomed him. They had seen all the things he did at the Passover[d] Feast in Jerusalem. They had been at the Passover Feast, too.

[46] Jesus went to visit Cana in Galilee again. This is where Jesus had changed the water into wine. One of the king's important officers lived in the city of Capernaum. This man's son was sick. [47] The man heard that Jesus

---

Look at . . . their work. As a farmer sends workers to harvest grain, Jesus sends his followers out to bring people to God.

had come from Judea and was now in Galilee. He went to Jesus and begged him to come to Capernaum and heal his son. His son was almost dead. [48] Jesus said to him, "You people must see signs and miracles[d] before you will believe in me."

[49] The officer said, "Sir, come before my child dies."

[50] Jesus answered, "Go. Your son will live."

The man believed what Jesus told him and went home. [51] On the way the man's servants came and met him. They told him, "Your son is well."

[52] The man asked, "What time did my son begin to get well?"

They answered, "It was about one o'clock yesterday when the fever left him."

[53] The father knew that one o'clock was the exact time that Jesus had said, "Your son will live." So the man and all the people of his house believed in Jesus.

[54] That was the second miracle that Jesus did after coming from Judea to Galilee.

Jesus Heals a Man at a Pool

5 Later Jesus went to Jerusalem for a special Jewish feast. [2] In Jerusalem there is a pool with five covered porches. In the Jewish language[n] it is called Bethesda.[n] This pool is near the Sheep Gate. [3] Many sick people were lying on the porches beside the pool. Some were blind, some were crippled, and some were paralysed.[n] [5] There was a man lying there who had been sick for 38 years. [6] Jesus saw the man and knew that he had been sick for a very long time. So Jesus asked him, "Do you want to be well?"

[7] The sick man answered, "Sir, there is no one to help me get into the pool when the water starts moving. I try to be the first one into the water. But when I try, someone else always goes in before I can."

[8] Then Jesus said, "Stand up. Pick up your mat and walk." [9] And immediately the man was well. He picked up his mat and began to walk.

The day all this happened was a Sabbath[d] day. [10] So the Jews said to the man who had been healed, "Today is the Sabbath. It is against our law for you to carry your mat on the Sabbath day."

[11] But he answered, "The man who made me well told me, 'Pick up your mat and walk'."

[12] Then they asked him, "Who is the man who told you to pick up your mat and walk?"

[13] But the man who had been healed did not know who it was. There were many people in that place, and Jesus had left.

[14] Later, Jesus found the man at the Temple.[d] Jesus said to him, "See, you are well now. But stop sinning or something worse may happen to you!"

[15] Then the man left and went back to the Jews. He told them that Jesus was the one who had made him well.

[16] Jesus was doing this on the Sabbath day. So the Jews began to do bad things to him. [17] But Jesus said to them, "My Father never stops working. And so I work, too."

Jewish language Aramaic, the language of the Jews in the first century.

Bethesda Also called Bethsaida or Bethzatha, a pool of water north of the Temple in Jerusalem.

Verse 3 Some Greek copies add "and they waited for the water to move". A few later copies add verse 4: "Sometimes an angel of the Lord came down to the pool and stirred up the water. After the angel did this, the first person to go into the pool was healed of any sickness he had."

[18] This made the Jews try harder to kill him. They said, "First Jesus was breaking the law about the Sabbath day. Then he said that God is his own Father! He is making himself equal with God!"

Jesus Has God's Authority

[19] But Jesus said, "I tell you the truth. The Son can do nothing alone. The Son does only what he sees his Father doing. The Son does whatever the Father does. [20] The Father loves the Son, and the Father shows the Son all the things he himself does. But the Father will show the Son greater things than this to do. Then you will all be amazed. [21] The Father raises the dead and gives them life. In the same way, the Son gives life to those he wants to. [22] Also, the Father judges no one. But the Father has given the Son power to do all the judging. [23] God did this so that all people will respect the Son the same way they respect the Father. He who does not respect the Son does not respect the Father. The Father is the One who sent the Son.

[24] "I tell you the truth. Whoever hears what I say and believes in the One who sent me has eternal life. He will not be judged guilty. He has already left death and has entered into life. [25] I tell you the truth. The time is coming and is already here when the dead will hear the voice of the Son of God. And those who hear will have life. [26] Life comes from the Father himself. So the Father has allowed the Son to give life. [27] And the Father has given the Son the power to judge because he is the Son of Man.[d] [28] Don't be surprised at this. A time is coming when all who are dead and in their graves will hear his voice. [29] Then they will come out of their graves. Those who did good will rise and have life for ever. But those who did evil will rise to be judged guilty.

Jesus Is God's Son

[30] "I can do nothing alone. I judge only the way I am told, so my judgement is right. I don't try to please myself. I try to please the One who sent me.

[31] "If I tell people about myself, then they will not accept what I say about myself. [32] But there is another who tells about me. And I know that the things he says about me are true.

[33] "You have sent men to John.[n] And he has told you about the truth. [34] But I don't need a man to tell about me. I tell you this so that you can be saved. [35] John was like a burning and shining lamp. And you were happy to enjoy his light for a while.

[36] "But I have a proof about myself that is greater than that of John. The things I do are my proof. These are the things my Father gave me to do. They show that the Father sent me. [37] And the Father who sent me has given proof about me himself. You have never heard his voice. You have never seen what he looks like. [38] His teaching does not live in you because you don't believe in the One that the Father sent. [39] You carefully study the Scriptures[d] because you think that they give you eternal life. Those are the same Scriptures that tell about me! [40] But you refuse to come to me to have that life.

[41] "I don't want praise from men. [42] But I know you – I know that you don't have God's love in you. [43] I have come from my Father – I speak for him. But you don't accept me. But when another person comes, speaking

John John the Baptist, who preached to people about Christ's coming (Matthew 3, Luke 3).

only for himself, you will accept him. [44]You like to have praise from each other. But you never try to get the praise that comes from the only God. So how can you believe? [45]Don't think that I will stand before the Father and say that you are wrong. Moses is the one who says that you are wrong. And he is the one that you hoped would save you. [46]If you really believed Moses, you would believe me because Moses wrote about me. [47]But you don't believe what Moses wrote. So how can you believe what I say?"

More than 5,000 People Fed

6 After this, Jesus went across Lake Galilee (or, Lake Tiberias). [2]Many people followed him because they saw the miracles[d] he did to heal the sick. [3]Jesus went up on a hill and there sat down with his followers. [4]It was almost the time for the Jewish Passover[d] Feast.

[5]Jesus looked up and saw a large crowd coming toward him. He said to Philip, "Where can we buy bread for all these people to eat?" [6](Jesus asked Philip this question to test him. Jesus already knew what he planned to do.)

[7]Philip answered, "We would all have to work a month to buy enough bread for each person here to have only a little piece."

[8]Another follower there was Andrew. He was Simon Peter's brother. Andrew said, [9]"Here is a boy with five loaves of barley bread and two little fish. But that is not enough for so many people."

[10]Jesus said, "Tell the people to sit down." This was a very grassy place. There were about 5,000 men who sat down there. [11]Then Jesus took the loaves of bread. He thanked God for the bread and gave it to the people who were sitting there. He did the same with the fish. He gave them as much as they wanted.

[12]They all had enough to eat. When they had finished, Jesus said to his followers, "Gather the pieces of fish and bread that were not eaten. Don't waste anything." [13]So they gathered up the pieces that were left. They filled 12 large baskets with the pieces that were left of the five barley loaves.

[14]The people saw this miracle that Jesus did. They said, "He must truly be the Prophet[n] who is coming into the world."

[15]Jesus knew that the people planned to come and take him by force and make him their king. So he left and went into the hills alone.

Jesus Walks on the Water

[16]That evening Jesus' followers went down to Lake Galilee. [17]It was dark now and Jesus had not yet come to them. The followers got into a boat and started across the lake to Capernaum. [18]By now a strong wind was blowing, and the waves on the lake were getting bigger. [19]They rowed the boat about four or five kilometres. Then they saw Jesus walking on the water, coming toward the boat. The followers were afraid. [20]But Jesus said to them, "Don't be afraid. It is I." [21]Then they were glad to take him into the boat. At once the boat came to land at the place where they wanted to go.

The People Seek Jesus

[22]The next day came. Some people had stayed on the other side of the lake. They knew that Jesus had not gone in the boat with his followers but that they had left without him. And

---

Prophet   They probably meant the prophet that God told Moses he would send (Deuteronomy 18:15–19).

they knew that only one boat had been there. [23]But then some boats came from Tiberias. They landed near the place where the people had eaten the bread after the Lord had given thanks. [24]The people saw that Jesus and his followers were not there now. So they got into boats and went to Capernaum. They wanted to find Jesus.

Jesus, the Bread of Life

[25]The people found Jesus on the other side of the lake. They asked him, "Teacher, when did you come here?"

[26]Jesus answered, "Are you looking for me because you saw me do miracles?[d] No! I tell you the truth. You are looking for me because you ate the bread and were satisfied. [27]Earthly food spoils and ruins. So don't work to get that kind of food. But work to get the food that stays good always and gives you eternal life. The Son of Man[d] will give you that food. God the Father has shown that he is with the Son of Man."

[28]The people asked Jesus, "What are the things God wants us to do?"

[29]Jesus answered, "The work God wants you to do is this: to believe in the One that God sent."

[30]So the people asked, "What miracle will you do? If we can see a miracle, then we will believe you. What will you do? [31]Our fathers ate the manna[d] in the desert. This is written in the Scriptures:[d] 'God gave them bread from heaven to eat'."[n]

[32]Jesus said, "I tell you the truth. Moses was not the one who gave you bread from heaven. But my Father gives you the true bread from heaven. [33]God's bread is the One who comes down from heaven and gives life to the world."

[34]The people said, "Sir, give us this bread always."

[35]Then Jesus said, "I am the bread that gives life. He who comes to me will never be hungry. He who believes in me will never be thirsty. [36]But as I told you before, you have seen me, and still you don't believe. [37]The Father gives me my people. Every one of them will come to me, and I will always accept them. [38]I came down from heaven to do what God wants me to do. I did not come to do what I want to do. [39]I must not lose even one of those that God has given me, but I must raise them up on the last day. This is what the One who sent me wants me to do. [40]Everyone who sees the Son and believes in him has eternal life. I will raise him up on the last day. This is what my Father wants."

'God gave . . . eat.'   Quotation from Psalm 78:24.

John 6:19 Then they saw Jesus walking on the water.

⁴¹The Jews began to complain about Jesus. They complained because he said, "I am the bread that comes down from heaven." ⁴²The Jews said, "This is Jesus. We know his father and mother. He is only Joseph's son. How can he say, 'I came down from heaven'?"

⁴³But Jesus answered, "Stop complaining to each other. ⁴⁴The Father is the One who sent me. No one can come to me unless the Father draws him to me. And I will raise him up on the last day. ⁴⁵It is written in the prophets,ᵈ 'God will teach all the people'.ⁿ Everyone who listens to the Father and learns from him comes to me. ⁴⁶No one has seen the Father except the One who is from God. Only he has seen the Father. ⁴⁷I tell you the truth. He who believes has eternal life. ⁴⁸I am the bread that gives life. ⁴⁹Your ancestors ate the manna in the desert. But still they died. ⁵⁰Here is the bread that comes down from heaven. If anyone eats this bread, he will never die. ⁵¹I am the living bread that came down from heaven. If anyone eats this bread, he will live for ever. This bread is my flesh. I will give my flesh so that the people in the world may have life."

⁵²Then the Jews began to argue among themselves. They said, "How can this man give us his flesh to eat?"

⁵³Jesus said, "I tell you the truth. You must eat the flesh of the Son of Man. And you must drink his blood. If you don't do this, then you won't have real life in you. ⁵⁴He who eats my flesh and drinks my blood has eternal life. I will raise him up on the last day. ⁵⁵My flesh is true food. My blood is true drink. ⁵⁶Whoever eats my flesh and drinks my blood lives in me, and I live in him. ⁵⁷The Father sent me. The Father lives, and I live because of

the Father. So he who eats me will live because of me. ⁵⁸I am not like the bread our ancestors ate. They ate that bread, but still they died. I am the bread that came down from heaven. He who eats this bread will live for ever." ⁵⁹Jesus said all these things while he was teaching in the synagogueᵈ in Capernaum.

The Words of Eternal Life

⁶⁰The followers of Jesus heard this. Many of them said, "This teaching is hard. Who can accept it?"

⁶¹Jesus knew that his followers were complaining about this. So he said, "Does this teaching bother you? ⁶²If so will it also bother you to see the Son of Manᵈ going back to the place where he came from? ⁶³It is not the flesh that gives a person life. It is the spirit that gives life. The words I told you are spirit, and so they give life. ⁶⁴But some of you don't believe." (Jesus knew who did not believe. He knew this from the beginning. And he knew who would turn against him.) ⁶⁵Jesus said, "That is the reason I said, 'If the Father does not let a person come to me, then he cannot come'."

⁶⁶After Jesus said this, many of his followers left him. They stopped following him.

⁶⁷Jesus asked the 12 followers, "Do you want to leave, too?"

⁶⁸Simon Peter answered Jesus, "Lord, where would we go? You have the words that give eternal life. ⁶⁹We believe in you. We know that you are the Holy One from God."

⁷⁰Then Jesus answered, "I chose all 12 of you. But one of you is a devil." ⁷¹Jesus was talking about Judas, the son of Simon Iscariot. Judas was one of the 12. But later he was going to turn against Jesus.

'God . . . people.' Quotation from Isaiah 54:13.

Jesus and His Brothers

7 After this, Jesus travelled around Galilee. He did not want to travel in Judea, because the Jews there wanted to kill him. [2] It was time for the Jewish Feast[d] of Shelters. [3] So Jesus' brothers said to him, "You should leave here and go to Judea. Then your followers there can see the miracles[d] you do. [4] Anyone who wants to be well known does not hide what he does. If you are doing these things, show yourself to the world." [5] (Even Jesus' brothers did not believe in him.)

[6] Jesus said to his brothers, "The right time for me has not yet come. But any time is right for you. [7] The world cannot hate you. But it hates me, because I tell about the evil things it does. [8] So you go to the feast. I will not go now. The right time for me has not yet come." [9] After saying this, Jesus stayed in Galilee.

[10] So Jesus' brothers left to go to the feast. When they had gone, Jesus went, too. But he did not let people see him. [11] At the feast the Jews were looking for him. They said, "Where is that man?"

[12] There was a large crowd of people there. Many of them were whispering to each other about Jesus. Some said, "He is a good man."

Others said, "No, he fools the people." [13] But no one was brave enough to talk about Jesus openly. They were afraid of the Jews.

Jesus Teaches at the Feast

[14] The feast was about half over. Then Jesus went to the Temple[d] and began to teach. [15] The Jews were amazed. They said, "This man has never studied in school. How did he learn so much?"

[16] Jesus answered, "The things I teach are not my own. My teaching comes from him who sent me. [17] If anyone chooses to do what God wants, then he will know that my teaching comes from God. He will know that this teaching is not my own. [18] He who teaches his own ideas is trying to get honour for himself. But he who tries to bring honour to the one who sent him – that person speaks the truth. There is nothing false in him. [19] Moses gave you the law,[n] but none of you obey that law. Why are you trying to kill me?"

[20] The people answered, "A demon[d] has come into you. We are not trying to kill you."

[21] Jesus said to them, "I did one miracle,[d] and you are all amazed. [22] Moses gave you the law about circumcision.[d] (But really Moses did not give you circumcision. Circumcision came from our ancestors.) And yet you circumcise a baby on a Sabbath[d] day. [23] This shows that a baby can be circumcised on a Sabbath day to obey the law of Moses. So why are you angry at me for healing a person's whole body on the Sabbath day? [24] Stop judging by the way things look! Be fair, and judge by what is really right."

Is Jesus the Christ?

[25] Then some of the people who lived in Jerusalem said, "This is the man they are trying to kill. [26] But he is teaching where everyone can see and hear him. And no one is trying to stop him. Perhaps the leaders have decided that he really is the Christ.[d] [27] But we know where this man is from. And when the real Christ comes, no one will know where he comes from."

---

law   Moses gave God's people the law that God gave him on Mount Sinai (Exodus 34:29–32).

²⁸Jesus was still teaching in the Temple.[d] He cried out, "Yes, you know me, and you know where I am from. But I have not come by my own authority. I was sent by the One who is true. You don't know him. ²⁹But I know him. I am from him, and he sent me."

³⁰When Jesus said this, the people tried to take him. But no one was able to touch him. It was not yet the right time. ³¹But many of the people believed in Jesus. They said, "When the Christ comes, will he do more miracles[d] than this man has done?"

Some Leaders Try to Arrest Jesus

³²The Pharisees[d] heard the crowd whispering these things about Jesus. So the leading priests and the Pharisees sent some Temple[d] guards to arrest him. ³³Then Jesus said, "I will be with you a little while longer. Then I will go back to the One who sent me. ³⁴You will look for me, but you will not find me. And you cannot come where I am."

³⁵The Jews said to each other, "Where will this man go so we cannot find him? Will he go to the Greek cities where our people live? Will he teach the Greek people there? ³⁶This man says, 'You will look for me but you will not find me'. He also says, 'You cannot come where I am'. What does this mean?"

Jesus Talks About the Spirit

³⁷The last day of the feast came. It was the most important day. On that day Jesus stood up and said in a loud voice, "If anyone is thirsty, let him come to me and drink. ³⁸If a person believes in me, rivers of living water will flow out from his heart. This is what the Scripture[d] says." ³⁹Jesus was talking about the Holy Spirit.[d] The Spirit had not yet been given because Jesus had not yet been raised to glory. But later, those who believed in Jesus would receive the Spirit.

The People Argue About Jesus

⁴⁰The people heard these things that Jesus said. Some of them said, "This man really is the Prophet."[n]

⁴¹Others said, "He is the Christ."[d]

Still others said, "The Christ will not come from Galilee. ⁴²The Scripture[d] says that the Christ will come from David's family. And the Scripture says that the Christ will come from Bethlehem, the town where David lived." ⁴³So the people did not agree with each other about Jesus. ⁴⁴Some of them wanted to arrest him, but no one was able to touch him.

The Leaders Won't Believe

⁴⁵The Temple[d] guards went back to the leading priests and the Pharisees.[d] The priests and the Pharisees asked, "Why didn't you bring Jesus?"

⁴⁶The Temple guards answered, "The things he says are greater than the words of any man!"

⁴⁷The Pharisees answered, "So Jesus has fooled you too! ⁴⁸Have any of the leaders or the Pharisees believed in him? No! ⁴⁹But those people, who know nothing about the law, are under God's curse!"

⁵⁰But Nicodemus was there in that group. He was the one who had gone to see Jesus before.[n] Nicodemus said, ⁵¹"Our law does not judge a man with-

---

Prophet They probably meant the prophet God told Moses he would send (Deuteronomy 18:15–19).
But Nicodemus . . . before The story about Nicodemus going and talking to Jesus is in John 3:1–21.

out hearing him. We cannot judge him until we know what he has done."

⁵²They answered, "Are you from Galilee too? Study the Scriptures.^d You will learn that no prophet^d comes from Galilee."

⁵³And everyone left and went home.ⁿ

The Woman Caught in Adultery

8 Jesus went to the Mount of Olives.^d ²But early in the morning he went back to the Temple.^d All the people came to Jesus, and he sat and taught them. ³The teachers of the law and the Pharisees^d brought a woman there. She had been caught in adultery.^d They forced the woman to stand before the people. ⁴They said to Jesus, "Teacher, this woman was caught having sexual relations with a man who is not her husband. ⁵The law of Moses commands that we kill with stones every woman who does this. What do you say we should do?" ⁶They were asking this to trick Jesus so that they could have some charge against him.

But Jesus knelt down and started writing on the ground with his finger. ⁷They continued to ask Jesus their question. So he stood up and said, "Is there anyone here who has never sinned? The person without sin can throw the first stone at this woman." ⁸Then Jesus knelt down again and wrote on the ground.

⁹Those who heard Jesus began to leave one by one. The older men left first, and then the others. Jesus was left there alone with the woman. She was standing before him. ¹⁰Jesus stood up again and asked her, "Woman, all of those people have gone. Has no one judged you guilty?"

¹¹She answered, "No one has judged me, sir."

Then Jesus said, "So I don't judge you either. You may go now, but don't sin again."

Jesus Is the Light of the World

¹²Later, Jesus talked to the people again. He said, "I am the light of the world. The person who follows me will

John 8:12 "I am the light of the world."

never live in darkness. He will have the light that gives life."

¹³But the Pharisees^d said to Jesus, "When you talk about yourself, you are the only one to say these things are true. We cannot accept these things you say."

¹⁴Jesus answered, "Yes, I am saying these things about myself, but they are true. I know where I came from. And I know where I am going. You don't know where I came from or where I am going. ¹⁵You judge me the way you would judge any man. I don't judge anyone. ¹⁶But if I judge, my judging is true. When I judge, I am

Verse 53 Some early Greek manuscripts do not contain 7:53–8:11.

not alone. The Father who sent me is with me. [17]Your own law says that when two witnesses say the same thing, then you must accept what they say. [18]I am one of the witnesses who speaks about myself. And the Father who sent me is my other witness."

[19]They asked, "Where is your father?"

Jesus answered, "You don't know me or my Father. But if you knew me, then you would know my Father, too." [20]Jesus said these things while he was teaching in the Temple.[d] He was near the place where the money that the people give is kept. But no one arrested him. The right time for Jesus had not yet come.

The People Misunderstand Jesus

[21]Again, Jesus said to the people, "I will leave you. You will look for me, but you will die in your sins. You cannot come where I am going."

[22]So the Jews asked, "Will Jesus kill himself? Is that why he said, 'You cannot come where I am going'?"

[23]But Jesus said, "You people are from here below, but I am from above. You belong to this world, but I don't belong to this world. [24]So I told you that you would die in your sins. Yes, you will die in your sins if you don't believe that I am he."

[25]They asked, "Then who are you?"

Jesus answered, "I am what I have told you from the beginning. [26]I have many things to say about you and to judge you for. But I tell people only the things I have heard from the One who sent me. And he speaks the truth."

[27]The people did not understand that Jesus was talking to them about the Father. [28]So Jesus said to them, "You will lift up the Son of Man.[d] Then you will know that I am he. You will know that these things I do are not by

my own authority. You will know that I say only what the Father has taught me. [29]The One who sent me is with me. I always do what is pleasing to him. So he has not left me alone." [30]While Jesus was saying these things, many people believed in him.

Freedom from Sin

[31]So Jesus said to the Jews who believed in him, "If you continue to obey my teaching, you are truly my followers. [32]Then you will know the truth. And the truth will make you free."

[33]The Jews answered, "We are Abraham's children. And we have never been slaves. So why do you say that we will be free?"

[34]Jesus answered, "I tell you the truth. Everyone who lives in sin is a slave to sin. [35]A slave does not stay with a family for ever, but a son belongs to the family for ever. [36]So if the Son makes you free, then you will be truly free. [37]I know you are Abraham's children. But you want to kill me because you don't accept my teaching. [38]I am telling you what my Father has shown me. But you do what your father has told you."

[39]They answered, "Our father is Abraham."

Jesus said, "If you were really Abraham's children, you would do the things that Abraham did. [40]I am a man who has told you the truth which I heard from God. But you are trying to kill me. Abraham did nothing like that. [41]So you are doing the things that your own father did."

But the Jews said, "We are not like children who never knew who their father was. God is our Father. He is the only Father we have."

[42]Jesus said to them, "If God were really your Father, you would love me. I came from God and now I am here.

I did not come by my own authority. God sent me. [43] You don't understand what I say because you cannot accept my teaching. [44] Your father is the devil. You belong to him and want to do what he wants. He was a murderer from the beginning. He was against the truth, for there is no truth in him. He is a liar, and he is like the lies he tells. He is the father of lies. [45] But I speak the truth. That is why you don't believe me. [46] Can any of you prove that I am guilty of sin? If I am telling the truth, why don't you believe me? [47] He who belongs to God accepts what God says. But you don't accept what God says, because you don't belong to God."

Jesus and Abraham

[48] The Jews answered, "We say you are a Samaritan![d] We say a demon[d] has come into you. Are we not right?"

[49] Jesus answered, "I have no demon in me. I give honour to my Father, but you dishonour me. [50] I am not trying to get honour for myself. There is One who wants this honour for me, and he is the judge. [51] I tell you the truth. If anyone obeys my teaching, he will never die."

[52] The Jews said to Jesus, "Now we know that you have a demon in you! Even Abraham and the prophets[d] died. But you say, 'Whoever obeys my teaching will never die'. [53] Do you think that you are greater than our father Abraham? Abraham died. And the prophets died, too. Who do you think you are?"

[54] Jesus answered, "If I give honour to myself, that honour is worth nothing. The One who gives me honour is my Father. And you say that he is your God. [55] But you don't really know him. I know him. If I said I did not know him, then I would be a liar as you are liars. But I do know him, and I obey what he says. [56] Your father Abraham was very happy that he would see my day. He saw that day and was glad."

[57] The Jews said to him, "What? You have seen Abraham! You are not even 50 years old!"

[58] Jesus answered, "I tell you the truth. Before Abraham was born, I am!" [59] When Jesus said this, the people picked up stones to throw at him. But Jesus hid himself, and then he left the Temple.[d]

Jesus Heals a Man Born Blind

9 As Jesus was walking along, he saw a man who had been born blind. [2] His followers asked him, "Teacher, whose sin caused this man to be born blind – his own sin or his parents' sin?"

[3] Jesus answered, "It is not this man's sin or his parents' sin that caused him be blind. This man was born blind so that God's power could be shown in him. [4] While it is day time, we must continue doing the work of the One who sent me. The night is coming. And no one can work at night. [5] While I am in the world, I am the light of the world."

[6] After Jesus said this, he spat on the ground and made some mud with it. He put the mud on the man's eyes. [7] Then he told the man, "Go and wash in the Pool of Siloam." (Siloam means Sent.) So the man went to the pool. He washed and came back. And he was able to see.

[8] Some people had seen this man begging before. They and the man's neighbours said, "Look! Is this the same man who always sits and begs?"

[9] Some said, "Yes! He is the one." But others said, "No, he's not the same man. He only looks like him."

So the man himself said, "I am the man."

¹⁰They asked, "What happened? How did you get your sight?"

¹¹He answered, "The man named Jesus made some mud and put it on my eyes. Then he told me to go to Siloam and wash. So I went and washed and came back seeing."

¹²They asked him, "Where is this man?"

The man answered, "I don't know."

Pharisees Question the Healing

¹³Then the people took to the Pharisees^d the man who had been blind. ¹⁴The day Jesus had made mud and healed his eyes was a Sabbath^d day. ¹⁵So now the Pharisees asked the man, "How did you get your sight?"

He answered, "He put mud on my eyes. I washed, and now I can see."

¹⁶Some of the Pharisees were saying, "This man does not keep the Sabbath day. He is not from God!"

Others said, "But a man who is a sinner can't do miracles^d like these." So they could not agree with each other.

¹⁷They asked the man again, "What do you say about him? It was your eyes he opened."

The man answered, "He is a prophet."^d

¹⁸The Jews did not believe that he had been blind and could now see again. So they sent for the man's parents ¹⁹and asked them, "Is this your son? You say that he was born blind. Then how does he see now?"

²⁰His parents answered, "We know that this is our son, and we know that he was born blind. ²¹But we don't know how he can see now. We don't know who opened his eyes. Ask him. He is old enough to answer for himself." ²²His parents said this because they were afraid of the Jews. The Jews had already decided that anyone who said that Jesus was the

Christ^d would be put out of the synagogue.^d ²³That is why his parents said, "He is old enough. Ask him."

²⁴So for the second time, the Jewish leaders called the man who had been blind. They said, "You should give God the glory by telling the truth. We know that this man is a sinner."

²⁵He answered, "I don't know if he is a sinner. But one thing I do know. I was blind, and now I can see."

²⁶The Jewish leaders asked, "What did he do to you? How did he make you see again?"

²⁷He answered, "I have already told you that. But you would not listen to me. Why do you want to hear it again? Do you want to become his followers, too?"

²⁸Then they insulted him and said, "You are his follower. We are followers of Moses. ²⁹We know that God spoke to Moses. But we don't even know where this man comes from!"

³⁰The man answered, "This is a very strange thing. You don't know where he comes from, and yet he opened my eyes. ³¹We all know that God does not listen to sinners. But God listens to anyone who worships and obeys him. ³²Nobody has ever heard of anyone giving sight to a man born blind. ³³If this man was not from God, he could do nothing."

³⁴They answered, "You were born full of sin! Are you trying to teach us?" And they threw the man out.

Spiritual Blindness

³⁵Jesus heard that they had thrown him out. So Jesus found him and said, "Do you believe in the Son of Man?"^d

³⁶He asked, "Who is the Son of Man, sir? Tell me, so I can believe in him!"

³⁷Jesus said to him, "You have already seen him. The Son of Man is the one talking with you now."

[38] He said, "Yes, Lord, I believe!" Then the man bowed and worshipped Jesus.

[39] Jesus said, "I came into this world so that the world could be judged. I came so that the blind[n] could see and so that those who see will become blind."

[40] Some of the Pharisees[d] were near Jesus. When they heard him say this, they asked, "What? Are you saying that we are blind, too?"

[41] Jesus said, "If you were really blind, you would not be guilty of sin. But now that you say you can see, your guilt remains."

The Shepherd and His Sheep

10 Jesus said, "I tell you the truth. The man who does not enter the sheep fold by the door, but climbs in some other way, is a thief and a robber. [2] The one who enters by the door is the shepherd of the sheep. [3] The man who guards the door opens it for him. And the sheep listen to the voice of the shepherd. He calls his own sheep, using their names, and he leads them out. [4] He brings all of his sheep out. Then he goes ahead of them and leads them. They follow him because they know his voice. [5] But they will never follow a stranger. They will run away from him because they don't know his voice." [6] Jesus told the people this story, but they did not understand what it meant.

Jesus Is the Good Shepherd

[7] So Jesus said again, "I tell you the truth. I am the door for the sheep. [8] All the people who came before me were thieves and robbers. The sheep did not listen to them. [9] I am the door. The person who enters through me will be saved. He will be able to come in and go out and find pasture. [10] A thief comes to steal and kill and destroy. But I came to give life – life in all its fullness.

[11] "I am the good shepherd. The

John 10:11 "I am the good shepherd."

good shepherd gives his life for the sheep. [12] The worker who is paid to keep the sheep is different from the shepherd who owns them. So when the worker sees a wolf coming, he runs away and leaves the sheep alone. Then the wolf attacks the sheep and scatters them. [13] The man runs away because he is only a paid worker. He does not really care for the sheep.

[14-15] "I am the good shepherd. I know my sheep, as the Father knows me. And my sheep know me, as I know the Father. I give my life for the sheep. [16] I have other sheep that are not in this flock here. I must bring them also. They will listen to my voice, and there will be one flock and one shepherd. [17] The Father loves me because I give

---

blind   Jesus is talking about people who are spiritually blind, not physically blind.

my life. I give my life so that I can take it back again. [18]No one takes it away from me. I give my own life freely. I have the right to give my life, and I have the right to take it back. This is what my Father commanded me to do."

[19]Again the Jews did not agree with each other because of these words Jesus said. [20]Many of them said, "A demon[d] has come into him and made him mad. Why listen to him?"

[21]But others said, "A man who is mad with a demon does not say things like this. Can a demon open the eyes of the blind?"

[22]The time came for the Feast[d] of Dedication at Jerusalem. This was during the winter. [23]Jesus was walking in the Temple[d] in Solomon's Porch.[d] [24]The Jews gathered around him and said, "How long will you make us wonder about you? If you are the Christ,[d] then tell us plainly."

Jesus Is the Son of God

[25]Jesus answered, "I have told you already, but you did not believe. I do miracles[d] in my Father's name. Those miracles show who I am. [26]But you don't believe because you are not my sheep. [27]My sheep listen to my voice. I know them, and they follow me. [28]I give them eternal life, and they will never die. And no person can steal them out of my hand. [29]My Father gave my sheep to me. He is greater than all, and no person can steal my sheep out of my Father's hand. [30]The Father and I are one."

[31]Again the Jews picked up stones to kill Jesus. [32]But Jesus said to them, "I have done many good works from the Father. Which of these good works are you killing me for?"

[33]The Jews answered, "We are not killing you for any good work you did. But you say things that are against God. You are only a man, but you say you are the same as God!"

[34]Jesus answered, "It is written in your law that God said, 'I have said you are gods!'[n] [35]This Scripture[d] called those people gods, the people who received God's message. And Scripture is always true. [36]So why do you say that I speak against God because I said, 'I am God's Son'? I am the one God chose and sent into the world. [37]If I don't do what my Father does, then don't believe me. [38]But if I do what my Father does, even though you don't believe in me, believe what I do. Then you will know and understand that the Father is in me and I am in the Father."

[39]The Jews tried to take Jesus again, but he escaped from them.

[40]Then Jesus went back across the Jordan River to the place where John[n] had first baptised. Jesus stayed there, [41]and many people came to him. They said, "John never did a miracle. But everything John said about this man is true." [42]And in that place many believed in Jesus.

The Death of Lazarus

11 There was a man named Lazarus who was sick. He lived in the town of Bethany, where Mary and her sister Martha lived. [2]Mary is the woman who later put perfume on the Lord and wiped his feet with her hair. Mary's brother was Lazarus, the man who was now sick. [3]So Mary and Martha sent someone to tell Jesus, "Lord, the one you love is sick."

[4]When Jesus heard this he said, "This sickness will not end in death.

'I . . . gods.' Quotation from Psalm 82:6.
John John the Baptist, who preached to people about Christ's coming (Matthew 3, Luke 3).

It is for the glory of God. This has happened to bring glory to the Son of God." [5] Jesus loved Martha and her sister and Lazarus. [6] But when he heard that Lazarus was sick, he stayed where he was for two more days. [7] Then Jesus said to his followers, "Let us go back to Judea."

[8] The followers said, "But Teacher, the Jews there tried to kill you with stones. That was only a short time ago. Now you want to go back there?" [9] Jesus answered, "Are there not 12 hours in the day? If anyone walks in the daylight, he will not stumble because he can see by this world's light. [10] But if anyone walks at night he stumbles because there is no light to help him see."

[11] After Jesus said this, he added, "Our friend Lazarus has fallen asleep. But I am going there to wake him." [12] The followers said, "But Lord, if he can sleep, he will get well." [13] Jesus meant that Lazarus was dead. But Jesus' followers thought that he meant Lazarus was really sleeping. [14] So then Jesus said plainly, "Lazarus is dead. [15] And I am glad for your sakes that I was not there so that you may believe. But let us go to him now."

[16] Then Thomas (the one called Didymus) said to the other followers, "Let us go, too. We will die with him."

Jesus in Bethany

[17] Jesus arrived in Bethany. There he learned that Lazarus had already been dead and in the tomb for four days. [18] Bethany was about three kilometres from Jerusalem. [19] Many Jews had come there to comfort Martha and Mary about their brother.

[20] Martha heard that Jesus was coming, and she went out to meet him. But Mary stayed at home. [21] Martha said to Jesus, "Lord, if you had been here, my brother would not have died. [22] But I know that even now God will give you anything you ask."

[23] Jesus said, "Your brother will rise and live again."

[24] Martha answered, "I know that he will rise and live again in the resurrection[n] on the last day."

[25] Jesus said to her, "I am the resurrection and the life. He who believes in me will have life even if he dies. [26] And he who lives and believes in me will never die. Martha, do you believe this?"

[27] Martha answered, "Yes, Lord. I believe that you are the Christ,[d] the Son of God. You are the One who was coming to the world."

Jesus Cries

[28] After Martha said this, she went back to her sister Mary. She talked to Mary alone. Martha said, "The Teacher is here and he is asking for you." [29] When Mary heard this, she got up quickly and went to Jesus. [30] Jesus had not yet come into the town. He was still at the place where Martha had met him. [31] The Jews were with Mary in the house, comforting her. They saw Mary stand and leave quickly. They followed her, thinking that she was going to the tomb to cry there. [32] But Mary went to the place where Jesus was. When she saw him, she fell at his feet and said, "Lord, if you had been here, my brother would not have died."

[33] Jesus saw that Mary was crying and that the Jews who came with her were crying, too. Jesus felt very sad in his heart and was deeply troubled. [34] He asked, "Where did you bury him?"

"Come and see, Lord," they said.

[35] Jesus cried.

---

resurrection   Being raised from death to live again.

36So the Jews said, "See how much he loved him."

37But some of them said, "If Jesus healed the eyes of the blind man, why didn't he keep Lazarus from dying?"

Jesus Raises Lazarus

38Again Jesus felt very sad in his heart. He came to the tomb. The tomb was a cave with a large stone covering the entrance. 39Jesus said, "Move the stone away."

Martha said, "But, Lord, it has been four days since he died. There will be a bad smell." Martha was the sister of the dead man.

40Then Jesus said to her, "Didn't I tell you that if you believed, you would see the glory of God?"

41So they moved the stone away from the entrance. Then Jesus looked up and said, "Father, I thank you that you heard me. 42I know that you always hear me. But I said these things because of the people here around me. I want them to believe that you sent me." 43After Jesus said this, he cried out in a loud voice, "Lazarus, come out!" 44The dead man came out. His hands and feet were wrapped with pieces of cloth, and he had a cloth around his face.

Jesus said to them, "Take the cloth off him and let him go."

The Leaders Plan to Kill Jesus

45There were many Jews who had come to visit Mary. They saw what Jesus did. And many of them believed in him. 46But some of the Jews went to the Pharisees.*d* They told the Pharisees what Jesus had done. 47Then the leading priests and Pharisees called a meeting of the Jewish council. They asked, "What should we do? This man is doing many miracles.*d* 48If we let him continue doing these things, everyone will believe in him. Then the Romans will come and take away our Temple*d* and our nation."

49One of the men there was Caiaphas. He was the high priest that year. Caiaphas said, "You people know nothing! 50It is better for one man to die for the people than for the whole nation to be destroyed. But you don't realise this."

51Caiaphas did not think of this himself. He was high priest that year. So he was really prophesying*d* that Jesus would die for the Jewish nation 52and for God's scattered children. This would bring them all together and make them one.

53That day the Jewish leaders started planning to kill Jesus. 54So Jesus no longer travelled openly among the Jews. He left there and went to a place near the desert. He went to a town called Ephraim and stayed there with his followers.

55It was almost time for the Jewish Passover*d* Feast. Many from the country went up to Jerusalem before the Passover. They went to do the special things to make themselves pure. 56The people looked for Jesus. They stood in the Temple and were asking each other, "Is he coming to the Feast? What do you think?" 57But the leading priests and the Pharisees had given orders about Jesus. They said that if anyone knew where Jesus was, he must tell them. Then they could arrest Jesus.

Jesus with Friends in Bethany

12 Six days before the Passover*d* Feast, Jesus went to Bethany, where Lazarus lived. (Lazarus is the man Jesus raised from death.) 2There they had a dinner for Jesus. Martha served the food. Lazarus was one of the people eating with Jesus. 3Mary brought in half a litre of very expensive perfume made from pure nard.*d*

She poured the perfume on Jesus'
feet, and then she wiped his feet with
her hair. And the sweet smell from the
perfume filled the whole house.

⁴Judas Iscariot, one of Jesus' followers, was there. (He was the one
who would later turn against Jesus.)
Judas said, ⁵"This perfume was worth
300 silver coins.ⁿ It should have been
sold and the money given to the poor."
⁶But Judas did not really care about
the poor. He said this because he was
a thief. He was the one who kept the
money box, and he often stole money
from it.

⁷Jesus answered, "Leave her alone.
It was right for her to save this perfume for today – the day for me to
be prepared for burial. ⁸The poor will
always be with you, but you will not
always have me."

The Plot Against Lazarus

⁹A large crowd of Jews heard that
Jesus was in Bethany. So they went
there to see not only Jesus but also
Lazarus. Lazarus was the one Jesus
raised from death. ¹⁰So the leading
priests made plans to kill Lazarus, too.
¹¹Because of Lazarus many Jews were
leaving them and believing in Jesus.

Jesus Enters Jerusalem

¹²The next day a great crowd in Jerusalem heard that Jesus was coming
there. These were the people who had
come to the Passoverᵈ Feast. ¹³They
took branches of palm trees and went
out to meet Jesus. They shouted,

"Praiseⁿ God!
God bless the One who comes in
     the name of the Lord!
God bless the King of Israel!"
                         Psalm 118:25–26

¹⁴Jesus found a colt and sat on it.
This was as the Scriptureᵈ says,
¹⁵"Don't be afraid, people of Jerusalem!
     Your king is coming.
     He is sitting on the colt of a
          donkey."   *Zechariah 9:9*
¹⁶The followers of Jesus did not
understand this at first. But after Jesus
was raised to glory, they remembered
that this had been written about him.
And they remembered that they had
done these things to him.

People Tell About Jesus

¹⁷There had been many people with
Jesus when he raised Lazarus from
death and told him to come out of the
tomb. Now they were telling others
about what Jesus did. ¹⁸Many people
went out to meet Jesus, because they
had heard about this miracle.ᵈ ¹⁹So
the Phariseesᵈ said to each other, "You
can see that nothing is going right for
us. Look! The whole world is following
him."

Jesus Talks About His Death

²⁰There were some Greek people,
too, who came to Jerusalem to worship
at the Passoverᵈ Feast. ²¹They went to
Philip. (Philip was from Bethsaida, in
Galilee.) They said, "Sir, we would like
to see Jesus." ²²Philip told Andrew.
Then Andrew and Philip told Jesus.

²³Jesus said to them, "The time has
come for the Son of Manᵈ to receive
his glory. ²⁴I tell you the truth. A grain
of wheat must fall to the ground and
die. Then it makes many seeds. But if
it never dies, it remains only a single
seed. ²⁵The person who loves his life
will give up true life. But the person
who hates his life in this world will
keep true life for ever. ²⁶Whoever

---

silver coin   One coin, a denarius, was the average pay for one day's work.
Praise   Literally, "Hosanna", a Hebrew word used at first in praying to God for help, but at this
     time it was probably a shout of joy used in praising God or his Messiah.

serves me must follow me. Then my servant will be with me everywhere I am. My Father will honour anyone who serves me.

27"Now I am very troubled. What should I say? Should I say, 'Father, save me from this time'? No, I came to this time so that I could suffer. 28Father, bring glory to your name!"

Then a voice came from heaven, "I have brought glory to it, and I will do it again."

29The crowd standing there heard the voice. They said it was thunder.

But others said, "An angel has spoken to him."

30Jesus said, "That voice was for you, not for me. 31Now is the time for the world to be judged. Now the ruler of this world will be thrown down. 32I will be lifted up from the earth. And when this happens, I will draw all people toward me." 33Jesus said this to show how he would die.

34The crowd said, "We have heard from the law that the Christ*d* will live for ever. So why do you say, 'The Son of Man must be lifted up'? Who is this 'Son of Man'?"

35Then Jesus said, "The light will be with you for a little longer. So walk while you have the light. Then the darkness will not catch you. He who walks in the darkness does not know where he is going. 36So believe in the light while you still have it. Then you will become sons of light." When Jesus had said this, he left and hid himself from them.

Some Don't Believe in Jesus

37Though Jesus had done many miracles*d* before the people, they still did not believe in him. 38This was to make clear the full meaning of what Isaiah the prophet*d* said:

"Lord, who believed the things we told them?

Who has seen the Lord's power?"   *Isaiah 53:1*

39This is why the people could not believe: Isaiah also said,

40"He has blinded their eyes.
He has closed their minds.
This is so that they will not see
    with their eyes
nor understand in their minds.
This is so they will not
    come back to me and be
        forgiven."   *Isaiah 6:10*

41Isaiah said this because he saw Jesus' glory and spoke about him.

42But many people believed in Jesus, even many of the Jewish leaders. But because of the Pharisees,*d* they did not say that they believed in him. They were afraid that they would be put out of the synagogue.*d* 43They loved praise from men more than praise from God.

44Then Jesus cried out, "He who believes in me is really believing in the One who sent me. 45He who sees me sees the One who sent me. 46I have come as light into the world. I came so that whoever believes in me would not stay in darkness.

47"If anyone hears my words and does not obey them, I do not judge him. For I did not come to judge the world, but to save the world. 48There is a judge for the one who refuses to believe in me and does not accept my words. The word I have taught will be his judge on the last day. 49The things I taught were not from myself. The Father who sent me told me what to say and what to teach. 50And I know that eternal life comes from what the Father commands. So whatever I say is what the Father told me to say."

Jesus Washes His Followers' Feet

13 It was almost time for the Jewish Passover*d* Feast. Jesus

knew that it was time for him to leave this world and go back to the Father. He had always loved those who were his own in the world, and he loved them all the way to the end. ²Jesus and his followers were at the evening meal. The devil had already persuaded Judas Iscariot to turn against Jesus. (Judas was the son of Simon.) ³Jesus knew that the Father had given him power over everything. He also knew that he had come from God and was going back to God. ⁴So during the meal Jesus stood up and took off his outer clothing. Taking a towel, he wrapped it around his waist. ⁵Then he poured water into a bowl and began to wash the followers' feet. He dried them with the towel that was wrapped around him.

⁶Jesus came to Simon Peter. But Peter said to Jesus, "Lord, are you going to wash my feet?"

John 13:6 "Lord, are you going to wash my feet?"

⁷Jesus answered, "You don't understand what I am doing now. But you will understand later."

⁸Peter said, "No! You will never wash my feet."

Jesus answered, "If I don't wash your feet, then you are not one of my people."

⁹Simon Peter answered, "Lord, after you wash my feet, wash my hands and my head, too!"

¹⁰Jesus said, "After a person has had a bath, his whole body is clean. He needs only to wash his feet. And you men are clean,ᵈ but not all of you." ¹¹Jesus knew who would turn against him. That is why Jesus said, "Not all of you are clean."

¹²When he had finished washing their feet, he put on his clothes and sat down again. Jesus asked, "Do you understand what I have just done for you? ¹³You call me 'Teacher' and 'Lord'. And this is right, because that is what I am. ¹⁴I, your Lord and Teacher, have washed your feet. So you also should wash each other's feet. ¹⁵I did this as an example for you. So you should do as I have done for you. ¹⁶I tell you the truth. A servant is not greater than his master. A messenger is not greater than the one who sent him. ¹⁷If you know these things, you will be happy if you do them.

¹⁸"I am not talking about all of you. I know those I have chosen. But what the Scriptureᵈ said must happen: 'The man who ate at my table has now turned against me'.ⁿ ¹⁹I am telling you this now before it happens. Then when it happens you will believe that I am he. ²⁰I tell you the truth. Whoever accepts anyone I send also accepts me. And whoever accepts me also accepts the One who sent me."

'The man . . . me.' Quotation from Psalm 41:9.

Jesus Talks About His Death

[21] After Jesus said this, he was very troubled. He said openly, "I tell you the truth. One of you will turn against me."

[22] The followers all looked at each other. They did not know whom Jesus was talking about. [23] One of the followers was sitting[n] next to Jesus. This was the follower Jesus loved. [24] Simon Peter made signs to him to ask Jesus who it was that he was talking about.

[25] That follower leaned closer to Jesus and asked, "Lord, who is it that will turn against you?"

[26] Jesus answered, "I will dip this bread into the dish. The man I give it to is the man who will turn against me." So Jesus took a piece of bread. He dipped it and gave it to Judas Iscariot, the son of Simon. [27] As soon as Judas took the bread, Satan entered him. Jesus said to Judas, "The thing that you will do – do it quickly!" [28] None of the men at the table understood why Jesus said this to Judas. [29] He was the one who kept the money box. So some of the followers thought that Jesus was telling Judas to buy what was needed for the feast. Or they thought that Jesus wanted Judas to give something to the poor.

[30] Judas accepted the bread Jesus gave him and immediately went out. It was night.

[31] When Judas was gone, Jesus said, "Now the Son of Man[d] receives his glory. And God receives glory through him. [32] If God receives glory through him, then God will give glory to the Son through himself. And God will give him glory quickly."

[33] Jesus said, "My children, I will be with you only a little longer. You will look for me. And what I told the Jews, I tell you now: where I am going you cannot come.

[34] "I give you a new command: love each other. You must love each other as I have loved you. [35] All people will know that you are my followers if you love each other."

Peter Will Say He Doesn't Know Jesus

[36] Simon Peter asked Jesus, "Lord, where are you going?"

Jesus answered, "Where I am going you cannot follow now. But you will follow later."

[37] Peter asked, "Lord, why can't I follow you now? I am ready to die for you!"

[38] Jesus answered, "Will you really die for me? I tell you the truth. Before the cock crows, you will say three times that you don't know me."

Jesus Comforts His Followers

14 Jesus said, "Don't let your hearts be troubled. Trust in God. And trust in me. [2] There are many rooms in my Father's house. I would not tell you this if it were not true. I am going there to prepare a place for you. [3] After I go and prepare a place for you, I will come back. Then I will take you to be with me so that you may be where I am. [4] You know the way to the place where I am going."

[5] Thomas said to Jesus, "Lord, we don't know where you are going. So how can we know the way?"

[6] Jesus answered, "I am the way. And I am the truth and the life. The only way to the Father is through me.

---

sitting Literally, "lying". The people of that time ate lying down and leaning on one arm.

[7] If you really knew me, then you would know my Father, too. But now you do know him, and you have seen him."

[8] Philip said to him, "Lord, show us the Father. That is all we need."

[9] Jesus answered, "I have been with you a long time now. Do you still not know me, Philip? He who has seen me has seen the Father. So why do you say, 'Show us the Father'? [10] Don't you believe that I am in the Father and the Father is in me? The words I say to you don't come from me. The Father lives in me, and he is doing his own work. [11] Believe me when I say that I am in the Father and the Father is in me. Or believe because of the miracles[d] I have done. [12] I tell you the truth. He who believes in me will do the same things that I do. He will do even greater things than these because I am going to the Father. [13] And if you ask for anything in my name, I will do it for you. Then the Father's glory will be shown through the Son. [14] If you ask me for anything in my name, I will do it.

The Promise of the Holy Spirit

[15] "If you love me, you will do the things I command. [16] I will ask the Father, and he will give you another Helper.[n] He will give you this Helper to be with you for ever. [17] The Helper is the Spirit[d] of truth. The world cannot accept him because it does not see him or know him. But you know him. He lives with you and he will be in you.

[18] "I will not leave you all alone like orphans. I will come back to you. [19] In a little while the world will not see me any more, but you will see me. Because I live, you will live, too. [20] On that day you will know that I am in my Father. You will know that you are in me and I am in you. [21] He who knows my commands and obeys them is the one who loves me. And my Father will love him who loves me. I will love him and will show myself to him."

[22] Then Judas (not Judas Iscariot) said, "But, Lord, why do you plan to show yourself to us, but not to the world?"

[23] Jesus answered, "If anyone loves me, then he will obey my teaching. My Father will love him, and we will come to him and make our home with him. [24] He who does not love me does not obey my teaching. This teaching that you hear is not really mine. It is from my Father, who sent me.

[25] "I have told you all these things while I am with you. [26] But the Helper will teach you everything. He will cause you to remember all the things I told you. This Helper is the Holy Spirit whom the Father will send in my name.

[27] "I leave you peace. My peace I give you. I do not give it to you as the world does. So don't let your hearts be troubled. Don't be afraid. [28] You heard me say to you, 'I am going, but I am coming back to you'. If you loved me, you should be happy that I am going back to the Father because he is greater than I am. [29] I have told you this now, before it happens. Then when it happens, you will believe. [30] I will not talk with you much longer. The ruler of this world is coming. He has no power over me. [31] But the world must know that I love the Father. So I do exactly what the Father told me to do.

"Come now, let us go."

Helper   "Counsellor", or "Comforter". Jesus is talking about the Holy Spirit.

Jesus Is Like a Vine

15 "I am the true vine; my Father is the gardener. ²He cuts off every branch of mine that does not produce fruit. And he trims and cleans every branch that produces fruit so that it will produce even more fruit. ³You are already clean*d* because of the words I have spoken to you. ⁴Remain in me, and I will remain in you. No branch can produce fruit alone. It must remain in the vine. It is the same with you. You cannot produce fruit alone. You must remain in me.

⁵"I am the vine, and you are the branches. If a person remains in me and I remain in him, then he produces much fruit. But without me he can do nothing. ⁶If anyone does not remain in me, then he is like a branch that is thrown away. That branch dies. People pick up dead branches, throw them into the fire, and burn them. ⁷Remain in me and follow my teachings. If you do this, then you can ask for anything you want, and it will be given to you. ⁸You should produce much fruit and show that you are my followers. This brings glory to my Father. ⁹I loved you as the Father loved me. Now remain in my love. ¹⁰I have obeyed my Father's commands, and I remain in his love. In the same way, if you obey my commands, you will remain in my love. ¹¹I have told you these things so that you can have the same joy I have. I want your joy to be the fullest joy.

¹²"This is my command: love each other as I have loved you. ¹³The greatest love a person can show is to die for his friends. ¹⁴You are my friends if you do what I command you. ¹⁵I don't call you servants now. A servant does not know what his master is doing. But now I call you friends because I have made known to you everything I heard from my Father. ¹⁶You did not choose me; I chose you. And I gave you this work, to go and produce fruit. I want you to produce fruit that will last. Then the Father will give you anything you ask for in my name. ¹⁷This is my command: love each other.

Jesus Warns His Followers

¹⁸"If the world hates you, remember that it hated me first. ¹⁹If you belonged to the world, then it would love you as it loves its own. But I have chosen you out of the world. So you don't belong to it. That is why the world hates you. ²⁰Remember what I told you: a servant is not greater than his master. If people did wrong to me,

John 15:1 "I am the true vine."

they will do wrong to you, too. And if they obeyed my teaching, they will obey yours, too. [21] They will do all this to you because of me. They don't know the One who sent me. [22] If I had not come and spoken to them, they would not be guilty of sin. But now they have no excuse for their sin. [23] He who hates me also hates my Father. [24] I did works among them that no one else has ever done. If I had not done those works, they would not be guilty of sin. But now they have seen what I did, and yet they have hated both me and my Father. [25] But this happened so that what is written in their law would be true: 'They hated me for no reason'.[n]

[26] "I will send you the Helper[n] from the Father. He is the Spirit of truth who comes from the Father. When he comes, he will tell about me. [27] And you also must tell people about me because you have been with me from the beginning.

16 "I have told you these things to keep you from giving up. [2] People will put you out of their synagogues.[d] Yes, the time is coming when whoever kills you will think that he is offering service to God. [3] They will do this because they have not known the Father and they have not known me. [4] I have told you these things now. So when the time comes, you will remember that I warned you.

The Work of the Holy Spirit

"I did not tell you these things at the beginning, because I was with you then. [5] Now I am going back to the One who sent me. But none of you asks me, 'Where are you going?' [6] Your hearts are filled with sadness because I have told you these things. [7] But I

tell you the truth. It is better for you that I go away. When I go away I will send the Helper[n] to you. If I do not go away, then the Helper will not come. [8] When the Helper comes, he will prove to the people of the world the truth about sin, about being right with God, and about judgement. [9] He will prove to them about sin, because they don't believe in me. [10] He will prove to them that I am right with God, because I am going to the Father. You will not see me any more. [11] And the Helper will prove to them the truth about judgement, because the ruler of this world is already judged.

[12] "I have many more things to say to you, but they are too much for you now. [13] But when the Spirit[d] of truth comes he will lead you into all truth. He will not speak his own words. He will speak only what he hears and will tell you what is to come. [14] The Spirit of truth will bring glory to me. He will take what I have to say and tell it to you. [15] All that the Father has is mine. That is why I said that the Spirit will take what I have to say and tell it to you.

Sadness Will Become Happiness

[16] "After a little while you will not see me. And then after a little while you will see me again."

[17] Some of the followers said to each other, "What does Jesus mean when he says, 'After a little while you will not see me, and then after a little while you will see me again'? And what does he mean when he says, 'Because I am going to the Father'?" [18] They also asked, "What does he mean by 'a little while'? We don't understand what he is saying."

'They . . . reason'   These words could be from Psalm 35:19 or Psalm 69:4.
Helper   "Counsellor", or "Comforter". Jesus is talking about the Holy Spirit.

¹⁹Jesus saw that the followers wanted to ask him about this. So Jesus said to the followers, "Are you asking each other what I meant when I said, 'After a little while you will not see me. And then after a little while you will see me again'? ²⁰I tell you the truth. You will cry and be sad, but the world will be happy. You will be sad, but your sadness will become joy. ²¹When a woman gives birth to a baby, she has pain, because her time has come. But when her baby is born, she forgets the pain. She forgets because she is so happy that a child has been born into the world. ²²It is the same with you. Now you are sad. But I will see you again and you will be happy. And no one will take away your joy. ²³In that day you will not ask me for anything. I tell you the truth. My Father will give you anything you ask for in my name. ²⁴You have never asked for anything in my name. Ask and you will receive. And your joy will be the fullest joy.

Victory over the World

²⁵"I have told you these things, using words that hide the meaning. But the time will come when I will not use words like that to tell you things. I will speak to you in plain words about the Father. ²⁶In that day you will ask the Father for things in my name. I am saying that I will not need to ask the Father for you. ²⁷No! The Father himself loves you. He loves you because you have loved me. And he loves you because you have believed that I came from God. ²⁸I came from the Father into the world. Now I am leaving the world and going back to the Father."

²⁹Then the followers of Jesus said, "You are speaking clearly to us now. You are not using words that are hard to understand. ³⁰We can see now that you know all things. You can answer a person's question even before he asks it. This makes us believe that you came from God."

³¹Jesus answered, "So now you believe? ³²Listen to me. A time is coming when you will be scattered. Each of you will be scattered to his own home. That time is now here. You will leave me. I will be alone. But I am never really alone. Why? Because the Father is with me.

³³"I told you these things so that you can have peace in me. In this world you will have trouble. But be brave! I have defeated the world!"

Jesus Prays for His Followers

17 After Jesus said these things he looked towards heaven. Jesus prayed, "Father, the time has come. Give glory to your Son so that the Son can give glory to you. ²You gave the Son power over all people so that the Son could give eternal life to all those people you have given to him. ³And this is eternal life: that men can know you, the only true God, and that men can know Jesus Christ, the One you sent. ⁴I have finished the work you gave me to do. I have brought you glory on earth. ⁵And now, Father, give me glory with you. Give me the glory I had with you before the world was made.

⁶"You gave me some men from the world. I have shown them what you are like. Those men belonged to you, and you gave them to me. They have obeyed your teaching. ⁷Now they know that everything you gave me comes from you. ⁸I gave these men the teachings that you gave me. They accepted those teachings. They know that I truly came from you. ⁹I pray for them now. I am not praying for the people in the world. But I am praying for those men you gave me, because they are yours. ¹⁰All I have is yours,

and all you have is mine. And my glory is shown through these men. ¹¹Now I am coming to you. I will not stay in the world now. But these men are still in the world. Holy Father, keep them safe. Keep them safe by the power of your name (the name you gave me), so that they will be one, the same as you and I are one. ¹²While I was with them, I kept them safe. I kept them safe by the power of your name – the name you gave me. I protected them. And only one of them, the one who is going to hell, was lost. He was lost so that what was said in the Scripture*d* would happen.

¹³"I am coming to you now. But I pray these things while I am still in the world. I say these things so that these men can have my joy. I want them to have all of my joy. ¹⁴I have given them your teaching. And the world has hated them. The world hated these men, because they don't belong to the world, just as I don't belong to the world. ¹⁵I am not asking you to take them out of the world. But I am asking that you keep them safe from the Evil One. ¹⁶They don't belong to the world, just as I don't belong to the world. ¹⁷Make them ready for your service through your truth. Your teaching is truth. ¹⁸I have sent them into the world, just as you sent me into the world. ¹⁹I am making myself ready to serve. I do this for them so that they can truly be ready for your service.

²⁰"I pray for these men. But I am also praying for all people who will believe in me because of the teaching of these men. ²¹Father, I pray that all people who believe in me can be one. You are in me and I am in you. I pray that these people can also be one in us, so that the world will believe that you sent me. ²²I have given these people the glory that you gave me. I

gave them this glory so that they can be one, just as you and I are one. ²³I will be in them and you will be in me. So they will be completely one. Then the world will know that you sent me. And the world will know that you loved these people just as you loved me.

²⁴"Father, I want those you have given me to be with me in every place I am. I want them to see my glory. This is the glory you gave me because you loved me before the world was made. ²⁵Father, you are the One who is good. The world does not know you, but I know you. And these people know that you sent me. ²⁶I showed them what you are like. And again I will show them what you are like. Then they will have the same love that you have for me. And I will live in them."

Jesus Is Arrested

18 When Jesus finished praying, he left with his followers. They went across the Kidron Valley. On the other side there was a garden of olive trees. Jesus and his followers went there.

²Judas knew where this place was, because Jesus met there often with his followers. Judas was the one who turned against Jesus. ³So Judas led a group of soldiers to the garden. Judas also brought some guards from the leading priests and the Pharisees.*d* They were carrying torches, lanterns, and weapons.

⁴Jesus knew everything that would happen to him. Jesus went out and asked, "Who is it you are looking for?"

⁵The men answered, "Jesus from Nazareth."

Jesus said, "I am Jesus." (Judas, the one who turned against Jesus, was standing there with them.) ⁶When Jesus said, "I am Jesus," the men moved back and fell to the ground.

[7]Jesus asked them again, "Who is it you are looking for?"

They said, "Jesus of Nazareth."

[8]Jesus said, "I told you that I am he. So if you are looking for me, then let these other men go." [9]This happened so that the words Jesus said before might come true: "I have not lost any of the men you gave me."

[10]Simon Peter had a sword. He took out the sword and struck the servant of the high priest, cutting off his right ear. (The servant's name was Malchus.) [11]Jesus said to Peter, "Put your sword back. Shall I not drink of the cup[n] the Father has given me?"

Jesus Is Brought Before Annas

[12]Then the soldiers with their commander and the Jewish guards arrested Jesus. They tied him [13]and led him first to Annas. Annas was the father-in-law of Caiaphas, the high priest that year. [14]Caiaphas was the one who had told the Jews that it would be better if one man died for all the people.

Peter Says He Doesn't Know Jesus

[15]Simon Peter and another one of Jesus' followers went along after Jesus. This follower knew the high priest. So he went with Jesus into the high priest's courtyard. [16]But Peter waited outside near the door. The follower who knew the high priest came back outside. He spoke to the girl at the door and brought Peter inside. [17]The girl at the door said to Peter, "Aren't you also one of that man's followers?"

Peter answered, "No, I am not!"

[18]It was cold, so the servants and guards had built a fire. They were standing around it and warming themselves. Peter was standing with them, warming himself.

The High Priest Questions Jesus

[19]The high priest asked Jesus questions about his followers and his teaching. [20]Jesus answered, "I have spoken openly to everyone. I have always taught in synagogues[d] and in the Temple,[d] where all the Jews come together. I never said anything in secret. [21]So why do you question me? Ask the people who heard my teaching. They know what I said."

[22]When Jesus said this, one of the guards standing there hit him. The guard said, "Is that the way you answer the high priest?"

[23]Jesus answered him, "If I said something wrong, then say what was wrong. But if what I said is true, why do you hit me?"

[24]Then Annas sent Jesus to Caiaphas, the high priest. Jesus was still tied.

Peter Says Again He Doesn't Know Jesus

[25]Simon Peter was standing and warming himself. They said to him, "Aren't you one of that man's followers?"

Peter denied it and said, "No, I am not."

[26]One of the servants of the high priest was there. This servant was a relative of the man whose ear Peter had cut off. The servant said, "Didn't I see you with him in the garden?"

[27]Again Peter said it wasn't true. Just then a cockerel crowed.

---

cup   Jesus is talking about the bad things that will happen to him. Accepting these things will be very hard, like drinking a cup of something that tastes very bitter.

John 18:27 Just then a cockerel crowed.

Jesus Is Brought Before Pilate

28 Then the Jews led Jesus from Caiaphas' house to the Roman governor's palace. It was early in the morning. The Jews would not go inside the palace. They did not want to make themselves unclean,[n] because they wanted to eat the Passover[d] meal. 29 So Pilate went outside to them. He asked, "What charges do you bring against this man?"

30 They answered, "He is a criminal. That is why we brought him to you."

31 Pilate said to the Jews, "Take him yourselves and judge him by your own law."

They answered, "But we are not allowed to put anyone to death." 32 (This happened so that what Jesus had said about how he would die would come true.)

33 Then Pilate went back inside the palace. He called Jesus to him and asked, "Are you the king of the Jews?"

34 Jesus said, "Is that your own question, or did others tell you about me?"

35 Pilate answered, "I am not a Jew. It was your own people and their leading priests who brought you before me. What have you done wrong?"

36 Jesus said, "My kingdom does not belong to this world. If it belonged to this world, my servants would fight so that I would not be given over to the Jews. But my kingdom is from another place."

37 Pilate said, "So you are a king!"

Jesus answered, "You say that I am a king. That is true. I was born for this: to tell people about the truth. That is why I came into the world. And everyone who belongs to the truth listens to me."

38 Pilate said, "What is truth?" After he said this, he went out to the Jews again. He said to them, "I can find nothing to charge against this man. 39 But it is your custom that I free one prisoner to you at the time of the Passover. Do you want me to free this 'King of the Jews'?"

40 They shouted back, "No, not him! Let Barabbas go free!" (Barabbas was a robber.)

19 Then Pilate ordered that Jesus be taken away and whipped. 2 The soldiers used some thorny branches to make a crown. They put this crown on Jesus' head and put a purple robe around him. 3 Then they came to Jesus many times and said, "Hail, King of the Jews!" They hit Jesus in the face.

4 Again Pilate came out and said to

---

unclean   Going into a non-Jewish place would make them unfit to eat the Passover Feast, according to Jewish law.

the Jews, "Look! I am bringing Jesus out to you. I want you to know that I find nothing I can charge against him." [5]Then Jesus came out, wearing the crown of thorns and the purple robe. Pilate said to the Jews, "Here is the man!"

[6]When the leading priests and the Jewish guards saw Jesus they shouted, "Kill him on a cross! Kill him on a cross!"

But Pilate answered, "Take him and nail him to a cross yourselves. I find nothing I can charge against him."

[7]The Jews answered, "We have a law that says he should die, because he said he is the Son of God."

[8]When Pilate heard this, he was even more afraid. [9]He went back inside the palace and asked Jesus, "Where are you from?" But Jesus did not answer him. [10]Pilate said, "You refuse to speak to me? Don't you know that I have power to set you free and power to have you killed on a cross?"

[11]Jesus answered, "The only power you have over me is the power given to you by God. The man who gave me to you is guilty of a greater sin."

[12]After this, Pilate tried to let Jesus go free. But the Jews cried out, "Anyone who makes himself king is against Caesar. If you let this man go free, you are not Caesar's friend."

[13]Pilate heard what the Jews were saying. So he brought Jesus out to the place called The Stone Pavement. (In the Jewish language[n] the name is Gabbatha.) Pilate sat down on the judge's seat there. [14]It was about six o'clock in the morning on Preparation[d] Day of Passover[d] week. Pilate said to the Jews, "Here is your king!"

[15]The Jews shouted, "Take him away! Take him away! Kill him on a cross!"

Pilate asked them, "Do you want me to kill your king on a cross?"

The leading priests answered, "The only king we have is Caesar!"

[16]So Pilate gave Jesus to them to be killed on a cross.

Jesus Is Killed on a Cross

The soldiers took charge of Jesus. [17]Carrying his own cross, Jesus went out to a place called The Place of the Skull. (In the Jewish language[n] this place is called Golgotha.) [18]There they nailed Jesus to the cross. They also put two other men on crosses, one on each side of Jesus with Jesus in the middle. [19]Pilate wrote a sign and put it on the cross. It read: "JESUS OF NAZARETH, THE KING OF THE JEWS." [20]The sign was written in the Jewish language, in Latin, and in Greek. Many of the Jews read the sign, because this place where they killed Jesus was near the city. [21]The leading Jewish priests said to Pilate, "Don't write, 'The King of the Jews'. But write, 'This man said, I am the King of the Jews'."

[22]Pilate answered, "What I have written, I have written!"

[23]After the soldiers nailed Jesus to the cross, they took his clothes. They divided them into four parts. Each soldier got one part. They also took his long shirt. It was all one piece of cloth, woven from top to bottom. [24]So the soldiers said to each other, "We should not tear this into parts. We should throw lots[d] to see who will get it." This happened to give full meaning to the Scripture:[d]

"They divided my clothes among
    them.
And they threw lots[d] for my
    clothing."   *Psalm 22:18*

So the soldiers did this.

Jewish language   Aramaic, the language of the Jews in the first century.

[25] Jesus' mother stood near his cross. His mother's sister was also standing there, with Mary the wife of Clopas, and Mary Magdalene. [26] Jesus saw his mother. He also saw the follower he loved standing there. He said to his mother, "Dear woman, here is your son." [27] Then he said to the follower, "Here is your mother." From that time on, this follower took her to live in his home.

Jesus Dies

[28] After this, Jesus knew that everything had been done. To make the Scripture[d] come true, he said, "I am thirsty."[n] [29] There was a jar full of vinegar there, so the soldiers soaked a sponge in it. Then they put the sponge on a branch of a hyssop plant and lifted it to Jesus' mouth. [30] Jesus tasted the vinegar. Then he said, "It is finished." He bowed his head and died.

[31] This day was Preparation[d] Day. The next day was a special Sabbath[d] day. The Jews did not want the bodies to stay on the cross on the Sabbath day. So they asked Pilate to order that the legs of the men be broken[n] and the bodies be taken away. [32] So the soldiers came and broke the legs of the first man on the cross beside Jesus. Then they broke the legs of the man on the other cross beside Jesus. [33] But when the soldiers came to Jesus, they saw that he was already dead. So they did not break his legs, [34] but one of the soldiers stuck his spear into Jesus' side. At once blood and water came out. [35] (The one who saw this happen has told about it. The things he says are true. He knows that he tells the truth. He told about it so that you also can believe.) [36] These things happened to make the Scripture come true: "Not one of his bones will be broken."[n] [37] And another Scripture said, "They will look at the one they have stabbed."[n]

Jesus Is Buried

[38] Later, a man named Joseph from Arimathea asked Pilate if he could take the body of Jesus. (Joseph was a secret follower of Jesus, because he was afraid of the Jews.) Pilate gave his permission. So Joseph came and took Jesus' body away. [39] Nicodemus went with Joseph. Nicodemus was the man who earlier had come to Jesus at night. He brought about 35 kilograms of spices. This was a mixture of myrrh[d] and aloes.[d] [40] These two men took Jesus' body and wrapped it with the spices in pieces of linen cloth. (This is how the Jews bury people.) [41] In the place where Jesus was killed, there was a garden. In the garden was a new tomb where no one had ever been buried. [42] The men laid Jesus in that tomb because it was near, and the Jews were preparing to start their Sabbath[d] day.

Jesus' Tomb Is Empty

20 Early on the first day of the week, Mary Magdalene went to the tomb. It was still dark. Mary saw that the large stone had been moved away from the tomb. [2] So Mary ran to Simon Peter and the other follower (the one Jesus loved). Mary said, "They have taken the Lord out of the tomb. We don't know where they have put him."

"I am thirsty."   Read Psalms 22:15; 69:21.
broken   The breaking of the men's bones would make them die sooner.
"Not one . . . broken."   Quotation from Psalm 34:20. The idea is from Exodus 12:46; Numbers 9:12.
"They . . . stabbed."   Quotation from Zechariah 12:10.

[3] So Peter and the other follower started for the tomb. [4] They were both running, but the other follower ran faster than Peter. So the other follower reached the tomb first. [5] He bent down and looked in. He saw the strips of linen cloth lying there, but he did not go in. [6] Then following him came Simon Peter. He went into the tomb and saw the strips of linen lying there. [7] He also saw the cloth that had been around Jesus' head. The cloth was folded up and laid in a different place from the strips of linen. [8] Then the other follower, who had reached the tomb first, also went in. He saw and believed. [9] (These followers did not yet understand from the Scriptures[d] that Jesus must rise from death.)

Jesus Appears to Mary Magdalene

[10] Then the followers went back home. [11] But Mary stood outside the tomb, crying. While she was still crying, she bent down and looked inside the tomb. [12] She saw two angels dressed in white. They were sitting where Jesus' body had been, one at the head and one at the feet.

[13] They asked her, "Woman, why are you crying?"

She answered, "They have taken away my Lord. I don't know where they have put him." [14] When Mary said this, she turned around and saw Jesus standing there. But she did not know that it was Jesus.

[15] Jesus asked her, "Woman, why are you crying? Whom are you looking for?"

Mary thought he was the gardener. So she said to him, "Did you take him away, sir? Tell me where you put him, and I will get him."

[16] Jesus said to her, "Mary."

Mary turned toward Jesus and said in the Jewish language,[n] "Rabboni." (This means Teacher.)

[17] Jesus said to her, "Don't hold me. I have not yet gone up to the Father. But go to my brothers and tell them this: 'I am going back to my Father and your Father. I am going back to my God and your God'."

[18] Mary Magdalene went and said to the followers, "I have seen the Lord!" And she told them what Jesus had said to her.

Jesus Appears to His Followers

[19] It was the first day of the week. That evening the followers were together. The doors were locked, because they were afraid of the Jews. Then Jesus came and stood among them. He said, "Peace be with you!" [20] After he said this, he showed them his hands and his side. The followers were very happy when they saw the Lord.

[21] Then Jesus said again, "Peace be with you! As the Father sent me, I now send you." [22] After he said this, he breathed on them and said, "Receive the Holy Spirit.[d] [23] If you forgive anyone his sins, they are forgiven. If you don't forgive them, they are not forgiven."

Jesus Appears to Thomas

[24] Thomas (called Didymus) was not with the followers when Jesus came. Thomas was one of the 12. [25] The other followers told Thomas, "We have seen the Lord."

But Thomas said, "I will not believe it until I see the nail marks in his hands. And I will not believe until I put my finger where the nails were and put my hand into his side."

[26] A week later the followers were

Jewish language   Aramaic, the language of the Jews in the first century.

in the house again. Thomas was with them. The doors were locked, but Jesus came in and stood among them. He said, "Peace be with you!" [27] Then he said to Thomas, "Put your finger here. Look at my hands. Put your hand here in my side. Stop doubting and believe."

John 20:27 "Stop doubting and believe."

[28] Thomas said to him, "My Lord and my God!"

[29] Then Jesus told him, "You believe because you see me. Those who believe without seeing me will be truly happy."

Why John Wrote This Book

[30] Jesus did many other miracles[d] in front of his followers that are not written in this book. [31] But these are written so that you can believe that Jesus is the Christ,[d] the Son of God. Then, by believing, you can have life through his name.

Jesus Appears to Seven Followers

21 Later, Jesus showed himself to his followers by Lake Galilee.[n] This is how it happened. [2] Some of the followers were together. They were Simon Peter, Thomas (called Didymus), Nathanael from Cana in Galilee, the two sons of Zebedee, and two other followers. [3] Simon Peter said, "I am going out to fish."

The other followers said, "We will go with you." So they went out and got into the boat. They fished that night but caught nothing.

[4] Early the next morning Jesus stood on the shore. But the followers did not know that it was Jesus. [5] Then he said to them, "Friends, have you caught any fish?"

They answered, "No".

[6] He said, "Throw your net into the water on the right side of the boat, and you will find some." So they did this. They caught so many fish that they could not pull the net back into the boat.

[7] The follower whom Jesus loved said to Peter, "It is the Lord!" When Peter heard him say this, he wrapped his coat around himself. (Peter had taken his clothes off.) Then he jumped into the water. [8] The other followers went to shore in the boat, dragging the net full of fish. They were not very far from shore, only about 100 metres. [9] When the followers stepped out of the boat and onto the shore, they saw a fire of hot coals. There were fish on the fire, and there was bread.

[10] Then Jesus said, "Bring some of the fish that you caught."

[11] Simon Peter went into the boat and pulled the net to the shore. It was full of big fish. There were 153. Even though there were so many, the net

Lake Galilee　Literally, "Sea of Tiberias".

did not tear. [12]Jesus said to them, "Come and eat." None of the followers dared ask him, "Who are you?" They knew it was the Lord. [13]Jesus came and took the bread and gave it to them. He also gave them the fish.

[14]This was now the third time that Jesus showed himself to his followers after he was raised from death.

Jesus Talks to Peter

[15]When they had finished eating, Jesus said to Simon Peter, "Simon, son of John, do you love me more than these?"

He answered, "Yes, Lord, you know that I love you."

Jesus said, "Take care of my lambs."

[16]Again Jesus said, "Simon, son of John, do you love me?"

He answered, "Yes, Lord, you know that I love you."

Jesus said, "Take care of my sheep."

[17]A third time he said, "Simon, son of John, do you love me?"

Peter was hurt because Jesus asked him the third time, "Do you love me?" Peter said, "Lord, you know everything. You know that I love you!"

He said to him, "Take care of my sheep. [18]I tell you the truth. When you were younger, you tied your own belt and went where you wanted. But when you are old, you will put out your hands and someone else will tie them. They will take you where you don't want to go." [19](Jesus said this to show how Peter would die to give glory to God.) Then Jesus said to Peter, "Follow me!"

[20]Peter turned and saw that the follower Jesus loved was walking behind them. (This was the follower who had leaned against Jesus at the supper and had said, "Lord, who will turn against you?") [21]When Peter saw him behind them he asked Jesus, "Lord, what about him?"

[22]Jesus answered, "Perhaps I want him to live until I come back. That should not be important to you. You follow me!"

[23]So a story spread among the brothers that this follower would not die. But Jesus did not say that he would not die. He only said, "Perhaps I want him to live until I come back. That should not be important to you."

[24]That follower is the one who is telling these things. He is the one who has now written them down. We know that what he says is true.

[25]There are many other things that Jesus did. If every one of them were written down, I think the whole world would not be big enough for all the books that would be written.

ACTS

The Good News of Jesus Spreads

Luke Writes Another Book

1 To Theophilus,
The first book I wrote was about everything that Jesus did and taught. ²I wrote about the whole life of Jesus, from the beginning until the day he was taken up into heaven. Before this, Jesus talked to the apostles*d* he had chosen. With the help of the Holy Spirit,*d* Jesus told them what they should do. ³After his death, he showed himself to them and proved in many ways that he was alive. The apostles saw Jesus during the 40 days after he was raised from death. He spoke to them about the kingdom of God. ⁴Once when he was eating with them, he told them not to leave Jerusalem. He said, "The Father has made you a promise which I told you about before. Wait here to receive this promise. ⁵John baptised people with water, but in a few days you will be baptised with the Holy Spirit."

Jesus Is Taken Up into Heaven

⁶The apostles*d* were all together. They asked Jesus, "Lord, are you at this time going to give the kingdom back to Israel?"

⁷Jesus said to them, "The Father is the only One who has the authority to decide dates and times. These things are not for you to know. ⁸But the Holy Spirit*d* will come to you. Then you will receive power. You will be my witnesses – in Jerusalem, in all of Judea, in Samaria, and in every part of the world."

⁹After he said this, as they were watching, he was lifted up. A cloud hid him from their sight. ¹⁰As he was going, they were looking into the sky. Suddenly, two men wearing white

Acts 1:9 As they were watching, he was lifted up.

clothes stood beside them. ¹¹They said, "Men of Galilee, why are you standing here looking into the sky? You saw Jesus taken away from you into heaven. He will come back in the same way you saw him go."

A New Apostle Is Chosen

¹²Then they went back to Jerusalem from the Mount of Olives.*d* (This mountain is about a kilometre from Jerusalem.) ¹³When they entered the city, they went to the upstairs room where they were staying. Peter, John,

James, Andrew, Philip, Thomas, Bartholomew, Matthew, James son of Alphaeus, Simon (known as the Zealot[d]), and Judas son of James were there. [14]They all continued praying together. Some women, including Mary the mother of Jesus, and Jesus' brothers were also there with the apostles.

[15]During this time there was a meeting of the believers. (There were about 120 of them.) Peter stood up and said, [16-17]"Brothers, in the Scriptures[d] the Holy Spirit[d] said through David that something must happen. The Spirit was talking about Judas, one of our own group, who served together with us. The Spirit said that Judas would lead men to arrest Jesus. [18]Judas bought a field with the money he got for his evil act. (But Judas fell to his death, his body burst open, and all his intestines poured out.) [19]Everyone in Jerusalem learned about this. This is why they named the field Akeldama. (In their language Akeldama means "field of blood".) [20]In the Book of Psalms, this is written:

'May his place be empty.
    Leave no one to live in it'.
                            Psalm 69:25

And it is also written:
'Let another man replace him as
    leader'.   *Psalm 109:8*

[21-22]"So now a man must join us and become a witness of Jesus' being raised from death. He must be one of the men who were part of our group during all the time the Lord Jesus was with us. He must have been with us from the time John began to baptise people until the day when Jesus was taken up from us to heaven."

[23]They put the names of two men before the group. One was Joseph Barsabbas, who was also called Justus. The other was Matthias. [24-25]The apostles prayed, "Lord, you know the minds of everyone. Show us which one of these two you have chosen to do this work. Judas turned away from it and went where he belongs. Lord, show us which one should take his place as an apostle!"[d] [26]Then they used lots[d] to choose between them, and the lots showed that Matthias was the one. So he became an apostle with the other 11.

The Coming of the Holy Spirit

2 When the day of Pentecost[d] came, they were all together in one place. [2]Suddenly a noise came from heaven. It sounded like a strong wind blowing. This noise filled the whole house where they were sitting. [3]They saw something that looked like flames of fire. The flames were separated and stood over each person there. [4]They were all filled with the Holy Spirit,[d] and they began to speak different languages.[n] The Holy Spirit was giving them the power to speak these languages.

[5]There were some religious Jews staying in Jerusalem who were from every country in the world. [6]When they heard this noise, a crowd came together. They were all surprised, because each one heard them speaking in his own language. [7]They were completely amazed at this. They said, "Look! Aren't all these men that we hear speaking from Galilee?[n] [8]But each of us hears them in his own language. How is this possible? We are from different places: [9]Parthia, Media, Elam, Mesopotamia, Judea, Cappa-

---

languages   This can also be translated "tongues".
from Galilee   The people were surprised because the men from Galilee were speaking other languages and not their own.

docia, Pontus, Asia, [10] Phrygia, Pamphylia, Egypt, the areas of Libya near Cyrene, Rome [11] (both Jews and those who had become Jews), Crete and Arabia. But we hear these men telling in our own languages about the great things God has done!" [12] They were all amazed and confused. They asked each other, "What does this mean?"

[13] But others were making fun of them, saying, "They have had too much wine."

Peter Speaks to the People

[14] But Peter stood up with the 11 apostles.[d] In a loud voice he spoke to the crowd: "My fellow Jews, and all of you who are in Jerusalem, listen to me. Pay attention to what I have to say. [15] These men are not drunk, as you think; it is only nine o'clock in the morning! [16] But Joel the prophet[d] wrote about what is happening here today:

[17] 'God says: In the last days
     I will give my Spirit[d] freely to all
          kinds of people.
     Your sons and daughters will
          prophesy.[d]
     Your old men will dream dreams.
     Your young men will see visions.
[18] At that time I will give my Spirit
          even to my servants, both men
          and women.
     And they will prophesy.
[19] I will show miracles[d]
          in the sky and on the earth:
          blood, fire and thick smoke.
[20] The sun will become dark.
     The moon will become red as
          blood.
     And then the great and glorious
          day of the Lord will come.
[21] Then anyone who asks the Lord
          for help
     will be saved'.   *Joel 2:28–32*

[22] "Men of Israel, listen to these words: Jesus from Nazareth was a very special man. God clearly showed this to you by the miracles,[d] wonders, and signs God did through him. You all know this, because it happened right here among you. [23] Jesus was given to you, and you killed him. With the help of evil men you nailed him to a cross. But God knew all this would happen. This was God's plan which he had made long ago. [24] God raised Jesus from death. God set him free from the pain of death. Death could not hold him. [25] For David said this about him:

'I keep the Lord before me
     always.
     Because he is close by my side,
     I will not be hurt.
[26] So I am glad, and I rejoice.
     Even my body has hope.
[27] This is because you will not leave
          me in the grave.
     You will not let your Holy One
          rot.
[28] You will teach me God's way to
          live.
     Being with you will fill me with
          joy'.   *Psalm 16:8–11*
[29] "Brothers, I can tell you truly about David, our ancestor. He died and was buried. His grave is still here with us today. [30] David was a prophet[d] and knew what God had said. God had promised David that he would make a person from David's family a king just as he was.[n] [31] David knew this before it happened. That is why he said:

'He was not left in the grave.
     His body did not rot'.
David was talking about the Christ[d] rising from death. [32] So Jesus is the One whom God raised from death! And we are all witnesses to this.

God . . . was. See 2 Samuel 7:13; Psalm 132:11.

[33] Jesus was lifted up to heaven and is now at God's right side. The Father has given the Holy Spirit[d] to Jesus as he promised. So now Jesus has poured out that Spirit. This is what you see and hear. [34] David was not the one who was lifted up to heaven. But he said:

'The Lord said to my Lord:

Sit by me at my right side,

[35] until I put your enemies under your control'.[n]   *Psalm 110:1*

[36] "So, all the people of Israel should know this truly: God has made Jesus both Lord and Christ. He is the man you nailed to the cross!"

[37] When the people heard this, they were sick at heart. They asked Peter and the other apostles, "What shall we do?"

[38] Peter said to them, "Change your hearts and lives and be baptised, each one of you, in the name of Jesus Christ for the forgiveness of your sins. And you will receive the gift of the Holy Spirit. [39] This promise is for you. It is also for your children and for all who are far away. It is for everyone the Lord our God calls to himself."

[40] Peter warned them with many other words. He begged them, "Save yourselves from the evil of today's people!" [41] Then those people who accepted what Peter said were baptised. About 3,000 people were added to the number of believers that day. [42] They spent their time learning the apostles' teaching. And they continued to share, to break bread,[n] and to pray together.

The Believers Share

[43] The apostles[d] were doing many miracles[d] and signs. And everyone felt great respect for God. [44] All the believers stayed together. They shared everything. [45] They sold their land and the things they owned. Then they divided the money and gave it to those people who needed it. [46] The believers met together in the Temple[d] every day. They all had the same purpose. They broke bread in their homes, happy to share their food with joyful hearts. [47] They praised God, and all the people liked them. More and more people were being saved every day; the Lord was adding those people to the group of believers.

Peter Heals a Crippled Man

3 One day Peter and John went to the Temple.[d] It was three o'clock in the afternoon. This was the time for the daily prayer service. [2] There, at the Temple gate called Beautiful Gate, was a man who had been crippled all his life. Every day he was carried to this gate to beg. He would ask for money from the people going into the Temple. [3] The man saw Peter and John going into the Temple and asked them for money. [4] Peter and John looked straight at him and said, "Look at us!" [5] The man looked at them; he thought they were going to give him some money. [6] But Peter said, "I don't have any silver or gold, but I do have something else I can give you: by the power of Jesus Christ from Nazareth – stand up and walk!" [7] Then Peter took the man's right hand and lifted him up. Immediately the man's feet and ankles became strong. [8] He jumped up, stood on his feet, and began to walk. He went into the Temple with them, walking and jumping, and praising God. [9-10] All the people recognised him. They knew he was the crippled man

---

until . . . control   Literally, "until I make your enemies a footstool for your feet".
break bread   This may mean a meal as in verse 46, or the Lord's Supper, the special meal Jesus told his followers to eat to remember him (Luke 22:14–20).

MATTHEW 9:21
*"If I can touch his coat,
then I will be healed."*

MARK 4:37–38
A very strong wind came up on the lake. The waves began coming over the sides and into the boat.

LUKE 19:5
"Zacchaeus, hurry and come down! I must stay at your house today."

who always sat by the Beautiful Gate begging for money. Now they saw this same man walking and praising God. The people were amazed. They could not understand how this could happen.

Peter Speaks to the People

[11] The man was holding on to Peter and John. All the people were amazed and ran to Peter and John at Solomon's Porch.[d] [12] When Peter saw this, he said to them, "Men of Israel, why are you surprised? You are looking at us as if it were our own power that made

Acts 3:11–26 Peter speaks to the people.

this man walk. Do you think this happened because we are good? No! [13] The God of Abraham, Isaac and Jacob, the God of our ancestors, gave glory to Jesus, his servant. But you gave him up to be killed. Pilate decided to let him go free. But you told Pilate you did not want Jesus.

[14] He was pure and good, but you said you did not want him. You told Pilate to give you a murderer[n] instead of Jesus. [15] And so you killed the One who gives life! But God raised him from death. We are witnesses to this. [16] It was the power of Jesus that made this crippled man well. This happened because we trusted in the power of Jesus. You can see this man, and you know him. He was made completely well because of trust in Jesus. You all saw it happen!

[17] "Brothers, I know you did those things to Jesus because you did not understand what you were doing. Your leaders did not understand either. [18] God said this would happen. He said through the prophets[d] that his Christ[d] would suffer and die. And now God has made these things come true in this way. [19] So you must change your hearts and lives! Come back to God, and he will forgive your sins. [20] Then the Lord will give you times of spiritual rest. He will give you Jesus, the One he chose to be the Christ. [21] But Jesus must stay in heaven until the time comes when all things will be made right again. God told of this time long ago when he spoke through his holy prophets. [22] Moses said, 'The Lord your God will give you a prophet like me. He will be one of your own people. You must obey everything he tells you. [23] Anyone who does not obey him will die, separated from God's people'.[n] [24] Samuel, and all the other prophets who spoke for God after Samuel, told of this time now. [25] You have received what the prophets talked about. You have received the agreement God made with your ancestors. He said to your father Abraham, 'Through your descendants[d] all the

---

murderer Barabbas, the man the Jews asked Pilate to set free instead of Jesus (Luke 23:18).
'The Lord ... people' Quotation from Deuteronomy 18:15,19 and Leviticus 23:39.

nations on the earth will be blessed'.[n] [26]God has raised up his servant and sent him to you first. He sent Jesus to bless you by turning each of you away from doing evil things."

Peter and John at the Council

4 While Peter and John were speaking to the people, a group of men came up to them. There were Jewish priests, the captain of the soldiers that guarded the Temple,[d] and some Sadducees.[d] [2]They were upset because the two apostles[d] were teaching the people. Peter and John were preaching that people will rise from death through the power of Jesus. [3]The Jewish leaders grabbed Peter and John and put them in jail. It was already night, so they kept them in jail until the next day. [4]But many of those who heard Peter and John preach believed the things they said. There were now about 5,000 men in the group of believers.

[5]The next day the Jewish leaders, the older Jewish leaders, and the teachers of the law met in Jerusalem. [6]Annas the high priest, Caiaphas, John, and Alexander were there. Everyone from the high priest's family was there. [7]They made Peter and John stand before them. The Jewish leaders asked them: "By what power or authority did you do this?"

[8]Then Peter was filled with the Holy Spirit.[d] He said to them, "Rulers of the people and you older leaders, [9]are you questioning us about a good thing that was done to a crippled man? Are you asking us who made him well? [10]We want all of you and all the Jewish people to know that this man was made well by the power of Jesus Christ from Nazareth! You nailed him

to a cross, but God raised him from death. This man was crippled, but he is now well and able to stand here before you because of the power of Jesus! [11]Jesus is

'the stone[n] that you builders did not want.

It has become the cornerstone'.[d]   *Psalm 118:22*

[12]Jesus is the only One who can save people. His name is the only power in the world that has been given to save people. And we must be saved through him!"

[13]The Jewish leaders saw that Peter and John were not afraid to speak. They understood that these men had no special training or education. So they were amazed. Then they realised that Peter and John had been with Jesus. [14]They saw the crippled man standing there beside the two apostles. They saw that the man was healed. So they could say nothing against them. [15]The Jewish leaders told them to leave the meeting. Then the leaders talked to each other about what they should do. [16]They said, "What shall we do with these men? Everyone in Jerusalem knows that they have done a great miracle![d] We cannot say it is not true. [17]But we must warn them not to talk to people any more using that name. Then this thing will not spread among the people."

[18]So they called Peter and John in again. They told them not to speak or to teach at all in the name of Jesus. [19]But Peter and John answered them, "What do you think is right? What would God want? Should we obey you or God? [20]We cannot keep quiet. We must speak about what we have seen and heard." [21-22]The Jewish leaders

---

'Through . . . blessed'   Quotation from Genesis 22:18; 26:24.
stone   A symbol meaning Jesus.

could not find a way to punish them because all the people were praising God for what had been done. (This miracle was a proof from God. The man who was healed was more than 40 years old!) So the Jewish leaders warned the apostles again and let them go free.

The Believers' Prayer

23 Peter and John left the meeting of Jewish leaders and went to their own group. They told them everything that the leading priests and the older Jewish leaders had said to them. 24 When the believers heard this, they prayed to God with one purpose. They prayed, "Lord, you are the One who made the sky, the earth, the sea, and everything in the world. 25 Our father David was your servant. With the help of the Holy Spirit[d] he said:

'Why are the nations so angry?
    Why are the people making
        useless plans?
26 The kings of the earth prepare to
        fight.
    Their leaders make plans
        together
against the Lord
    and against his Christ'.[d]

Psalm 2:1–2

27 These things really happened when Herod, Pontius Pilate, the non-Jewish people, and the Jewish people all came together against Jesus here in Jerusalem. Jesus is your holy Servant. He is the One you made to be the Christ. 28 These people made your plan happen; it happened because of your power and your will. 29 And now, Lord, listen to what they are saying. They are trying to make us afraid! Lord, we are your servants. Help us to speak your word without fear. 30 Help us to be brave by showing us your power; make sick people well, give proofs, and make miracles[d] happen

by the power of Jesus, your holy servant."

31 After they had prayed, the place where they were meeting was shaken. They were all filled with the Holy Spirit,[d] and they spoke God's word without fear.

The Believers Share

32 The group of believers were joined in their hearts, and they had the same spirit. No person in the group said that the things he had were his own. Instead, they shared everything. 33 With great power the apostles[d] were telling people that the Lord Jesus was truly raised from death. And God blessed all the believers greatly. 34 They all received the things they needed. Everyone that owned fields or houses sold them. They brought the money 35 and gave it to the apostles. Then each person was given the things he needed.

36 One of the believers was named Joseph. The apostles called him Barnabas. (This name means "one who encourages".) He was a Levite, born in Cyprus. 37 Joseph owned a field. He sold it, brought the money, and gave it to the apostles.

Ananias and Sapphira

5 A man named Ananias and his wife Sapphira sold some land. 2 But he gave only part of the money to the apostles.[d] He secretly kept some of it for himself. His wife knew about this, and she agreed to it. 3 Peter said, "Ananias, why did you let Satan rule your heart? You lied to the Holy Spirit.[d] Why did you keep part of the money you received for the land for yourself? 4 Before you sold the land, it belonged to you. And even after you sold it, you could have used the money any way you wanted. Why did you think of doing this? You lied to God,

Acts 5:2 He secretly kept some of it for himself.

Proofs from God

[12]The apostles[d] did many signs and miracles[d] among the people. And they would all meet together on Solomon's Porch.[d] [13]None of the others dared to stand with them. All the people were saying good things about them. [14]More and more men and women believed in the Lord and were added to the group of believers. [15]As Peter was passing by, the people brought their sick into the streets. They put their sick on beds and mats so at least Peter's shadow might fall on them. [16]Crowds came from all the towns around Jerusalem. They brought their sick and those who were bothered by evil spirits. All of them were healed.

The Apostles Obey God

[17]The high priest and all his friends (a group called the Sadducees[d]) became very jealous. [18]They took the apostles[d] and put them in jail. [19]But during the night, an angel of the Lord opened the doors of the jail. He led the apostles outside and said, [20]"Go and stand in the Temple.[d] Tell the people everything about this new life." [21]When the apostles heard this, they obeyed and went into the Temple. It was early in the morning, and they began to teach.

The high priest and his friends arrived. They called a meeting of the Jewish leaders and all the important older men of the Jews. They sent some men to the jail to bring the apostles to them. [22]When the men went to the jail, they could not find the apostles. So they went back and told the Jewish leaders about this. [23]They said, "The jail was closed and locked. The guards were standing at the doors. But when we opened the doors, the jail was empty!" [24]Hearing this, the captain of the Temple guards and the leading

not to men!" [5-6]When Ananias heard this, he fell down and died. Some young men came in, wrapped up his body, carried it out, and buried it. And everyone who heard about this was filled with fear.

[7]About three hours later his wife came in. She did not know what had happened. [8]Peter said to her, "Tell me how much money you got for your field. Was it this much?"

Sapphira answered, "Yes, that was the price."

[9]Peter said to her, "Why did you and your husband agree to test the Spirit of the Lord? Look! The men who buried your husband are at the door! They will carry you out." [10]At that moment Sapphira fell down by his feet and died. The young men came in and saw that she was dead. They carried her out and buried her beside her husband. [11]The whole church and all the others who heard about these things were filled with fear.

priests were confused. They wondered, "What will happen because of this?"

25 Then someone came and told them, "Listen! The men you put in jail are standing in the Temple. They are teaching the people!" 26 Then the captain and his men went out and brought the apostles back. But the soldiers did not use force, because they were afraid that the people would kill them with stones.

27 The soldiers brought the apostles to the meeting and made them stand before the Jewish leaders. The high priest questioned them. 28 He said, "We gave you strict orders not to go on teaching in that name. But look what you have done! You have filled Jerusalem with your teaching. You are trying to make us responsible for this man's death."

29 Peter and the other apostles answered, "We must obey God, not men! 30 You killed Jesus. You hung him on a cross. But God, the same God our ancestors had, raised Jesus up from death! 31 Jesus is the One whom God raised to be on his right side. God made Jesus our Leader and Saviour. God did this so that all Jews could change their hearts and lives and have their sins forgiven. 32 We saw all these things happen. The Holy Spirit[d] also proves that these things are true. God has given the Spirit to all who obey him."

33 When the Jewish leaders heard this, they became very angry and wanted to kill them. 34 A Pharisee[d] named Gamaliel stood up in the meeting. He was a teacher of the law, and all the people respected him. He ordered the apostles to leave the meeting for a little while. 35 Then he said to them, "Men of Israel, be careful of what you are planning to do to these men! 36 Remember when Theudas appeared? He said that he was a great man, and about 400 men joined him. But he was killed. And all his followers were scattered. They were able to do nothing. 37 Later, a man named Judas came from Galilee at the time of the registration.[n] He led a group of followers, too. He was also killed, and all his followers were scattered. 38 And so now I tell you: stay away from these men. Leave them alone. If their plan comes from men, it will fail. 39 But if it is from God, you will not be able to stop them. You might even be fighting against God himself!"

The Jewish leaders agreed with what Gamaliel said. 40 They called the apostles in again. They beat the apostles and told them not to speak in the name of Jesus again. Then they let them go free. 41 The apostles left the meeting full of joy because they were given the honour of suffering disgrace for Jesus. 42 The apostles did not stop teaching people. Every day in the Temple and in people's homes they continued to tell the Good News – that Jesus is the Christ.[d]

Seven Men Are Chosen

6 More and more people were becoming followers of Jesus. But during this same time, the Greek-speaking followers had an argument with the other Jewish followers. The Greek-speaking Jews said that their widows were not getting their share of the food that was given out every day. 2 The 12 apostles[d] called the whole group of followers together. They said, "It is not right for us to stop our work of teaching God's word in order to serve tables. 3 So, brothers, choose seven of your own men. They

registration   Census. A counting of all the people and the things they own.

must be men who are good. They must be full of wisdom and full of the Spirit.*d* We will put them in charge of this work. ⁴Then we can use all our time to pray and to teach the word of God."

⁵The whole group liked the idea. So they chose these seven men: Stephen (a man with great faith and full of the Holy Spirit), Philip,*n* Procorus, Nicanor, Timon, Parmenas, and Nicolas (a man from Antioch who had become a Jew). ⁶Then they put these men before the apostles. The apostles prayed and laid their hands on*n* the men.

⁷The word of God was reaching more and more people. The group of followers in Jerusalem became larger and larger. A great number of the Jewish priests believed and obeyed.

Stephen Is Arrested

⁸Stephen was richly blessed by God. God gave him the power to do great miracles*d* and signs among the people. ⁹But some Jews were against him. They belonged to a synagogue*d* of Free Men*n* (as it was called). (This synagogue was also for Jews from Cyrene and from Alexandria.) Jews from Cilicia and Asia were also with them. They all came and argued with Stephen. ¹⁰But the Spirit*d* was helping him to speak with wisdom. His words were so strong that the Jews could not argue with him. ¹¹So they paid some men to say, "We heard him say things against Moses and against God!"

¹²This upset the people, the older Jewish leaders, and the teachers of the law. They came to Stephen, grabbed

him and brought him to a meeting of the Jewish leaders. ¹³They brought in some men to tell lies about Stephen. They said, "This man is always saying things against this holy place and the law of Moses. ¹⁴We heard him say that Jesus from Nazareth will destroy this place. He also said that Jesus will change the things that Moses told us to do." ¹⁵All the people in the meeting were watching Stephen closely. His face looked like the face of an angel.

Stephen's Speech

7 The high priest said to Stephen, "Are these things true?"

²Stephen answered, "Brothers and fathers, listen to me. Our glorious God appeared to Abraham, our ancestor. Abraham was in Mesopotamia before he lived in Haran. ³God said to Abraham, 'Leave your country and your relatives. Go to the land I will show you'.*n* ⁴So Abraham left the country of Chaldea and went to live in Haran. After Abraham's father died, God sent him to this place where you now live. ⁵God did not give Abraham any of this land, not even a foot of it. But God promised that he would give him and his descendants*d* this land. (This was before Abraham had any descendants.) ⁶This is what God said to him: 'Your descendants will be strangers in a land they don't own. The people there will make them slaves. And they will do cruel things to them for 400 years. ⁷But I will punish the nation where they are slaves. Then your descendants will leave that land. Then they will worship me in this place'.*n* ⁸God made an agreement with Abraham; the sign for this agreement was

---

Philip Not the apostle named Philip.
laid their hands on Here, doing this showed that these men were given a special work of God.
Free Men Jews who had been slaves or whose fathers had been slaves, but were now free.
'Leave ... you' Quotation from Genesis 12:1.
'Your descendants ... place' Quotation from Genesis 15:13–14 and Exodus 12.

circumcision.[d] And so when Abraham had his son Isaac, Abraham circumcised him when he was eight days old. Isaac also circumcised his son Jacob. And Jacob did the same for his sons, the 12 ancestors[n] of our people.

9 "These sons became jealous of Joseph. They sold him to be a slave in Egypt. But God was with him. 10 Joseph had many troubles there, but God saved him from all those troubles. The king of Egypt liked Joseph and respected him because of the wisdom that God gave him. The king made him governor of Egypt. He put Joseph in charge of all the people in his palace.

11 "Then all the land of Egypt and of Canaan became so dry that nothing would grow there. This made the people suffer greatly. The sons could not find anything to eat. 12 But when Jacob heard that there was grain in Egypt, he sent his sons, our ancestors, there. This was their first trip to Egypt. 13 Then they went there a second time. This time, Joseph told his brothers who he was. And the king learned about Joseph's family. 14 Then Joseph sent some men to invite Jacob, his father, to come to Egypt. He also invited all his relatives (75 persons altogether). 15 So Jacob went down to Egypt, where he and his sons died. 16 Later their bodies were moved to Shechem and put in a grave there. (It was the same grave that Abraham had bought in Shechem from the sons of Hamor for a sum of money.)

17 "The number of people in Egypt grew large. There were more and more of our people there. (The promise that God made to Abraham was soon to come true.) 18 Then a new king began to rule Egypt. He did not know who Joseph was. 19 This king tricked our people and was cruel to our ancestors. He forced them to put their babies outside to die. 20 This was the time when Moses was born. He was a fine child. For three months Moses was cared for in his father's house. 21 When they put Moses outside, the king's daughter took him. She raised him as if he were her own son. 22 The Egyptians taught Moses all the things they knew. He was a powerful man in the things he said and did.

23 "When Moses was about 40 years old, he thought it would be good to visit his brothers, the people of Israel. 24 Moses saw an Egyptian doing wrong to a Jew. So he defended the Jew and punished the Egyptian for hurting him. Moses killed the Egyptian. 25 Moses thought that his fellow Jews would understand that God was using him to save them. But they did not understand. 26 The next day, Moses saw two Jewish men fighting. He tried to make peace between them. He said, 'Men, you are brothers! Why are you hurting each other?' 27 The man who was hurting the other man pushed Moses away. He said, 'Who made you our ruler and judge? 28 Are you going to kill me as you killed the Egyptian yesterday?'[n] 29 When Moses heard him say this, he left Egypt. He went to live in the land of Midian where he was a stranger. While Moses lived in Midian, he had two sons.

30 "After 40 years Moses was in the desert near Mount Sinai. An angel appeared to him in the flames of a burning bush. 31 When Moses saw this, he was amazed. He went near to look closer at it. Moses heard the Lord's voice. 32 The Lord said, 'I am the God of your ancestors. I am the

---

12 ancestors   Important ancestors of the Jews; the leaders of the 12 Jewish tribes.
'Who . . . yesterday?'   Quotation from Exodus 2:14.

God of Abraham, Isaac and Jacob'.[n] Moses began to shake with fear and was afraid to look. [33]The Lord said to him, 'Take off your sandals. You are standing on holy ground. [34]I have seen the troubles my people have suffered in Egypt. I have heard their cries. I have come down to save them. And now, Moses, I am sending you back to Egypt'.[n]

[35]"This Moses was the same man the Jews said they did not want. They had said to him, 'Who made you our ruler and judge?'[n] Moses is the same man God sent to be a ruler and saviour, with the help of an angel. This was the angel Moses saw in the burning bush. [36]So Moses led the people out of Egypt. He worked miracles[d] and signs in Egypt, at the Red Sea,[d] and then in the desert for 40 years. [37]This is the same Moses that said to the Jewish people: 'God will give you a prophet[d] like me. He will be one of your own people'.[n] [38]This is the same Moses who was with the gathering of the Jews in the desert. He was with the angel that spoke to him at Mount Sinai, and he was with our ancestors. He received commands from God that give life, and he gave those commands to us.

[39]"But our fathers did not want to obey Moses. They rejected him. They wanted to go back to Egypt again. [40]They said to Aaron, 'Moses led us out of Egypt. But we don't know what has happened to him. So make us gods who will lead us'.[n] [41]So the people made an idol that looked like a calf. Then they brought sacrifices to it. The people were proud of what they had made with their own hands! [42]But God turned against them. He did not try to stop them from worshipping the sun, moon and stars. This is what is written in the book of the prophets: God says,

'People of Israel, you did not bring
me sacrifices and offerings
while you travelled in the desert
for 40 years.
[43]But now you will have to carry
with you
the tent to worship the false god
Molech[d]
and the idols of the star god
Rephan that you made to
worship.
This is because I will send you
away beyond Babylon'.
Amos 5:25–27

[44]"The Holy Tent[d] where God spoke to our fathers was with the Jews in the desert. God told Moses how to make this Tent. He made it like the plan God showed him. [45]Later, Joshua led our fathers to capture the lands of the other nations. Our people went in, and God drove the other people out. When our people went into this new land, they took with them this same Tent. They received this Tent from their fathers and kept it until the time of David. [46]God was very pleased with David. He asked God to let him build a house for him, the God of Jacob. [47]But Solomon was the one who built the Temple.[d]

[48]"But the Most High does not live in houses that men build with their hands. This is what the prophet says:
[49]'Heaven is my throne.
The earth is my footstool.
So do you think you can build a
house for me? says the Lord.

'I am . . . Jacob' Quotation from Exodus 3:6.
'Take . . . Egypt' Quotation from Exodus 3:5–10.
'Who . . . judge?' Quotation from Exodus 2:14.
'God . . . people' Quotation from Deuteronomy 18:15.
'Moses . . . us' Quotation from Exodus 32:1.

There is no place where I need to rest.
⁵⁰ Remember, I made all these things!' "   *Isaiah 66:1–2*

⁵¹ Stephen continued speaking: "You stubborn Jewish leaders! You have not given your hearts to God! You won't listen to him! You are always against what the Holy Spirit*ᵈ* is trying to tell you. Your ancestors were like this, and you are just like them! ⁵² Your fathers tried to hurt every prophet who ever lived. Those prophets said long ago that the Righteous One would come. But your fathers killed them. And now you have turned against the Righteous One and killed him. ⁵³ You received the law of Moses, which God gave you through his angels. But you don't obey it!"

Stephen Is Killed

⁵⁴ When the Jewish leaders heard Stephen saying all these things, they became very angry. They were so angry that they were grinding their teeth at Stephen. ⁵⁵ But Stephen was full of the Holy Spirit.*ᵈ* He looked up to heaven and saw the glory of God. He saw Jesus standing at God's right side. ⁵⁶ He said, "Look! I see heaven open. And I see the Son of Man*ᵈ* standing at God's right side!"

⁵⁷ Then the Jewish leaders all shouted loudly. They covered their ears with their hands and all ran at Stephen. ⁵⁸ They took him out of the city and threw stones at him until he was dead. The men who told lies against Stephen left their coats with a young man named Saul. ⁵⁹ While they were throwing stones, Stephen prayed, "Lord Jesus, receive my spirit!" ⁶⁰ He fell on his knees and cried in a loud voice, "Lord, do not hold this sin against them!" After Stephen said this, he died.

8 Saul agreed that the killing of Stephen was a good thing.

Trouble for the Believers

²⁻³ Some religious men buried Stephen. They cried very loudly for him. On that day the Jews began trying to hurt the church in Jerusalem. The Jews made them suffer very much. Saul was also trying to destroy the church. He went from house to house. He dragged out men and women and put them in jail. All the believers, except the apostles,*ᵈ* went to different places in Judea and Samaria. ⁴ And everywhere they were scattered, they told people the Good News.*ᵈ*

Acts 7:58 They took him out of the city and threw stones at him until he was dead.

Philip Preaches in Samaria

[5] Philip[n] went to the city of Samaria and preached about the Christ.[d] [6] The people there heard Philip and saw the miracles[d] he was doing. They all listened carefully to the things he said. [7] Many of these people had evil spirits in them. But Philip made the evil spirits leave them. The spirits made a loud noise when they came out. There were also many weak and crippled people there. Philip healed them, too. [8] So the people in that city were very happy.

[9] But there was a man named Simon in that city. Before Philip came there, Simon had practised magic. He amazed all the people of Samaria with his magic. He boasted and called himself a great man. [10] All the people – the least important and the most important – paid attention to what Simon said. They said, "This man has the power of God, called 'the Great Power'!" [11] Simon had amazed them with his magic tricks so long that the people became his followers. [12] But Philip told them the Good News[d] about the kingdom of God and the power of Jesus Christ. Men and women believed Philip and were baptised. [13] Simon himself believed and was baptised. He stayed very close to Philip. When he saw the miracles and the very powerful things that Philip did, Simon was amazed.

[14] The apostles[d] were still in Jerusalem. They heard that the people of Samaria had accepted the word of God. So they sent Peter and John to them. [15] When Peter and John arrived, they prayed that the Samaritan believers might receive the Holy Spirit.[d] [16] These people had been baptised in the name of the Lord Jesus. But the Holy Spirit had not yet entered any of them. [17] Then, when the two apostles began laying their hands on[n] the people, they received the Holy Spirit.

[18] Simon saw that the Spirit was given to people when the apostles laid their hands on them. So he offered the apostles money. [19] He said, "Give me also this power so that when I lay my hands on a person, he will receive the Holy Spirit."

[20] Peter said to him, "You and your money should both be destroyed! You thought you could buy God's gift with money. [21] You cannot share with us in this work. Your heart is not right before God. [22] Change your heart! Turn away from this evil thing you have done. Pray to the Lord. Maybe he will forgive you for thinking this. [23] I see that you are full of bitter jealousy and ruled by sin."

[24] Simon answered, "Both of you pray for me to the Lord. Pray that the things you have said will not happen to me!"

[25] Then the two apostles told the people the things they had seen Jesus do. And after the apostles had given the message of the Lord, they went back to Jerusalem. On the way, they went through many Samaritan towns and preached the Good News to the people.

Philip Teaches an Ethiopian

[26] An angel of the Lord spoke to Philip. The angel said, "Get ready and go south. Go to the road that leads down to Gaza from Jerusalem – the desert road." [27] So Philip got ready and went. On the road he saw a man from

Philip   Not the apostle named Philip.
laying their hands on   Here, doing this showed that these men were given a special work of God.

Ethiopia, a eunuch.[d] He was an important officer in the service of Candace, the queen of the Ethiopians. He was responsible for taking care of all her money. He had gone to Jerusalem to worship, and [28] now he was on his way home. He was sitting in his chariot and reading from the book of Isaiah, the prophet.[d] [29] The Spirit[d] said to Philip, "Go to that chariot and stay near it."

[30] So Philip ran toward the chariot. He heard the man reading from Isaiah, the prophet. Philip asked, "Do you understand what you are reading?"

[31] He answered, "How can I understand? I need someone to explain it to me!" Then he invited Philip to climb

Acts 8:31 He invited Philip to climb in and sit with him.

in and sit with him. [32] The verse of Scripture[d] that he was reading was this:

"He was like a sheep being led to be killed.

He was quiet, as a sheep is quiet while its wool is being cut.

He said nothing.
[33]   He was shamed and was treated unfairly.

He died without children to continue his family.

His life on earth has ended."

Isaiah 53:7–8

[34] The officer said to Philip, "Please tell me, who is the prophet talking about? Is he talking about himself or about someone else?" [35] Philip began to speak. He started with this same Scripture and told the man the Good News[d] about Jesus.

[36] While they were travelling down the road, they came to some water. The officer said, "Look! Here is water! What is stopping me from being baptised?" [37 n] [38] Then the officer commanded the chariot to stop. Both Philip and the officer went down into the water, and Philip baptised him. [39] When they came up out of the water, the Spirit of the Lord took Philip away; the officer never saw him again. The officer continued on his way home, full of joy. [40] But Philip appeared in a city called Azotus and preached the Good News in all the towns on the way from Azotus to Caesarea.

Saul Is Converted

9 In Jerusalem Saul was still trying to frighten the followers of the Lord by saying he would kill them. So he went to the high priest [2] and asked him to write letters to the synagogues[d] in the city of Damascus. Saul wanted the high priest to give him the authority to find people in Damascus who

---

Verse 37 Some late copies of Acts add verse 37: "Philip answered, 'If you believe with all your heart, you can'. The officer said, 'I believe that Jesus Christ is the Son of God'."

were followers of Christ's Way. If he found any there, men or women, he would arrest them and bring them back to Jerusalem.

[3] So Saul went to Damascus. As he came near the city, a bright light from heaven suddenly flashed around him. [4] Saul fell to the ground. He heard a voice saying to him, "Saul, Saul! Why are you doing things against me?"

[5] Saul said, "Who are you, Lord?"

The voice answered, "I am Jesus. I am the One you are trying to hurt. [6] Get up now and go into the city. Someone there will tell you what you must do."

[7] The men travelling with Saul stood there, but they said nothing. They heard the voice, but they saw no one. [8] Saul got up from the ground. He opened his eyes, but he could not see. So the men with Saul took his hand and led him into Damascus. [9] For three days Saul could not see, and he did not eat or drink.

[10] There was a follower of Jesus in Damascus named Ananias. The Lord spoke to Ananias in a vision, "Ananias!"

Ananias answered, "Here I am, Lord."

[11] The Lord said to him, "Get up and go to the street called Straight Street. Find the house of Judas.[n] Ask for a man named Saul from the city of Tarsus. He is there now, praying. [12] Saul has seen a vision. In it a man named Ananias comes to him and lays his hands on him. Then he sees again."

[13] But Ananias answered, "Lord, many people have told me about this man and the terrible things he did to your people in Jerusalem. [14] Now he has come here to Damascus. The leading priests have given him the power to arrest everyone who worships you."

[15] But the Lord said to Ananias, "Go! I have chosen Saul for an important work. He must make me known to non-Jews, to kings, and to the people of Israel. [16] I will show him how much he must suffer for my name."

[17] So Ananias went to the house of Judas. He laid his hands on Saul and said, "Brother Saul, the Lord Jesus sent me. He is the one you saw on the road on your way here. He sent me so that you can see again and be filled with the Holy Spirit."[d] [18] Immediately, something that looked like fish scales fell from Saul's eyes. He was able to see again! Then Saul got up and was baptised. [19] After eating some food, his strength returned.

Saul Preaches in Damascus

Saul stayed with the followers of Jesus in Damascus for a few days. [20] Soon he began to preach about Jesus in the synagogues,[d] saying, "Jesus is the Son of God!"

[21] All the people who heard him were amazed. They said, "This is the man who was in Jerusalem. He was trying to destroy those who trust in this name! He came here to do the same thing. He came here to arrest the followers of Jesus and take them back to the leading priests."

[22] But Saul became more and more powerful. His proofs that Jesus is the Christ[d] were so strong that the Jews in Damascus could not argue with him.

Saul Escapes from Damascus

[23] After many days, the Jews made plans to kill Saul. [24] They were watching the city gates day and night. They wanted to kill him, but Saul learned about their plan. [25] One night some followers of Saul helped him leave the

---

Judas   This is not either of the apostles named Judas.

city. They lowered him in a basket through an opening in the city wall.

Saul in Jerusalem

²⁶Then Saul went to Jerusalem. He tried to join the group of followers, but they were all afraid of him. They did not believe that he was really a follower. ²⁷But Barnabas accepted Saul and took him to the apostles.ᵈ Barnabas told them that Saul had seen the Lord on the road. He explained how the Lord had spoken to Saul. Then he told them how boldly Saul had preached in the name of Jesus in Damascus.

²⁸And so Saul stayed with the followers. He went everywhere in Jerusalem, preaching boldly in the name of Jesus. ²⁹He would often talk and argue with the Jews who spoke Greek. But they were trying to kill him. ³⁰When the brothers learned about this, they took Saul to Caesarea. From there they sent him to Tarsus.

³¹The church everywhere in Judea, Galilee, and Samaria had a time of peace. With the help of the Holy Spirit,ᵈ the group became stronger. The believers showed that they respected the Lord by the way they lived. Because of this, the group of believers grew larger and larger.

Peter Heals Aeneas

³²As Peter was travelling through all the area, he visited God's people who lived in Lydda. ³³There he met a paralysed man named Aeneas. Aeneas had not been able to leave his bed for the past eight years. ³⁴Peter said to him, "Aeneas, Jesus Christ heals you. Stand up and make your bed!" Aeneas stood up immediately. ³⁵All the people living in Lydda and on the Plain of Sharon saw him. These people turned to the Lord.

Peter in Joppa

³⁶In the city of Joppa there was a follower named Tabitha. (Her Greek name, Dorcas, means "a deer".) She was always doing good and helping the poor. ³⁷While Peter was in Lydda, Tabitha became sick and died. Her body was washed and put in a room upstairs. ³⁸The followers in Joppa heard that Peter was in Lydda. (Lydda is near Joppa.) So they sent two men to Peter. They begged him, "Hurry, please come to us!" ³⁹Peter got ready and went with them. When he arrived, they took him to the upstairs room. All the widows stood around Peter, crying. They showed him the shirts and coats that Tabitha had made when she was still alive. ⁴⁰Peter sent everyone out of the room. He kneeled and prayed. Then he turned to the body and said, "Tabitha, stand up!" She opened her eyes, and when she saw Peter, she sat up. ⁴¹He gave her his hand and helped her up. Then he called the saintsᵈ and the widows into the room. He showed them Tabitha; she was alive! ⁴²People everywhere in Joppa learned about this, and many believed in the Lord. ⁴³Peter stayed in Joppa for many days with a man named Simon who was a leatherworker.

Peter and Cornelius

10 At Caesarea there was a man named Cornelius. He was an officer in the Italian group of the Roman army. ²Cornelius was a religious man. He and all the other people who lived in his house worshipped the true God. He gave much of his money to the poor and prayed to God often. ³One afternoon about three o'clock, Cornelius saw a vision clearly. In the vision an angel of God came to him and said, "Cornelius!"

⁴Cornelius stared at the angel. He became afraid and said, "What do you want, Lord?"

The angel said, "God has heard your prayers. He has seen what you give to the poor. And God remembers you. ⁵Send some men now to Joppa to bring back a man named Simon. Simon is also called Peter. ⁶Simon is staying with a man, also named Simon, who is a leatherworker. He has a house beside the sea." ⁷Then the angel who spoke to Cornelius left. Cornelius called two of his servants and a soldier. The soldier was a religious man who worked for Cornelius. ⁸Cornelius explained everything to these three men and sent them to Joppa.

⁹The next day as they came near Joppa, Peter was going up to the roof^n to pray. It was about noon. ¹⁰Peter was hungry and wanted to eat. But while the food was being prepared, he had a vision. ¹¹He saw heaven opened and something coming down. It looked like a big sheet being lowered to earth by its four corners. ¹²In it were all kinds of animals, reptiles, and birds. ¹³Then a voice said to Peter, "Get up, Peter; kill and eat."

¹⁴But Peter said, "No, Lord! I have never eaten food that is unholy or unclean."^{d}

¹⁵But the voice said to him again, "God has made these things clean. Don't call them 'unholy'!" ¹⁶This happened three times. Then the sheet was taken back to heaven.

¹⁷While Peter was wondering what this vision meant, the men Cornelius sent had found Simon's house. They were standing at the gate. ¹⁸They asked, "Is Simon Peter staying here?"

¹⁹Peter was still thinking about the vision. But the Spirit^d said to him, "Listen! Three men are looking for you. ²⁰Get up and go downstairs. Go with them and don't ask questions. I have sent them to you."

²¹So Peter went down to the men. He said, "I am the man you are looking for. Why have you come here?"

²²They said, "A holy angel spoke to Cornelius, an army officer. He is a good man; he worships God. All the Jewish people respect him. The angel told Cornelius to ask you to his house so that he can hear what you have to say." ²³Peter asked the men to come in and spend the night.

The next day Peter got ready and went with them. Some of the brothers from Joppa joined him. ²⁴On the following day they came to Caesarea. Cornelius was waiting for them. He had called together his relatives and close friends. ²⁵When Peter entered, Cornelius met him. He fell at Peter's feet and worshipped him. ²⁶But Peter helped him up, saying, "Stand up! I too am only a man." ²⁷Peter went on talking with Cornelius as they went inside. There Peter saw many people together. ²⁸He said, "You people understand that it is against our Jewish law for a Jew to associate with or visit anyone who is not a Jew. But God has shown me that I should not call any person 'unholy' or 'unclean'. ²⁹That is why I did not argue when I was asked to come here. Now, please tell me why you sent for me."

³⁰Cornelius said, "Four days ago, I was praying in my house. It was at this same time – three o'clock in the afternoon. Suddenly, there was a man standing before me wearing shining

---

roof In Bible times houses were built with flat roofs. The roof was used for drying things such as flax and fruit. It was also used as an extra room, as a place for worship and as a place to sleep in the summer.

clothes. [31]He said, 'Cornelius! God has heard your prayer. He has seen what you give to the poor. And God remembers you. [32]So send some men to Joppa and ask Simon Peter to come. Peter is staying in the house of a man, also named Simon, who is a leather-worker. His house is beside the sea'. [33]So I sent for you immediately, and it was very good of you to come. Now we are all here before God to hear everything the Lord has commanded you to tell us."

Peter's Speech

[34]Peter began to speak: "I really understand now that to God every person is the same. [35]God accepts any-one who worships him and does what is right. It is not important what country a person comes from. [36]You know that God has sent his message to the people of Israel. That message is the Good News[d] that peace has come through Jesus Christ. Jesus is the Lord of all people! [37]You know what has happened all over Judea. It began in Galilee after John[n] preached to the people about baptism. [38]You know about Jesus from Nazareth. God made him the Christ[d] by giving him the Holy Spirit[d] and power. You know how Jesus went everywhere doing good. He healed those who were ruled by the devil, for God was with Jesus. [39]We saw all the things that Jesus did in Judea and in Jerusalem. But they killed him by nailing him to a cross. [40]Yet, on the third day, God raised Jesus to life and caused him to be seen. [41]But he was not seen by all the people. Only the witnesses that God had already chosen saw him, and we are those witnesses. We ate and drank with him after he was raised from

death. [42]He told us to preach to the people and to tell them that he is the one whom God chose to be the judge of the living and the dead. [43]Everyone who believes in Jesus will be forgiven. God will forgive his sins through Jesus. All the prophets[d] say this is true."

Non-Jews Receive the Holy Spirit

[44]While Peter was still saying this, the Holy Spirit[d] came down on all those who were listening. [45]The Jew-ish believers who came with Peter were amazed that the gift of the Holy Spirit had been given even to the non-Jewish people. [46]These Jewish be-lievers heard them speaking in different languages[n] and praising God. Then Peter said, [47]"Can anyone keep these people from being baptised with water? They have received the Holy Spirit just as we did!" [48]So Peter ordered that they be baptised in the name of Jesus Christ. Then they asked Peter to stay with them for a few days.

Peter Returns to Jerusalem

11 The apostles[d] and the believers in Judea heard that non-Jewish people had accepted God's teaching too. [2]But when Peter came to Jerusa-lem, some Jewish believers argued with him. [3]They said, "You went into the homes of people who are not Jews and are not circumcised![d] You even ate with them!"

[4]So Peter explained the whole story to them. [5]He said, "I was in the city of Joppa. While I was praying, I had a vision. In the vision, I saw something which looked like a big sheet coming down from heaven. It was being low-ered to earth by its four corners. It came down very close to me, and [6]I

John John the Baptist, who preached to people about Christ's coming (Matthew 3, Luke 3).
languages This can also be translated "tongues".

looked inside it. I saw animals, wild beasts, reptiles, and birds. [7] I heard a voice say to me, 'Get up, Peter. Kill and eat'. [8] But I said, 'No, Lord! I have never eaten anything that is unholy or unclean'.[d] [9] But the voice from heaven answered again, 'God has made these things clean. Don't call them unholy!' [10] This happened three times. Then the whole thing was taken back to heaven. [11] Right then three men came to the house where I was staying. They were sent to me from Caesarea. [12] The Spirit[d] told me to go with them without doubting. These six believers here also went with me. We went to the house of Cornelius. [13] He told us about the angel he saw standing in his house. The angel said to him, 'Send some men to Joppa and invite Simon Peter to come. [14] He will speak to you. The things he will say will save you and all your family'. [15] When I began my speech, the Holy Spirit came on them just as he came on us at the beginning. [16] Then I remembered the words of the Lord. He said, 'John baptised in water, but you will be baptised in the Holy Spirit!' [17] God gave to them the same gift that he gave to us who believed in the Lord Jesus Christ. So could I stop the work of God? No!"

[18] When the Jewish believers heard this, they stopped arguing. They praised God and said, "So God is allowing the non-Jewish people also to turn to him and live."

The Good News Comes to Antioch

[19] Many of the believers were scattered by the terrible things that happened after Stephen was killed. Some of them went to places as far away as Phoenicia, Cyprus, and Antioch. They were telling the message to others, but only to Jews. [20] Some of these believers were men from Cyprus and Cyrene. When they came to Antioch, they spoke also to Greeks, telling them the Good News[d] about the Lord Jesus. [21] The Lord was helping the believers. And a large group of people believed and turned to the Lord.

[22] The church in Jerusalem heard about all of this, so they sent Barnabas to Antioch. [23-24] Barnabas was a good man, full of the Holy Spirit[d] and full of faith. When he reached Antioch and saw how God had blessed the people, he was glad. He encouraged all the believers in Antioch. He told them, "Never lose your faith. Always obey the Lord with all your hearts." Many people became followers of the Lord.

[25] Then Barnabas went to the city of Tarsus to look for Saul. [26] When he found Saul, he brought him to Antioch. And for a whole year Saul and

Acts 11:6 "I saw animals, wild beasts, reptiles, and birds."

Barnabas met with the church. They taught many people there. In Antioch the followers were called Christians for the first time.

[27] About that time some prophets[d] came from Jerusalem to Antioch. [28] One of them was named Agabus. He stood up and spoke with the help of the Holy Spirit. He said, "A very hard time is coming to the whole world. There will be no food for people to eat." (This happened when Claudius ruled.) [29] The followers all decided to help their brothers who lived in Judea. Each one planned to send them as much as he could. [30] They gathered the money and gave it to Barnabas and Saul, who brought it to the elders[d] in Judea.

Herod Agrippa Hurts the Church

12 During that same time King Herod began to do terrible things to some who belonged to the church. [2] He ordered James, the brother of John, to be killed by the sword. [3] Herod saw that the Jews liked this, so he decided to arrest Peter, too. (This happened during the time of the Feast[d] of Unleavened Bread.)

[4] After Herod arrested Peter, he put him in jail and handed him over to be guarded by 16 soldiers. Herod planned to bring Peter before the people for trial after the Passover[d] Feast. [5] So Peter was kept in jail. But the church kept on praying to God for him.

Peter Leaves the Jail

[6] The night before Herod was to bring him to trial, Peter was sleeping. He was between two soldiers, bound with two chains. Other soldiers were guarding the door of the jail. [7] Suddenly, an angel of the Lord stood there. A light shined in the room. The angel touched Peter on the side and

woke him up. The angel said, "Hurry! Get up!" And the chains fell off Peter's hands. [8] The angel said to him, "Get dressed and put on your sandals." And so Peter did this. Then the angel said, "Put on your coat and follow me." [9] So the angel went out, and Peter followed him. Peter did not know if what the angel was doing was real. He thought he might be seeing a vision. [10] They went past the first and the second guard. They came to the iron gate that separated them from the city. The gate opened itself for them. They went through the gate and walked down a street. And the angel suddenly left him.

[11] Then Peter realised what had happened. He thought, "Now I know that the Lord really sent his angel to me. He rescued me from Herod and from all the things the Jewish people thought would happen."

[12] When he realised this, he went to the home of Mary. She was the mother of John. (John was also called Mark.) Many people were gathered there, praying. [13] Peter knocked on the outside door. A servant girl named Rhoda came to answer it. [14] She recognised Peter's voice, and she was very happy. She even forgot to open the door. She ran inside and told the group, "Peter is at the door!"

[15] They said to her, "You are insane!" But she kept on saying that it was true. So they said, "It must be Peter's angel."

[16] Peter continued to knock. When they opened the door, they saw him and were amazed. [17] Peter made a sign with his hand to tell them to be quiet. He explained how the Lord led him out of the jail. And he said, "Tell James and the other believers what happened." Then he left to go to another place.

[18] The next day the soldiers were

very upset. They wondered what had happened to Peter. [19] Herod looked everywhere for Peter but could not find him. So he questioned the guards and ordered that they be killed.

The Death of Herod Agrippa

Later Herod moved from Judea and went to the city of Caesarea, where he stayed for a while. [20] Herod was very angry with the people of Tyre and Sidon. But the people of those cities all came in a group to Herod. They were able to get Blastus, the king's personal servant, on their side. They asked Herod for peace because their country got its food from his country.

[21] On a chosen day Herod put on his royal robes. He sat on his throne and made a speech to the people. [22] They shouted, "This is the voice of a god, not a man!" [23] Herod did not give the glory to God. So an angel of the Lord caused him to become sick. He was eaten by worms and died.

[24] God's message continued to spread and reach more and more people.

[25] After Barnabas and Saul finished their task in Jerusalem, they returned to Antioch. John, also called Mark, was with them.

Barnabas and Saul Are Chosen

13 In the church at Antioch there were these prophets[d] and teachers: Barnabas, Simeon (also called Niger), Lucius (from the city of Cyrene), Manaen (who had grown up with Herod, the ruler) and Saul. [2] They were all worshipping the Lord and giving up eating.[n] The Holy Spirit[d] said to them, "Give Barnabas and Saul to

me to do a special work. I have chosen them for it."

[3] So they gave up eating and prayed. They laid their hands on[n] Barnabas and Saul and sent them out.

Barnabas and Saul in Cyprus

[4] Barnabas and Saul were sent out by the Holy Spirit.[d] They went to the city of Seleucia. From there they sailed to the island of Cyprus. [5] When they came to Salamis, they preached the Good News[d] of God in the Jewish synagogues.[d] John Mark was with them to help.

[6] They went across the whole island to Paphos. In Paphos they met a Jew who was a magician. His name was Bar-Jesus. He was a false prophet,[d] [7] who always stayed close to Sergius Paulus, the governor. Sergius Paulus was a clever man. He asked Barnabas and Saul to come to him, because he wanted to hear the message of God. [8] But Elymas, the magician, was against them. (Elymas is the name for Bar-Jesus in the Greek language.) He tried to stop the governor from believing in Jesus. [9] But Saul was filled with the Holy Spirit. (Saul's other name was Paul.) He looked straight at Elymas [10] and said, "You son of the devil! You are an enemy of everything that is right! You are full of evil tricks and lies. You are always trying to change the Lord's truths into lies! [11] Now the Lord will touch you, and you will be blind. For a time you will not be able to see anything – not even the light from the sun."

Then everything became dark for Elymas. He walked around, trying to find someone to lead him by the hand.

---

giving up eating This is called "fasting". The people would give up eating for a special time of prayer and worship to God. It was also done to show sadness.
laid their hands on Here, this was a sign to show that these men were given a special work of God.

[12] When the governor saw this, he believed. He was amazed at the teaching about the Lord.

Paul and Barnabas Leave Cyprus

[13] Paul and those with him sailed away from Paphos. They came to Perga, in Pamphylia. But John Mark left them and returned to Jerusalem. [14] They continued their trip from Perga and went to Antioch, a city in Pisidia. On the Sabbath[d] day they went into the synagogue[d] and sat down. [15] The law of Moses and the writings of the prophets[d] were read. Then the leaders of the synagogue sent a message to Paul and Barnabas: "Brothers, if you have any message that will encourage the people, please speak!"

[16] Paul stood up. He raised his hand and said, "Men of Israel and you other people who worship God, please listen! [17] The God of the people of Israel chose our ancestors. He made the people great during the time they lived in Egypt. He brought them out of that country with great power. [18] And he was patient with them for 40 years in the desert. [19] God destroyed seven nations in the land of Canaan and gave the land to his people. [20] All this happened in about 450 years.

"After this, God gave them judges until the time of Samuel the prophet. [21] Then the people asked for a king. God gave them Saul son of Kish. Saul was from the tribe[d] of Benjamin. He was king for 40 years. [22] After God took him away, God made David their king. This is what God said about him: 'I have found David son of Jesse. He is the kind of man I want. He will do all that I want him to do'. [23] So God has brought one of David's descendants[d] to Israel to be their Saviour.[d] That descendant is Jesus. And God

promised to do this. [24] Before Jesus came, John[n] preached to all the people of Israel. He told them about a baptism of changed hearts and lives. [25] When he was finishing his work, he said, 'Who do you think I am? I am not the Christ.[d] He is coming later. I am not worthy to untie his sandals'.

[26] "Brothers, sons in the family of Abraham, and you non-Jews who worship God, listen! The news about this salvation has been sent to us. [27] Those who live in Jerusalem and their leaders did not realise that Jesus was the Saviour. They did not understand the words that the prophets wrote, which are read every Sabbath[d] day. But they made them come true when they said Jesus was guilty. [28] They could not find any real reason for Jesus to die, but they asked Pilate to have him killed. [29] They did to him all that the Scriptures[d] had said. Then they took him down from the cross and laid him in a tomb. [30] But God raised him up from death! [31] After this, for many days, the people who had gone with Jesus from Galilee to Jerusalem saw him. They are now his witnesses to the people. [32] We tell you the Good News[d] about the promise God made to our ancestors. [33] We are their children, and God has made this promise come true for us. God did this by raising Jesus from death. We read about this also in Psalm 2:

'You are my Son.
    Today I have become your
        Father'.   *Psalm 2:7*

[34] God raised Jesus from death. He will never go back to the grave and become dust. So God said:

'I will give you the holy and sure
        blessings
    that I promised to David'.
                            Isaiah 55:3

John   John the Baptist, who preached to people about Christ's coming (Matthew 3, Luke 3).

[35] But in another place God says:

'You will not let your Holy One
    rot in the grave'.   *Psalm 16:10*

[36] David did God's will during his lifetime. Then he died and was buried with his fathers. And his body did rot in the grave! [37] But the One God raised from death did not rot in the grave. [38-39] Brothers, you must understand what we are telling you: you can have forgiveness of your sins through Jesus. The law of Moses could not free you from your sins. But everyone who believes is free from all sins through him. [40] Be careful! Don't let what the prophets said happen to you:

[41] 'Listen, you people who doubt!

You can wonder, and then die.

I will do something in your
    lifetime that will amaze you.

You won't believe it even when
    you are told about it!' "

Habakkuk 1:5

[42] While Paul and Barnabas were leaving the synagogue, the people asked them to tell them more about these things on the next Sabbath. [43] After the meeting, many Jews followed Paul and Barnabas from that place. With the Jews there were many who had changed to the Jewish religion and worshipped God. Paul and Barnabas were persuading them to continue trusting in God's kindness.

[44] On the next Sabbath day, almost all the people in the city came to hear the word of the Lord. [45] Seeing the crowd, the Jews became very jealous. They said insulting things and argued against what Paul said. [46] But Paul and Barnabas spoke very boldly. They said, "We must speak the message of God to you first. But you refuse to listen. You are judging yourselves not worthy of having eternal life! So we will now go to the people of other nations! [47] This is what the Lord told us to do. The Lord said:

'I have made you a light for the
    non-Jewish nations.

You will show people all over
    the world the way to be
    saved'."   *Isaiah 49:6*

[48] When the non-Jewish people heard Paul say this, they were happy. They gave honour to the message of the Lord. And many of the people believed the message. They were the ones chosen to have life for ever.

[49] And so the message of the Lord was spreading through the whole country. [50] But the Jews stirred up some of the important religious women and the leaders of the city against Paul and Barnabas. They started trouble against Paul and Barnabas and drove them out of their area. [51] So Paul and Barnabas shook the dust off their feet[n] and went to Iconium. [52] But the followers were filled with joy and the Holy Spirit.[d]

Paul and Barnabas in Iconium

14 In Iconium, Paul and Barnabas went as usual to the Jewish synagogue.[d] They spoke so well that a great many Jews and Greeks believed. [2] But some of the Jews who did not believe excited the non-Jewish people and turned them against the believers. [3] But Paul and Barnabas stayed in Iconium a long time and spoke bravely for the Lord. The Lord showed that their message about his grace was true by giving them the power to work miracles[d] and signs. [4] But some of the people in the city agreed with the Jews. Others believed the apostles.[d] So the city was divided.

[5] Some non-Jewish people, some Jews, and some of their rulers wanted to harm Paul and Barnabas by killing

shook . . . feet   A warning. It showed that they had finished talking to these people.

them with stones. [6]When Paul and Barnabas learned about this, they went to Lystra and Derbe, cities in Lycaonia, and to the areas around those cities. [7]They announced the Good News[d] there, too.

Paul in Lystra and Derbe

[8]In Lystra there sat a man who had been born crippled; he had never walked. [9]This man was listening to Paul speak. Paul looked straight at him and saw that the man believed God could heal him. [10]So he cried out, "Stand up on your feet!" The man

Acts 14:10 "Stand up on your feet!"

jumped up and began walking around. [11]When the crowds saw what Paul did, they shouted in their own Lycaonian language. They said, "The gods have become like men! They have come down to us!" [12]And the people began to call Barnabas "Zeus".[n] They called Paul "Hermes",[n] because he was the

main speaker. [13]The temple of Zeus was near the city. The priest of this temple brought some bulls and flowers to the city gates. The priest and the people wanted to offer a sacrifice to Paul and Barnabas. [14]But when the apostles,[d] Barnabas and Paul, understood what they were about to do, they tore their clothes in anger. Then they ran in among the people and shouted, [15]"Men, why are you doing these things? We are only men, human beings like you! We are bringing you the Good News.[d] We are telling you to turn away from these worthless things and turn to the true living God. He is the One who made the sky, the earth, the sea, and everything that is in them. [16]In the past, God let all the nations do what they wanted. [17]Yet he did things to prove he is real: He shows kindness to you. He gives you rain from heaven and crops at the right times. He gives you food and fills your hearts with joy." [18]Even with these words, they were barely able to keep the crowd from offering sacrifices to them.

[19]Then some Jews came from Antioch and Iconium. They persuaded the people to turn against Paul. And so they threw stones at Paul and dragged him out of town. They thought that they had killed him. [20]But the followers gathered around him, and he got up and went back into the town. The next day, he and Barnabas left and went to the city of Derbe.

The Return to Antioch in Syria

[21]Paul and Barnabas told the Good News[d] in Derbe and many became followers. Paul and Barnabas returned to Lystra, Iconium, and Antioch. [22]In those cities they made the followers

---

"Zeus"   The Greeks believed in many gods. Zeus was their most important god.
"Hermes"   The Greeks believed he was a messenger for the other gods.

of Jesus stronger. They helped them to stay in the faith. They said, "We must suffer many things to enter God's kingdom." ²³ They chose elders[d] for each church, by praying and giving up eating.[n] These elders were men who had trusted the Lord. So Paul and Barnabas put them in the Lord's care.

²⁴ Then they went through Pisidia and came to Pamphylia. ²⁵ They preached the message in Perga, and then they went down to Attalia. ²⁶ And from there they sailed away to Antioch. This is where the believers had put them into God's care and had sent them out to do this work. And now they had finished the work.

²⁷ When they arrived in Antioch, they gathered the church together. Paul and Barnabas told them all about what God had done with them. They told how God had made it possible for the non-Jews to believe! ²⁸ And they stayed there a long time with the followers.

The Meeting at Jerusalem

15 Then some men came to Antioch from Judea. They began teaching the non-Jewish brothers: "You cannot be saved if you are not circumcised.[d] Moses taught us to do this." ² Paul and Barnabas were against this teaching and argued with the men about it. So the group decided to send Paul, Barnabas, and some other men to Jerusalem. There they could talk more about this with the apostles[d] and elders.[d]

³ The church helped the men leave on the trip. They went through the countries of Phoenicia and Samaria, telling all about how the non-Jewish people had turned to God. This made all the believers very happy. ⁴ When they arrived in Jerusalem, the apostles, the elders, and the church welcomed them. Paul, Barnabas, and the others told of all the things that God had done with them. ⁵ But some of the believers who had belonged to the Pharisee[d] group came forward. They said, "The non-Jewish believers must be circumcised. We must tell them to obey the law of Moses!"

⁶ The apostles and the elders gathered to study this problem. ⁷ There was a long debate. Then Peter stood up and said to them, "Brothers, you know what happened in the early days. God chose me from among you to preach the Good News[d] to the non-Jewish people. They heard the Good News from me, and they believed. ⁸ God, who knows the thoughts of all men, accepted them. He showed this to us by giving them the Holy Spirit,[d] just as he did to us. ⁹ To God, those people are not different from us. When they believed, he made their hearts pure. ¹⁰ So now why are you testing God? You are putting a heavy load around the necks of the non-Jewish brothers. It is a load that neither we nor our fathers were able to carry. ¹¹ But we believe that we and they too will be saved by the grace of the Lord Jesus!"

¹² Then the whole group became quiet. They listened to Paul and Barnabas speak. Paul and Barnabas told about all the miracles[d] and signs that God did through them among the non-Jewish people. ¹³ After they finished speaking, James spoke. He said, "Brothers, listen to me. ¹⁴ Simon has told us how God showed his love for the non-Jewish people. For the first time he has accepted them and made

---

giving up eating This is called "fasting". The people would give up eating for a special time of prayer and worship to God. It was also done to show sadness.

them his people. ¹⁵The words of the prophets*d* agree with this too:
¹⁶'After these things I will return.
The kingdom of David is like a fallen tent.
But I will rebuild it.
And I will again build its ruins.
And I will set it up.
¹⁷Then those people who are left alive may ask the Lord for help.
And all people from other nations may worship me,
says the Lord.
And he will make it happen.
¹⁸ And these things have been known for a long time'.

Amos 9:11–12

¹⁹"So I think we should not bother the non-Jewish brothers who have turned to God. ²⁰Instead, we should write a letter to them. We should tell them these things: Do not eat food that has been offered to idols. (This makes the food unclean.*d*) Do not take part in any kind of sexual sin. Do not taste blood. Do not eat animals that have been strangled. ²¹They should not do these things, because there are still men in every city who teach the law of Moses. For a long time the words of Moses have been read in the synagogue*d* every Sabbath*d* day."

Letter to Non-Jewish Believers

²²The apostles,*d* the elders,*d* and the whole church decided to send some of their men with Paul and Barnabas to Antioch. They chose Judas Barsabbas and Silas, who were respected by the believers. ²³They sent the following letter with them:

From the apostles and elders, your brothers.
To all the non-Jewish brothers in Antioch, Syria and Cilicia:

Dear Brothers,
²⁴We have heard that some of our men have come to you and said things that trouble and upset you. But we did not tell them to do this! ²⁵We have all agreed to choose some men and send them to you. They will be with our dear friends Barnabas and Paul – ²⁶men who have given their lives to serve our Lord Jesus Christ. ²⁷So we have sent Judas and Silas with them. They will tell you the same things. ²⁸It has pleased the Holy Spirit*d* that you should not have a heavy load to carry, and we agree. You need to do only these things: ²⁹do not eat any food that has been offered to idols. Do not taste blood. Do not eat any animals that have been strangled. Do not take part in any kind of sexual sin. If you stay away from these things, you will do well.
Good bye.

³⁰So the men left Jerusalem and went to Antioch. There they gathered the church and gave them the letter. ³¹When they read it, they were very happy because of the encouraging letter. ³²Judas and Silas were also prophets,*d* who said many things to encourage the believers and make them stronger. ³³After some time Judas and Silas were sent off in peace by the believers. They went back to those who had sent them. ³⁴ *n*
³⁵But Paul and Barnabas stayed in Antioch. They and many others preached the Good News*d* and taught the people the message of the Lord.

Paul and Barnabas Separate

³⁶After some time, Paul said to Barnabas, "We preached the message of the Lord in many towns. We should go back to all those towns to

visit the believers and see how they are doing."

37 Barnabas wanted to take John Mark with them too. 38 But John Mark had left them at Pamphylia; he did not continue with them in the work. So Paul did not think it was a good idea to take him. 39 Paul and Barnabas had a serious argument about this. They separated and went different ways. Barnabas sailed to Cyprus and took Mark with him. 40 But Paul chose Silas and left. The believers in Antioch put Paul into the Lord's care. 41 And he went through Syria and Cilicia, giving strength to the churches.

Timothy Goes with Paul and Silas

16 Paul came to Derbe and Lystra. A follower named Timothy was there. Timothy's mother was Jewish and a believer. His father was a Greek. 2 The brothers in Lystra and Iconium respected Timothy and said good things about him. 3 Paul wanted Timothy to travel with him. But all the Jews living in that area knew that Timothy's father was Greek. So Paul circumcised[d] Timothy to please the Jews. 4 Paul and the men with him travelled from town to town. They gave the decisions made by the apostles[d] and elders[d] in Jerusalem for the people to obey. 5 So the churches became stronger in the faith and grew larger every day.

Paul Is Called Out of Asia

6 Paul and the men with him went through the areas of Phrygia and Galatia. The Holy Spirit[d] did not let them preach the Good News[d] in the country of Asia. 7 When they came near the country of Mysia, they tried

to go into Bithynia. But the Spirit of Jesus did not let them. 8 So they passed by Mysia and went to Troas. 9 That night Paul had a vision. In the vision, a man from Macedonia came to him. The man stood there and begged, "Come over to Macedonia. Help us!" 10 After Paul had seen the vision, we immediately prepared to leave for Macedonia. We understood that God had called us to tell the Good News to those people.

Lydia Becomes a Christian

11 We left Troas in a ship, and we sailed straight to the island of Samothrace. The next day we sailed to Neapolis.[n] 12 Then we went by land to Philippi, the leading city in that part of Macedonia. It is also a Roman colony.[n] We stayed there for several days. 13 On the Sabbath[d] day we went outside the city gate to the river. There we thought we would find a special place for prayer. Some women had gathered there, so we sat down and talked with them. 14 There was a woman named Lydia from the city of Thyatira. Her job was selling purple cloth. She worshipped the true God. The Lord opened her mind to pay attention to what Paul was saying. 15 She and all the people in her house were baptised. Then Lydia invited us to her home. She said, "If you think I am truly a believer in the Lord, then come and stay in my house." And she persuaded us to stay with her.

Paul and Silas in Jail

16 Once, while we were going to the place for prayer, a servant girl met us. She had a special spirit[n] in her. She

earned a lot of money for her owners by telling fortunes. [17]This girl followed Paul and us. She said loudly, "These men are servants of the Most High God! They are telling you how you can be saved!"

[18]She kept this up for many days. This bothered Paul, so he turned and said to the spirit, "By the power of Jesus Christ, I command you to come out of her!" Immediately, the spirit came out.

[19]The owners of the servant girl saw this. These men knew that now they could not use her to make money. So they grabbed Paul and Silas and dragged them before the city rulers in the marketplace. [20]Here they brought Paul and Silas to the Roman rulers and said, "These men are Jews and are making trouble in our city. [21]They are teaching things that are not right for us as Romans to do."

[22]The crowd joined the attack against them. The Roman officers tore the clothes of Paul and Silas and had them beaten with rods again and again. [23]Then Paul and Silas were thrown into jail. The jailer was ordered to guard them carefully. [24]When he heard this order, he put them far inside the jail. He pinned down their feet between large blocks of wood.

[25]About midnight Paul and Silas were praying and singing songs to God. The other prisoners were listening to them. [26]Suddenly, there was a big earthquake. It was so strong that it shook the foundation of the jail. Then all the doors of the jail broke open. All the prisoners were freed from their chains. [27]The jailer woke up and saw that the jail doors were open. He thought that the prisoners had already escaped. So he got his

Acts 16:25 Paul and Silas were praying and singing songs to God.

sword and was about to kill himself.[n] [28]But Paul shouted, "Don't hurt yourself! We are all here!"

[29]The jailer told someone to bring a light. Then he ran inside. Shaking with fear, he fell down before Paul and Silas. [30]Then he brought them outside and said, "Men, what must I do to be saved?"

[31]They said to him, "Believe in the Lord Jesus and you will be saved – you and all the people in your house." [32]So Paul and Silas told the message of the Lord to the jailer and all the people in his house. [33]At that hour of the night the jailer took Paul and Silas and washed their wounds. Then he and all his people were baptised immediately. [34]After this the jailer took Paul and Silas home and gave them food. He and his family were very happy because they now believed in God.

---

kill himself He thought the leaders would kill him for letting the prisoners escape.

[35]The next morning, the Roman officers sent the police to tell the jailer, "Let these men go free!"

[36]The jailer said to Paul, "The officers have sent an order to let you go free. You can leave now. Go in peace."

[37]But Paul said to the police, "They beat us in public without a trial, even though we are Roman citizens.[n] And they threw us in jail. Now they want to make us go away quietly. No! Let them come themselves and bring us out!"

[38]The police told the Roman officers what Paul said. When the officers heard that Paul and Silas were Roman citizens, they were afraid. [39]So they came and told Paul and Silas they were sorry. They took Paul and Silas out of jail and asked them to leave the city. [40]So when they came out of the jail, they went to Lydia's house. There they saw some of the believers and encouraged them. Then they left.

Paul and Silas in Thessalonica

17 Paul and Silas travelled through Amphipolis and Apollonia and came to Thessalonica. In that city there was a Jewish synagogue.[d] [2]Paul went into the synagogue as he always did. On each Sabbath[d] day for three weeks, Paul talked with the Jews about the Scriptures.[d] [3]He explained and proved that the Christ[d] must die and then rise from death. He said, "This Jesus I am telling you about is the Christ." [4]Some of the Jews were convinced and joined Paul and Silas. Many of the Greeks who worshipped the true God and many of the important women joined them.

[5]But the Jews became jealous. They got some evil men from the market-place, formed a mob and started a riot. They ran to Jason's house, looking for Paul and Silas. The men wanted to bring Paul and Silas out to the people. [6]But they did not find them. So they dragged Jason and some other believers to the leaders of the city. The people were yelling, "These men have made trouble everywhere in the world. And now they have come here too! [7]Jason is keeping them in his house. All of them do things against the laws of Caesar.[d] They say that there is another king called Jesus."

[8]When the people and the leaders of the city heard these things, they became very upset. [9]They made Jason and the others put up a sum of money. Then they let the believers go free.

Paul and Silas Go to Berea

[10]That same night the believers sent Paul and Silas to Berea. There Paul and Silas went to the Jewish synagogue.[d] [11]These Jews were better than the Jews in Thessalonica. They were eager to hear the things Paul and Silas said. These Jews in Berea studied the Scriptures[d] every day to find out if these things were true. [12]So, many of them believed. Many important Greek men and women also believed. [13]But when the Jews in Thessalonica learned that Paul was preaching the word of God in Berea, they came there, too. They upset the people and made trouble. [14]So the believers quickly sent Paul away to the coast. But Silas and Timothy stayed in Berea. [15]The men who took Paul went with him to Athens. Then they carried a message from Paul back to Silas and Timothy. It said, "Come to me as soon as you can."

Roman citizens   Roman law said that Roman citizens must not be beaten before they had a trial.

Paul in Athens

[16]Paul was waiting for Silas and Timothy in Athens. He was troubled because he saw that the city was full of idols. [17]In the synagogue,[d] he talked with the Jews and the Greeks who worshipped the true God. He also talked every day with people in the marketplace.

[18]Some of the Epicurean and Stoic philosophers[n] argued with him. Some of them said, "This man doesn't know what he is talking about. What is he trying to say?" Paul was telling them the Good News[d] of Jesus' rising from death. They said, "He seems to be telling us about some other gods." [19]They got Paul and took him to a meeting of the Areopagus.[n] They said, "Please explain to us this new idea that you have been teaching. [20]The things you are saying are new to us. We want to know what this teaching means." [21](All the people of Athens and those from other countries always used their time talking about all the newest ideas.)

[22]Then Paul stood before the meeting of the Areopagus. He said, "Men of Athens, I can see that you are very religious in all things. [23]I was going through your city, and I saw the things you worship. I found an altar that had these words written on it: "TO A GOD WHO IS NOT KNOWN". You worship a god that you don't know. This is the God I am telling you about! [24]He is the God who made the whole world and everything in it. He is the Lord of the land and the sky. He does not live in temples that men build! [25]This God is the One who gives life, breath, and everything else to people. He does not need any help from them. He has everything he needs. [26]God began by making one man. From him came all the different people who live everywhere in the world. He decided exactly when and where they must live. [27]God wanted them to look for him and perhaps search all around for him and find him. But he is not far from any of us: [28]'We live in him. We walk in him. We are in him'. Some of your own poets have said: 'For we are his children'. [29]We are God's children. So, you must not think that God is like something that people imagine or make. He is not like gold, silver, or rock. [30]In the past, people did not understand God, but God ignored this. But now, God tells everyone in the world to change his heart and life. [31]God has decided on a day that he will judge all the world. He will be fair. He will use a man to do this. God chose that man long ago. And God has proved this to everyone by raising that man from death!"

[32]When the people heard about Jesus being raised from death, some of them laughed. They said, "We will hear more about this from you later." [33]So Paul went away from them. [34]But some of the people believed Paul and joined him. One of those who believed was Dionysius, a member of the Areopagus. Also a woman named Damaris and some others believed.

Paul in Corinth

18 Later, Paul left Athens and went to Corinth. [2]Here he met a Jew named Aquila. Aquila was born in the country of Pontus. But Aquila and his wife, Priscilla, had recently moved to

---

Epicurean and Stoic philosophers Philosophers were those who searched for truth. Epicureans believed that pleasure, especially pleasures of the mind, were the goal of life. Stoics believed that life should be without feelings of joy or grief.
Areopagus A council or group of important leaders in Athens. They were like judges.

Corinth from Italy. They left Italy because Claudius[n] commanded that all Jews must leave Rome. Paul went to visit Aquila and Priscilla. [3]They were tentmakers, just as he was. He stayed with them and worked with them. [4]Every Sabbath[d] day he talked with the Jews and Greeks in the synagogue.[d] Paul tried to persuade these people to believe in Jesus.

[5]Silas and Timothy came from Macedonia and joined Paul in Corinth. After this, Paul used all his time telling people the Good News.[d] He showed the Jews that Jesus is the Christ.[d] [6]But they would not accept Paul's teaching and said some evil things. So he shook off the dust from his clothes.[n] He said to them, "If you are not saved, it will be your own fault! I have done all I can do! After this, I will go only to non-Jewish people!" [7]Paul left the synagogue and moved into the home of Titius Justus. It was next to the synagogue. This man worshipped the true God. [8]Crispus was the leader of that synagogue. He and all the people living in his house believed in the Lord. Many others in Corinth also listened to Paul. They too believed and were baptised.

[9]During the night, Paul had a vision. The Lord said to him, "Don't be afraid! Continue talking to people and don't be quiet! [10]I am with you. No one will hurt you because many of my people are in this city." [11]Paul stayed there for a year and a half, teaching God's word to the people.

Paul Is Brought Before Gallio

[12]Gallio became the governor of the country of Southern Greece. At that time, some of the Jews came together against Paul and took him to the court. [13]They said to Gallio, "This man is teaching people to worship God in a way that is against our law!"

[14]Paul was about to say something, but Gallio spoke to the Jews. Gallio said, "I would listen to you Jews if you were complaining about a crime or some wrong. [15]But the things you are saying are only questions about words and names – arguments about your own law. So you must solve this problem yourselves. I don't want to be a judge of these things!" [16]Then Gallio made them leave the court.

[17]Then they all grabbed Sosthenes. (Sosthenes was now the leader of the synagogue.[d]) They beat him there before the court. But this did not bother Gallio.

Paul Returns to Antioch

[18]Paul stayed with the believers for many more days. Then he left and sailed for Syria. Priscilla and Aquila went with him. At Cenchrea, Paul cut off his hair.[n] This showed that he had made a promise to God. [19]Then they went to Ephesus, where Paul left Priscilla and Aquila. While Paul was there, he went into the synagogue[d] and talked with the Jews. [20]When they asked him to stay with them longer, he refused. [21]He left them, but he said, "I will come back to you again if God wants me to." And so he sailed away from Ephesus.

[22]Paul landed at Caesarea. Then he went and gave greetings to the church in Jerusalem. After that, Paul went to Antioch. [23]He stayed there for a while and then left and went through the countries of Galatia and Phrygia. He travelled from town to town in these

---

Claudius The emperor (ruler) of Rome, A.D. 41–54.
shook . . . clothes This was a warning. It showed that Paul had finished talking to the Jews.
cut . . . hair Jews did this to show that the time of a special promise to God was finished.

countries, giving strength to all the followers.

Apollos in Ephesus and Corinth

24 A Jew named Apollos came to Ephesus. He was born in the city of Alexandria. He was an educated man who knew the Scriptures[d] well. 25 He had been taught about the Lord. He was always very excited when he spoke and taught the truth about Jesus. But the only baptism that Apollos knew about was the baptism that John[n] taught. 26 Apollos began to speak very boldly in the synagogue,[d] and Priscilla and Aquila heard him. So they took him to their home and helped him better understand the way of God. 27 Now Apollos wanted to go to the country of Southern Greece, so the believers helped him. They wrote a letter to the followers there, asking them to accept him. These followers had believed in Jesus because of God's grace. When Apollos went there, he helped them very much. 28 He argued very strongly with the Jews before all the people. Apollos clearly proved that the Jews were wrong. Using the Scriptures, he proved that Jesus is the Christ.[d]

Paul in Ephesus

19 While Apollos was in Corinth, Paul was visiting some places on the way to Ephesus. There he found some followers. 2 Paul asked them, "Did you receive the Holy Spirit[d] when you believed?"

They said, "We have never even heard of a Holy Spirit!"

3 So he asked, "What kind of baptism did you have?"

They said, "It was the baptism that John[n] taught."

4 Paul said, "John's baptism was a baptism of changed hearts and lives. He told people to believe in the One who would come after him. That One is Jesus."

5 When they heard this, they were baptised in the name of the Lord Jesus. 6 Then Paul laid his hands on them,[n] and the Holy Spirit came upon them. They began speaking different languages[n] and prophesying.[d] 7 There were about 12 men in this group.

8 Paul went into the synagogue[d] and spoke out boldly for three months. He talked with the Jews and persuaded them to accept the things he said about the kingdom of God. 9 But some of the Jews became stubborn and refused to believe. These Jews said evil things about the Way of Jesus. All the people heard these things. So Paul left them and took the followers with him. He went to a place where a man named Tyrannus had a school. There Paul talked with people every day 10 for two years. Because of his work, every Jew and Greek in the country of Asia heard the word of the Lord.

The Sons of Sceva

11 God used Paul to do some very special miracles.[d] 12 Some people took handkerchiefs and clothes that Paul had used and put them on the sick. When they did this, the sick were healed and evil spirits left them.

13-14 But some Jews also were travelling around and making evil spirits go out of people. The seven sons of Sceva were doing this. (Sceva was a leading Jewish priest.) These Jews tried to use

John John the Baptist, who preached to people about Christ's coming (Matthew 3, Luke 3).
laid his hands on them Here, doing this was a sign to show that Paul had God's authority or power to give these people special powers of the Holy Spirit.
languages This can also be translated "tongues".

the name of the Lord Jesus to force the evil spirits out. They would say, "By the same Jesus that Paul talks about, I order you to come out!"

[15] But once an evil spirit said to these Jews, "I know Jesus, and I know about Paul, but who are you?"

[16] Then the man, who had the evil spirit in him, jumped on these Jews. He was much stronger than all of them. He beat them and tore their clothes off, so they ran away from the house. [17] All the people in Ephesus, Jews and Greeks, learned about this. They were filled with fear. And the people gave great honour to the Lord Jesus. [18] Many of the believers began to confess openly and tell all the evil things they had done. [19] Some of them had used magic. These believers brought their magic books and burned them before everyone. Those books were worth about 50,000 silver coins.[n]

[20] So in a powerful way the word of the Lord kept spreading and growing.

Paul Plans a Trip

[21] After these things, Paul made plans to go to Jerusalem. He planned to go through the countries of Macedonia and Southern Greece, and then on to Jerusalem. He said, "After I have been to Jerusalem, I must also visit Rome." [22] Paul sent Timothy and Erastus, two of his helpers, ahead to Macedonia. He himself stayed in Asia for a while.

Trouble in Ephesus

[23] But during that time, there was some serious trouble in Ephesus about the Way of Jesus. [24] There was a man named Demetrius, who worked with silver. He made little silver models that looked like the temple of the goddess Artemis.[n] The men who did this work made much money. [25] Demetrius had a meeting with these men and some others who did the same kind of work. He told them, "Men, you know that we make a lot of money from our business. [26] But look at what this man Paul is doing! He has convinced and turned away many people in Ephesus and in almost all of Asia! He says the gods that men make are not real. [27] There is a danger that our business will lose its good name. But there is also another danger: people will begin to think that the temple of the great goddess Artemis is not important! Her greatness will be destroyed. And

Acts 19:19 These believers brought their magic books and burned them.

50,000 silver coins Probably drachmas. One coin was enough to pay a man for working one day.
Artemis A Greek goddess that the people of Asia Minor worshipped.

Artemis is the goddess that ever one in Asia and the whole world worships."

[28] When the men heard this, they became very angry. They shouted, "Artemis, the goddess of Ephesus, is great!" [29] The whole city became confused. The people grabbed Gaius and Aristarchus. (These two men were from Macedonia and were travelling with Paul.) Then all the people ran to the theatre. [30] Paul wanted to go in and talk to the crowd, but the followers did not let him. [31] Also, some leaders of Asia were friends of Paul. They sent him a message, begging him not to go into the theatre. [32] Some people were shouting one thing, and some were shouting another. The meeting was completely confused. Most of the people did not know why they had come together. [33] The Jews put a man named Alexander in front of the people. Some of them had told him what to do. Alexander waved his hand because he wanted to explain things to the people. [34] But when they saw that Alexander was a Jew, they all began shouting the same thing. They continued shouting for two hours: "Great is Artemis of Ephesus!"

[35] Then the city clerk made the crowd be quiet. He said, "Men of Ephesus, everyone knows that Ephesus is the city that keeps the temple of the great goddess Artemis. All people know that we also keep her holy stone[n] that fell from heaven. [36] No one can say that this is not true. So you should be quiet. You must stop and think before you do anything. [37] You brought these men here, but they have not said anything evil against our goddess. They have not stolen anything from her temple. [38] We have courts of law, and there are judges. Do Demetrius and the men who work with him have a charge against anyone? They should go to the courts! That is where they can argue with each other! [39] Is there something else you want to talk about? It can be decided at the regular town meeting of the people. [40] I say this because some people might see this trouble today and say that we are rioting. We could not explain this because there is no real reason for this meeting." [41] After the city clerk said these things, he told the people to go home.

Paul in Macedonia and Greece

20 When the trouble stopped, Paul sent for the followers to come to him. He encouraged them and then told them good bye. Paul left and went to the country of Macedonia. [2] He said many things to strengthen the followers in the different places on his way through Macedonia. Then he went to Southern Greece. [3] He stayed there three months. He was ready to sail for Syria, but some Jews were planning something against him. So Paul decided to go back through Macedonia to Syria. [4] Some men went with him. They were Sopater son of Pyrrhus, from the city of Berea; Aristarchus and Secundus, from the city of Thessalonica; Gaius, from Derbe; and Timothy; and Tychicus and Trophimus, two men from the country of Asia. [5] These men went first, ahead of Paul, and waited for us at Troas. [6] We sailed from Philippi after the Feast[d] of Unleavened Bread and we met them in Troas five days later. We stayed there seven days.

---

holy stone   Probably a meteorite or stone that the people thought looked like Artemis.

Paul's Last Visit to Troas

[7] On the first day of the week,[n] we all met together to break bread.[n] Paul spoke to the group. Because he was planning to leave the next day, he kept on talking till midnight. [8] We were all together in a room upstairs, and there were many lamps in the room. [9] A young man named Eutychus was sitting in the window. As Paul continued talking, Eutychus was falling into a deep sleep. Finally, he went sound asleep and fell to the ground from the third floor. When they picked him up, he was dead. [10] Paul went down to Eutychus. He knelt down and put his arms around him. He said, "Don't worry. He is alive now." [11] Then Paul went upstairs again, broke bread, and ate. He spoke to them a long time, until it was early morning. Then he left. [12] They took the young man home alive and were greatly comforted.

The Trip from Troas to Miletus

[13] We sailed for the city of Assos. We went first, ahead of Paul. He wanted to join us on the ship there. Paul planned it this way because he wanted to go to Assos by land. [14] When he met us at Assos, we took him aboard and went to Mitylene. [15] The next day, we sailed from Mitylene and came to a place near Chios. The next day, we sailed to Samos. A day later, we reached Miletus. [16] Paul had already decided not to stop at Ephesus. He did not want to stay too long in the country of Asia. He was hurrying to be in Jerusalem on the day of Pentecost,[d] if that was possible.

The Elders from Ephesus

[17] Now from Miletus Paul sent to Ephesus and called for the elders[d] of the church. [18] When they came to him, he said, "You know about my life from the first day I came to Asia. You know the way I lived all the time I was with you. [19] The Jews plotted against me. This troubled me very much. But you know that I always served the Lord. I never thought of myself first, and I often cried. [20] You know I preached to you, and I did not hold back anything that would help you. You know that I taught you in public and in your homes. [21] I warned both Jews and Greeks to change their lives and turn to God. And I told them all to believe in our Lord Jesus. [22] But now I must obey the Holy Spirit[d] and go to Jerusalem. I don't know what will happen to me there. [23] I know only that in every city the Holy Spirit tells me that troubles and even jail wait for me. [24] I don't care about my own life. The most important thing is that I complete my mission. I want to finish the work that the Lord Jesus gave me – to tell people the Good News[d] about God's grace.

[25] "And now, I know that none of you will ever see me again. All the time I was with you, I was preaching the kingdom of God. [26] So today I can tell you one thing that I am sure of: if any of you should be lost, I am not responsible. [27] This is because I have told you everything God wants you to know. [28] Be careful for yourselves and for all the people God has given you. The Holy Spirit gave you the work of caring for this flock. You must be like

---

first day of the week   Sunday, which for the Jews began at sunset on our Saturday. But if in this part of Asia a different system of time was used, then the meeting was on our Sunday night.
break bread   Probably the Lord's Supper, the special meal that Jesus told his followers to eat to remember him (Luke 22:14–20).

shepherds to the church of God.*ⁿ* This is the church that God bought with his own death. ²⁹I know that after I leave, some men will come like wild wolves and try to destroy the flock. ³⁰Also, men from your own group will rise up and twist the truth. They will lead away followers after them. ³¹So be careful! Always remember this: for three years I never stopped warning each of you. I taught you night and day. I often cried over you.

³²"Now I am putting you in the care of God and the message about his grace. That message is able to give you strength, and it will give you the blessings that God has for all his holy people. ³³When I was with you, I never wanted anyone's money or fine clothes. ³⁴You know that I always worked to take care of my own needs and the needs of those who were with me. ³⁵I showed you in all things that you should work as I did and help the weak. I taught you to remember the words of Jesus. He said, 'It is more blessed to give than to receive'."

³⁶When Paul had said this, he knelt down with all of them and prayed. ³⁷⁻³⁸And they all cried because Paul had said that they would never see him again. They put their arms around him and kissed him. Then they went with him to the ship.

Paul Goes to Jerusalem

21 We all said good bye to them and left. We sailed straight to Cos. The next day, we reached Rhodes, and from Rhodes we went to Patara. ²There we found a ship that was going to Phoenicia. We went aboard and sailed away. ³We sailed near the island of Cyprus. We could see it to the north, but we sailed on

to Syria. We stopped at Tyre because the ship needed to unload its cargo there. ⁴We found some followers in Tyre, and we stayed with them for seven days. Through the Holy Spirit*ᵈ* they warned Paul not to go to Jerusalem. ⁵When we finished our visit, we left and continued our trip. All the followers, even the women and children, came outside the city with us. We all knelt down on the beach and prayed. ⁶Then we said good bye and got on the ship. The followers went back home.

⁷We continued our trip from Tyre and arrived at Ptolemais. We greeted the believers there and stayed with them for a day. ⁸We left Ptolemais and went to the city of Caesarea. There we went into the home of Philip and stayed with him. Philip had the work of telling the Good News.*ᵈ* He was one of the seven helpers.*ⁿ* ⁹He had four unmarried daughters who had the gift of prophesying.*ᵈ* ¹⁰After we had been there for some time, a prophet named Agabus arrived from Judea. ¹¹He came to us and borrowed Paul's belt. Then he used the belt to tie his own hands and feet. He said, "The Holy Spirit says, 'This is how the Jews in Jerusalem will tie up the man who wears this belt. Then they will give him to the non-Jewish people'."

¹²We all heard these words. So we and the people there begged Paul not to go to Jerusalem. ¹³But he said, "Why are you crying and making me so sad? I am ready to be tied up in Jerusalem. And I am ready to die for the Lord Jesus!"

¹⁴We could not persuade him to stay away from Jerusalem. So we stopped begging him and said, "We pray that what the Lord wants will be done."

of God Some Greek copies say, "of the Lord".
helpers The seven men chosen for a special work described in Acts 6:1–6.

[15]After this, we got ready and started on our way to Jerusalem. [16]Some of the followers from Caesarea went with us. They took us to the home of Mnason, a man from Cyprus. Mnason was one of the first followers. They took us to his home so that we could stay with him.

Paul Visits James

[17]In Jerusalem the believers were glad to see us. [18]The next day, Paul went with us to visit James. All the elders[d] were there, too. [19]Paul greeted them and told them everything that God had done among the non-Jewish people through him. [20]When they heard this, they praised God. Then they said to Paul, "Brother, you can see that many thousands of Jews have become believers. But they think it is very important to obey the law of Moses. [21]These Jews have heard about your teaching. They heard that you tell the Jews who live among non-Jews to leave the law of Moses. They heard that you tell them not to circumcise[d] their children and not to obey Jewish customs. [22]What should we do? The Jewish believers here will learn that you have come. [23]So we will tell you what to do: four of our men have made a promise to God. [24]Take these men with you and share in their cleansing ceremony.[n] Pay their expenses. Then they can shave their heads.[n] Do this and it will prove to everyone that what they have heard about you is not true. They will see that you follow the law of Moses in your own life. [25]We have already sent a letter to the non-Jewish believers. The letter said: 'Do not eat food that has been offered to idols. Do not taste blood. Do not eat animals that have been strangled. Do not take part in any kind of sexual sin'."

[26]Then Paul took the four men with him. The next day, he shared in the cleansing ceremony. Then he went to the Temple.[d] Paul announced the time when the days of the cleansing ceremony would be finished. On the last day an offering would be given for each of the men.

[27]The seven days were almost over. But some Jews from Asia saw Paul at the Temple. They caused all the people to be upset, and they grabbed Paul. [28]They shouted, "Men of Israel, help us! This is the man who goes everywhere teaching things that are against the law of Moses, against our people, and against this Temple. And now he has brought some Greek men into the Temple. He has made this holy place unclean!"[d] [29](The Jews said this because they had seen Trophimus with Paul in Jerusalem. Trophimus was a man from Ephesus. The Jews thought that Paul had brought him into the Temple.)

[30]All the people in Jerusalem became very upset. They ran and took Paul and dragged him out of the Temple. The Temple doors were closed immediately. [31]The people were about to kill Paul. Now the commander of the Roman army in Jerusalem learned that there was trouble in the whole city. [32]Immediately he ran to the place where the crowd was gathered. He brought officers and soldiers with him, and the people saw them. So they stopped beating Paul. [33]The commander went to Paul and arrested him. He told his soldiers to tie Paul with two chains. Then he asked, "Who is this man? What has he done wrong?" [34]Some in the crowd were

---

cleansing ceremony   The special things Jews did to end the Nazirite promise.
shave their heads   The Jews did this to show that their promise was finished.

Acts 21:33 The commander went to Paul and arrested him.

yelling one thing, and some were yelling another. Because of all this confusion and shouting, the commander could not learn what had happened. So he ordered the soldiers to take Paul to the army barracks. 35-36The whole mob was following them. When the soldiers came to the steps, they had to carry Paul. They did this because the people were ready to hurt him. They were shouting, "Kill him!"

37The soldiers were about to take Paul into the army barracks. But he spoke to the commander, "May I say something to you?"

The commander said, "Do you speak Greek? 38I thought you were the Egyptian who started some trouble against the government not long ago. He led 4,000 killers out to the desert."

39Paul said, "No, I am a Jew from Tarsus in the country of Cilicia. I am a citizen of that important city. Please, let me speak to the people."

40The commander gave permission, so Paul stood on the steps. He waved with his hand so that the people would be quiet. When there was silence, Paul spoke to them in the Jewish language.*n*

Paul Speaks to the People

22 Paul said, "Brothers and fathers, listen to me! I will make my defence to you." 2When the Jews heard him speaking the Jewish language,*n* they became very quiet. Paul said, 3"I am a Jew. I was born in Tarsus in the country of Cilicia. I grew up in this city. I was a student of Gamaliel.*n* He carefully taught me everything about the law of our ancestors. I was very serious about serving God, just as are all of you here today. 4I hurt the people who followed the Way of Jesus. Some of them were even killed. I arrested men and women and put them in jail. 5The high priest and the whole council of older Jewish leaders can tell you that this is true. These leaders gave me letters to the Jewish brothers in Damascus. So I was going there to arrest these people and bring them back to Jerusalem to be punished.

6"But something happened to me on my way to Damascus. It was about noon when I came near Damascus. Suddenly a bright light from heaven flashed all around me. 7I fell to the ground and heard a voice saying, 'Saul, Saul, why are you doing things against me?' 8I asked, 'Who are you, Lord?' The voice said, 'I am Jesus from Nazareth. I am the One you are trying to hurt'. 9The men who were with me

Jewish language Aramaic, the language of the Jews in the first century.
Gamaliel A very important teacher of the Pharisees, a Jewish religious group (Acts 5:34).

did not understand the voice. But they saw the light. ¹⁰I said, 'What shall I do, Lord?' The Lord answered, 'Get up and go to Damascus. There you will be told about all the things I have planned for you to do'. ¹¹I could not see, because the bright light had made me blind. So the men led me into Damascus.

¹²"There a man named Ananias came to me. He was a religious man; he obeyed the law of Moses. All the Jews who lived there respected him. ¹³Ananias came to me, stood by me, and said, 'Brother Saul, see again!' Immediately I was able to see him. ¹⁴Ananias told me, 'The God of our fathers chose you long ago. He chose you to know his plan. He chose you to see the Righteous One and to hear words from him. ¹⁵You will be his witness to all people. You will tell them about the things you have seen and heard. ¹⁶Now, why wait any longer? Get up, be baptised, and wash your sins away. Do this, trusting in him to save you'.

¹⁷"Later, I returned to Jerusalem. I was praying in the Temple,^{d} and I saw a vision. ¹⁸I saw the Lord saying to me, 'Hurry! Leave Jerusalem now! The people here will not accept the truth about me'. ¹⁹But I said, 'Lord, they know that in every synagogue^d I put the believers in jail and beat them. ²⁰They also know that I was there when Stephen, your witness, was killed. I stood there and agreed that they should kill him. I even held the coats of the men who were killing him!' ²¹But the Lord said to me, 'Leave now. I will send you far away to the non-Jewish people'."

²²The crowd listened to Paul until he said this. Then they began shouting, "Kill him! Get him out of the world! A man like this should not be allowed to live!" ²³They shouted and threw off their coats.^{n} They threw dust into the air.^{n}

²⁴Then the commander ordered the soldiers to take Paul into the army barracks and beat him. The commander wanted to make Paul tell why the people were shouting against him like this. ²⁵So the soldiers were tying him up, preparing to beat him. But Paul said to an officer there, "Do you have the right to beat a Roman citizen^n who has not been proved guilty?"

²⁶When the officer heard this, he went to the commander and told him about it. The officer said, "Do you know what you are doing? This man is a Roman citizen!"

²⁷The commander came to Paul and said, "Tell me, are you really a Roman citizen?"

He answered, "Yes."

²⁸The commander said, "I paid a lot of money to become a Roman citizen."

But Paul said, "I was born a citizen."

²⁹The men who were preparing to question Paul moved away from him immediately. The commander was frightened because he had already tied Paul, and Paul was a Roman citizen.

Paul Speaks to Jewish Leaders

³⁰The next day the commander decided to learn why the Jews were accusing Paul. So he ordered the leading priests and the Jewish council to meet. The commander took Paul's chains off. Then he brought Paul out and stood him before their meeting.

---

threw off their coats This showed that the Jews were very angry at Paul.
threw dust into the air This showed even greater anger.
Roman citizen Roman law said that Roman citizens must not be beaten before they had a trial.

23 Paul looked at the Jewish council and said, "Brothers, I have lived my life in a good way before God up to this day." [2] Ananias,[n] the high priest, heard this and told the men who were standing near Paul to hit him on his mouth. [3] Paul said to Ananias, "God will hit you too! You are like a dirty wall that has been painted white! You sit there and judge me, using the law of Moses. But you are telling them to hit me, and that is against the law."

[4] The men standing near Paul said to him, "You cannot talk like that to God's high priest! You are insulting him!"

[5] Paul said, "Brothers, I did not know this man was the high priest. It is written in the Scriptures,[d] 'You must not curse a leader of your people'."[n]

[6] Some of the men in the meeting were Sadducees,[d] and others were Pharisees.[d] So Paul shouted to them, "My brothers, I am a Pharisee and my father was a Pharisee! I am on trial here because I hope that people will rise from death!"

[7] When Paul said this, there was an argument between the Pharisees and the Sadducees. The group was divided. [8] (The Sadducees believe that after people die, they cannot live again. The Sadducees also teach that there are no angels or spirits. But the Pharisees believe in them all.) [9] So there was a great uproar. Some of the teachers of the law, who were Pharisees, stood up and argued, "We find nothing wrong with this man! Maybe an angel or a spirit did speak to him."

[10] The argument was beginning to turn into a fight. The commander was afraid that the Jews would tear Paul to pieces. So the commander told the soldiers to go down and take Paul away and put him in the army barracks.

[11] The next night the Lord came and stood by Paul. He said, "Be brave! You have told people in Jerusalem about me. You must do the same in Rome also."

[12] In the morning some of the Jews made a plan to kill Paul. They made a promise that they would not eat or drink anything until they had killed him. [13] There were more than 40 Jews who made this plan. [14] They went and talked to the leading priests and the older Jewish leaders. They said, "We have made a promise to ourselves that we will not eat or drink until we have killed Paul! [15] So this is what we want you to do: send a message to the commander to bring Paul out to you. Tell him you want to ask Paul more questions. We will be waiting to kill him while he is on the way here."

[16] But Paul's nephew heard about this plan. He went to the army barracks and told Paul about it. [17] Then Paul called one of the officers and said, "Take this young man to the commander. He has a message for him."

[18] So the officer brought Paul's nephew to the commander. The officer said, "The prisoner, Paul, asked me to bring this young man to you. He wants to tell you something."

[19] The commander led the young man to a place where they could be alone. The commander asked, "What do you want to tell me?"

[20] The young man said, "The Jews have decided to ask you to bring Paul down to their council meeting tomorrow. They want you to think that they are going to ask him more questions. [21] But don't believe them! There

Ananias   This is not the same man as the one named Ananias in Acts 22:12.
'You ... people.'   Quotation from Exodus 22:28.

are more than 40 men who are hiding and waiting to kill Paul. They have all made a promise not to eat or drink until they have killed him! Now they are waiting for you to agree."

²²The commander sent the young man away. He said to him, "Don't tell anyone that you have told me about their plan."

Paul Is Sent to Caesarea

²³Then the commander called two officers. He said to them, "I need some men to go to Caesarea. Get 200 soldiers ready. Also, get 70 horsemen and 200 men with spears. Be ready to leave at nine o'clock tonight. ²⁴Get some horses for Paul to ride. He must be taken to Governor Felix safely." ²⁵And he wrote a letter that said:

²⁶From Claudius Lysias.

To the Most Excellent Governor Felix:

Greetings.

²⁷The Jews had taken this man, and they planned to kill him. But I learned that he is a Roman citizen, so I went with my soldiers and saved him. ²⁸I wanted to know why they were accusing him. So I brought him before their council meeting. ²⁹I learned that the Jews said Paul did some

things that were wrong. But these charges were about their own laws. And no charge was worthy of jail or death. ³⁰I was told that some of the Jews were planning to kill Paul. So I sent him to you at once. I also told those Jews to tell you what they have against him.

³¹So the soldiers did what they were told. They took Paul and brought him to the city of Antipatris that night. ³²The next day the horsemen went with Paul to Caesarea. But the other soldiers went back to the army barracks in Jerusalem. ³³The horsemen came to Caesarea and gave the letter to the governor. Then they turned Paul over to him. ³⁴The governor read the letter. Then he asked Paul, "What area are you from?" He learned that Paul was from Cilicia. ³⁵He said, "I will hear your case when those who are against you come here too." Then the governor gave orders for Paul to be kept under guard in the palace. (This building had been built by Herod.)

The Jews Accuse Paul

24 Five days later Ananias, the high priest, went to the city of Caesarea. With him were some of the older Jewish leaders and a lawyer

Acts 24:1–23 The Jews accuse Paul.

named Tertullus. They had come to make charges against Paul before the governor. [2]Paul was called into the meeting, and Tertullus began to accuse him, saying: "Most Excellent Felix! Our people enjoy much peace because of you, and many wrong things in our country are being made right through your wise help. [3]We accept these things always and in every place. And we are thankful for them. [4]But I do not want to take any more of your time. I beg you to be kind and listen to our few words. [5]This man is a troublemaker. He makes trouble among the Jews everywhere in the world. He is a leader of the Nazarene[d] group. [6]Also, he was trying to make the Temple[d] unclean,[d] but we stopped him.[n] [8]You can decide if all these things are true. Ask him some questions yourself." [9]The other Jews agreed and said that all of this was true.

[10]The governor made a sign for Paul to speak. So Paul said, "Governor Felix, I know that you have been a judge over this nation for a long time. So I am happy to defend myself before you. [11]I went to worship in Jerusalem only 12 days ago. You can learn for yourself that this is true. [12]Those who are accusing me did not find me arguing with anyone in the Temple. I was not stirring up the people. And I was not making trouble in the Temple or in the synagogues[d] or in the city. [13]They cannot prove the things they are saying against me now. [14]But I will tell you this: I worship the God of our ancestors as a follower of the Way of Jesus. The Jews say that the Way of Jesus is not the right way. But I believe everything that is taught in the law of Moses and that is written in the books of the Prophets.[d] [15]I have the same hope in God that they have – the hope that all people, good and bad, will be raised from death. [16]This is why I always try to do what I believe is right before God and men.

[17]"I was away from Jerusalem for several years. I went back there to bring money to my people and to offer sacrifices. [18]I was doing this when they found me in the Temple. I had finished the cleansing ceremony. I had not made any trouble; no people were gathering around me. [19]But some Jews from the country of Asia were there. They should be here, standing before you. If I have really done anything wrong, they are the ones who should accuse me. [20]Or ask these Jews here if they found any wrong in me when I stood before the Jewish council in Jerusalem. [21]But I did say one thing when I stood before them: 'You are judging me today because I believe that people will rise from death!'"

[22]Felix already understood much about the Way of Jesus. He stopped the trial and said, "When commander Lysias comes here, I will decide about your case." [23]Felix told the officer to keep Paul guarded. But he told the officer to give Paul some freedom and to let his friends bring what he needed.

Paul Speaks to Felix and His Wife

[24]After some days Felix came with his wife, Drusilla, who was a Jew. He asked for Paul to be brought to him. He listened to Paul talk about believing in Christ Jesus. [25]But Felix

---

Verse 6   Some Greek copies add 6b–8a: "And we wanted to judge him by our own law. [7]But the officer Lysias came and used much force to take him from us. [8]And Lysias commanded his people to come to you to accuse us."

became afraid when Paul spoke about things like right living, self-control, and the time when God will judge the world. He said, "Go away now. When I have more time, I will call for you." ²⁶ At the same time Felix hoped that Paul would give him some money. So he sent for Paul often and talked with him.

²⁷ But after two years, Porcius Festus became governor. Felix was no longer governor, but he had left Paul in prison to please the Jews.

Paul Asks to See Caesar

25 Three days after Festus became governor, he went from Caesarea to Jerusalem. ² There the leading priests and the important Jewish leaders made charges against Paul before Festus. ³ They asked Festus to do something for them. They wanted him to send Paul back to Jerusalem. (They had a plan to kill Paul on the way.) ⁴ But Festus answered, "No! Paul will be kept in Caesarea. I will return there soon myself. ⁵ Some of your leaders should go with me. They can accuse the man there in Caesarea, if he has really done something wrong."

⁶ Festus stayed in Jerusalem another eight or ten days. Then he went back to Caesarea. The next day he told the soldiers to bring Paul before him. Festus was seated on the judge's seat ⁷ when Paul came into the room. The Jews who had come from Jerusalem stood around him. They started making serious charges against Paul. But they could not prove any of them. ⁸ This is what Paul said to defend himself: "I have done nothing wrong against the Jewish law, against the Temple,^d or against Caesar!"^d

⁹ But Festus wanted to please the Jews. So he asked Paul, "Do you want to go to Jerusalem? Do you want me to judge you there on these charges?"

¹⁰ Paul said, "I am standing at Caesar's judgment seat now. This is where I should be judged! I have done nothing wrong to the Jews; you know this is true. ¹¹ If I have done something wrong and the law says I must die, I do not ask to be saved from death. But if these charges are not true, then no one can give me to them. No! I want Caesar to hear my case!"

¹² Festus talked about this with the people who advised him. Then he said, "You have asked to see Caesar; so you will go to Caesar!"

Paul Before King Agrippa

¹³ A few days later King Agrippa and Bernice came to Caesarea to visit Festus. ¹⁴ They stayed there for some time, and Festus told the king about Paul's case. Festus said, "There is a man that Felix left in prison. ¹⁵ When I went to Jerusalem, the leading priests and the older Jewish leaders there made charges against him. They wanted me to sentence him to death. ¹⁶ But I answered, 'When a man is accused of a crime, Romans do not hand him over just to please someone. The man must be allowed to face his accusers and defend himself against their charges'. ¹⁷ So these Jews came here to Caesarea for the trial. And I did not waste time. The next day I sat on the judge's seat and commanded that the man be brought in. ¹⁸ The Jews stood up and accused him. But they did not accuse him of any serious crime as I thought they would. ¹⁹ The things they said were about their own religion and about a man named Jesus. Jesus died, but Paul said that he is still alive. ²⁰ I did not know much about these things; so I did not ask questions. But I asked Paul, 'Do you want to go to Jerusalem and be judged

there?' [21] But he asked to be kept in Caesarea. He wants a decision from the Emperor.[n] So I ordered that Paul be held until I could send him to Caesar[d] in Rome."

[22] Agrippa said to Festus, "I would like to hear this man, too."

Festus said, "Tomorrow you will hear him!"

[23] The next day Agrippa and Bernice appeared. They dressed and acted like very important people. Agrippa and Bernice, the army leaders, and the important men of Caesarea went into the judgement room. Then Festus ordered the soldiers to bring Paul in. [24] Festus said, "King Agrippa and all who are gathered here with us, you see this man. All the Jewish people, here and in Jerusalem, have complained to me about him. They shout that he should not live any longer. [25] When I judged him, I could find nothing wrong. I found no reason to order his death. But he asked to be judged by Caesar. So I decided to send him. [26] But I have nothing definite to write to the Emperor about him. So I have brought him before all of you – especially you, King Agrippa. I hope that you can question him and give me something to write. [27] I think it is foolish to send a prisoner to Caesar without saying what the charges are against him."

Paul Defends Himself

26 Agrippa said to Paul, "You may now speak to defend yourself." Then Paul raised his hand and began to speak. [2] He said, "King Agrippa, I will answer all the charges that the Jews make against me. I think it is a blessing that I can stand here before you today. [3] I am very happy to talk to you, because you know so much about all the Jewish customs and the things that the Jews argue about. Please listen to me patiently.

[4] "All the Jews know about my whole life. They know the way I lived from the beginning in my own country and later in Jerusalem. [5] They have known me for a long time. If they want to, they can tell you that I was a good Pharisee.[d] And the Pharisees obey the laws of the Jewish religion more carefully than any other group of Jewish people. [6] Now I am on trial because I hope for the promise that God made to our ancestors. [7] This is the promise that the 12 tribes[d] of our people hope to receive. For this hope the Jews serve God day and night. My king, the Jews have accused me because I hope for this same promise! [8] Why do any of you people think it is impossible for God to raise people from death?

[9] "I too thought I ought to do many things against Jesus from Nazareth. [10] And in Jerusalem I did many things against God's people. The leading priests gave me the power to put many of them in jail. When they were being killed, I agreed that it was a good thing. [11] In every synagogue,[d] I often punished them. I tried to make them say evil things against Jesus. I was so angry against them that I even went to other cities to find them and punish them.

[12] "One time the leading priests gave me permission and the power to go to Damascus. [13] On the way there, at noon, I saw a light from heaven. The light was brighter than the sun. It flashed all around me and the men who were travelling with me. [14] We all fell to the ground. Then I heard a voice speaking to me in the Jewish lan-

Emperor The ruler of the Roman Empire, which was Europe, North Africa and the Middle East.

guage.*n* The voice said, 'Saul, Saul, why are you doing things against me? You are only hurting yourself by fighting me'. [15] I said, 'Who are you, Lord?' The Lord said, 'I am Jesus. I am the One you are trying to hurt. [16] Stand up! I have chosen you to be my servant. You will be my witness – you will tell people the things that you have seen and the things that I will show you. This is why I have come to you today. [17] I will not let your own people hurt you. And I will keep you safe from the non-Jewish people too. These are the people I am sending you to. [18] I send you to open their eyes that they may turn away from darkness to the light. I send you that they may turn away from the power of Satan and turn to God. Then their sins can be forgiven and they can have a place with those people who have been made holy by believing in me'.

[19] "King Agrippa, after I had this vision from heaven, I obeyed it. [20] I began telling people that they should change their hearts and lives and turn to God. I told them to do things to show that they really had changed. I told this first to those in Damascus, then in Jerusalem and in every part of Judea, and also to the non-Jewish people. [21] This is why the Jews took me and were trying to kill me in the Temple.*d* [22] But God helped me and is still helping me today. With God's help I am standing here today and telling all people what I have seen. But I am saying nothing new. I am saying what Moses and the prophets*d* said would happen. [23] They said that the Christ*d* would die and be the first to rise from death. They said that the Christ would

bring light to the Jewish and non-Jewish people."

Paul Tries to Persuade Agrippa

[24] While Paul was saying these things to defend himself, Festus said loudly, "Paul, you are out of your mind! Too much study has driven you insane!"

[25] Paul said, "Most Excellent Festus, I am not insane. My words are true. They are not the words of a foolish man. [26] King Agrippa knows about these things. I can speak freely to him. I know that he has heard about all of these things. They did not happen in a corner. [27] King Agrippa, do you believe what the prophets*d* wrote? I know you believe!"

[28] King Agrippa said to Paul, "Do you think you can persuade me to become a Christian in such a short time?"

[29] Paul said, "Whether it is a short or a long time, I pray to God that not only you but every person listening to me today would be saved and be like me – except for these chains I have!"

[30] Then King Agrippa, Governor Festus, Bernice, and all the people sitting with them stood up [31] and left the room. They were talking to each other. They said, "There is no reason why this man should die or be put in jail." [32] And Agrippa said to Festus, "We could let this man go free, but he has asked Caesar*d* to hear his case."

Paul Sails for Rome

27 It was decided that we would sail for Italy. An officer named Julius, who served in the Emperor's*n* army, guarded Paul and some other prisoners. [2] We got on a ship and left.

Jewish language   Aramaic, the language of the Jews in the first century.
Emperor   The ruler of the Roman Empire, which was Europe, North Africa and the Middle East.

The ship was from the city of Adramyttium and was about to sail to different ports in the country of Asia. Aristarchus, a man from the city of Thessalonica in Macedonia, went with us. [3] The next day we came to Sidon. Julius was very good to Paul. He gave Paul freedom to go and visit his friends, who took care of his needs. [4] We left Sidon and sailed close to the island of Cyprus because the wind was blowing against us. [5] We went across the sea by Cilicia and Pamphylia. Then we came to the city of Myra, in Lycia. [6] There the officer found a ship from Alexandria that was going to Italy. So he put us on it.

[7] We sailed slowly for many days. We had a hard time reaching Cnidus because the wind was blowing against us. We could not go any farther that way. So we sailed by the south side of the island of Crete near Salmone. [8] We sailed along the coast, but the sailing was hard. Then we came to a place called Safe Harbours, near the city of Lasea.

[9] But we had lost a lot of time. It was now dangerous to sail, because it was already after the Day of Cleansing.[n] So Paul warned them, [10] "Men, I can see there will be a lot of trouble on this trip. The ship and the things in the ship will be lost. Even our lives may be lost!" [11] But the captain and the owner of the ship did not agree with Paul. So the officer did not believe Paul. Instead, the officer believed what the captain and owner of the ship said. [12] And that harbour was not a good place for the ship to stay for the winter. So most of the men decided that the ship should leave. The men hoped we could go to Phoenix. The ship could stay there for the winter. (Phoenix was a city on the island of Crete. It had a harbour which faced south west and north west.)

The Storm

[13] Then a good wind began to blow from the south. The men on the ship thought, "This is the wind we wanted, and now we have it!" So they pulled up the anchor. We sailed very close to the island of Crete. [14] But then a very strong wind named the "north-easter" came from the island. [15] This wind took the ship and carried it away. The ship could not sail against it. So we stopped trying and let the wind blow us. [16] We went below a small island named Cauda. Then we were able to bring in the lifeboat, but it was very hard to do. [17] After the men took the lifeboat in, they tied ropes around the ship to hold it together. The men were afraid that the ship would hit the sandbanks of Syrtis.[n] So they lowered the sail and let the wind carry the ship. [18] The next day the storm was blowing us so hard that the men threw out some of the cargo. [19] A day later they threw out the ship's equipment. [20] For many days we could not see the sun or the stars. The storm was very bad. We lost all hope of staying alive – we thought we would die.

[21] The men had gone without food for a long time. Then one day Paul stood up before them and said, "Men, I told you not to leave Crete. You should have listened to me. Then you would not have all this trouble and loss. [22] But now I tell you to cheer up. None of you will die! But the ship will be lost. [23] Last night an angel from God came to me. This is the God I worship.

Day of Cleansing An important Jewish holy day in the Autumn. This was the time of year that bad storms happened on the sea.
Syrtis Shallow area in the sea near the Libyan coast.

I am his. ²⁴God's angel said, 'Paul, do not be afraid! You must stand before Caesar.*d* And God has given you this promise: He will save the lives of all those men sailing with you'. ²⁵So men, be cheerful! I trust in God. Everything will happen as his angel told me. ²⁶But we will go aground on an island."

²⁷On the fourteenth night we were floating around in the Adriatic Sea.*n* The sailors thought we were close to land. ²⁸They threw a rope into the water with a weight on the end of it. They found that the water was 20 fathoms deep. They went a little farther and threw the rope in again. It was 15 fathoms deep. ²⁹The sailors were afraid that we would hit the rocks, so they threw four anchors into the water. Then they prayed for daylight to come. ³⁰Some of the sailors wanted to leave the ship, and they lowered the lifeboat. These sailors wanted the other men to think that they were throwing more anchors from the front of the ship. ³¹But Paul told the officer and the other soldiers, "If these men do not stay in the ship, your lives cannot be saved!" ³²So the soldiers cut the ropes and let the lifeboat fall into the water.

³³Just before dawn Paul began persuading all the people to eat something. He said, "For the past 14 days you have been waiting and watching. You have not eaten. ³⁴Now I beg you to eat something. You need it to stay alive. None of you will lose even one hair off your heads." ³⁵After he said this, Paul took some bread and thanked God for it before all of them. He broke off a piece and began eating. ³⁶All the men felt better. They all started eating too. ³⁷(There were 276 people on the ship.) ³⁸We ate all we wanted. Then we began making the ship lighter by throwing the grain into the sea.

The Ship Is Destroyed

³⁹When daylight came, the sailors saw land. They did not know what land it was, but they saw a bay with a beach. They wanted to sail the ship to the beach, if they could. ⁴⁰So they cut the ropes to the anchors and left the anchors in the sea. At the same time, they untied the ropes that were holding the rudders. Then they raised the front sail into the wind and sailed toward the beach. ⁴¹But the ship hit a sandbank. The front of the ship stuck there and could not move. Then the big waves began to break the back of the ship to pieces.

⁴²The soldiers decided to kill the prisoners so that none of them could swim away and escape. ⁴³But Julius, the officer, wanted to let Paul live. He did not allow the soldiers to kill the prisoners. Instead he ordered everyone who could swim to jump into the water and swim to land. ⁴⁴The rest used wooden boards or pieces of the ship. And this is how all the people made it safely to land.

Paul on the Island of Malta

28 When we were safe on land, we learned that the island was called Malta. ²It was raining and very cold. But the people who lived there were very good to us. They made us a fire and welcomed all of us. ³Paul gathered a pile of sticks for the fire. He was putting them on the fire when a poisonous snake came out because of the heat and bit him on the hand. ⁴The people living on the island saw the snake hanging from Paul's hand. They said to each other, "This man must be a murderer! He did not die

---

Adriatic Sea   The sea between Greece and Italy, including the central Mediterranean.

*Acts 28:3 A poisonous snake came out
. . . and bit him on the hand.*

in the sea, but Justice*n* does not want him to live." [5] But Paul shook the snake off into the fire. He was not hurt. [6] The people thought that Paul would swell up or fall down dead. The people waited and watched him for a long time, but nothing bad happened to him. So they changed their minds about Paul. Now they said, "He is a god!"

[7] There were some fields around there owned by a very important man on the island. His name was Publius. He welcomed us into his home and was very good to us. We stayed in his house for three days. [8] Publius' father was very sick with a fever and dysentery.*n* But Paul went to him and prayed. Then he put his hands on the man and healed him. [9] After this, all

the other sick people on the island came to Paul, and he healed them, too. [10-11] The people on the island gave us many honours. We stayed there three months. When we were ready to leave, they gave us the things we needed.

Paul Goes to Rome

We got on a ship from Alexandria. The ship had stayed on the island during the winter. On the front of the ship was the sign of the twin gods.*n* [12] We stopped at Syracuse for three days and then left. [13] From there we sailed to Rhegium. The next day a wind began to blow from the southwest, so we were able to leave. A day later we came to Puteoli. [14] We found some believers there, and they asked us to stay with them for a week. Finally, we came to Rome. [15] The believers in Rome heard that we were there. They came out as far as the Market of Appius*n* and the Three Inns*n* to meet us. When Paul saw them, he was encouraged and thanked God.

Paul in Rome

[16] Then we arrived at Rome. There, Paul was allowed to live alone. But a soldier stayed with him to guard him.

[17] Three days later Paul sent for the Jewish leaders there. When they came together, he said, "Brothers, I have done nothing against our people. I have done nothing against the customs of our fathers. But I was arrested in Jerusalem and given to the Romans. [18] The Romans asked me many questions. But they could find no reason why I should be killed. They wanted to let me go free, [19] but the Jews there did not want that. So I had to ask to

Justice   The people thought there was a god named Justice who would punish bad people.
dysentery   A sickness like diarrhoea.
twin gods   Statues of Castor and Pollux, gods in old Greek tales.
Market of Appius   A town about 43 kilometres from Rome.
Three Inns   A town about 48 kilometres from Rome.

come to Rome to have my trial before Caesar.[d] But I have no charge to bring against my own people. [20]That is why I wanted to see you and talk with you. I am bound with this chain because I believe in the hope of Israel."

[21]The Jews answered Paul, "We have received no letters from Judea about you. None of our Jewish brothers who have come from there brought news about you or told us anything bad about you. [22]We want to hear your ideas. We know that people everywhere are speaking against this religious group."

[23]Paul and the Jews chose a day for a meeting. On that day many more of the Jews met with Paul at the place he was staying. Paul spoke to them all day long, explaining the kingdom of God to them. He tried to persuade them to believe these things about Jesus. He used the law of Moses and the writings of the prophets[d] to do this. [24]Some of the Jews believed what Paul said, but others did not. [25]So they argued, and the Jews were ready to leave. But Paul said one more thing to them: "The Holy Spirit[d] spoke the truth to your fathers through Isaiah the prophet. He said,

[26]'Go to this people and say:
You will listen and listen, but you
     will not understand.
You will look and look, but you
     will not learn.
[27]For these people have become
     stubborn.
They don't hear with their ears.
And they have closed their
     eyes.
Otherwise, they might really
     understand
what they see with their eyes
and hear with their ears.
They might really understand in
     their minds.
If they did this, they would come
     back to me and be forgiven'.
                    Isaiah 6:9–10

[28]"I want you Jews to know that God has also sent his salvation to the non-Jewish people. They will listen!" [29][n]

[30]Paul stayed two full years in his own rented house. He welcomed all people who came and visited him. [31]He preached about the kingdom of God and taught about the Lord Jesus Christ. He was very bold, and no one tried to stop him from speaking.

Verse 29 Some late Greek copies add verse 29: "After Paul said this, the Jews left. They were arguing very much with each other."

ROMANS

God's Plan to Save Us

1 From Paul, a servant of Christ Jesus. God called me to be an apostle[d] and chose me to tell the Good News.[d]

2 God promised this Good News long ago through his prophets.[d] That promise is written in the Holy Scriptures.[d] 3-4 The Good News is about God's Son, Jesus Christ our Lord. As a man, he was born from the family of David. But through the Spirit[d] of holiness he was appointed to be God's Son with great power by rising from death. 5 Through Christ, God gave me the special work of an apostle. This was to lead people of all nations to believe and obey. I do this work for Christ. 6 And you who are in Rome are also called to belong to Jesus Christ.

7 This letter is to all of you in Rome whom God loves and has called to be his holy people.

May God our Father and the Lord Jesus Christ show you kindness and give you peace.

A Prayer of Thanks

8 First I want to say that I thank my God through Jesus Christ for all of you. I thank God because people everywhere in the world are talking about your great faith. 9-10 God knows that every time I pray I always mention you. God is the One I serve with my whole heart by telling the Good News[d] about his Son. I pray that I will be allowed to come to you, and this will happen if God wants it. 11 I want very much to see you, to give you some spiritual gift to make you strong. 12 I mean that I want us to help each other with the faith that we have. Your faith will help me, and my faith will help you. 13 Brothers, I want you to know that I planned many times to come to you. But this has not been possible. I wanted to come so that I could help you grow spiritually. I wanted to help you as I have helped the other non-Jewish people.

14 I must serve all people – Greeks and non-Greeks, the wise and the foolish. 15 That is why I want so much to preach the Good News to you in Rome.

16 I am proud of the Good News. It is the power God uses to save

Romans 1:7 "This letter is to all of you in Rome . . ."

everyone who believes – to save the Jews first, and also to save the non-Jews. [17]The Good News shows how God makes people right with himself. God's way of making people right with him begins and ends with faith. As the Scripture[d] says, "The person who is made right with God by faith will live for ever."[n]

All People Have Done Wrong

[18]God's anger is shown from heaven against all the evil and wrong things that people do. By their own evil lives they hide the truth. [19]God shows his anger because everything that may be known about God has been made clear. Yes, God has clearly shown them everything that may be known about him. [20]There are things about God that people cannot see – his eternal power and all the things that make him God. But since the beginning of the world those things have been easy to understand. They are made clear by what God has made. So people have no excuse for the bad things they do. [21]They knew God. But they did not give glory to God, and they did not thank him. Their thinking became useless. Their foolish minds were filled with darkness. [22]They said they were wise, but they became fools. [23]They gave up the glory of God who lives for ever. They traded that glory for the worship of idols made to look like earthly people. They traded God's glory for things that look like birds, animals, and snakes.

[24]People were full of sin, wanting only to do evil. So God let them go their sinful way. They became full of sexual sin, using their bodies wrongly with each other. [25]They traded the truth of God for a lie and worshipped and served things that were made by

man. But they did not worship and serve the God who made those things. God should be praised for ever. Amen.

[26]Because people did those things, God left them and let them do the shameful things they wanted to do. Women stopped having natural sex and started having sex with other women. [27]In the same way, men stopped having natural sex and began wanting each other. Men did shameful things with other men. And in their bodies they received the punishment for those wrongs.

[28]People did not think it was important to have a true knowledge of God. So God left them and allowed them to have their own worthless thinking. And so those people do the things that they should not do. [29]They are filled with every kind of sin, evil, selfishness, and hatred. They are full of jealousy, murder, fighting, lying, and thinking the worst about each other. They gossip [30]and say evil things about each other. They hate God. They are rude and conceited and boast about themselves. They invent ways of doing evil. They do not obey their parents. [31]They are foolish, they do not keep their promises, and they show no kindness or mercy to other people. [32]They know God's law says that those who live like this should die. But they continue to do these evil things. And they also feel that those who do these things are doing right.

You People Also Are Sinful

2 If you think that you can judge others, then you are wrong. You too are guilty of sin. You judge people, but you do the same bad things they do. So when you judge them, you are really judging yourself guilty. [2]God judges those who do wrong things.

"The person . . . for ever."   Quotation from Habakkuk 2:4.

And we know that God's judging is right. [3] You judge those who do wrong, but you do wrong yourselves. Do you think you will be able to escape the judgement of God? [4] God has been very kind to you, and he has been patient with you. God has been waiting for you to change. But you think nothing of his kindness. Perhaps you do not understand that God is kind to you so that you will change your hearts and lives. [5] But you are hard and stubborn and refuse to change. So you are making your own punishment greater and greater on the day God shows his anger. On that day all people will see God's right judgements. [6] God will reward or punish every person for what he has done. [7] Some people live for God's glory, for honour, and for life that has no end. They live for those things by always continuing to do good. God will give life for ever to them. [8] But other people are selfish and refuse to follow truth. They follow evil. God will give them his punishment and anger. [9] He will give trouble and suffering to everyone who does evil – to the Jews first and also to the non-Jews. [10] But God will give glory, honour, and peace to everyone who does good – to the Jews first and also to the non-Jews. [11] For God judges all people in the same way.

[12] People who have God's law and those who have never heard of the law are all the same when they sin. Those who do not have the law and are sinners will be lost. And, in the same way, people who have the law and are sinners will be judged by the law. [13] Hearing the law does not make people right with God. The law makes people right with God only if they obey what the law says. [14] (The non-Jews do not have the law. But when they freely do things that the law commands, then they are the law for themselves. This is true even though they do not have the law. [15] They show that in their hearts they know what is right and wrong, just as the law commands. And they also show this by the way they feel about right and wrong. Sometimes their thoughts tell them they did wrong. And sometimes their thoughts tell them they did right.) [16] All these things will happen on the day when God will judge the secret thoughts of people's hearts. The Good News[d] that I preach says that God will judge everyone through Christ Jesus.

The Jews and the Law

[17] What about you? You call yourself a Jew. You trust in the law of Moses and boast that you are close to God. [18] You know what God wants you to do. And you know the things that are important because you have learned the law. [19] You think you are a guide for the blind and a light for those who are in darkness. [20] You think you can show foolish people what is right and teach those who know nothing. You have the law; so you think you know everything and have all truth. [21] You teach other people. So why don't you teach yourself? You tell others not to steal. But you yourselves steal. [22] You say that others must not take part in adultery.[d] But you yourselves are guilty of that sin. You hate idols. But you steal from temples. [23] You boast about having God's law. But you bring shame to God by breaking his law. [24] It is written in the Scriptures:[d] "The non-Jews speak against God's name because of you Jews."[n]

[25] If you follow the law, then your circumcision[d] has meaning. But if you break the law, then it is as if you were

---

"The non-Jews . . . Jews." Quotation from Isaiah 52:5; Ezekiel 36:20.

never circumcised. ²⁶The non-Jews are not circumcised. But if they do what the law says, then it is as if they were circumcised. ²⁷You Jews have the written law and circumcision, but you break the law. So those who are not circumcised in their bodies, but still obey the law, will show that you are guilty.

²⁸A person is not a true Jew if he is only a Jew in his physical body. True circumcision is not only on the outside of the body. ²⁹A person is a true Jew only if he is a Jew inside. True circumcision is done in the heart by the Spirit,^d not by the written law. Such a person gets praise from God, not from other people.

3 So, do Jews have anything that other people do not have? Is there anything special about being circumcised? ²Yes, of course, there is in every way. The most important thing is this: God trusted the Jews with his teachings. ³It is true that some Jews were not faithful to God. But will that stop God from doing what he promised? ⁴No! God will continue to be true even when every person is false. As the Scriptures^d say:

"So your words may be shown to
be right.
You are fair when you judge
me."   *Psalm 51:4*

⁵When we do wrong, that shows more clearly that God is right. So can we say that God is wrong to punish us? (I am talking as men might talk.) ⁶No! If God could not punish us, then God could not judge the world.

⁷A person might say, "When I lie, it really gives God glory, because my lie shows God's truth. So why am I judged a sinner?" ⁸It would be the same to say, "We should do evil so that good will come." Some people find fault with us and say that we teach this. Those who say such things about

us are wrong, and they should be punished.

All People Are Guilty

⁹So are we Jews better than others? No! We have already said that Jews and non-Jews are the same. They are all guilty of sin. ¹⁰As the Scriptures^d say:

"There is no one without sin.
None!
¹¹ There is no one who
understands.
There is no one who looks to
God for help.
¹²All have turned away.
Together, everyone has become
evil.
None of them does anything
good."   *Psalm 14:1–3*
¹³"Their throats are like open
graves.
They use their tongues for
telling lies."   *Psalm 5:9*
"Their words are like snake's
poison."   *Psalm 140:3*
¹⁴ "Their mouths are full of
cursing and hate." *Psalm 10:7*
¹⁵"They are always ready to kill
people.
¹⁶ Everywhere they go they cause
ruin and misery.
¹⁷They don't know how to live in
peace."   *Isaiah 59:7–8*
¹⁸ "They have no fear of or respect
for God."   *Psalm 36:1*

¹⁹The law commands many things. We know that those commands are for those who are under the law. This stops all excuses and brings the whole world under God's judgement, ²⁰because no one can be made right with God by following the law. The law only shows us our sin.

How God Makes People Right

²¹But God has a way to make people right with him without the law. And

God has now shown us that way which the law and the prophets[d] told us about. [22] God makes people right with himself through their faith in Jesus Christ. This is true for all who believe in Christ, because all are the same. [23] All people have sinned and are not good enough for God's glory. [24] People are made right with God by his grace, which is a free gift. They are made right with God by being made free from sin through Jesus Christ. [25] God gave Jesus as a way to forgive sin through faith. And all of this is because of the blood of Jesus' death. This showed that God always does what is right and fair. God was right in the past when he was patient and did not punish people for their sins. [26] And God gave Jesus to show today that God does what is right. God did this so that he could judge rightly and also make right any person who has faith in Jesus.

[27] So do we have a reason to boast about ourselves? No! And why not? It is the way of faith that stops all boasting, not the way of following the law. [28] A person is made right with God through faith, not through what he does to follow the law. [29] Is God only the God of the Jews? Is he not also the God of the non-Jews? [30] Of course he is, for there is only one God. He will make Jews right with him by their faith. And he will also make non-Jews right with him through their faith. [31] So do we destroy the law by following the way of faith? No! Faith causes us to be what the law truly wants.

The Example of Abraham

4 So what can we say about Abraham,[n] the father of our people? What did he learn about faith? [2] If Abraham was made right by the things he did, then he had a reason to boast. But he could not boast before God. [3] The Scripture[d] says, "Abraham believed God. And that faith made him right with God."[n]

[4] When a person works, his pay is not given to him as a gift. He earns the pay he gets. [5] But a person cannot do any work that will make him right with God. So he must trust in God. Then God accepts his faith, and that makes him right with God. God is the One who can make even those who are evil right in his sight. [6] David said the same thing. He said that a person is truly blessed when God does not look at what he has done but accepts him as good:

[7] "Happy are they
    whose sins are forgiven,
    whose wrongs are pardoned.
[8] Happy is the person
    whom the Lord does not
        consider guilty."   *Psalm 32:1–2*

[9] Is this blessing only for those who are circumcised?[d] Or is it also for those who are not circumcised? We have already said that God accepted Abraham's faith, and that faith made him right with God. [10] So how did this happen? Did God accept Abraham before or after he was circumcised? God accepted him before his circumcision. [11] Abraham was circumcised later to show that God accepted him. His circumcision was proof that he was right with God through faith before he was circumcised. So Abraham is the father of all those who believe but are not circumcised. He is the father of all believers who are accepted as being right with God. [12] And Abraham is also the father of those who have been circumcised. But

---

Abraham   Most respected ancestor of the Jews. Every Jew hoped to see Abraham.
"Abraham . . . God."   Quotation from Genesis 15:6.

it is not their circumcision that makes him their father. He is their father only if they live following the faith that our father Abraham had before he was circumcised.

God Keeps His Promise

[13] Abraham[n] and his descendants[d] received the promise that the whole world would belong to them. But Abraham did not receive that promise through the law. He received it because he was right with God through his faith. [14] If people could receive what God promised by following the law, then faith is worthless. And God's promise to Abraham is worthless, [15] because the law can only bring God's anger. But if there is no law, then there is nothing to disobey.

[16] So people receive God's promise by having faith. This happens so that the promise can be a free gift. And if the promise is a free gift, then all of Abraham's children can have that promise. The promise is not only for those people that live under the law of Moses. It is for anyone who lives with faith like Abraham. He is the father of us all. [17] As it is written in the Scriptures:[d] "I am making you a father of many nations."[n] This is true before God. Abraham believed in God – the God who gives life to the dead and decides that things will happen that have not yet happened.

[18] There was no hope that Abraham would have children. But Abraham believed God and continued hoping. And that is why he became the father of many nations. As God told him, "Your descendants will also be too many to count."[n] [19] Abraham was almost 100 years old, well past the age for having children. Also, Sarah could not have children. Abraham thought about all this. But his faith in God did not become weak. [20] He never doubted that God would keep his promise. Abraham never stopped believing. He grew stronger in his faith and gave praise to God. [21] Abraham felt sure that God was able to do the thing that God promised. [22] So, "God accepted Abraham's faith, and that made him right with God."[n] [23] Those words ("God accepted Abraham's faith") were written not only for Abraham. [24] They were written also for us. God

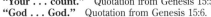

Abraham   Most respected ancestor of the Jews. Every Jew hoped to see Abraham.
"I . . . nations."   Quotation from Genesis 17:5.
"Your . . . count."   Quotation from Genesis 15:5.
"God . . . God."   Quotation from Genesis 15:6.

Romans 4:18 Abraham believed God and continued hoping.

will accept us also because we believe. We believe in the One who raised Jesus our Lord from death. [25]Jesus was given to die for our sins. And he was raised from death to make us right with God.

Right with God

5 We have been made right with God because of our faith. So we have peace with God through our Lord Jesus Christ. [2]Through our faith, Christ has brought us into that blessing of God's grace that we now enjoy. And we are happy because of the hope we have of sharing God's glory. [3]And we also have joy with our troubles because we know that these troubles produce patience. [4]And patience produces character, and character produces hope. [5]And this hope will never disappoint us, because God has poured out his love to fill our hearts. God gave us his love through the Holy Spirit,[d] whom God has given to us.

[6]Christ died for us while we were still weak. We were living against God, but at the right time, Christ died for us. [7]Very few people will die to save the life of someone else. Although perhaps for a good man someone might possibly die. [8]But Christ died for us while we were still sinners. In this way God shows his great love for us.

[9]We have been made right with God by the blood of Christ's death. So through Christ we will surely be saved from God's anger. [10]I mean that while we were God's enemies, God made friends with us through the death of his Son. Surely, now that we are God's friends, God will save us through his Son's life. [11]And not only that, but now we are also very happy in God through our Lord Jesus Christ. Through Jesus we are now God's friends again.

Adam and Christ

[12]Sin came into the world because of what one man did. And with sin came death. And this is why all men must die – because all men sinned. [13]Sin was in the world before the law of Moses. But God does not judge people guilty of sin if there is no law. [14]But from the time of Adam to the time of Moses, everyone had to die. Adam died because he sinned by not obeying God's command. But even those who did not sin in the same way had to die.

Adam was like the One who was coming in the future. [15]But God's free gift is not like Adam's sin. Many people died because of the sin of that one man. But the grace that they received from God was much greater. Many people received God's gift of life by the grace of the one man, Jesus Christ. [16]After Adam sinned once, he was judged guilty. But the gift of God is different. God's free gift came after many sins. And the gift makes people right with God. [17]One man sinned, and so death ruled all people because of that one man. But now some people accept God's full grace and the great gift of being made right with him. They will surely have true life and rule through the one man, Jesus Christ.

[18]So one sin of Adam brought the punishment of death to all people. But in the same way, one good act that Christ did makes all people right with God. And that brings true life for all. [19]One man disobeyed God, and many became sinners. But in the same way, one man obeyed God, and many will be made right. [20]The law came to make people have more sin. But when people had more sin, God gave them more of his grace. [21]Sin once used death to rule us. But God gave people more of his grace so that grace could

rule by making people right with him. And this brings life for ever through Jesus Christ our Lord.

Dead to Sin but Alive in Christ

6 So do you think that we should continue sinning so that God will give us more and more grace? [2] No! We died to our old sinful lives. So how can we continue living with sin? [3] Did you forget that all of us became part of Christ when we were baptised? We shared his death in our baptism. [4] So when we were baptised, we were buried with Christ and shared his death. We were buried with him so that we could live a new life, just as Christ was raised from death by the wonderful power of the Father.

[5] Christ died, and we have been joined with Christ by dying too. So we will also be joined with him by rising from death as he did. [6] We know that our old life died with Christ on the cross. This was so that our sinful selves would have no power over us, and we would not be slaves to sin. [7] Anyone who has died is made free from sin's control.

[8] If we died with Christ, we know that we will also live with him. [9] Christ was raised from death. And we know that he cannot die again. Death has no power over him now. [10] Yes, when Christ died, he died to defeat the power of sin once – enough for all time. He now has a new life, and his new life is with God. [11] In the same way, you should see yourselves as being dead to the power of sin and alive with God through Christ Jesus.

[12] So, do not let sin control you in your life here on earth. You must not be ruled by the things your sinful self makes you want to do. [13] Do not offer the parts of your body to serve sin. Do not use your bodies as things to do evil with, but offer yourselves to God. Be like people who have died and now live. Offer the parts of your body to God to be used for doing good. [14] Sin will not be your master, because you are not under law but under God's grace.

Slaves of Righteousness

[15] So what should we do? Should we sin because we are under grace and not under law? No! [16] Surely you know that when you give yourselves like slaves to obey someone, then you are really slaves of that person. The person you obey is your master. You can follow sin, or obey God. Sin brings spiritual death. But obeying God makes you right with him. [17] In the past you were slaves to sin – sin controlled you. But thank God, you fully obeyed the things that were taught to you. [18] You were made free from sin, and now you are slaves to goodness. [19] I use this example because this is hard for you to understand. In the past you offered the parts of your body to be slaves to sin and evil. You lived only for evil. In the same way now you must give yourselves to be slaves of goodness. Then you will live only for God.

[20] In the past you were slaves to sin, and goodness did not control you. [21] You did evil things, and now you are ashamed of them. Those things only bring death. [22] But now you are free from sin and have become slaves of God. This brings you a life that is only for God. And this gives you life for ever. [23] When someone sins, he earns what sin pays – death. But God gives us a free gift – life for ever in Christ Jesus our Lord.

An Example from Marriage

7 Brothers, all of you understand the law of Moses. So surely you know that the law rules over a person only while he is alive. [2] For example, a

woman must stay married to her husband as long as he is alive. But if her husband dies, then she is free from the law of marriage. ³But if she marries another man while her husband is still alive, the law says she is guilty of adultery.*ᵈ* But if her husband dies, then the woman is free from the law of marriage. So if she marries another man after her husband dies, she is not guilty of adultery.

⁴In the same way, my brothers, your old selves died, and you became free from the law through the body of Christ. Now you belong to someone else. You belong to the One who was raised from death. We belong to Christ so that we can be used in service to God. ⁵In the past, we were ruled by our sinful selves. The law made us want to do sinful things. And those sinful things we wanted to do controlled our bodies, so that the things we did were only bringing us death. ⁶In the past, the law held us like prisoners. But our old selves died, and we were made free from the law. So now we serve God in a new way, not in the old way with written rules. Now we serve God in the new way, with the Spirit.*ᵈ*

Our Fight Against Sin

⁷You might think that I am saying that sin and the law are the same thing. That is not true. But the law was the only way I could learn what sin meant. I would never have known what it means to want something wrong if the law had not said, "You must not want to take your neighbour's things."*ⁿ* ⁸And sin found a way to use that command and cause me to want every kind of wrong thing. So sin came to me because of that command. But without the law, sin has no power.

⁹I was alive without the law before I knew the law. But when the law's command came to me, then sin began to live. ¹⁰And I died because of sin. The command was meant to bring life, but for me that command brought death. ¹¹Sin found a way to fool me by using the command. Sin used the command to make me die.

¹²So the law is holy, and the command is holy and right and good. ¹³Does this mean that something that is good brought death to me? No! Sin used something that is good to bring death to me. This happened so that I could see what sin is really like. The command was used to show that sin is something very evil.

The War Within Man

¹⁴We know that the law is spiritual. But I am not spiritual. Sin rules me as if I were its slave. ¹⁵I do not understand the things I do. I do not do the good things I want to do. And I do the bad things I hate to do. ¹⁶And if I do not want to do the bad things I do, then that means that I agree that the law is good. ¹⁷But I am not really the one who is doing these bad things. It is sin living in me that does these things. ¹⁸Yes, I know that nothing good lives in me – I mean nothing good lives in the part of me that is earthly and sinful. I want to do the things that are good. But I do not do them. ¹⁹I do not do the good things that I want to do. I do the bad things that I do not want to do. ²⁰So if I do things I do not want to do, then I am not the one doing those things. It is sin living in me that does those bad things.

²¹So I have learned this rule: when I want to do good, evil is there with me. ²²In my mind, I am happy with

---

"You . . . things." Quotation from Exodus 20:13,15–17.

God's law. [23] But I see another law working in my body. That law makes war against the law that my mind accepts. That other law working in my body is the law of sin, and that law makes me its prisoner. [24] What a miserable man I am! Who will save me from this body that brings me death? [25] God will. I thank him for saving me through Jesus Christ our Lord!

So in my mind I am a slave to God's law. But in my sinful self I am a slave to the law of sin.

Life in the Spirit

8 So now, those who are in Christ Jesus are not judged guilty. [2] I am not judged guilty because in Christ Jesus the law of the Spirit[d] that brings life made me free. It made me free from the law that brings sin and death. [3] The law was without power, because the law was made weak by our sinful selves. But God did what the law could not do. He sent his own Son to earth with the same human life that others use for sin. He sent his Son to be an offering to pay for sin. So God used a human life to destroy sin. [4] He did this so that we could be right as the law said we must be. Now we do not live following our sinful selves, but we live following the Spirit.

[5] Those who live following their sinful selves think only about things that their sinful selves want. But those who live following the Spirit are thinking about the things that the Spirit wants them to do. [6] If a person's thinking is controlled by his sinful self, then there is death. But if his thinking is controlled by the Spirit, then there is life and peace. [7] This is true because if a person's thinking is controlled by his sinful self, then he is against God. He refuses to obey God's law. And really

he is not able to obey God's law. [8] Those people who are ruled by their sinful selves cannot please God.

[9] But you are not ruled by your sinful selves. You are ruled by the Spirit, if that Spirit of God really lives in you. But if anyone does not have the Spirit of Christ, then he does not belong to Christ. [10] Your body will always be dead because of sin. But if Christ is in you, then the Spirit gives you life, because Christ made you right with God. [11] God raised Jesus from death. And if God's Spirit is living in you, then he will also give life to your bodies that die. God is the One who raised Christ from death. And he will give life through his Spirit that lives in you.

[12] So, my brothers, we must not be ruled by our sinful selves. We must not live the way our sinful selves want. [13] If you use your lives to do the wrong things your sinful selves want, then you will die spiritually. But if you use the Spirit's help to stop doing the wrong things you do with your body, then you will have true life.

[14] The true children of God are those who let God's Spirit lead them. [15] The Spirit that we received is not a spirit that makes us slaves again to fear. The Spirit that we have makes us children of God. And with that Spirit we say, "Father, dear Father."[n] [16] And the Spirit himself joins with our spirits to say that we are God's children. [17] If we are God's children, then we will receive the blessings God has for us. We will receive these things from God together with Christ. But we must suffer as Christ suffered, and then we will have glory as Christ has glory.

Our Future Glory

[18] We have sufferings now. But the sufferings we have now are nothing

---

"Father, dear Father" Literally, "Abba, Father". Jewish children called their fathers "Abba".

compared to the great glory that will be given to us. [19]Everything that God made is waiting with excitement for

Romans 8:19 Everything that God made is waiting . . .

the time when God will show the world who his children are. The whole world is longing for that to happen. [20]Everything that God made was changed to become useless. This was not by its own wish. It happened because God wanted it. But there was this hope: [21]that everything God made would be set free from ruin. There was hope that everything God made would have the freedom and glory that belong to God's children.

[22]We know that everything God made has been waiting until now in pain, like a woman ready to give birth. [23]Not only the world, but we also have been waiting with pain inside us. We have the Spirit[d] as the first part of God's promise. So we are waiting for

God to finish making us his own children. I mean we are waiting for our bodies to be made free. [24]We were saved, and we have this hope. If we see what we are waiting for, then that is not really hope. People do not hope for something they already have. [25]But we are hoping for something that we do not have yet. We are waiting for it patiently.

[26]Also, the Spirit helps us. We are very weak, but the Spirit helps us with our weakness. We do not know how to pray as we should. But the Spirit himself speaks to God for us, even begs God for us. The Spirit speaks to God with deep feelings that words cannot explain. [27]God can see what is in people's hearts. And he knows what is in the mind of the Spirit, because the Spirit speaks to God for his people in the way that God wants.

[28]We know that in everything God works for the good of those who love him. They are the people God called, because that was his plan. [29]God knew them before he made the world. And God decided that they would be like his Son. Then Jesus would be the firstborn[n] of many brothers. [30]God planned for them to be like his Son. And those he planned to be like his Son, he also called. And those he called, he also made right with him. And those he made right, he also glorified.

God's Love in Christ Jesus

[31]So what should we say about this? If God is with us, then no one can defeat us. [32]God let even his own Son suffer for us. God gave his Son for us all. So with Jesus, God will surely give us all things. [33]Who can accuse the people that God has chosen? No one!

---

firstborn   Here this probably means that Christ was the first in God's family to share God's glory.

God is the One who makes them right. [34] Who can say that God's people are guilty? No one! Christ Jesus died, but that is not all. He was also raised from death. And now he is on God's right side and is begging God for us. [35] Can anything separate us from the love Christ has for us? Can troubles or problems or sufferings? If we have no food or clothes, if we are in danger, or even if death comes – can any of these things separate us from Christ's love? [36] As it is written in the Scriptures:[d]

> "For you we are in danger of
>   death all the time.
> People think we are worth no
>   more than sheep to be
>   killed."   *Psalm 44:22*

[37] But in all these things we have full victory through God who showed his love for us. [38-39] Yes, I am sure that nothing can separate us from the love God has for us. Not death, not life, not angels, not ruling spirits, nothing now, nothing in the future, no powers, nothing above us, nothing below us, or anything else in the whole world will ever be able to separate us from the love of God that is in Christ Jesus our Lord.

God and the Jewish People

9 I am in Christ, and I am telling you the truth. I do not lie. My feelings are ruled by the Holy Spirit,[d] and they tell me that I am not lying. [2] I have great sorrow and always feel much sadness for the Jewish people. [3] I wish I could help my Jewish brothers, my people. I would even wish that I were cursed and cut off from Christ if that would help them. [4] They are the people of Israel. They were God's chosen children. They have the glory of God and the agreements that God made between himself and his people. God gave them the law of Moses and the right way of worship. And God gave his promises to them. [5] They are the descendants[d] of our great ancestors, and they are the earthly family of Christ. Christ is God over all. Praise him for ever![n] Amen.

[6] I do not mean that God failed to keep his promise to them. But only some of the people of Israel are truly God's people.[n] [7] And only some of Abraham's[n] descendants are true children of Abraham. But God said to Abraham: "The descendants I promised you will be from Isaac."[n] [8] This means that not all of Abraham's descendants are God's true children. Abraham's true children are those who become God's children because of the promise God made to Abraham. [9] God's promise to Abraham was this: "At the right time I will return, and Sarah will have a son."[n] [10] And that is not all. Rebekah also had sons. And those sons had the same father, our father Isaac. [11-12] But before the two boys were born, God told Rebekah, "The older will serve the younger."[n] This was before the boys had done anything good or bad. God said this before they were born so that the one chosen would be chosen because of God's own plan. He was chosen because he was the one God wanted to call, not because of anything he did.

Christ . . . for ever!   This can also mean, "May God, who rules over all things, be praised for ever!"

God's people   Literally, "Israel", the people God chose to bring his blessings to the world.

Abraham   Most respected ancestor of the Jews. Every Jew hoped to see Abraham.

"The descendants . . . Isaac."   Quotation from Genesis 21:12.

"At . . . son."   Quotation from Genesis 18:10,14.

"The older . . . younger."   Quotation from Genesis 25:23.

[13] As the Scripture[d] says, "I loved Jacob, but I hated Esau."[n]

[14] So what should we say about this? Is God unfair? In no way. [15] God said to Moses, "I will show kindness to anyone I want to show kindness. I will show mercy to anyone I want to show mercy."[n] [16] So God will choose the one he decides to show mercy to. And his choice does not depend on what people want or try to do. [17] The Scripture says to the king of Egypt: "I made you king so I might show my power in you. In this way my name will be talked about in all the earth."[n] [18] So God shows mercy where he wants to show mercy. And he makes stubborn the people he wants to make stubborn.

[19] So one of you will ask me: "If God controls the things we do, then why does he blame us for our sins? Who can fight his will?" [20] Do not ask that. You are only human. And human beings have no right to question God. An object cannot tell the person who made it, "Why did you make me like this?" [21] The man who makes a jar can make anything he wants to make. He can use the same clay to make different things. He can make one thing for special use and another thing for daily use.

[22] It is the same way with what God has done. God wanted to show his anger and to let people see his power. But God patiently stayed with those people he was angry with – people who were ready to be destroyed. [23] God waited with patience so that he could make known his rich glory. He wanted to give that glory to the people who receive his mercy. He has prepared these people to have his glory,

and [24] we are those people whom God called. He called us from the Jews and from the non-Jews. [25] As the Scripture says in Hosea:

"I will say, 'You are my people'
  to those I had called 'not my
  people'.
And I will show my love
  to those people I did not love."
Hosea 2:1,23

[26] "Now it is said to Israel,
  'You are not my people'.
But later they will be called
  'children of the living God'."
Hosea 1:10

[27] And Isaiah cries out about Israel:
"There are so many people of
  Israel.
  They are like the grains of sand
  by the sea.
But only a few of them will be
  saved.
[28] For the Lord will quickly and
  completely punish the people
  on the earth."   *Isaiah 10:22–23*

[29] It is as Isaiah said:
"The Lord of heaven's armies
  allowed a few of our
  descendants to live.
Otherwise we would have been
  completely destroyed
  like the cities of Sodom and
  Gomorrah."[n]   *Isaiah 1:9*

[30] So what does all this mean? It means this: the non-Jews were not trying to make themselves right with God. But they were made right with God because of their faith. [31] And the people of Israel tried to follow a law to make themselves right with God. But they did not succeed, [32] because they tried to make themselves right by the things they did. They did not

---

"I . . . Esau."   Quotation from Malachi 1:2–3.
"I . . . mercy."   Quotation from Exodus 33:19.
"I . . . earth."   Quotation from Exodus 9:16.
Sodom, Gomorrah   Two cities that God destroyed because the people were so evil.

trust in God to make them right. They fell over the stone that causes people to fall. ³³As it is written in the Scripture:

"I will put in Jerusalem a stone
   that causes people to
   stumble.
It is a rock that makes them fall.
Anyone who trusts in him will not
   be disappointed."

Isaiah 8:14; 28:16

10 Brothers, the thing I want most is for all the Jews to be saved. That is my prayer to God. ²I can say this about them: they really try to follow God. But they do not know the right way. ³They did not know the way that God makes people right with him. And they tried to make themselves right in their own way. So they did not accept God's way of making people right. ⁴Christ ended the law, so that everyone who believes in him may be right with God.

⁵Moses writes about being made right by following the law. He says, "A person who does these things will have life for ever because of them."ⁿ ⁶But this is what the Scripture says about being made right through faith: "Don't say to yourself, 'Who will go up into heaven?'" (That means, "Who will go up to heaven to get Christ and bring him down to earth?") ⁷"And do not say, 'Who will go down into the world below?'" (That means, "Who will go down to get Christ and bring him up from death?") ⁸This is what the Scripture says: "God's teaching is near you; it is in your mouth and in your heart."ⁿ That is the teaching of faith that we tell. ⁹If you use your mouth to say, "Jesus is Lord", and if

you believe in your heart that God raised Jesus from death, then you will be saved. ¹⁰We believe with our

Romans 10:9 If you use your mouth to say, "Jesus is Lord", and if you believe in your heart . . .

hearts, and so we are made right with God. And we use our mouths to say that we believe, and so we are saved. ¹¹As the Scripture says, "Anyone who trusts in him will never be disappointed."ⁿ ¹²That Scripture says "anyone" because there is no difference between Jew and non-Jew. The same Lord is the Lord of all and gives many blessings to all who trust in him. ¹³The Scripture says, "Anyone who asks the Lord for help will be saved."ⁿ

¹⁴But before people can trust in the Lord for help, they must believe in him. And before they can believe in the Lord, they must hear about him.

"A person . . . them." Quotation from Leviticus 18:5.
Verses 6–8 Quotations from Deuteronomy 9:4; 30:12–14; Psalm 107:26.
"Anyone . . . disappointed." Quotation from Isaiah 28:16.
"Anyone . . . saved." Quotation from Joel 2:32.

And for them to hear about the Lord, someone must tell them. [15]And before someone can go and tell them, he must be sent. It is written, "How beautiful is the person who comes to bring Good News."[n]

[16]But not all the Jews accepted the good news. Isaiah said, "Lord, who believed what we told them?"[n] [17]So faith comes from hearing the Good News.[d] And people hear the Good News when someone tells them about Christ.

[18]But I ask: Didn't people hear the Good News? Yes, they heard – as the Scripture says:

"Their message went out through
    all the world.
It goes everywhere on earth."
                    Psalm 19:4

[19]Again I ask: Didn't the people of Israel understand? Yes, they did understand. First, Moses says:

"I will use those who are not a
    nation to make you jealous.
I will use a nation that does not
    understand to make you
    angry."   *Deuteronomy 32:21*

[20]Then Isaiah is bold enough to say:

"I was found by those who were
    not asking me for help.
I made myself known to people
    who were not looking for
    me."   *Isaiah 65:1*

[21]But about Israel God says,

"All day long I stood ready to
    accept
people who disobey and are
    stubborn."   *Isaiah 65:2*

God Shows Mercy to All People

11 So I ask: Did God throw out his people? No! I myself am an Israelite. I am from the family of Abraham, from the tribe[d] of Benjamin. [2]God chose the Israelites to be his people before they were born. And God did not leave his people. Surely you know what the Scripture[d] says about Elijah, how he prayed to God against the people of Israel. Elijah said, [3]"They have killed your prophets,[d] and they have destroyed your altars. I am the only prophet left. And now they are trying to kill me, too."[n] [4]But what answer did God give Elijah? He said, "But I have left 7,000 people in Israel. Those 7,000 have never bowed down before Baal."[n] [5]It is the same now. There are a few people that God has chosen by his grace. [6]And if God chose them by grace, then it is not for the things they have done. If they could be made God's people by what they did, then God's gift of grace would not really be a gift.

[7]So this is what has happened: the people of Israel tried to be right with God. But they did not succeed. But the ones God chose did become right with him. The others became hard and refused to listen to God. [8]As it is written in the Scriptures:[d]

"God gave the people a dull mind
    so they could not
    understand."   *Isaiah 29:10*
"God closed their eyes so they
    could not see,
and God closed their ears so
    they could not hear.
This continues until today."
                    Deuteronomy 29:4

[9]And David says:

"Let their own feasts trap them
    and cause their ruin.

"How . . . news." Quotation from Isaiah 52:7.
"Lord, . . . them?" Quotation from Isaiah 53:1.
"They . . . too." Quotation from 1 Kings 19:10,14.
"But . . . Baal." Quotation from 1 Kings 19:18.

Let their feasts cause them to sin and be paid back.

[10] Let their eyes be closed so they cannot see.

Let their backs be for ever weak from troubles."   *Psalm 69:22–23*

[11] So I ask: when the Jews fell, did that fall destroy them? No! But their mistake brought salvation to the non-Jews. This took place to make the Jews jealous. [12] The Jews' mistake brought rich blessings for the world. And what the Jews lost brought rich blessings for the non-Jewish people. So surely the world will get much richer blessings when enough Jews become the kind of people God wants.

[13] Now I am speaking to you who are not Jews. I am an apostle[d] to the non-Jews. So while I have that work, I will do the best I can. [14] I hope I can make my own people jealous. That way, maybe I can help some of them to be saved. [15] God turned away from the Jews. When that happened, God became friends with the other people in the world. So when God accepts the Jews, then surely that will bring to them life after death.

[16] If the first piece of bread is offered to God, then the whole loaf is made holy. If the roots of a tree are holy, then the tree's branches are holy too.

[17] Some of the branches from an olive tree have been broken off, and the branch of a wild olive tree has been joined to that first tree. You non-Jews are the same as that wild branch, and you now share the strength and life of the first tree, the Jews. [18] So do not boast about those branches that were broken off. You have no reason to boast. Why? You do not give life to the root. The root gives life to you. [19] You will say, "Branches were broken off so that I could be joined to their

tree." [20] That is true. But those branches were broken off because they did not believe. And you continue to be part of the tree only because you believe. Do not be proud, but be afraid. [21] If God did not let the natural branches of that tree stay, then he will not let you stay if you don't believe.

[22] So you see that God is kind, but he can also be very strict. God punishes those who stop following him. But God is kind to you, if you continue following in his kindness. If you do not continue following him, you will be cut off from the tree. [23] And if the Jews will believe in God again, then God will accept the Jews back again. God is able to put them back where they were. [24] It is not natural for a wild branch to be part of a good tree. But you non-Jews are like a branch cut from a wild olive tree. And you were joined to a good olive tree. But those Jews are like a branch that grew from the good tree. So surely they can be joined to their own tree again.

[25] I want you to understand this secret truth, brothers. This truth will help you understand that you do not know everything. The truth is this: part of Israel has been made stubborn. But that will change when many non-Jews have come to God. [26] And that is how all Israel will be saved. It is written in the Scriptures:

"The Saviour will come from Jerusalem;

he will take away all evil from the family of Jacob.[n]

[27] And I will make this agreement with those people

when I take away their sins."

Isaiah 59:20–21; 27:9

[28] The Jews refuse to accept the Good News,[d] so they are God's enemies. This has happened to help

---

Jacob   Father of the 12 family groups of Israel, the people God chose to be his people.

you non-Jews. But the Jews are still God's chosen people, and God loves them very much. He loves them because of the promises he made to their ancestors. ²⁹God never changes his mind about the people he calls and the things he gives them. ³⁰At one time you refused to obey God. But now you have received mercy, because those people refused to obey. ³¹And now the Jews refuse to obey, because God showed mercy to you. But this happened so that they also can receive mercy from God. ³²All people have refused to obey God. God has given them all over to their stubborn ways, so that God can show mercy to all.

Praise to God

³³Yes, God's riches are very great! God's wisdom and knowledge have no end! No one can explain the things God decides. No one can understand God's ways. ³⁴As the Scripture*ᵈ* says,

"Who has known the mind of the
Lord?
Who has been able to give the
Lord advice?" *Isaiah 40:13*
³⁵"No one has ever given God
anything
that he must pay back." *Job 41:11*
³⁶Yes, God made all things. And

everything continues through God and for God. To God be the glory for ever! Amen.

Give Your Lives to God

12 So brothers, since God has shown us great mercy, I beg you to offer your lives as a living sacrifice to him. Your offering must be only for God and pleasing to him. This is the spiritual way for you to worship. ²Do not change yourselves to be like the people of this world. But be changed within by a new way of thinking. Then you will be able to decide what God wants for you. And you will be able to know what is good and pleasing to God and what is perfect. ³God has given me a special gift. That is why I have something to say to everyone among you. Do not think that you are better than you are. You must see yourself as you really are. Decide what you are by the amount of faith God has given you. ⁴Each one of us has a body, and that body has many parts. These parts all have different uses. ⁵In the same way, we are many, but in Christ we are all one body. Each one is a part of that body. And each part belongs to all the other parts. ⁶We all have different gifts. Each gift came because of the grace that God gave us. If one has the gift of prophecy,*ᵈ* he

Romans 12:6 We all have different gifts.

should use that gift with the faith he has. [7] If one has the gift of serving, he should serve. If one has the gift of teaching, he should teach. [8] If one has the gift of encouraging others, he should encourage. If one has the gift of giving to others, he should give freely. If one has the gift of being a leader, he should try hard when he leads. If one has the gift of showing kindness to others, that person should do so with joy.

[9] Your love must be real. Hate what is evil. Hold on to what is good. [10] Love each other like brothers and sisters. Give your brothers and sisters more honour than you want for yourselves. [11] Do not be lazy but work hard. Serve the Lord with all your heart. [12] Be joyful because you have hope. Be patient when trouble comes. Pray at all times. [13] Share with God's people who need help. Bring strangers in need into your homes.

[14] Wish good for those who do bad things to you. Wish them well and do not curse them. [15] Be happy with those who are happy. Be sad with those who are sad. [16] Live together in peace with each other. Do not be proud, but make friends with those who seem unimportant. Do not think how clever you are.

[17] If someone does wrong to you, do not pay him back by doing wrong to him. Try to do what everyone thinks is right. [18] Do your best to live in peace with everyone. [19] My friends, do not try to punish others when they wrong you. Wait for God to punish them with his anger. It is written: "I am the One who punishes; I will pay people back," [n] says the Lord. [20] But you should do this:

"If your enemy is hungry, feed him;
    if your enemy is thirsty, give
        him a drink.

Doing this will be like pouring
    burning coals on his head."
                        Proverbs 25:21–22
[21] Do not let evil defeat you. Defeat evil by doing good.

Christians Should Obey the Law

13 All of you must obey the government rulers. No one rules unless God has given him the power to rule. And no one rules now without that power from God. [2] So if anyone is against the government, he is really against what God has commanded. And so he brings punishment on himself. [3] Those who do right do not have to fear the rulers. But people who do wrong must fear them. Do you want to be unafraid of the rulers? Then do what is right, and the ruler will praise you. [4] He is God's servant to help you. But if you do wrong, then be afraid. The ruler has the power to punish; he is God's servant to punish those who do wrong. [5] So you must obey the government. You must obey not only because you might be punished, but because you know it is the right thing to do.

[6] And this is also why you pay taxes. Rulers are working for God and give their time to their work. [7] Pay everyone, then, what you owe him. If you owe any kind of tax, pay it. Show respect and honour to them all.

Loving Others

[8] Do not owe people anything. But you will always owe love to each other. The person who loves others has obeyed all the law. [9] The law says, "You must not be guilty of adultery. [d] You must not murder anyone. You must not steal. You must not want to take your neighbour's things." [n] All these commands and all others are really

---

"I ... back," Quotation from Deuteronomy 32:35.
"You ... things." Quotation from Exodus 20:13–15,17.

JOHN 12:13
They took branches of palm trees and went out to meet Jesus.

LUKE 22:47
One of the 12 apostles was leading them. He was Judas. He came close to Jesus so that he could kiss him.

JOHN 19:17–18
Jesus went out to a place called
The Place of the Skull. There
they nailed Jesus to the cross.

only one rule: "Love your neighbour as you love yourself."[n] [10]Love never hurts a neighbour. So loving is obeying all the law.

[11]I say this because we live in an important time. Yes, it is now time for you to wake up from your sleep. Our salvation is nearer now than when we first believed. [12]The "night"[n] is almost finished. The "day"[n] is almost here. So we should stop doing things that belong to darkness and take up the weapons used for fighting in the light. [13]Let us live in a right way, like people who belong to the day. We should not have wild parties or get drunk. There should be no sexual sins of any kind, no fighting or jealousy. [14]But clothe yourselves with the Lord Jesus Christ. Forget about satisfying your sinful self.

Do Not Criticise Other People

14 Do not refuse to accept into your group someone who is weak in faith. And do not argue with him about opinions. [2]One person believes that he can eat all kinds of food.[n] But if another man's faith is weak, then he believes he can eat only vegetables. [3]The one who knows that he can eat any kind of food must not feel that he is better than the one who eats only vegetables. And the person who eats only vegetables must not think that the one who eats all foods is wrong. God has accepted him. [4]You cannot judge another man's servant. His own master decides if he is doing well or not. And the Lord's servant will do well because the Lord helps him do well.

[5]One person thinks that one day is more important than another. And someone else thinks that every day is the same. Each one should be sure in his own mind. [6]The person who thinks one day is more important than other days is doing that for the Lord. And the one who eats all kinds of food is doing that for the Lord. Yes, he gives thanks to God for that food. And the man who refuses to eat some foods does that for the Lord, and he gives thanks to God. [7]For we do not live or die for ourselves. [8]If we live, we are living for the Lord. And if we die, we are dying for the Lord. So living or dying, we belong to the Lord.

[9]That is why Christ died and rose from death to live again. He did this so that he would be Lord over both the dead and the living. [10]So why do you judge your brother in Christ? And

Romans 14:10 Why do you judge your brother in Christ?

"Love . . . yourself." Quotation from Leviticus 19:18.
"night" This is used as a symbol of the sinful world we live in. This world will soon end.
"day" This is used as a symbol of the good time that is coming, when we will be with God.
all . . . food The Jewish law said there were some foods Jews should not eat. When Jews became Christians, some of them did not understand they could now eat all foods.

why do you think that you are better than he is? We will all stand before God, and he will judge us all. [11] Yes, it is written in the Scriptures:[d]

"Everyone will bow before me;
    everyone will say that I am
      God.
As surely as I live, these things
    will happen, says the Lord."

Isaiah 45:23

[12] So each of us will have to answer to God for what he has done.

Do Not Cause Others to Sin

[13] So we should stop judging each other. We must make up our minds not to do anything that will make a Christian brother sin. [14] I am in the Lord Jesus, and I know that there is no food that is wrong to eat. But if a person believes that something is wrong, then that thing is wrong for him. [15] If you hurt your brother's faith because of something you eat, then you are not really following the way of love. Do not destroy his faith by eating food that he thinks is wrong. Christ died for him. [16] Do not allow what you think is good to become what others say is evil. [17] In the kingdom of God, eating and drinking are not important. The important things are living right with God, peace, and joy in the Holy Spirit.[d] [18] Anyone who serves Christ by living this way is pleasing God and will be accepted by other people.

[19] So let us try to do what makes peace and helps one another. [20] Do not let the eating of food destroy the work of God. All foods are all right to eat, but it is wrong to eat food that causes someone else to sin. [21] It is better not to eat meat or drink wine or do anything that will cause your brother to sin.

[22] Your beliefs about these things should be kept secret between you and God. A person is blessed if he can do what he thinks is right without feeling guilty. [23] But if he eats something without being sure that it is right, then he is wrong because he did not believe that it was right. And if he does anything without believing that it is right, then it is a sin.

15 We who are strong in faith should help those who are weak. We should help them with their weaknesses, and not please only ourselves. [2] Let each of us please his neighbour for his good, to help him be stronger in faith. [3] Even Christ did not live to please himself. It was as the Scriptures[d] said: "When people insult you, it hurts me."[n] [4] Everything that was written in the past was written to teach us, so that we could have hope. That hope comes from the patience and encouragement that the Scriptures give us. [5] Patience and encouragement come from God. And I pray that God will help you all agree with each other the way Christ Jesus wants. [6] Then you will all be joined together, and you will give glory to God the Father of our Lord Jesus Christ. [7] Christ accepted you, so you should accept each other. This will bring glory to God. [8] I tell you that Christ became a servant of the Jews. This was to show that God's promises to the Jewish ancestors are true. [9] And he also did this so that the non-Jews could give glory to God for the mercy he gives to them. It is written in the Scriptures:

"So I will praise you among the
    non-Jewish people.
I will sing praises to your
    name."   *Psalm 18:49*

"When . . . me." Quotation from Psalm 69:9.

[10] The Scripture also says,
"Be happy, you non-Jews, together
with God's people."
Deuteronomy 32:43
[11] Again the Scripture says,
"All you non-Jews, praise the
Lord.
All you people, sing praises to
him." *Psalm 117:1*
[12] And Isaiah says,
"A new king will come from
Jesse's family.[n]
He will come to rule over the
non-Jews;
and the non-Jews will have hope
because of him." *Isaiah 11:10*
[13] I pray that the God who gives
hope will fill you with much joy and
peace while you trust in him. Then
your hope will overflow by the power
of the Holy Spirit.[d]

Paul Talks About His Work

[14] My brothers, I am sure that you
are full of goodness. I know that you
have all the knowledge you need and
that you are able to teach each other.
[15] But I have written to you very openly
about some things that I wanted you
to remember. I did this because God
gave me this special gift: [16] to be a minister of Christ Jesus to the non-Jewish
people. I served God by teaching his
Good News,[d] so that the non-Jewish
people could be an offering that God
would accept – an offering made holy
by the Holy Spirit.[d]
[17] So I am proud of what I have done
for God in Christ Jesus. [18] I will not
talk about anything I did myself. I will
talk only about what Christ has done
through me in leading the non-Jewish
people to obey God. They have obeyed
God because of what I have said and
done. [19] And they have obeyed God
because of the power of miracles[d] and

the great things they saw, and the
power of the Holy Spirit. I preached
the Good News from Jerusalem all the
way around to Illyricum. And so I have
finished that part of my work. [20] I
always want to preach the Good News
in places where people have never
heard of Christ. I do this because I
do not want to build on the work that
someone else has already started.
[21] But it is written in the Scriptures:[d]
"Those who were not told about
him will see,
and those who have not heard
about him will understand."
Isaiah 52:15

Paul's Plan to Visit Rome

[22] That is why many times I was
stopped from coming to you. [23] Now I
have finished my work here. Since for
many years I have wanted to come to
you, [24] I hope to visit you on my way
to Spain. I will enjoy being with you,
and you can help me on my trip.
[25] Now I am going to Jerusalem to help
God's people. [26] The believers in
Macedonia and Southern Greece were
happy to give their money to help the
poor among God's people at Jerusalem. [27] They were happy to do this,
and really they owe it to them. These
non-Jews have shared in the Jews'
spiritual blessings. So they should use
their material possessions to help the
Jews. [28] I must be sure that the poor
in Jerusalem get the money that has
been given for them. After I do this, I
will leave for Spain and stop and visit
you. [29] I know that when I come to you,
I will bring Christ's full blessing.
[30] Brothers, I beg you to help me in
my work by praying for me to God.
Do this because of our Lord Jesus and
the love that the Holy Spirit[d] gives us.
[31] Pray that I will be saved from the

Jesse's family Jesse was the father of David, king of Israel. Jesus was from their family.

non-believers in Judea. And pray that this help I bring to Jerusalem will please God's people there. [32]Then, if God wants me to, I will come to you. I will come with joy, and together you and I will have a time of rest. [33]The God who gives peace be with you all. Amen.

Greetings to the Christians

16 I recommend to you our sister Phoebe. She is a helper[n] in the church in Cenchrea. [2]I ask you to accept her in the Lord in the way God's people should. Help her with anything she needs because she has helped me and many other people too.

[3]Give my greetings to Priscilla and Aquila, who work together with me in Christ Jesus. [4]They risked their own lives to save my life. I am thankful to them, and all the non-Jewish churches are thankful to them as well. [5]Also, greet for me the church that meets at their house.

Greetings to my dear friend Epenetus. He was the first person in the country of Asia to follow Christ. [6]Greetings to Mary, who worked very hard for you. [7]Greetings to Andronicus and Junias, my relatives, who were in prison with me. The apostles feel they are very important. They were believers in Christ before I was. [8]Greetings to Ampliatus, my dear friend in the Lord. [9]Greetings to Urbanus. He is a worker together with me for Christ. And greetings to my dear friend Stachys. [10]Greetings to Apelles. He was tested and proved that he truly loves Christ. Greetings to all those who are in the family of Aristobulus. [11]Greetings to Herodion, my relative. Greetings to all those in the

family of Narcissus who belong to the Lord. [12]Greetings to Tryphena and Tryphosa. Those women work very hard for the Lord. Greetings to my dear friend Persis. She also has worked very hard for the Lord. [13]Greetings to Rufus who is a special person in the Lord. Greetings to his mother, who has been a mother to me also. [14]Greetings to Asyncritus, Phlegon, Hermes, Patrobas, Hermas, and all the brothers who are with them. [15]Greetings to Philologus and Julia, Nereus and his sister, and Olympas. And greetings to all God's people with them. [16]Greet each other with a holy kiss. All of Christ's churches send greetings to you.

[17]Brothers, I ask you to look out for those who cause people to be against each other and who upset other people's faith. They are against the true teaching you learned. Stay away from them. [18]For such people are not serving our Lord Christ. They are only doing what pleases themselves. They use fancy talk and fine words to fool the minds of those who do not know about evil. [19]All the believers have heard that you obey. So I am very happy because of you. But I want you to be wise in what is good and innocent in what is evil.

[20]The God who brings peace will soon defeat Satan and give you power over him.

The grace of our Lord Jesus be with you.

[21]Timothy, a worker together with me, sends greetings, as well as Lucius, Jason, and Sosipater, my relatives.

[22]I am Tertius, and I am writing this letter from Paul. I send greetings to you in the Lord.

[23]Gaius is letting me and the whole

---

helper   Literally, "deaconess". This might mean the same as one of the special women helpers in 1 Timothy 3:11.

church here use his home. He also sends greetings to you, as do Erastus and our brother Quartus. Erastus is the city treasurer here. [24] *n*

[25] Glory to God! God is the One who can make you strong in faith by the Good News[d] that I tell people and by the message about Jesus Christ. The message about Christ is the secret truth that was hidden for long ages past, but is now made known. [26] It has been made clear through the writings of the prophets.[d] And by the command of the eternal God it is made known to all nations, that they might believe and obey.

[27] To the only wise God be glory for ever through Jesus Christ! Amen.

Verse 24   Some Greek copies add verse 24: "The grace of our Lord Jesus Christ be with all of you. Amen."

1 CORINTHIANS

Help for a Church with Problems

1 From Paul. I was called to be an apostle*d* of Christ Jesus because that is what God wanted. Also from Sosthenes, our brother in Christ.

[2] To the church of God in Corinth, to those people who have been made holy in Christ Jesus. You were called to be God's holy people with all people everywhere who trust in the name of the Lord Jesus Christ – their Lord and ours:

[3] Grace and peace to you from God our Father and the Lord Jesus Christ.

Paul Gives Thanks to God

[4] I always thank my God for you because of the grace that God has given you in Christ Jesus. [5] In Jesus you have been blessed in every way, in all your speaking and in all your knowledge. [6] The truth about Christ has been proved in you. [7] So you have every gift from God while you wait for our Lord Jesus Christ to come again. [8] Jesus will keep you strong until the end. He will keep you strong, so that there will be no wrong in you on the day our Lord Jesus Christ comes again. [9] God is faithful. He is the One who has called you to share life with his Son, Jesus Christ our Lord.

Problems in the Church

[10] I beg you, brothers, in the name of our Lord Jesus Christ. I beg that all of you agree with each other, so that you will not be divided. I beg that you be completely joined together by having the same kind of thinking and the same purpose. [11] My brothers, some people from Chloe's family have told me that there are arguments among you. [12] This is what I mean: one of you says, "I follow Paul"; another says, "I follow Apollos"; another says, "I follow Peter"; and another says, "I follow Christ". [13] Christ cannot be divided into different groups! Did Paul die on the cross for you? No! Were you baptised in the name of Paul? No! [14] I am thankful that I did not baptise any of you except Crispus and Gaius. [15] I am thankful, because now no one can say

1 Corinthians 1:10 Agree with each other, so that you will not be divided.

that you were baptised in my name. [16] (I also baptised the family of Stephanas. But I do not remember that I myself baptised any others.) [17] Christ did not give me the work of baptising people. He gave me the work of preaching the Good News,*d* and he sent me to preach the Good News without using words of worldly wisdom. If I used worldly wisdom to tell the Good News, the cross*n* of Christ would lose its power.

Christ Is God's Power and Wisdom

[18] The teaching about the cross seems foolish to those who are lost. But to us who are being saved it is the power of God. [19] It is written in the Scriptures:*d*

"I will cause the wise men to lose
    their wisdom.
I will make the wise men unable
    to understand."   *Isaiah 29:14*

[20] Where is the wise person? Where is the educated person? Where is the philosopher*n* of our times? God has made the wisdom of the world foolish. [21] The world did not know God through its own wisdom. So God chose to use the message that sounds foolish to save those who believe it. [22] The Jews ask for miracles*d* as proofs. The Greeks want wisdom. [23] But we preach Christ on the cross. This is a big problem to the Jews. And it seems foolish to the non-Jews. [24] But Christ is the power of God and the wisdom of God to those people God has called – Jews and Greeks. [25] Even the foolishness of God is wiser than men. Even the weakness of God is stronger than men.

[26] Brothers, look at what you were when God called you. Not many of you were wise in the way the world judges wisdom. Not many of you had great influence. Not many of you came from important families. [27] But God chose the foolish things of the world to shame the wise. He chose the weak things of the world to shame the strong. [28] And he chose what the world thinks is not important. He chose what the world hates and thinks is nothing. He chose these to destroy what the world thinks is important. [29] God did this so that no man can boast before him. [30] It is God who has made you part of Christ Jesus. Christ has become wisdom for us from God. Christ is the reason we are right with God and have freedom from sin; Christ is the reason we are holy. [31] So, as the Scripture*d* says, "If a person boasts, he should boast only about the Lord."*n*

The Message of Christ's Death

2 Dear brothers, when I came to you, I did not come as a proud man. I preached God's truth, but not with fancy words or a show of great learning. [2] I decided that while I was with you I would forget about everything except Jesus Christ and his death on the cross. [3] When I came to you, I was weak and shook with fear. [4] My teaching and my speaking were not with wise words that persuade people. But the proof of my teaching was the power that the Spirit*d* gives. [5] I did this so that your faith would be in God's power, not in the wisdom of a man.

---

cross   Paul uses the cross as a picture of the gospel, the story of Christ's death and rising from death to pay for men's sins. The cross, or Christ's death, was God's way to save men.
philosopher   Philosophers were those who searched for truth.
"If . . . Lord."   Quotation from Jeremiah 9:24.

God's Wisdom

⁶Yet I speak wisdom to those who are mature. But this wisdom is not from this world or of the rulers of this world. (These rulers are losing their power.) ⁷But I speak God's secret wisdom, which he has kept hidden. God planned this wisdom for our glory, before the world began. ⁸None of the rulers of this world understood it. If they had, they would not have killed the Lord of glory on a cross. ⁹But as it is written in the Scriptures:ᵈ

"no one has ever seen this.
No one has ever heard about it.
No one has ever imagined
what God has prepared for
those
who love him."   *Isaiah 64:4*

¹⁰But God has shown us these things through the Spirit.ᵈ

The Spirit knows all things, even the deep secrets of God. ¹¹It is like this: no one knows the thoughts that another person has. Only a person's spirit that lives in him knows his thoughts. It is the same with God. No one knows the thoughts of God. Only the Spirit of God knows God's thoughts. ¹²We did not receive the spirit of the world, but we received the Spirit that is from God. We received this Spirit so that we can know all that God has given us. ¹³When we speak, we do not use words taught to us by the wisdom that men have. We use words taught to us by the Spirit. We use spiritual words to explain spiritual things. ¹⁴A person who is not spiritual does not accept the gifts that come from the Spirit of God. That person thinks they are foolish. He cannot understand the Spirit's gifts, because they can only be judged spiritually. ¹⁵But the spiritual person is able to judge all things. Yet no one can judge him. The Scripture says:

¹⁶"Who has known the mind of the
Lord?
Who has been able to teach
him?"   *Isaiah 40:13*

But we have the mind of Christ.

Following Men Is Wrong

3 Brothers, in the past I could not talk to you as I talk to spiritual people. I had to talk to you as I would to people of the world – babies in Christ. ²The teaching I gave you was like milk, not solid food. I did this because you were not ready for solid food. And even now you are not ready. ³You are still not spiritual. You have jealousy and arguing among you. This shows that you are not spiritual. You are acting like people of the world. ⁴One of you says, "I follow Paul," and another says, "I follow Apollos." When you say things like this, you are acting like worldly people.

⁵Is Apollos important? No! Is Paul important? No! We are only servants of God who helped you believe. Each one of us did the work God gave us to do. ⁶I planted the seed of the teaching in you, and Apollos watered it. But God is the One who made the seed grow. ⁷So the one who plants is not important, and the one who waters is not important. Only God is important, because he is the One who makes things grow. ⁸The one who plants and the one who waters have the same purpose. And each will be rewarded for his own work. ⁹We are workers together for God. And you are like a farm that belongs to God.

And you are a house that belongs to God. ¹⁰Like an expert builder I built the foundation of that house. I used the gift that God gave me to do this. Others are building on that foundation. But everyone should be careful how he builds. ¹¹The foundation has already been built. No one can build any other foundation. The foundation that has already been laid is Jesus Christ. [12] Anyone can build on that foundation, using gold, silver, jewels, wood, grass, or straw. [13] But the work that each person does will be clearly seen, because the Day[n] will make it plain. That Day will appear with fire, and the fire will test every man's work. [14] If the building that a man puts on the foundation still stands, he will get his reward. [15] But if his building is burned up, he will suffer loss. The man will be saved, but it will be as if he escaped from a fire.

[16] You should know that you yourselves are God's temple. God's Spirit[d] lives in you. [17] If anyone destroys God's temple, God will destroy him, because God's temple is holy. You yourselves are God's temple.

[18] Do not fool yourselves. If anyone among you thinks he is wise in this world, he should become a fool. Then he can become truly wise, [19] because the wisdom of this world is foolishness to God. It is written in the Scriptures,[d] "He catches wise men in their own clever traps."[n] [20] It is also written in the Scriptures, "The Lord knows what people think. He knows they are just a puff of wind."[n] [21] So you should not boast about men. All things are yours: [22] Paul, Apollos and Peter; the world, life, death, the present, and the future – all these things are yours. [23] And you belong to Christ, and Christ belongs to God.

Apostles of Christ

4 This is what people should think about us: we are servants of Christ. We are the ones God has trusted with his secret truths. [2] A person who is trusted with something must show that he is worthy of that trust. [3] I do not care if I am judged by you or if I am judged by any human court. I do not even judge myself. [4] I know of no wrong that I have done. But this does not make me innocent. The Lord is the One who judges me. [5] So do not judge before the right time; wait until the Lord comes. He will bring to light things that are now hidden in darkness. He will make known the secret purposes of people's hearts. Then God will give everyone the praise he should get.

[6] Brothers, I have used Apollos and myself as examples. I did this so that you could learn from us the meaning of the words, "Follow only what is written in the Scriptures."[d] Then you will not be proud of one man and hate another. [7] Who says that you are better than others? Everything you have was given to you. And if this is so, why do you boast as if you got these things by your own power?

[8] You think you have everything you need. You think you are rich. You think you have become kings without us. I wish you really were kings! Then we could be kings together with you. [9] But it seems to me that God has given me and the other apostles[d] the last place. We are like men sentenced to die. We are like a show for the whole world to see – angels and people. [10] We are fools for Christ's sake. But you think you are very wise in Christ. We are weak, but you think you are strong. You receive honour, but we are hated. [11] Even now we still do not have enough to eat or drink or enough clothes. We are often beaten. We have no homes. [12] We work hard with our

---

Day The day Christ will come to judge all people and take his people home to live with him.
"He ... traps." Quotation from Job 5:13.
"The Lord ... wind." Quotation from Psalm 94:11.

own hands for our food. People curse us, but we bless them. They hurt us, and we accept it. [13]They say evil things against us, but we say only kind things to them. Even today, we are treated as though we are the rubbish of the world – the scum of the earth.

[14]I am not trying to make you feel ashamed. I am writing this to give you a warning as if you were my own dear children. [15]For though you may have 10,000 teachers in Christ, you do not have many fathers. Through the Good News[d] I became your father in Christ Jesus. [16]So I beg you, please be like me. [17]That is why I am sending Timothy to you. He is my son in the Lord. I love Timothy, and he is faithful. He will help you remember the way I live in Christ Jesus. This way of life is what I teach in all the churches everywhere.

[18]Some of you have become proud, thinking that I will not come to you again. [19]But I will come very soon if the Lord wants me to. Then I will see what those who are proud can do, not what they say. [20]I want to see this because the kingdom of God is not talk but power. [21]Which do you want: that I come to you with punishment, or that I come with love and gentleness?

Wickedness in the Church

5 Now, it is actually being said that there is sexual sin among you. And it is of such a bad kind that it does not happen even among those who do not know God. A man there has his father's wife. [2]And still you are proud of yourselves! You should have been filled with sadness. And the man who did that sin should be put out of your group. [3]My body is not there with you, but I am with you in spirit. And I have already judged the man who did that

sin. I judged him just as I would if I were really there. [4]Meet together as the people of our Lord Jesus. I will be with you in spirit, and you will have the power of our Lord Jesus with you. [5]Then give this man to Satan, so that his sinful self[n] will be destroyed. And then his spirit can be saved on the day of the Lord.

[6]Your boasting is not good. You know the saying, "Just a little yeast makes the whole batch of dough rise." [7]Take out all the old yeast so that you will be a new batch of dough. And you really are new dough without yeast. For Christ, our Passover[d] lamb, was killed to cleanse us. [8]So let us continue our feast, but not with the bread that has the old yeast. That old yeast is the yeast of sin and wickedness. But let us eat the bread that has no yeast. This is the bread of goodness and truth.

[9]I wrote to you in my letter that you should not associate with those who take part in sexual sin. [10]But I did not mean that you should not associate with the sinful people of this world. People of the world do take part in sexual sin, or they are selfish and they cheat each other, or they worship idols. But to get away from them you would have to leave this world. [11]I am writing to tell you that the person you must not associate with is this: anyone who calls himself a brother in Christ but who takes part in sexual sin, or is selfish, or worships idols, or lies about others, or gets drunk, or cheats people. Do not even eat with someone like that.

[12-13]It is not my business to judge those who are not part of the church. God will judge them. But you must judge the people who are part of the church. The Scripture[d] says, "You

---

sinful self   Literally, "flesh". This could also mean his body.

must get rid of the evil person among you."[n]

Judging Problems Among Christians

6 When one of you has something against a brother in Christ, why do you go to the judges in the law courts?

1 Corinthians 6:1 When one of you has something against a brother . . .

Those people are not right with God. So why do you let them decide who is right? You should be ashamed! Why do you not let God's people decide who is right? [2] Surely you know that God's people will judge the world. So if you are to judge the world, then surely you are able to judge small things as well. [3] You know that in the future we will judge angels. So surely we can judge things in this life. [4] So if you have disagreements that must be judged, why do you take them to those who are not part of the church? They mean nothing to the church. [5] I say this to shame you. Surely there is someone among you wise enough to judge a complaint between two brothers in Christ. [6] But now one brother goes to court against another brother. And you let men who are not believers judge their case!

[7] The lawsuits that you have against each other show that you are already defeated. It would be better for you to let someone wrong you! It would be better for you to let someone cheat you! [8] But you yourselves do wrong and cheat! And you do this to your own brothers in Christ!

[9-10] Surely you know that the people who do wrong will not receive God's kingdom. Do not be fooled. These people will not receive God's kingdom: those who sin sexually, or worship idols, or take part in adultery,[d] or men who have sexual relations with other men, or steal, or are selfish, or get drunk, or lie about others, or cheat. [11] In the past, some of you were like that. But you were washed clean. You were made holy. And you were made right with God in the name of the Lord Jesus Christ and by the Spirit of our God.

Use Your Bodies for God's Glory

[12] "I am allowed to do all things." But all things are not good for me to do. "I am allowed to do all things." But I must not do those things that will make me their slave. [13] "Food is for the stomach, and the stomach for food." Yes. But God will destroy them both. The body is not for sexual sin. The body is for the Lord, and the Lord is for the body. [14] By God's power God raised the Lord Jesus from death. And God will also raise us from death. [15] Surely you know that your bodies are parts of Christ himself. So I must

"**You . . . you.**"   Quotation from Deuteronomy 17:7; 19:19; 22:21,24; 24:7.

never take parts of Christ and join them to a prostitute![d] [16]It is written in the Scriptures,[d] "The two people will become one body."[n] So you should know that a man who joins himself with a prostitute becomes one with her in body. [17]But the one who joins himself with the Lord is one with the Lord in spirit.

[18]So run away from sexual sin. Every other sin that a man does is outside his body. But the one who sins sexually sins against his own body. [19]You should know that your body is a temple for the Holy Spirit.[d] The Holy Spirit is in you. You have received the Holy Spirit from God. You do not own yourselves. [20]You were bought by God for a price. So honour God with your bodies.

About Marriage

7 Now I will discuss the things you wrote to me about. It is good for a man not to marry. [2]But sexual sin is a danger. So each man should have his own wife. And each woman should have her own husband. [3]The husband should give his wife all that she should have as his wife. And the wife should give her husband all that he should have as her husband. [4]The wife does not have power over her own body. Her husband has the power over her body. And the husband does not have power over his own body. His wife has the power over his body. [5]Do not refuse to give your bodies to each other. But you might both agree to stay away from sexual relations for a time. You might do this so that you can give your time to prayer. Then come together again. This is so that Satan cannot tempt you in your weakness. [6]I say this to give you permission. It is not a command. [7]I wish everyone

were like me. But each person has his own gift from God. One has one gift, another has another gift.

[8]Now for those who are not married and for the widows I say this: it is good for them to stay single as I am. [9]But if they cannot control their bodies, then they should marry. It is better to marry than to burn with sexual desire.

[10]Now I give this command for the married people. (The command is not from me; it is from the Lord.) A wife should not leave her husband. [11]But if she does leave, she must not marry again. Or she should go back to her husband. Also the husband should not divorce his wife.

[12]For all the others I say this (I am saying this, not the Lord): a brother in Christ might have a wife who is not a believer. If she will live with him, he must not divorce her. [13]And a woman might have a husband who is not a believer. If he will live with her, she must not divorce him. [14]The husband who is not a believer is made holy through his believing wife. And the wife who is not a believer is made holy through her believing husband. If this were not true, then your children would not be clean.[d] But now your children are holy.

[15]But if the person who is not a believer decides to leave, let him leave. When this happens, the brother or sister in Christ is free. God called us to a life of peace. [16]Wife, maybe you will save your husband; and husband, maybe you will save your wife. You do not know now what will happen later.

Live as God Called You

[17]But each one should continue to live the way God has given him to live – the way he was when God called him. This is a rule I make in all the

---

"The two . . . body." Quotation from Genesis 2:24.

churches. ¹⁸If a man was already circumcised^d when he was called, he should not change his circumcision. If a man was without circumcision when he was called, he should not be circumcised. ¹⁹It is not important if a man is circumcised or not circumcised. The important thing is obeying God's commands. ²⁰Each one should stay the way he was when God called him. ²¹If you were a slave when God called you, do not let that bother you. But if you can be free, then become free. ²²The person who was a slave when the Lord called him is free in the Lord. He belongs to the Lord. In the same way, the one who was free when he was called is now Christ's slave. ²³You all were bought for a price. So do not become slaves of men. ²⁴Brothers, in your new life with God each one of you should continue the way you were when you were called.

Questions About Getting Married

²⁵Now I write about people who are not married. I have no command from the Lord about this, but I give my opinion. And I can be trusted, because the Lord has given me mercy. ²⁶This is a time of trouble. So I think that it is good for you to stay the way you are. ²⁷If you have a wife, then do not try to become free from her. If you are not married, then do not try to find a wife. ²⁸But if you decide to marry, this is not a sin. And it is not a sin for a girl who has never married to get married. But those who marry will have trouble in this life. And I want you to be free from this trouble.

²⁹Brothers, this is what I mean: we do not have much time left. So starting now, those who have wives should use their time to serve the Lord as if they had no wives. ³⁰Those who are sad should live as if they are not sad. Those who are happy should live as if they are not happy. Those who buy things should live as if they own nothing. ³¹Those who use the things of the world should live as if those things are not important to them. You should live like this, because this world, the way it is now, will soon be gone.

1 Corinthians 7:25–40 Questions about getting married.

³²I want you to be free from worry. A man who is not married is busy with the Lord's work. He is trying to please the Lord. ³³But a man who is married is busy with things of the world. He is trying to please his wife. ³⁴He must think about two things – pleasing his wife and pleasing the Lord. A woman who is not married or a girl who has never married is busy with the Lord's work. She wants to give herself fully – body and soul – to the Lord. But a married woman is busy with things of the world. She is trying to please her husband. ³⁵I am saying this to help you. I am not trying to limit you. But I want you to live in the right way. And I want you to give yourselves fully to

the Lord without giving your time to other things.

³⁶ A man might think that he is not doing the right thing with the girl he is engaged to. The girl might be almost past the best age to marry. So he might feel that he should marry her. He should do what he wants. They should get married. It is no sin. ³⁷ But another man might be more sure in his mind. There may be no need for marriage, so he is free to do what he wants. If he has decided in his own heart not to marry, he is doing the right thing. ³⁸ So the man who marries his girl does right. And the man who does not marry does even better.

³⁹ A woman must stay with her husband as long as he lives. If the husband dies, she is free to marry any man she wants. But she must marry in the Lord. ⁴⁰ The woman is happier if she does not marry again. This is my opinion, and I believe that I have God's Spirit.

About Food Offered to Idols

8 Now I will write about meat that is sacrificed to idols. We know that "we all have knowledge". Knowledge puffs you up with pride, but love builds up. ² Whoever thinks he knows something does not yet know anything as he should. ³ But he who loves God is known by God.

⁴ So this is what I say about eating meat sacrificed to idols: we know that an idol is really nothing in the world. And we know that there is only one God. ⁵ It is really not important if there are things called gods, in heaven or on earth. (And there are many things that people call "gods" and "lords".) ⁶ But for us there is only one God. He is our Father. All things came from him, and we live for him. And there

is only one Lord – Jesus Christ. All things were made through Jesus, and we also have life through him.

⁷ But not all people know this. Until now, some people have had the habit of worshipping idols. So now when they eat meat, they still feel as if it belongs to an idol. They are not sure that it is right to eat this meat. When they eat it, they feel guilty. ⁸ But food will not make us closer to God. Refusing to eat does not make us less pleasing to God. And eating does not make us better in God's sight.

⁹ But be careful with your freedom. Your freedom may cause those who are weak in faith to fall into sin. ¹⁰ You have "knowledge", so you might eat in an idol's temple.^{n} Someone who is weak in faith might see you eating there. This would encourage him to eat meat sacrificed to idols. But he really thinks it is wrong. ¹¹ So this weak brother is ruined because of your "knowledge". And Christ died for this brother. ¹² When you sin against your brothers in Christ like this and cause them to do what they feel is wrong, you are also sinning against Christ. ¹³ So if the food I eat makes my brother fall into sin, I will never eat meat again. I will stop eating meat, so that I will not cause my brother to sin.

Paul Is like the Other Apostles

9 I am a free man. I am an apostle.^{d} I have seen Jesus our Lord. You people are all an example of my work in the Lord. ² Others may not accept me as an apostle, but surely you accept me. You are proof that I am an apostle in the Lord.

³ Some people want to judge me. So this is the answer I give them: ⁴ do we not have the right to eat and drink? ⁵ Do we not have the right to bring a

---

idol's temple   Building where a false god is worshipped.

believing wife with us when we travel? The other apostles, the Lord's brothers, and Peter all do this. [6]And are Barnabas and I the only ones who must work to earn our living? [7]No soldier ever serves in the army and pays his own salary. No one ever plants a vineyard without eating some of the grapes himself. No person takes care of a flock of sheep without drinking some of the milk himself.

[8]This is not only what men think. God's law says the same thing. [9]Yes, it is written in the law of Moses: "When an ox is working in the grain, do not cover its mouth and keep it from eating."[n] When God said this, was he thinking only about oxen? No. [10]He was really talking about us. Yes, that Scripture[d] was written for us. The one who ploughs and the one who works in the grain should hope to get some of the grain for their work. [11]We planted spiritual seed among you. So we should be able to harvest from you some things for this life. Surely this is not asking too much. [12]Other men have the right to receive something from you. So surely we have this right, too. But we do not use this right. No, we put up with everything ourselves so that we will not stop anyone from obeying the Good News[d] of Christ. [13]Surely you know that those who work at the Temple[d] get their food from the Temple. And those who serve at the altar get part of what is offered at the altar. [14]It is the same with those who tell the Good News. The Lord has commanded that those who tell the Good News should get their living from this work.

[15]But I have not used any of these rights. And I am not writing this now to get anything from you. I would rather die than to have my reason for boasting taken away. [16]Telling the Good News is not my reason for boasting. Telling the Good News is my duty – something I must do. And how bad it will be for me if I do not tell the Good News. [17]If I preach because it is my own choice, I should get a reward. But I have no choice. I must tell the Good News. I am only doing the duty that was given to me. [18]So what reward do I get? This is my reward: that when I tell the Good News I can offer it freely. In this way I do not use my right to be paid in my work for the Good News.

[19]I am free. I belong to no man. But I make myself a slave to all people. I do this to help save as many people as I can. [20]To the Jews I became like a Jew. I did this to help save the Jews. I myself am not ruled by the law. But to those who are ruled by the law I became like a person who is ruled by the law. I did this to help save those who are ruled by the law. [21]To those who are without the law I became like a person who is without the law. I did this to help save those people who are without the law. (But really, I am not without God's law – I am ruled by Christ's law.) [22]To those who are weak, I became weak so that I could help save them. I have become all things to all people. I did this so that I could save some of them in any way possible. [23]I do all this because of the Good News. I do it so that I can share in the blessings of the Good News.

[24]You know that in a race all the runners run. But only one gets the prize. So run like that. Run to win! [25]All those who compete in the games use strict training. They do this so that they can win a crown. That crown is an earthly thing that lasts only a short time. But our crown will continue for

"When an ox . . . eating." Quotation from Deuteronomy 25:4.

ever. [26] So I do not run without a goal. I fight like a boxer who is hitting something – not just the air. [27] It is my own body that I hit. I make it my slave. I do this so that I myself will not be rejected after I have preached to others.

Don't Be like the Jews

10 Brothers, I want you to know what happened to our ancestors who followed Moses. They were all under the cloud, and they all went through the sea. [2] They were all baptised as followers of Moses in the cloud and in the sea. [3] They all ate the same spiritual food. [4] And they all drank the same spiritual drink. They drank from that spiritual rock that was with them. That rock was Christ. [5] But God was not pleased with most of them. They died in the desert.

[6] And these things that happened are examples for us. They should stop us from wanting evil things as those people did. [7] Do not worship idols, as some of them did. It is written in the Scriptures:[d] "The people sat down to eat and drink. Then they got up and sinned sexually."[n] [8] We should not take part in sexual sins, as some of them did. In one day 23,000 of them died because of their sins. [9] We should not test the Lord as some of them did. They were killed by snakes. [10] And do not complain as some of them did. They were killed by the angel that destroys.

[11] The things that happened to those people are examples. And they were written down to be warnings for us. For we live in a time when all these things of the past have reached their goal. [12] So anyone who thinks he is

standing strong should be careful not to fall. [13] The only temptations that you have are the temptations that all people have. But you can trust God. He will not let you be tempted more than you can stand. But when you are tempted, God will also give you a way to escape that temptation. Then you will be able to stand it.

[14] So, my dear friends, stay away from worshipping idols. [15] I am speaking to you, as to intelligent people; judge for yourselves what I say. [16] We give thanks for the cup of blessing.[n] It is a sharing in the blood of Christ's death. And the bread that we break is a sharing in the body of Christ. [17] There is one loaf of bread. And we are many people. But we all share from that one loaf. So we are really one body.

[18] Think about the people of Israel: do not those who eat the sacrifices share in the altar? [19] I do not mean that the food sacrificed to an idol is something important. And I do not mean that an idol is anything at all. [20] But I say that what is sacrificed to idols is offered to demons,[d] not to God. And I do not want you to share anything with demons. [21] You cannot drink the cup of the Lord and the cup of demons, too. You cannot share in the Lord's table and the table of demons, too. [22] Do we want to make the Lord jealous? We are not stronger than he is, are we?

How to Use Christian Freedom

[23] "We are allowed to do all things." Yes. But all things are not good for us to do. "We are allowed to do all things." Yes. But not all things help others grow stronger. [24] No one

---

"The people . . . sexually." Quotation from Exodus 32:6.
cup of blessing The cup of the fruit of the vine that Christians thank God for and drink at the Lord's Supper.

should try to do what will help only himself. He should try to do what is good for others.

[25] Eat any meat that is sold in the meat market. Do not ask questions about the meat to see if it is something you think is wrong to eat. [26] You can eat it, "because the earth and everything on it belong to the Lord."[n]

[27] Someone who is not a believer may invite you to eat with him. If you want to go, eat anything that is put before you. Do not ask questions to see if it is something you think might be wrong to eat. [28] But if anyone says to you, "That food was offered to idols," then do not eat it. Do not eat it because of that person who told you and because eating it would be something that might be thought wrong. [29] I don't mean that you think it is wrong. But the other person might think it is wrong. My own freedom should not be judged by what someone else thinks. [30] I eat the meal with thankfulness. And I do not want to be criticised because of something I thank God for.

[31] So if you eat, or if you drink, or if you do anything, do everything for the glory of God. [32] Never do anything that might make others do wrong – Jews, Greeks, or God's church. [33] I do the same thing. I try to please everybody in every way. I am not trying to do what is good for me. I try to do what is good for the most people. I do this so that they can be saved.

11 Follow my example, as I follow the example of Christ.

Being Under Authority

[2] I praise you because you remember me in everything. You follow closely the teachings that I gave you.

[3] But I want you to understand this: the head of every man is Christ. And the head of a woman is the man.[n] And the head of Christ is God. [4] Every man who prophesies[d] or prays with his head covered brings shame to his head. [5] But every woman who prays or prophesies should have her head covered. If her head is not covered, she brings shame to her head. She is the same as a woman who has her head shaved. [6] If a woman does not cover her head, it is the same as cutting off all her hair. But it is shameful for a woman to cut off her hair or to shave her head. So she should cover her head. [7] But a man should not cover his head, because he is made like God and is God's glory. But woman is man's glory. [8] Man did not come from woman, but woman came from man. [9] And man was not made for woman. Woman was made for man. [10] So that is why a woman should have her head covered with something to show that she is under authority. And also she should do this because of the angels.

[11] But in the Lord the woman is important to the man, and the man is important to the woman. [12] This is true because woman came from man, but also man is born from woman. Really, everything comes from God. [13] Decide this for yourselves: is it right for a woman to pray to God without something on her head? [14] Even nature itself teaches you that wearing long hair is shameful for a man. [15] But wearing long hair is a woman's honour. Long hair is given to the woman to cover her head. [16] Some people may still want to argue about this. But I would add that neither we nor the churches of God accept any other practice.

"because . . . Lord."   Quotation from Psalms 24:1; 50:12; 89:11.
the man   This could also mean "her husband".

The Lord's Supper

[17] In the things I tell you now I do not praise you. Your meetings hurt you more than they help you. [18] First, I hear that when you meet together as a church you are divided. And I believe some of this. [19] (It is necessary for there to be differences among you. That is the way to make it clear which of you are really doing right.) [20] When you all come together, you are not really eating the Lord's Supper.[n] [21] This is because when you eat, each person eats without waiting for the others. Some people do not get enough to eat, while others have too much to drink. [22] You can eat and drink in your own homes! It seems that you think God's church is not important. You embarrass those who are poor. What should I tell you? Should I praise you for doing this? I do not praise you.

[23] The teaching that I gave you is the same teaching that I received from the Lord: on the night when Jesus was handed over to be killed, he took bread [24] and gave thanks for it. Then he broke the bread and said, "This is my body; it is for you. Do this to remember me." [25] In the same way, after they ate, Jesus took the cup. He said, "This cup shows the new agreement from God to his people. This new agreement begins with the blood of my death. When you drink this, do it to remember me." [26] Every time you eat this bread and drink this cup, you show others about the Lord's death until he comes.

[27] So a person should not eat the bread or drink the cup of the Lord in a way that is not worthy of it. If he does he is sinning against the body and the blood of the Lord. [28] Everyone should look into his own heart before he eats the bread and drinks the cup. [29] If someone eats the bread and drinks the cup without recognising the body, then he is judged guilty by eating and drinking. [30] That is why many in your group are sick and weak. And many have died. [31] But if we judged ourselves in the right way, then God would not judge us. [32] But when the Lord judges us, he punishes us to show us the right way. He does this so that we will not be destroyed along with the world.

[33] So my brothers, when you come together to eat, wait for each other. [34] If anyone is too hungry, he should eat at home. Do this so that your meeting together will not bring God's judgement on you. I will tell you what to do about the other things when I come.

Gifts from the Holy Spirit

12 Now, brothers, I want you to understand about spiritual gifts. [2] You remember the lives you lived before you were believers. You let yourselves be influenced and led away to worship idols – things that have no life. [3] So I tell you that no one who is speaking with the help of God's Spirit says, "Jesus be cursed." And no one can say, "Jesus is Lord," without the help of the Holy Spirit.[d]

[4] There are different kinds of gifts; but they are all from the same Spirit. [5] There are different ways to serve; but all these ways are from the same Lord. [6] And there are different ways that God works in people; but all these ways are from the same God. God works in us all in everything we do. [7] Something from the Spirit can be seen in each person, to help everyone. [8] The Spirit gives one person the ability to speak

---

Lord's Supper   The meal Jesus told his followers to eat to remember him (Luke 22:14–20).

with wisdom. And the same Spirit gives another the ability to speak with knowledge. [9]The same Spirit gives faith to one person. And that one Spirit gives another gifts of healing. [10]The Spirit gives to another person the power to do miracles,[d] to another the ability to prophesy.[d] And he gives to another the ability to know the difference between good and evil spirits. The Spirit gives one person the ability to speak in different kinds of languages[n] and to another the ability to interpret those languages. [11]One Spirit, the same Spirit, does all these things. The Spirit decides what to give each person.

The Body of Christ

[12]A person's body is only one thing, but it has many parts. Yes, there are many parts to a body, but all those parts make only one body. Christ is like that too. [13]Some of us are Jews, and some of us are Greeks. Some of us are slaves, and some of us are free. But we were all baptised into one body through one Spirit.[d] And we were all made to share in the one Spirit.

[14]And a person's body has more than one part. It has many parts. [15]The foot might say, "I am not a hand. So I am not part of the body." But saying this would not stop the foot from being a part of the body. [16]The ear might say, "I am not an eye. So I am not part of the body." But saying this would not make the ear stop being a part of the body. [17]If the whole body were an eye, the body would not be able to hear. If the whole body were an ear, the body would not be able to smell anything. [18-19]If each part of the body were the same part, there would be no body. But truly God put the parts in the body as he wanted them.

He made a place for each one of them. [20]And so there are many parts, but only one body.

[21]The eye cannot say to the hand, "I don't need you!" And the head cannot say to the foot, "I don't need you!" [22]No! Those parts of the body that seem to be weaker are really very important. [23]And the parts of the body that we think are not worth much are the parts that we give the most care to. And we give special care to the parts of the body that we want to hide. [24]The more beautiful parts of our body need no special care. But God put the body together and gave more honour to the parts that need it. [25]God did this so that our body would not be divided. God wanted the different parts to care the same for each other. [26]If one part of the body suffers, then all the other parts suffer with it. Or if one part of our body is honoured, then all the other parts share its honour.

[27]All of you together are the body of Christ. Each one of you is a part of that body. [28]And in the church God has given a place first to apostles,[d] second to prophets,[d] and third to teachers. Then God has given a place to those who do miracles,[d] those who have gifts of healing, those who can help others, those who are able to lead, and those who can speak in different languages.[n] [29]Not all are apostles. Not all are prophets. Not all are teachers. Not all do miracles. [30]Not all have gifts of healing. Not all speak in different languages.[n] Not all interpret those languages. [31]But you should truly want to have the greater gifts.

Love

And now I will show you the best way of all.

---

languages　This can also be translated "tongues".

13 I may speak in different languages[n] of men or even angels. But if I do not have love, then I am only a noisy bell or a ringing cymbal. [2] I may have the gift of prophecy;[d] I may understand all the secret things of God and all knowledge; and I may have faith so great that I can move mountains. But even if I have all these things, if I do not have love, then I am nothing. [3] I may give everything I own to feed the poor. And I may even give my body as an offering to be burned. But I gain nothing by doing these things if I do not have love.

[4] Love is patient and kind. Love is not jealous, it does not boast, and it is not proud. [5] Love is not rude, is not selfish, and does not become angry easily. Love does not remember wrongs done against it. [6] Love is not happy with evil, but is happy with the truth. [7] Love patiently accepts all things. It always trusts, always hopes, and always continues strong.

[8] Love never ends. There are gifts of prophecy,[d] but they will be ended. There are gifts of speaking in different languages,[n] but those gifts will end. There is the gift of knowledge, but it will be ended. [9] These things will end, because this knowledge and these prophecies we have are not complete. [10] But when perfection comes, the things that are not complete will end. [11] When I was a child, I talked like a child; I thought like a child; I made plans like a child. When I became a man, I stopped those childish ways. [12] It is the same with us. Now we see as if we are looking into a dark mirror. But at that time, in the future, we shall see clearly. Now I know only a part. But at that time I will know fully, as God has known me. [13] So these three things continue for ever: faith, hope and love. And the greatest of these is love.

1 Corinthians 13:13 And the greatest of these is love.

Spiritual Gifts

14 Love, then, is what you should try for. And you should truly want to have the spiritual gifts. And the gift you should want most is to be able to prophesy.[d] [2] I will explain why. One who has the gift of speaking in a different language[n] is not speaking to people. He is speaking to God. No one understands him – he is speaking secret things through the Spirit.[d] [3] But one who prophesies is speaking to people. He gives people strength, encouragement, and comfort. [4] The one who speaks in a different language is helping only himself. But the one who prophesies is helping the whole church. [5] I would like all of you to have

---

languages This can also be translated "tongues".
language This can also be translated "tongue".

the gift of speaking in different kinds of languages. But more, I want you to prophesy. The person who prophesies is greater than the one who can only speak in different languages – unless someone is there who can explain what he says. Then the whole church can be helped.

6 Brothers, will it help you if I come to you speaking in different languages? No! It will help you only if I bring you a new truth or some knowledge, or some prophecy, or some teaching. 7 It is the same as with non-living things that make sounds – like a flute or a harp. If different musical notes are not made clear, you will not know what song is being played. Each note must be played clearly for you to be able to understand the tune. 8 And in a war, if the trumpet does not sound clearly, the soldiers will not know it is time to prepare for fighting. 9 It is the same with you. The words you speak with your tongue must be clear. Unless you speak clearly, no one can understand what you are saying. You will be talking in the air! 10 It is true that there are many kinds of speech in the world. And they all have meaning. 11 So unless I understand the meaning of what someone says to me, I am a stranger to him, and he is a stranger to me. 12 It is the same with you. You want spiritual gifts very much. So try most to have the gifts that help the church grow stronger.

13 The one who has the gift of speaking in a different language should pray that he can also interpret what he says. 14 If I pray in a different language, my spirit is praying, but my mind does nothing. 15 So what should I do? I will pray with my spirit, but I will also pray with my mind. I will sing with my spirit, but I will also sing with my

mind. 16 You might be praising God with your spirit. But a person there without understanding cannot say "Amen"[n] to your prayer of thanks. He does not know what you are saying. 17 You may be thanking God in a good way, but the other person is not helped.

18 I thank God that my gift of speaking in different kinds of languages is greater than any of yours. 19 But in the church meetings I would rather speak five words that I understand than thousands of words in a different language. I would rather speak with my understanding, so that I can teach others.

20 Brothers, do not think like children. In evil things be like babies. But in your thinking you should be like full-grown men. 21 It is written in the Scriptures:[d]

"I will use strange words and
　　foreign languages
to speak to these people.
But even then they will not listen."

Isaiah 28:11–12

That is what the Lord says.

22 So the gift of speaking in different kinds of languages is a proof for those who do not believe, not for those who believe. And prophecy is for people who believe, not for those who do not believe. 23 Suppose the whole church meets together and everyone speaks in different languages. If some people come in who are without understanding or do not believe, they will say you are mad. 24 But suppose everyone is prophesying and someone comes in who does not believe or is without understanding. If everyone is prophesying, his sin will be shown to him, and he will be judged by all that he hears. 25 The secret things in his heart will be made known. So he will bow

---

"Amen"   When a person says "Amen", it means he agrees with the things that were said.

down and worship God. He will say, "Truly, God is with you."

Meetings Should Help the Church

26 So, brothers, what should you do? When you meet together, one person has a song. Another has a teaching. Another has a new truth from God. Another speaks in a different language,[n] and another person interprets that language. The purpose of all these things should be to help the church grow strong. 27 When you meet together, if anyone speaks in a different language, then it should be only two, or not more than three, who speak. They should speak one after the other. And someone else should interpret what they say. 28 But if there is no interpreter, then anyone who speaks in a different language should be quiet in the church meeting. He should speak only to himself and to God.

29 And only two or three prophets[d] should speak. The others should judge what they say. 30 And if a message from God comes to another person who is sitting, then the first speaker should stop. 31 You can all prophesy one after the other. In this way all the people can be taught and encouraged. 32 The spirits of prophets are under the control of the prophets themselves. 33 God is not a God of confusion but a God of peace.

This is true in all the churches of God's people. 34 Women should keep quiet in the church meetings. They are not allowed to speak. They must be under control. This is also what the law of Moses says. 35 If there is something the women want to know, they should ask their own husbands at home. It is shameful for a woman to speak in the church meeting. 36 Did God's teaching come from you? Or are you the only ones who have received that teaching?

37 If anyone thinks that he is a prophet or that he has a spiritual gift, then he should understand that what I am writing to you is the Lord's command. 38 If that person does not know this, then he is not known by God.

39 So my brothers, you should truly want to prophesy. And do not stop people from using the gift of speaking in different kinds of languages. 40 But let everything be done in a way that is right and orderly.

The Good News About Christ

15 Now, brothers, I want you to remember the Good News[d] I brought to you. You received this Good News, and you continue strong in it. 2 And you are saved by this Good News. But you must continue believing what I told you. If you do not, then you believed for nothing.

3 I passed on to you what I received. And this was the most important: that Christ died for our sins, as the Scriptures[d] say; 4 that he was buried and was raised to life on the third day as the Scriptures say; 5 and that he showed himself to Peter and then to the twelve apostles.[d] 6 After that, Jesus showed himself to more than 500 of the believers at the same time. Most of them are still living today. But some have died. 7 Then Jesus showed himself to James and later to all the apostles. 8 Last of all he showed himself to me – as to a person not born at the normal time. 9 All the other apostles are greater than I am. This is because I persecuted the church of God. And this is why I am not even good enough to be called an apostle. 10 But God's grace has made me what

---

language   This can also be translated "tongue".

I am. And his grace to me was not wasted. I worked harder than all the other apostles. (But I was not really the one working. It was God's grace that was with me.) [11]So then it is not important if I preached to you or if the other apostles preached to you. We all preach the same thing, and this is what you believed.

We Will Be Raised from Death

[12]It is preached that Christ was raised from death. So why do some of you say that people will not be raised from death? [13]If no one will ever be raised from death, then Christ was not raised from death. [14]And if Christ was not raised, then our preaching is worth nothing. And your faith is worth nothing. [15]And also, we will be guilty of lying about God. Because we have preached about him by saying that he raised Christ from death. And if people are not raised from death, then God never raised Christ from death. [16]If the dead are not raised, Christ has not been raised either. [17]And if Christ has not been raised, then your faith is for nothing; you are still guilty of your sins. [18]And also, those in Christ who have already died are lost. [19]If our hope in Christ is for this life only, we should be pitied more than anyone else in the world.

[20]But Christ has truly been raised from death – the first one and proof that those who are asleep in death will also be raised. [21]Death comes to everyone because of what one man did. But the rising from death also happens because of one man. [22]In Adam all of us die. In the same way, in Christ all of us will be made alive again. [23]But everyone will be raised to life in the right order. Christ was first to be raised. When Christ comes again, those who belong to him will be raised to life. [24]Then the end will come. Christ will destroy all rulers, authorities, and powers. And he will give the kingdom to God the Father. [25]Christ must rule until God puts all enemies under Christ's control. [26]The last enemy to be destroyed will be death. [27]The Scripture[d] says, "God put all things under his control."[n] When it says that "all things" are put under him, it is clear that this does not include God himself. God is the one putting everything under Christ's control. [28]After everything has been put under Christ, then the Son himself will be put under God. God is the One who put all things under Christ. And Christ will be put under God, so that God will be the complete ruler over everything.

[29]If the dead are never raised, then what will people do who are baptised for those who have died? If the dead are not raised at all, why are people baptised for them?

[30]And what about us? Why do we put ourselves in danger every hour? [31]I die every day. That is true, brothers, just as it is true that I boast about you in Christ Jesus our Lord. [32]If I fought wild animals in Ephesus only for human reasons, I have gained nothing. If the dead are not raised, then, "Let us eat and drink, because tomorrow we will die."[n]

[33]Do not be fooled: "Bad friends will ruin good habits." [34]Come back to your right way of thinking and stop sinning. I say this to shame you – some of you do not know God.

What Kind of Body Will We Have?

[35]But someone may ask, "How are the dead raised? What kind of body

"God put . . . control." Quotation from Psalm 8:6.
"Let us . . . die." Quotation from Isaiah 22:13; 56:12.

will they have?" ³⁶Those are stupid questions. When you plant something, it must die in the ground before it can live and grow. ³⁷And when you plant it, what you plant does not have the same "body" that it will have later. What you plant is only a seed, maybe wheat or something else. ³⁸But God gives it a body that he has planned for it. And God gives each kind of seed its own body. ³⁹All things made of flesh are not the same kinds of flesh: people have one kind of flesh, animals have another kind, birds have another, and fish have another. ⁴⁰Also there are heavenly bodies and earthly bodies. But the beauty of the heavenly bodies is one kind. The beauty of the earthly bodies is another kind. ⁴¹The sun has one kind of beauty. The moon has another beauty, and the stars have another. And each star is different in its beauty.

⁴²It is the same with the dead who are raised to life. The body that is "planted" will ruin and decay. But that body is raised to a life that cannot be destroyed. ⁴³When the body is "planted", it is without honour. But it is raised in glory. When the body is "planted", it is weak. But when it is raised, it has power. ⁴⁴The body that is "planted" is a physical body.

When it is raised, it is a spiritual body.

There is a physical body. And there is also a spiritual body. ⁴⁵It is written in the Scriptures:ᵈ "The first man became a living person."ⁿ But the last Adam became a spirit that gives life. ⁴⁶The spiritual man did not come first. It was the physical man who came first; then came the spiritual. ⁴⁷The first man came from the dust of the earth. The second man came from heaven. ⁴⁸People belong to the earth. They are like the first man of earth. But those people who belong to heaven are like the man of heaven. ⁴⁹We were made like the man of earth. So we will also be made like the man of heaven.

⁵⁰I tell you this, brothers: flesh and blood cannot have a part in the kingdom of God. A thing that will die cannot have a part in something that never dies. ⁵¹But listen, I tell you this secret: we will not all die, but we will all be changed. ⁵²It will only take a second. We will be changed as quickly as an eye blinks. This will happen when the last trumpet sounds. The trumpet will sound and those who have died will be raised to live for ever. And we will all be changed. ⁵³This body that will decay must clothe itself

"**The first . . . person.**"   Quotation from Genesis 2:7.

1 Corinthians 15:38 God gives it a body that he has planned for it.

with something that will never decay. And this body that dies must clothe itself with something that will never die. ⁵⁴So this body that decays will clothe itself with that which never decays. And this body that dies will clothe itself with that which never dies. When this happens, then this Scripture will be made true:

"Death is destroyed for ever in
victory."   *Isaiah 25:8*
⁵⁵"Death, where is your victory?
Death, where is your power to
hurt?"   *Hosea 13:14*
⁵⁶Death's power to hurt is sin. The power of sin is the law. ⁵⁷But we thank God! He gives us the victory through our Lord Jesus Christ.

⁵⁸So my dear brothers, stand strong. Do not let anything change you. Always give yourselves fully to the work of the Lord. You know that your work in the Lord is never wasted.

The Gift for Other Believers

16 Now I will write about the collection of money for God's people. Do the same thing that I told the Galatian churches to do: ²on the first day of every week, each one of you should put aside as much money as you can from what you are blessed with. You should save it up, so that you will not have to collect money after I come. ³When I arrive, I will send some men to take your gift to Jerusalem. These will be men who you all agree should go. I will send them with letters of introduction. ⁴If it seems good for me to go also, these men will go along with me.

Paul's Plans

⁵I plan to go through Macedonia. So I will come to you after I go through there. ⁶Maybe I will stay with you for a time. I might even stay all winter.

Then you can help me on my trip, wherever I go. ⁷I do not want to come to see you now, because I would have to leave to go on to other places. I hope to stay a longer time with you if the Lord allows it. ⁸But I will stay at Ephesus until Pentecost.*ᵈ* ⁹I will stay, because a good opportunity for a great and growing work has been given to me now. And there are many people working against me.

¹⁰Timothy might come to you. Try to make him feel comfortable with you. He is working for the Lord just as I am. ¹¹So none of you should refuse to accept Timothy. Help him on his trip in peace, so that he can come back to me. I am expecting him to come back with the brothers.

¹²Now about our brother Apollos: I strongly encouraged him to visit you with the other brothers. But he was sure that he did not want to go now. But when he has the opportunity, he will go to you.

Paul Ends His Letter

¹³Be careful. Continue strong in the faith. Have courage, and be strong. ¹⁴Do everything in love.

¹⁵You know that the family of Stephanas were the first believers in Southern Greece. They have given themselves to the service of God's people. I ask you, brothers, ¹⁶to follow the leading of people like these and anyone else who works and serves with them.

¹⁷I am happy that Stephanas, Fortunatus, and Achaicus have come. You are not here, but they have filled your place. ¹⁸They have given rest to my spirit and to yours. You should recognise the value of men like these.

¹⁹The churches in the country of Asia send greetings to you. Aquila and Priscilla greet you in the Lord. Also

the church that meets in their house greets you. [20]All the brothers here send greetings. Give each other a holy kiss when you meet.

[21]I am Paul, and I am writing this greeting with my own hand.

[22]If anyone does not love the Lord, then let him be separated from God – lost for ever!

Come, O Lord!

[23]The grace of the Lord Jesus be with you.

[24]My love be with all of you in Christ Jesus.

2 CORINTHIANS

Paul Answers Those Who Accuse Him

1 From Paul, an apostle*d* of Christ Jesus. I am an apostle because that is what God wanted.

Also from Timothy our brother in Christ.

To the church of God in Corinth, and to all of God's people in the whole country of Southern Greece:

² Grace and peace to you from God our Father and the Lord Jesus Christ.

Paul Gives Thanks to God

³ Praise be to the God and Father of our Lord Jesus Christ. God is the Father who is full of mercy. And he is the God of all comfort. ⁴ He comforts us every time we have trouble, so that we can comfort others when they have

2 Corinthians 1:4 He comforts us . . . so that we can comfort others.

trouble. We can comfort them with the same comfort that God gives us. ⁵ We share in the many sufferings of Christ. In the same way, much comfort comes to us through Christ. ⁶ If we have troubles, it is for your comfort and salvation. If we have comfort, then you also have comfort. This helps you to accept patiently the same sufferings that we have. ⁷ Our hope for you is strong. We know that you share in our sufferings. So we know that you also share in the comfort we receive.

⁸ Brothers, we want you to know about the trouble we suffered in the country of Asia. We had great burdens there that were greater than our own strength. We even gave up hope for life. ⁹ Truly, in our own hearts we believed that we would die. But this happened so that we would not trust in ourselves. It happened so that we would trust in God, who raises people from death. ¹⁰ God saved us from these great dangers of death. And he will continue to save us. We have put our hope in him, and he will save us again. ¹¹ And you can help us with your prayers. Then many people will give thanks for us – that God blessed us because of their many prayers.

The Change in Paul's Plans

¹² This is what we are proud of, and I can say with all my heart that it is true: in all the things we have done in the world, we have done everything with an honest and pure heart from God. And this is even more true in what we have done with you. We did this by God's grace, not by the kind

of wisdom the world has. [13] For we write to you only what you can read and understand. And I hope that [14] as you have understood some things about us, you may come to know everything about us. Then you can be proud of us, as we will be proud of you on the day our Lord Jesus Christ comes again.

[15] I was very sure of all this. That is why I made plans to visit you first. Then you could be blessed twice. [16] I planned to visit you on my way to Macedonia. Then I planned to visit you again on my way back. I wanted to get help from you for my trip to Judea. [17] Do you think that I made these plans without really thinking? Or maybe you think I make plans as the world does, so that I say "Yes, yes", and at the same time "No, no".

[18] But if you can believe God, then you can believe that what we tell you is never both "Yes" and "No". [19] The Son of God, Jesus Christ, that Silas and Timothy and I preached to you, was not "Yes" and "No". In Christ it has always been "Yes". [20] The "Yes" to all of God's promises is in Christ. And that is why we say "Amen"[n] through Christ to the glory of God. [21] And God is the One who makes you and us strong in Christ. God made us his chosen people. [22] He put his mark on us to show that we are his. And he put his Spirit[d] in our hearts to be a guarantee for all he has promised.

[23] I tell you this, and I ask God to be my witness that this is true: the reason I did not come back to Corinth was that I did not want to punish or hurt you. [24] I do not mean that we are trying to control your faith. You are strong in faith. But we are workers with you for your own happiness.

2 So I decided that my next visit to you would not be another visit to make you sad. [2] If I make you sad, who will make me happy? Only you can make me happy – you whom I made sad. [3] I wrote you a letter for this reason: that when I came to you I would not be made sad by the people who should make me happy. I felt sure of all of you. I felt sure that you would share my joy. [4] When I wrote to you before, I was very troubled and unhappy in my heart. I wrote with many tears. I did not write to make you sad, but to let you know how much I love you.

Forgive the Sinner

[5] Someone there among you has caused sadness. He caused this not to me, but to all of you – I mean he caused sadness to all in some way. (I do not want to make it sound worse than it really is.) [6] The punishment that most of you gave him is enough for him. [7] But now you should forgive him and comfort him. This will keep him from having too much sadness and giving up completely. [8] So I beg you to show him that you love him. [9] This is why I wrote to you. I wanted to test you and see if you obey in everything. [10] If you forgive someone, I also forgive him. And what I have forgiven – if I had anything to forgive – I forgave it for you, and Christ was with me. [11] I did this so that Satan would not win anything from us. We know very well what Satan's plans are.

Paul's Concern in Troas

[12] I went to Troas to preach the Good News[d] of Christ. The Lord gave me a good opportunity there. [13] But I had no peace because I did not find

---

"Amen"   When a person says "Amen", it means he agrees with the things that were said.

my brother Titus there. So I said good bye and went to Macedonia.

Victory Through Christ

[14] But thanks be to God, who always leads us in victory through Christ. God uses us to spread his knowledge everywhere like a sweet-smelling perfume. [15] Our offering to God is this: we are the sweet smell of Christ among those who are being saved and among those who are lost. [16] To those who are lost, we are the smell of death that brings death. But to those who are being saved, we are the smell of life that brings life. So who is able to do this work? [17] We do not sell the word of God for a profit as many other people do. But in Christ we speak the truth before God. We speak as men sent from God.

Servants of the New Agreement

3 Are we starting to boast about ourselves again? Do we need letters of introduction to you or from you, like some other people? [2] You yourselves are our letter, written on our hearts. It is known and read by everyone. [3] You show that you are a letter from Christ that he sent through us. This letter is not written with ink, but with the Spirit[d] of the living God. It is not written on stone tablets.[n] It is written on human hearts.

[4] We can say this, because through Christ we feel sure before God. [5] I do not mean that we are able to say that we can do this work ourselves. It is God who makes us able to do all that we do. [6] God made us able to be servants of a new agreement from himself to his people. This new agreement is not a written law. It is of the Spirit. The written law brings death, but the Spirit gives life.

[7] The law that brought death was written in words on stone. It came with God's glory. Moses' face was so bright with glory that the people of Israel could not continue to look at his face. And that glory later disappeared. [8] So surely the new way that brings the Spirit has even more glory. [9] That law judged people guilty of sin, but it had glory. So surely the new way that makes people right with God has much greater glory. [10] That old law had glory. But it really loses its glory when it is compared to the much greater glory of this new way. [11] If that law which disappeared came with glory, then this new way which continues for ever has much greater glory.

[12] We have this hope, so we are very brave. [13] We are not like Moses. He put a covering over his face so that the people of Israel would not see it. The glory was disappearing, and Moses did not want them to see it end. [14] But their minds were closed. Even today that same covering hides the meaning when they read the old agreement. That covering is taken away only through Christ. [15] But even today, when they read the law of Moses, there is a covering over their minds. [16] But when a person changes and follows the Lord, that covering is taken away. [17] The Lord is the Spirit. And where the Spirit of the Lord is, there is freedom. [18] Our faces, then, are not covered. We all show the Lord's glory, and we are being changed to be like him. This change in us brings more and more glory. And it comes from the Lord, who is the Spirit.

stone tablets   Meaning the law of Moses that was written on stone tablets (Exodus 24:12; 25:16).

Preaching the Good News

4 God, with his mercy, gave us this work to do. So we don't give up. [2] But we have turned away from secret and shameful ways. We use no trickery, and we do not change the teaching of God. We teach the truth plainly. This is how we show everyone who we are. And this is how they can know in their hearts what kind of people we are before God. [3] The Good News[d] that we preach may be hidden. But it is hidden only to those who are lost. [4] The devil who rules this world has blinded the minds of those who do not believe. They cannot see the light of the Good News – the Good News about the glory of Christ, who is exactly like God. [5] We do not preach about ourselves. But we preach that Jesus Christ is Lord; and we preach that we are your servants for Jesus. [6] God once said, "Let the light shine out of the darkness!" And this is the same God who made his light shine in our hearts. He gave us light by letting us know the glory of God that is in the face of Christ.

Spiritual Treasure in Clay Jars

[7] We have this treasure from God. But we are only like clay jars that hold the treasure. This shows that this great power is from God, not from us. [8] We have troubles all around us, but we are not defeated. We do not know what to do, but we do not give up. [9] We are persecuted, but God does not leave us. We are hurt sometimes, but we are not destroyed. [10] We carry the death of Jesus in our own bodies, so that the life of Jesus can also be seen in our bodies. [11] We are alive, but for Jesus we are always in danger of death. This is so that the life of Jesus can be seen in our bodies that die. [12] So death is working in us, but life is working in you.

[13] It is written in the Scriptures,[d] "I believed, so I spoke."[n] Our faith is like this, too. We believe, and so we speak. [14] God raised the Lord Jesus from death. And we know that God will also raise us with Jesus. God will bring us together with you, and we will stand before him. [15] All these things are for you. And so the grace of God is being given to more and more people. This will bring more and more thanks to God for his glory.

Living by Faith

[16] So we do not give up. Our physical body is becoming older and weaker,

"I ... spoke."   Quotation from Psalm 116:10.

2 Corinthians 4:7 We are only like clay jars.

but our spirit inside us is made new every day. [17] We have small troubles for a while now, but they are helping us gain an eternal glory. That glory is much greater than the troubles. [18] So we set our eyes not on what we see but on what we cannot see. What we see will last only a short time. But what we cannot see will last for ever.

5 We know that our body – the tent we live in here on earth – will be destroyed. But when that happens, God will have a house for us to live in. It will not be a house made by men. It will be a home in heaven that will last for ever. [2] But now we are tired of this body. We want God to give us our heavenly home. [3] It will clothe us, and we will not be naked. [4] While we live in this body, we have burdens, and we complain. We do not want to be naked. We want to be clothed with our heavenly home. Then this body that dies will be fully covered with life. [5] This is what God made us for. And he has given us the Spirit[d] to be a guarantee for this new life.

[6] So we always have courage. We know that while we live in this body, we are away from the Lord. [7] We live by what we believe, not by what we can see. [8] So I say that we have courage. And we really want to be away from this body and be at home with the Lord. [9] Our only goal is to please God. We want to please him whether we live here or there. [10] For we must all stand before Christ to be judged. Each one will receive what he should get – good or bad – for the things he did when he lived in the earthly body.

Becoming Friends with God

[11] We know what it means to fear the Lord. So we try to help people accept the truth. God knows what we really are. And I hope that in your hearts you know, too. [12] We are not trying to prove ourselves to you again. But we are telling you about ourselves, so you will be proud of us. Then you will have an answer for those who are proud about things that can be seen. They do not care about what is in the heart. [13] If we are out of our minds, it is for God. If we have our right mind, then it is for you. [14] The love of Christ controls us. Because we know that One died for all. So all have died. [15] Christ died for all so that those who live would not continue to live for themselves. He died for them and was raised from death so that they would live for him.

[16] From this time on we do not think of anyone as the world does. It is true that in the past we thought of Christ as the world thinks. But we no longer think of him in that way. [17] If anyone belongs to Christ, then he is made new. The old things have gone; everything is made new! [18] All this is from God. Through Christ, God made peace between us and himself. And God gave us the work of bringing everyone into peace with him. [19] I mean that God was in Christ, making peace between the world and himself. In Christ, God did not hold the world guilty of its sins. And he gave us this message of peace. [20] So we have been sent to speak for Christ. It is as if God is calling to you through us. We speak for Christ when we beg you to be at peace with God. [21] Christ had no sin. But God made him become sin. God did this for us so that in Christ we could become right with God.

6 We are workers together with God. So we beg you: do not let the grace that you received from God be for nothing. [2] God says,

"I heard your prayers at the right time,
　　and I gave you help on the day
　　of salvation."　　*Isaiah 49:8*

I tell you that the "right time" is now. The "day of salvation" is now.

[3] We do not want anyone to find anything wrong with our work. So we do nothing that will be a problem for anyone. [4] But in every way we show that we are servants of God: in accepting many hard things, in troubles, in difficulties, and in great problems. [5] We are beaten and thrown into prison. Men become upset and fight us. We work hard, and sometimes we get no sleep or food. [6] We show that we are servants of God by living a pure life, by our understanding, by our patience, and by our kindness. We show this by the Holy Spirit,[d] by true love, [7] by speaking the truth, and by God's power. We use our right living to defend ourselves against everything. [8] Some people honour us, but other people shame us. Some people say good things about us, but other people say bad things. Some people say we are liars, but we speak the truth. [9] We are not known, but we are well known. We seem to be dying, but look – we continue to live. We are punished, but we are not killed. [10] We have much sadness, but we are always rejoicing. We are poor, but we are making many people rich in faith. We have nothing, but really we have everything.

[11] We have spoken freely to you in Corinth. We have opened our hearts to you. [12] Our feelings of love for you have not stopped. It is you that have stopped your feelings of love for us. [13] I speak to you as if you were my children. Do to us as we have done – open your hearts to us.

Warning About Non-Christians

[14] You are not the same as those who do not believe. So do not join yourselves to them. Good and bad do not belong together. Light and darkness cannot share together. [15] How can Christ and Belial, the devil, have any agreement? What can a believer have together with a non-believer? [16] The temple of God cannot have any agreement with idols. And we are the temple of the living God. As God said:

"I will live with them and walk with them. And I will be their God. And they will be my people."[n]

[17] "Leave those people,
    and make yourselves pure, says the Lord.
Touch nothing that is unclean,[d]
    and I will accept you."

Isaiah 52:11; Ezekiel 20:34,41

[18] "I will be your father,
    and you will be my sons and daughters,
    says the Lord All-Powerful."

2 Samuel 7:14; 7:8

7 Dear friends, we have these promises from God. So we should make ourselves pure – free from anything that makes body or soul unclean. We should try to become perfect in the way we live, because we respect God.

Paul's Joy

[2] Open your hearts to us. We have not done wrong to anyone. We have not ruined the faith of any person, and we have cheated no one. [3] I do not say this to blame you. I told you before that we love you so much that we would live or die with you. [4] I feel very sure of you. I am very proud of you. You give me much comfort. And in all of our troubles I have great joy.

[5] When we came into Macedonia, we had no rest. We found trouble all around us. We had fighting on the out-

---

"I . . . people." Quotation from Leviticus 26:11–12; Jeremiah 32:38; Ezekiel 37:27.

side and fear on the inside. ⁶But God comforts those who are troubled. And God comforted us when Titus came. ⁷We were comforted by his coming and also by the comfort that you gave him. Titus told us about your wish to see me. He told us that you are very sorry for what you did. And he told me about your great care for me. When I heard this, I was much happier.

⁸Even if the letter I wrote you made you sad, I am not sorry I wrote it. I know it made you sad, and I was sorry for that. But it made you sad only for a short time. ⁹Now I am happy, but not because you were made sad. I am happy because your sorrow made you change your hearts. You became sad in the way God wanted you to. So you were not hurt by us in any way. ¹⁰Being sorry in the way God wants makes a person change his heart and life. This leads to salvation, and we cannot be sorry for that. But the kind of sorrow the world has will bring death. ¹¹You had the kind of sorrow God wanted you to have. Now see what this sorrow has brought you: it has made you very serious. It made you want to prove that you were not wrong. It made you angry and afraid. It made you want to see me. It made you care. It made you want the right thing to be done. You proved that you were not guilty in any part of the problem. ¹²I wrote that letter, but not because of the one who did the wrong. And it was not written because of the person who was hurt. But I wrote the letter so that you could see, before God, the great care that you have for us. ¹³That is why we were comforted. We were very comforted. And we were even happier to see that Titus was so happy. All of you made him feel much better. ¹⁴I boasted to Titus about you. And you showed that I was right. Everything that we said to you

was true. And you have proved that what we boasted about to Titus is true. ¹⁵And his love for you is stronger when he remembers that you were all ready to obey. You welcomed him with respect and fear. ¹⁶I am very happy that I can trust you fully.

Christian Giving

8 And now, brothers, we want you to know about the grace that God gave the churches in Macedonia. ²They have been tested by great troubles. And they are very poor. But they gave much because of their great joy. ³I can tell you that they gave as much as they were able. They gave even more than they could afford. No one told them to do it. ⁴But they asked us again and again – they begged us to let them share in this service for God's people. ⁵And they gave in a way that we did not expect: they first gave themselves to the Lord and to us. This is what God wants. ⁶So we asked Titus to help you finish this special work of grace. He is the one who started this work. ⁷You are rich in everything – in faith, in speaking, in knowledge, in truly wanting to help, and in the love you learned from us. And so we want you to be rich also in this gift of giving.

⁸I am not commanding you to give. But I want to see if your love is true love. I do this by showing you that others really want to help. ⁹You know the grace of our Lord Jesus Christ. You know that Christ was rich, but for you he became poor. Christ did this so that by his being poor you might become rich.

¹⁰This is what I think you should do: Last year you were the first to want to give. And you were the first who gave. ¹¹So now finish the work that you started. Then your "doing" will be equal to your "wanting to do". Give from what you have. ¹²If you want to

give, your gift will be accepted. Your gift will be judged by what you have, not by what you do not have. [13]We do not want you to have troubles while other people are at ease. We want everything to be equal. [14]At this time you have plenty. What you have can help others who are in need. Then

2 Corinthians 8:14 What you have can help others.

later, when they have plenty, they can help you when you are in need. Then all will be equal. [15]As it is written in the Scriptures,[d] "The person who gathered more did not have too much. The person who gathered less did not have too little."[n]

Titus and His Companions

[16]I thank God because he gave Titus the same love for you that I have. [17]Titus accepted what we asked him to do. He wanted very much to go to you. This was his own idea. [18]We are sending with him the brother who is praised by all the churches. This brother is praised because of his service in preaching the Good News.[d] [19]Also, this brother was chosen by the churches to go with us when we deliver this gift of money. We are doing this service to bring glory to the Lord and to show that we really want to help.

[20]We are being careful so that no one will criticise us about the way we are handling this large gift. [21]We are trying to do what is right. We want to do what the Lord accepts as right and also what people think is right.

[22]Also, we are sending with them our brother who is always ready to help. He has proved this to us in many ways. And he wants to help even more now because he has much faith in you.

[23]Now about Titus – he is my partner who is working with me to help you. And about the other brothers – they are sent from the churches, and they bring glory to Christ. [24]So show these men that you really have love. Show them why we are proud of you. Then all the churches can see it.

Help for Fellow Christians

9 I really do not need to write to you about this help for God's people. [2]I know that you want to help. I have been boasting about this to the people in Macedonia. I have told them that you in Southern Greece have been ready to give since last year. And your wanting to give has made most of them here ready to give also. [3]But I am sending the brothers to you. I do not want our boasting about you in this to be for nothing. I want you to be ready, as I said you would be. [4]If any of the people from Macedonia

"The person . . . little." Quotation from Exodus 16:18.

come with me and find that you are not ready, we will be ashamed. We will be ashamed that we were so sure of you. (And you will be ashamed, too!) [5]So I thought that I should ask these brothers to go to you before we come. They will finish getting in order the gift you promised. Then the gift will be ready when we come, and it will be a gift you wanted to give – not a gift that you hated to give.

[6]Remember this: the person who plants a little will have a small harvest. But the person who plants a lot will have a big harvest. [7]Each one should give, then, what he has decided in his heart to give. He should not give if it makes him sad. And he should not give if he thinks he is forced to give. God loves the person who gives happily. [8]And God can give you more blessings than you need. Then you will always have plenty of everything. You will have enough to give to every good work. [9]It is written in the Scriptures:[d]

"He gives freely to the poor.
The things he does are right
and will continue for ever."

Psalm 112:9

[10]God is the One who gives seed to the farmer. And he gives bread for food. And God will give you all the seed you need and make it grow. He will make a great harvest from your goodness. [11]God will make you rich in every way so that you can always give freely. And your giving through us will cause many to give thanks to God. [12]This service that you do helps the needs of God's people. It is also bringing more and more thanks to God. [13]This service you do is a proof of your faith. Many people will praise God because of it. They will praise God because you follow the Good News[d] of Christ – the gospel you say you believe. They will praise God

because you freely share with them and with all others. [14]And when they pray, they will wish they could be with you. They will feel this because of the great grace that God has given you. [15]Thanks be to God for his gift that is too wonderful to explain.

Paul Defends His Ministry

10 I, Paul, am begging you with the gentleness and the kindness of Christ. Some people say that I am easy on you when I am with you and strict when I am away. [2]They think that we live in a worldly way. I plan to be very strict against them when I come. I beg you that when I come I will not need to use that same strictness with you. [3]We do live in the world. But we do not fight in the same way that the world fights. [4]We fight with weapons that are different from those the world uses. Our weapons have power from God. These weapons can destroy the enemy's strong places. We destroy men's arguments. [5]And we destroy every proud thing that raises itself against the knowledge of God. We capture every thought and make it give up and obey Christ. [6]We are ready to punish anyone there who does not obey. But first we want you to obey fully.

[7]You must look at the facts before you. If anyone feels sure that he belongs to Christ, then he must remember that we belong to Christ just as he does. [8]It is true that we boast freely about the authority the Lord gave us. But he gave us this authority to strengthen you, not to hurt you. So I will not be ashamed of the boasting we do. [9]I don't want you to think that I am trying to scare you with my letters. [10]Some people say, "Paul's letters are powerful and sound important. But when he is with us, he is weak. And his speaking is nothing."

¹¹They should know this: we are not there with you now, so we say these things in letters. But when we are there with you, we will show the same authority that we show in our letters.

¹²We do not dare to put ourselves in the same group with those who think that they are very important. We do not compare ourselves to them. They use themselves to measure themselves, and they judge themselves by what they themselves are. This shows that they know nothing. ¹³But we will not boast about things outside the work that was given us to do. We will limit our boasting to the work that God gave us. And this work includes our work with you. ¹⁴We are not boasting too much. We would be boasting too much if we had not already come to you. But we have come to you with the Good News[d] of Christ. ¹⁵We limit our boasting to the work that is ours. We do not boast in the work other men have done. We hope that your faith will continue to grow. And we hope that you will help our work to grow much larger. ¹⁶We want to tell the Good News in the areas beyond your city. We do not want to boast about work that has already been done in another man's area. ¹⁷But, "If a person boasts, he should boast only about the Lord."[n] ¹⁸It is not the one who says he is good who is accepted but the one that the Lord thinks is good.

Paul and the False Apostles

11 I wish you would be patient with me even when I am a little foolish. But you are already doing that. ²I am jealous over you. And this jealousy comes from God. I promised to give you to Christ. He must be your only husband. I want to give you to Christ to be his pure bride. ³But I am afraid that your minds will be led away from your true and pure following of Christ. This might happen just as Eve was tricked by the snake with his evil ways. ⁴You are very patient with anyone who comes to you and preaches a different Jesus than the one we preached. You are very willing to accept a spirit or good news that is different from the Spirit[d] and Good News[d] that you received from us.

⁵I do not think that those "great apostles" are any better than I am. ⁶I may not be a trained speaker, but I do have knowledge. We have shown this to you clearly in every way.

⁷I preached God's Good News to you without pay. I made myself unimportant to make you important. Do you think that was wrong? ⁸I accepted pay from other churches. I took their money so that I could serve you. ⁹If I needed something when I was with you, I did not trouble any of you. The brothers who came from Macedonia gave me all that I needed. I did not allow myself to depend on you in any way. And I will never depend on you. ¹⁰No one in Southern Greece will stop me from boasting about that. I say this with the truth of Christ in me. ¹¹And why do I not depend on you? Do you think it is because I do not love you? No. God knows that I love you.

¹²And I will keep on doing what I am doing now. I will continue because I want to stop those people from having a reason to boast. They would like to say that the work they boast about is the same as ours. ¹³Such men are not true apostles.[d] They are workers who lie. And they change themselves to look like apostles of Christ. ¹⁴This does not surprise us. Even Satan changes himself to look like an angel

---

"If a person . . . Lord." Quotation from Jeremiah 9:24.

of light.ⁿ ¹⁵So it does not surprise us if Satan's servants also make themselves look like servants who work for what is right. But in the end they will be punished for the things they do.

Paul Tells About His Sufferings

¹⁶I tell you again: No one should think that I am a fool. But if you think that I am a fool, then accept me as you would accept a fool. Then I can boast a little, too. ¹⁷I boast because I feel sure of myself. But I am not talking as the Lord would talk. I am boasting like a fool. ¹⁸Many people are boasting about their lives in the world. So I will boast, too. ¹⁹You are wise, so you will gladly be patient with fools! ²⁰You are even patient with someone who orders you around and uses you! You are patient with those who trick you, or think they are better than you, or hit you in the face! ²¹It is shameful to me to say this, but we were too "weak" to do those things to you!

But if anyone else is brave enough to boast, then I also will be brave and boast. (I am talking like a fool.) ²²Are they Hebrews?ⁿ So am I. Are they Israelites? So am I. Are they from Abraham's family? So am I. ²³Are they serving Christ? I am serving him more. (I am insane to talk like this.) I have worked much harder than they. I have been in prison more often. I have been hurt more in beatings. I have been near death many times. ²⁴Five times the Jews have given me their punishment of 39 lashes with a whip. ²⁵Three different times I was beaten with rods. Once they tried to kill me with stones. Three times I was in ships that were wrecked, and one of those times I spent the night and the next day in the sea. ²⁶I have gone

on many travels. And I have been in danger from rivers, from thieves, from my own people, the Jews, and from those who are not Jews. I have been in danger in cities, in places where no one lives, and on the sea. And I have been in danger with false brothers. ²⁷I have done hard and tiring work, and many times I did not sleep. I have been hungry and thirsty. Many times I have been without food. I have been cold and without clothes. ²⁸Besides all this, there is on me every day the load of my concern for all the churches. ²⁹I feel weak every time someone is weak. I feel upset every time someone is led into sin.

³⁰If I must boast, I will boast about the things that show I am weak. ³¹God knows that I am not lying. He is the God and Father of the Lord Jesus

2 Corinthians 11:33 They put the basket through a hole in the wall and lowered me down.

---

angel of light Messenger from God. The devil fools people so that they think he is from God.
Hebrews A name for the Jews that some Jews were very proud of.

Christ, and he is to be praised for ever. [32]When I was in Damascus, the governor under King Aretas wanted to arrest me. So he put guards around the city. [33]But my friends put me in a basket. Then they put the basket through a hole in the wall and lowered me down. So I escaped from the governor.

A Special Blessing in Paul's Life

12 I must continue to boast. It will do no good, but I will talk now about visions and revelations[n] from the Lord. [2]I know a man in Christ who was taken up to the third heaven. This happened 14 years ago. I do not know whether the man was in his body or out of his body. But God knows. [3-4]And I know that this man was taken up to paradise.[n] I don't know if he was in his body or away from his body. But he heard things he is not able to explain. He heard things that no man is allowed to tell. [5]I will boast about a man like that. But I will not boast about myself, except about my weaknesses. [6]But if I wanted to boast about myself, I would not be a fool. I would not be a fool, because I would be telling the truth. But I will not boast about myself. I do not want people to think more of me than what they see me do or hear me say.

[7]But I must not become too proud of the wonderful things that were shown to me. So a painful problem[n] was given to me. This problem is a messenger from Satan. It is sent to beat me and keep me from being too proud. [8]I begged the Lord three times to take this problem away from me. [9]But the Lord said to me, "My grace is enough for you. When you are weak, then my power is made perfect in you." So I am very happy to boast about my weaknesses. Then Christ's power can live in me. [10]So I am happy when I have weaknesses, insults, hard times, sufferings, and all kinds of troubles. All these things are for Christ. And I am happy, because when I am weak, then I am truly strong.

Paul's Love for the Christians

[11]I have been talking like a fool. But you made me do it. You are the ones who should say good things about me. I am worth nothing, but those "great apostles" are not worth any more than I am! [12]When I was with you, I did what proves that I am an apostle[d] – signs, wonders, and miracles.[d] And I did these things with much patience. [13]So you received everything that the other churches have received. Only one thing was different: I was not a burden to you. Forgive me for this!

[14]I am now ready to visit you the third time. And I will not be a burden to you. I want nothing from you, I only want you. Children should not have to save up to give to their parents. Parents should save to give to their children. [15]So I am happy to give everything I have for you. I will even give myself for you. If I love you more, will you love me less?

[16]It is clear that I was not a burden to you. But you think that I was sly and used lies to catch you. [17]Did I cheat you by using any of the men I sent to you? No, you know I did not. [18]I asked Titus to go to you. And I sent our brother with him. Titus did not cheat you, did he? No, you know that Titus and I did the same thing and with the same spirit.

---

revelations   Revelation is making known a truth that was hidden.
paradise   A place where good people go when they die.
painful problem   Literally, "thorn in the flesh".

[19] Do you think that we have been defending ourselves to you all this time? We have been speaking in Christ and before God. You are our dear friends. And everything that we do is to make you stronger. [20] I do this because I am afraid that when I come, you will not be what I want you to be. And I am afraid that I will not be what you want me to be. I am afraid that among you there may be arguing, jealousy, anger, selfish fighting, evil talk, gossip, pride, and confusion. [21] I am afraid that when I come to you again, my God will make me ashamed before you. I may be saddened by many of those who have sinned. I may be saddened because they have not changed their hearts and have not turned away from their sexual sins and from the shameful things they have done.

Final Warnings and Greetings

13 I will come to you for the third time. And remember, "Every case must be proved by two or three witnesses."[n] [2] When I was with you the second time, I gave a warning to those who had sinned. Now I am away from you, and I give a warning to all the others. When I come to you again, I will not be easy on them. [3] You want proof that Christ is speaking through me. My proof is that he is not weak among you, but he is powerful. [4] It is true that he was weak when he was killed on the cross. But he lives now by God's power. It is true that we are weak in Christ. But for you we will be alive in Christ by God's power.

[5] Look closely at yourselves. Test yourselves to see if you are living in the faith. You know that Christ Jesus is in you – unless you fail the test. [6] But I hope you will see that we ourselves have not failed the test. [7] We pray to God that you will not do anything wrong. It is not important to see that we have passed the test. But it is important that you do what is right, even if it seems that we have failed. [8] We cannot do anything against the truth, but only for the truth. [9] We are happy to be weak, if you are strong. And we pray that you will grow stronger and stronger. [10] I am writing this while I am away from you. I am writing so that when I come I will not have to be harsh in my use of authority. The Lord gave me this authority to use to make you stronger, not to destroy you.

[11] Now, brothers, I say good-bye. Try to be perfect. Do what I have asked you to do. Agree with each other, and live in peace. Then the God of love and peace will be with you.

[12] Give each other a holy kiss when you greet each other. [13] All of God's holy people send greetings to you.

[14] The grace of the Lord Jesus Christ, the love of God, and the fellowship of the Holy Spirit[d] be with you all.

"Every . . . witnesses." Quotation from Deuteronomy 19:15.

GALATIANS

Christians Are Saved by Grace

1 From Paul, an apostle.*ᵈ*
I was not chosen to be an apostle by men. I was not sent from men. It was Jesus Christ and God the Father who made me an apostle. God is the One who raised Jesus from death.

Galatians 1:1–2 From Paul . . . to the churches in Galatia.

²This letter is also from all the brothers who are with me.

To the churches in Galatia.*ⁿ*

³I pray that God our Father and the Lord Jesus Christ will be good to you and give you peace. ⁴Jesus gave himself for our sins to free us from this evil world we live in. This is what God the Father wanted. ⁵The glory belongs to God for ever and ever. Amen.

The Only Good News

⁶A short time ago God called you to follow him. He called you by his grace that came through Christ. But now I am amazed at you! You are already turning away and believing something different from the Good News.*ᵈ* ⁷Really, there is no other Good News. But some people are confusing you and want to change the Good News of Christ. ⁸We preached to you the Good News. So if we ourselves, or even an angel from heaven, preach to you something different from the Good News, he should be condemned! ⁹I said this before. Now I say it again: you have already accepted the Good News. If anyone tells you another way to be saved, he should be condemned!

¹⁰Do you think I am trying to make people accept me? No! God is the One I am trying to please. Am I trying to please men? If I wanted to please men, I would not be a servant of Christ.

Paul's Authority Is from God

¹¹Brothers, I want you to know that the Good News*ᵈ* I preached to you was not made by men. ¹²I did not get it from men, nor did any man teach it to me. Jesus Christ showed it to me.

¹³You have heard about my past life. I belonged to the Jewish religion. I hurt the church of God very much and

---

Galatia Probably the same country where Paul preached and began churches on his first missionary trip. Read the book of Acts, chapters 13 and 14.

tried to destroy it. [14]I was becoming a leader in the Jewish religion. I did better than most other Jews of my age. I tried harder than anyone else to follow the old rules. These rules were the customs handed down by our ancestors.

[15]But God had special plans for me even before I was born. So he called me through his grace that I might [16]tell the Good News about his Son to the non-Jewish people. So God told me about his Son. When God called me, I did not get advice or help from any man. [17]I did not go to Jerusalem to see those who were apostles[d] before I was. But, without waiting, I went away to Arabia and later went back to Damascus.

[18]After three years I went to Jerusalem to meet Peter and stayed with him for 15 days. [19]I met no other apostles, except James, the brother of the Lord. [20]God knows that these things I write are not lies. [21]Later, I went to the areas of Syria and Cilicia.

[22]In Judea the churches in Christ had never met me. [23]They had only heard this about me: "This man was trying to hurt us. But now he is preaching the same faith that he once tried to destroy." [24]And these believers praised God because of me.

Other Apostles Accepted Paul

2 After 14 years, I went to Jerusalem again, this time with Barnabas. I also took Titus with me. [2]I went because God showed me that I should go. I met with those men who were the leaders of the believers. When we were alone, I told them the Good News[d] that I preach to the non-Jewish people. I did not want my past work and the work I am now doing to be wasted. [3]Titus was with me. But Titus was not forced to be circumcised,[d] even though he was a Greek. [4]We

talked about this problem because some false brothers had come into our group secretly. They came in like spies to find out about the freedom we have in Christ Jesus. They wanted to make us slaves. [5]But we did not agree with anything those false brothers wanted! We wanted the truth of the Good News to continue for you.

[6]Those men who seemed to be important did not change the Good News that I preach. (It doesn't matter to me if they were "important" or not. To God all men are the same.) [7]But these leaders saw that God had given me special work, just as he had to Peter. God gave Peter the work of telling the Good News to the Jews. But God gave me the work of telling the Good News to the non-Jewish people. [8]God gave Peter the power to work as an apostle[d] for the Jewish people. But he also gave me the power to work as an apostle for those who are not Jews. [9]James, Peter, and John, who seemed to be the leaders, saw that God had given me this special grace. So they accepted Barnabas and me. They said, "Paul and Barnabas, we agree that you should go to the people who are not Jews. We will go to the Jews." [10]They asked us to do only one thing – to remember to help the poor. And this was something that I really wanted to do.

Paul Shows that Peter Was Wrong

[11]When Peter came to Antioch, I was against him because he was wrong. [12]This is what happened: when Peter first came to Antioch, he ate with the non-Jewish people. But then some Jewish men were sent from James. When they arrived, Peter stopped eating with the non-Jewish people and separated himself from them. He was afraid of the Jews who believe that all non-Jewish people must

be circumcised.*d* [13]So Peter was a hypocrite.*d* The other Jewish believers joined with him and were hypocrites, too. Even Barnabas was influenced by what these Jewish believers did. [14]I saw what they did. They were not following the truth of the Good News.*d* So I spoke to Peter in front of them all. I said: "Peter, you are a Jew, but you are not living like a Jew. You are living like the non-Jewish people. So why do you now try to force the non-Jewish people to live like Jews?"

[15]We were not born as non-Jewish "sinners", but we were born as Jews. [16]Yet we know that a person is not made right with God by following the law. No! It is trusting in Jesus Christ that makes a person right with God. So we, too, have put our faith in Christ Jesus, that we might be made right with God. And we are right with God because we trusted in Christ – not because we followed the law. For no one can be made right with God by following the law.

[17]We Jews came to Christ to be made right with God. So it is clear that we were sinners too. Does this mean that Christ makes us sinners? No! [18]But I would really be wrong to begin teaching again those things of the law of Moses that I gave up. [19]I stopped living for the law. It was the law that put me to death. I died to the law so that I can now live for God. I was put to death on the cross with Christ. [20]I do not live any more – it is Christ living in me. I still live in my body, but I live by faith in the Son of God. He loved me and gave himself to save me. [21]This gift is from God, and it is very important to me. If the law could make us right with God, then Christ did not have to die.

Blessing Comes Through Faith

3 You people in Galatia were told very clearly about the death of Jesus Christ on the cross. But you were very foolish. You let someone trick you. [2]Tell me this one thing: how did you receive the Holy Spirit?*d* Did you receive the Spirit by following the law? No! You received the Spirit because you heard the Good News*d* and believed it. [3]You began your life in Christ by the Spirit. Now do you try to continue it by your own power? That is foolish. [4]You have experienced many things. Were all those experiences wasted? I hope not! [5]Does God give you the Spirit because you follow the law? No! Does God work miracles*d* among you because you follow the law? No! God gives you his Spirit and works miracles among you because you heard the Good News and believed it.

[6]The Scriptures*d* say the same thing about Abraham: "Abraham believed God, and God accepted Abraham's faith, and that faith made him right with God."*n* [7]So you should know that the true children of Abraham are those who have faith. [8]The Scriptures told what would happen in the future. They said that God would make the non-Jewish people right through their faith. This Good News was told to Abraham beforehand, as the Scripture says: "All nations will be blessed through you."*n* [9]Abraham believed this, and because he believed, he was blessed. It is the same today. All who believe today are blessed just as Abraham was blessed. [10]But those who depend on following the law to make them right are under a curse because the Scriptures say, "Anyone will be cursed who does not always obey what

"**Abraham . . . God.**" Quotation from Genesis 15:6.
"**All . . . you.**" Quotation from Genesis 12:3.

is written in the Book of the Law!"[n] [11]So it is clear that no one can be made right with God by the law. The Scriptures say, "He who is right with God by faith will live." [12]The law does not use faith. It says, "A person who does these things will live for ever because of them."[n] [13]So the law put a curse on us, but Christ took away that curse. He changed places with us and put himself under that curse. It is written in the Scriptures, "Everyone whose body is displayed on a tree[n] is cursed." [14]Christ did this so that God's blessing promised to Abraham might come to the non-Jews. This blessing comes through Jesus Christ. Jesus died so that we could have the Spirit that God promised and receive this promise by believing.

The Law and the Promise

[15]Brothers, let me give you an example: think about an agreement that a person makes with another person. After that agreement is accepted by both people, no one can stop that agreement or add anything to it. [16]God made promises to Abraham and his descendant.[d] God did not say, "and to your descendants". That would mean many people. But God said, "and to your descendant". That means only one person; that person is Christ. [17]This is what I mean: God had an agreement with Abraham and promised to keep it. The law, which came 430 years later, cannot change God's promise to Abraham. [18]Can following the law give us what God promised? No! If this is so, it is not God's promise that brings us the blessings. Instead God freely gave his blessings to Abraham through the promise he had made.

[19]So what was the law for? The law was given to show the wrong things people do. It continued until the special descendant of Abraham came. God's promise was about this descendant. The law was given through angels who used Moses as a mediator[n] to give the law to men. [20]But a mediator is not needed when there is only one side. And God is only one.

The Purpose of the Law of Moses

[21]Does this mean that the law is against God's promises? Never! If there were a law that could give men life, then we could be made right by following that law. [22]But this is not true, because the Scriptures[d] showed that the whole world is bound by sin. This was so that the promise would be given through faith. And it is given to people who believe in Jesus Christ.

[23]Before this faith came, we were all held prisoners by the law. We had no freedom until God showed us the way of faith that was coming. [24]So the law was our master until Christ came. After Christ came, we could be made right with God through faith. [25]Now the way of faith has come, and we no longer live under the law.

[26-27]You were all baptised into Christ, and so you were all clothed with Christ. This shows that you are all children of God through faith in Christ Jesus. [28]Now, in Christ, there is no difference between Jew and Greek. There is no difference between slaves

---

"Anyone . . . Law!"   Quotation from Deuteronomy 27:26.
"A person . . . them."   Quotation from Leviticus 18:5.
displayed on a tree   Deuteronomy 21:22–23 says that when a person was killed for doing wrong, his body was hung on a tree to show shame. Paul means that the cross of Jesus was like that.
mediator   A person who helps one person talk to or give something to another person.

and free men. There is no difference between male and female. You are all the same in Christ Jesus. [29] You belong to Christ. So you are Abraham's descendants.[d] You receive all of God's blessings because of the promise that God made to Abraham.

4 I want to tell you this: while the one who will inherit his father's property is still a child, he is no different from a slave. It does not matter that the child owns everything. [2] While he is a child, he must obey those who are chosen to care for him. But when the child reaches the age set by his father, he is free. [3] It is the same for us. We were once like children. We were slaves to the useless rules of this world. [4] But when the right time came, God sent his Son. His Son was born of a woman and lived under the law. [5] God did this so that he could buy freedom for those who were under the law. His purpose was to make us his children.

[6] And you are God's children. That is why God sent the Spirit of his Son into your hearts. The Spirit[d] cries out, "Father, dear Father."[n] [7] So now you are not a slave; you are God's child, and God will give you what he promised, because you are his child.

Paul's Love for the Christians

[8] In the past you did not know God. You were slaves to gods that were not real. [9] But now you know the true God. Really, it is God who knows you. So why do you turn back to those weak and useless rules you followed before? Do you want to be slaves to those things again? [10] You still follow teachings about special days, months,

Galatians 4:7 So now you are not a slave; you are God's child.

seasons, and years. [11] I am afraid for you. I fear that my work for you has been wasted.

[12] Brothers, I was like you; so I beg you to become like me. You were very good to me before. [13] You remember that I came to you the first time because I was sick. That was when I preached the Good News[d] to you. [14] Though my sickness was a trouble for you, you did not hate me or make me leave. But you welcomed me as an angel from God, as if I were Jesus Christ himself! [15] You were very happy then. Where is that joy now? I remember that you would have taken out your eyes and given them to me if that were possible. [16] Now am I your enemy because I tell you the truth?

[17] Those people[n] are working hard to persuade you. But this is not good for you. They want to persuade you to

---

"Father, dear Father" Literally, "Abba, Father". Jewish children called their fathers "Abba".
Those people They are the false teachers who were bothering the believers in Galatia (Galatians 1:7).

turn against us. They want you to follow only them. [18]It is good for people to show interest in you, but only if their purpose is good. This is always true. It is true when I am with you and when I am away. [19]My little children, again I feel pain for you as a mother feels when she gives birth. I will feel this until you truly become like Christ. [20]I wish I could be with you now. Then perhaps I could change the way I am talking to you. Now I do not know what to do about you.

The Example of Hagar and Sarah

[21]Some of you people still want to be under the law of Moses. Tell me, do you know what the law says? [22]The Scriptures[d] say that Abraham had two sons. The mother of one son was a slave woman. The mother of the other son was a free woman. [23]Abraham's son from the slave woman was born in the normal human way. But the son from the free woman was born because of the promise God made to Abraham. [24]This makes a picture for us. The two women are like the two agreements between God and men. One agreement is the law that God made on Mount Sinai.[n] The people who are under this agreement are like slaves. The mother named Hagar is like that agreement. [25]She is like Mount Sinai in Arabia and is a picture of the earthly Jewish city of Jerusalem. This city is a slave, and all its people, the Jews, are slaves to the law. [26]But the heavenly Jerusalem which is above is like the free woman. She is our mother. [27]It is written in the Scriptures:

"Be happy, Jerusalem.
    You are like a woman who never
       gave birth to children.
Start singing and shout for joy.
    You never felt the pain of giving
       birth to children.
But you will have more children
    than the woman who has a
       husband."   *Isaiah 54:1*

[28]My brothers, you are God's children because of his promise, as Isaac was then. [29]The son who was born in the normal way treated the other son badly. It is the same today. [30]But what does the Scripture say? "Throw out the slave woman and her son! The son of the free woman will receive everything his father has. But the son of the slave woman will receive nothing."[n] [31]So, my brothers, we are not children of the slave woman. We are children of the free woman.

Keep Your Freedom

5 We have freedom now because Christ made us free. So stand strong. Do not change and go back into the slavery of the law. [2]Listen! I am Paul. I tell you that if you go back to the law by being circumcised,[d] then Christ is no good for you. [3]Again, I warn every man: if you allow yourselves to be circumcised, then you must follow all the law. [4]If you try to be made right with God through the law, then your life with Christ is over – you have left God's grace. [5]But we hope to be made right with God through faith, and we wait for this hope anxiously with the Spirit's[d] help. [6]When we are in Christ Jesus, it is not important if we are circumcised or not. The important thing is faith – the kind of faith that works through love.

[7]You were running a good race. You were obeying the truth. Who stopped you from following the true way?

Mount Sinai   Mountain in Arabia where God gave his laws to Moses (Exodus 19 and 20).
"Throw . . . nothing."   Quotation from Genesis 21:10.

[8] Whatever way he used did not come from the One who chose you. [9] Be careful! "Just a little yeast makes the whole batch of dough rise." [10] But I trust in the Lord that you will not believe those different ideas. Someone is confusing you with such ideas. And he will be punished, whoever he is.

[11] My brothers, I do not teach that a man must be circumcised. If I teach circumcision, then why am I still being treated badly? If I still taught circumcision, my preaching about the cross would not be a problem. [12] I wish the people who are bothering you would castrate[n] themselves!

[13] My brothers, God called you to be free. But do not use your freedom as an excuse to do the things that please your sinful self. Serve each other with love. [14] The whole law is made complete in this one command: "Love your neighbour as you love yourself."[n] [15] If you go on hurting each other and tearing each other apart, be careful! You will completely destroy each other.

The Spirit and Human Nature

[16] So I tell you: live by following the Spirit.[d] Then you will not do what your sinful selves want. [17] Our sinful selves want what is against the Spirit. The Spirit wants what is against our sinful selves. The two are against each other. So you must not do just what you please. [18] But if you let the Spirit lead you, you are not under the law.

[19] The wrong things the sinful self does are clear: being sexually unfaithful, not being pure, taking part in sexual sins, [20] worshipping false gods, doing witchcraft,[d] hating, making trouble, being jealous, being angry, being selfish, making people angry with each other, causing divisions among people, [21] having envy, being drunk, having wild and wasteful parties, and doing other things like this. I warn you now as I warned you before: those who do these things will not be in God's kingdom. [22] But the Spirit gives love, joy, peace, patience, kindness, goodness, faithfulness, [23] gentleness, self-control. There is no law that says these things are wrong. [24] Those who belong to Christ Jesus have crucified their own sinful selves. They have given up their old selfish feelings and the evil things they wanted to do. [25] We get our new life from the Spirit. So we should follow the Spirit. [26] We must not be proud. We must not make trouble with each other. And we must not be jealous of each other.

Help Each Other

6 Brothers, someone in your group might do something wrong. You who are spiritual should go to him and help make him right again. You should do this in a gentle way. But be careful! You might be tempted to sin, too. [2] Help each other with your troubles. When you do this, you truly obey the law of Christ. [3] If anyone thinks that he is important when he is really not important, he is only fooling himself. [4] He should not compare himself with others. Each person should judge his own actions. Then he can be proud for what he himself has done. [5] Each person must be responsible for himself.

[6] Anyone who is learning the teaching of God should share all the good things he has with his teacher.

---

castrate To cut off part of the male sex organ. Paul uses this word because it is similar to "circumcision". Paul wanted to show that he is very upset with the false teachers.
"Love . . . yourself." Quotation from Leviticus 19:18.

Life Is like Planting a Field

⁷Do not be fooled: you cannot cheat God. A person harvests only what he plants. ⁸If he plants to satisfy his sinful self, his sinful self will bring him eternal death. But if he plants to please the Spirit,ᵈ he will receive eternal life from the Spirit. ⁹We must not become tired of doing good. We will receive our harvest of eternal life at the right time. We must not give up! ¹⁰When we have the opportunity to help anyone, we should do it. But we should give special attention to those who are in the family of believers.

Paul Ends His Letter

¹¹I am writing this myself. See what large letters I use. ¹²Some men are trying to force you to be circumcised.ᵈ They do these things so that the Jews will accept them. They are afraid that they will be treated badly if they follow only the cross of Christ.ⁿ ¹³Those who are circumcised do not obey the law themselves, but they want you to be circumcised. Then they can boast about what they forced you to do. ¹⁴I hope I will never boast about things like that. The cross of our Lord Jesus Christ is my only reason for boasting. Through the cross of Jesus my world was crucified and I died to the world. ¹⁵It is not important if a man is circumcised or not circumcised. The important thing is being the new people God has made. ¹⁶Peace and mercy to those who follow this rule – to all of God's people.

¹⁷So do not give me any more trouble. I have scars on my body. These showⁿ I belong to Christ Jesus.

¹⁸My brothers, I pray that the grace of our Lord Jesus Christ will be with your spirit. Amen.

cross of Christ Paul uses the cross as a picture of the gospel, the story of Christ's death and rising from death to pay for men's sins. The cross, or Christ's death, was God's way to save men.
These show Many times Paul was beaten and whipped by people who were against him because he was teaching about Christ. The scars were from these beatings.

EPHESIANS

God Unites His People

1 From Paul, an apostle[d] of Christ Jesus. I am an apostle because that is what God wanted.

To God's holy people living in Ephesus, believers in Christ Jesus.

[2] Grace and peace to you from God our Father and the Lord Jesus Christ.

Spiritual Blessings in Christ

[3] Praise be to the God and Father of our Lord Jesus Christ. In Christ, God has given us every spiritual blessing in heaven. [4] In Christ, he chose us before the world was made. In his love he chose us to be his holy people – people without blame before him. [5] And before the world was made, God decided to make us his own children through Jesus Christ. That was what he wanted and what pleased him. [6] This brings praise to God because of his wonderful grace. God gave that grace to us freely, in Christ, the One he loves. [7] In Christ we are set free by the blood of his death. And so we have forgiveness of sins because of God's rich grace. [8] God gave us that grace fully and freely. God, with full wisdom and understanding, [9] let us know his secret purpose. This was what God wanted, and he planned to do it through Christ. [10] His goal was to carry out his plan when the right time came. He planned that all things in heaven and on earth would be joined together in Christ as the head.

[11] In Christ we were chosen to be God's people. God had already chosen us to be his people, because that is what he wanted. And God is the One who makes everything agree with what he decides and wants. [12] We are the first people who hoped in Christ. And we were chosen so that we would bring praise to God's glory. [13] So it is with you. You heard the true teaching – the Good News[d] about your salvation. When you heard it, you believed in Christ. And in Christ, God put his special mark on you by giving you the Holy Spirit[d] that he had promised. [14] That Holy Spirit is the guarantee that we will get what God promised for his people. This will

Ephesians 1:12 We were chosen so that we would bring praise to God's glory.

bring full freedom to the people who belong to God, to bring praise to God's glory.

Paul's Prayer

[15-16]That is why I always remember you in my prayers and always thank God for you. I have always done this since the time I heard about your faith in the Lord Jesus and your love for all God's people. [17]I always pray to the God of our Lord Jesus Christ – to the glorious Father. I pray that he will give you a spirit that will make you wise in the knowledge of God – the knowledge that he has shown you. [18]I pray that you will have greater understanding in your heart. Then you will know the hope that God has chosen to give us. I pray that you will know that the blessings God has promised his holy people are rich and glorious. [19]And you will know that God's power is very great for us who believe. That power is the same as the great strength [20]God used to raise Christ from death and put him at his right side in heaven. [21]God made Christ more important than all rulers, authorities, powers, and kings. Christ is more important than anything in this world or in the next world. [22]God put everything under his power. And God made him the head over everything for the church. [23]The church is Christ's body. The church is filled with Christ, and Christ fills everything in every way.

From Death to Life

2 In the past your spiritual lives were dead because of your sins and the things you did wrong against God. [2]Yes, in the past you lived the way the world lives. You followed the ruler of the evil powers that are above the earth. That same spirit is now working in those who refuse to obey God. [3]In the past all of us lived like them. We lived trying to please our sinful selves. We did all the things our bodies and minds wanted. We should have suffered God's anger because of the way we were. We were the same as all other people.

[4]But God's mercy is great, and he loved us very much. [5]We were spiritually dead because of the things we did wrong against God. But God gave us new life with Christ. You have been saved by God's grace. [6]And he raised us up with Christ and gave us a seat with him in the heavens. He did this for those of us who are in Christ Jesus. [7]He did this so that for all future time he could show the very great riches of his grace. He shows that grace by being kind to us in Christ Jesus. [8]I mean that you have been saved by grace because you believe. You did not save yourselves. It was a gift from God. [9]You cannot boast that you are saved by the work you have done. [10]God has made us what we are. In Christ Jesus, God made us new people so that we would do good works. God had planned in advance those good works for us. He had planned for us to live our lives doing them.

One in Christ

[11]You were born non-Jews. You are the people the Jews call "uncircumcised".[n] Those who call you "uncircumcised" call themselves "circumcised".[d] (Their circumcision is only something they themselves do to their bodies.) [12]Remember that in the past you were without Christ. You were not citizens of Israel. And you had no part in the agreements[n] with

---

uncircumcised   People not having the mark of circumcision as the Jews have.
agreements   The agreements that God gave to his people in the Old Testament.

the promise that God made to his people. You had no hope, and you did not know God. [13]Yes, at one time you were far away from God. But now in Christ Jesus you are brought near to God through the blood of Christ's death. [14]Because of Christ we now have peace. Christ made both Jews and non-Jews one people. They were separated as if there were a wall between them. But Christ broke down that wall of hate by giving his own body. [15]The Jewish law had many commands and rules. But Christ ended that law. Christ's purpose was to make the two groups of people become one new people in him. By doing this Christ would make peace. [16]Through the cross Christ ended the hatred between the two groups. And after Christ made the two groups to be one body, he wanted to bring them back to God. Christ did this with his death on the cross. [17]Christ came and preached peace to you non-Jews who were far away from God. And he preached peace to those Jews who were near to God. [18]Yes, through Christ we all have the right to come to the Father in one Spirit.[d]

[19]So now you non-Jews are not visitors or strangers. Now you are citizens together with God's holy people. You belong to God's family. [20]You believers are like a building that God owns. That building was built on the foundation of the apostles[d] and prophets.[d] Christ Jesus himself is the most important stone[n] in that building. [21]That whole building is joined together in Christ. And Christ makes it grow and become a holy temple in the Lord. [22]And in Christ you, too, are being built together with the Jews. You are being built into a place where God lives through the Spirit.

Paul's Work for the Non-Jews

3 So I, Paul, am a prisoner of Christ Jesus. I am a prisoner for you who are not Jews. [2]Surely you know that God gave me this work through his grace to help you. [3]God let me know his secret plan. He showed it to me. I have already written a little about this. [4]And if you read what I wrote, then you can see that I truly understand the secret truth about the Christ.[d] [5]People who lived in other times were not told that secret truth. But now, through the Spirit,[d] God has shown that secret truth to his holy apostles[d] and prophets.[d] [6]This is that secret truth: that the non-Jews will receive what God has for his people, just as the Jews will. The non-Jews are together with the Jews as part of the same body. And they share together in the promise that God made in Christ Jesus. The non-Jews have all of this because of the Good News.[d]

[7]By God's special gift of grace, I became a servant to tell that Good News. God gave me that grace through his power. [8]I am the least important of all God's people. But God gave me this gift – to tell the non-Jewish people the Good News about the riches of Christ. Those riches are too great to understand fully. [9]And God gave me the work of telling all people about the plan for God's secret truth. That secret truth has been hidden in God since the beginning of time. God is the One who created everything. [10]His purpose was that through the church all the rulers and powers in the heavenly world will now know God's wisdom, which has so

---

most important stone Literally, "cornerstone". The first and most important stone in a building.

many forms. [11]This agrees with the purpose God had since the beginning of time. And God carried out his plan through Christ Jesus our Lord. [12]In Christ we can come before God with freedom and without fear. We can do this through faith in Christ. [13]So I ask you not to become discouraged because of the sufferings I am having for you. My sufferings bring honour to you.

The Love of Christ

[14]So I bow in prayer before the Father. [15]Every family in heaven and on earth gets its true name from him. [16]I ask the Father in his great glory to give you the power to be strong in spirit. He will give you that strength through his Spirit.[d] [17]I pray that Christ will live in your hearts because of your faith. I pray that your life will be strong in love and be built on love. [18]And I pray that you and all God's holy people will have the power to understand the greatness of Christ's love. I pray that you can understand how wide and how long and how high and how deep that love is. [19]Christ's love is greater than any person can ever know. But I pray that you will be able to know that love. Then you can be filled with the fullness of God.

[20]With God's power working in us, God can do much, much more than anything we can ask or think of. [21]To him be glory in the church and in Christ Jesus for all time, for ever and ever. Amen.

The Unity of the Body

4 I am in prison because I belong to the Lord. God chose you to be his people. I tell you now to live the way God's people should live. [2]Always be humble and gentle. Be patient and accept each other with love. [3]You are joined together with peace through the Spirit.[d] Do all you can to continue together in this way. Let peace hold you together. [4]There is one body and one Spirit. And God called you to have one hope. [5]There is one Lord, one faith, and one baptism. [6]There is one God and Father of everything. He rules everything. He is everywhere and in everything.

[7]Christ gave each one of us a special gift. Each one received what Christ wanted to give him. [8]That is why it says in the Scriptures,[d]

"When he went up to the heights,
　he led a parade of captives.
And he gave gifts to people."

Psalm 68:18

[9]When it says, "He went up", what does it mean? It means that he first came down to the earth. [10]So Jesus came down, and he is the same One who went up. He went up above all the heavens. Christ did that to fill everything with himself. [11]And Christ gave gifts to men – he made some to be apostles,[d] some to be prophets,[d] some to go and tell the Good News,[d] and some to have the work of caring for and teaching God's people. [12]Christ gave those gifts to prepare God's holy people for the work of serving. He gave those gifts to make the body of Christ stronger. [13]This work must continue until we are all joined together in the same faith and in the same knowledge about the Son of God. We must become like a mature person – we must grow until we become like Christ and have all his perfection.

[14]Then we will no longer be babies. We will not be tossed about like a ship that the waves carry one way and then another. We will not be influenced by every new teaching we hear from men who are trying to fool us. Those men make plans and try any kind of trick to fool people into following the wrong

path. [15]No! We will speak the truth with love. We will grow up in every way to be like Christ, who is the head. [16]The whole body depends on Christ. And all the parts of the body are joined and held together. Each part of the body does its own work. And this makes the whole body grow and be strong with love.

The Way You Should Live

[17]In the Lord's name, I tell you this. I warn you: do not continue living like those who do not believe. Their thoughts are worth nothing. [18]They do not understand. They know nothing, because they refuse to listen. So they cannot have the life that God gives. [19]They have lost their feeling of shame. And they use their lives for doing evil. More and more they want to do all kinds of evil things. [20]But the things you learned in Christ were not like this. [21]I know that you heard about him, and you are in him; so you were taught the truth. Yes, the truth is in Jesus. [22]You were taught to leave your old self – to stop living the evil way you lived before. That old self becomes worse and worse because people are fooled by the evil things they want to do. [23]But you were taught to be made new in your hearts. [24]You were taught to become a new person. That new person is made to be like God – made to be truly good and holy.

[25]So you must stop telling lies. Tell each other the truth because we all belong to each other in the same body.[n] [26]When you are angry, do not sin. And do not go on being angry all day. [27]Do not give the devil a way to defeat you. [28]If a person is stealing, he must stop stealing and start working. He must use his hands for doing

something good. Then he will have something to share with those who are poor.

[29]When you talk, do not say harmful things. But say what people need – words that will help others become stronger. Then what you say will help those who listen to you. [30]And do not make the Holy Spirit[d] sad. The Spirit is God's proof that you belong to him. God gave you the Spirit to show that God will make you free when the time comes. [31]Do not be bitter or angry or cross. Never shout angrily or say things to hurt others. Never do anything evil. [32]Be kind and loving to each other. Forgive each other just as God forgave you in Christ.

Living in the Light

5 You are God's children whom he loves. So try to be like God. [2]Live a life of love. Love other people just as Christ loved us. Christ gave himself for us – he was a sweet-smelling offering and sacrifice to God.

[3]But there must be no sexual sin among you. There must not be any kind of evil or greed. Those things are not right for God's holy people. [4]Also, there must be no evil talk among you. You must not speak foolishly or tell evil jokes. These things are not right for you. But you should be giving thanks to God. [5]You can be sure of this: no one will have a place in the kingdom of Christ and of God if he does sexual sins, or does evil things, or is greedy. Anyone who is greedy is serving a false god.

[6]Do not let anyone fool you by telling you things that are not true. These things will bring God's anger on those who do not obey him. [7]So have nothing to do with them. [8]In the past you were full of darkness, but now you are

Tell . . . body.   Quotation from Zechariah 8:16.

full of light in the Lord. So live like children who belong to the light. [9] Light brings every kind of goodness, right living, and truth. [10] Try to learn what pleases the Lord. [11] Do not do the things that people in darkness do. That brings nothing good. But do good things to show that the things done in darkness are wrong. [12] It is shameful even to talk about what those people do in secret. [13] But the light makes all things easy to see. [14] And everything that is made easy to see can become light. This is why it is said:

"Wake up, sleeper!
    Rise from death,
and Christ will shine on you."

[15] So be very careful how you live. Do not live like those who are not wise. Live wisely. [16] I mean that you should use every chance you have for doing good, because these are evil times. [17] So do not be foolish with your lives. But learn what the Lord wants you to do. [18] Do not be drunk with wine. That will ruin you spiritually. But be filled with the Spirit.[d] [19] Speak to each other with psalms, hymns, and spiritual songs. Sing and make music in your hearts to the Lord. [20] Always give thanks to God the Father for everything, in the name of our Lord Jesus Christ.

Wives and Husbands

[21] Be willing to obey each other. Do this because you respect Christ.

[22] Wives, be under the authority of your husbands, as of the Lord. [23] The husband is the head of the wife, as Christ is the head of the church. The church is Christ's body – Christ is the Saviour of the body. [24] The church is under the authority of Christ. So it is the same with you wives. You should be under the authority of your husbands in everything.

[25] Husbands, love your wives as Christ loved the church. Christ died for the church [26] to make it belong to God. Christ used the word to make the church clean by washing it with water. [27] Christ died so that he could give the church to himself like a bride in all her beauty. He died so that the church could be pure and without fault, with no evil or sin or any other wrong thing in it. [28] And husbands should love their wives in the same way. They should love their wives as they love their own bodies. The man who loves his wife loves himself. [29] No person ever hates his own body, but feeds and takes care of it. And that is what Christ does for the church, [30] because we are parts of his body. [31] The Scripture says, "So a man will leave his father and mother and be united with his wife. And the two people will become one body."[n] [32] That secret truth is very important – I am talking about Christ and the church. [33] But each one of you must love his wife as he loves himself. And a wife must respect her husband.

Children and Parents

6 Children, obey your parents the way the Lord wants. This is the right thing to do. [2] The command says, "Honour your father and mother."[n] This is the first command that has a promise with it. [3] The promise is: "Then everything will be well with you, and you will have a long life on the earth."[n]

[4] Fathers, do not make your children

"So . . . body." Quotation from Genesis 2:24.
"Honour . . . mother." Quotation from Exodus 20:12; Deuteronomy 5:16.
"Then . . . earth." Quotation from Exodus 20:12; Deuteronomy 5:16.

angry, but raise them with the training and teaching of the Lord.

Slaves and Masters

⁵Slaves, obey your masters here on earth with fear and respect. And do that with a heart that is true, just as you obey Christ. ⁶You must do more than obey your masters to please them only while they are watching you. You must obey them as you are obeying Christ. With all your heart you must do what God wants. ⁷Do your work, and be happy to do it. Work as if you were serving the Lord, not as if you were serving only men. ⁸Remember that the Lord will give a reward to everyone, slave or free, for doing good.

⁹Masters, in the same way, be good to your slaves. Do not say things to scare them. You know that the One who is your Master and their Master is in heaven. And that Master treats everyone alike.

Wear the Full Armour of God

¹⁰Finally, be strong in the Lord and in his great power. ¹¹Wear the full armour of God. Wear God's armour so that you can fight against the devil's evil tricks. ¹²Our fight is not against people on earth. We are fighting against the rulers and authorities and the powers of this world's darkness. We are fighting against the spiritual powers of evil in the heavenly world. ¹³That is why you need to put on God's full armour. Then on the day of evil you will be able to stand strong. And when you have finished the whole fight, you will still be standing. ¹⁴So stand strong, with the belt of truth tied around your waist. And on your chest wear the protection of right living. ¹⁵And on your feet wear the Good News*ᵈ* of peace to help you stand strong. ¹⁶And also use the shield of

Ephesians 6:11 Wear the full armour of God.

faith. With that you can stop all the burning arrows of the Evil One. ¹⁷Accept God's salvation to be your helmet. And take the sword of the Spirit*ᵈ* – that sword is the teaching of God. ¹⁸Pray in the Spirit at all times. Pray with all kinds of prayers, and ask for everything you need. To do this you must always be ready. Never give up. Always pray for all God's people.

¹⁹Also pray for me. Pray that when I speak, God will give me words so that I can tell the secret truth of the Good News without fear. ²⁰I have the work of speaking that Good News. I am doing that now, here in prison. Pray that when I preach the Good News I will speak without fear, as I should.

Final Greetings

²¹I am sending to you Tychicus, our brother whom we love. He is a faithful servant of the Lord's work. He will tell you everything that is happening with

me. Then you will know how I am and what I am doing. ²²That is why I am sending him. I want you to know how we are. I am sending him to encourage you.

²³Peace and love with faith to you from God the Father and the Lord Jesus Christ. ²⁴God's grace to all of you who love our Lord Jesus Christ with love that never ends.

PHILIPPIANS

Serve Others with Joy

1 From Paul and Timothy, servants of Jesus Christ.

To all of God's holy people in Christ Jesus who live in Philippi. And to your elders*d* and deacons.*d*

²Grace and peace to you from God our Father and the Lord Jesus Christ.

Paul's Prayer

³I thank God every time I remember you. ⁴And I always pray for all of you with joy. ⁵I thank God for the help you gave me while I preached the Good News.*d* You helped from the first day you believed until now. ⁶God began doing a good work in you. And he will continue it until it is finished when Jesus Christ comes again. I am sure of that.

⁷And I know that I am right to think like this about all of you. I am sure because I have you in my heart. All of you share in God's grace with me. You share in God's grace with me while I am in prison, while I am defending the Good News, and while I am proving the truth of the Good News. ⁸God knows that I want to see you very much. I love all of you with the love of Christ Jesus.

⁹This is my prayer for you: that your love will grow more and more; that you will have knowledge and understanding with your love; ¹⁰that you will see the difference between good and bad and choose the good; that you will be pure and without wrong for the coming of Christ; ¹¹that you will do many good things with the help of Christ to bring glory and praise to God.

Paul's Troubles Help the Work

¹²Brothers, I want you to know that what has happened to me has helped to spread the Good News.*d* ¹³I am in prison because I am a believer in Christ. All the palace guards and everyone else knows this. ¹⁴I am still in prison, but most of the believers feel better about this now. And so they are much braver about telling the Good News about Christ.

¹⁵It is true that some preach about Christ because they are jealous and bitter. But others preach about Christ because they want to help. ¹⁶They preach because they have love, and they know that God gave me the work of defending the Good News. ¹⁷But others preach about Christ because they are selfish. Their reason for preaching is wrong. They want to make trouble for me in prison.

¹⁸But I do not care if they make trouble for me. The important thing is that they are preaching about Christ. They should do it for the right reasons. But I am happy even if they do it for wrong reasons. And I will continue to be happy. ¹⁹You are praying for me, and the Spirit of Jesus Christ helps me. So I know that this trouble will bring my freedom. ²⁰The thing I want and hope for is that I will not fail Christ in anything. I hope that I will have the courage now, as always, to show the greatness of Christ in my life here on earth. I want to do that if I die or if I live. ²¹To me the only important thing about living is Christ. And even death would be profit for me. ²²If I

continue living in the body, I will be able to work for the Lord. But what should I choose – living or dying? I do not know. ²³It is hard to choose between the two. I want to leave this life and be with Christ. That is much better. ²⁴But you need me here in my body. ²⁵I know that you need me, and so I know that I will stay with you. I will help you grow and have joy in your faith. ²⁶You will be very happy in Christ Jesus when I am with you again.

²⁷Be sure that you live in a way that brings honour to the Good News of Christ. Then whether I come and visit you or am away from you, I will hear good things about you. I will hear that you continue strong with one purpose and that you work together as a team for the faith of the Good News. ²⁸And you will not be afraid of those who are against you. All of these things are proof from God that you will be saved and that your enemies will be lost. ²⁹God gave you the honour both of believing in Christ and suffering for Christ. Both these things bring glory to Christ. ³⁰When I was with you, you saw the struggles I had. And you hear about the struggles I am having now. You yourselves are having the same kind of struggles.

2 Does your life in Christ give you strength? Does his love comfort you? Do we share together in the Spirit?ᵈ Do you have mercy and kindness? ²If so, make me very happy by having the same thoughts, sharing the same love, and having one mind and purpose. ³When you do things, do not let selfishness or pride be your guide. Be humble and give more honour to others than to yourselves. ⁴Do not be interested only in your own life, but be interested in the lives of others.

Be Unselfish like Christ

⁵In your lives you must think and act like Christ Jesus.
⁶Christ himself was like God in
  everything.
 He was equal with God.
 But he did not think that being
  equal with God was
  something to be held on to.
⁷He gave up his place with God
  and made himself nothing.
 He was born to be a man
 and became like a servant.
⁸And when he was living as a man,
  he humbled himself and was
  fully obedient to God.
 He obeyed even when it caused
  his death – death on a cross.
⁹So God raised Christ to the
  highest place.
 God made the name of Christ
  greater than every other
  name.
¹⁰God wants every knee to bow to
  Jesus –
 everyone in heaven, on earth,
  and under the earth.
¹¹Everyone will say, "Jesus Christ is
  Lord"
 and bring glory to God the
  Father.

Be the People God Wants You to Be

¹²My dear friends, you have always obeyed. You obeyed God when I was with you. It is even more important that you obey now while I am not with you. Keep on working to complete your salvation, and do it with fear and trembling. ¹³Yes, God is working in you to help you want to do what pleases him. Then he gives you the power to do it.

¹⁴Do everything without complaining or arguing. ¹⁵Then you will

Philippians 2:14 Do everything without complaining.

be innocent and without anything wrong in you. You will be God's children without fault. But you are living with crooked and mean people all around you. Among them you shine like stars in the dark world. ¹⁶You offer to them the teaching that gives life. So when Christ comes again, I can be happy because my work was not wasted. I ran in the race and won.

¹⁷Your faith makes you offer your lives as a sacrifice in serving God. Perhaps I will have to offer my own blood with your sacrifice. But if that happens, I will be happy and full of joy with all of you. ¹⁸You also should be happy and full of joy with me.

Timothy and Epaphroditus

¹⁹I hope in the Lord Jesus to send Timothy to you soon. I will be happy to learn how you are. ²⁰I have no other person like Timothy. He truly cares for you. ²¹Other people are interested only in their own lives. They are not interested in the work of Christ Jesus. ²²You know the kind of person Timothy is. You know that he has served with me in telling the Good News,ᵈ as a son serves his father. ²³I plan to send him to you quickly when I know what will happen to me. ²⁴I am sure that the Lord will help me to come to you soon.

²⁵Epaphroditus is my brother in Christ. He works and serves with me in the army of Christ. When I needed help, you sent him to me. I think now that I must send him back to you ²⁶because he wants very much to see all of you. He is worried because you heard that he was sick. ²⁷Yes, he was sick, and nearly died. But God helped him and me too, so that I would not have more sadness. ²⁸So I want very much to send him to you. When you see him, you can be happy. And I can stop worrying about you. ²⁹Welcome him in the Lord with much joy. Give honour to people like Epaphroditus. ³⁰He should be honoured because he almost died for the work of Christ. He put his life in danger so that he could help me. This was help that you could not give me.

The Importance of Christ

3 My brothers, be full of joy in the Lord. It is no trouble for me to write the same things to you again, and it will help you to be more ready. ²Be careful of those who do evil. They are like dogs. They demand that we cutⁿ the body. ³But we are the ones who are truly circumcised.ᵈ We worship God through his Spirit.ᵈ We are proud to be in Christ Jesus. And we do not trust in ourselves or anything

cut   The word in Greek is like the word "circumcise", but it means "to cut completely off".

we can do. [4]Even if I am able to trust in myself, still I do not. If anyone thinks that he has a reason to trust in himself, he should know that I have greater reason for trusting in myself. [5]I was circumcised eight days after my birth. I am from the people of Israel and the tribe[d] of Benjamin. I am a Hebrew, and my parents were Hebrews. The law of Moses was very important to me. That is why I became a Pharisee.[d] [6]I was so enthusiastic that I tried to hurt the church. No one could find fault with the way I obeyed the law of Moses. [7]At one time all these things were important to me. But now I think those things are worth nothing because of Christ. [8]Not only those things, but I think that all things are worth nothing compared with the greatness of knowing Christ Jesus my Lord. Because of Christ, I have lost all those things. And now I know that all those things are worthless rubbish. This allows me to have Christ [9]and to belong to him. Now that I belong to Christ, I am right with God and this being right does not come from my following the law. It comes from God through faith. God uses my faith in Christ to make me right with him. [10]All I want is to know Christ and the power of his rising from death. I want to share in Christ's sufferings and become like him in his death. [11]If I have those things, then I have hope that I myself will be raised from death.

Continuing Towards Our Goal

[12]I do not mean that I am already as God wants me to be. I have not yet reached that goal. But I continue trying to reach it and to make it mine. Christ wants me to do that. That is the reason Christ made me his. [13]Brothers, I know that I have not yet reached that goal. But there is one thing I always do: I forget the things that are past. I try as hard as I can to reach the goal that is before me. [14]I keep trying to reach the goal and get the prize. That prize is mine because God called me through Christ to the life above.

[15]All of us who have grown spiritually to be mature should think this way, too. And if there are things you do not agree with, God will make them clear to you. [16]But we should continue following the truth we already have.

[17]Brothers, all of you should try to follow my example and to copy those who live the way we showed you. [18]Many people live like enemies of the cross of Christ. I have often told you about them, and it makes me cry to tell you about them now. [19]The way they live is leading them to destruction. Instead of serving God, they do whatever their bodies want. They do shameful things, and they are proud of it. They think only about earthly things. [20]But our homeland is in heaven, and we are waiting for our Saviour, the Lord Jesus Christ, to come from heaven. [21]He will change our simple bodies and make them like his own glorious body. Christ can do this by his power. With that power he is able to rule all things.

What the Christians Are to Do

4 My dear brothers, I love you and want to see you. You bring me joy and make me proud of you. Continue following the Lord as I have told you.

[2]I ask Euodia and Syntyche to agree in the Lord. [3]And because you serve faithfully with me, my friend, I ask you to help these women to do this. They served with me in telling people the Good News.[d] They served together with Clement and others who worked

with me. Their names are written in the book of life.[n]

[4] Be full of joy in the Lord always. I will say again, be full of joy.

[5] Let all men see that you are gentle and kind. The Lord is coming soon. [6] Do not worry about anything. But pray and ask God for everything you need. And when you pray, always give thanks. [7] And God's peace will keep your hearts and minds in Christ Jesus. The peace that God gives is so great that we cannot understand it.

[8] Brothers, continue to think about the things that are good and worthy of praise. Think about the things that are true and honourable and right and pure and beautiful and respected. [9] And do what you learned and received from me. Do what I told you and what you saw me do. And the God who gives peace will be with you.

Paul Thanks the Christians

[10] I am very happy in the Lord that you have shown your care for me again. You continued to care about me, but there was no way for you to show it. [11] I am telling you this, but it is not because I need anything. I have learned to be satisfied with the things I have and with everything that happens. [12] I know how to live when I am poor. And I know how to live when I have plenty. I have learned the secret of being happy at any time in every-thing that happens. I have learned to be happy when I have enough to eat and when I do not have enough to eat. I have learned to be happy when I have all that I need and when I do not have the things I need. [13] I can do all things through Christ because he gives me strength.

[14] But it was good that you helped me when I needed help. [15] You people in Philippi remember when I first preached the Good News[d] there. When I left Macedonia, you were the only church that gave me help. [16] Several times you sent me things I needed when I was in Thessalonica. [17] Really, it is not that I want to receive gifts from you. But I want you to have the good that comes from giving. [18] And now I have everything, and more. I have all I need because Epaphroditus brought your gift to me. Your gift is like a sweet-smelling sacrifice offered to God. God accepts that sacrifice, and it pleases him. [19] My God will use his wonderful riches in Christ Jesus to give you everything you need. [20] Glory to our God and Father for ever and ever! Amen.

[21] Greet each of God's people in Christ. God's people who are with me send greetings to you. [22] All of God's people greet you. And those believers from the palace of Caesar[d] greet you, too.

[23] The grace of the Lord Jesus Christ be with you all.

---

book of life   God's book that has the names of all God's chosen people (Revelation 3:5; 21:27).

COLOSSIANS

Only Christ Can Save People

1 From Paul, an apostle[d] of Christ Jesus. I am an apostle because that is what God wanted.

Also from Timothy, our brother.

[2] To the holy and faithful brothers in Christ that live in Colosse. Grace and peace from God our Father.

[3] In our prayers for you we always thank God, the Father of our Lord Jesus Christ. [4] We thank God because we have heard about the faith you have in Christ Jesus and the love you have for all of God's people. [5] You have this faith and love because of your hope, and what you hope for is saved for you in heaven. You learned about this hope when you heard the true teaching, the Good News[d] [6] that was told to you. Everywhere in the world that Good News is bringing blessings and is growing. This has happened with you, too, since you heard the Good News and understood the truth about the grace of God. [7] You learned about God's grace from Epaphras, whom we love. Epaphras works together with us and is a faithful servant of Christ for us. [8] He also told us about the love you have from the Holy Spirit.[d]

[9] Since the day we heard this about you, we have continued praying for you. We ask God that you will know fully what God wants. We pray that you will also have great wisdom and understanding in spiritual things. [10] Then you will live the kind of life that honours and pleases the Lord in every way. You will produce fruit in every good work and grow in the knowledge of God. [11] Then God will strengthen you with his own great power. And you will not give up when troubles come, but you will be patient. [12] Then you will joyfully give thanks to the Father. He has made you able to have all that he has prepared for his people who live in the light. [13] God made us free from the power of darkness, and he brought us into the kingdom of his dear Son. [14] The Son paid

Colossians 1:10 You will produce fruit in every good work and grow in the knowledge of God.

for our sins, and in him we have forgiveness.

The Importance of Christ

[15] No one has seen God, but Jesus is exactly like him. Christ ranks higher than all the things that have been made. [16] Through his power all things were made – things in heaven and on earth, things seen and unseen, all powers, authorities, lords, and rulers. All things were made through Christ and for Christ. [17] Christ was there before anything was made. And all things continue because of him. [18] He is the head of the body. (The body is the church.) Everything comes from him. And he is the first one who was raised from death. So in all things Jesus is most important. [19] God was pleased for all of himself to live in Christ. [20] And through Christ, God decided to bring all things back to himself again – things on earth and things in heaven. God made peace by using the blood of Christ's death on the cross.

[21] At one time you were separated from God. You were God's enemies in your minds because the evil deeds you did were against God. [22] But now Christ has made you God's friends again. He did this by his death while he was in the body, that he might bring you into God's presence. He brings you before God as people who are holy, with no wrong in you, and with nothing that God can judge you guilty of. [23] And Christ will do this if you continue to believe in the Good News[d] you heard. You must continue strong and sure in your faith. You must not be moved away from the hope that Good News gave you. That same Good News has been told to everyone in the world. I, Paul, help in preaching that Good News.

Paul's Work for the Church

[24] I am happy in my sufferings for you. There are many things that Christ must still suffer through his body, the church. I am accepting my part of these things that must be suffered. I accept these sufferings in my body. I suffer for his body, the church. [25] I became a servant of the church because God gave me a special work to do that helps you. My work is to tell fully the teaching of God. [26] This teaching is the secret truth that was hidden since the beginning of time. It was hidden from everyone, but now it is made known to God's holy people. [27] God decided to let his people know this rich and glorious truth which he has for all people. This truth is Christ himself, who is in you. He is our only hope for glory. [28] So we continue to preach Christ to all men. We use all wisdom to warn and to teach everyone. We are trying to bring each one into God's presence as a mature person in Christ. [29] To do this, I work and struggle, using Christ's great strength that works so powerfully in me.

2 I want you to know that I am trying very hard to help you. And I am trying to help those in Laodicea and others who have never seen me. [2] I want them to be strengthened and joined together with love. I want them to be rich in the strong belief that comes from understanding. I mean I want you to know fully God's secret truth. That truth is Christ himself. [3] And in him all the treasures of wisdom and knowledge are safely kept.

[4] I say this so that no one can fool you by arguments that seem good, but are false. [5] I am not there with you, but my heart is with you. I am happy to see your good lives and your strong faith in Christ.

Continue to Live in Christ

⁶As you received Christ Jesus the Lord, so continue to live in him. ⁷Keep your roots deep in him and have your lives built on him. Be strong in the faith, just as you were taught. And always be thankful.

⁸Be sure that no one leads you away with false ideas and words that mean nothing. Those ideas come from men. They are the worthless ideas of this world. They are not from Christ. ⁹All of God lives in Christ fully (even when Christ was on earth). ¹⁰And in him you have a full and true life. He is ruler over all rulers and powers.

¹¹In Christ you had a different kind of circumcision.ᵈ That circumcision was not done by hands. I mean, you were made free from the power of your sinful self. That is the kind of circumcision Christ does. ¹²When you were baptised, you were buried with Christ and you were raised up with Christ because of your faith in God's power. That power was shown when he raised Christ from death. ¹³You were spiritually dead because of your sins and because you were not free from the power of your sinful self. But God made you alive with Christ. And God forgave all our sins. ¹⁴We owed a debt because we broke God's laws. That debt listed all the rules we failed to follow. But God forgave us that debt. He took away that debt and nailed it to the cross. ¹⁵God defeated the spiritual rulers and powers. With the cross God won the victory and defeated them. He showed the world that they were powerless.

Don't Follow People's Rules

¹⁶So do not let anyone make rules for you about eating and drinking or about a religious feast, a New Moonᵈ Festival, or a Sabbathᵈ day. ¹⁷In the past, these things were like a shadow of what was to come. But the new things that were coming are found in Christ. ¹⁸Some enjoy acting as if they were humble and love to worship angels. They are always talking about the visions they have seen. Do not let them tell you that you are wrong. They are full of foolish pride because of their human way of thinking. ¹⁹They do not keep themselves under the control of Christ, the head. The whole body depends on Christ. Because of him all the parts of the body care for each other and help each other. This strengthens the body and holds it together. And so the body grows in the way God wants.

²⁰You died with Christ and were made free from the worthless rules of the world. So why do you act as if you still belong to this world? I mean, why do you follow rules like these: ²¹"Don't eat this", "Don't taste that", "Don't touch that thing"? ²²These rules are talking about earthly things that are gone as soon as they are used. They are only man-made commands and teachings. ²³These rules seem to be wise. But they are only part of a man-made religion. They make people pretend not to be proud and make them punish their bodies. But they do not really control the evil desires of the sinful self.

Your New Life in Christ

3 You were raised from death with Christ. So aim at what is in heaven, where Christ is sitting at the right hand of God. ²Think only about the things in heaven, not the things on earth. ³Your old sinful self has died, and your new life is kept with Christ in God. ⁴Christ is your life. When he comes again, you will share in his glory.

⁵So put all evil things out of your life: sexual sinning, doing evil, letting evil thoughts control you, wanting things that are evil, and always selfishly wanting more and more. This really means living to serve a false god. ⁶These things make God angry.ⁿ ⁷In your evil life in the past, you also did these things.

⁸But now put these things out of your life: anger, bad temper, doing or saying things to hurt others, and using evil words when you talk. ⁹Do not lie to each other. You have left your old sinful life and the things you did before. ¹⁰You have begun to live the new life. In your new life you are being made new. You are becoming like the One who made you. This new life brings you the true knowledge of God. ¹¹In the new life there is no difference between Greeks and Jews. There is no difference between those who are circumcisedᵈ and those who are not circumcised, or people that are foreigners, or Scythians.ⁿ There is no difference between slaves and free people. But Christ is in all believers. And Christ is all that is important.

¹²God has chosen you and made you his holy people. He loves you. So always do these things: show mercy to others; be kind, humble, gentle, and patient. ¹³Do not be angry with each other, but forgive each other. If someone does wrong to you, then forgive him. Forgive each other because the Lord forgave you. ¹⁴Do all these things; but most important, love each other. Love is what holds you all together in perfect unity. ¹⁵Let the peace that Christ gives control your thinking. You were all called together in one bodyⁿ to have peace. Always be thankful. ¹⁶Let the teaching of Christ live in you richly. Use all wisdom to teach and strengthen each other. Sing psalms, hymns, and spiritual songs with thankfulness in your hearts to God. ¹⁷Everything you say and everything you do should all be done for Jesus your Lord. And in all you do, give thanks to God the Father through Jesus.

Your New Life with Other People

¹⁸Wives, be under the authority of your husbands. This is the right thing to do in the Lord.

¹⁹Husbands, love your wives, and be gentle to them.

²⁰Children, obey your parents in all things. This pleases the Lord.

²¹Fathers, do not nag your children.

Colossians 3:21 Fathers, do not nag your children.

These . . . angry Some Greek copies add: "against the people who do not obey God."
Scythians The Scythians were known as very wild and cruel people.
body The spiritual body of Christ, meaning the church or his people.

JOHN 21:6
They caught so many fish that they could not pull the net back onto the boat.

ACTS 2:3–4
They saw something that looked like flames of fire... They were all filled with the Holy Spirit, and they began to speak in different languages.

ACTS 9:4
Saul fell to the ground. He heard a voice saying to him, "Saul, Saul! Why are you doing things against me?"

If you are too hard to please, they may want to stop trying.

22 Slaves, obey your masters in all things. Do not obey just when they are watching you, to gain their favour. But serve them honestly, because you respect the Lord. 23 In all the work you are doing, work the best you can. Work as if you were working for the Lord, not for men. 24 Remember that you will receive your reward from the Lord, which he promised to his people. You are serving the Lord Christ. 25 But remember that anyone who does wrong will be punished for that wrong. And the Lord treats everyone the same.

4 Masters, give the things that are good and fair to your slaves. Remember that you have a Master in heaven.

What the Christians Are to Do

2 Continue praying and keep alert. And when you pray, always thank God. 3 Also pray for us. Pray that God will give us an opportunity to tell people his message. Pray that we can preach the secret truth that God has made known about Christ. I am in prison because I preach this truth. 4 Pray that I can speak in a way that will make it clear as I should.

5 Be wise in the way you act with people who are not believers. Use your time in the best way you can. 6 When you talk, you should always be kind and wise. Then you will be able to answer everyone in the way you should.

News About the People with Paul

7 Tychicus is my dear brother in Christ. He is a faithful minister and servant with me in the Lord. He will tell you all the things that are happening to me. 8 That is why I am sending him. I want you to know how we are. I am sending him to encourage you. 9 I send him with Onesimus. Onesimus is a faithful and dear brother in Christ. He is one of your group. They will tell you all that has happened here.

10 Aristarchus greets you. He is a prisoner with me. And Mark, the cousin of Barnabas, also greets you. (I have already told you what to do about Mark. If he comes, welcome him.) 11 Jesus, who is called Justus, also greets you. These are the only Jewish believers who work with me for the kingdom of God. They have been a comfort to me.

12 Epaphras also greets you. He is a servant of Jesus Christ. And he is from your group. He always prays for you. He prays that you will grow to be spiritually mature and have everything that God wants for you. 13 I know that he has worked hard for you and the people in Laodicea and in Hierapolis. 14 Demas and our dear friend Luke, the doctor, greet you.

15 Greet the brothers in Laodicea. And greet Nympha and the church that meets in her house. 16 After this letter is read to you, be sure that it is also read to the church in Laodicea. And you must read the letter that I wrote to Laodicea. 17 Tell Archippus, "Be sure to do the work the Lord gave you."

18 I, Paul, greet you and write this with my own hand. Remember me in prison. God's grace be with you.

1 THESSALONIANS

Paul Encourages New Christians

1 From Paul, Silas, and Timothy.
To the church in Thessalonica, the church in God the Father and the Lord Jesus Christ. May God's grace and peace be yours.

The Faith of the Thessalonians

2 We always remember you when we pray and thank God for all of you. 3 When we pray to God our Father, we always thank him for the things you have done because of your faith. And we thank him for the work you have done because of your love. And we thank him that you continue to be strong because of your hope in our Lord Jesus Christ.

4 Brothers, God loves you. And we know that he has chosen you to be his. 5 We brought the Good News[d] to you. But we did not use only words. We brought the Good News with power, with the Holy Spirit,[d] and with sure knowledge that it is true. Also you know how we lived when we were with you. We lived that way to help you. 6 And you became like us and like the Lord. You suffered much, but still you accepted the teaching with the joy that comes from the Holy Spirit. 7 So you became an example to all the believers in Macedonia and Southern Greece. 8 The Lord's teaching spread from you in Macedonia and Southern Greece. And your faith in God has become known everywhere. So we do not need to say anything about your faith. 9 People everywhere are telling of the good way you accepted us when we were there with you. They tell about how you stopped worshipping idols and changed to serving the living and true God. 10 And you changed to wait for God's Son to come from heaven. God raised that Son from death. He is Jesus, who saves us from God's angry judgement that is sure to come.

Paul's Work in Thessalonica

2 Brothers, you know that our visit to you was not a failure. 2 Before we came to you, we suffered in Philippi. People there insulted us. You know about that. And when we came to you, many people were against us. But our God helped us to be brave and to tell you his Good News.[d] 3 Our message was a message to encourage you. We were not trying to lie. We had no evil plan. We were not trying to trick you. 4 But we speak the Good News because God tested us and trusted us to do it. When we speak, we are not trying to please men. But we are trying to please God, who tests our hearts. 5 You know that we never tried to influence you by saying nice things about you. We were not trying to get your money. We had no selfishness to hide from you. God knows that this is true. 6 We were not looking for praise from you or anyone else. We are apostles[d] of Christ. When we were with you, we could have used our authority to make you do things.

7 But we were very gentle with you. We were like a mother caring for her little children. 8 Because we loved you, we were happy to share God's Good News with you. But not only that, we were also happy to share even our own

lives with you. [9]Brothers, I know that you remember how hard we worked. We worked night and day so that we would not burden any of you while we preached God's Good News to you.

[10]When we were with you, we lived in a holy and right way, without fault. You know that this is true, and God knows that this is true. [11]You know that we treated each of you as a father treats his own children. [12]We strengthened you, we comforted you, and we told you to live good lives for God. It is God who calls you to his glorious kingdom.

[13]Also, we always thank God because of the way you accepted his message. You heard his message from us, and you accepted it as the word of God, not the words of men. And it really is God's message. And that message works in you who believe. [14]Brothers, you have been like God's churches in Christ that are in Judea.[n] God's people suffered bad things from the other Jews there. And you suffered the same bad things from the people of your own country. [15]Those Jews killed both the Lord Jesus and the prophets.[d] And they forced us to leave that country. They do not please God. They are against all people. [16]They try to stop us from teaching the non-Jews so that they may be saved. But those Jews are adding more and more sins to the sins they already have. The anger of God has come to them at last.

Paul Wants to Visit Them Again

[17]Brothers, we were separated from you for a short time, but our thoughts were still with you. We wanted very much to see you, and tried very hard to do so. [18]I, Paul, tried to come many times, but Satan stopped us. [19]For you are our hope, our joy, and the crown we will be proud of when our Lord Jesus Christ comes. [20]Truly you are our glory and our joy.

3 We could not come to you, but it was very hard to wait any longer. So we decided to stay in Athens alone [2]and send Timothy to you. Timothy is our brother, who works with us for God. He helps us tell people the Good News[d] about Christ. We sent Timothy to strengthen and comfort you in your faith. [3]We sent him so that none of you would be upset by these troubles we have now. You yourselves know that we must have these troubles. [4]Even when we were with you, we told you that we all would have to suffer. And you know that it has happened the way we said. [5]This is why I sent Timothy to you, so that I could know about your faith. I sent him when I could not wait any longer. I was afraid that the devil had tempted you, and then our hard work would have been wasted.

[6]But Timothy now has come back to us from you and has brought us good news about your faith and love. He told us that you always remember us in a good way. He told us that you want to see us just as much as we want to see you. [7]So, brothers, we are comforted about you, because of your faith. We have much trouble and suffering, but still we are comforted. [8]For our life is really full if you stand strong in the Lord. [9]We have so much joy before our God because of you, and we thank him for you. But we cannot thank him enough for all the joy we feel. [10]And we continue praying with all our heart for you night and day. We pray that we can see you again and give you all the things you need to make your faith strong.

[11]We pray that our God and Father

Judea   The Jewish land where Jesus lived and taught and where the church first began.

and our Lord Jesus will prepare the way for us to come to you. [12]We pray that the Lord will make your love grow more and more for each other and for all people. We pray that you will love others as we love you and [13]that your hearts will be made strong. Then you will be holy and without fault before our God and Father when our Lord Jesus comes with all his holy people.

A Life that Pleases God

4 Brothers, now I have some other things to tell you. We taught you how to live in a way that will please God. And you are living that way. Now we ask you and encourage you in the Lord Jesus to live that way more and more. [2]You know what we told you to do by the authority of the Lord Jesus. [3]God wants you to be holy and to stay away from sexual sins. [4]He wants each one of you to learn how to take a wife[n] in a way that is holy and honourable. [5]Don't use your body for sexual sin. The people who do not know God use their bodies for that. [6]So do not wrong your brother or cheat him in this way. The Lord will punish people who do those things. We have already told you and warned you about that. [7]God called us to be holy and does not want us to live in sin. [8]So the person who refuses to obey this teaching is refusing to obey God, not man. And God is the One who gives us his Holy Spirit.[d]

[9]We do not need to write to you about having love for your brothers and sisters in Christ. God has already taught you to love each other. [10]And truly you do love the brothers in all of Macedonia. Brothers, now we encourage you to love them more and more. [11]Do all you can to live a peaceful life. Take care of your own business.

Do your own work. We have already told you to do these things. [12]If you do, then people who are not believers will respect you. And you will not have to depend on others for what you need.

The Lord's Coming

[13]Brothers, we want you to know about those who have died. We do not want you to be sad as others who have no hope. [14]We believe that Jesus died and that he rose again. So, because of Jesus, God will bring together with Jesus those who have died. [15]What we tell you now is the Lord's own message. We who are living now may still be living when the Lord comes again. We who are living at that time will be with the Lord, but not before those who have already died. [16]The Lord himself will come down from heaven. There will be a loud command with the voice of the archangel[n] and with the trumpet call of God. And those who have died and were in Christ will rise first. [17]After that, those who are still alive at that time will be gathered up with them. We will be taken up in the clouds to meet the Lord in the air. And we will be with the Lord for ever. [18]So comfort each other with these words.

Be Ready for the Lord's Coming

5 Now, brothers, we do not need to write to you about times and dates. [2]You know very well that the day the Lord comes again will be a surprise like a thief that comes in the night. [3]People will say, "We have peace and we are safe." At that time they will be destroyed quickly, as pains come quickly to a woman having a baby. And those people will not escape. [4]But you,

---

learn . . . wife   This might also mean "learn to control your own body".
archangel   The leader among God's angels or messengers.

1 Thessalonians 5:2 The day the Lord comes again will be a surprise like a thief that comes in the night.

brothers, are not living in darkness. And so that day will not surprise you like a thief. [5]You are all people who belong to the light. You belong to the day. We do not belong to the night or to darkness. [6]So we should not be like other people. We should not be sleeping, but we should be awake and have self-control. [7]Those who sleep, sleep at night. Those who get drunk, get drunk at night. [8]But we belong to the day; so we should control ourselves. We should wear faith and love to protect us. And the hope of salvation should be our helmet. [9]God did not choose us to suffer his anger, but to have salvation through our Lord Jesus Christ. [10]Jesus died for us so that we can live together with him. It is not important if we are alive or dead when

Jesus comes. [11]So comfort each other and give each other strength, just as you are doing now.

Final Instructions and Greetings

[12]Now, brothers, we ask you to respect those people who work hard with you, who lead you in the Lord and teach you. [13]Respect them with a very special love because of the work they do with you.

Live in peace with each other. [14]We ask you, brothers, to warn those who do not work. Encourage the people who are afraid. Help those who are weak. Be patient with every person. [15]Be sure that no one pays back wrong for wrong. But always try to do what is good for each other and for all people.

[16]Always be happy. [17]Never stop praying. [18]Give thanks whatever happens. That is what God wants for you in Christ Jesus.

[19]Do not stop the work of the Holy Spirit.[d] [20]Do not treat prophecy[d] as if it were not important. [21]But test everything. Keep what is good. [22]And stay away from everything that is evil.

[23]We pray that God himself, the God of peace, will make you pure, belonging only to him. We pray that your whole self – spirit, soul, and body – will be kept safe and be without wrong when our Lord Jesus Christ comes. [24]The One who calls you will do that for you. You can trust him.

[25]Brothers, please pray for us.

[26]Give all the brothers a holy kiss when you meet. [27]I tell you by the authority of the Lord to read this letter to all the brothers.

[28]The grace of our Lord Jesus Christ be with you.

2 THESSALONIANS

The Problems of New Christians

1 From Paul, Silas, and Timothy.
To the church in Thessalonica in God our Father and the Lord Jesus Christ.

² Grace and peace to you from God the Father and the Lord Jesus Christ.

Paul Talks About God's Judgement

³ We must always thank God for you. And we should do this because it is right. It is right because your faith is growing more and more. And the love that every one of you has for each other is also growing. ⁴ So we boast about you to the other churches of God. We tell them about the way you continue to be strong and have faith. You are being treated badly and are suffering many troubles, but you continue with strength and faith.

⁵ This is proof that God is right in his judgement. God wants you to be worthy of his kingdom. Your suffering is for that kingdom. ⁶ And God will do what is right. He will give trouble to those who trouble you. ⁷ And he will give peace to all of you who are troubled and to us also. God will give us this help when the Lord Jesus is shown to us from heaven with his powerful angels. ⁸ He will come from heaven with burning fire to punish those who do not know God. He will punish those who do not obey the Good News*d* of our Lord Jesus Christ. ⁹ Those people will be punished with a destruction that continues for ever. They will not be allowed to be with the Lord, and they will be kept away from his great power. ¹⁰ This will hap-

pen on the day when the Lord Jesus comes to receive glory with his holy people. And all the people who have believed will be amazed at Jesus. You will be in that group of believers because you believed what we told you.

¹¹ That is why we always pray for you. We ask our God to help you live the good way that he called you to live. The goodness you have makes you want to do good, and the faith you have makes you work. We pray that with his power God will help you do these things more and more. ¹² We pray all this so that the name of our Lord Jesus Christ can have glory in you. And you can have glory in him. That glory comes from the grace of our God and the Lord Jesus Christ.

Evil Things Will Happen

2 Brothers, we have something to say about the coming of our Lord Jesus Christ. We want to talk to you about that time when we will meet together with him. ² Do not become easily upset in your thinking or afraid if you hear that the day of the Lord has already come. Someone may say this in a prophecy*d* or in a message. Or you may read it in a letter that someone tells you came from us. ³ Do not let any person fool you in any way. That day of the Lord will not come until the turning away from God happens. And that day will not come until the Man of Evil appears. He belongs to hell. ⁴ He is against anything called God or anything that people worship. And the Man of Evil puts himself above anything called God or anything that people worship. And that Man of Evil even goes into God's Temple[d] and sits there. Then he says that he is God.

[5] I told you when I was with you that all this would happen. Do you not remember? [6] And you know what is stopping that Man of Evil now. He is being stopped now so that he will appear at the right time. [7] The secret power of evil is already working in the world now. But there is one who is stopping that power. And he will continue to stop it until he is taken out of the way. [8] Then that Man of Evil will appear. And the Lord Jesus will kill him with the breath that comes from his mouth and will destroy him with the glory of his coming. [9] The Man of Evil will come by the power of Satan. He will have great power, and he will do many different false miracles,[d] signs, and wonders. [10] He will use every kind of evil to trick those who are lost. They are lost because they refused to love the truth. (If they loved the truth, they would be saved.) [11] But they refused to love the truth; so God sends them something powerful that leads them away from the truth. He sends them that power so they will believe something that is not true. [12] So all those who do not believe the truth will be judged guilty. They did not believe the truth, and they enjoyed doing evil.

You Are Chosen for Salvation

[13] Brothers, the Lord loves you. God chose you from the beginning to be saved. So we must always thank God for you. You are saved by the Spirit[d] that makes you holy and by your faith in the truth. [14] God used the Good News[d] that we preached to call you to be saved. He called you so that you can share in the glory of our Lord Jesus Christ. [15] So, brothers, stand strong and continue to believe the teachings we gave you. We taught you those things in our speaking and in our letter to you.

[16-17] We pray that the Lord Jesus Christ himself and God our Father will comfort you and strengthen you in every good thing you do and say. God loved us. Through his grace he gave us a good hope and comfort that continues for ever.

Pray for Us

3 And now, brothers, pray for us. Pray that the Lord's teaching will continue to spread quickly. And pray that people will give honour to that teaching, just as happened with you. [2] And pray that we will be protected from bad and evil people. (Not all people believe in the Lord.)

[3] But the Lord is faithful. He will give you strength and protect you from the Evil One. [4] The Lord makes us feel sure that you are doing the things we told you. And we know that you will continue to do those things. [5] We pray that the Lord will lead your hearts into God's love and Christ's patience.

The Duty to Work

[6] Brothers, by the authority of our Lord Jesus Christ we command you to stay away from any believer who refuses to work. People who refuse to work are not following the teaching that we gave them. [7] You yourselves know that you should live as we live. We were not lazy when we were with you. [8] And when we ate another person's food, we always paid for it. We worked and worked so that we would not be a trouble to any of you. We worked night and day. [9] We had the right to ask you to help us. But we worked to take care of ourselves so that we would be an example for you

to follow. [10] When we were with you, we gave you this rule: "If anyone will not work, he will not eat."

[11] We hear that some people in your group refuse to work. They do nothing. And they busy themselves in other people's lives. [12] We command those people to work quietly and earn their own food. In the Lord Jesus Christ we beg them to do this. [13] Brothers, never become tired of doing good.

[14] If anyone does not obey what we tell you in this letter, then remember who he is. Do not associate with him. Then maybe he will feel ashamed. [15] But do not treat him as an enemy. Warn him as a brother.

Final Words

[16] We pray that the Lord of peace will give you peace at all times and in every way. May the Lord be with all of you.

[17] I am Paul, and I end this letter now in my own handwriting. All my letters have this to show they are from me. This is the way I write.

[18] May our Lord Jesus Christ show all of you his grace.

1 TIMOTHY

Advice to a Young Preacher

1 From Paul, an apostle*d* of Christ Jesus, by the command of God our Saviour and Christ Jesus our hope.

²To Timothy, a true son to me because you believe.

Grace, mercy, and peace from God the Father and Christ Jesus our Lord.

Warning Against False Teaching

³I want you to stay in Ephesus. I asked you to do that when I went into Macedonia. Some people there in Ephesus are teaching false things. Stay there so that you can command them to stop. ⁴Tell them not to spend their time on stories that are not true and on long lists of names in family histories. These things only bring arguments; they do not help God's work. God's work is done by faith. ⁵The purpose of this command is for people to have love. To have this love they must have a pure heart, they must do what they know is right, and they must have true faith. ⁶Some people have wandered away from these things. They talk about things that are worth nothing. ⁷They want to be teachers of the law, but they do not know what they are talking about. They do not even understand what they say they are sure about.

⁸We know that the law is good if a man uses it correctly. ⁹We also know that the law is not made for good men. The law is made for people who are against the law and for those who refuse to follow the law. It is for people who are against God and are sinful, who are not holy and have no religion, who kill their fathers and mothers, who murder, ¹⁰who take part in sexual sins, men who have sexual relations with other men, those who sell slaves, who tell lies, who speak falsely, and who do anything against the true teaching of God. ¹¹That teaching is part of the Good News*d* that God gave me to tell. That glorious Good News is from the blessed God.

Thanks for God's Mercy

¹²I thank Christ Jesus our Lord because he trusted me and gave me this work of serving him. And he gives me strength. ¹³In the past I spoke against Christ and persecuted him and did all kinds of things to hurt him. But God showed mercy to me because I did not know what I was doing. I did those things when I did not believe. ¹⁴But the grace of our Lord was fully given to me. And with that grace came the faith and love that are in Christ Jesus.

¹⁵What I say is true, and you should fully accept it: Christ Jesus came into the world to save sinners. And I am the worst of those sinners. ¹⁶But I was given mercy. I was given mercy so that in me Christ Jesus could show that he has patience without limit. And he showed his patience with me, the worst of all sinners. Christ wanted me to be an example for those who would believe in him and have life for ever. ¹⁷Honour and glory to the King that rules for ever! He cannot be destroyed and cannot be seen. Honour and glory for ever and ever to the only God. Amen.

¹⁸Timothy, you are like a son to me.

I am giving you a command that agrees with the prophecies[d] that were given about you in the past. I tell you this so that you can follow those prophecies and fight the good fight of faith. [19] Continue to have faith and do what you know is right. Some people have not done this. Their faith has been destroyed. [20] Hymenaeus and Alexander are men who have done that. I have given them to Satan so that they will learn not to speak against God.

Some Rules for Men and Women

2 First, I tell you to pray for all people. Ask God for the things people need, and be thankful to him.

1 Timothy 2:1 Pray for all people.

[2] You should pray for kings and for all who have authority. Pray for the leaders so that we can have quiet and peaceful lives – lives full of worship and respect for God. [3] This is good, and it pleases God our Saviour. [4] God wants all people to be saved. And he wants everyone to know the truth.

[5] There is only one God. And there is only one way that people can reach God. That way is through Jesus Christ, who is also a man. [6] Jesus gave himself to pay for the sins of all people. Jesus is proof that God wants all people to be saved. And that proof came at the right time. [7] That is why I was chosen to tell the Good News[d] and was chosen to be an apostle.[d] (I am telling the truth. I am not lying.) I was chosen to teach the non-Jewish people to believe and to know the truth.

[8] I want men everywhere to pray. These men who lift up their hands in prayer must be holy. They must not be men who become angry and have arguments.

[9] I also want women to wear clothes that are right for them. They should dress with respect and right thinking. They should not use fancy braided hair or gold or pearls or expensive clothes to make themselves beautiful. [10] But they should make themselves beautiful by doing good deeds. Women who say they worship God should make themselves beautiful in that way.

[11] A woman should learn by listening quietly and being fully ready to obey. [12] I do not allow a woman to teach a man or to have authority over a man. She must remain silent. [13] For Adam was made first; Eve was made later. [14] Also, Adam was not the one who was tricked by the devil. It was the woman who was tricked and became a sinner. [15] But women will be saved through having children. They will be saved if they continue in faith, love, holiness, and self-control.

Leaders in the Church

3 What I say is true: if anyone wants to become an elder,[d] he is wanting a good work. [2] An elder must be so

good that people cannot rightly criticise him. He must have only one wife. He must have self-control and be wise. He must be respected by other people and must be ready to help people by accepting them into his home. He must be a good teacher. [3]He must not drink too much wine, and he must not be a man who likes to fight. He must be gentle and peaceful. He must not love money. [4]He must be a good leader of his own family so that his children obey him with full respect. [5](If a man does not know how to be a leader over his own family, he will not be able to take care of God's church.) [6]But an elder must not be a new believer. A new believer might be too proud of himself. Then he would be judged guilty for his pride just as the devil was. [7]An elder must also have the respect of people who are not in the church. Then he will not be criticised by others and caught in the devil's trap.

Helpers in the Church

[8]In the same way, deacons[d] must be men that people can respect. They must not say things they do not mean. They must not use their time drinking too much wine, and they must not be men who are always trying to get rich by cheating others. [9]They must follow the faith that God made known to us and always do what they know is right. [10]You should test those men first. If you find nothing wrong in them, then they can serve as deacons. [11]In the same way, the women[n] must have the respect of other people. They must not be women who repeat evil gossip about other people. They must have self-control and be women who can be trusted in everything. [12]Deacons

must have only one wife. They must be good leaders of their children and their own families. [13]Those who serve well as deacons are making an honourable place for themselves. And they will feel very sure of their faith in Christ Jesus.

The Secret of Our Life

[14]I hope I can come to you soon. But I am writing these things to you now. [15]Then, even if I cannot come soon, you will know about the things that people must do in the family of God. That family is the church of the living God, the support and foundation of the truth. [16]Without doubt, the secret of our life of worship is great:

He was shown to us in a human body,
proved right by the Spirit,[d]
and seen by angels.
He was preached to the nations,
believed in by the world,
and taken to heaven in glory.

A Warning About False Teachers

4 The Holy Spirit[d] clearly says that in the later times some people will stop believing the true faith. They will obey spirits that lie and will follow the teachings of demons.[d] [2]Such teachings come from hypocrites,[d] men who cannot see what is right and what is wrong. It is as if their understanding were destroyed by a hot iron. [3]They tell people that it is wrong to marry. And they tell people that there are some foods that must not be eaten. But God made those foods, and the people who believe and who know the truth can eat those foods with thanks. [4]Everything that God made is good. Nothing that God made should be

women This might mean the wives of the deacons, or it might mean women who serve in the same way as deacons.

refused if it is accepted with thanks to God. [5]Everything God made is made holy by what God has said and by prayer.

Be a Good Servant of Christ

[6]Tell these things to the brothers. This will show that you are a good servant of Christ Jesus. You will show that you are made strong by the words of faith and good teaching that you have been following. [7]People tell silly stories that do not agree with God's truth. Do not follow what those stories teach. But teach yourself only to serve God. [8]Training your body helps you in some ways, but serving God helps you in every way. Serving God brings you blessings in this life and in the future life, too. [9]What I say is true, and you should fully accept it. [10]For this is why we work and struggle: we hope in the living God. He is the Saviour of all people. And in a very special way, he is the Saviour of all who believe in him.

[11]Command and teach these things. [12]You are young, but do not let anyone treat you as if you were not important. Be an example to show the believers how they should live. Show them with your words, with the way you live, with your love, with your faith, and with your pure life. [13]Continue to read the Scriptures[d] to the people, strengthen them, and teach them. Do these things until I come. [14]Remember to use the gift that you have. That gift was given to you through a prophecy[d] when the group of elders[d] laid their hands on[n] you. [15]Continue to do those things. Give your life to doing them. Then everyone can see that your work is progressing. [16]Be careful in your life and in your teaching. Continue to live and teach rightly. Then you will save yourself and those people who listen to you.

Rules for Living with Others

5 Do not speak angrily to an older man, but talk to him as if he were your father. Treat younger men like brothers. [2]Treat older women like mothers, and younger women like sisters. Always treat them in a pure way.

[3]Take care of widows who are all alone. [4]But if a widow has children or grandchildren, the first thing they need to learn is to do their duty to their own family. When they do this, they will be repaying their parents or grandparents. That pleases God. [5]If a widow is all alone and without help, then she puts her hope in God and prays night and day for God's help. [6]But the widow who uses her life to please herself is really dead while she is still living. [7]Tell the believers there to do these things so that no one can say they are doing wrong. [8]A believer should take care of his own relatives, especially his own family. If he does not do that, he has turned against the faith. He is worse than a person who does not believe in God.

[9]To be on your list of widows, a woman must be 60 years old or older. She must have been faithful to her husband. [10]She must be known as a woman who has done good works. By this, I mean good works such as raising her children, accepting visitors in her home, washing the feet of God's people, helping those in trouble, and using her life to do all kinds of good deeds.

[11]But do not put younger widows on that list. After they give themselves to Christ, they are often pulled away from him by their physical needs. And then they want to marry again. [12]And

---

laid their hands on   A sign to show that Timothy was being given a special work of God.

they will be judged for not doing what they first promised to do. [13]Also, those younger widows begin to waste their time going from house to house. They begin to gossip and busy themselves with other people's lives. They say things that they should not say. [14]So I want the younger widows to marry, have children, and take care of their homes. If they do this, then no enemy will have any reason to criticise them. [15]But some of the younger widows have already turned away to follow Satan.

[16]If any woman who is a believer has widows in her family, then she should care for them herself. The church should not have to care for them. Then the church will be able to care for the widows who have no living family.

[17]The elders[d] who lead the church well should receive great honour. Those who work hard by speaking and teaching especially should receive great honour. [18]For the Scripture[d] says, "When an ox is working in the grain, do not cover its mouth to keep it from eating."[n] And the Scripture also says, "A worker should be given his pay."[n]

[19]Do not listen to someone who accuses an elder, unless there are two or three other persons who say he did wrong. [20]Tell those who keep on sinning that they are wrong. Do this in front of the whole church so that the others will have a warning.

[21]Before God and Jesus Christ and the chosen angels, I command you to do these things. Be careful to do them without showing favour to anyone.

[22]Think carefully before you lay your hands on[n] anyone for the Lord's service. Do not share in the sins of others. Keep yourself pure.

[23]Timothy, stop drinking only water and drink a little wine. This will help your stomach, and you will not be sick so often.

[24]The sins of some people are easy to see even before they are judged. But the sins of others are seen only later. [25]So also good deeds are easy to see. But even when they are not easy to see, they cannot stay hidden.

6 All who are slaves should show full respect to their masters. Then no one will speak against God's name and our teaching. [2]Some slaves have masters who are believers. This means they are all brothers. But the slaves should not show their masters any less respect. They should serve their masters even better, because they are helping believers they love.

False Teaching and True Riches

You must teach and preach these things. [3]If anyone has a different teaching, he does not accept the true teaching of our Lord Jesus Christ. And that teaching shows him the true way to serve God. [4]The person who teaches falsely is full of pride and understands nothing. He is sick with a love for arguing and fighting about words. And that brings jealousy, quarrels, insults, and evil mistrust. [5]And that also brings arguments from men who have evil minds. They have lost the truth. They think that serving God is a way to get rich.

[6]It is true that serving God makes a person very rich, if he is satisfied with what he has. [7]When we came into the world, we brought nothing. And when we die, we can take nothing out.

"When . . . eating." Quotation from Deuteronomy 25:4.
"A worker . . . pay." Quotation from Luke 10:7.
lay your hands on A sign of giving authority or power to another person.

8 So, if we have food and clothes, we will be satisfied with that. 9 Those who want to become rich bring temptation to themselves. They are caught in a trap. They begin to want many foolish things that will hurt them, things that ruin and destroy people. 10 The love of money causes all kinds of evil. Some people have left the true faith because they want to get more and more money. But they have caused themselves a great deal of sorrow.

Some Things to Remember

11 But you are a man of God. So you should stay away from all those things. Try to live in the right way, serve God, have faith, love, patience, and gentleness. 12 Keeping your faith is like running a race. Try as hard as you can to win. Be sure you receive the life that continues for ever. You were called to have that life. And you confessed the great truth about Christ in a way that many people heard. 13 Before God and Christ Jesus I give you a command. Christ Jesus confessed that same great truth when he stood before Pontius Pilate. And God gives life to everything. Now I tell you: 14 do the things you were commanded to do. Do them without wrong or blame until the time when our Lord Jesus Christ comes again. 15 God will make that happen at the right time. He is the blessed and only Ruler. He is the King of all kings and the Lord of all lords. 16 God is the only One who never dies. He lives in light so bright that men cannot go near it. No one has ever seen God, or can see him. May honour and power belong to God for ever. Amen.

17 Give this command to those who are rich with things of this world. Tell them not to be proud. Tell them to hope in God, not their money. Money cannot be trusted, but God takes care of us richly. He gives us everything to enjoy. 18 Tell the rich people to do good and to be rich in doing good deeds. Tell them to be happy to give and ready to share. 19 By doing that, they will be saving a treasure for themselves in heaven. That treasure will be a strong foundation. Their future life can be built on that treasure. Then they will be able to have the life that is true life.

20 Timothy, God has trusted you with many things. Keep those things safe. Stay away from people who say foolish things that are not from God. Stay away from those who argue against the truth. They use something they call "knowledge", but it is really not knowledge. 21 They say that they have that "knowledge", but they have left the true faith.

God's grace be with you.

1 Timothy 6:10 The love of money causes all kinds of evil.

2 TIMOTHY

Paul Encourages Timothy

1 From Paul, an apostle*d* of Christ Jesus by the will of God. God sent me to tell of the promise of life that is in Christ Jesus.

²To Timothy, a dear son to me. Grace, mercy, and peace to you from God the Father and Christ Jesus our Lord.

Encouragement for Timothy

³I always remember you in my prayers, day and night. And I thank God for you in these prayers. He is the God my ancestors served. And I serve him, doing what I know is right. ⁴I remember that you cried for me. And I want very much to see you so that I can be filled with joy. ⁵I remember your true faith. That kind of faith first belonged to your grandmother Lois and to your mother Eunice. And I know that you now have that same faith. ⁶That is why I remind you to use the gift God gave you. God gave you that gift when I laid my hands on*n* you. Now let it grow, as a small flame grows into a fire. ⁷God did not give us a spirit that makes us afraid. He gave us a spirit of power and love and self-control.

⁸So do not be ashamed to tell people about our Lord Jesus. And do not be ashamed of me. I am in prison for the Lord. But suffer with me for the Good News.*d* God gives us the strength to do that. ⁹God saved us and made us his holy people. That was not because of anything we did ourselves but because of what he wanted and because of his grace. That grace was given to us through Christ Jesus before time began. ¹⁰It was not shown to us until our Saviour Christ Jesus came. Jesus destroyed death. And through the Good News, he showed us the way to have life that cannot be destroyed. ¹¹I was chosen to tell that Good News and to be an apostle*d* and a teacher. ¹²And I suffer now because I tell the Good News. But I am not ashamed. I know Jesus, the One I have believed in. And I am sure that he is able to protect what he has trusted me with until that Day.*n* ¹³Follow the true teachings you heard from me. Follow them as an example of the faith and love we have in Christ Jesus. ¹⁴Protect the truth that you were given. Protect it with the help of the Holy Spirit*d* who lives in us.

¹⁵You know that everyone in the country of Asia has left me, even Phygelus and Hermogenes. ¹⁶I pray that the Lord will show mercy to the family of Onesiphorus. He has often helped me and was not ashamed that I was in prison. ¹⁷When he came to Rome, he looked for me until he found me. ¹⁸I pray that the Lord will allow Onesiphorus to have mercy from the Lord on that Day. You know how many ways Onesiphorus helped me in Ephesus.

---

laid . . . on A sign to show that Paul had power from God to give Timothy a special blessing.

Day The day Christ will come to judge all people and take his people to live with him.

A Loyal Soldier of Christ Jesus

2 Timothy, you are like a son to me. Be strong in the grace that we have in Christ Jesus. [2] You and many others have heard what I have taught. You should teach the same thing to some people you can trust. Then they will be able to teach it to others. [3] Share in the troubles that we have. Accept them like a true soldier of Christ Jesus. [4] A soldier wants to please his commanding officer, so he does not waste his time doing the things that most people do. [5] If an athlete is running a race, he must obey all the rules in order to win. [6] The farmer who works hard should be the first person to get some of the food that he grew. [7] Think about these things that I am saying. The Lord will give you the ability to understand all these things.

[8] Remember Jesus Christ. He is from the family of David. After Jesus died, he was raised from death. This is the Good News[d] that I preach, [9] and I am suffering because of that Good News. I am even bound with chains like a criminal. But God's teaching is not in chains. [10] So I patiently accept all these troubles. I do this so that those whom God has chosen can have the salvation that is in Christ Jesus. With that salvation comes glory that never ends.

[11] This teaching is true:
If we died with him,
    then we will also live with
        him.
[12] If we accept suffering,
    then we will also rule with
        him.
If we refuse to accept him,
    then he will refuse to accept
        us.
[13] If we are not faithful,
    he will still be faithful,
    because he cannot be false to
        himself.

A Worker Pleasing to God

[14] Continue teaching these things. And warn people before God not to argue about words. Arguing about words does not help anyone, and it ruins those who listen. [15] Do the best you can to be the kind of person that God will accept, and give yourself to him. Be a worker who is not ashamed of his work – a worker who uses the true teaching in the right way. [16] Stay away from those who talk about useless worldly things. That kind of talk will lead a person more and more away from God. [17] Their evil teaching will spread like a sickness inside the body. Hymenaeus and Philetus are men like that. [18] They have left the true teaching. They say that the rising from death of all men has already taken place. And those two men are destroying the faith of some people. [19] But God's strong foundation continues to stand. These words are written on that foundation: "The Lord knows those who belong to him."[n] And also these words are written on that foundation, "Everyone who says that he believes in the Lord must stop doing wrong."

[20] In a large house there are things made of gold and silver. But also there are things made of wood and clay. Some things are used for special purposes, and others are made for ordinary jobs. [21] If anyone makes himself clean[d] from evil things, he will be used for special purposes. He will

"**The Lord . . . him.**" Quotation from Numbers 16:5.

be made holy, and the Master can use him. He will be ready to do any good work.

²²Stay away from the evil things young people love to do. Try hard to live right and to have faith, love, and peace. Work for these things together with those who have pure hearts and who trust in the Lord. ²³Stay away from foolish and stupid arguments. You know that such arguments grow into bigger arguments. ²⁴And a servant of the Lord must not quarrel! He must be kind to everyone. He must be a good teacher. He must be patient. ²⁵The Lord's servant must gently teach those who do not agree with him. Maybe God will let them change their hearts so that they can accept the truth. ²⁶The devil has trapped them and causes them to do what he wants. But maybe they can wake up and free themselves from the devil's trap.

The Last Days

3 Remember this! There will be many troubles in the last days. ²In those times people will love only themselves and money. They will boast and be proud. They will say evil things against others. They will not obey their parents. People will not be thankful or be the kind of people God wants. ³They will not have love for others. They will refuse to forgive others and will speak bad things. They will not control themselves. They will be cruel and will hate what is good. ⁴In the last days, people will turn against their friends. They will do foolish things without thinking. They will be conceited and proud. They will love pleasure. They will not love God. ⁵They will continue to act as if they serve God, but they will not really serve God. Stay away from those

people. ⁶Some of them go into homes and get control of weak women who are full of sin. They are led to sin by the many evil desires they have. ⁷Those women always try to learn new teachings, but they are never able to understand the truth fully. ⁸Just as Jannes and Jambres were against Moses, these people are against the truth. They are people whose thinking has been confused. They have failed in trying to follow the faith. ⁹But they will not be successful in what they do. Everyone will see that they are foolish. That is what happened to Jannes and Jambres.

Obey the Teachings

¹⁰But you know all about me. You know what I teach and the way I live. You know my goal in life. You know my faith, my patience, and my love. You know that I never stop trying. ¹¹You know how I have been hurt and have suffered. You know all that happened to me in Antioch, Iconium, and Lystra. You know the hurts I suffered in those places. But the Lord saved me from all those troubles. ¹²Everyone who wants to live the way God wants, in Christ Jesus, will be hurt. ¹³People who are evil and cheat other people will go from bad to worse. They will fool others, but they will also be fooling themselves.

¹⁴But you should continue following the teachings that you learned. You know that these teachings are true. And you know you can trust those who taught you. ¹⁵You have known the Holy Scriptures^d since you were a child. The Scriptures are able to make you wise. And that wisdom leads to salvation through faith in Christ Jesus. ¹⁶All Scripture is

2 Timothy 3:16 All Scripture is given by God.

are pleasing to them, teachers who say the things they want to hear. [4]They will stop listening to the truth. They will begin to follow the teaching in false stories. [5]But you should control yourself at all times. When troubles come, accept them. Do the work of telling the Good News. Do all the duties of a servant of God.

[6]My life is being given as an offering to God. The time has come for me to leave this life. [7]I have fought the good fight. I have finished the race. I have kept the faith. [8]Now, a crown is waiting for me. I will get that crown for being right with God. The Lord is the judge who judges rightly, and he will give me the crown on that Day.[n] He will give that crown not only to me but to all those who have waited with love for him to come again.

Personal Words

[9]Do your best to come to me as soon as you can. [10]Demas loved this world too much. He left me and went to Thessalonica. Crescens went to Galatia. And Titus went to Dalmatia. [11]Luke is the only one still with me. Get Mark and bring him with you when you come. He can help me in my work here. [12]I sent Tychicus to Ephesus.

[13]When I was in Troas, I left my coat there with Carpus. So when you come, bring it to me. Also, bring my books, particularly the ones written on parchment.[n]

[14]Alexander the metalworker did many harmful things against me. The Lord will punish him for the things he did. [15]You should be careful that he does not hurt you too. He fought strongly against our teaching.

[16]The first time I defended myself,

given by God and is useful for teaching and for showing people what is wrong in their lives. It is useful for correcting faults and teaching us how to live correctly. [17]Using the Scriptures, the person who serves God will be ready and will have everything he needs to do every good work.

4 Before God and Jesus Christ I give you a command. Christ Jesus is the One who will judge all who are living and all who have died. Jesus has a kingdom, and he is coming again. So I give you this command: [2]preach the Good News.[d] Be ready at all times. Tell people what they need to do, tell them when they are wrong, and encourage them. Do these things with great patience and careful teaching. [3]The time will come when people will not listen to the true teaching. They will find more and more teachers who

---

Day   The day Christ will come to judge all people and take his people to live with him.
parchment   Something like paper made from the skins of sheep and used for writing on.

no one helped me. Everyone left me. I pray that God will forgive them. [17] But the Lord stayed with me. He gave me strength so that I could fully tell the Good News[d] to the non-Jews. The Lord wanted all the non-Jews to hear it. So I was saved from the lion's mouth. [18] The Lord will save me when anyone tries to hurt me. The Lord will bring me safely to his heavenly kingdom. Glory for ever and ever to the Lord. Amen.

Final Greetings

[19] Greet Priscilla and Aquila and the family of Onesiphorus. [20] Erastus stayed in Corinth. And I left Trophimus sick in Miletus. [21] Try as hard as you can to come to me before winter.

Eubulus sends greetings to you. Also Pudens, Linus, Claudia, and all the brothers in Christ greet you.

[22] The Lord be with your spirit. Grace be with you.

TITUS

Paul Instructs Titus

1 From Paul, a servant of God and an apostle[d] of Jesus Christ. I was sent to help the faith of God's chosen people. I was sent to help them to know the truth. And that truth shows people how to serve God. [2] That faith and that knowledge come from our hope for life for ever. God promised that life to us before time began, and God does not lie. [3] At the right time God let the world know about that life through preaching. He trusted me with that work, and I preached because God our Saviour commanded me to.

[4] To Titus. You are like a true son to me in the faith we share.

Grace and peace to you from God the Father and Christ Jesus our Saviour.

Titus' Work in Crete

[5] I left you in Crete so that you could finish doing the things that still needed to be done. I left you there also so that you could choose men to be elders[d] in every town. [6] To be an elder, a man must not be guilty of doing wrong. He must have only one wife. His children must be believers. They must not be known as children who are wild and who do not obey. [7] An elder has the job of taking care of God's work. So he must not be guilty of doing wrong. He must not be a man who is proud and selfish or who becomes angry quickly. He must not drink too much wine. He must not be a person who likes to fight. And he must not be a person who always tries to get rich by cheating people. [8] An elder must be ready to help others by accepting them into his home. He must love what is good. He must be wise. He must live right. He must be holy. And he must be able to control himself. [9] An elder must faithfully follow the truth just as we teach it. He must be able to help people by using true and right teaching. And he must be able to show those who are against the true teaching that they are wrong.

[10] There are many people who refuse to obey – people who talk about worthless things and lead others into the wrong way. I am talking mostly about those who say that all non-Jews must be circumcised.[d] [11] These people must be stopped from talking. They are destroying whole families by teaching things that they should not teach. They teach them only to cheat people and make money. [12] Even one of their own prophets from Crete said, "Cretan people are always liars. They are evil animals and lazy people who do nothing but eat." [13] The words that prophet said are true. So tell those people that they are wrong. You must be strict with them. Then they will become strong in the faith [14] and stop accepting Jewish stories. And they will stop following the commands of others who do not accept the truth. [15] To those who are pure, all things are pure. But to those who are full of sin and do not believe, nothing is pure. The thinking of those people has become evil and their knowledge of what is right has been ruined. [16] They say they know God, but the evil things they do show that they do not accept God. They are terrible people, they

refuse to obey, and they are useless for doing anything good.

Following the True Teaching

2 You must speak things that make the true teaching attractive. ²Teach older men to have self-control, to be serious, and to be wise. They should be strong in faith, strong in love, and strong in patience.

³Also, teach older women to be holy in the way they live. Teach them not to speak against others or have the habit of drinking too much wine. They should teach what is good. ⁴In that way they can teach younger women to love their husbands and children. ⁵They can teach younger women to be wise and pure, to take care of their homes, to be kind, and to obey their husbands. Then no one will be able to criticise the teaching God gave us.

⁶In the same way, tell young men to be wise. ⁷You should do good deeds to be an example in every way for young men. When you teach, be

Titus 2:8 When you speak, speak the truth.

honest and serious. ⁸And when you speak, speak the truth so that you cannot be criticised. Then anyone who is against you will be ashamed because there is nothing bad that he can say against us.

⁹And tell slaves to obey their masters at all times. They should try to please them and not argue with them. ¹⁰They should not steal from them. And they should show their masters that they can be fully trusted. Then, in everything they do they will make the teaching of God our Saviour attractive.

¹¹That is the way we should live, because God's grace has come. That grace can save every person. ¹²It teaches us not to live against God and not to do the evil things the world wants to do. That grace teaches us to live on earth now in a wise and right way – a way that shows that we serve God. ¹³We should live like that while we are waiting for the coming of our great God and Saviour Jesus Christ. He is our great hope, and he will come with glory. ¹⁴He gave himself for us; he died to free us from all evil. He died to make us pure people who belong only to him – people who are always wanting to do good things.

¹⁵Tell everyone these things. You have full authority. So use that authority to strengthen the people and tell them what they should do. And do not let anyone treat you as if you were not important.

The Right Way to Live

3 Remind the believers to do these things: to be under the authority of rulers and government leaders, to obey them and be ready to do good, ²to speak no evil about anyone, to live in peace with all, to be gentle and polite to all people.

³In the past we were foolish people,

too. We did not obey, we were wrong, and we were slaves to many things our bodies wanted and enjoyed. We lived doing evil and being jealous. People hated us and we hated each other. ⁴But then the kindness and love of God our Saviour was shown. ⁵He saved us because of his mercy, not because of good deeds we did to be right with God. He saved us through the washing that made us new people. He saved us by making us new through the Holy Spirit.*ᵈ* ⁶God poured out to us that Holy Spirit fully through Jesus Christ our Saviour. ⁷We were made right with God by His grace. And God gave us the Spirit so that we could receive the life that never ends. That is what we hope for.

⁸This teaching is true. And I want you to be sure that the people understand these things. Then those who believe in God will be careful to use their lives for doing good. These things are good and will help all people.

⁹Stay away from those who have foolish arguments, who talk about useless family histories, who make trouble and fight about what the law of Moses teaches. Those things are worth nothing and will not help anyone. ¹⁰If someone causes arguments, then give him a warning. If he continues to cause arguments, warn him again. If he still continues causing arguments, then do not be around him. ¹¹You know that such a person is evil and sinful. His sins prove that he is wrong.

Some Things to Remember

¹²I will send Artemas and Tychicus to you. When I send them, try hard to come to me at Nicopolis. I have decided to stay there this winter. ¹³Zenas the lawyer and Apollos will be travelling from there. Do all that you can to help them on their way. Be sure that they have everything they need. ¹⁴Our people must learn to use their lives for doing good deeds. They should do good to those in need. Then our people will not have useless lives.

¹⁵All who are with me greet you. Greet those who love us in the faith.

Grace be with you all.

PHILEMON

A Slave Becomes a Christian

[1] From Paul, a prisoner for Jesus Christ, and from Timothy, our brother.

To Philemon, our dear friend and worker with us; [2] to Apphia, our sister; to Archippus, a worker with us; and to the church that meets in your home.

[3] Grace and peace to you from God our Father and the Lord Jesus Christ.

Philemon's Love and Faith

[4] I remember you in my prayers. And I always thank my God for you. [5] I hear about the love you have for all God's holy people and the faith you have in the Lord Jesus. [6] I pray that the faith you share will make you understand every blessing that we have in Christ. [7] My brother, you have shown love to God's people. You have made them feel happy. This has given me great joy and comfort.

Accept Onesimus as a Brother

[8] There is something that you should do. And because of your love in Christ, I feel free to order you to do it. [9] But because I love you, I am asking you instead. I, Paul, am an old man now, and a prisoner for Christ Jesus. [10] I am asking you a favour for my son Onesimus. He became my son while I was in prison. [11] In the past he was useless to you. But now he has become useful for both you and me.

[12] I am sending him back to you, and with him I am sending my own heart. [13] I wanted to keep him with me to help me while I am in prison for the Good News.[d] By helping me he would be serving you. [14] But I did not want to do anything without asking you first. Then any favour you do for me will be because you want to do it, not because I forced you to do it.

[15] Onesimus was separated from you for a short time. Maybe that happened so that you could have him back for ever – [16] not to be a slave, but better than a slave, to be a loved brother. I love him very much. But you will love him even more. You will love him as a man and as a brother in the Lord.

[17] If you think of me as your friend, then accept Onesimus back. Welcome him as you would welcome me. [18] If Onesimus has done anything wrong to you, charge that to me. If he owes you anything, charge that to me. [19] I, Paul, am writing this with my own hand. I will pay back anything Onesimus owes. And I will say nothing about what you owe me for your own life. [20] So, my brother, I ask that you do this for me in the Lord. Comfort my heart in Christ. [21] I write this letter, knowing that you will do what I ask you and even more.

[22] Also, please prepare a room for me to stay in. I hope that God will answer your prayers and I will be able to come to you.

Final Greetings

[23] Epaphras is a prisoner with me for Christ Jesus. He sends greetings to you. [24] And also Mark, Aristarchus, Demas, and Luke send greetings. They are workers together with me.

[25] The grace of our Lord Jesus Christ be with your spirit.

HEBREWS

A Better Life Through Christ

God Spoke Through His Son

1 In the past God spoke to our ancestors through the prophets.[d] He spoke to them many times and in many different ways. [2]And now in these last days God has spoken to us through his Son. God has chosen his Son to own all things. And he made the world through the Son. [3]The Son reflects the glory of God. He is an exact copy of God's nature. He holds everything together with his powerful word. The Son made people clean from their sins. Then he sat down at the right side of God, the Great One in heaven. [4]The Son became much greater than the angels. And God gave him a name that is much greater than theirs.

[5]This is because God never said to any of the angels,

"You are my Son.
　Today I have become your
　　Father." *Psalm 2:7*

Nor did God say of any angel,

"I will be his Father,
　and he will be my Son."
　　　　　　　2 Samuel 7:14

[6]And when God brings his firstborn Son into the world, he says,

"Let all God's angels worship
　him."[n] *Psalm 97:7*

[7]This is what God said about the angels:

"God makes his angels become
　like winds.

He makes his servants become
　like flames of fire." *Psalm 104:4*

[8]But God said this about his Son:

"God, your throne will last for ever
　and ever.
You will rule your kingdom with
　fairness.
[9]You love what is right and hate
　evil.
So God has chosen you to rule
　those with you.
Your God has given you much
　joy." *Psalm 45:6–7*

[10]God also says,

"Lord, in the beginning you made
　the earth.
And your hands made the
　skies.
[11]They will be destroyed, but you
　will remain.
They will all wear out like
　clothes.
[12]You will fold them like a coat.
And, like clothes, you will
　change them.
But you never change.
And your life will never end."
　　　　　　Psalm 102:25–27

[13]And God never said this to an angel:

"Sit by me at my right side
until I put your enemies under
　your control."[n] *Psalm 110:1*

[14]All the angels are spirits who serve God and are sent to help those who will receive salvation.

"Let . . . him."　These words are found in Deuteronomy 32:43 in the Septuagint, the Greek version of the Old Testament, and in a Hebrew copy among the Dead Sea Scrolls.
until . . . control　Literally, "until I make your enemies a footstool for your feet."

Our Salvation Is Great

2 So we must be more careful to follow what we were taught. Then we will not be pulled away from the truth. [2]The teaching that God spoke through angels was shown to be true. And anyone who did not follow it or obey it received the punishment he earned. [3]The salvation that was given to us is very great. So surely we also will be punished if we live as if this salvation were not important. It was the Lord himself who first told about this salvation. And those who heard him proved to us that this salvation is true. [4]God also proved it by using wonders, great signs, and many kinds of miracles.[d] And he proved it by giving people gifts through the Holy Spirit,[d] just as he wanted.

Christ Became like Men

[5]God did not choose angels to be the rulers of the new world that was coming. It is that future world we have been talking about. [6]It is written somewhere in the Scriptures,[d]

"Why is man important to you?
    Why do you take care of the son
        of man?[n]
[7]For a short time you made him
        lower than the angels.
    But you crowned him with glory
        and honour.
[8]   You put all things under his
        control."   *Psalm 8:4–6*

If God put everything under his control, there was nothing left that he did not rule. But we do not yet see him ruling over everything. [9]But we see Jesus! For a short time he was made lower than the angels. But now we see him wearing a crown of glory and honour because he suffered and died. Because of God's grace, he died for everyone.

[10]God is the One who made all things. And all things are for his glory. God wanted to have many sons share his glory. So God made perfect the One who leads people to salvation. He made Jesus a perfect Saviour through Jesus' suffering.

[11]Jesus, who makes people holy, and those who are made holy are from the same family. So he is not ashamed to call them his brothers. [12]He says,

"Then, I will tell my fellow
        Israelites about you.
    I will praise you when your
        people meet to worship you."
                                    Psalm 22:22

[13]He also says,

"I will trust in God."   *Isaiah 8:17*

And he also says,

"I am here. And with me are the
        children that God has given
        me."   *Isaiah 8:18*

[14]These children are people with physical bodies. So Jesus himself became like them and had the same experiences they have. He did this so that, by dying, he could destroy the one who has the power of death. That one is the devil. [15]Jesus became like men and died so that he could free them. They were like slaves all their lives because of their fear of death. [16]Clearly, it is not angels that Jesus helps, but the people who are from Abraham.[n] [17]For this reason Jesus had to be made like his brothers in every way. He became like men so that he could be their merciful and faithful high priest in service to God. Then Jesus could bring forgiveness for their sins. [18]And now he can help those who

---

son of man   This can mean any, but the name "Son of Man" is often used to mean Jesus. When Jesus became a man, he showed what God planned for all people to be.
Abraham   Most respected ancestor of the Jews. Every Jew hoped to see Abraham.

are tempted. He is able to help because he himself suffered and was tempted.

Jesus Is Greater than Moses

3 So all of you, holy brothers, should think about Jesus. You were all called by God. God sent Jesus to us, and he is the high priest of our faith. [2]And Jesus was faithful to God as Moses was. Moses did everything God wanted him to do in God's family. [3]A man who is the head of a family receives more honour than others in the family. It is the same with Jesus. Jesus should have more honour than Moses. [4]Every family has its head, but God is the head of everything. [5]Moses was faithful in God's family as a servant. He told what God would say in the future. [6]But Christ is faithful as a Son who is the head of God's family. And we are God's family if we hold on to our faith and are proud of the great hope we have.

We Must Continue to Follow God

[7]So it is as the Holy Spirit[d] says:
"Today listen to what he says.
[8]   Do not be stubborn as in the
        past
    when you turned against God.
There you tested God in the
        desert.
[9]   For 40 years in the desert your
        ancestors saw the things I
        did.
    But they tested me and my
        patience.
[10]I was angry with them.
    I said, 'They are not loyal to me.
    They have not understood my
        ways'.
[11]So I was angry and made a
    promise.

'They will never enter my land
        of rest'."[n]   Psalm 95:7–11
[12]So brothers, be careful that none of you has an evil, unbelieving heart. This will stop you from following the living God. [13]But encourage each other every day. Do this while it is "today".[n] Help each other so that none of you will become hardened because of sin and its tricks. [14]We all share in Christ. This is true if we keep till the end the sure faith we had in the beginning. [15]This is what the Scripture[d] says:

"Today listen to what he says.
    Do not be stubborn as in the
        past
    when you turned against God."
                        Psalm 95:7–8
[16]Who heard God's voice and was against him? It was all those people Moses led out of Egypt. [17]And whom was God angry with for 40 years? He was angry with those who sinned, who died in the desert. [18]And whom was God talking to when he promised that they would never enter and have his rest? He was talking to those who did not obey him. [19]So we see that they were not allowed to enter and have God's rest because they did not believe.

4 Now God has left us that promise that we may enter and have his rest. Let us be very careful, then, so that none of you will fail to get that rest. [2]The Good News[d] was preached to us just as it was to them. But the teaching they heard did not help them. They heard it but did not accept it with faith. [3]We who have believed are able to enter and have God's rest. As God has said,

"So I was angry and made a
    promise.

---

rest A place of rest God promised to give his people.
"today" This word is taken from verse 7. It means that it is important to do these things now.

'They will never enter my land of rest'."

Psalm 95:11

But God's work was finished from the time he made the world. [4]Somewhere in the Scriptures[d] he talked about the seventh day of the week: "And on the seventh day God rested from all his work."[n] [5]And again in the Scripture God said, "They will never enter my land of rest."

[6]It is still true that some people will enter and have God's rest. But those who first heard the way to be saved did not enter. They did not enter because they did not obey. [7]So God planned another day, called "today". He spoke about that day through David a long time later. It is the same Scripture used before:

"Today listen to what he says.

Do not be stubborn." *Psalm 95:7–8*

[8]We know that Joshua[n] did not lead the people into that rest. We know this because God spoke later about another day. [9]This shows that the seventh-day rest[n] for God's people is still coming. [10]For anyone who enters and has God's rest will rest from his work as God did. [11]So let us try as hard as we can to enter God's rest. We must try hard so that no one will be lost by following the example of those who refused to obey.

[12]God's word is alive and working. It is sharper than a sword sharpened on both sides. It cuts all the way into us, where the soul and the spirit are joined. It cuts to the centre of our joints and our bones. And God's word judges the thoughts and feelings in our hearts. [13]Nothing in all the world can be hidden from God. Everything is clear and lies open before him. And to him we must explain the way we have lived.

Jesus Is Our High Priest

[14]We have a great high priest who has gone into heaven. He is Jesus the Son of God. So let us hold on to the faith we have. [15]For our high priest is able to understand our weaknesses. When he lived on earth, he was tempted in every way that we are, but he did not sin. [16]Let us, then, feel free to come before God's throne. Here there is grace. And we can receive

"And . . . work."   Quotation from Genesis 2:2.

Joshua   After Moses died, Joshua became leader of the Jewish people. Joshua led them into the land that God promised to give them.

seventh-day rest   Literally, "sabbath rest", meaning a sharing in the rest that God began after he created the world.

Hebrews 4:12 God's word is alive and working. It is sharper than a sword sharpened on both sides.

mercy and grace to help us when we need it.

5 Every high priest is chosen from among men. He is given the work of going before God for them. He must offer gifts and sacrifices for sins. [2] He himself is weak. So he is able to be gentle with those who do not understand and who are doing wrong things. [3] Because he is weak the high priest must offer sacrifices for his own sins. And then he offers sacrifices for the sins of the people.

[4] To be a high priest is an honour. But no one chooses himself for this work. He must be called by God as Aaron[n] was. [5] So also Christ did not choose himself to have the honour of being a high priest. But God chose him. God said to him,

"You are my Son;
   today I have become your
      Father."   *Psalm 2:7*

[6] And in another Scripture[d] God says,

"You are a priest for ever,
   a priest like Melchizedek."[n]
                    Psalm 110:4

[7] While Jesus lived on earth, he prayed to God and asked God for help. He prayed with loud cries and tears to the One who could save him from death. And his prayer was heard because he left it all up to God. [8] Even though Jesus was the Son of God, he learned to obey by what he suffered. [9] And he became our perfect high priest. He gives eternal salvation to all who obey him. [10] And God made Jesus high priest, a priest like Melchizedek.

Warning Against Falling Away

[11] We have much to say about this. But it is hard to explain because you are so slow to understand. [12] You have had enough time so that by now you should be teachers. But you need someone to teach you again the first lessons of God's message. You still need the teaching that is like milk. You are not ready for solid food. [13] Anyone who lives on milk is still a baby. He knows nothing about right teaching. [14] But solid food is for those who are grown up. They have practised in order to know the difference between good and evil.

6 So let us go on to grown-up teaching. Let us not go back over the lessons we learned about Christ at the beginning. We should not start over again with teaching about turning from acts that lead to death and about believing in God. [2] We should not return to the teaching of baptisms,[n] of laying on of hands,[n] of the raising of the dead and eternal judgement. [3] And we will go on to grown-up teaching if God allows.

[4] Some people cannot be brought back again to a changed life. They were once in God's light. They enjoyed heaven's gift, and they shared in the Holy Spirit.[d] [5] They found out how good God's word is, and they received the powers of his new world. [6] And then they fell away from Christ! It is not possible to keep on bringing them back to a changed life again. For they are nailing the Son of God to a cross again and are shaming him in front of others.

Aaron   Aaron was the first Jewish high priest. He was Moses' brother.

Melchizedek   A priest and king who lived in the time of Abraham. (Read Genesis 14:17–24.)

baptisms   The word here may refer to Christian baptism, or it may refer to the Jewish ceremonial washings.

laying . . . hands   Putting the hands on people showed that they were being given some special work or some spiritual gift or blessing.

[7] Some people are like land that gets plenty of rain. The land produces a good crop for those who work it, and it receives God's blessings. [8] Other people are like land that grows thorns and weeds and is worthless. It is in danger of being cursed by God. It will be destroyed by fire.

[9] Dear friends, we are saying this to you. But we really expect better things from you that will lead to your salvation. [10] God is fair. He will not forget the work you did and the love you showed for him by helping his people. And he will remember that you are still helping them. [11] We want each of you to go on with the same hard work all your lives. Then you will surely get what you hope for. [12] We do not want you to become lazy. Be like those who have faith and patience. They will receive what God has promised.

[13] God made a promise to Abraham. And as there is no one greater than God, he used himself when he swore to Abraham. [14] He said, "I will surely bless you and give you many descendants."[n] [15] Abraham waited patiently for this to happen. And he received what God promised.

[16] People always use the name of someone greater than themselves when they swear. The oath proves that what they say is true. And this ends all arguing about what they say. [17] God wanted to prove that his promise was true. He wanted to prove this to those who would get what he promised. He wanted them to understand clearly that his purposes never change. So God proved his promise by also making an oath. [18] These two things cannot change. God cannot lie when he makes a promise, and he cannot lie when he makes an oath. These things encourage us who came to God for safety. They give us strength to hold on to the hope we have been given. [19] We have this hope as an anchor for the soul, sure and strong. It enters behind the curtain in the Most Holy Place in heaven. [20] Jesus has gone in there ahead of us and for us. He has become the high priest for ever, a priest like Melchizedek.[n]

The Priest Melchizedek

[7] Melchizedek[n] was the king of Salem and a priest for the Most High God. He met Abraham when Abraham was coming back after defeating the kings. When they met, Melchizedek blessed Abraham. [2] And Abraham gave Melchizedek a tenth of everything he had brought back from the battle. First, Melchizedek's name means "king of goodness". Also, he is king of Salem, which means "king of peace". [3] No one knows who Melchizedek's father or mother was.[n] No one knows where he came from. And no one knows when he was born or when he died. Melchizedek is like the Son of God; he continues being a priest for ever.

[4] You can see that Melchizedek was very great. Abraham, the great father, gave Melchizedek a tenth of everything that Abraham won in battle. [5] Now the law says that those in the tribe[d] of Levi who become priests must get a tenth from the people. The priests collect it from their own people, even though the priests and the people are both from the family of Abraham. [6] Melchizedek was not from the tribe of Levi. But he got a tenth from Abraham. And he blessed

---

"I . . . descendants." Quotation from Genesis 22:17.
Melchizedek A priest and king who lived in the time of Abraham. (Read Genesis 14:17–24.)
No . . . was Literally, "Melchizedek was without father, without mother, without genealogy."

Abraham, the man who had God's promises. [7]And everyone knows that the more important person blesses the less important person. [8]Those priests get a tenth, but they are only men who live and then die. But Melchizedek, who got a tenth from Abraham, continues living, as the Scripture[d] says. [9]It is Levi who gets a tenth from the people. But we might even say that when Abraham paid Melchizedek a tenth, then Levi also paid it. [10]Levi was not yet born. But Levi was in the body of his ancestor Abraham when Melchizedek met Abraham.

[11]The people were given the law[n] based on a system of priests from the tribe of Levi. But they could not be made spiritually perfect through that system of priests. So there was a need for another priest to come. I mean a priest like Melchizedek, not Aaron. [12]And when a different kind of priest comes, the law must be changed, too. [13]We are saying these things about Christ. He belonged to a different tribe. No one from that tribe ever served as a priest at the altar. [14]It is clear that our Lord came from the tribe of Judah. And Moses said nothing about priests belonging to that tribe.

Jesus Is like Melchizedek

[15]And this becomes even more clear. We see that another priest comes, who is like Melchizedek.[n] [16]He was not made a priest by human rules and laws. He became a priest through the power of his life, which continues for ever. [17]In the Scriptures,[d] this is said about him:

"You are a priest for ever,
a priest like Melchizedek."

Psalm 110:4

[18]The old rule is now set aside because it was weak and useless. [19]The law of Moses could not make anything perfect. But now a better hope has been given to us. And with this hope we can come near to God.

[20]Also, it is important that God made an oath when he made Jesus high priest. When the others became priests, there was no oath. [21]But Christ became a priest with God's oath. God said:

"The Lord has made a promise
and will not change his mind.
'You are a priest for ever'."

Psalm 110:4

[22]So this means that Jesus is the guarantee of a better agreement[n] from God to his people.

[23]Also, when one of the other priests died, he could not continue being a priest. So there were many priests. [24]But Jesus lives for ever. He will never stop serving as priest. [25]So he is always able to save those who come to God through him. He can do this, because he always lives, ready to help those who come before God.

[26]So Jesus is the kind of high priest that we need. He is holy; he has no sin in him. He is pure and not influenced by sinners. And he is raised above the heavens. [27]He is not like the other priests. They had to offer sacrifices every day, first for their own sins, and then for the sins of the people. But Christ does not need to do that. He offered his sacrifice only once and for all time. Christ offered himself! [28]The law chooses high

---

The . . . law This refers to the people of Israel who were given the law of Moses.
Melchizedek A priest and king who lived in the time of Abraham. (Read Genesis 14:17–24.)
agreement God gives a contract or agreement to his people. For the Jews, this agreement was the law of Moses. But now God has given a better agreement to his people through Christ.

priests who are men with all their weaknesses. But the word of God's oath came later than the law. It made God's Son to be the high priest. And that Son has been made perfect for ever.

Jesus Is Our High Priest

8 Here is the point of what we are saying: we do have a high priest who sits on the right side of God's throne in heaven. ²Our high priest serves in the Most Holy Place. He serves in the true place of worship that was made by God, not by men.

³Every high priest has the work of offering gifts and sacrifices to God. So our high priest must also offer something to God. ⁴If our high priest were now living on earth, he would not be a priest. I say this because there are already priests here who follow the law by offering gifts to God. ⁵The work that they do as priests is only a dim copy of what is in heaven. For when Moses was ready to build the Holy Tent,*d* God warned him: "Be very careful to make everything by the plan I showed you on the mountain."*n* ⁶But the priestly work that has been given to Jesus is much greater than the work that was given to the other priests. In the same way, the new agreement that Jesus brought from God to his people is much greater than the old one. And the new agreement is based on promises of better things.

⁷If there was nothing wrong with the first agreement,*n* there would be no need for a second agreement. ⁸But God found something wrong with his people. He says:

"The time is coming, says the
        Lord,
when I will make a new
        agreement.
It will be with the people of
        Israel
and the people of Judah.
⁹It will not be like the agreement
        I made with their ancestors.
That was when I took them by the
        hand
to bring them out of Egypt.
But they broke that agreement,
        and I turned away from them,
        says the Lord.
¹⁰In the future I will make this
        agreement
with the people of Israel, says
        the Lord.
I will put my teachings in their
        minds.
And I will write them on their
        hearts.
I will be their God,
        and they will be my people.
¹¹People will no longer have to
        teach
their neighbours and relatives to
        know the Lord.
This is because all will know
        me,
from the least to the most
        important.
¹²I will forgive them for the wicked
        things they did.
I will not remember their sins
        any more."   *Jeremiah 31:31–34*

¹³God called this a new agreement, so he has made the first agreement old. And anything that is old and worn out is ready to disappear.

Worship Under the Old Agreement

9 The first agreement*n* had rules for worship. And it had a man-made

---

"Be . . . mountain." Quotation from Exodus 25:40.
first agreement The contract God gave the Jewish people when he gave them the law of Moses.

place for worship. [2]The Holy Tent[d] was set up for this. The first area in the Tent was called the Holy Place. In it were the lamp and the table with the bread that was made holy for God. [3]Behind the second curtain was a room called the Most Holy Place. [4]In it was a golden altar for burning incense.[d] Also there was the Holy Ark[d] that held the old agreement. The Holy Ark was covered with gold. Inside this Holy Ark was a golden jar of manna[d] and Aaron's rod – the rod that once grew leaves. Also in it were the stone tablets of the old agreement. [5]Above the Holy Ark were the creatures with wings that showed God's glory. The wings of the creatures reached over the lid. But we cannot tell everything about these things now.

[6]Everything in the Tent was made ready in this way. Then the priests went into the first room every day to do their worship. [7]But only the high priest could go into the second room, and he did that only once a year. He could never enter the inner room without taking blood with him. He offered that blood to God for himself and for the people's sins. These were sins people did without knowing that they were sinning. [8]The Holy Spirit[d] uses this to show that the way into the Most Holy Place was not open. This was while the system of the old Holy Tent was still being used. [9]This is an example for the present time. It shows that the gifts and sacrifices offered cannot make the worshipper perfect in his heart. [10]These gifts and sacrifices were only about food and drink and special washings. They were rules for

the body, to be followed until the time of God's new way.

Worship Under the New Agreement

[11]But Christ has come as the high priest of the good things we now have. The tent he entered is greater and more perfect. It is not made by men. It does not belong to this world. [12]Christ entered the Most Holy Place only once – and for all time. He did not take with him the blood of goats and calves. His sacrifice was his own blood. He entered the Most Holy Place and set us free from sin for ever. [13]The blood of goats and bulls and the ashes of a cow are sprinkled on the people who are unclean[d] and this makes their bodies clean again.

[14]How much more is done by the blood of Christ. He offered himself through the eternal Spirit[n] as a perfect sacrifice to God. His blood will make our hearts clean from useless acts. We are made pure so that we may serve the living God.

[15]So Christ brings a new agreement from God to his people. Those who are called by God can now receive the blessings that God has promised. These blessings will last for ever. They can have those things because Christ died so that the people who lived under the first agreement could be set free from sin.

[16]When there is a will,[n] it must be proven that the man who wrote that will is dead. [17]A will means nothing while the man is alive. It can be used only after he dies. [18]This is why even the first agreement could not begin without blood to show death. [19]First,

---

Spirit This refers to the Holy Spirit; to Christ's own spirit; or to the spiritual and eternal nature of his sacrifice.

will A legal document that shows how a person's money and property are to be distributed at the time of his death. This is the same word in Greek as "agreement" in verse 15.

Moses told all the people every command in the law. Next he took the blood of calves and mixed it with water. Then he used red wool and a branch of the hyssop plant to sprinkle the blood and water on the book of the law and on all the people. [20]He said, "This is the blood which begins the agreement that God commanded you to obey."[n] [21]In the same way, Moses sprinkled the blood on the Holy Tent[d] and over all the things used in worship. [22]The law says that almost everything must be made clean by blood. And sins cannot be forgiven without blood to show death.

Christ's Death Takes Away Sins

[23]So the copies of the real things in heaven had to be made clean[d] by animal sacrifices. But the real things in heaven need much better sacrifices. [24]For Christ did not go into the Most Holy Place made by men. It is only a copy of the real one. He went into heaven itself. He is there now before God to help us. [25]The high priest enters the Most Holy Place once every year. He takes with him blood that is not his own blood. But Christ did not go into heaven to offer himself many times. [26]Then he would have had to suffer many times since the world was made. But Christ came only once and for all time. He came at just the right time to take away all sin by sacrificing himself. [27]Everyone must die once. After a person dies, he is judged. [28]So Christ was offered as a sacrifice once to take away the sins of many people. And he will come a second time, but not to offer himself for sin. He will come again to bring salvation to those who are waiting for him.

10 The law is only an unclear picture of the good things coming in the future. It is not a perfect picture of the real things. The people under the law offered the same sacrifices every year. These sacrifices can never make perfect those who come near to worship God. [2]If the law could make them perfect, the sacrifices would have already stopped. The worshippers would be made clean, and they would no longer feel guilty for their sins. [3]These sacrifices remind them of their sins every year, [4]because it is not possible for the blood of bulls and goats to take away sins.

[5]So when Christ came into the world, he said:
"You do not want sacrifices and
offerings.
But you have prepared a body
for me.
[6]You do not ask for burnt
offerings
and offerings to take away
sins.
[7]Then I said, 'Look, I have come.
It is written about me in the
book.
My God, I have come to do
what you want'." *Psalm 40:6-8*
[8]In this Scripture[d] he first said, "You do not want sacrifices and offerings. You do not ask for burnt offerings and offerings to take away sins." (These are all sacrifices that the law commands.) [9]Then he said, "Here I am. I have come to do what you want." So God ends the first system of sacrifices so that he can set up the new system. [10]Jesus Christ did what God wanted him to do. And because of this, we are made holy through the sacrifice of his body. Christ made this sacrifice only once, and for all time.

[11]Every day the priests stand and do their religious service. Again and

"This . . . obey." Quotation from Exodus 24:8.

again they offer the same sacrifices. But those sacrifices can never take away sins. [12]But Christ offered one sacrifice for sins, and it is good for ever. Then he sat down at the right side of God. [13]And now Christ waits there for his enemies to be put under his power. [14]With one sacrifice he made perfect for ever those who are being made holy.

[15]The Holy Spirit[d] also tells us about this. First he says:

[16]"In the future I will make this
       agreement[n]
    with the people of Israel, says
       the Lord.
I will put my teachings in their
       hearts.
And I will write them on their
       minds."   *Jeremiah 31:33*

[17]Then he says:
    "Their sins and the evil things
       they do –
    I will not remember any more."
                           Jeremiah 31:34

[18]And when these have been forgiven, there is no more need for a sacrifice for sins.

Continue to Trust God

[19]So, brothers, we are completely free to enter the Most Holy Place. We can do this without fear because of the blood of Jesus' death. [20]We can enter through a new way that Jesus opened for us. It is a living way. It leads through the curtain – Christ's body. [21]And we have a great priest over God's house. [22]So let us come near to God with a sincere heart and a sure faith. We have been cleansed and made free from feelings of guilt. And our bodies have been washed with pure water. [23]Let us hold firmly to the hope that we have confessed. We can trust God to do what he promised.

[24]Let us think about each other and help each other to show love and do good deeds. [25]You should not stay away from the church meetings, as some are doing. But you should meet together and encourage each other. Do this even more as you see the Day[n] coming.

Hebrews 10:25 You should meet together and encourage each other.

[26]If we decide to go on sinning after we have learned the truth, there is no longer any sacrifice for sins. [27]There is nothing but fear in waiting for the judgement and the angry fire that will destroy all those who live against God. [28]Any person who refused to obey the law of Moses was found guilty from

---

agreement God gives a contract or agreement to his people. For the Jews, this agreement was the law of Moses. But now God has given a better agreement to his people through Christ.

Day The day Christ will come to judge all people and take his people to live with him.

the proof given by two or three witnesses. He was put to death without mercy. [29] So what do you think should be done to a person who does not respect the Son of God? He looks at the blood of the agreement, the blood that made him holy, as no different from other men's blood. He insults the Spirit[d] of God's grace. Surely he should have a much worse punishment. [30] We know that God said, "I will punish those who do wrong. I will repay them."[n] And he also said, "The Lord will judge his people."[n] [31] It is a terrible thing to fall into the hands of the living God.

[32] Remember those days in the past when you first learned the truth. You had a hard struggle with many sufferings, but you continued strong. [33] Sometimes you were hurt and persecuted before crowds of people. And sometimes you shared with those who were being treated that way. [34] You helped the prisoners. And you even had joy when all that you owned was taken from you. You were joyful because you knew that you had something better and more lasting.

[35] So do not lose the courage that you had in the past. It has a great reward. [36] You must hold on, so you can do what God wants and receive what he has promised. [37] For in a very short time,

"The One who is coming will
    come.
He will not be late.
[38] The person who is right with me
    will have life because of his
    faith.
But if he turns back with fear,
    I will not be pleased with him."

Habakkuk 2:3–4

[39] But we are not those who turn back

and are lost. We are people who have faith and are saved.

Faith

11 Faith means being sure of the things we hope for. And faith means knowing that something is real even if we do not see it. [2] People who lived in the past became famous because of faith.

[3] It is by faith we understand that the whole world was made by God's command. This means that what we see was made by something that cannot be seen.

[4] It was by faith that Abel offered God a better sacrifice than Cain did. God said he was pleased with the gifts Abel offered. So God called Abel a good man because of his faith. Abel died, but through his faith he is still speaking.

[5] It was by faith that Enoch was taken to heaven. He never died. He could not be found, because God had taken him away. Before he was taken, the Scripture[d] says that he was a man who truly pleased God. [6] Without faith no one can please God. Anyone who comes to God must believe that he is real and that he rewards those who truly want to find him.

[7] It was by faith that Noah heard God's warnings about things that he could not yet see. He obeyed God and built a large boat to save his family. By his faith, Noah showed that the world was wrong. And he became one of those who are made right with God through faith.

[8] It was by faith that Abraham obeyed God's call to go to another place that God promised to give him. He left his own country, not knowing where he was to go. [9] It was by faith

that he lived in the country God promised to give him. He lived there like a visitor who did not belong. He lived in tents with Isaac and Jacob, who had received that same promise from God. [10] Abraham was waiting for the city[n] that has real foundations – the city planned and built by God.

[11] He was too old to have children, and Sarah was not able to have children. It was by faith that Abraham was made able to become a father. Abraham trusted God to do what he had promised. [12] This man was so old that he was almost dead. But from him came as many descendants as there are stars in the sky. They are as many as the grains of sand on the seashore that cannot be counted.

[13] All these great men died in faith. They did not get the things that God promised his people. But they saw them coming far in the future and were glad. They said that they were like visitors and strangers on earth. [14] When people say such things, they show that they are looking for a country that will be their own country. [15] If they had been thinking about that country they had left, they could have gone back. [16] But those men were waiting for a better country – a heavenly country. So God is not ashamed to be called their God, for he has prepared a city for them.

[17] It was by faith that Abraham offered his son Isaac as a sacrifice. God made the promises to Abraham. But God tested him. And Abraham was ready to offer his own son as a sacrifice. [18] God had said, "The descendants I promised you will be from Isaac."[n] [19] Abraham believed that God could raise the dead. And really, it

was as if Abraham brought Isaac back from death.

[20] It was by faith that Isaac blessed the future of Jacob and Esau. [21] It was by faith that Jacob blessed each one of Joseph's sons. He did this while he was dying. Then he worshipped as he leaned on the top of his staff.

[22] It was by faith that Joseph spoke about the Israelites leaving Egypt while he was dying. He told them what to do with his body.

[23] It was by faith that Moses' parents hid him for three months after he was born. They saw that Moses was a beautiful baby. And they were not afraid to disobey the king's order.

[24] It was by faith that Moses, when he grew up, refused to be called the son of the king of Egypt's daughter. [25] He chose to suffer with God's people instead of enjoying sin for a short time. [26] He thought that it was better to suffer for the Christ[d] than to have all the treasures of Egypt. He was looking only for God's reward. [27] It was by faith that Moses left Egypt. He was not afraid of the king's anger. Moses continued strong as if he could see the God that no one can see. [28] It was by faith that Moses prepared the Passover[d] and spread the blood on the doors. It was spread so that the one who brings death would not kill the firstborn[d] sons of Israel.

[29] It was by faith that the people crossed the Red Sea as if it were dry land. The Egyptians also tried to do it, but they were drowned.

[30] It was by faith that the walls of Jericho fell. They fell after the people had marched around the walls of Jericho for seven days.

[31] It was by faith that Rahab, the

city   The spiritual "city" where God's people live with him. Also called "the heavenly Jerusalem". (See Hebrews 12:22.)

"The descendants . . . Isaac."   Quotation from Genesis 21:12.

prostitute,*ᵈ* welcomed the spies and was not killed with those who refused to obey God.

³² Do I need to give more examples? I do not have time to tell you about Gideon, Barak, Samson, Jephthah, David, Samuel, and the prophets.*ᵈ* ³³ Through their faith they defeated kingdoms. They did what was right and received what God promised. They shut the mouths of lions, ³⁴ stopped great fires and were saved from being killed with swords. They were weak, and yet were made strong. They were powerful in battle and defeated other armies. ³⁵ Women received their dead relatives raised back to life. Others were tortured and refused to accept their freedom. They did this so that they could be raised from death to a better life. ³⁶ Some were laughed at and beaten. Others were tied and put into prison. ³⁷ They were killed with stones and they were cut in half. They were killed with swords. Some wore the skins of sheep and goats. They were poor, abused, and treated badly. ³⁸ The world was not good enough for them! They wandered in deserts and mountains, living in caves and holes in the earth.

³⁹ All these people are known for their faith. But none of them received what God had promised. ⁴⁰ God planned to give us something better. Then they would be made perfect, but only together with us.

Follow Jesus' Example

12 So we have many people of faith around us. Their lives tell us what faith means. So let us run the race that is before us and never give up. We should remove from our lives anything that would get in the way. And we should remove the sin that so easily catches us. ² Let us look only to Jesus. He is the one who began our

Hebrews 12:1 Let us run the race.

faith, and he makes our faith perfect. Jesus suffered death on the cross. But he accepted the shame of the cross as if it were nothing. He did this because of the joy that God put before him. And now he is sitting at the right side of God's throne. ³ Think about Jesus. He held on patiently while sinful men were doing evil things against him. Look at Jesus' example so that you will not get tired and stop trying.

God Is Like a Father

⁴ You are struggling against sin, but your struggles have not yet caused you to be killed. ⁵ You have forgotten his encouraging words for his sons:
> "My son, don't think the Lord's
>   discipline of you is worth
>   nothing.
> And don't stop trying when the
>   Lord corrects you.
> ⁶ The Lord corrects those he loves.
> And he punishes everyone he
>   accepts as his child."
>   *Proverbs 3:11–12*

[7]So accept your sufferings as if they were a father's punishment. God does these things to you like a father punishing his sons. All sons are punished by their fathers. [8]If you are never punished (and every son must be punished), you are not true children and not really sons. [9]We have all had fathers here on earth who punished us. And we respected our fathers. So it is even more important that we accept punishment from the Father of our spirits. If we do this, we will have life. [10]Our fathers on earth punished us for a short time. They punished us in the way they thought was best. But God punishes us to help us, so that we can become holy as he is. [11]We do not enjoy punishment. Being punished is painful. But later, after we have learned from being punished, we have peace, because we start living in the right way.

Be Careful How You Live

[12]You have become weak. So make yourselves strong again. [13]Live in the right way so that you will be saved and your weakness will not cause you to be lost.

[14]Try to live in peace with all people. And try to live lives free from sin. If anyone's life is not holy, he will never see the Lord. [15]Be careful that no one fails to get God's grace. Be careful that no one becomes like a bitter weed growing among you. A person like that can ruin all of you. [16]Be careful that no one takes part in sexual sin. And be careful that no person is like Esau and never thinks about God. Esau was the oldest son, and he would have received everything from his father. But Esau sold all that for a single meal. [17]You remember that after Esau did this, he wanted to get his father's blessing. He wanted this blessing so much that he cried. But his father refused to give him the blessing, because Esau could find no way to change what he had done.

[18]You have not come to a mountain that can be touched and that is burning with fire. You have not come to darkness, sadness and storms. [19]You have not come to the noise of a trumpet or to the sound of a voice. When the people of Israel heard the voice, they begged not to have to hear another word. [20]They did not want to hear the command: "If anything, even an animal, touches the mountain, it must be put to death with stones."[n] [21]What they saw was so terrible that Moses said, "I am shaking with fear."[n]

[22]But you have not come to that kind of place. The new place you have come to is Mount Zion.[n] You have come to the city of the living God, the heavenly Jerusalem. You have come to thousands of angels gathered together with joy. [23]You have come to the meeting of God's firstborn[n] children. Their names are written in heaven. You have come to God, the judge of all people. And you have come to the spirits of good people who have been made perfect. [24]You have come to Jesus, the One who brought the new agreement from God to his people. You have come to the sprinkled blood[n] that has

"If . . . stones." Quotation from Exodus 19:12–13.
"I . . . fear." Quotation from Deuteronomy 9:19.
Mount Zion Another name for Jerusalem, here meaning the spiritual city of God's people.
firstborn The first son born in a Jewish family was given the most important place in the family and received special blessings. All of God's children are like that.
sprinkled blood The blood of Jesus' death.

a better message than the blood of Abel.[n]

[25] So be careful and do not refuse to listen when God speaks. They refused to listen to him when he warned them on earth. And they did not escape. Now God is warning us from heaven. So it will be worse for us if we refuse to listen to him. [26] When he spoke before, his voice shook the earth. But now he has promised, "Once again I will shake not only the earth but also the heavens."[n] [27] The words "once again" clearly show us that everything that was made will be destroyed. These are the things that can be shaken. And only the things that cannot be shaken will remain.

[28] So let us be thankful because we have a kingdom that cannot be shaken. We should worship God in a way that pleases him. So let us worship him with respect and fear, [29] because our God is like a fire that burns things up.

13 Keep on loving each other as brothers in Christ. [2] Remember to welcome strangers into your homes. Some people have done this and have welcomed angels without knowing it. [3] Do not forget those who are in prison. Remember them as if you were in prison with them. Remember those who are suffering as if you were suffering with them.

[4] Marriage should be honoured by everyone. Husband and wife should keep their marriage pure. God will judge guilty those who take part in sexual sins. [5] Keep your lives free from the love of money. And be satisfied with what you have. God has said,

"I will never leave you;
    I will never forget you."

Deuteronomy 31:6

[6] So we can feel sure and say,

"I will not be afraid because the
    Lord is my helper.
People can't do anything to me."

Psalm 118:6

[7] Remember your leaders. They taught God's message to you. Remember how they lived and died, and copy their faith. [8] Jesus Christ is the same yesterday, today, and for ever.

[9] Do not let all kinds of strange teachings lead you into the wrong way. Your hearts should be strengthened by God's grace, not by obeying rules about foods. Obeying such rules does not help anyone.

[10] We have a sacrifice. But the priests who serve in the Holy Tent[d] cannot eat from it. [11] The high priest carries the blood of animals into the Most Holy Place. There he offers this blood for sins. But the bodies of the animals are burned outside the camp. [12] So Jesus also suffered outside the city. He died to make his people holy with his own blood. [13] So let us go to Jesus outside the camp. We should accept the same shame that Jesus had.

[14] Here on earth we do not have a city that lasts for ever. But we are looking for the city that we will have in the future. [15] So through Jesus let us always offer our sacrifice to God. This sacrifice is our praise, coming from lips that speak his name. [16] Do not forget to do good to others. And share with them what you have. These are the sacrifices that please God.

[17] Obey your leaders and be under their authority. These men are watching you because they are responsible for your souls. Obey them so that they will do this work with joy, not sadness. It will not help you to make their work hard.

Abel   The son of Adam and Eve, who was killed by his brother Cain (Genesis 4:8).
"Once . . . heavens."   Quotation from Haggai 2:6,21.

[18] Continue praying for us. We feel sure about what we are doing, because we always want to do the right thing. [19] And I beg you to pray that God will send me back to you soon.

[20–21] I pray that the God of peace will give you every good thing you need so that you can do what he wants. God is the One who raised from death our Lord Jesus, the Great Shepherd of the sheep. God raised him because of the blood of his death. His blood began the agreement that God made with his people. And this agreement is eternal. I pray that God, through Christ, will do in us what pleases him. And to Jesus Christ be glory for ever and ever. Amen.

[22] My brothers, I beg you to listen patiently to this message I have written to encourage you. This letter is not very long. [23] I want you to know that our brother Timothy has been let out of prison. If he arrives soon, we will both come to see you.

[24] Greet all your leaders and all of God's people. Those from Italy send greetings to you.

[25] God's grace be with you all.

JAMES

How to Live as a Christian

1 From James, a servant of God and of the Lord Jesus Christ. To all of God's people who are scattered everywhere in the world:

Greetings.

Faith and Wisdom

² My brothers, you will have many kinds of troubles. But when these things happen, you should be very happy. ³ You know that these things are testing your faith. And this will give you patience. ⁴ Let your patience show itself perfectly in what you do. Then you will be perfect and complete. You will have everything you need. ⁵ But if any of you needs wisdom, you should ask God for it. God is generous. He enjoys giving to all people, so God will give you wisdom. ⁶ But when you ask God, you must believe. Do not doubt God. Anyone who doubts is like a wave in the sea. The wind blows the wave up and down. ⁷⁻⁸ He who doubts is thinking two different things at the same time. He cannot decide about anything he does. A person like that should not think that he will receive anything from the Lord.

True Riches

⁹ If a believer is poor, he should be proud because God has made him spiritually rich. ¹⁰ If he is rich, he should be proud because God has shown him that he is spiritually poor. The rich person will die like a wild flower in the grass. ¹¹ The sun rises and becomes hotter and hotter. The heat makes the plants very dry, and the flower falls off. The flower was beautiful, but now it is dead. It is the same with a rich person. While he is still taking care of his business, he will die.

Temptation Is Not from God

¹² When a person is tempted and still continues strong, he should be happy. After he has proved his faith, God will reward him with life for ever. God promised this to all people who love him. ¹³ When someone is being tempted, he should not say, "God is tempting me." Evil cannot tempt God, and God himself does not tempt anyone. ¹⁴ It is the evil that a person wants that tempts him. His own evil desire

James 1:6 Anyone who doubts is like a wave in the sea.

leads him away and holds him. [15] This desire causes sin. Then the sin grows and brings death.

[16] My dear brothers, do not be fooled about this. [17] Every good action and every perfect gift is from God. These good gifts come down from the Creator of the sun, moon, and stars. God does not change like their shifting shadows. [18] God decided to give us life through the word of truth. He wanted us to be the most important of all the things he made.

Listening and Obeying

[19] My dear brothers, always be willing to listen and slow to speak. Do not become angry easily. [20] Anger will not help you live a good life as God wants. [21] So put out of your life every evil thing and every kind of wrong you do. Don't be proud but accept God's teaching that is planted in your hearts. This teaching can save your souls.

[22] Do what God's teaching says; do not just listen and do nothing. When you only sit and listen, you are fooling yourselves. [23] A person who hears God's teaching and does nothing is like a man looking in a mirror. [24] He sees his face, then goes away and quickly forgets what he looked like. [25] But the truly happy person is the one who carefully studies God's perfect law that makes people free. He continues to study it. He listens to God's teaching and does not forget what he has heard. Then he obeys what God's teaching says. When he does this, it makes him happy.

The True Way to Worship God

[26] A person might think he is religious. But if he says things he should not say, then he is just fooling himself. His "religion" is worth noth-ing. [27] Religion that God accepts is this: caring for orphans or widows who need help; and keeping yourself free from the world's evil influence. This is the kind of religion that God accepts as pure and good.

Love All People

2 My dear brothers, you are believers in our glorious Lord Jesus Christ. So never think that some people are more important than others. [2] Suppose someone comes into your church meeting wearing very nice clothes and a gold ring. At the same time a poor man comes in wearing old, dirty clothes. [3] You show special attention to the one wearing nice clothes. You say, "Please, sit here in this good seat." But you say to the poor man, "Stand over there," or "Sit on the floor by my feet!" [4] What are you doing? You are making some people more important than others. With evil thoughts you are deciding which person is better.

[5] Listen, my dear brothers! God chose the poor in the world to be rich in faith. He chose them to receive the kingdom God promised to people who love him. [6] But you show no respect to the poor man. And you know that it is the rich who are always trying to control your lives. And they are the ones who take you to court. [7] They are the ones who say bad things against Jesus, who owns you.

[8] One law rules over all other laws. This royal law is found in the Scriptures:[d] "Love your neighbour as you love yourself."[n] If you obey this law, then you are doing right. [9] But if you are treating one person as if he were more important than another, then you are sinning. That royal law proves that you are guilty of breaking God's

---

"Love . . . yourself." Quotation from Leviticus 19:18.

law. [10]A person might follow all of God's law. But if he fails to obey even one command, he is guilty of breaking all the commands in that law. [11]God said, "You must not be guilty of adultery."[d][n] The same God also said, "You must not murder anyone."[n] So if you do not take part in adultery, but you murder someone, then you are guilty of breaking all of God's law. [12]You will be judged by the law that makes people free. You should remember this in everything you say and do. [13]Yes, you must show mercy to others, or God will not show mercy to you when he judges you. But the person who shows mercy can stand without fear when he is judged.

Faith and Good Works

[14]My brothers, if someone says he has faith, but does nothing, his faith is worth nothing. Can faith like that save him? [15]A brother or sister in Christ might need clothes or might need food. [16]And you say to him, "God be with you! I hope you stay warm and get plenty to eat." You say this, but you do not give that person the things he needs. Unless you help him, your words are worth nothing. [17]It is the same with faith. If faith does nothing, then that faith is dead, because it is alone.

[18]Someone might say, "You have faith, but I do things. Show me your faith! Your faith does nothing. I will show you my faith by the things I do." [19]You believe there is one God. Good! But the demons[d] believe that, too! And they shake with fear.

[20]You foolish person! Must you be shown that faith that does nothing is worth nothing? [21]Abraham is our father. He was made right with God by the things he did. He offered his son Isaac to God on the altar. [22]So you see that Abraham's faith and the things he did worked together. His faith was made perfect by what he did. [23]This shows the full meaning of the Scripture[d] that says: "Abraham believed God, and God accepted Abraham's faith, and that faith made him right with God."[n] And Abraham was called "God's friend."[n] [24]So you see that a person is made right with God by the things he does. He cannot be made right by faith only.

[25]Another example is Rahab, who was a prostitute.[d] But she was made right with God by something she did: she helped the spies for God's people. She welcomed them into her home and helped them escape by a different road.

[26]A person's body that does not have a spirit is dead. It is the same with faith. Faith that does nothing is dead!

Controlling the Things We Say

3 My brothers, not many of you should become teachers. You know that we who teach will be judged more strictly than others. [2]We all make many mistakes. If there were a person who never said anything wrong, he would be perfect. He would be able to control his whole body, too. [3]We put bits into the mouths of horses to make them obey us. We can control their whole bodies. [4]It is the same with ships. A ship is very big, and it is pushed by strong winds. But a very small rudder controls that big ship.

"You . . . adultery."   Quotation from Exodus 20:14 and Deuteronomy 5:18.
"You . . . anyone."   Quotation from Exodus 20:13 and Deuteronomy 5:17.
"Abraham . . . God."   Quotation from Genesis 15:6.
"God's friend"   These words about Abraham are found in 2 Chronicles 20:7 and Isaiah 41:8.

The man who controls the rudder decides where the ship will go. The ship goes where the man wants. [5] It is the same with the tongue. It is a small part of the body, but it boasts about doing great things.

A big forest fire can be started with only a little flame. [6] And the tongue is like a fire. It is a whole world of evil among the parts of our bodies. The tongue spreads its evil through the whole body. It starts a fire that influences all of life. The tongue gets this fire from hell. [7] People can tame every kind of wild animal, bird, reptile, and fish, and they have tamed them. [8] But no one can tame the tongue. It is wild and evil. It is full of poison that can kill. [9] We use our tongues to praise our Lord and Father, but then we curse people. And God made them like himself. [10] Praises and curses come from the same mouth! My brothers, this should not happen. [11] Do good and bad water flow from the same spring? [12] My brothers, can a fig tree make olives? Can a grapevine make figs? No! And a well full of salty water cannot give good water.

True Wisdom

[13] Is there anyone among you who is truly wise and understanding? Then he should show his wisdom by living right. He should do good things without being proud. A wise person does not boast. [14] But if you are selfish and have bitter jealousy in your hearts, you have no reason to boast. Your boasting is a lie that hides the truth. [15] That kind of "wisdom" does not come from God. That "wisdom" comes from the world. It is not spiritual. It is from the devil. [16] Where there is jealousy and selfishness, there will be confusion and every kind of evil. [17] But the wisdom that comes from God is like this: first, it is pure. Then it is also peaceful, gentle, and easy to please. This wisdom is always ready to help those who are troubled and to do good for others. This wisdom is always fair and honest. [18] When people work for peace in a peaceful way, they receive the good result of their good living.

Give Yourselves to God

4 Do you know where your fights and arguments come from? They come from the selfish desires that make war inside you. [2] You want things, but you do not have them. So you are ready to kill and are jealous of other people. But you still cannot get what you want. So you argue and fight. You do not get what you want because you do not ask God. [3] Or when you ask, you do not receive because the reason you ask is wrong. You want things only so that you can use them for your own pleasures.

[4] So, you people are not loyal to God! You should know that loving the world is the same as hating God. So if a person wants to be a friend of the world, he makes himself God's enemy. [5] Do you think the Scripture[d] means nothing? It says, "The Spirit[d] that God made to live in us wants us for himself alone."[n] [6] But God gives us even more grace, as the Scripture says,

"God is against the proud,
but he gives grace to the
humble."   *Proverbs 3:34*

[7] So give yourselves to God. Stand against the devil, and the devil will run away from you. [8] Come near to God, and God will come near to you. You are sinners. So clean sin out of your lives. You are trying to follow God and the world at the same time. Make your

---

"The Spirit . . . alone." These words may be from Exodus 20:5.

thinking pure. [9]Be sad, cry, and weep! Change your laughter into crying. Change your joy into sadness. [10]Don't be too proud before the Lord, and he will make you great.

You Are Not the Judge

[11]Brothers, do not say bad things about each other. If you say bad things about your brother in Christ or judge him, then you are saying bad things about the law he follows. You are also judging the law he follows. And when you are judging the law, you are not a follower of the law. You have become a judge! [12]God is the only One who makes laws, and he is the only Judge. He is the only One who can save and destroy. So it is not right for you to judge your neighbour.

Let God Plan Your Life

[13]Some of you say, "Today or tomorrow we will go to some city. We will stay there a year, do business, and make money." [14]But you do not know what will happen tomorrow! Your life is like a mist. You can see it for a short time, but then it goes away. [15]So you should say, "If the Lord wants, we will live and do this or that." [16]But now you are proud and you boast. All of this boasting is wrong. [17]And when a person knows the right thing to do, but does not do it, then he is sinning.

A Warning to the Rich

5 You rich people, listen! Cry and be very sad because of the trouble that will come to you. [2]Your riches will rot, and your clothes will be eaten by moths. [3]Your gold and silver will rust, and rust will be a proof that you were wrong. It will eat your bodies like fire. You saved your treasure for the last days. [4]Men worked in your fields, but you did not pay them. They harvested your crops and are crying out against you. Now the Lord of heaven's armies has heard their cries. [5]Your life on earth was full of rich living. You pleased yourselves with everything you wanted. You made yourselves fat, like an animal ready to be killed. [6]You showed no mercy to the innocent man. You murdered him. He cannot stand against you.

Be Patient

[7]Brothers, be patient until the Lord comes again. A farmer is patient. He waits for his valuable crop to grow from the earth. He waits patiently for it to receive the first rain and the last rain. [8]You, too, must be patient. Do not give up hope. The Lord is coming soon. [9]Brothers, do not complain

James 5:2 Your riches will rot, and your clothes will be eaten by moths.

against each other. If you do not stop complaining, you will be judged guilty. And the Judge is ready to come! [10] Brothers, follow the example of the prophets[d] who spoke for the Lord. They suffered many hard things, but they were patient. [11] We say they are happy because they were able to do this. You have heard about Job's patience. You know that after all his trouble, the Lord helped him. This shows that the Lord is full of mercy and is kind.

Be Careful What You Say

[12] My brothers, it is very important that you do not use an oath when you make a promise. Don't use the name of heaven, earth, or anything else to prove what you say. When you mean yes, say only "yes". When you mean no, say only "no". Do this so that you will not be judged guilty.

The Power of Prayer

[13] If one of you is having troubles, he should pray. If one of you is happy, he should sing praises. [14] If one of you is sick, he should call the church's elders.[d] The elders should pour oil on him[n] in the name of the Lord and pray for him. [15] And the prayer that is said with faith will make the sick person well. The Lord will heal him. And if he has sinned, God will forgive him. [16] Confess your sins to each other and pray for each other. Do this so that God can heal you. When a good man prays, great things happen. [17] Elijah was a man just like us. He prayed that it would not rain. And it did not rain on the land for three and a half years! [18] Then Elijah prayed again. And the rain came down from the sky, and the land grew crops again.

Saving a Soul

[19] My brothers, one of you may wander away from the truth. And someone may help him come back. [20] Remember this: anyone who brings a sinner back from the wrong way will save that sinner's soul from death. By doing this, that person will cause many sins to be forgiven.

---

pour oil on him   Oil was used like medicine, so that is probably how the believers used it.

1 PETER

Encouragement for Suffering Christians

1 From Peter, an apostle*d* of Jesus Christ.

To God's chosen people who are away from their homes. You are scattered all around the countries of Pontus, Galatia, Cappadocia, Asia, and Bithynia. ²God planned long ago to choose you by making you his holy people. Making you holy is the Spirit's*d* work. God wanted you to obey him and to be made clean by the blood of the death of Jesus Christ. Grace and peace be yours more and more.

A Living Hope

³Praise be to the God and Father of our Lord Jesus Christ. God has great mercy, and because of his mercy he gave us a new life. He gave us a living hope because Jesus Christ rose from death. ⁴Now we hope for the blessings God has for his children. These blessings are kept for you in heaven. They cannot be destroyed or be spoiled or lose their beauty. ⁵God's power protects you through your faith, and it keeps you safe until your salvation comes. That salvation is ready to be given to you at the end of time. ⁶This makes you very happy. But now for a short time different kinds of troubles may make you sad. ⁷These troubles come to prove that your faith is pure. This purity of faith is worth more than gold. Gold can be proved to be pure by fire, but gold can be destroyed. But the purity of your faith will bring you praise and glory and honour when Jesus Christ comes again. ⁸You have not seen Christ, but still you love him.

You cannot see him now, but you believe in him. You are filled with a joy that cannot be explained. And that joy is full of glory. ⁹Your faith has a goal, to save your souls. And you are receiving that goal – your salvation.

¹⁰The prophets*d* searched carefully and tried to learn about this salvation.They spoke about the grace that was coming to you. ¹¹The Spirit*d* of Christ was in the prophets. And the Spirit was telling about the sufferings that would happen to Christ and about the glory that would come after those sufferings. The prophets tried to learn about what the Spirit was showing them. They tried to learn when those things would happen and what the world would be like at that time. ¹²It was shown to them that their service was not for themselves. It was for you. They were serving you when they told about the truths you have now heard. The men who preached the Good News*d* to you told you those things. They did it with the help of the Holy Spirit that was sent from heaven. These are truths that even the angels long to know about.

A Call to Holy Living

¹³So prepare your minds for service and have self-control. All your hope should be for the gift of grace that will be yours when Jesus Christ comes again. ¹⁴In the past you did not understand, so you did the evil things you wanted. But now you are children of God who obey. So do not live as you lived in the past. ¹⁵But be holy in all

that you do, just as God is holy. God is the One who called you. [16]It is written in the Scriptures:[d] "You must be holy, because I am holy."[n]

[17]You pray to God and call him Father. And this Father judges each man's work equally. So while you are here on earth, you should live with respect for God. [18]You know that in the past you were living in a worthless way. You got that way of living from the people who lived before you. But you were saved from that useless life. You were bought, but not with something that can be destroyed like gold or silver. [19]You were bought with the precious blood of the death of Christ, who was like a pure and perfect lamb. [20]Christ was chosen before the world was made. But he was shown to the world in these last times for you. [21]You believe in God through Christ. God raised Christ from death and gave him glory. So your faith and your hope are in God.

[22]Now you have made yourselves pure by obeying the truth. Now you can have true love for your brothers. So love each other deeply with all your heart. [23]You have been born again. This new life did not come from something that dies, but from something that cannot die. You were born again through God's living message that continues for ever. [24]The Scripture says,

"All people are like the grass.
    And all their strength is like the
        flowers of the field.
The grass dies and the flowers
        fall,
[25]but the word of the Lord will live
        for ever."   *Isaiah 40:6–8*
And this is the word that was preached to you.

Jesus Is the Living Stone

2 So then, get rid of all evil and all lying. Do not be a hypocrite.[d] Do not be jealous or speak evil of others. Put all these things out of your life. [2]As newborn babies want milk, you should want the pure and simple teaching. By it you can grow up and be saved. [3]For you have already examined and seen how good the Lord is.

[4]The Lord Jesus is the "stone"[n] that lives. The people of the world did not want this stone. But he was the stone God chose. To God he was worth much. So come to him. [5]You also are like living stones. Let yourselves be used to build a spiritual temple – to be holy priests who offer spiritual sacrifices to God. He will accept those sacrifices through Jesus Christ. [6]The Scripture[d] says:

"I will put a stone in the ground in
    Jerusalem.
Everything will be built on this
    important and precious rock.
Anyone who trusts in him
    will never be disappointed."
                          Isaiah 28:16
[7]This stone is worth a great deal to you who believe. But to the people who do not believe, he is

"the stone that the builders did
    not want.
It has become the
    cornerstone."[d]   *Psalm 118:22*
[8]To people who do not believe, he is

"a stone that causes people to
    stumble.
It is a rock that makes them
    fall."   *Isaiah 8:14*
They stumble because they do not obey what God says. This is what God planned to happen to them.

"You must be . . . holy." Quotation from Leviticus 11:45; 19:2; 20:7.
"stone" The most important stone in God's spiritual temple or house (his people).

[9] But you are chosen people. You are the King's priests. You are a holy nation. You are a nation that belongs to God alone. God chose you to tell of the wonderful things he has done. He called you out of darkness into his wonderful light. [10] At one time you were not God's people, but now you are his people. In the past you had never received mercy, but now you have received God's mercy.

Live for God

[11] Dear friends, you are like visitors and strangers in this world. So I beg you to stay away from the evil things your bodies want to do. These things fight against your soul. [12] People who do not believe are living all around you. They might say that you are doing wrong. So live good lives. Then they will see the good things you do, and they will give glory to God on the day when Christ comes again.

Obey Every Human Authority

[13] Obey the people who have authority in this world. Do this for the Lord. Obey the king, who is the highest authority. [14] And obey the leaders who are sent by the king. They are sent to punish those who do wrong and to praise those who do right. [15] So when you do good, you stop foolish people from saying stupid things about you. This is what God wants. [16] Live as free men. But do not use your freedom as an excuse to do evil. Live as servants of God. [17] Show respect for all people. Love the brothers and sisters of God's family. Respect God. Honour the king.

Follow Christ's Example

[18] Slaves, accept the authority of your masters. Do this with all respect. You should obey masters who are good and kind, and you should obey masters who are bad. [19] A person might have to suffer even when he has done nothing wrong. But if he thinks of God and bears the pain, this pleases God. [20] If you are punished for doing wrong, there is no reason to praise you for bearing punishment. But if you suffer for doing good, and you are patient, then that pleases God. [21] That is what you were called to do. Christ suffered for you. He gave you an example to follow. So you should do as he did.

[22] "He did no sin.
      He never lied."   *Isaiah 53:9*
[23] People insulted Christ, but he did not insult them in return. Christ suffered, but he did not threaten. He let God take care of him. God is the One who judges rightly. [24] Christ carried our sins in his body on the cross. He did this so that we would stop living for sin and start living for what is right. And we are healed because of his wounds. [25] You were like sheep that went the wrong way. But now you have come back to the Shepherd and Protector of your souls.

Wives and Husbands

3 In the same way, you wives should accept the authority of your husbands. Then, if some husbands have not obeyed God's teaching, they will be persuaded to believe. You will not need to say a word to them. They will be persuaded by the way their wives live. [2] Your husbands will see the pure lives that you live with your respect for God. [3] It is not fancy hair, gold jewellery, or fine clothes that should make you beautiful. [4] No, your beauty should come from within you – the beauty of a gentle and quiet spirit. This beauty will never disappear, and it is worth a great deal to God. [5] It was the same with the holy women who lived long ago and followed God. They

1 Peter 3:3 It is not fancy hair, gold jewellery, or fine clothes that should make you beautiful.

made themselves beautiful in this way. They accepted the authority of their husbands. ⁶Sarah obeyed Abraham, her husband, and called him her master. And you women are true children of Sarah if you always do what is right and are not afraid.

⁷In the same way, you husbands should live with your wives in an understanding way. You should show respect to them. They are weaker than you. But God gives them the same blessing that he gives you – the grace that gives true life. Do this so that nothing will stop your prayers.

Suffering for Doing Right

⁸Finally, all of you should live together in peace. Try to understand each other. Love each other as brothers. Be kind and humble. ⁹Do not do wrong to a person to pay him back for doing wrong to you. Or do not insult someone to pay him back for insulting you. But ask God to bless that person. Do this, because you yourselves were called to receive a blessing. ¹⁰The Scripture*ᵈ* says,

"A person must do these things
to enjoy life and have many,
happy days.
He must not say evil things.
He must not tell lies.
¹¹He must stop doing evil and do
good.
He must look for peace and
work for it.
¹²The Lord sees the good people.
He listens to their prayers.
But the Lord is against
those who do evil." *Psalm 34:12–16*
¹³If you are always trying to do good, no one can really hurt you. ¹⁴But you may suffer for doing right. Even if that happens, you are blessed.
"Don't be afraid of the things they
fear.
Do not dread those things.
¹⁵But respect Christ as the holy
Lord in your hearts."
Isaiah 8:12–13
Always be ready to answer everyone who asks you to explain about the hope you have. ¹⁶But answer in a gentle way and with respect. Always feel that you are doing right. Then, those who speak evil of your good life in Christ will be made ashamed. ¹⁷It is better to suffer for doing good than for doing wrong. Yes, it is better, if that is what God wants. ¹⁸Christ himself died for you. And that one death paid for your sins. He was not guilty, but he died for those who are guilty. He did this to bring you all to God. His body was killed, but he was made alive in the spirit. ¹⁹And in the spirit he went and preached to the spirits in prison. ²⁰These were the spirits who refused to obey God long ago in the time of

Noah. God was waiting patiently for them while Noah was building the boat. Only a few people – eight in all – were saved by water. [21]That water is like baptism that now saves you – not the washing of dirt from the body, but the promise made to God from a good heart. And this is because Jesus Christ was raised from death. [22]Now Jesus has gone into heaven and is at God's right side. He rules over angels, authorities, and powers.

Changed Lives

4 Christ suffered while he was in his body. So you should strengthen yourselves with the same way of thinking Christ had. The person who has suffered in his body is finished with sin. [2]Strengthen yourselves so that you will live your lives here on earth doing what God wants, not doing the evil things that people want. [3]In the past you wasted too much time doing what the non-believers like to do. You were guilty of sexual sins and had evil desires. You were getting drunk, you had wild and drunken parties, and you did wrong by worshipping idols. [4]Non-believers think it is strange that you do not do the many wild and wasteful things that they do. And so they insult you. [5]But they will have to explain about what they have done. They must explain to God who is ready to judge the living and the dead. [6]The Good News[d] was preached to those who are now dead. By their dying, they were judged like all men. But the Good News was preached to them so that they could live in the spirit as God lives.

Use God's Gifts Wisely

[7]The time is near when all things will end. So keep your minds clear, and control yourselves. Then you will be able to pray. [8]Most importantly, love each other deeply. Love has a way of not looking at others' sins. [9]Open your homes to each other, without complaining. [10]Each of you received a spiritual gift. God has shown you his grace in giving you different gifts. And you are like servants who are responsible for using God's gifts. So be good servants and use your gifts to serve each other. [11]Anyone who speaks should speak words from God. The person who serves should serve with the strength that God gives. You should do these things so that in everything God will be praised through Jesus Christ. Power and glory belong to him for ever and ever. Amen.

Suffering as a Christian

[12]My friends, do not be surprised at the painful things you are now suffering. These things are testing your faith. So do not think that something strange is happening to you. [13]But you should be happy that you are sharing in Christ's sufferings. You will be happy and full of joy when Christ comes again in glory. [14]When people insult you because you follow Christ, then you are blessed. You are blessed because the glorious Spirit,[d] the Spirit of God, is with you. [15]Do not suffer for murder, theft, or any other crime, nor because you trouble other people. [16]But if you suffer because you are a Christian, then do not be ashamed. You should praise God because you wear that name. [17]It is time for judgement to begin, and it will begin with God's family. If that judging begins with us, what will happen to those people who do not obey the Good News[d] of God?

[18]"It is very hard for a good person
        to be saved.
    Then the wicked person and

the sinner will surely be lost!"[n]

[19] So then those who suffer as God wants them to should trust their souls to him. God is the One who made them, and they can trust him. So they should continue to do what is right.

The Flock of God

5 Now I have something to say to the elders[d] in your group. I am also an elder. I myself have seen Christ's sufferings. And I will share in the glory that will be shown to us. I beg you to [2] take care of God's flock, his people, that you are responsible for. Watch over it because you want to, not because you are forced to do it. That is how God wants it. Do it because you are happy to serve, not because you want money. [3] Do not be like a ruler over people you are responsible for. Be good examples to them. [4] Then when Christ, the Head Shepherd, comes, you will

1 Peter 5:4 You will get a crown . . . and it will never lose its beauty.

get a crown. This crown will be glorious, and it will never lose its beauty.

[5] In the same way, younger men should be willing to be under older men. And all of you should be very humble with each other.

"God is against the proud,
but he gives grace to the
humble."   *Proverbs 3:34*

[6] So be humble under God's powerful hand. Then he will lift you up when the right time comes. [7] Give all your worries to him, because he cares for you.

[8] Control yourselves and be careful! The devil is your enemy. And he goes around like a roaring lion looking for someone to eat. [9] Refuse to give in to the devil. Stand strong in your faith. You know that your Christian brothers and sisters all over the world are having the same sufferings you have.

[10] Yes, you will suffer for a short time. But after that, God will make everything right. He will make you strong. He will support you and keep you from falling. He is the God who gives all grace. He called you to share in his glory in Christ. That glory will continue for ever. [11] All power is his for ever and ever. Amen.

Final Greetings

[12] I wrote this short letter with the help of Silas. I know that he is a faithful brother in Christ. I wrote to comfort and encourage you. I wanted to tell you that this is the true grace of God. Stand strong in that grace.

[13] The church in Babylon sends you greetings. They were chosen the same as you. Mark, my son in Christ, also greets you. [14] Give each other a kiss of Christian love when you meet.

Peace to all of you who are in Christ.

"It . . . lost!"   Quotation from Proverbs 11:31 in the Septuagint, the Greek version of the Old Testament.

2 PETER

Correcting False Teachings

1 From Simon Peter, a servant and apostle[d] of Jesus Christ.

To you who have received a faith as valuable as ours. You received that faith because our God and Saviour Jesus Christ is fair and does what is right.

[2] Grace and peace be given to you more and more. You will have grace and peace because you truly know God and Jesus our Lord.

God Has Given Us Blessings

[3] Jesus has the power of God. His power has given us everything we need to live and to serve God. We have these things because we know him. Jesus called us by his glory and goodness. [4] Through his glory and goodness, he gave us the very great and rich gifts he promised us. With those gifts you can share in being like God. And so the world will not ruin you with its evil desires.

[5] Because you have these blessings, you should try as much as you can to add these things to your lives: to your faith, add goodness; and to your goodness, add knowledge; [6] and to your knowledge, add self-control; and to your self-control, add the ability to hold on; and to your ability to hold on, add service for God; [7] and to your service for God, add kindness for your brothers and sisters in Christ; and to this kindness, add love. [8] If all these things are in you and are growing, they will help you never to be useless. They will help your knowledge of our Lord Jesus Christ make your lives better. [9] But if anyone does not have these things, he cannot see clearly. He is blind. He has forgotten that he was made clean from his past sins.

[10] My brothers, God called you and chose you to be his. Try hard to show that you really are God's chosen people. If you do all these things, you will never fall. [11] And you will be given a very great welcome into the kingdom of our Lord and Saviour Jesus Christ. That kingdom continues for ever.

[12] You know these things, and you are very strong in the truth. But I will always help you to remember these things. [13] I think it is right for me to help you remember while I am still living here on earth. [14] I know that I must soon leave this body. Our Lord Jesus Christ has shown me that. [15] I will try the best I can to help you remember these things always. I want you to be able to remember them even after I am gone.

We Saw Christ's Glory

[16] We have told you about the powerful coming of our Lord Jesus Christ. What we told you were not just clever stories that someone invented. But we saw the greatness of Jesus with our own eyes. [17] Jesus heard the voice of God, the Greatest Glory. That was when Jesus received honour and glory from God the Father. The voice said, "This is my Son, and I love him. I am very pleased with him." [18] We heard that voice. It came from heaven while we were with Jesus on the holy mountain.

[19] This makes us more sure about

the message the prophets[d] gave. And it is good for you to follow closely what they said. Their message is like a light shining in a dark place. That light shines until the day begins and the morning star rises in your hearts. [20]Most of all, you must understand this: no prophecy in the Scriptures[d] ever comes from the prophet's own interpretation. [21]No prophecy ever came from what a man wanted to say. But men led by the Holy Spirit[d] spoke words from God.

False Teachers

2 There used to be false prophets[d] among God's people, just as there are now. And you will have some false teachers in your group. They will secretly teach things that are wrong – teachings that will cause people to be lost. They will even refuse to accept the Master, Jesus, who bought their freedom. And so they will quickly destroy themselves. [2]Many will follow their evil ways and say evil things about the Way of truth. [3]Those false teachers only want your money. So they will use you by telling you what is not true. But God has already judged them guilty. And they will not escape the One who will destroy them.

[4]When angels sinned, God did not let them go free without punishment. God sent them to hell and put them in caves of darkness. They are being held there to be judged. [5]And God punished the evil people who lived long ago. He brought a flood to the world that was full of people who were against him. But God saved Noah and seven other people with him. Noah was a man who preached about being right with God. [6]And God also punished the evil cities of Sodom and Gomorrah.[n] He burned those cities

until there was nothing left but ashes. He made those cities an example to show what will happen to those who are against God. [7]But God saved Lot from those cities. Lot, a good man, was troubled because of the dirty lives of evil people. [8](Lot was a good man, but he lived with evil people every day. His good heart was hurt by the evil things that he saw and heard.) [9]And so the Lord knows how to save those who serve him. He will save them when troubles come. And the Lord will hold evil people and punish them, while waiting for the Judgement Day. [10]That punishment is especially for those who live by doing the evil things their sinful selves want, and for those who hate the Lord's authority.

These false teachers do anything they want and boast about it. They are not afraid to say bad things about the glorious angels. [11]The angels are much stronger and more powerful than false teachers. But even the angels do not accuse them with insults before the Lord. [12]But these men say bad things about what they do not understand. They are like animals that act without thinking. These animals are born to be caught and killed. And, like wild animals, these false teachers will be destroyed. [13]They have caused many people to suffer; so they themselves will suffer. That is their pay for what they have done. They take pleasure in doing evil things openly. So they are like dirty spots and stains among you. They bring shame to you in the meals that you eat together. [14]Every time they look at a woman they want her. Their desire for sin is never satisfied. They lead weak people into the trap of sin. They have taught their hearts to be selfish. God will punish them. [15]These false teachers left

Sodom and Gomorrah   Two cities God destroyed because the people were so evil.

the right road and lost their way. They followed the way that Balaam went. Balaam was the son of Beor, who loved being paid for doing wrong. [16]But a donkey told Balaam that he was sinning. And the donkey is an animal that cannot talk. But the donkey spoke with a man's voice and stopped the prophet's mad thinking.

[17]Those false teachers are like rivers that have no water. They are like clouds blown by a storm. A place in the blackest darkness has been kept for them. [18]They boast with words that mean nothing. By their evil desires they lead people into the trap of sin. They lead away people who are just beginning to escape from other people who live in error. [19]They promise them freedom, but they themselves are not free. They are slaves of things that will be destroyed. For a person is a slave of anything that controls him. [20]They were made free from the evil in the world by knowing our Lord and Saviour Jesus Christ. But if they return to evil things and those things control them, then it is worse for them than it was before. [21]Yes, it would be better for them to have never known the right way. That would be better than to know the right way and then to turn away from the holy teaching that was given to them. [22]What they did is like this true saying: "A dog eats what it throws up."[n] And, "After a pig is washed, it goes back and rolls in the mud."

Jesus Will Come Again

3 My friends, this is the second letter I have written to you. I wrote both letters to you to help your honest minds remember something. [2]I want you to remember the words that the

2 Peter 2:22 "After a pig is washed, it goes back and rolls in the mud."

holy prophets[d] spoke in the past. And remember the command that our Lord and Saviour gave us through your apostles.[d] [3]It is important for you to understand what will happen in the last days. People will laugh at you. They will live doing the evil things they want to do. [4]They will say, "Jesus promised to come again. Where is he? Our fathers have died. But the world continues the way it has been since it was made." [5]But they do not want to remember what happened long ago. God spoke and made heaven and earth. He made the earth from water and with water. [6]Then the world was flooded and destroyed with water. [7]And that same word of God is keeping heaven and earth that we have now. They are being kept to be destroyed by fire. They are being kept for the Judgement Day and the destruction of all who are against God.

⁸But do not forget this one thing, dear friends: to the Lord one day is as a thousand years, and a thousand years is as one day. ⁹The Lord is not slow in doing what he promised – the way some people understand slowness. But God is being patient with you. He does not want anyone to be lost. He wants everyone to change his heart and life.

¹⁰But the day the Lord comes again will be a surprise, like a thief. The skies will disappear with a loud noise. Everything in the skies will be destroyed by fire. And the earth and everything in it will be burned up.ⁿ ¹¹In that way everything will be destroyed. So what kind of people should you be? You should live holy lives and serve God. ¹²You should wait for the day of God and look forward to its coming. When that day comes, the skies will be destroyed with fire, and everything in the skies will melt with heat. ¹³But God made a promise to us. And we are waiting for what he promised – a new

heaven and a new earth where goodness lives.

¹⁴Dear friends, we are waiting for this to happen. So try as hard as you can to be without sin and without fault. Try to be at peace with God. ¹⁵Remember that we are saved because our Lord is patient. Our dear brother Paul told you the same thing when he wrote to you with the wisdom that God gave him. ¹⁶Paul writes about this in all his letters. Sometimes there are things in Paul's letters that are hard to understand. And some people explain these things falsely. They are ignorant and weak in faith. They also falsely explain the other Scriptures.ᵈ But they are destroying themselves by doing that.

¹⁷Dear friends, you already know about this. So be careful. Do not let those evil people lead you away by the wrong they do. Be careful so that you will not fall from your strong faith. ¹⁸But grow in the grace and knowledge of our Lord and Saviour Jesus Christ. Glory be to him now and for ever! Amen.

---

will be burned up Many Greek copies say, "will be found". One copy says, "will disappear".

1 JOHN

Love One Another

1 We write to you now about something that has always existed.
We have heard.
We have seen with our own eyes.
We have watched,
and we have touched with our hands.
We write to you about the Word[n] that gives life. [2] He who gives life was shown to us. We saw him, and we can give proof about it. And now we tell you that he has life that continues for ever. The One who gives this life was with God the Father. God showed him to us. [3] Now we tell you what we have seen and heard because we want you to have fellowship with us. The fellowship we share together is with God the Father and his Son, Jesus Christ. [4] We write this to you so that you can be full of joy with us.

God Forgives Our Sins

[5] Here is the message we have heard from God and now tell to you: God is light,[n] and in him there is no darkness at all. [6] So if we say that we have fellowship with God, but we continue living in darkness, then we are liars. We do not follow the truth. [7] God is in the light. We should live in the light, too. If we live in the light, we share fellowship with each other. And when we live in the light, the blood of the death of Jesus, God's Son, is making us clean from every sin.
[8] If we say that we have no sin, we are fooling ourselves, and the truth is not in us. [9] But if we confess our sins, he will forgive our sins. We can trust God. He does what is right. He will make us clean from all the wrongs we have done. [10] If we say that we have not sinned, then we make God a liar. We do not accept God's true teaching.

Jesus Is Our Helper

2 My dear children, I write this letter to you so that you will not sin. But if anyone does sin, we have Jesus Christ to help us. He is the Righteous One. He defends us before God the Father. [2] Jesus is the way our sins are taken away. And Jesus is the way that all people can have their sins taken away, too.
[3] If we obey what God has told us to do, then we are sure that we truly know God. [4] If someone says, "I know God!" but does not obey God's commands, then he is a liar. The truth is not in him. [5] But if someone obeys God's teaching, then God's love has truly arrived at its goal in him. This is how we know that we are following God: [6] whoever says that God lives in him must live as Jesus lived.

The Command to Love Others

[7] My dear friends, I am not writing a new command to you. It is the same command you have had since the beginning. It is the teaching you have already heard. [8] But I am writing a new

---

Word The Greek word is "logos", meaning any kind of communication. It could be translated "message". Here, it means Christ. Christ was the way God told people about himself.
light This word is used to show what God is like. It means goodness or truth.

command to you. This command is true; you can see its truth in Jesus and in yourselves. The darkness is passing away, and the true light is already shining.

[9] Someone says, "I am in the light."[n] But if he hates his brother, he is still in the darkness. [10] Whoever loves his brother lives in the light, and there is nothing in him that will cause him to do wrong. [11] But whoever hates his brother is in darkness. He lives in darkness and does not know where he is going. The darkness has made him blind.

[12] I write to you, dear children,
　　because your sins are forgiven
　　　　through Christ.
[13] I write to you, fathers,
　　because you know the One
　　　　who existed from the
　　　　beginning.
　I write to you, young men,
　　because you have defeated the
　　　　Evil One.
[14] I write to you, children,
　　because you know the Father.
　I write to you, fathers,
　　because you know the One
　　　　who existed from the
　　　　beginning.
　I write to you, young men,
　　because you are strong;
　the word of God lives in you,
　and you have defeated the Evil
　　　　One.

[15] Do not love the world or the things in the world. If anyone loves the world, the love of the Father is not in him. [16] These are the evil things in the world: wanting things to please our sinful selves; wanting the sinful things we see; being too proud of the things we have. But none of those things comes from the Father. All of them come from the world. [17] The world is passing away. And everything that people want in the world is passing away. But the person who does what God wants lives for ever.

Reject the Enemies of Christ

[18] My dear children, the end is near! You have heard that the Enemy of Christ[d] is coming. And now many enemies of Christ are already here. So we know that the end is near. [19] Those enemies of Christ were in our group. But they left us. They did not really belong with us. If they were really part of our group, then they would have stayed with us. But they left. This shows that none of them really belonged with us.

[20] You have the gift[n] that the Holy One gave you. So you all know the truth. [21] Why do I write to you? Do I write because you do not know the truth? No, I write this letter because you do know the truth. And you know that no lie comes from the truth.

[22] So who is the liar? It is the person who says Jesus is not the Christ. A person who says Jesus is not the Christ is the enemy of Christ. He does not believe in the Father or in his Son. [23] If anyone does not believe in the Son, he does not have the Father. But whoever accepts the Son has the Father, too.

[24] Be sure that you continue to follow the teaching that you heard from the beginning. If you continue in that teaching, you will stay in the Son and in the Father. [25] And this is what the Son promised to us – life for ever.

[26] I am writing this letter about those people who are trying to lead you the wrong way. [27] Christ gave you a special gift. You still have this gift in you. So

---

light This word is used to show what God is like. It means goodness or truth.
gift This might mean the Holy Spirit. Or it might mean teaching or truth as in verse 24.

you do not need any other teacher. The gift he gave you teaches you about everything. This gift is true, not false. So continue to live in Christ, as his gift taught you.

²⁸Yes, my dear children, live in him. If we do this, we can be without fear on the day when Christ comes back. We will not need to hide and be ashamed when he comes. ²⁹You know that Christ is righteous. So you know that all who do what is right are God's children.

We Are God's Children

3 The Father has loved us so much! He loved us so much that we are called children of God. And we really are his children. But the people in the world do not understand that we are God's children, because they have not known him. ²Dear friends, now we are children of God. We have not yet been shown what we will be in the future. But we know that when Christ comes again, we will be like him. We will see him as he really is. ³Christ is pure. And every person who has this hope in Christ keeps himself pure like Christ.

⁴When a person sins, he breaks God's law. Yes, sinning is the same as living against God's law. ⁵You know that Christ came to take away sins. There is no sin in Christ. ⁶So the person who lives in Christ does not go on sinning. If he goes on sinning, he has never really understood Christ and has never known him.

⁷Dear children, do not let any person lead you the wrong way. Christ is righteous. To be like Christ, a person must do what is right. ⁸The devil has been sinning since the beginning. Anyone who continues to sin

belongs to the devil. The Son of God came for this purpose: to destroy the devil's work.

⁹When God makes someone his child, that person does not go on sinning. The new life God gave that person stays in him. So he is not able to go on sinning, because he has become a child of God. ¹⁰So we can see who God's children are and who the devil's children are. Those who do not do what is right are not children of God, and anyone who does not love his brother is not a child of God.

We Must Love Each Other

¹¹This is the teaching you have heard from the beginning: we must love each other. ¹²Do not be like Cain who belonged to the Evil One. Cain killed his brother. He killed his brother because the things Cain did were evil, and the things his brother did were good.

¹³Brothers, do not be surprised when the people of this world hate you. ¹⁴We know that we have left death and have come into life. We know this because we love our brothers in Christ. Whoever does not love is still in death. ¹⁵Everyone who hates his brother is a murderer.ⁿ And you know that no murderer has eternal life in him. ¹⁶This is how we know what real love is: Jesus gave his life for us. So we should give our lives for our brothers. ¹⁷Suppose a believer is rich enough to have all that he needs. He sees his brother in Christ who is poor and does not have what he needs. What if the believer does not help the poor brother? Then the believer does not have God's love in his heart. ¹⁸My children, our love should not be only words and talk. Our love must be true

Everyone ... murderer. If a person hates his brother in Christ, then in his mind he has killed his brother. Jesus explained this sin to his followers (Matthew 5:21–26).

love. And we should show that love by what we do.

[19-20]This is the way we know that we belong to the way of truth. When our hearts make us feel guilty, we can still have peace before God. God is greater than our hearts, and he knows everything.

[21]My dear friends, if we do not feel that we are doing wrong, we can be without fear when we come to God. [22]And God gives us the things we ask for. We receive these things because we obey God's commands, and we do what pleases him. [23]This is what God commands: that we believe in his Son, Jesus Christ, and that we love each other, just as he commanded. [24]The person who obeys God's commands lives in God. And God lives in him. How do we know that God lives in us? We know because of the Spirit[d] God gave us.

Warning Against False Teachers

4 My dear friends, many false prophets[d] are in the world now. So do not believe every spirit. But test the spirits to see if they are from God. [2]This is how you can know God's Spirit:[d] one spirit says, "I believe that Jesus is the Christ who came to earth and became a man." That Spirit is from God. [3]Another spirit refuses to say this about Jesus. That spirit is not from God but is the spirit of the Enemy of Christ. You have heard that the Enemy of Christ is coming. And now he is already in the world.

[4]My dear children, you belong to God. So you have defeated them because God's Spirit, who is in you, is greater than the devil, who is in the world. [5]And they belong to the world. What they say is from the world, and the world listens to them. [6]But we are from God, and those who know God listen to us. But those who are not from God do not listen to us. That is how we know the Spirit that is true and the spirit that is false.

Love Comes from God

[7]Dear friends, we should love each other, because love comes from God. The person who loves has become God's child and knows God. [8]Whoever does not love does not know God, because God is love. [9]This is how God showed his love to us: he sent his only Son into the world to give us life through him. [10]True love is God's love for us, not our love for God. God sent his Son to be the way to take away our sins.

[11]That is how much God loved us, dear friends! So we also must love each other. [12]No one has ever seen God. But if we love each other, God lives in us. If we love each other, God's love has reached its goal. It is made perfect in us.

[13]We know that we live in God and God lives in us. We know this because God gave us his Spirit.[d] [14]We have seen that the Father sent his Son to be the Saviour of the world. That is what we teach. [15]If someone says, "I believe that Jesus is the Son of God," then God lives in him. And he lives in God. [16]And so we know the love that God has for us, and we trust that love.

God is love. Whoever lives in love lives in God, and God lives in him. [17]If God's love is made perfect in us, then we can be without fear on the day God judges us. We will be without fear, because in this world we are like him. [18]Where God's love is, there is no fear, because God's perfect love takes away fear. It is punishment that makes a person fear. So love is not made perfect in the person who has fear.

[19]We love because God first loved us. [20]If someone says, "I love God," but hates his brother, he is a liar. He

can see his brother, but he hates him. So he cannot love God, whom he has never seen. [21]And God gave us this command: whoever loves God must also love his brother.

Faith in the Son of God

5 Everyone who believes that Jesus is the Christ[d] is God's child. The person who loves the Father also loves the Father's children. [2]How do we know that we love God's children? We know because we love God and we obey his commands. [3]Loving God means obeying his commands. And God's commands are not too hard for us. [4]Everyone who is a child of God has the power to win against the world. It is our faith that wins the victory against the world. [5]So the one who wins against the world is the person who believes that Jesus is the Son of God.

[6]Jesus Christ is the One who came with water[n] and with blood.[n] He did not come by water only. He came by both water and blood. And the Spirit[d] says that this is true. The Spirit is the truth. [7]So there are three witnesses that tell us about Jesus: [8]the Spirit, the water, and the blood. These three witnesses agree. [9]We believe people when they say something is true. But what God says is more important. And he has told us the truth about his own Son. [10]Anyone who believes in the Son of God has the truth that God told us. Anyone who does not believe makes God a liar. He does not believe what God told us about his Son. [11]This is what God told us: God has given us eternal life, and this life is in his Son. [12]Whoever has the Son has life. But the person who does not have the Son of God does not have life.

We Have Eternal Life Now

[13]I write this letter to you who believe in the Son of God. I write so that you will know that you have eternal life now. [14]We can come to God with no doubts. This means that when we ask God for things (and those things agree with what God wants for us), then God cares about what we say. [15]God listens to us every time we ask him. So we know that he gives us the things that we ask from him.

1 John 5:15 God listens to us every time we ask him.

[16]Suppose someone sees his brother in Christ sinning (sin that does not lead to eternal death). That person should pray for his brother who is sinning. Then God will give the brother life. I am talking about people whose sin does not lead to eternal death. There is sin that leads to death. I do not mean that a person should pray about that sin. [17]Doing wrong is

---

water This probably means the water of Jesus' baptism.
blood This probably means the blood of Jesus' death.

always sin. But there is sin that does not lead to eternal death.

[18] We know that anyone who is God's child does not continue to sin. The Son of God keeps him safe, and the Evil One cannot hurt him. [19] We know that we belong to God. But the Evil One controls the whole world.

[20] And we know that the Son of God has come and has given us understanding. Now we can know God, the One who is true. And our lives are in that true God and in his Son, Jesus Christ. He is the true God, and he is eternal life. [21] So, dear children, keep yourselves away from false gods.

2 JOHN

Do Not Help False Teachers

[1] From the Elder.[n]

To the chosen lady[n] and to her children:

I love all of you in the truth.[n] Also, all those who know the truth love you. [2] We love you because of the truth – the truth that lives in us and will be with us for ever.

[3] Grace, mercy, and peace will be with us from God the Father and from his Son, Jesus Christ. And may we have these blessings in truth and love.

[4] I was very happy to learn about some of your children. I am happy that they are following the way of truth, as the Father commanded us. [5] And now, dear lady, I tell you: we should all love each other. This is not a new command. It is the same command we have had from the beginning. [6] And loving means living the way he commanded us to live. And God's command is this: that you live a life of love. You have heard this command from the beginning.

[7] Many false teachers are in the world now. They refuse to say that Jesus Christ came to earth and became a man. Anyone who refuses to say this is a false teacher and an enemy of Christ. [8] Be careful! Do not lose the reward that you have worked for. Be careful, so that you will receive your full reward.

[9] A person must continue to follow only the teaching of Christ. If he goes beyond Christ's teaching, then he does not have God. But if he continues following the teaching of Christ, then he has both the Father and the Son. [10] If someone comes to you, but does not bring this teaching, then do not accept him into your house. Do not welcome him. [11] If you accept him, you are helping him with his evil work.

[12] I have much to say to you, but I do not want to use paper and ink. Instead, I hope to come and visit you. Then we can be together and talk. That will make us very happy. [13] The children of your chosen sister[n] send you their love.

Elder This is probably John the apostle. "Elder" means an older man. It can also mean a special leader in the church (as in Titus 1:5).

lady This might mean a woman. Or, in this letter, it might mean a church. If it is a church, then "her children" would be the people of the church.

truth The truth or "Good News" about Jesus Christ that joins all believers together.

sister Sister of the "lady" in verse 1. This might be another woman or another church.

3 JOHN

Help Christians Who Teach Truth

[1] From the Elder.[n]

To my dear friend Gaius whom I love in the truth:[n]

[2] My dear friend, I know your soul is doing well. I pray that you are doing fine in every way and that your health is good. [3] Some brothers in Christ came and told me about the truth in your life. They said that you are following the way of truth. This made me very happy. [4] It always gives me the greatest joy when I hear that my children are following the way of truth.

[5] My dear friend, it is good that you continue to help the brothers. You are helping those that you do not even know! [6] These brothers told the church about the love you have. Please help them to continue their mission. Help them in a way that will please God. [7] They started out on their mission to serve Christ. They did not accept any help from those who are not believers. [8] So we should help these brothers. And when we do, we share in their work for the truth.

[9] I wrote a letter to the church. But Diotrephes will not listen to what we say. He always wants to be their leader. [10] When I come, I will talk about what Diotrephes is doing. He lies and says evil things about us. But that is not all he does. He refuses to help those who are working to serve Christ. He also stops those who want to help the brothers and puts them out of the church.

[11] My dear friend, do not follow what is bad; follow what is good. He who does what is good is from God. But he who does evil has never known God.

[12] Everyone says good things about Demetrius. And the truth agrees with what they say. Also, we say good about him. And you know that what we say is true.

[13] I have many things I want to tell you, but I do not want to use pen and ink. [14] I hope to visit you soon. Then we can be together and talk. [15] Peace to you. The friends here with me send their love. Please give our love to each one of the friends there.

Elder This is probably John the apostle. "Elder" means an older man. It can also mean a special leader in the church (as in Titus 1:5).

truth The truth or "Good News" about Jesus Christ that joins all believers together.

ACTS 12:7
The angel said, "Hurry! Get up!!"
And the chains fell off Peter's hands.

JUDE

Warnings About False Teachers

[1] From Jude, a servant of Jesus Christ and a brother of James.

To all who have been called by God. God the Father loves you, and you have been kept safe in Jesus Christ.

[2] All mercy, peace, and love be yours.

God Will Punish Sinners

[3] Dear friends, I wanted very much to write to you about the salvation we all share together. But I felt the need to write to you about something else: I want to encourage you to fight hard for the faith that God gave his holy people. God gave this faith once, and it is good for all time. [4] Some people have secretly entered your group. They have already been judged guilty for the things they are doing. Long ago the prophets[d] wrote about these people. They are against God. They have used the grace of our God in the wrong way – to do sinful things. They refuse to accept Jesus Christ, our only Master and Lord.

[5] I want to remind you of some things that you already know: remember that the Lord saved his people by bringing them out of the land of Egypt. But later the Lord destroyed all those who did not believe. [6] And remember the angels who had power but did not keep it. They left their own home. So the Lord has kept these angels in darkness. They are bound with everlasting chains, to be judged on the great day. [7] Also remember the cities of Sodom and Gomorrah[n] and the other towns around them. They acted as the angels who did not obey God. Their towns were full of sexual sin and men having sexual relations with men. They suffer the punishment of eternal fire, as an example for all to see.

[8] It is the same with these people who have entered your group. They are guided by dreams. They make themselves dirty with sin. They reject God's authority and say bad things against the glorious angels. [9] Not even the archangel[n] Michael did this. He argued with the devil about who would have the body of Moses. Michael did not dare to accuse the devil with insults. He said, "The Lord punish you." [10] But these people say bad things about what they do not understand. They do understand some things. But they understand them not by thinking, but by feeling, the way dumb animals understand things. And these are the very things that destroy them. [11] It will be bad for them. They have followed the way that Cain went. To make money, they have given themselves to doing the wrong that Balaam did. They have fought against God as Korah did. And like Korah, they will be destroyed. [12] They are like dirty spots in the special meals you share together. They eat with you and have no fear. They take care only of themselves. They are clouds without rain. The wind blows them around. They are trees that have no fruit when

---

Sodom and Gomorrah Two cities God destroyed because the people were so evil.
archangel The leader among God's angels or messengers.

it is time and are pulled out of the ground. So they are dead twice over. [13]They are like wild waves in the sea. These people do shameful things in the same way that waves make foam. They are like stars that wander in the sky. A place in the blackest darkness has been kept for them for ever.

[14]Enoch, the seventh descendant[d] from Adam, said this about these people: "Look, the Lord is coming with thousands and thousands of his holy angels. [15]The Lord will judge every person. He is coming to judge everyone and to punish all who are against God. He will punish them for all the evil they have done against him. And he will punish the sinners who are against God. He will punish them for all the evil things they have said against him."

[16]These people always complain and blame others. They always do the evil things they want to do. They boast about themselves. The only reason they say good things about other people is to get what they want.

A Warning and Things to Do

[17]Dear friends, remember what the apostles[d] of our Lord Jesus Christ said before. [18]They said to you, "In the last times there will be people who laugh about God. They will do only what they want to do – things that are against God." [19]These are the people who divide you. They do only what their sinful selves want. They do not have the Spirit.[d]

[20]But dear friends, use your most holy faith to build yourselves up strong. Pray with the Holy Spirit. [21]Keep yourselves in God's love. Wait for the Lord Jesus Christ with his mercy to give you life for ever.

[22]Show mercy to people who have doubts. [23]Save them. Take them out of the fire. Show mercy mixed with fear to others. Hate even their clothes which are dirty from sin.

Praise God

[24]God is strong and can help you not to fall. He can bring you before his glory without any wrong in you and give you great joy. [25]He is the only God. He is the One who saves us. To him be glory, greatness, power, and authority through Jesus Christ our Lord for all time past, now, and for ever. Amen.

REVELATION

Christ Will Win over Evil

John Tells About This Book

1 This is the revelation[n] of Jesus Christ. God gave this revelation to Jesus, to show his servants what must soon happen. And Jesus sent his angel to show it to his servant John. [2]John has told everything that he has seen. It is the truth that Jesus Christ told him; it is the message from God. [3]The one who reads the words of God's message is happy. And the people who hear this message and do what is written in it are happy. The time is near when all of this will happen.

Jesus' Message to the Churches

[4]From John,

To the seven churches in the country of Asia:

Grace and peace to you from the One who is and was and is coming, and from the seven spirits before his throne, [5]and from Jesus Christ. Jesus is the faithful witness. He is first among those raised from death. He is the ruler of the kings of the earth.

He is the One who loves us. And he is the One who made us free from our sins with the blood of his death. [6]He made us to be a kingdom of priests who serve God his Father. To Jesus Christ be glory and power for ever and ever! Amen.

[7]Look, Jesus is coming with the clouds! Everyone will see him, even those who stabbed him. And all peoples of the earth will cry loudly because of him. Yes, this will happen! Amen.

[8]The Lord God says, "I am the Alpha and the Omega.[n] I am the One who is and was and is coming. I am the All-Powerful."

[9]I am John, and I am your brother in Christ. We are together in Jesus, and we share in these things: in suffering, in the kingdom, and in patience. I was on the island of Patmos[n] because I had preached God's message and the truth about Jesus. [10]On the Lord's Day the Spirit[d] took control of me. I heard a loud voice behind me that sounded like a trumpet. [11]The voice said, "Write what you see and send that book to the seven churches: to Ephesus, Smyrna, Pergamum, Thyatira, Sardis, Philadelphia, and Laodicea."

[12]I turned to see who was talking to me. When I turned, I saw seven golden lampstands. [13]I saw someone among the lampstands who was "like a Son of Man".[n] He was dressed in a long robe. He had a gold band around his chest. [14]His head and hair were white like wool, as white as snow. His eyes were like flames of fire. [15]His feet were like bronze that glows hot in a furnace. His voice was like the noise

---

revelation   A making known of truth that has been hidden.
Alpha and the Omega   The first and last letters in the Greek alphabet. This means "the beginning and the end".
Patmos   A small island in the Aegean Sea, near the coast of Asia Minor (modern Turkey).
"like ... Man"   "Son of Man" is a name Jesus called himself. It showed he was God's Son, but he was also a man. See dictionary.

of flooding water. ¹⁶He held seven stars in his right hand. A sharp two-edged sword came out of his mouth. He looked like the sun shining at its brightest time.

¹⁷When I saw him, I fell down at his feet like a dead man. He put his right hand on me and said, "Do not be afraid! I am the First and the Last. ¹⁸I am the One who lives. I was dead, but look: I am alive for ever and ever! And I hold the keys of death and where the dead are. ¹⁹So write the things you see, what is now and what will happen later. ²⁰Here is the hidden meaning of the seven stars that you saw in my right hand and the seven golden lamp-stands that you saw. The seven lamp-stands are the seven churches. The seven stars are the angels of the seven churches.

To the Church in Ephesus

2 "Write this to the angel of the church in Ephesus:

"The One who holds the seven stars in his right hand and walks among the seven golden lamp-stands says this to you. ²I know what you do. You work hard, and you never give up. I know that you do not accept evil people. You have tested those who say that they are apostles*d* but really are not. You found that they are liars. ³You continue to serve me. You have suffered troubles for my name, and you have not given up.

⁴"But I have this against you: you have left the love you had in the beginning. ⁵So remember where you were before you fell. Change your hearts and do what you did at first. If you do not change, I will come to you. I will take away your lampstand from its place. ⁶But there is something you do that is right: you hate what the Nicolaitans*n* practise, as much as I.

⁷"Every person who has ears should listen to what the Spirit*d* says to the churches. To him who wins the victory I will give the right to eat the fruit from the tree of life. This tree is in the garden of God.

To the Church in Smyrna

⁸"Write this to the angel of the church in Smyrna:

"The One who is the First and the Last says this to you. He is the One who died and came to

Nicolaitans This is the name of a religious group that followed false beliefs and ideas.

Revelation 1:17 When I saw him, I fell down at his feet like a dead man.

life again. [9] I know your troubles. I know that you are poor, but really you are rich! I know the bad things that some people say about you. They say they are Jews, but they are not true Jews. They are a synagogue[d] that belongs to Satan. [10] Do not be afraid of what will happen to you. I tell you, the devil will put some of you in prison to test you. You will suffer for ten days. But be faithful, even if you have to die. If you are faithful, I will give you the crown of life.
[11] "Everyone who has ears should listen to what the Spirit[d] says to the churches. He who wins the victory will not be hurt by the second death.

To the Church in Pergamum

[12] "Write this to the angel of the church in Pergamum:

"The One who has the sharp two-edged sword says this to you. [13] I know where you live. You live where Satan has his throne. But you are true to me. You did not refuse to tell about your faith in me even during the time of Antipas. Antipas was my faithful witness who was killed in your city. Your city is where Satan lives.
[14] "But I have a few things against you: you have some there who follow the teaching of Balaam. Balaam taught Balak how to cause the people of Israel to sin. They sinned by eating food offered to idols and by taking part in sexual sins. [15] You also have some who follow the teaching of the Nicolaitans.[n] [16] So change your hearts and lives! If you do

not, I will come to you quickly and fight against them with the sword that comes out of my mouth.
[17] "Everyone who has ears should listen to what the Spirit[d] says to the churches!
"I will give the hidden manna[d] to everyone who wins the victory. I will also give him a white stone with a new name written on it. No one knows this new name except the one who receives it.

To the Church in Thyatira

[18] "Write this to the angel of the church in Thyatira:

"The Son of God is saying these things. He is the One who has eyes that blaze like fire and feet like shining bronze. He says this to you: [19] I know what you do. I know about your love, your faith, your service, and your patience. I know that you are doing more now than you did at first. [20] But I have this against you: you let that woman Jezebel do what she wants. She says that she is a prophetess.[d] But she is leading my people away with her teaching. Jezebel leads them to take part in sexual sins and to eat food that is offered to idols. [21] I have given her time to change her heart and turn away from her sin. But she does not want to change. [22] And so I will throw her on a bed of suffering. And all those who take part in adultery[d] with her will suffer greatly. I will do this now if they do not turn away from the wrongs she does. [23] I will also kill her followers. Then all the churches will know that I am the One who knows what people feel

Nicolaitans This is the name of a religious group that followed false beliefs and ideas.

and think. And I will repay each of you for what you have done.

²⁴"But others of you in Thyatira have not followed her teaching. You have not learned what some call Satan's deep secrets. This is what I say to you: I will not put any other load on you. ²⁵Only continue the way you are until I come.

²⁶"I will give power to everyone who wins the victory and continues to the end to do what I want. I will give him power over the nations:

²⁷ 'You will make them obey you by punishing them with an iron rod.

You will break them into pieces like pottery'. *Psalm 2:9*
²⁸This is the same power I received from my Father. I will also give him the morning star. ²⁹Everyone who has ears should listen to what the Spirit*ᵈ* says to the churches.

To the Church in Sardis

3 "Write this to the angel of the church in Sardis:

"The One who has the seven spirits and the seven stars says this to you. I know what you do. People say that you are alive, but really you are dead. ²Wake up! Make yourselves stronger while you still have something left and before it dies completely. I have found that what you are doing is not good enough for my God. ³So do not forget what you have received and heard. Obey it. Change your hearts and lives! You must wake up, or I will come to you and surprise you like a thief. And you will not know when I will come. ⁴But you have a few there in Sardis who have kept them-

selves clean. They will walk with me. They will wear white clothes, because they are worthy. ⁵He who wins the victory will be dressed in white clothes like them. I will not take away his name from the book of life. I will say that he belongs to me before my Father and before his angels. ⁶Everyone who has ears should listen to what the Spirit*ᵈ* says to the churches.

To the Church in Philadelphia

⁷"Write this to the angel of the church in Philadelphia:

"The One who is holy and true says this to you. He holds the key of David. When he opens something, it cannot be closed. And when he closes something, it cannot be opened. ⁸I know what you do. I have put an open door before you, and no one can close it. I know that you have a little strength. But you have followed my teaching. And you were not afraid to speak my name. ⁹Listen! There is a synagogue*ᵈ* that belongs to Satan. Those in this synagogue say they are Jews, but they are liars. They are not true Jews. I will make them come before you and bow at your feet. They will know that I have loved you. ¹⁰You have followed my teaching about not giving up. So I will keep you from the time of trouble that will come to the whole world. This trouble will test those who live on earth.

¹¹"I am coming soon. Continue the way you are now. Then no one will take away your crown. ¹²I will make the one who wins the victory a pillar in the temple of my God. He will never have to leave

it. I will write on him the name of my God and the name of the city of my God. This city is the new Jerusalem.[n] It comes down out of heaven from my God. I will also write on him my new name. [13] Every person who has ears should listen to what the Spirit[d] says to the churches.

To the Church in Laodicea

[14] "Write this to the angel of the church in Laodicea:

"The Amen[n] is the One who is the faithful and true witness. He is the ruler of all that God has made. He says this to you: [15] I know what you do. You are not hot or cold. I wish that you were hot or cold! [16] But you are only warm – not hot, not cold. So I am ready to spit you out of my mouth. [17] You say you are rich. You think you have become wealthy and do not need anything. But you do not know that you are really miserable, pitiful, poor, blind, and naked. [18] I advise you to buy gold from me – gold made pure in fire. Then you can be truly rich. Buy from me clothes that are white. Then you can cover your shameful nakedness. Buy from me medicine to put on your eyes. Then you can truly see.

[19] "I correct and punish those whom I love. So be eager to do right. Change your hearts and lives. [20] Here I am! I stand at the door and knock. If anyone hears my voice and opens the door, I will come in and eat with him. And he will eat with me.

[21] "He who wins the victory will

Revelation 3:20 "I stand at the door and knock. If anyone hears my voice and opens the door . . .

sit with me on my throne. It was the same with me. I won the victory and sat down with my Father on his throne. [22] Everyone who has ears should listen to what the Spirit[d] says to the churches."

John Sees Heaven

4 After this I looked, and there before me was an open door in heaven. And I heard the same voice that spoke to me before. It was the voice that sounded like a trumpet. The voice said, "Come up here, and I will show you what must happen after this." [2] Then the Spirit[d] took control of me. There before me was a throne in heaven. Someone was sitting on the throne. [3] The One who sat on the throne looked like precious stones,

---

Jerusalem This name is used to mean the spiritual city God built for his people.
Amen Used here as a name for Jesus, it means to agree fully that something is true.

like jasper and carnelian. All around the throne was a rainbow the colour of an emerald. [4]Around the throne there were 24 other thrones. There were 24 elders[n] sitting on the 24 thrones. The elders were dressed in white, and they had golden crowns on their heads. [5]Lightning flashes and noises of thunder came from the throne. Before the throne there were seven lamps burning. These lamps are the seven spirits of God. [6]Also before the throne there was something that looked like a sea of glass. It was clear like crystal.

Around the throne, on each side, there were four living things. These living things had eyes all over them, in front and behind. [7]The first living thing was like a lion. The second was like a calf. The third had a face like a man. The fourth was like a flying eagle. [8]Each of these four living things had six wings. The living things were covered all over with eyes, inside and out. Day and night they never stop saying:

"Holy, holy, holy is the Lord God All-Powerful.

He was, he is, and he is coming."

[9]These living things give glory and honour and thanks to the One who sits on the throne. He is the One who lives for ever and ever. And every time the living things do this, [10]the 24 elders bow down before the One who sits on the throne. The elders worship him who lives for ever and ever. They put their crowns down before the throne and say:

[11]"Our Lord and God! You are worthy

to receive glory and honour and power.

You made all things.

Everything existed and was made

because you wanted it."

5 Then I saw a scroll in the right hand of the One sitting on the throne. The scroll had writing on both sides. It was kept closed with seven seals. [2]And I saw a powerful angel. He called in a loud voice, "Who is worthy to break the seals and open the scroll?" [3]But there was no one in heaven or on earth or under the earth who could open the scroll or look inside it. [4]I cried and cried because there was no one who was worthy to open the scroll or look inside. [5]But one of the elders said to me, "Do not cry! The Lion[n] from the tribe[d] of Judah has won the victory. He is David's descendant.[d] He is able to open the scroll and its seven seals."

[6]Then I saw a Lamb standing in the centre of the throne with the four living things around it. The elders were also around the Lamb. The Lamb looked as if he had been killed. He had seven horns and seven eyes. These are the seven spirits of God that were sent into all the world. [7]The Lamb came and took the scroll from the right hand of the One sitting on the throne. [8]After he had taken the scroll, the four living things and the 24 elders bowed down before the Lamb. Each one of them had a harp. Also, they were holding golden bowls full of incense.[d] These bowls of incense are the prayers of God's holy people. [9]And they all sang a new song to the Lamb:

"You are worthy to take the scroll and to open its seals,

because you were killed;

and with the blood of your death you bought men for God

---

24 elders   Elder means "older". Here the elders probably represent God's people.
Lion   Here refers to Christ.

from every tribe, language, people, and nation.

¹⁰ You made them to be a kingdom of priests for our God. And they will rule on the earth."

¹¹ Then I looked, and I heard the voices of many angels. The angels were around the throne, the four living things, and the elders. There were thousands and thousands of angels – there were 10,000 times 10,000. ¹² The angels said in a loud voice:

"The Lamb who was killed is worthy
to receive power, wealth, wisdom and strength,
honour, glory, and praise!"

¹³ Then I heard every living thing in heaven and on earth and under the earth and in the sea. I heard every thing in all these places, saying:

"All praise and honour and glory and power
for ever and ever
to the One who sits on the throne and to the Lamb!"

¹⁴ The four living things said, "Amen!" And the elders bowed down and worshipped.

6 Then I watched while the Lamb opened the first of the seven seals. I heard one of the four living things speak with a voice like thunder. It said, "Come!" ² I looked and there before me was a white horse. The rider on the horse held a bow, and he was given a crown. And he rode out, defeating the enemy. He rode out to win the victory.

³ The Lamb opened the second seal. Then I heard the second living thing say, "Come!" ⁴ Then another horse came out. This was a red horse. Its rider was given power to take away peace from the earth. He was given

power to make people kill each other. And he was given a big sword.

⁵ The Lamb opened the third seal. Then I heard the third living thing say, "Come!" I looked, and there before me was a black horse. Its rider held a pair of scales in his hand. ⁶ Then I heard something that sounded like a voice. It came from where the four living things were. The voice said, "A litre of wheat for a day's pay. And three litres of barley for a day's pay. And do not damage the olive oil and wine!"

⁷ The Lamb opened the fourth seal. Then I heard the voice of the fourth living thing say, "Come!" ⁸ I looked, and there before me was a pale horse. Its rider was named death. Hades[n] was following close behind him. They were given power over a quarter of the earth. They were given power to kill people by war, by starving them, by disease, and by the wild animals of the earth.

⁹ The Lamb opened the fifth seal. Then I saw some souls under the altar. They were the souls of those who had been killed because they were faithful to God's message and to the truth they had received. ¹⁰ These souls shouted in a loud voice, "Holy and true Lord, how long until you judge the people of the earth and punish them for killing us?" ¹¹ Then each one of these souls was given a white robe. They were told to wait a short time longer. There were still some of their brothers in the service of Christ who must be killed as they were. They were told to wait until all of this killing was finished.

¹² Then I watched while the Lamb opened the sixth seal. There was a great earthquake. The sun became black like rough black cloth. The full moon became red like blood. ¹³ The

---

Hades   The unseen world where the dead are.

stars in the sky fell to the earth like figs falling from a fig tree when the wind blows. [14]The sky disappeared. It was rolled up like a scroll. And every mountain and island was moved from its place.

[15]Then all people hid in caves and behind the rocks on the mountains. There were the kings of the earth, the rulers, the generals, the rich people and the powerful people. Everyone, slave and free, hid himself. [16]They called to the mountains and the rocks, "Fall on us. Hide us from the face of the One who sits on the throne. Hide us from the anger of the Lamb! [17]The great day for their anger has come. Who can stand against it?"

The 144,000 People of Israel

7 After this I saw four angels standing at the four corners of the earth. The angels were holding the four winds of the earth. They were stopping the wind from blowing on the land or on the sea or on any tree. [2]Then I saw another angel coming from the east. This angel had the seal of the living God. He called out in a loud voice to the four angels. These were the four angels that God had given power to harm the earth and the sea. He said to the four angels, [3]"Do not harm the land or the sea or the trees before we put the sign on the people who serve our God. We must put the sign on their foreheads." [4]Then I heard how many people were marked with the sign. There were 144,000. They were from every tribe[d] of the people of Israel.

[5]From the tribe of Judah 12,000 were marked with the sign,

from the tribe of Reuben 12,000,

from the tribe of Gad 12,000,
[6]from the tribe of Asher 12,000,
from the tribe of Naphtali 12,000,
from the tribe of Manasseh 12,000,
[7]from the tribe of Simeon 12,000,
from the tribe of Levi 12,000,
from the tribe of Issachar 12,000,
[8]from the tribe of Zebulun 12,000,
from the tribe of Joseph 12,000,
from the tribe of Benjamin 12,000.

The Great Crowd

[9]Then I looked, and there was a great number of people. There were so many people that no one could count them. They were from every nation, tribe,[d] people, and language of the earth. They were all standing before the throne and before the Lamb. They wore white robes and had palm branches in their hands. [10]They were shouting in a loud voice, "Salvation belongs to our God, who sits on the throne, and to the Lamb." [11]The elders[n] and the four living things were there. All the angels were standing around them and the throne. The angels bowed down on their faces before the throne and worshipped God. [12]They were saying, "Amen! Praise, glory, wisdom, thanks, honour, power, and strength belong to our God for ever and ever. Amen!"

[13]Then one of the elders asked me, "Who are these people in white robes? Where did they come from?"

[14]I answered, "You know who they are, sir."

And the elder said, "These are the people who have come out of the great suffering. They have washed their robes[n] with the blood of the Lamb. Now they are clean and white. [15]And they are before the throne of God.

---

elders   Elder means "older". Here the elders probably represent God's people.
washed their robes   This means they believed in Jesus so that their sins could be forgiven by Christ's blood.

They worship God day and night in his temple. And the One who sits on the throne will protect them. [16]Those people will never be hungry again. They will never be thirsty again. The sun will not hurt them. No heat will burn them. [17]For the Lamb at the centre of the throne will be their shepherd. He will lead them to springs of water that give life. And God will wipe away every tear from their eyes."

The Seventh Seal

8 The Lamb opened the seventh seal. Then there was silence in heaven for about half an hour. [2]And I saw the seven angels who stand before God. They were given seven trumpets. [3]Another angel came and stood at the altar. This angel had a golden incense burner.[d] The angel was given a lot of incense to offer with the prayers of all God's holy people. The angel put this offering on the golden altar before the throne. [4]The smoke from the incense went up from the angel's hand to God. It went up with the prayers of God's people. [5]Then the angel filled the incense burner with fire from the altar and threw it on the earth. There were flashes of lightning, thunder and loud noises, and an earthquake.

The Seven Angels and Trumpets

[6]Then the seven angels who had the seven trumpets prepared to blow them.

[7]The first angel blew his trumpet. Then hail and fire mixed with blood was poured down on the earth. And a third of the earth and all the green grass and a third of the trees were burned up.

[8]The second angel blew his trumpet. Then something that looked like a big mountain burning with fire was thrown into the sea. And a third of the sea became blood. [9]And a third of the living things in the sea died, and a third of the ships were destroyed.

[10]The third angel blew his trumpet. Then a large star, burning like a torch, fell from the sky. It fell on a third of the rivers and on the springs of water. [11]The name of the star is Wormwood.[n] And a third of all the water became bitter. Many people died from drinking the water that was bitter.

[12]The fourth angel blew his trumpet. Then a third of the sun and a third of the moon and a third of the stars were hit. So a third of them became dark. A third of the day was without light.

[13]While I watched, I heard an eagle that was flying high in the air. The

Revelation 8:13 I heard an eagle that was flying high in the air.

eagle said with a loud voice, "Trouble! Trouble! Trouble for those who live

---

Wormwood   Name of a very bitter plant, used here to give the idea of bitter sorrow.

on the earth! The trouble will begin with the sounds of the trumpets that the other three angels are about to blow."

9 Then the fifth angel blew his trumpet. And I saw a star fall from the sky to the earth. The star was given the key to the deep hole that leads down to the bottomless pit. ²Then it opened the bottomless pit. Smoke came up from the hole like smoke from a big furnace. The sun and sky became dark because of the smoke from the hole. ³Then locusts[d] came down to the earth out of the smoke. They were given the power to sting like scorpions.[n] ⁴They were told not to harm the grass on the earth or any plant or tree. They could harm only the people who did not have the sign of God on their foreheads. ⁵These locusts were given the power to cause pain to the people for five months. But they were not given the power to kill anyone. And the pain they felt was like the pain that a scorpion gives when it stings a person. ⁶During those days people will look for a way to die, but they will not find it. They will want to die, but death will run away from them.

⁷The locusts looked like horses prepared for battle. On their heads they wore things that looked like crowns of gold. Their faces looked like human faces. ⁸Their hair was like women's hair, and their teeth were like lions' teeth. ⁹Their chests looked like iron breastplates. The sound their wings made was like the noise of many horses and chariots hurrying into battle. ¹⁰The locusts had tails with stingers like scorpions. The power they had to hurt people for five months was in their tails. ¹¹The

locusts had a king who was the angel of the bottomless pit. His name in the Hebrew language is Abaddon. In the Greek language his name is Apollyon.[n]

¹²The first great trouble is past. There are still two other great troubles that will come.

¹³The sixth angel blew his trumpet. Then I heard a voice coming from the horns on the golden altar that is before God. ¹⁴The voice said to the sixth angel who had the trumpet, "Free the four angels who are tied at the great river Euphrates." ¹⁵These four angels had been kept ready for this hour and day and month and year. They were freed to kill a third of all people on the earth. ¹⁶I heard how many troops on horses were in their army. There were 200,000,000.

¹⁷In my vision I saw the horses and their riders. They looked like this: they had breastplates that were fiery red, dark blue, and yellow like sulphur. The heads of the horses looked like heads of lions. The horses had fire, smoke, and sulphur coming out of their mouths. ¹⁸A third of all the people on earth were killed by these three terrible things coming out of the horses' mouths: the fire, the smoke, and the sulphur. ¹⁹The horses' power was in their mouths and also in their tails. Their tails were like snakes that have heads to bite and hurt people.

²⁰The other people on the earth were not killed by these terrible things. But they still did not change their hearts and turn away from what they had made with their own hands. They did not stop worshipping demons[d] and idols made of gold, silver, bronze, stone, and wood – things that cannot see or hear or walk.

scorpions   A scorpion is an insect that stings with a poison.
Abaddon, Apollyon   Both names mean "Destroyer".

[21]These people did not change their hearts and turn away from murder or evil magic, from their sexual sins or stealing.

The Angel and the Little Scroll

10 Then I saw another powerful angel coming down from heaven. He was dressed in a cloud and had a rainbow around his head. His face was like the sun, and his legs were like poles of fire. [2]The angel was holding a small scroll open in his hand. He put his right foot on the sea and his left foot on the land. [3]He shouted loudly like the roaring of a lion. When he shouted, the voices of seven thunders spoke. [4]The seven thunders spoke, and I started to write. But then I heard a voice from heaven. The voice said, "Do not write what the seven thunders said. Keep these things secret."

[5]Then the angel I saw standing on the sea and on the land raised his right hand to heaven. [6]He made a promise by the power of the One who lives for ever and ever. He is the One who made the skies and all that is in them. He made the earth and all that is in it, and he made the sea and all that is in it. The angel said, "There will be no more waiting! [7]In the days when the seventh angel is ready to blow his trumpet, God's secret plan will be finished. This plan is the Good News[d] God told to his servants, the prophets."[d]

[8]Then I heard the same voice from heaven again. The voice said to me, "Go and take the open scroll that is in the angel's hand. This is the angel that is standing on the sea and on the land."

[9]So I went to the angel and asked him to give me the little scroll. He said to me, "Take the scroll and eat it. It will be sour in your stomach. But in your mouth it will be sweet as honey." [10]So I took the little scroll from the angel's hand and I ate it. In my mouth it tasted sweet as honey. But after I had eaten it, it was sour in my stomach. [11]Then I was told, "You must prophesy[d] again about many peoples, nations, languages, and kings."

The Two Witnesses

11 Then I was given a measuring stick like a rod. I was told, "Go and measure the temple[n] of God and the altar, and count the number of people worshipping there. [2]But do not measure the yard outside the temple. Leave it alone. It has been given to the people who are not Jews. They will walk on the holy city for 42 months. [3]And I will give power to my two witnesses to prophesy[d] for 1,260 days. They will be dressed in rough cloth to show how sad they are."

[4]These two witnesses are the two olive trees and the two lampstands that stand before the Lord of the earth. [5]If anyone tries to hurt the witnesses, fire comes from their mouths and kills their enemies. Anyone who tries to hurt them will die like this. [6]These witnesses have the power to stop the sky from raining during the time they are prophesying. They have power to make the waters become blood. They have power to send every kind of trouble to the earth. They can do this as many times as they want.

[7]When the two witnesses have finished telling their message, the beast will fight against them. This is the beast that comes up from the bottomless pit. He will defeat them

---

temple   God's house – the place where God's people worship and serve him. Here, John sees it pictured as the special building in Jerusalem where God commanded the Jews to worship him.

and kill them. [8]The bodies of the two witnesses will lie in the street of the great city. This city is named Sodom[n] and Egypt. These names for the city have a special meaning. It is the city where the Lord was killed. [9]Men from every race of people, tribe,[d] language, and nation will look at the bodies of the two witnesses for three and a half days. They will refuse to bury them. [10]People who live on the earth will be happy because these two are dead. They will have parties and send each other gifts. They will do these things because these two prophets brought much suffering to those who live on the earth.

[11]But after three and a half days, God put the breath of life into the two prophets again. They stood on their feet. Everyone who saw them was filled with fear. [12]Then the two prophets heard a loud voice from heaven say, "Come up here!" And they went up into heaven in a cloud. Their enemies watched them go.

[13]At that same time there was a great earthquake. A tenth of the city was destroyed. And 7,000 people were killed in the earthquake. Those who did not die were very afraid. They gave glory to the God of heaven.

[14]The second great trouble is finished. The third great trouble is coming soon.

The Seventh Trumpet

[15]Then the seventh angel blew his trumpet. And there were loud voices in heaven. The voices said:

"The power to rule the world
    now belongs to our Lord and his
    Christ.[d]

And he will rule for ever and
    ever."

[16]Then the 24 elders[n] bowed down on their faces and worshipped God. These are the elders who sit on their thrones before God. [17]They said:

"We give thanks to you, Lord God
    All-Powerful.
You are the One who is and
    who was.
We thank you because you have
    used your great power
and have begun to rule!
[18]The people of the world were
    angry;
but now is the time for your
    anger.
Now is the time for the dead to
    be judged.
It is time to reward your servants
    the prophets[d]
and to reward your holy people,
all who respect you, great and
    small.
It is time to destroy those who
    destroy the earth!"

[19]Then God's temple[n] in heaven was opened. The Holy Ark[d] that holds the agreement that God gave to his people could be seen in his temple. Then there were flashes of lightning, noises, thunder, an earthquake, and a great hailstorm.

The Woman and the Dragon

12 And then a great wonder appeared in heaven. There was a woman who was clothed with the sun. The moon was under her feet. She had a crown of 12 stars on her head. [2]The woman was pregnant. She cried out

---

Sodom   City that God destroyed because the people were so evil.
24 elders   Elder means "older". Here the elders probably represent God's people.
temple   God's house – the place where God's people worship and serve him. John sees the heavenly temple pictured to be like the Temple of God's people in the Old Testament.

Revelation 12:1 There was a woman who was clothed with the sun.

with pain because she was about to give birth. ³Then another wonder appeared in heaven. There was a giant red dragon. He had seven heads with seven crowns on each head. He also had ten horns. ⁴The dragon's tail swept a third of the stars out of the sky and threw them down to the earth. The dragon stood in front of the woman who was ready to give birth to a baby. He wanted to eat the woman's baby as soon as it was born. ⁵The woman gave birth to a son. He will rule all the nations with an iron sceptre.*d* But her child was taken up to God and to his throne. ⁶The woman ran away into the desert to a place God prepared for her. There she would be taken care of for 1,260 days.

⁷Then there was a war in heaven. Michael*n* and his angels fought against the dragon. The dragon and his angels fought back. ⁸But the dragon was not strong enough. He and his angels lost their place in heaven. ⁹He was thrown down out of heaven. (The giant dragon is that old snake called the devil or Satan. He leads the whole world the wrong way.) The dragon with his angels was thrown down to the earth.

¹⁰Then I heard a loud voice in heaven say:

"The salvation and the power and
    the kingdom of our God
and the authority of his Christ*d*
    have now come.
They have come because the
    accuser of our brothers has
    been thrown out.
He accused our brothers day
    and night before our God.
¹¹And our brothers defeated him
    by the blood of the Lamb's
    death
and by the truth they preached.
They did not love their lives so
    much
that they were afraid of death.
¹²So be happy, you heavens
    and all who live there!
But it will be terrible for the earth
    and the sea,
    because the devil has come
        down to you!
He is filled with anger.
    He knows that he does not have
        much time."

¹³The dragon saw that he had been thrown down to the earth. So he hunted down the woman who had given birth to the son. ¹⁴But the woman was given the two wings of a great eagle. Then she could fly to the place that was prepared for her in the desert. There she would be taken care of for three and a half years. There she would be away from the snake. ¹⁵Then the snake poured water out of

Michael   The archangel – leader among God's angels or messengers (Jude 9).

its mouth like a river. He poured the water towards the woman, so that the flood would carry her away. ¹⁶But the earth helped her. The earth opened its mouth and swallowed the river that came from the mouth of the dragon. ¹⁷Then the dragon was very angry at the woman. He went off to make war against all her other children. Her children are those who obey God's commands and have the truth that Jesus taught. ¹⁸And the dragon stood on the seashore.

The Two Beasts

13 Then I saw a beast coming up out of the sea. It had ten horns and seven heads. There was a crown on each horn. A name against God was written on each head. ²This beast looked like a leopard, with feet like a bear's feet. He had a mouth like a lion's mouth. The dragon gave the beast all of his power and his throne and great authority. ³One of the heads of the beast looked as if it had been wounded and killed. But this death wound was healed. The whole world was amazed and followed the beast. ⁴People worshipped the dragon because he had given his power to the beast. And they also worshipped the beast. They asked, "Who is as powerful as the beast? Who can make war against him?"

⁵The beast was allowed to speak proud words and words against God. He was allowed to use his power for 42 months. ⁶He used his mouth to speak against God. He spoke against God's name, against the place where God lives, and against all those who live in heaven. ⁷He was given power to make war against God's holy people and to defeat them. He was given power over every tribe,ᵈ people, language, and nation. ⁸All who live on earth will wor-

ship the beast. These are all the people since the beginning of the world whose names are not written in the Lamb's book of life. The Lamb is the One who was killed.

⁹If anyone has ears, he should listen:

¹⁰If anyone is to be a prisoner,
    then he will be a prisoner.
If anyone is to be killed with the
        sword,
    then he will be killed with the
        sword.

This means that God's holy people must have patience and faith.

¹¹Then I saw another beast coming up out of the earth. He had two horns like a lamb, but he talked like a dragon. ¹²This beast stands before the first beast and uses the same power that the first beast has. He uses this power to make everyone living on earth worship the first beast. The first beast was the one that had the death wound that was healed. ¹³The second one does great miracles.ᵈ He even makes fire come down from heaven to earth while people are watching. ¹⁴This second beast fools those who live on earth. He fools them by the miracles he has been given the power to do. He does these miracles to serve the first beast. The second beast ordered people to make an idol to honour the first beast. This was the one that was wounded by the sword but did not die. ¹⁵The second beast was given power to give life to the idol of the first one. Then the idol could speak and order all who did not worship it to be killed. ¹⁶The second animal also forced all people, small and great, rich and poor, free and slave, to have a mark on their right hand or on their forehead. ¹⁷No one could buy or sell without this mark. This mark is the name of the beast or the number of his name. ¹⁸Whoever has under-

standing can find the meaning of the number. This requires wisdom. This number is the number of a man. His number is 666.

The Song of the Saved

14 Then I looked, and there before me was the Lamb. He was standing on Mount Zion.[n] There were 144,000 people with him. They all had his name and his Father's name written on their foreheads. [2]And I heard a sound from heaven like the noise of flooding water and like the sound of loud thunder. The sound I heard was like people playing harps. [3]And they sang a new song before the throne and before the four living things and the elders.[n] The only ones who could learn the new song were the 144,000 who had been saved from the earth. No one else could learn the song. [4]These 144,000 are the ones who did not do sinful things with women. They kept themselves pure. They follow the Lamb everywhere he goes. These 144,000 were saved from among the people of the earth. They are the first people to be offered to God and the Lamb. [5]They were not guilty of telling lies. They are without fault.

The Three Angels

[6]Then I saw another angel flying high in the air. The angel had the eternal Good News[d] to preach to those who live on earth – to every nation, tribe,[d] language, and people. [7]The angel said in a loud voice, "Fear God and give him praise. The time has come for God to judge all people. Worship God. He made the heavens, the earth, the sea, and the springs of water."

[8]Then the second angel followed the first angel and said, "She is destroyed! The great city of Babylon is destroyed! She made all the nations drink the wine of her adultery[d] and of God's anger."

[9]A third angel followed the first two angels. This third angel said in a loud voice: "It will be bad for the person who worships the beast and his idol and gets the beast's mark on the forehead or on the hand. [10]He will drink the wine of God's anger. This wine is prepared with all its strength in the cup of God's anger. He will be put in pain with burning sulphur before the holy angels and the Lamb. [11]And the smoke from their burning pain will rise for ever and ever. There will be no rest, day or night, for those who worship the beast and his idol or who get the mark of his name." [12]This means that God's holy people must be patient. They must obey God's commands and keep their faith in Jesus.

[13]Then I heard a voice from heaven. It said, "Write this: from now on, the dead who were in the Lord when they died are happy."

The Spirit[d] says, "Yes, that is true. They will rest from their hard work. The reward of all they have done stays with them."

The Earth Is Harvested

[14]I looked and there before me was a white cloud. Sitting on the white cloud was One who looked like a Son of Man.[n] He had a gold crown on his head and a sharp sickle[n] in his hand.

Mount Zion   Another name for Jerusalem, here meaning the spiritual city of God's people.
elders   Elder means "older". Here the elders probably represent God's people.
Son of Man   "Son of Man" is a name Jesus called himself. It showed he was God's Son, but he was also a man. See dictionary.
sickle   A farming tool with a curved blade. It was used to harvest grain.

¹⁵Then another angel came out of the temple. This angel called to the One who was sitting on the cloud, "Take your sickle and gather from the earth. The time to harvest has come. The fruit of the earth is ripe." ¹⁶So the One that was sitting on the cloud swung his sickle over the earth. And the earth was harvested.

¹⁷Then another angel came out of the temple in heaven. This angel also had a sharp sickle. ¹⁸And then another angel came from the altar. This angel had power over the fire. This angel called to the angel with the sharp sickle. He said, "Take your sharp sickle and gather the bunches of grapes from the earth's vine. The earth's grapes are ripe." ¹⁹The angel swung his sickle over the earth. He gathered the earth's grapes and threw them into the great winepress*d* of God's anger. ²⁰The grapes were crushed in the winepress outside the city. And blood flowed out of the winepress. It rose as high as the heads of the horses for a distance of 300 kilometres.

The Last Troubles

15 Then I saw another wonder in heaven. It was great and amazing. There were seven angels bringing seven troubles. These are the last troubles, because after these troubles God's anger is finished.

²I saw what looked like a sea of glass mixed with fire. All of those who had won the victory over the beast and his idol and over the number of his name were standing by the sea. They had harps that God had given them. ³They sang the song of Moses, the servant of God, and the song of the Lamb:

"You do great and wonderful
    things,   *Psalm 111:2*
Lord God, the God of heaven's
    armies.   *Amos 3:13*

Everything the Lord does is right
    and true,   *Psalm 145:17*
  King of the nations.
⁴Everyone will respect you, Lord.
               Jeremiah 10:7
  They will honour you.
  Only you are holy.
  All people will come
    and worship you.   *Psalm 86:9,10*
This is because he is a faithful
    God who does no wrong.
  He is right and fair."
             Deuteronomy 32:4

⁵After this I saw the temple (the Tent*d* of the Agreement) in heaven. The temple was opened. ⁶And the seven angels bringing the seven troubles came out of the temple. They were dressed in clean, shining linen. They wore golden bands tied around their chests. ⁷Then one of the four living things gave seven golden bowls to the seven angels. The bowls were filled with the anger of God, who lives for ever and ever. ⁸The temple was filled with smoke from the glory and the power of God. No one could enter the temple until the seven troubles of the seven angels were finished.

The Bowls of God's Anger

16 Then I heard a loud voice from the temple. The voice said to the seven angels, "Go and pour out the seven bowls of God's anger on the earth."

²The first angel left. He poured out his bowl on the land. Then ugly and painful sores came upon all those who had the mark of the beast and who worshipped his idol.

³The second angel poured out his bowl on the sea. Then the sea became blood like that of a dead man. Every living thing in the sea died.

⁴The third angel poured out his bowl on the rivers and the springs of water. And they became blood. ⁵Then

I heard the angel of the waters say to God:

"Holy One, you are the One who
　　is and who was.
You are right to decide to
　　punish these evil people.
[6] They have spilled the blood of
　　your holy people and your
　　prophets.[d]
Now you have given them blood
　　to drink as they deserve."

[7] And I heard the altar say:

"Yes, Lord God All-Powerful,
　　the way you punish evil people
　　is right and fair."

[8] The fourth angel poured out his bowl on the sun. The sun was given power to burn the people with fire. [9] They were burned by the great heat, and they cursed the name of God. God is the One who had control over these troubles. But the people refused to change their hearts and lives and give glory to God.

[10] The fifth angel poured out his bowl on the throne of the beast. And darkness covered the beast's kingdom. People bit their tongues because of the pain. [11] They cursed the God of heaven because of their pain and the sores they had. But they refused to change their hearts and turn away from the evil things they did.

[12] The sixth angel poured out his bowl on the great river Euphrates. The water in the river was dried up. This prepared the way for the kings from the east to come. [13] Then I saw three evil spirits that looked like frogs. They came out of the mouth of the dragon, out of the mouth of the beast, and out of the mouth of the false prophet.[d] [14] These evil spirits are the spirits of demons.[d] They have power to do miracles.[d] They go out to the kings of the whole world. They go out to gather the kings for battle on the great day of God All-Powerful.

[15] "Listen! I will come as a thief comes! Happy is the person who stays awake and keeps his clothes with him. Then he will not have to go without clothes and be ashamed because he is naked."

[16] Then the evil spirits gathered the kings together to the place that is called Armageddon[n] in the Hebrew language.

[17] The seventh angel poured out his bowl into the air. Then a loud voice came out of the temple from the throne. The voice said, "It is finished!" [18] Then there were flashes of lightning, noises, thunder, and a big earthquake. This was the worst earthquake that has ever happened since people have been on earth. [19] The great city split into three parts. The cities of the nations were destroyed. And God did not forget to punish Babylon the Great. He gave that city the cup filled with the wine of his terrible anger. [20] Every island disappeared, and there were no more mountains. [21] Giant hailstones fell on people from the sky. The hailstones weighed about 50 kilograms each. People cursed God because of the hail. This trouble was a terrible thing.

The Woman on the Animal

17 One of the seven angels came and spoke to me. This was one of the angels that had the seven bowls. He said, "Come, and I will show you the punishment that will be given to the famous prostitute.[d] She is the one sitting over many waters. [2] The kings of the earth sinned sexually with her. And the people of the earth became drunk from the wine of her sexual sin."

Armageddon This word means "Hill of Megiddo", where many battles were fought long ago.

[3]Then the angel carried me away by the Spirit[d] to the desert. There I saw a woman sitting on a red beast. He was covered with names against God written on him. He had seven heads and ten horns. [4]The woman was dressed in purple and red. She was shining with the gold, jewels, and pearls she was wearing. She had a golden cup in her hand. This cup was filled with evil things and the uncleanness of her sexual sin. [5]She had a title written on her forehead. This title has a hidden meaning. This is what was written:

THE GREAT BABYLON
MOTHER OF PROSTITUTES
AND THE EVIL THINGS OF THE EARTH

[6]I saw that the woman was drunk. She was drunk with the blood of God's holy people. She was drunk with the blood of those who were killed because of their faith in Jesus.

When I saw the woman, I was totally amazed. [7]Then the angel said to me, "Why are you amazed? I will tell you the hidden meaning of this woman and the beast she rides – the one with seven heads and ten horns. [8]The beast that you saw was once alive. He is not alive now. But he will be alive and come up out of the bottomless pit and go away to be destroyed. The people who live on earth will be amazed when they see the beast. They will be amazed because he was once alive, is not alive now, but will come again. These are the people whose names have never been written in the book of life since the beginning of the world.

[9]"You need a wise mind to understand this. The seven heads on the beast are the seven hills where the woman sits. They are also seven kings. [10]Five of the kings have already died. One of the kings lives now. And the last king is coming. When he comes, he will stay only a short time. [11]The beast that was once alive but is not alive now is an eighth king. This eighth king also belongs to the first seven kings. And he will go away to be destroyed.

[12]"The ten horns you saw are ten kings. These ten kings have not yet begun to rule. But they will receive power to rule with the beast for one hour. [13]All ten of these kings have the same purpose. And they will give their power and authority to the beast. [14]They will make war against the Lamb. But the Lamb will defeat them, because he is Lord of lords and King of kings. He will defeat them with his chosen and faithful followers – the people that he has called."

[15]Then the angel said to me, "You saw the water where the prostitute sits. These waters are the many peoples, the different races, nations, and languages. [16]The beast and the ten horns you saw will hate the prostitute. They will take everything she has and leave her naked. They will eat her body and burn her with fire. [17]God made the ten horns want to carry out his purpose: they agreed to give the beast their power to rule. They will rule until what God has said is completed. [18]The woman you saw is the great city that rules over the kings of the earth."

Babylon Is Destroyed

18 Then I saw another angel coming down from heaven. This angel had great power. The angel's glory made the earth bright. [2]The angel shouted in a powerful voice:

"The great city of Babylon is
destroyed!
She has become a home for
demons.[d]

She has become a city for every
evil spirit,
a city for every unclean[d] and
hated bird.

[3] All the peoples of the earth have
drunk
the strong wine of her sexual sin.
The kings of the earth have
sinned sexually with her,
and the businessmen of the
world have grown rich from
the great wealth of her
luxury."

[4] Then I heard another voice from
heaven say:
"Come out of that city, my people,
so that you will not share in her
sins.
Then you will not receive the
terrible things that will
happen to her.
[5] The city's sins are piled up as
high as the sky.
God has not forgotten the
wrongs she has done.
[6] Give that city the same as she
gave to others.
Pay her back twice as much as
she did.
Prepare wine for her that is twice
as strong
as the wine she prepared for
others.

[7] She gave herself much glory and
rich living.
Give her that much suffering
and sadness.
She says to herself, 'I am a queen
sitting on my throne.
I am not a widow; I will never
be sad'.
[8] So these terrible things will come
to her in one day:
death, crying, and great hunger.
She will be destroyed by fire,
because the Lord God who
judges her is powerful."

[9] The kings of the earth who sinned
sexually with her and shared her
wealth will see the smoke from her
burning. Then they will cry and weep
because of her death. [10] They will be
afraid of her suffering and stand far
away. They will say:
"Terrible! How terrible, great city,
powerful city of Babylon!
Your punishment has come in one
hour!"

[11] And the businessmen of the earth
will cry and weep for her. They will
be sad because now there is no one
to buy the things they sell. [12] They sell
gold, silver, jewels, pearls, fine linen
cloth, purple cloth, silk, and red cloth.
They sell all kinds of citron wood and
all kinds of things made from ivory,

Revelation 18:2 "The great city of Babylon is destroyed!"

expensive wood, bronze, iron, and marble. [13]They also sell cinnamon, spice, incense,[d] myrrh,[d] frankincense,[d] wine, and olive oil; fine flour, wheat, cattle, sheep, horses, and carriages. They sell the bodies and souls of men.

[14]They will say,

"Babylon, the good things you
    wanted are gone from you.
All your rich and fancy things
    have disappeared.
You will never have them
    again."

[15]The businessmen will be afraid of her suffering and stand far away from her. These are the men who became rich from selling those things to her. The men will cry and be sad. [16]They will say:

"Terrible! How terrible for the
    great city!
She was dressed in fine linen,
    purple and red cloth.
She was shining with gold,
    jewels, and pearls!
[17]All these riches have been
    destroyed in one hour!"

Every sea captain, all those who travel on ships, the sailors, and all the people who earn money from the sea stood far away from Babylon. [18]They saw the smoke from her burning. They said loudly, "There was never a city like this great city!" [19]They threw dust on their heads and cried to show how sad they were. They said:

"Terrible! How terrible for the
    great city!
All the people who had ships on
    the sea
    became rich because of her
        wealth!
But she has been destroyed in one
    hour!
[20]Be happy because of this, heaven!

Be happy, God's holy people and
    apostles[d] and prophets![d]
God has punished her because of
    what she did to you."

[21]Then a powerful angel picked up a stone like a large stone for grinding grain. The angel threw the stone into the sea and said:

"That is how the great city of
    Babylon will be thrown
    down.
The city will never be found
    again.
[22]The music of people playing harps
    and other instruments, flutes
    and trumpets,
    will never be heard in you again.
No workman doing any job
    will ever be found in you again.
The sound of grinding grain
    will never be heard in you again.
[23]The light of a lamp
    will never shine in you again.
The voices of a bridegroom and
    bride
    will never be heard in you
        again.
Your businessmen were the
    world's great men.
All the nations were tricked by
    your magic.
[24]She is guilty of the death
    of the prophets and God's holy
        people
    and of all who have been killed
        on earth."

People in Heaven Praise God

19 After this I heard what sounded like a great many people in heaven. They were saying:

"Hallelujah![n]
Salvation, glory, and power belong
    to our God.
[2]   His judgements are true and
        right.

Hallelujah   This means "praise God!"

Our God has punished the
    prostitute.[d]
  She is the one who made the
    earth evil with her sexual
    sin.
God has punished the prostitute to
    pay her for the death of his
    servants."
  [3]Again they said:
"Hallelujah!
She is burning, and her smoke
    will rise for ever and ever."
[4]Then the 24 elders[n] and the four
living things bowed down. They wor-
shipped God, who sits on the throne.
They said:
"Amen, Hallelujah!"
  [5]Then a voice came from the
    throne:
"Praise our God, all you who
    serve him!
Praise our God, all you who
    honour him, both small and
    great!"
[6]Then I heard what sounded like a
great many people. It sounded like the
noise of flooding water and like loud
thunder. The people were saying:
  "Hallelujah!
  Our Lord God rules. He is the
    All-Powerful.
[7]Let us rejoice and be happy
    and give God glory!
Give God glory, because the
    wedding of the Lamb has
    come.
  And the Lamb's bride has made
    herself ready.
[8]Fine linen was given to the bride
    for her to wear.
  The linen was bright and clean."
(The fine linen means the good things
done by God's holy people.)
  [9]Then the angel said to me, "Write
this: those who are invited to the wedding meal of the Lamb are happy!"

Then the angel said, "These are the
true words of God."
  [10]Then I bowed down at the angel's
feet to worship him. But he said to me,
"Do not worship me! I am a servant
like you and your brothers who have
the truth of Jesus. Worship God!
Because the truth about Jesus is the
spirit that gives all prophecy."[d]

The Rider on the White Horse

  [11]Then I saw heaven open. There
before me was a white horse. The
rider on the horse is called Faithful
and True. He is right when he judges
and makes war. [12]His eyes are like
burning fire, and on his head are many
crowns. He has a name written on
him, but he is the only one who knows
the name. No other person knows the
name. [13]He is dressed in a robe
dipped in blood. His name is the Word
of God. [14]The armies of heaven were
following him on white horses. They
were dressed in fine linen, white and
clean. [15]A sharp sword comes out of
the rider's mouth. He will use this
sword to defeat the nations. He will
rule them with a sceptre[d] of iron. He
will crush out the wine in the winepress[d] of the terrible anger of God All-
Powerful. [16]On his robe and on his
leg was written this name: "KING OF
KINGS AND LORD OF LORDS".
  [17]Then I saw an angel standing in
the sun. The angel called with a loud
voice to all the birds flying in the sky,
"Come together for the great feast of
God. [18]Come together so that you can
eat the bodies of kings and generals
and famous men. Come to eat the
bodies of the horses and their riders
and the bodies of all people – free,
slave, small, and great."
  [19]Then I saw the beast and the
kings of the earth. Their armies were

24 elders Elder means "older". Here the elders probably represent God's people.

gathered together to make war against the rider on the horse and his army. [20]But the beast was captured and with him the false prophet.[d] This false prophet was the one who did the miracles[d] for the beast. The false prophet had used these miracles to trick those who had the mark of the beast and worshipped his idol. The false prophet and the beast were thrown alive into the lake of fire that burns with sulphur. [21]Their armies were killed with the sword that came out of the mouth of the rider on the horse. All the birds ate the bodies until they were full.

The 1,000 Years

20 I saw an angel coming down from heaven. He had the key to the bottomless pit. He also held a large chain in his hand. [2]The angel grabbed the dragon, that old snake who is the devil. The angel tied him up for 1,000 years. [3]Then he threw him into the bottomless pit and closed it and locked it over him. The angel did this so that he could not trick the people of the earth any more until the 1,000 years were ended. After 1,000 years he must be set free for a short time.

[4]Then I saw some thrones and people sitting on them. They had been given the power to judge. And I saw the souls of those who had been killed because they were faithful to the truth of Jesus and the message from God. They had not worshipped the beast or his idol. They had not received the mark of the beast on their foreheads or on their hands. They came back to life and ruled with Christ for 1,000 years. [5](The others that were dead did not live again until the 1,000 years were ended.) This is the first raising of the dead. [6]Blessed and holy are those who share in this first raising of the dead. The second death has no power over them. They will be priests for God and for Christ. They will rule with him for 1,000 years.

[7]When the 1,000 years are over, Satan will be set free from his prison. [8]He will go out to trick the nations in all the earth – Gog and Magog. Satan will gather them for battle. There will be so many people that they will be like sand on the seashore. [9]And Satan's army marched across the earth and gathered around the camp of God's people and the city that God loves. But fire came down from heaven and burned them up. [10]And Satan, who tricked them, was thrown into the lake of burning sulphur with the beast and the false prophet.[d] There they will be punished day and night for ever and ever.

People of the World Are Judged

[11]Then I saw a great white throne and the One who was sitting on it. Earth and sky ran away from him and disappeared. [12]And I saw the dead, great and small, standing before the throne. And the book of life was opened. There were also other books opened. The dead were judged by what they had done, which was written in the books. [13]The sea gave up the dead who were in it. Death and Hades[n] gave up the dead who were in them. Each person was judged by what he had done. [14]And Death and Hades were thrown into the lake of fire. This lake of fire is the second death. [15]And if anyone's name was not found written in the book of life, he was thrown into the lake of fire.

Hades   Where the dead are.

The New Jerusalem

21 Then I saw a new heaven and a new earth. The first heaven and the first earth had disappeared. Now there was no sea. [2]And I saw the holy city coming down out of heaven from God. This holy city is the new Jerusalem.[n] It was prepared like a bride dressed for her husband. [3]I heard a loud voice from the throne. The voice said, "Now God's home is with men. He will live with them, and they will be his people. God himself will be with them and will be their God. [4]He will wipe away every tear from their eyes. There will be no more death, sadness, crying, or pain. All the old ways are gone."

[5]The One who was sitting on the throne said, "Look! I am making everything new!" Then he said, "Write this, because these words are true and can be trusted."

[6]The One on the throne said to me: "It is finished! I am the Alpha and the Omega,[n] the Beginning and the End. I will give free water from the spring of the water of life to anyone who is thirsty. [7]Anyone who wins the victory will receive this. And I will be his God, and he will be my son. [8]But those who are cowards, who refuse to believe, who do evil things, who kill, who sin sexually, who do evil magic, who worship idols, and who tell lies – all these will have a place in the lake of burning sulphur. This is the second death."

[9]One of the seven angels came to me. This was one of the angels who had the seven bowls full of the seven last troubles. He said, "Come with me.

I will show you the bride, the wife of the Lamb." [10]The angel carried me away by the Spirit[d] to a very large and high mountain. He showed me the holy city, Jerusalem. It was coming down out of heaven from God. [11]It was shining with the glory of God. It was shining bright like a very expensive jewel, like a jasper. It was clear as crystal. [12]The city had a great high wall with 12 gates. There were 12 angels at the gates. On each gate was written the name of one of the 12 tribes[d] of Israel. [13]There were three gates on the east, three on the north, three on the south, and three on the west. [14]The walls of the city were built on 12 foundation stones. On the stones were written the names of the 12 apostles[d] of the Lamb.

[15]The angel who talked with me had a measuring rod made of gold. He had this rod to measure the city, its gates, and its wall. [16]The city was built in a square. Its length was equal to its width. The angel measured the city with the rod. The city was 12,000 stadia[n] long, 12,000 stadia wide, and 12,000 stadia high. [17]The angel also measured the wall. It was 144 cubits[n] high, by man's measurement. That was the measurement the angel was using. [18]The wall was made of jasper. The city was made of pure gold, as pure as glass. [19]The foundation stones of the city walls had every kind of jewel in them. The first cornerstone was jasper, the second was sapphire, the third was chalcedony, the fourth was emerald, [20]the fifth was onyx, the sixth was carnelian, the seventh was chrysolite, the eighth was beryl, the

new Jerusalem   The spiritual city where God's people live with him.
Alpha and the Omega   The first and last letters in the Greek alphabet. This means "the beginning and the end".
stadia   One stadion was a distance of about 200 metres. It was one-eighth of a Roman mile.
cubits   A cubit is about half a metre, the length from the elbow to the tip of the little finger.

ninth was topaz, the tenth was chryso-prase, the eleventh was jacinth, and the twelfth was amethyst. ²¹The 12 gates were 12 pearls. Each gate was made from a single pearl. The street of the city was made of pure gold. The gold was clear as glass.

²²I did not see a temple in the city. The Lord God All-Powerful and the Lamb are the city's temple. ²³The city does not need the sun or the moon to shine on it. The glory of God is its light, and the Lamb is the city's lamp. ²⁴By its light the people of the world will walk. The kings of the earth will bring their glory into it. ²⁵The city's gates will never be shut on any day, because there is no night there. ²⁶The greatness and the honour of the nations will be brought into it. ²⁷Nothing unclean*d* will ever enter the city. No one who does shameful things or tells lies will ever go into it. Only those whose names are written in the Lamb's book of life will enter the city.

22 Then the angel showed me the river of the water of life. The river was shining like crystal. It flows from the throne of God and of the Lamb ²down the middle of the street of the city. The tree of life was on each side of the river. It produces fruit 12 times a year, once each month. The leaves of the tree are for the healing of all people. ³Nothing that God judges guilty will be in that city. The throne of God and of the Lamb will be there. And God's servants will worship him. ⁴They will see his face, and his name will be written on their foreheads. ⁵There will never be night again. They will not need the light of a lamp or the light of the sun. The Lord God will give them light. And they will rule like kings for ever and ever.

⁶The angel said to me, "These words are true and can be trusted. The Lord is the God of the spirits of

Revelation 22:2 The tree of life was on each side of the river.

the prophets.*d* He sent his angel to show his servants the things that must happen soon."

⁷"Listen! I am coming soon! He who obeys the words of prophecy in this book will be happy."

⁸I am John. I am the one who heard and saw these things. When I heard and saw them, I bowed down to worship at the feet of the angel who showed these things to me. ⁹But the angel said to me, "Do not worship me! I am a servant like you and your brothers the prophets. I am a servant like all those who obey the words in this book. Worship God!"

¹⁰Then the angel told me, "Do not keep secret the words of prophecy in this book. The time is near for all this to happen. ¹¹Whoever is doing evil, let him continue to do evil. Whoever is unclean, let him continue to be unclean. Whoever is doing right, let him continue to do right. Whoever is holy, let him continue to be holy.

[12] "Listen! I am coming soon! I will bring rewards with me. I will repay each one for what he has done. [13] I am the Alpha and the Omega,[n] the First and the Last, the Beginning and the End.

[14] "Those who wash their robes[n] will be blessed. They will have the right to eat the fruit from the tree of life. They may go through the gates into the city. [15] Outside the city are the evil people, those who do evil magic, who sin sexually, who murder, who worship idols, and who love lies and tell lies.

[16] "I, Jesus, have sent my angel to tell you these things for the churches. I am the descendant[d] from the family of David. I am the bright morning star."

[17] The Spirit[d] and the bride say, "Come!" Everyone who hears this should also say, "Come!" If anyone is thirsty, let him come; whoever wishes it may have the water of life as a free gift.

[18] I warn everyone who hears the words of the prophecy of this book: if anyone adds anything to these words, God will give him the troubles written about in this book. [19] And if anyone takes away from the words of this book of prophecy, God will take away his share of the tree of life and of the holy city, which are written about in this book.

[20] Jesus is the One who says that these things are true. Now he says, "Yes, I am coming soon."

Amen. Come, Lord Jesus!

[21] The grace of the Lord Jesus be with you all. Amen.

Alpha and the Omega   The first and last letters in the Greek alphabet. This means "the beginning and the end".
wash their robes   This means they believed in Jesus so that their sins could be forgiven by Christ's blood.

DICTIONARY

A

Abba (AB-uh) was a child's word for "father" in the Aramaic language. Early Christians used this word in speaking to God. This shows how close we can feel to him. (Mark 14:36; Romans 8:15; Galatians 4:6)

ABRAHAM

Abraham (AY-brah-ham) was the most respected man in the Jewish nation. The Jews called him "father Abraham". He was known for his great faith. (John 8:39; Romans 4:1, 16; Hebrews 11:11, 12)

Adam (AD-um) means "out of the earth". He was the first man God created. He was made from the dust of the ground. (1 Corinthians 15:45)

adultery (ah-DUL-ter-ee) is breaking a marriage promise by having sexual relations with someone other than your husband or wife. (Mark 10:11, 12; John 8:3–5)

agreement (uh-GREE-ment) is a contract or promise. It is sometimes called a covenant. God made agreements with his people. One agreement was the "Law of Moses". God has given a new agreement to his people through Christ in the New Testament. Hebrews 8–10 explains the differences between the two agreements. (Hebrews 9:15–22)

Agrippa (uh-GRIP-pah) See "Herod Agrippa II".

alabaster (AL-a-bas-ter) is a light-coloured stone with streaks or stripes through it. Perfume was often kept in beautiful containers made of alabaster. (Matthew 26:7; Luke 7:37)

aloes (AL-ohs) were oils from sweet-smelling sap of certain trees. They were used for perfume, medicine and to prepare bodies for burial. (John 19:39)

altar (ALL-ter) was a place where sacrifices, gifts or prayers were offered to God. Altars were often made of earth, grass or rocks piled up in the shape of a table on which the gift could be placed. (Matthew 5:23, 24; James 2:21)

amen (AH-MEN) is a Hebrew word for "that is right". A person says "amen" to show he agrees with what has been said. (1 Corinthians 14:16; Revelation 7:11, 12)

Andrew (AN-droo) was a fisherman and the brother of the apostle Peter. Andrew was also one of the 12 apostles of Jesus. (Mark 1:16–18; 3:14–19; John 1:40–44; Acts 1:13)

angel (AIN-jel) is a Greek word that means "messenger". Angels are heavenly beings. They can sometimes look like people. God used angels to help his people and to announce important events. (Matthew 25:31; Luke 2:8–15; Hebrews 1:14; 12:22; 13:2; 2 Peter 2:4)

Annas (AN-us) was a high priest of the Jews during Jesus' lifetime. He served as the high priest in Jerusalem from A.D. 7 to 14. (Luke 3:2; John 18:12–23; Acts 4:6) See also "priest".

apostle (uh-POS-'l) is a Greek word that means "someone who is sent off". Jesus gave the name to the 12 men he chose as his special followers. He sent them to tell the good news about him to the whole world. Later, after Judas killed himself, Matthias became an apostle. Paul was also called an apostle. (Matthew 10:1–4; Mark 3:14–19; Acts 1:2–26; 1 Corinthians 15:8–10)

Aquila (AK-wi-lah) was a Jewish Christian from the city of Rome. He and his wife Priscilla (or Prisca) worked as tentmakers and travelled with Paul. When they were at home in Rome or working in Ephesus, the Christians worshipped in their home. (Acts 18:2, 3, 18, 26; Romans 16:3–5; 1 Corinthians 16:19)

Aramaic (AR-uh-MAY-ik) was the language of the people in the nation of Aram. The Jews in the country of Palestine started speaking Aramaic when they were taken as slaves by the Babylonian people. Jesus probably spoke Aramaic. (John 19:20)

NOAH'S ARK

ark, Noah's In this Bible it is called Noah's boat. (1 Peter 3:20)

Ark of God or Holy Box is often called Ark of the Covenant. It was a special box made of acacia wood and gold. Gold creatures with wings covered the top. Inside were the stone tablets where the Ten Commandments were written. Later, a pot of manna and Aaron's staff were also put into the Box. It was to remind the people of Israel of God's promise to be with them. In this Bible it is also called the Holy Ark or the Holy Ark of God. (Hebrews 9:4)

Augustus Caesar (aw-GUS-tus SEE-zer) or Caesar Augustus was the first Roman emperor. He was the ruler when Jesus was born. He was a nephew to the famous Julius Caesar. (Luke 2:1, 2)

B

baptise (BAP-tise) is from a Greek word that in New Testament times meant to dip or immerse. Baptism as practised by Christians was in water. Baptism reminds us of Jesus' death, burial and rising to live again. It shows our death to sin and our being raised to new life with Christ. (Acts 2:38, 41; 8:36–39; 10:47; 16:15, 33; 18:8; Romans 6:3, 4)

Baptist (BAP-tist) means "someone who baptises". John, a relative of Jesus, was called this because he baptised many people. (Matthew 3:1)

Barabbas (bah-RAB-us) means "son of a father". He was a robber who had murdered someone in Jerusalem. He was in jail when Jesus was on trial. It was the time of year when a criminal would be freed from prison. The people cried out to have Barabbas freed and Jesus killed on the cross. Pilate, the Roman governor, did as they demanded. (Matthew 27:16–26; Mark 15:6–11)

Barnabas (BAR-nah-bus) means "one who encourages". The apostles gave this name to Joseph because he helped others. Barnabas, who was from Cyprus, often travelled with Paul to teach about Jesus. The journeys of Barnabas with Paul are told in Acts 13–15. (Acts 4:36, 37; 11:22–26)

Bartholomew (bar-THOL-oh-mew) was one of the 12 apostles of Jesus. He may also have been called Nathanael. (Matthew 10:2, 3; Luke 6:13–15; John 1:43–50)

beatitude (bee-A-ti-tyood) means "blessed" or "happy". This name is often used for Jesus' teaching in Matthew 5:3–12 and Luke 6:20–22. In these verses Jesus described a blessed or happy person.

Beelzebul (bee-EL-ze-bull), also spelled Beelzebub, came from the name Baal-Zebub. This was the name of the false god of the Philistines. In the New Testament Beelzebul is a name sometimes used for the devil. (Matthew 12:24; Mark 3:22, 23)

believers (be-LEE-vers) is a word used in the New Testament to describe the followers of Jesus. (Acts 2:41–47; 5:14)

Bethlehem (BETH-le-hem) means "house of bread". It is a small town five miles from Jerusalem in the country of Judea. It was the home town of King David in the Old Testament. Jesus was born there. (Matthew 2:1; Luke 2:15–18)

Bible (BY-bul) means "the book". The Bible is a group of books and letters that Christians accept as the word of God. It

BIBLE

is divided into two parts. The Old Testament contains 39 books, and the New Testament contains 27 books. See also "Scriptures".

blasphemy (BLAS-feh-mee) is saying things against God. Jesus was often accused of blasphemy because he said he was the Son of God. The people who accused him did not understand that he really was God's Son. (Matthew 9:3; 26:65; John 10:36)

blessing (BLES-ing) is a good gift from God to his people. (Luke 6:28; 24:50, 51; Acts 3:26; Hebrews 6:7; 1 Peter 3:9)

bread that shows we are in God's presence is also called Bread of the Presence, or showbread. It was a group of 12 loaves of bread that were kept on the table in the Holy Tent and later in the Temple. This special bread reminded the people that they were always in God's presence. (Luke 6:1–4)

Caesar (SEE-zer) was the name of a famous Roman family. In New Testament times it was used as the title of the Roman emperors. (Luke 2:1; 3:1; 20:22–25) See "Augustus Caesar".

Caiaphas (KY-uh-fus) was the Jewish high priest from A.D. 18 to 36. He was one of those who planned to kill Jesus. (Matthew 26:57–68; John 11:49–53; 18:12–28)

CENTURION

centurion (sen-TYUR-ree-un) was a Roman army officer who commanded 100 soldiers. (Matthew 8:5; Luke 7:2)

Cephas (SEE-fus) See "Peter".

chariot (CHA-re-ut) was a kind of fast, two-wheeled cart usually pulled by two horses. It was used for battles, travelling and parades. (Acts 8:28–31)

Christ (KRYST) means "anointed (or chosen) one" in Greek. In Hebrew the word is "Messiah". Jesus is the Christ. He was chosen by God to save people from their sins. (Mark 8:29; 14:61, 62; Luke 23:2; Acts 2:36; 17:3; 18:28)

Christian (KRIS-chun) means "belonging to Christ". Christ's followers are called Christians. (Acts 11:26; 26:28; 1 Peter 4:16)

church in the New Testament means a group of Christians. In those times the church often met in someone's home. (Matthew 16:18; Acts 2:47; 14:27; Romans 16:5)

circumcision (SIR-kum-SIH-zhun) This means to cut off the foreskin of the male sex organ. Each Jewish baby boy was circumcised on the eighth day after he was born. This act was done as a sign of the agreement God had made with his people, the Jews. Because of this, the Jews sometimes are called "the circumcision" and non-Jews are called "the uncircumcision". (John 7:22; Acts 7:8)

confess (kun-FES) means to admit that something is true. The New Testament teaches a believer to confess that Jesus is the Son of God. Christians are also told to confess their sins, to admit that they have done wrong. (Romans 10:9, 10; Philippians 2:11; 1 John 1:9)

cornerstone This was the most important stone at a corner in the base of a building. The cornerstone had to be perfect so the building's walls would be straight. The other stones were fitted against the cornerstone. Jesus is called the cornerstone of the new law. (Ephesians 2:20)

council (KOWN-s'l), or meeting, was the highest Jewish court in the days of Jesus.

Its proper name was the "Sanhedrin". The men of the council sat in a half circle to hear the people who came to speak to them. The trials of Jesus and Stephen were held in front of this council. (Matthew 26:57–68, Acts 6:13–15)

covenant (KUV-eh-nant) See "agreement".

cross refers to a cruel way of killing criminals in New Testament times. The person was tied or nailed to two rough beams of wood nailed together in the shape of an "x" or "t". Then, he was left hanging in a public place to die. Jesus was killed by the Roman soldiers this way. In the New Testament the word "cross" is often used to remind us that Christ's death on the cross was God's way of saving us from our sins. (John 19:17–31; 1 Corinthians 1:18–25; Galatians 6:12; Ephesians 2:15, 16)

CROSS

D

David (DAY-vid) was Israel's greatest king. Jesus is called the "Son of David" because he was born to members of David's family. (Luke 1:69; 2:4; 18:38; Acts 2:29–31; 13:22)

deacon (DEE-kun) is a Greek word meaning "servant". Deacons are people chosen to serve the church in special ways. The men named in Acts 6:1–6 may have been the first deacons. Deacons are described in 1 Timothy 3:8–13.

demon (DEE-mun) was an evil spirit from the devil. Sometimes a demon lived in a person. But Jesus has more power than demons and could make them come out of people. (Matthew 12:22; Luke 8:26–39)

descendants (de-SEN-dants) are family members who are born to a person and his children. They would include grandchildren, great-grandchildren, great-great-grandchildren and so on. (Romans 4:18)

devil (DEV-'l) means "one who accuses". In the New Testament, the devil is often called Satan or Beelzebul. He is a spirit and the enemy of God and man. (Matthew 4:1–11; John 13:2; Ephesians 4:27; 6:10–17) See "Beelzebul".

disciple (dih-SYE-p'l) See "follower".

E

elder (EL-der) means "older". In the New Testament elders are appointed leaders in the church. (Acts 20:17–38; 1 Timothy 3:1–7; 1 Peter 5:1–4)

Elijah (e-LIE-juh) was a man who spoke for God in the Old Testament. He was a prophet about 800 years before Jesus was born. (Matthew 16:14; 17:3, 4; 27:47; Luke 1:17; James 5:17)

epistle (e-PIS-'l) is a Greek word meaning "letter". Many books of the New Testament were actually letters written to Christians in various cities. Some of these letters are Ephesians, Galatians, Romans, 1 and 2 Corinthians, Philippians and Colossians. (Colossians 4:16; 1 Thessalonians 5:27; 2 Thessalonians 3:17; 2 Peter 3:16)

eternal life (e-TER-nul LIFE) is the new kind of life promised to those who follow Jesus. It is living with a new help from God. It is also life that will never end. (John 3:16; 4:14; Galatians 2:20; 1 John 5:11–15)

eunuch (YOU-nuk) is a man who cannot have sexual relations. In the Bible eunuchs were often high officers in royal palaces or armies. (Acts 8:26–40)

Eutychus (YOU-ti-cus) means "lucky". Eutycus was a young man in the city of Troas. As he was sitting in an upstairs window listening to Paul preach, he went to sleep. He fell out of the window and died. But Paul, by God's power, brought him back to life. (Acts 20:7–12)

F

faith (FAYTH) is belief and trust. People who have great faith in God do what he says to do, even when they do not understand why. They do it because they believe in him and trust him. Faith in Jesus means believing he is the Son of God and trusting in him. (Matthew 8:10; Luke 8:24, 25; Romans 4:16–22; 5:1, 2; Ephesians 4:13; Hebrews 11)

fasting (FAST-ing) means giving up food for a while. People sometimes fast during a special time of prayer and worship to God. Jesus fasted for 40 days before he began preaching. It was also done to show sadness. (Matthew 4:1–11; 6:16–18; 9:14, 15; Acts 13:2, 3; 14:23)

feast (FEEST) is a special meal and celebration for a certain purpose. There were many different feasts in Bible times.

FEAST

Feast of Dedication was an eight-day celebration for the Jews. It was a way of being thankful that the Temple had been cleansed again. This was done in 164 B.C. after the Greeks had spoiled and ruined it. The celebration is called Hanukkah today by the Jews. (John 10:22)

Feast of Harvest See "Feast of Weeks".

Feast of Weeks was also called Pentecost, the Feast of Harvest and the Day of First Fruits. It was held seven weeks and one day after Passover. This was a feast of thanksgiving for the summer harvest. (Acts 2) See "Pentecost".

Felix (FEE-lix) was the Roman governor of Judea from A.D. 52 to 54. He was a cruel ruler. He kept the apostle Paul in prison for two years to please the Jews who hated Jesus and Paul. His full name was Marcus Antonius Felix. (Acts 23:24–24:27)

fellowship (FEL-o-ship) is sharing friendship and love with others. Christians have a very special fellowship with God and his people. (Acts 2:42; 1 John 1:3–7)

Festus (FES-tus) was the governor of Judea after Felix. His full name was Porcius (POR-shus) Festus. He allowed Paul to go to Rome to be tried by Caesar. (Acts 24:27–25:27; 26:24–32)

firstborn (FIRST-born) is the oldest child in a family. The son born first to a Jewish family received a double share of his father's wealth. Then he became the leader of the family when his father died. The Israelite people were called God's firstborn because he gave them special privileges. Jesus was also called God's firstborn son. He is now ruling over all creation. (Romans 8:29; Colossians 1:18; Hebrews 1:6)

follower (FOL-o-wer) is a person who is learning from someone. Jesus' followers are those who believe and obey his teaching. Another word for "follower" is "disciple". During his ministry, Jesus chose 12 special followers and made them his apostles. (Matthew 15:32–39; John 19:38; Acts 6:1–7; 11:26)

forgiveness (for-GIV-ness) means to be pardoned and not punished for a wrong thing done. A sinner who is sorry for his sin and stops doing that sin will be forgiven when he comes to God. That person will not be punished. Christians are also to forgive others for wrong things done to them. (Matthew 6:12–15; 9:2–8; 18:21, 22; Acts 8:22; Romans 4:7; 1 John 1:9)

frankincense (FRANK-in-sens) is a very expensive, sweet-smelling perfume. It comes from inside the terebinth tree that grows in the country of Arabia. Some wise men gave frankincense to Jesus when he was born. (Matthew 2:11; Revelation 18:13)

GABRIEL

G

Gabriel (GAY-bree-el) is God's angel who announced that John the Baptist and Jesus would be born. (Luke 1:11–20, 26–35)

Galilee (GAL-i-lee) was the country between the Jordan River and the Mediterranean Sea. It had lots of water and trees, and the land was good for growing grains like wheat and barley. Jesus grew up in the city of Nazareth in Galilee and, so, was often called "the Galilean". (Matthew 4:23–25; 21:11; John 2:1, 2; 7:1, 9, 41)

Galilee, Lake (GAL-i-lee) is also called the "Sea of Galilee". It is really a lake 20 kilometres long and about 13 kilometres wide. Storms often come up very quickly on this lake. Jesus spent much time around Lake Galilee. (Matthew 4:18–22; 8:23–27; 14:22–36; John 6:1, 2, 16–21)

Gentiles (JEN-tiles) means "nations". The Jews called anyone who was not a Jew a Gentile. The Jews thought all non-Jewish people were enemies. The Good News of Jesus is for all people, both Jews and non-Jewish people. (Acts 10:44–48; 11:18; 13:46–48; Romans 1:5; 11:11–13; Ephesians 3:6–8)

Gethsemane (geth-SEM-uh-nee) was a garden of olive trees just outside Jerusalem. It was at the bottom of the Mount of Olives. The night before Jesus was killed, he prayed in this garden. Jesus was there when Judas brought the soldiers to arrest him. (Matthew 26:36–50; Mark 14:32)

God is the One who made the world and everything in it. He is a spirit and does not have a body as man does. But people can know what God is like because he sent Jesus into the world to show them. God hates evil, but he loves his people so much that he let his Son die for them. God is the wisest and most powerful being in the universe. He has always been alive, and he will always be alive. He is love. Christians are called "children of God" because they have been given a spirit like God. (Matthew 5:9; John 4:24; 14:9; Romans 1:18; 5:8–11; 8:16; 11:36; Hebrews 1:1–4; 1 John 4:7–12)

LAKE GALILEE

GOLGOTHA

Golgotha (GOL-goh-thuh) is an Aramaic word meaning "skull". The Latin word for it is "Calvary". This is the hill where Jesus was killed on the cross by the Roman soldiers. It may have been called the "place of the skull" because many people died there. Or it may have been called that because the hill looks like a giant skull. (Matthew 27:32–35; Mark 15:22–24; John 19:17, 18)

Good News is also called the gospel. In the New Testament, the Good News is that Jesus died for us on the cross, was buried in a tomb and came back to life. Because he did these things for us, we can be saved. That is good news. (Mark 1:1; Acts 20:24; Colossians 1:21–23; 2 Timothy 1:10) See "gospel".

gospel (GOS-p'l) means "good news". It refers to Jesus' life, death and rising to live again. The first four books of the New Testament are called the gospels because they tell the good news of what Jesus has done for us. (Philippians 1:5, 7, 12; 2 Thessalonians 1:8) See "Good News".

grace is God's kindness and love shown to us, even though we do not deserve them. Part of God's grace is his forgiveness. He forgives us for the wrong things we do. He even let Jesus take the

punishment for our sins. (John 1:14; Acts 15:11; Romans 5:1, 2, 8; 1 Corinthians 15:10; 2 Corinthians 6:1, 2; Ephesians 2:4, 5, 8; Titus 3:3–7; Hebrews 4:16)

Greek is the language of the people of Greece. The New Testament was first written in the Greek language. Also, a person from the country of Greece is called a Greek. (John 19:20; Acts 14:1; 16:1, 3; 21:37; Colossians 3:11)

Hades (HAY-deez) is where the dead, both good and bad, are. (Acts 2:27, 31; Revelation 1:18)

heart in the Bible usually means the mind or feelings. It is not talking about the physical heart that pumps blood through the body. (Mark 12:30; Luke 2:19; 6:45; 12:34; Acts 2:46)

heaven (HEV-'n) is the home of God. In the New Testament it is said to be a place where there is no pain, no crying, no sadness, no night and no death. Jesus showed us his love by leaving heaven and coming to earth to die on a cross. God's people will live in heaven with him for ever. (John 3:13; 6:38–40; Acts 7:56; 2 Corinthians 5:1–10; 1 Peter 1:4; Revelation 21:4)

Hebrews (HEE-brooz) is another name for the Jewish people. The book of Hebrews is a letter written to Jewish Christians. (2 Corinthians 11:22; Philippians 3:5; Hebrews)

heir (AIR) is the person who is supposed to inherit what belongs to a relative. The heir usually receives these things when the relative dies. Because through Christ we can be adopted children of God, Christians are heirs of God's riches. (Galatians 4:1)

hell is the home of the devil. It is the place of punishment for ever for those who turn against God. Hell is described in the New Testament as a place of fire, pain, sorrow and sadness. (Matthew 23:33; 25:41; 2 Peter 2:4, 9; Revelation 20:14, 15; 21:8)

Herod (HEH-rud) was the name of four different rulers in the New Testament:

Herod I (Herod the Great) was king of the country of Palestine from the year 40 B.C. until about 4 B.C. He tried to kill the baby Jesus because Jesus was called a "king". Herod thought Jesus was an earthly king and would take away his throne. (Matthew 2:1–16; Luke 1:5)

Herod Antipas was the son of Herod I. He had John the Baptist's head cut off. Later, Jesus was sent to this man for trial. He ruled from the year 4 B.C. to about A.D. 39. (Matthew 14:1; Mark 6:14; Luke 23:6–12)

Herod Agrippa I was the king of Palestine for about three years (A.D. 41 to 44). He was the grandson of Herod I. He had the apostle James killed and the apostle Peter arrested. He did it to please the Jews who hated Jesus' followers. Later, this man was eaten by worms and died because he let the people treat him like a god. (Acts 12:1–21)

Herod Agrippa II was king of Palestine from the year A.D. 48 to 93. He was a great-grandson of Herod I. He heard the apostle Paul speak. He sent Paul to Caesar for trial. (Acts 25:13, 26; 26:1–32)

high priest was the most important religious leader of the Jewish people. He was often as important as the king. Caiaphas was the high priest when Jesus was killed. Annas was another high priest at that time. (Matthew 26:3, 57; Acts 23:2–5)

HIGH PRIEST

holy (HO-lee) means pure, belonging to and willing to serve God. God's people are called "holy people". (1 Corinthians 1:2; Ephesians 1:4; Philemon 5; 1 Peter 1:15, 16)

Holy Spirit (HO-lee SPIH-rit) is one of the three persons of God. The other two persons are God the Father and God the Son (Jesus). The Holy Spirit helped the apostles do miracles. He led men to write God's word. The Holy Spirit lives in Christians today. He is also called the Spirit of Christ, the Spirit of God, and the Comforter. (John 3:5–8; 16:13; Acts 2:1–4; 5:32; Romans 5:5; 8:9–16; 2 Peter 1:20, 21)

hypocrite (HIP-oh-krit) comes from the word for an actor on a stage. In the Bible it is a person who acts as if he is good but isn't. (Matthew 6:2, 5, 16; 7:3–5; Luke 13:15–17) idol (EYE-d'l) is a false god. The non-Jewish people often worshipped statues they made from wood, stone or metal. They worshipped these idols instead of the true God of heaven. (Acts 7:40–43; 17:16–23; 1 Thessalonians 1:9)

IDOL

incense (IN-sens) was a spice burned to make a sweet smell. This was done by the priests in the Meeting Tent and the Temple. A special altar was used to burn incense as worship to God. Since the smoke seemed to go up to God, this reminded people of prayer. (Luke 1:9; Revelation 8:3–4)

Isaac (EYE-zak) means "laughter". He was the son of Abraham and Sarah. He was named Isaac because Sarah laughed when the angel told her she would have a baby. She thought she was too old. God tested Abraham by asking him to offer Isaac as a sacrifice on an altar. When God saw that Abraham would obey him, he saved Isaac's life. (Mark 12:26; Hebrews 11:17–20)

Israel (IZ-ray-el) is a Hebrew word that means "he who wrestles with God". When Jacob struggled with an angel at Bethel, God named him Israel. The 12 tribes of the Jewish nation were descendants of Jacob. They were called Israelites. (Luke 1:68; Acts 2:36; 5:33–36)

J

Jacob (JAY-cub) was one of the sons of Isaac. He was the father of the 12 tribes of God's chosen people. He had 12 sons, and each son was the head of a tribe. (Matthew 1:2; 8:11; John 4:6)

James was the name of several men in the New Testament:

James, the son of Zebedee, was an apostle of Jesus and a brother of the apostle John. He was killed by Herod Agrippa I. (Matthew 10:2; Mark 10:35, 41; Acts 12:2)

James, the son of Alphaeus, was also one of Jesus' apostles. He may have been a cousin to Jesus. (Matthew 10:3)

James, the brother of Jesus, was a respected leader in the church in Jerusalem. He probably wrote the book of James in the New Testament. (Matthew 13:55; John 7:5; Acts 12:17; 21:18; Galatians 1:19)

Jerusalem (jeh-ROO-suh-lem) is sometimes called "Zion" or the "City of David". It was the greatest city of the country of Palestine. It was the centre of the Jewish religion because the Temple was there. Jesus was killed on the cross near Jerusalem. The city was destroyed by the Roman army in the year A.D. 70. Later, it was rebuilt in the same place by the

Moslems and is a great city today in the Middle East. (Luke 2:22–45; 13:34; 24:13, 18, 33, 47, 49; Acts 2:5, 14) See "Zion".

JESUS

Jesus (JEE-zus) means "saviour". He is the Son of God. He was born to Mary, a young Jewish woman. Mary was told by the angel Gabriel that she would have a baby boy. She was to name him "Jesus" because he would save his people from their sins. He is also called "Christ" and "Messiah". He lived a perfect life and never sinned. But he was killed by Roman soldiers on a cross near Jerusalem. Then, he came back to life and now lives in heaven with his father, God. He is one of the three persons of God. The other two persons are God the Father, and God the Holy Spirit. (Matthew 1:21; Luke 2:21; 3:23; John 20:19; Acts 2:19, 36; 4:10; Philippians 2:10–11) See "Christ" and "Messiah".

Jesus was a common name among Jewish people, so there were other, less important men in the New Testament named Jesus, too. (Colossians 4:11)

Jew (JOO) at first meant someone from the tribe of Judah. Judah was one of Jacob's 12 sons and the head of one of the 12 tribes of Israel. Later, the word Jew meant any person in any of the 12 tribes (Hebrews 1–13). A person who is not a Jew is called a Gentile or non-Jew.

Jesus was a Jew. (Matthew 2:2; 28:11–15; Acts 2:5; Romans 1:16; 10:12)

John was the name of several men in the New Testament:

> **John the Baptist** was Jesus' relative and the son of Elizabeth and Zechariah the priest. He lived in the desert and ate locusts and wild honey. He preached that the Saviour, Jesus, was coming soon. Jesus came to John the Baptist to be baptised in the Jordan River. Herod Antipas had John killed by cutting off his head. (Matthew 3:1–17; 11:11–13; 14:3–12; Luke 1:13–17)

> **John, the apostle,** was one of the sons of Zebedee. He and his brother James were fishermen. He wrote the gospel of John, the books of 1, 2 and 3 John and probably Revelation. He is sometimes referred to as "the one Jesus loved". John, Peter and James were Jesus' closest friends. (Mark 1:19, 20; 9:2; 14:33, 34; Acts 3:1–11; Revelation 1:1–4, 9)

> **John Mark** see "Mark".

Jordan (JOR-d'n) is the only large river in the country of Palestine. It runs about 75 miles from Mount Hermon to the Dead Sea. It also makes two lakes – Lake Huleh and Lake Galilee. Jesus was baptised in the Jordan River near the city of Jericho. (Matthew 3:5–17)

Joseph (JOZ-uf) was the name of several men in the Bible:

> **Joseph, the son of Jacob,** was one of the 12 sons of Israel. His two sons, Ephraim and Manasseh, each started a tribe. (Acts 7:10–14)

Joseph of Nazareth was the husband of Mary, Jesus' mother. He was a carpenter. He may have died when Jesus was a young man because he is not mentioned after Jesus' childhood. The New Testament says he was "a good man". (Matthew 1:18–24; 2:13–23)

Joseph of Arimathea took the body of Jesus down from the cross and buried it in a tomb he had dug for himself. He was a member of the Jewish religious court called the Sanhedrin. He was probably a Christian. (Matthew 27:57–60; Mark 15:43–46)

Judas Iscariot (JOO-dus is-CAH-ree-ut) was the apostle who turned against Jesus and handed him over to the Roman soldiers to be killed. For this he was paid only 30 pieces of silver, the price of a slave. Later, Judas killed himself. (Matthew 26:47–50; 27:3–5; John 13:26–30)

Jude (JOOD) was possibly a brother of Jesus and James. In Jesus' early ministry, Jude did not believe Jesus was the Son of God. Later, he believed and became a leader in Christ's church. He wrote the book of Jude in the New Testament. (John 7:5; Jude)

Judea (joo-DEE-uh) was the land of the Jews. It was a district in the country of Palestine. Both Jerusalem and Bethlehem were cities in Judea. John the Baptist began his preaching in the desert of Judea. (Matthew 2:1; Luke 1:5; 2:4; Acts 1:8)

Judgement Day (JUJ-ment DAY) is the day Christ will judge all people. He will take his followers to live with him for ever in heaven. Those who have followed the

devil will be sent to live with him in hell for ever. (Matthew 11:20–24; Hebrews 9:27, 28; 2 Peter 2:9, 10; 3:7)

LAMB

L

lamb (LAM) is an animal that the Jews often offered as a sacrifice (gift) to God. Since Jesus died as a sacrifice for us, he is called the Lamb of God that takes away the sins of the world. (John 1:29, 36; 1 Corinthians 5:7)

Lazarus (LAZ-uh-rus) was the name of two men in the New Testament:

> **Lazarus of Bethany** was a brother to Mary and Martha. He was also a very dear friend of Jesus. When he died, Jesus brought him back to life. (John 11:1–45; 12:1–11)

> **Lazarus, the beggar**, was the name of a person in a story Jesus told his followers. (Luke 16:19–31)

leprosy (LEH-prah-see) is a name for some bad skin diseases. A person with leprosy was called a leper and had to live outside the city. When other people came by, the lepers had to warn them by crying out "Unclean! Unclean!" (Matthew 8:1–3; Luke 17:11–19)

Levites (LEE-vites) were descendants of Levi, one of Jacob's sons. The priests all came from this tribe. But not all Levites were priests. Those who were not priests worked in the Meeting Tent or Temple in other ways. (Luke 10:32)

lid on the Holy Ark is also called the mercy seat. This was the beautiful gold lid on the Ark of God. It had a gold creature with wings on each end of it. This Holy Ark was kept in the Most Holy Place of the Meeting Tent and later in the Temple. (Hebrews 9:5)

locust (LO-cust) is an insect that looks like a grasshopper. Locusts travel in large groups. They eat crops and other green plants. Locusts were sometimes eaten as food. (Matthew 3:4)

lord means "master" or one who is in control. Jesus is called Lord because he rules over all the world and universe. Christians let Jesus be the Lord of their lives. (Acts 2:36; 21:12–14; Romans 10:9; 1 Corinthians 6:11; Colossians 3:17–24)

Lord's Prayer is the name often given to the model prayer Jesus taught his followers. (Matthew 6:9–13; Luke 11:1–4)

LORD'S SUPPER

Lord's Supper is the meal Jesus' followers eat to remember how he died for them. The bread reminds us of his body. The fruit of the vine reminds us of his blood. The Lord's Supper also shows that Jesus came back to life and now lives in heaven with God. (Matthew 26:26–30; Luke 22:14–20; 1 Corinthians 10:17; 11:23–32)

lots were sticks, stones or pieces of bone thrown like dice to decide something. Often God controlled the result of the

LOCUST

lots to let the people know what he wanted them to do. (Luke 1:9; 23:34; Acts 1:26)

Luke was a non-Jewish doctor who often travelled with the apostle Paul. He was a very educated man. He wrote the books of Luke and Acts in the New Testament. Luke tells many acts of Jesus that are not told in the other three gospels. (Colossians 4:14; 2 Timothy 4:11)

M

manna (MAN-ah) means "what is it?" It was the white, sweet-tasting food God gave the people of Israel in the wilderness. It appeared on the ground during the night so they could gather it in the morning. (Hebrews 9:4)

Mark, sometimes called John Mark, was a cousin to Barnabas. Mark travelled with Paul and Barnabas on part of their first missionary journey. He also wrote the gospel of Mark. Christians met in the home of Mark's mother, Mary, to pray for Peter to be freed from prison. (Acts 12:12, 25; 13:5, 13; 15:36–41; Colossians 4:10; 2 Timothy 4:11)

Martha (MAR-thuh) was the sister of Mary and Lazarus. They lived in the village of Bethany, which is very near Jerusalem. Jesus often stayed in their home when he was in that area. Martha and her brother and sister loved Jesus very much. (Luke 10:38–41; John 11:1–39; 12:2)

martyr (MAR-ter) is a Greek word that means "witness". Being a witness means telling what you know about something. Later, martyr came to mean a person who was killed for being a witness.

Stephen was the first Christian martyr. He was killed because he told people that Jesus is the Son of God. It is believed that all the apostles, except one, were martyrs for being witnesses about Jesus. (Acts 7:54–60; 12:2; 22:20; Revelation 2:13)

Mary is the name of several women in the New Testament:

MARY, THE MOTHER OF JESUS

Mary, the mother of Jesus, was a Jewish woman whom God chose to give birth to his only Son. This was a great honour and blessing from God. She married a man named Joseph. Mary stood at the foot of the cross when Jesus was killed. (Matthew 1:18–25; Luke 1:27–45; John 19:25–27)

Mary Magdalene was from the town of Magdala. She was a follower of Jesus. She watched the men put Jesus' body in the tomb. She was the first person to see Jesus after he came back to life. (Matthew 27:56, 61; Mark 15:40, 47; 16:1, 9; John 20:1–18)

Mary of Bethany was the sister of Martha and Lazarus. She was a dear friend of Jesus. Mary sat at Jesus' feet and listened to him teach. Once she poured some expensive perfume on his feet and dried them with her hair. (Luke 10:39–42)

Matthew (MATH-you), also called Levi, was a tax collector. He was one of Jesus' 12 apostles. He wrote the gospel of Matthew. (Matthew 9:9, 10; 10:3)

Melchizedek (mel-KIZ-ih-dek) means "king of righteousness". He was a priest and king who worshipped God in the time of Abraham. Jesus is now the Christian's king and high priest. In this way, Jesus is a priest and a king like Melchizedek. (Hebrews 5:4–10; 7:1–17)

mercy (MUR-see) is kindness and forgiveness. God had mercy on us. He sent his only Son, Jesus, to die on the cross for our sins. We, too, are taught to have mercy on other people. God says he will be as merciful to us as we are to others. (Matthew 5:7; Romans 11:32; James 2:13; 5:11; 1 Peter 2:10)

mercy seat See "lid on the Holy Ark".

Messiah (muh-SY-uh) is a Hebrew word for "appointed one" or "one chosen by God". The Greek word for Messiah is "Christ". Christians believe that Jesus is the Messiah or Christ. (John 1:41; 4:25)

minister (MIN-i-ster) means "servant". It also means one who lives serving God and others. Christians are taught to minister to each other and to non-Christians. (Romans 15:16)

miracle (MYR-ih-k'l) is a Latin word that means "wonderful thing". It is a great event which can be done only by God's help. Miracles are special signs to show God's power. In the Old Testament God used miracles to rescue his people. Jesus did miracles to prove that he was God's Son. The Bible tells us of many miracles. The sick were healed, the

blind were given sight, the crippled were able to walk and people could speak languages they had never studied. Sometimes people were even brought back to life after they had died. The best miracle was Jesus' coming back to life after he was killed on the cross. (Matthew 28:5–7; Luke 23:8; John 2:1–11; 3:2; 20:30, 31; Acts 4:16–22; 8:13)

Moses (MO-zez) in Hebrew means "saved from the water". Moses led God's people out of the land of Egypt where they had been slaves for 400 years. Moses wrote the first five books of the Old Testament. On Mount Sinai God gave to Moses the law for the Israelite people. It is called "the Law of Moses". (John 1:17, 45; 3:14; Hebrews 11:23, 24; Revelation 15:3)

Most Holy Place was the inner and most special room in the Meeting Tent and the Temple. The Ark of God was kept here. Only the high priest could go into this room, and he could enter only once a year. This was when he sprinkled blood on the lid of the Holy Ark to remind the people that their sins needed to be forgiven. (Hebrews 9:3–25)

MOUNT OF OLIVES

Mount of Olives is a hill covered with olive trees near Jerusalem. The garden of Gethsemane is on one side of the

Mount of Olives. Jesus was praying there when the Roman soldiers came to arrest him. Some of the same olive trees that were in the garden when Jesus was on earth may still be there today. (Luke 22:39–52; Acts 1:12)

Mount Zion (ZI-on) at first meant one of the hills on which Jerusalem was built. Later Zion became another name for the whole city of Jerusalem. In the New Testament, Zion is also used as a name for heaven. (Hebrews 12:22)

myrrh (MUR) was a sweet-smelling liquid taken from certain trees and shrubs. It was used as a perfume and as a pain reliever. It was one of the gifts the wise men gave Jesus when he was born. (Matthew 2:11; Mark 15:23; John 19:39)

NARD

N

nard was an expensive perfume. It was expensive because it had to be imported from India. (Mark 14:3; John 12:3)

Nazarene (NAZ-uh-reen) is a person from the town of Nazareth. Jesus grew up in Nazareth and was called a Nazarene. Sometimes Christians also were called Nazarenes, since they followed Jesus. (Matthew 2:23; Acts 24:5)

New Moon was a Jewish feast held on the first day of the month. It was celebrated with animal sacrifices and the blowing of trumpets. It was a way for the Israelites to dedicate the month to the Lord. (Colossians 2:16)

Noah (NO-uh) and his family were the only people of their time who served God. So God told them about the great flood that was coming. They built a large boat (often called an ark) about 450 feet long. Noah's family and every kind of animal were saved to start the world all over again. (1 Peter 3:20)

P

parable (PAR-uh-b'l) is a story that teaches a lesson by comparing two things. Jesus often used parables to teach the people. Some examples of parables can be found in Mark 12:1–12; Luke 10:29–37 and Luke 15:1–31.

Passover Feast (PASS-o-ver FEEST) was an important holy day for the Jews in the spring of each year. They ate a special meal on this day to remind them that God had freed them from being slaves in Egypt. Jesus was killed at Passover time. (Matthew 26:2, 17–19)

Paul is the Roman name for "Saul". Saul was a Jew, born in the city of Tarsus. He studied under Gamaliel, a famous teacher of God's law. At first, Paul tried to destroy Christ's church by putting Christians in jail and killing them. But Jesus appeared to him and changed his life completely. He was then called Paul. And he became an apostle and a great servant of God. He travelled to many countries, teaching about Jesus. Paul wrote many of the books of the New Testament as letters to Christians in different cities, such as Romans, Colossians and Corinthians. (Acts 7:58–60; 9:1–31; Philippians 3:5–7)

Pentecost (PEN-tee-cost) means "fifty". Pentecost was a Jewish feast day celebrating the summer harvest. It took place 50 days after the Passover Feast. The apostles began telling the Good News on Pentecost after Jesus died. (Acts 2; 20:16; 1 Corinthians 16:8)

persecute (PUR-seh-cute) means to hurt people. Christians in the New Testament times were often persecuted. Saul persecuted Christians by dragging them from their homes, putting them in jail and killing them. (Matthew 5:11, 12; Acts 8:1–4; Galatians 6:12; 1 Peter 3:13–15)

PETER

Peter (PEE-ter) was a fisherman. He and his brother, Andrew, were the first two apostles Jesus chose. He was first named Simon, but Jesus changed his name to Cephas, which means "rock" in Aramaic. In Greek the name is Peter. Peter, James and John were Jesus' closest friends. Peter was the first to tell the Good News of Jesus to the non-Jewish people. Later in his life, Peter wrote the New Testament books of 1 and 2 Peter. He probably died as a martyr for Christ. (Matthew 14:25–33; 16:13–18; Mark 14:27–39; Luke 22:54–62; John 20:1–6; Acts 3:1–26; 10:1–48)

Pharisees (FA-rih-seez) means "the separate people". They were a Jewish religious group who followed the religious laws and customs very strictly. Jesus often spoke against the Pharisees for their religious teachings and traditions. Many of the Pharisees did not like Jesus because he did not follow all of their rules. (Matthew 5:20; 23:23–36; Mark 7:1–13; Luke 18:9–14)

Philip (FIL-ip) was the name of several men in the New Testament:

> **Philip, the apostle,** was from the city of Bethsaida and was a friend of Peter and Andrew. He brought Nathanael to Jesus. (Matthew 10:2, 3; John 1:43–48; 12:21; 14:8, 9)

> **Philip, the evangelist,** was a Greek-speaking Jew. He was one of the seven men chosen to serve in the church in Jerusalem. Later, he preached the Good News in many places. (Acts 6:1–6; 8:5–40; 21:8, 9)

> **Philip, the tetrarch (ruler),** was the son of Herod I and Cleopatra. He built the city of Caesarea Philippi. (Luke 3:1)

Pontius Pilate (PON-shus PIE-lut) means "armed with a spear". Pilate was the Roman governor of Judea from A.D. 26 to 36. The Jews who wanted Jesus killed brought him to Pilate. He did not find Jesus guilty of any crime. But Pilate allowed the Jews to crucify Jesus because he was afraid of the people. (Luke 13:1; 23:1–52; Acts 3:13; 4:27; 1 Timothy 6:13)

Preparation Day (prep-a-RAY-shun DAY) was the day before the Sabbath day. On that day the Jews prepared or got everything ready for the Sabbath. (Luke 23:54; John 19:14, 31)

priest (PREEST) in the Old Testament was a servant of God who worked in the Meeting Tent or Temple. Priests helped the people offer their gifts and sacrifices to God. Jesus is the Christian's high priest. He brings man and God together. Because of this all Christians are now priests. (Hebrews 7:26–28; 1 Peter 2:5, 9; Revelation 1:5, 6) See "high priest".

Priscilla (prih-SIL-uh) See "Aquila".

prophecy (PROH-feh-see) means "message". It is God speaking through chosen people called prophets. The Old Testament has many prophecies about the Saviour who was to come into the world. Jesus was the answer to these prophecies. (2 Peter 1:20, 21; Revelation 22:18, 19) See "prophet".

prophesy (PROH-fes-sy) is to speak a prophecy. See "prophecy".

prophet (PROH-fet) means "messenger" or one who speaks for someone else. With God's help, a prophet was able to tell the people God's message correctly. Sometimes prophets told what would happen in the future. A woman who spoke God's message was called a prophetess. (Matthew 2:5, 6; Luke 2:36; 16:29–31; 24:25–27; Romans 1:2; 1 Corinthians 12:28, 29; 1 Peter 1:10–12)

prophetess See "prophet".

prostitute (PROH-sti-tyou-t) is a person who sells his or her body for sexual relations with someone to whom he or she is not married. This is a sin. (1 Corinthians 6:15)

R

Rahab (RAY-hab) was the name of a woman in Jericho. She hid the Israelite spies and helped them escape. (Matthew 1:5; Hebrews 11:31; James 2:25)

repent (rih-PENT) means being sorry for doing something wrong and not continuing to do that wrong thing. To repent is to "change your heart and life". (Matthew 3:2; 4:17; Mark 1:15; Luke 15:7, 10; Acts 2:38; 3:19)

resurrection (REZ-uh-REK-shun) is a dead person's coming back to life. In the New Testament several people came back to life with God's help. Some of them were Lazarus (John 11:38–45), Tabitha (Acts 9:36–42), the widow's son in the town of Nain (Luke 7:11–17) and Eutychus (Acts 20:8–12). Jesus, the Son of God, came back to life after being dead three days. This was the most important resurrection. His resurrection from death means we can be saved and live in heaven for ever. (Matthew 28:1–10; 1 Corinthians 15; 1 Peter 3:21, 22)

RESURRECTION

revelation (rev-uh-LAY-shun) means to show plainly something that has been hidden. The last book in the New Testament is called the Revelation to John. God showed the apostle John what to write to Christians to give them hope and faith even though they were being persecuted. (2 Corinthians 12:1; Revelation 1:1–3)

S

Sabbath (SAB-uth) means "rest". It was the seventh day of the Jewish week, their day of worship to God. The Jews were not allowed to work on this day. Some Jews became angry with Jesus because he healed people on the Sabbath. They thought this was breaking the Old Testament law of the Sabbath. (Matthew 12:9–14; Luke 6:1–11; Acts 18:4; Colossians 2:16, 17)

Sadducees (SAD-you-seez) were a Jewish religious group. They were rich and important men. They believed that only the first five books of the Old Testament were true. They did not believe in angels or life after death (resurrection). The Sadducees lost their power and importance after Jerusalem was destroyed by the Romans about the year A.D. 70. (Matthew 22:23–33; Acts 4:1, 2; 5:17, 18; 23:6–9)

saint is another word for Christian. God has set Christians apart to serve him. They live to please God and be like him – pure and holy. (Acts 9:13, 32, 41; 26:10; Romans 1:7; 1 Corinthians 1:2; Ephesians 1:1)

Samaritan (suh-MAR-ih-t'n) was a person from the area of Samaria in Palestine. Samaria was between Galilee and Judea.

These people were only part Jewish, so the Jews did not accept them. They hated the Samaritans. But Jesus showed love and concern for the Samaritans. One story that Jesus told is known as the story of "the good Samaritan". (Luke 10:30–37; John 4:1–42)

Sanhedrin (san-HEE-drin) See "council".

Satan (SAY-t'n) in Hebrew means "enemy". It is a name for the devil, the enemy of God and man. (Matthew 4:10; Luke 10:18, 19; Acts 5:3; 26:18) See "devil".

Saul (SAWL) in the New Testament was a man whose name was changed to Paul. See "Paul".

saviour (SAVE-yur) is someone who saves people from danger. The name Jesus means "saviour". Jesus is the Saviour of the people of this world. His life, death and resurrection made it possible for people to be saved from death and punishment for their sins. (Luke 2:11; John 4:42; Ephesians 5:23; Philippians 3:20; Titus 1:4; 1 John 4:14)

SCRIBE

scribe is a Hebrew word that means to write, to count and to put in order. In New Testament times scribes were men who wrote copies of the Scriptures. They were very careful when they copied the words of God. To be sure they had not made a mistake in copying, they would count the number of letters on each line they wrote. Scribes were educated, and some of them served as secretaries, royal assistants and teachers. (Matthew 7:29; 15:1–9; 23:1–36; Luke 22:2)

Scriptures (SCRIP-churs) means "writings". They are the special writings of God's word for man. When the word Scriptures is used in the New Testament, it usually means the Old Testament. Later, it came to mean the whole Bible (Luke 24:27, 32, 45; Acts 8:32–35; 17:2, 11; 2 Timothy 3:16; 2 Peter 1:20; 3:16) See "Bible".

scroll is a long roll of paper used for writing. In Bible times books were written on scrolls. These scrolls were rolled up from each end to the middle. They were made of papyrus (a plant) or parchment (an animal skin). Some scrolls were as long as 11.6 metres. (Luke 4:17–20; 2 Timothy 4:13; Revelation 5:1–5)

Sea of Galilee See "Galilee, Lake".

seal was a tool with a design or picture carved on it. Kings pressed this seal into wax which would be placed on important papers which would to close them. It was like a person's signature. If the seal was broken, it showed that someone else had looked at the papers. A seal also showed who owned something. Sometimes these seals were worn as rings. (2 Corinthians 1:22)

shepherd (SHEP-'rd) is a person who cares for and protects sheep. A shepherd loves his sheep and gives them food and water. He guides them to

a quiet place to rest. He protects the sheep from wolves and other wild animals. A good shepherd will even die trying to protect his sheep.

Jesus is called the Good Shepherd because he loves and cares for his followers who are often called sheep. Jesus was willing to die for his followers to save them. (Mark 6:34; John 10:1–30; 1 Peter 2:25; 5:4)

SHEPHERD

Silas (SY-lus) is sometimes called Silvanus. He was a teacher in the church in Jerusalem who often travelled with Paul. He became one of Paul's most trusted helpers. He may have written down some of Peter's and Paul's letters for them. (Acts 15:22, 30–17:16; 18:5; 1 Thessalonians 1:1; 1 Peter 5:12)

Simeon (SIM-ee-un) is a name that means "God has heard". Simeon was a godly man who lived in Jerusalem. When he saw the baby Jesus in the Temple, he knew that this child would save his people from their sins. He held the baby

Jesus in his arms and said a prayer of thanks to God. (Luke 2:25–35)

Simon (SY-mun), sometimes called Simeon, is a name that means "God has heard". The apostle Peter was first named Simon. Other men named Simon are also mentioned in the New Testament:

> **Simon of Cyrene** carried the cross of Jesus to the hill of Calvary. (Matthew 27:32)
>
> **Simon, the magician,** tried to buy the power of the Holy Spirit to do miracles. (Acts 8:9–24)
>
> **Simon, the Zealot,** was one of the 12 apostles. (Matthew 10:4)
>
> **Simon, the brother of Jesus,** (Matthew 13:55)

sin is a word, thought or act against the law of God. Sin is doing something God said not to do, or it could be not doing something he said to do. Jesus came to save us from being punished for our sins. (Romans 3:23; 5:12; 1 Corinthians 15:3; Galatians 1:4; Hebrews 4:15, 16; 1 John 1:8–10; 2:1, 2)

Solomon's Porch (SOL-o-mon's PORCH) was a covered courtyard on the east side of the Temple. People gathered here to sell animals and exchange money. Others met to discuss the Law of Moses. (John 10:23; Acts 3:11; 5:12)

Son of David was a name the Jews used for the Christ who was to save the world. This was because the Saviour was to come from the family of King David. Jesus was the "Son of David". (Matthew 9:27; 20:30; 21:9)

Son of Man was a name Jesus called himself. It showed that he was God's Son,

but he was also a man. (Matthew 24:30; 26:64; Mark 13:26; 14:62; Luke 21:27; 22:69)

soul (SOLE) is what makes a person alive. Sometimes the Bible writers used words like heart and soul to mean a person's whole being or the person himself. (Matthew 10:28)

Spirit See "Holy Spirit".

spirit (SPIH-rit) is the part of man that was made to be like God because God is spirit. The New Testament also talks about evil spirits. (John 4:23, 24; James 2:24–26) See "demon", "Holy Spirit" and "soul".

STEPHEN

Stephen (STEE-ven) was one of the seven men chosen to serve the church in Jerusalem. The New Testament says he was a man who had great faith. He was able to do miracles. Stephen was the first martyr for Christ. The Jews killed him by throwing stones at him because he taught that Jesus was the Son of God. (Acts 6:5–15; 7:54–60; 22:20)

synagogue (SIN-uh-gog) is a Greek word that means "a meeting". By the first century, the Jews met in synagogues to read and study the Scriptures. The building was also used as the Jewish court and as a school. Both Jesus and Paul often went to the Jewish synagogues to teach and discuss the Scriptures. (Matthew 4:23; Luke 4:16, 17; Acts 15:21; 17:1, 10)

Syria (SIH-ree-uh) is a Hebrew word that means "plain". In New Testament times it was the area north of Galilee and east of the Mediterranean Sea. Damascus was its capital city. In Old Testament times, this country was called Aram. (Matthew 4:24; 15:23)

T

tax collector was a Jew hired by the Romans to collect taxes. Most people did not like tax collectors because they worked for the Romans and often cheated people. The apostle Matthew was a tax collector before he became an apostle. Zacchaeus was also a tax collector. (Matthew 9:10, 11; 10:3; Luke 5:27; 19:1–8)

temple (TEM-p'l) is a building where people worship their gods. God told the Jewish people to worship him at the Temple in Jerusalem. This Temple had been built by King Solomon. It was later destroyed by the Babylonians. It was rebuilt by Zerubbabel. This Temple was destroyed by a Roman general, Pompey. Herod built a third Temple which was used in Jesus' time. (Mark 11:15–17; Acts 7:47; 19:27)

The New Testament also speaks of a Christian's body as a temple. That is because God's Spirit lives in the Christian. (Acts 7:48;19:27; 1 Corinthians 6:19)

temptation (temp-TAY-shun) is the devil's trying to get us to do something wrong. God has promised to help us when we are tempted, so we can choose to do the right thing. (Matthew 4:1-11; 1 Corinthians 10:13; Hebrews 2:18; 4:15, 16; James 1:12–14)

testament (TES-tuh-ment) See "agreement".

Thaddaeus (THAD-ee-us) was one of the 12 apostles. Little else is known about him. (Matthew 10:3; Mark 3:18)

THOMAS

Thomas (TOM-us) or Didymus, is a name that means "twin". He was one of Jesus' 12 apostles. His courage and love for Jesus are shown in John 11:16. Sometimes people call him "doubting Thomas". The other apostles told him Jesus had been raised from death. But Thomas did not believe it until he saw Jesus himself. (John 14:5–7; 20:24–29; 21:2)

Tiberius Caesar (ty-BEER-ee-us SEE-zur) was the Roman emperor during the last half of Jesus' life. He ruled from A.D. 14 to 37. The city of Tiberias was named after him. (Luke 3:1)

Timothy

Timothy (TIM-oh-thee) means "one who honours God". Timothy was a close friend and helper of the apostle Paul. He was the son of a Greek father and Jewish Christian mother. His mother Eunice and his grandmother Lois taught him the Scriptures. Paul wrote two letters, called 1 and 2 Timothy, to him. (Acts 16:1–3; 17:13–16; 1 Corinthians 4:17; 1 Thessalonians 3:1–6; 2 Timothy 1:2–5)

tithe (TIETH) means "tenth". In the Old Testament the Jewish people were told to give one-tenth of what they earned to God. (Luke 11:42; 18:12)

TITHE

Titus (TY-tus) was a trusted friend and helper of the apostle Paul. He often travelled with or for Paul. Paul wrote the book of Titus to him while Titus was on the island of Crete. (2 Corinthians 2:13; 7:6, 7, 13–15; 8:6, 16, 23; Titus 1:4, 5)

tomb (TOOM) is a place where a dead person's body is buried. Some tombs were underground. More often, in biblical times they were dug out of the side of a huge rock or mountain. A large stone was then rolled in front of the tomb to seal it. (Luke 23:53–55; 24:1, 2; John 11:38–41 ; 20:1–9)

transfiguration (tranz-fig-uh-RAY-shun) means "to change". Jesus was transfigured in front of Peter, James and John. Jesus had taken them up on a mountain with him. There his face and clothes began to shine brightly. God spoke to the apostles. He said that Jesus is his Son and that they should obey only him. (Matthew 17:1–9)

U

uncircumcised See "circumcision".

unclean is used to describe the state of a person, animal or action that was not pleasing to God. In the Old Testament God said certain animals were unclean. They were not to be eaten. If a person disobeyed this (or some other rule about being clean), that person was called unclean. He could not serve God until he was made clean again. (Romans 14:14)

unleavened bread (un-LEV-'nd bred) is bread made without yeast. This kind of bread is like a flat, thin cracker because it does not rise when it is baked. God told the Jews to use unleavened bread for the Passover Feast. (Matthew 26:17–29; Mark 14:12–25)

Unleavened Bread, Day of was the first day of the Feast of Unleavened Bread or Passover. (Luke 22:7)

V

virgin (VUR-jin) is a woman or girl who has not had sexual relations. (Matthew 1:23; Luke 1:34)

vision (VIH-zhun) is like a dream. A vision may come to a person when he is awake or asleep. God used visions to tell people what he wanted them to do, to teach them something or to let them know something that was going to happen. Peter had a vision of a sheet filled with animals. (Acts 9:10–12; 10:3–19; 11:5; 16:9, 10; 18:9)

WISE MEN

wise men, or "magi", was a name for men who studied the stars. Some wise men followed a star from the East and brought gifts to Jesus when he was born. (Matthew 2:1–12)

witchcraft means using the power of the devil to do magic. (Galatians 5:20)

witness (WIT-ness) is someone who tells what he has seen or what he knows. The apostles were witnesses for Christ because they told people that Jesus is the Son of God. (Acts 1:8, 22; 2:32; 22:14, 15)

word in the Bible often means God's message to us in the Scriptures. (1 Peter 1:24, 25; 1 John 2:14) Jesus is called the "Word" because he shows us what God is like. (John 1:1–5, 14)

yoke is a wooden frame that fits on the necks of animals to hold them together while working. Two oxen were often yoked together to pull a farmer's plough. The word yoke is also used to mean the work a person is to do. (Matthew 11:29)

Z

Zealots (ZEL-ots) were a group of Jewish men who were also called "Enthusiasts". They hated the Romans for controlling their home country and planned to force them out. Simon, the apostle, was a Zealot. (Luke 6:15; Acts 1:13)

Zion (ZY-on) was a hill inside the city of Jerusalem. Later, the name Zion, or Sion, was used to mean all of Jerusalem. In the New Testament, Mount Zion is sometimes even used as a name for heaven. (Hebrews 12:22; Revelation 14:1)

TABLE
OF WEIGHTS
AND MEASURES

METRIC CONVERSION

METRIC	IMPERIAL
LINEAR MEASUREMENTS	
1 centimetre	0.4 inch
1 metre	36 inches or 3 feet = 1 yard
1 kilometre	0.6 mile
LAND MEASURE	
1 hectare	2.5 acres = 100 acres
WEIGHTS	
1 gram	0.035 ounce
1 kilogram	2.2 pounds
1 ton	2200 pounds
LIQUID AND DRY MEASURES	
0.15 litre	5 fluid ounces = 1 gill
0.5 litre	1 pint
1.1 litres	2 pints = 1 quart
4.5 litres	1 gallon = 4 quarts
9 litres	2 gallons = 1 peck
36 litres	1 bushel = 4 pecks
AVOIRDUPOIS WEIGHT	
453 grams	1 pound
6 kilograms	14 pounds = 1 stone
1016 kilograms	2240 pounds = 1 ton

The figures of this table are not mathematically precise; but merely give approximate amounts and lengths. Weights and measures differed during biblical times and different places and the units are not always consistent throughout the books. Further research may well bring to light more accurate details.

BIBLE DIARY

EVENT	CHARACTER(S)	BOOK	DATE
Birth	Jesus	Mt 1–2	6 B.C.
Baptism	John & Jesus	Mk 1	
Temptation	Jesus	Lk 4	
Jairus' daughter	Jesus	Lk 8	
Feeding 5000	Jesus	Lk 9	
Calming the storm	Jesus & disciples	Mk 4	
Man with leprosy	Jesus	Mt 8	
Walking on water	Jesus	Mk 6	
Transfiguration	Jesus	Mt 17	
Withering fig tree	Jesus	Mt 21	
Triumphal entry	Jesus	Mk 11	
Jesus gets angry	Jesus	Jn 2	
Wedding of Cana	Jesus	Jn 2	
Bethesda Pool	Jesus	Jn 5	
The widow's two coins		Lk 21	
The Last Supper	Jesus & disciples	Mt 26	
Lazarus rises	Jesus & Lazarus	Jn 11	
Washing of feet	Jesus & disciples	Jn 13	
Garden of Gethsemane	Jesus	Mk 14	
Judas betrays Jesus	Judas, Jesus & the disciples	Lk 22	
Peter denies Jesus	Peter & Jesus	Mt 26	
The Crucifixion	Jesus	Mk 15	
The Resurrection	Jesus	Lk 24	
Baptism by Fire	The disciples	Acts 2	
Conversion of Saul	Saul to Paul	Acts 9	
A new heaven and a new earth	John	Rev 21	100 A.D.

THE MIRACLES OF JESUS

Miracle	Scripture	Where performed
Power over nature		
Turns water into wine	John 2:1–11	Cana
First catch of fish	Luke 5:1–11	Lake Galilee
Stills the storm	Matthew 8:23–27 Mark 4:35–41 Luke 8:22–25	Lake Galilee
Feeds 5,000	Matthew 14:15–21 Mark 6:35–44 Luke 9:12–17 John 6:5–15	near Bethsaida
Walks on sea	Matthew 14:22–23 Mark 6:45–52 John 6:16–21	Lake Galilee
Feeds 4,000	Matthew 15:32–39 Mark 8:1–9	near Bethsaida
Money from fish	Matthew 17:24–27	Capernaum
Withers fig tree	Matthew 21:17–22 Mark 11:12–14; 20–25	Jerusalem
Second catch of fish	John 21:1–14	Lake Galilee
Power over sickness		
Heals nobleman's son	John 4:46–54	Cana
Cures man with harmful skin disease	Matthew 8:1–4 Mark 1:40–45 Luke 5:12–15	Galilean city
Heals soldier's servant	Matthew 8:5–13 Luke 7:1–10	Capernaum
Heals Peter's mother-in-law	Matthew 8:14–17 Mark 1:29–31 Luke 4:38–89	Capernaum
Heals paralysed men	Matthew 9:1–8 Mark 2:1–12 Luke 5:17–26	Capernaum
Cures woman of bleeding	Matthew 9:20–22 Mark 5:25–34 Luke 8:43–48	Capernaum

Miracle	Scripture	Where performed
Power over sickness		
Gives blind their sight	Matthew 9:27–31	Capernaum
Heals crippled hand	Matthew 12:9–14 Mark 3:1–6 Luke 6:6–11	Galilee
Heals non-Jewish girl	Matthew 15:21–28 Mark 7:24–30	Tyre
Heals a deaf man who cannot talk	Mark 7:31–37	Decapolis
Heals a man at a pool	John 5:1–18	Bethsaida
Gives back sight	Mark 8:22–26	Bethsaida
Gives sight to a man born blind	John 9:1–41	Jerusalem
Heals man with dropsy	Luke 14:1–6	Jerusalem
Heals ten of harmful skin disease	Luke 17:11–19	Galilee
Replaces ear of high priest's servant	Luke 22:49–51 John 18:10–11	Garden of Gethsemane
Power over evil spirits		
Heals man who could not talk because of a demon	Matthew 9:32–34	Capernaum
Sends evil spirit from man	Mark 1:23–27 Luke 4:33–36	Capernaum
Heals man who was blind and could not talk	Matthew 12:22 Luke 11:14	Galilee
Heals child with demon	Matthew 17:14–20 Mark 9:14–29	Mt.Tabor
Heals woman crippled for 18 years	Luke 13:10–17	Jerusalem
Power over death		
Raises Jairus' daughter	Matthew 9:18–26 Mark 5:35–43 Luke 8:41–42, 49–56	Capernaum
Raises widow's only son	Luke: 7:11–16	Nain
Raises Lazarus	John 11:1–45	Bethany

STORIES JESUS TOLD

Parable	Passage	Subject	Lesson
New winebags	Matthew 9:16–17	Jesus' message	Jesus has a new message from God
Farmer and the seed	Matthew 13:1–8 Mark 4:3–8 Luke 8:5–8	God's Word	We must hear and obey God's word
Weeds	Matthew 13:24–30	God's people	The good and bad will be separated
Mustard seed	Matthew 13:31–32 Mark 4:30–32 Luke 13:18–19	God's people	Small beginnings can lead to big things
Yeast	Matthew 13:33 Luke 13:20–21	God's people	Small beginnings can lead to big things
Hidden treasure	Matthew 13:44	God's people	Choose what is truly valuable in life
Very valuable pearl	Matthew 13:45–46	God's people	Choose what is truly valuable in life
Fishing net	Matthew 13:47–50	God's people	The good and bad will be separated
Lost sheep	Matthew 18:12–14 Luke 15:3–7	God's love	God loves each person deeply
Servant who would not forgive	Matthew 18:23–25	God's people	We forgive because God forgave us
Workers in a vineyard	Matthew 20:1–16	Service	God rewards us generously
Two sons	Matthew 21:28–32	God's love	God welcomes the sinner who comes to him
Evil renters	Matthew 21:33–46 Mark 12:1–12	Punishment	People who hate God's Son will be punished
Wedding dinner	Matthew 22:1–14	Punishment	People who do not accept God's invitation will be punished
Ten virgins	Matthew 25:1–13	Jesus' return	We must be ready when he comes back

Parable	Passage	Subject	Lesson
Talents	Matthew 25:14–30	Service	We must use our abilities to serve God
Wise and evil servants	Matthew 24:45–51 Luke 12:42–48	Service	We are to serve God and others as we wait for Jesus to return
Two men who owed money	Luke 7:41–43	God's people	We love God more when we realise we are sinners
Good Samaritan	Luke 10:30–37	Service	Do good to all in need
Friend at midnight	Luke 11:5–8	God's love	God is always willing to help
Unimportant seat at party	Luke 14:7–11	Humility	Don't be proud: let God reward
Lost coin	Luke 15:8–10	God's love	Each one is important to God
Son who left home	Luke 15:11–32	God's love	God forgives all who change their hearts and minds and return to him
Clever manager	Luke 16:1–10	God's people	We are to use money to do good and prepare for the future
Rich man and Lazarus	Luke 16:19–31	Punishment	People who love money more than God are foolish
Unworthy servants	Luke 17:7–10	Service	Serve God because we are thankful
Unfair judge	Luke 18:1–8	God's love	God will answer our prayers if we ask him
Pharisee and tax collector	Luke 18:9–14	God's love	Anyone who changes his heart and life can be forgiven
Bags of money	Luke 19:11–27	Service	Use our talents to serve God

NOTES

NOTES

NOTES

NOTES

NOTES

PAUL'S MISSIONARY JOURNEYS

Acts and New Testament Letters

Crucifixion of Jesus	A.D.30	Paul's visit to Jerusalem (Acts 21)	A.D.57
Pentecost (Acts 2)	A.D.30	Paul's arrest (Acts 21–24)	A.D.57
Stephen martyred (Acts 7)	early A.D.30	Paul in prison	A.D.57–59
Paul converted	summer A.D.35	Paul's sea voyage to Rome	A.D.59–60
Paul in Damascus (Acts 9)	A.D.35–37	Paul's first Roman imprisonment	A.D.60–62
		Ephesians written	A.D.60
Paul to Jerusalem (Acts 9)	summer A.D.37	*Colosssians written*	A.D.61
		Philemon written	A.D.61
Paul in Tarsus	A.D.37–43	*Philippians written*	A.D.62
Paul in Antioch	A.D.43–48	Paul released and travelling	A.D.62–64
		1 Timothy written	A.D.62
Paul's first missionary journey	A.D.48–49	Paul travels to Spain	A.D.64–66
Galatians written	A.D.49	*Titus written*	A.D.66
Jerusalem Council (Acts 15)	A.D.49	Paul in Greece	A.D.67
Paul's second missionary journey	A.D.50–52	Paul arrested and taken to Rome	A.D.68
1 Thessalonians written	A.D.51	City of Jerusalem destroyed	A.D.70
2 Thessalonians written	A.D.51		
Paul's third missionary journey	A.D.53–57		
1 Corinthians written	A.D.56		
2 Corinthians written	A.D.56		
Romans written	A.D.57		

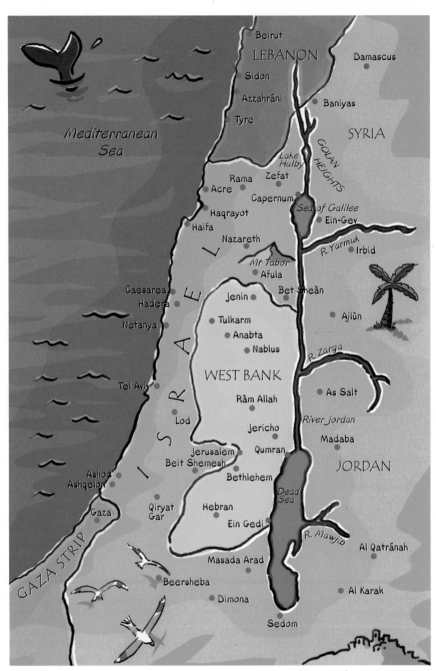

The Holy Land Today

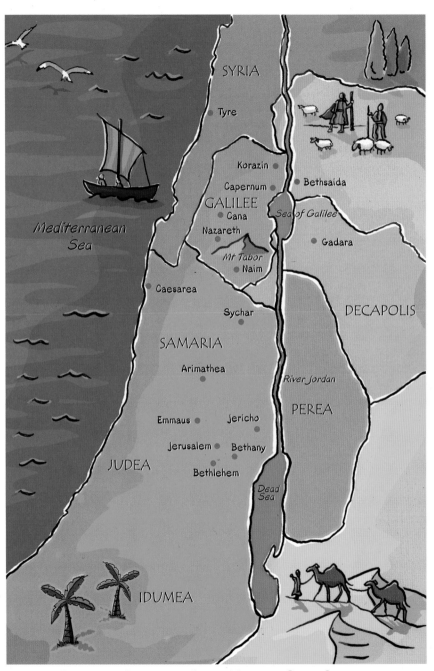

The Holy Land in the Life of Jesus

Paul's Journeys 1 and 2

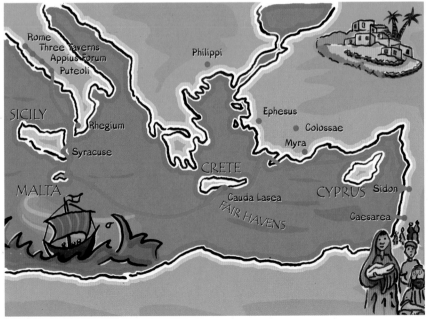

Paul's Journeys 3 and 4